The New York Times

STORY OF THE

YANKEES

The New York Times

STORY OF THE

YANKEES

1903–Present: 390 Articles, Profiles & Essays

Edited by

Dave Anderson

★

Foreword by

Alec Baldwin

BLACK DOG
& LEVENTHAL
PUBLISHERS
NEW YORK

Black Dog & Leventhal Publishers
Hachette Book Group
1290 Avenue of the Americas
New York, NY 10104

www.hachettebookgroup.com
www.blackdogandleventhal.com

First Trade Paperback Edition: April 2017

Black Dog & Leventhal Publishers is an imprint of Hachette Books, a division of Hachette Book Group. The Black Dog & Leventhal Publishers name and logo are trademarks of Hachette Book Group, Inc.

The publisher is not responsible for websites (or their content) that are not owned by the publisher.

The Hachette Speakers Bureau provides a wide range of authors for speaking events. To find out more, go to www.HachetteSpeakersBureau.com or call (866) 376-6591.

Print book interior design by Sheila Hart Design

Library of Congress Control Number: 2016959626

ISBNs: 978-1-579-12892-0 (hardcover); 978-0-316-46386-7 (paperback); 978-1-60376-370-7 (ebook)

Printed in the United States of America

LSC-C

10 9 8 7 6 5 4 3 2

CONTENTS

★ ★ ★

★ ★ ★

FOREWORD

MY INTRO TO SPORTS WRITING

by Alec Baldwin

In August of 1976, I left my home in Massapequa, Long Island, and moved to Washington, D.C. to attend George Washington University. This was the first time I had ever lived in a city and picking up a daily copy of The Washington Post was essential for political science undergrads. (This was, after all, the paper that a mere two years earlier had sent Nixon packing on that helicopter.) As I came to realize in other cities that I would either visit or live in, a tattered copy of a newspaper under one's arm meant you meant business.

The fall of 1976 was an unusual time in the nation's capital. The first post-Watergate presidential election was nearing its conclusion, and Jimmy Carter was on his way to defeating President Ford. But something equally dramatic was developing. Billy Kilmer's years as the Washington Redskins quarterback were winding down. A month after Carter was elected, the Post reported that Kilmer had been arrested for drunk driving. In Washington, it was difficult to discern which was the more significant story.

When I was a kid there was no ESPN, no Yankee or Red Sox channels. We didn't read Sports Illustrated because we couldn't afford magazines. We played ball and we watched ball games on TV. In fact, we watched anything that was on, especially on weekends. We watched Wide World of Sports and if Jim McKay was covering figure skating from Switzerland, we didn't care, as long as it kept us from mowing the lawn. In the summer, we'd lay on the couch, sutured to it actually, and nod our heads in agreement with Phil Rizzuto's or Ralph Kiner's every

utterance. Meanwhile, the grass in the yard seemed to grow by the hour, the mower poised just outside the door.

As I discovered in Washington, and would discover in Los Angeles and New York, sports media is a powerful and sensitive part of a city's psychology. Billy Kilmer alternately thrilled, exasperated and titillated Washington, a city where baseball then meant a team in Baltimore. When I moved to Los Angeles in the early 80s LA belonged to the Lakers. Football fans there seemed to love the college game as much as the pros. When Al Davis took the Raiders back to Oakland, he left a hundred-yard hole in the city's psyche that has not been filled since, so per- haps you understand why. It's the same with the Dodgers, who always seem like a transplant to some Angelenos. Sports fans want stability. They crave tradition.

In 1979, I was off to New York to attend New York University. The New York Times was waiting for me there, in the days when 10:30 A.M. was the unofficial cut-off time for getting an actual copy of paper. With no Internet back then, by late morning you either borrowed someone else's used Times or pulled an unsoiled copy out of a subway wastebasket. New York City is the place where day and night people of every stripe rub shoulders on the avenues. And there are newspapers for every taste and demographic. When I moved here, the word was that The Times had the best international and national coverage, The Daily News had the best metro, The Wall Street Journal had the best financial pages and the Post ruled gossip and sports.

The New York metro-area sports world is like a Chinese menu: Nets, Jets, Mets; Giants, Islanders, Rangers,

Devils, Knicks; and, above all, the Yankees. The Yankees, and their place in New York, are unique in American sports. They are not a team so much as a physical piece of the landscape that identifies their home town, like the Statue of Liberty, hot dog carts, or the subway. The Yankees and their logo are seemingly everywhere and on everyone. Forget T-shirts and key chains, jackets and bumper stickers. The Yanks are in the hearts of countless doormen and doctors, cops and cab drivers, bankers and bike messengers. And so they are examined, exposed, excoriated, exhumed, and extolled by all of the city's sports media.

Those who read The New York Times may well be able to find Yemen on a map or tell a Pollock from a Picasso or know which Albariño goes with scallops. But they can just as easily recite the details of A-Rod's latest injury, Derek Jeter's latest big hit or big play, or Mariano Rivera's latest save.

Yankee history is rich and deep, with players so iconic their first or last name, or their nickname, is identification enough. Billy Kilmer showed me how devotion to a team becomes a passion, and how a newspaper can feed it. But as colorful and entertaining as he was, Kilmer was no match for The Babe or The Iron Horse or the Yankee Clipper, Scooter, Yogi and Whitey, the Ol' Perfessor, the Mick and Maris, Reggie, Goose, or the oddest couple of all: George and Billy. For more than a century those names and dozens of others have been up there at Yankee Stadium on the grandest sports stage, and in The New York Times, the grandest sports pages.

INTRODUCTION

by Dave Anderson

One of the oldest stories in the daily jousting between New York baseball teams and New York newspapers has endured since one day nearly a century ago, when several reporters arrived at the West 42nd Street offices of the New York Giants demanding comment on the club's latest crisis. Dutifully, the receptionist hurried toward the desk of the owner or general manager whose identity has been lost in time.

"Sir," the receptionist was heard to say, "there are some newspapermen here and a gentleman from The Times."

That story is always good for a laugh but, then or now, not every newspaper gets or deserves such respect. The Times likes to think that its baseball writers always are gentlemen or gentlewomen, even when their reporting may not be so gentle. In our ever-changing world, most of the newspapers of that long-ago era are long gone. So are the Giants and the Brooklyn Dodgers, who departed for California after the 1957 season to be replaced by the Mets in 1962. But the Yankees have been around since 1903, and The Times—now online as well as on newsstands and on your doorstep—appears every morning, usually with a story or two (or three) about the Yankees. No other newspaper has recorded Yankees history so thoroughly.

After a slow start, the Yankees have reigned as America's most dominant sports franchise, with 27 World Series championships, 40 American League pennants, and 52 postseason appearances. Of the dozens of teams in North America's three other professional sports, only ice hockey's Montreal Canadiens are close, with 24 Stanley Cup celebrations. Pro basketball's Boston Celtics display 17 championship banners. When pro football's Green Bay Packers won Super Bowl XLV, they had 13 titles.

One of journalism's basic tenets is that names make news, and the Yankees have had many of baseball's most headline-friendly news makers: Babe Ruth, Lou Gehrig, Joe DiMaggio, Mickey Mantle, Yogi Berra, Whitey Ford, Reggie Jackson, Derek Jeter, Mariano Rivera, and Alex Rodriguez—not to forget George Steinbrenner, the blustery principal owner, and his five-time foil as the dugout manager, Billy Martin. Whenever any of them did or said something newsworthy, Times writers were there to report or comment on it. Six of those writers—more than that of any other newspaper—have their names on the J.G. Taylor Spink Award for "meritorious contributions to baseball writing" at the National Baseball Hall of Fame and Museum in Cooperstown, New York. The honored six include Red Smith and John Kieran, two Sports of the Times columnists whose commentaries were legendary literature, as well as John Drebinger, Leonard Koppett, Joe Durso, Murray Chass, and Claire Smith.

Red Smith was awarded a Pulitzer Prize in 1976 for his columns, as were Sports of the Times columnists Arthur Daley in 1956 and Dave Anderson in 1981. Other Times award winners over the years include columnists Robert Lipsyte, George Vecsey, Ira Berkow, William C. Rhoden, Harvey Araton and Selena Roberts, as well as beat writers James P. Dawson, Roscoe McGowen, Louis Effrat, Jack Curry, Buster Olney, Tyler Kepner, Ben Shpigel, and David Waldstein.

As you'll see, baseball writing, in adjusting to radio

and then television, has evolved from the no-byline era, to Drebinger's virtual play-by-play description of a World Series game from the 1920s through the '50s, to the Koppett and Durso analytical assessments in the '60s, to the Chass police-like details of the turbulent '70s and '80s. With more depth and features, Times writers excelled in covering the day-to-day developments of the team, not merely the games. So have the Times photographers, notably Ernest Sisto, Larry Morris, Barton Silverman, and Chang Lee. Once, when he was assigned to get a photo of Phil Rizzuto bunting during a game, Sisto mentioned it to the Yankees shortstop who told him, "When I'm going to bunt, I'll slide my right hand along my bat before the pitch." Rizzuto did, and Sisto clicked.

And what a team to cover. Even when the Yankees didn't win or lose the World Series, they usually were in the pennant races of past decades, and the postseason play-offs of more recent seasons. The Yankees won their World Series in bunches—four from 1923 to '32; six from '36 to '43; ten from '47 to '62; two in '77 and '78; and four from '96 to '00, before the '09 title. At last count, the National Baseball Hall of Fame includes 51 members who played, managed, or were an executive for the Yankees, the most for any major league franchise.

To appreciate the Yankees' mix of talent and success, no other club has had a Hall of Fame player at every position on at least one World Series winner: starting pitchers Whitey Ford, Herb Pennock, Waite Hoyt, Red Ruffing, Lefty Gomez, Catfish Hunter, and relief pitcher Rich (Goose) Gossage. Catchers Yogi Berra and Bill Dickey. First basemen Lou Gehrig and Johnny Mize. Second basemen Tony Lazzeri and Joe Gordon. Shortstop Phil Rizzuto. Third baseman Wade Boggs. Left fielder Enos Slaughter. Center fielders Joe DiMaggio, Mickey Mantle, and Earle Combs. Right fielders Babe Ruth and Reggie Jackson (also a designated hitter). Plus two certain future Hall of Famers in shortstop Derek Jeter and relief pitcher Mariano Rivera.

Four Yankees managers—Miller Huggins, Joe McCarthy, Casey Stengel, and Joe Torre—are in the Hall of Fame. Two general managers are there, Ed Barrow and George Weiss. Sooner or later, George Steinbrenner might join Jacob Ruppert as a longtime Yankees owner with a bronze plaque.

With so many World Series rings and American League pennants, the Yankees have created much more history than any of their New York–area colleagues. The pro football Giants have won eight NFL titles (including four Super Bowls); the Jets, one Super Bowl; the departed baseball Giants, five World Series; the departed Dodgers, one World Series; the Knicks, two NBA championships; the Nets, two American Basketball Association titles; the Rangers, five Stanley Cups; the Islanders, four; and the New Jersey Devils, three.

Love them or hate them, there has been no sports franchise quite like the Yankees, whose history the New York Times tells so well.

★ ★ ★

The New York Times front page reporting the Yankees 1996 World Series championship.

"All the News That's Fit to Print"

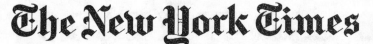

The New York Times

Late Edition
New York: **Today**, variable clouds, very mild. High 70. **Tonight**, scattered showers. Low 57. **Tomorrow**, becoming sunny, windy. High 64. **Yesterday**, high 65, low 49. Details, page 43.

VOL. CXLVI . . No. 50,593 NEW YORK, SUNDAY, OCTOBER 27, 1996 — $3 beyond the greater New York metropolitan area. — $2.50

DOLE IS CONTINUING ATTACKS ON PRESS AND THE PRESIDENT

EFFORT TO STIR 'OUTRAGE'

Republican Turning Attention to First Lady and Clinton's Lack of Military Service

By KATHARINE Q. SEELYE

FRESNO, Calif., Oct. 26 — On a bus trip through the verdant Central Valley of California, where 10 percent of this state's voters live, Bob Dole continued trying to stir up "outrage" today at the Clinton Administration, offered a rare mention of Hillary Rodham Clinton and harshly criticized the President's lack of military service.

Mr. Dole, traveling with Gov. Pete Wilson and met here by the actress Bo Derek, also continued trying to appeal to families, saying his tax-cut plan would give "more money for soccer moms, more money for day care." President Clinton's policies, Mr. Dole asserted, amounted to a "war on families."

"Wake up, America! Wake up, America! Wake up, America!" the Republican Presidential nominee thundered at a rally here. "Give America back to the people!"

As Mr. Clinton winds down his campaign, he is talking about crime more than his Republican opponent. In his weekly radio address today, the President called for more Federal assistance to crime victims. [Page 28.]

Mr. Dole, suggesting a media bias against Republicans, said today that members of his party "were punished in the 1970's because of Watergate — we probably deserved it." He added, "Now it's taken all this time to get back on our feet."

But if a Republican did only a fraction of the things the Clinton Administration had done, he said, "there would be outrage."

"They'd be putting out special editions of The New York Times," he went on. "They would be so outraged. And now it appears in Section D or later, if they got a later section."

While Mr. Dole's criticism of the news media ebbed today from its intense level of the previous two days, it was the third day in a row that he singled out The New York Times. Earlier, in the city of Visalia, he said: "I know that with a crowd this size, The New York Times will write not many people showed up, but the other papers will get it right."

The Secret Service estimated the crowd at 3,000 in Visalia, which has a population of about 75,000.

At the rally here in Fresno, 40 miles up the highway from Visalia, Mr. Dole also ridiculed the President

Continued on Page 26, Column 1

TODAY'S SECTIONS

Arts and Leisure/Section 2
Once a basket case, the Lincoln Center Theater today is anything but. A string of critical hits, a big budget, a huge membership and a just-finished major renovation have made it the pre-eminent nonprofit theatrical institution in the country. And yet many wonder, is it all that it can be?

Automobiles/Section 11*†

Book Review/Section 7
Alice Munro's "Selected Stories," from the last 20 years, is a work imbued with Canadian weather and Northern austerity, testing the gap between the real world and the pursuit of happiness.

The City/Section 13§

Editorials and Op-Ed/Section 4

Magazine/Section 6
The school reform that really matters is not vouchers or charter schools or breaking the unions or wiring the classrooms. It's a curriculum set in Washington, monitored in every town and city.

Money and Business/Section 3
The House of Rothschild, a banking family divided and in decline for decades, took a historic step toward unification.

Real Estate/Section 9*
Group buying Helmsley's holdings at Parkchester plans a restoration.

Regional Weeklies/Section 13¶

SportsSunday/Section 8

Television/Section 12*

Travel/Section 5
In the Caribbean this winter, you can loll on a private terrace (in Petit St. Vincent), dive off St. Thomas, visit gardens in Barbados or eat (and drink) royally in Anguilla.

WORLD SERIES '96

Comeback Is Complete: Yanks Win the Series

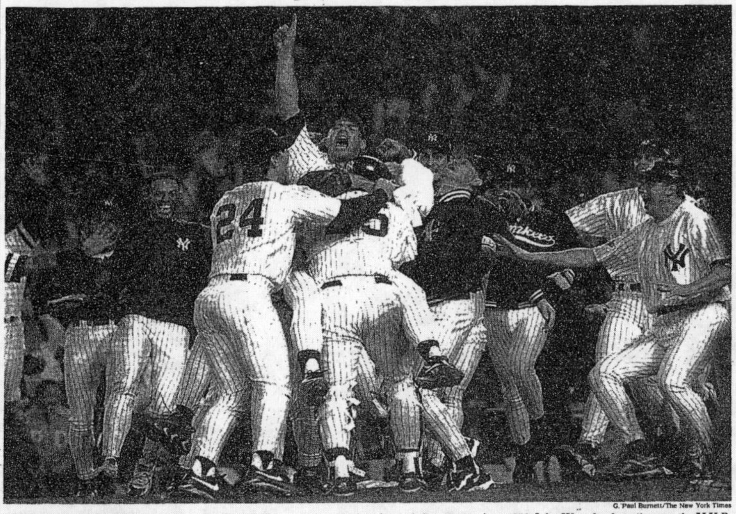

G. Paul Burnett/The New York Times

The Yankees lost the first two games to the Braves, then won four straight for their first crown since 1978. John Wetteland, center, was the M.V.P.

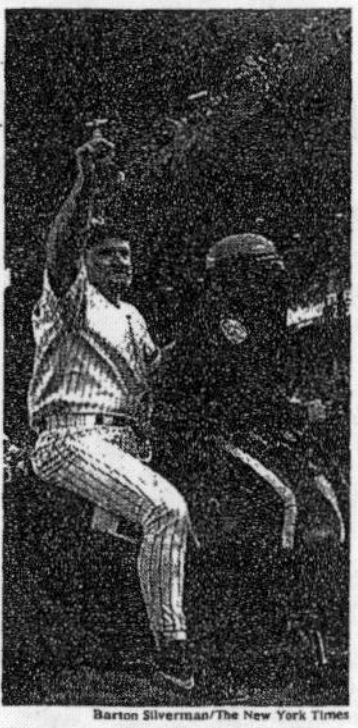

Barton Silverman/The New York Times

Better than a police escort: Wade Boggs celebrates the victory.

Team's 18-Year Wait Is Over

By N. R. KLEINFIELD

Ending years of futility and self-doubt, the Yankees defeated the Atlanta Braves 3-2 in a taut thriller last night to win their first World Series title in 18 years.

Crowning a magical season of many small miracles, the Yankees dropped the first two games at home and then stormed back to snatch four straight from the defending champions and claim a destiny that once seemed their very birthright.

The spellbinding six-game triumph over the Braves bestowed on the Yankees their 23d world championship, by far the most of any team, and perhaps their sweetest. Never since the Yankees began winning World Series titles in 1923 with a perfunctoriness that became an autumn habit had this storied franchise waited so long between victories. Before now, the team's lengthiest interlude stretched between 1962 and 1977. Before the 1970's, world championships arrived in the South Bronx every few years, if not every year.

The last time either of New York's baseball franchises had captured the world title was a decade ago, when the Mets mounted their improbable comeback over the Boston Red Sox.

GAME 6
Yankees 3, Braves 2

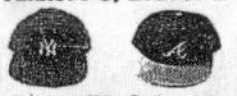

Yankees Win Series, 4-2

This was also only the third time that a team had lost the first two games at home and then gone on to take the championship. The last team to do it was the Mets in their 1986 victory.

On the last night of a long baseball year, before a raucous and expectant crowd, a team that has illuminated the imagination and touched the hearts of New Yorkers scored all of its runs in the third inning off Greg Maddux, the four-time Cy Young winner who shut down the Yankees with captivating artistry in Game 2. The Yankees got a lead-off double by Paul O'Neill, a triple by Joe Girardi and singles by Derek Jeter and Bernie Williams. Then, drawing on their domineering bullpen, they made the three-run lead stand up.

The Yankees managed to survive a spine-tingling fourth inning, when

Continued on Page 37, Column 1

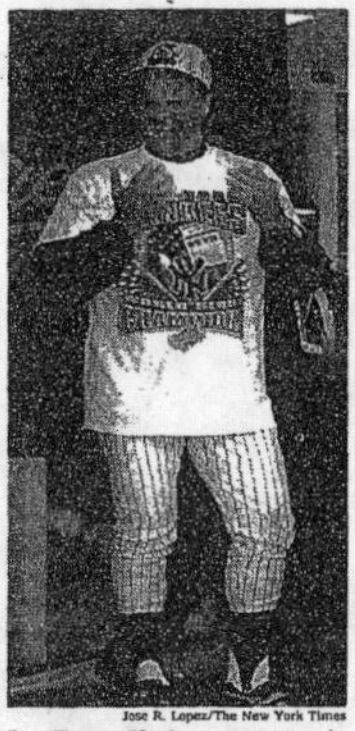

Jose R. Lopez/The New York Times

Joe Torre, Yankees manager, in the usual champagne shower.

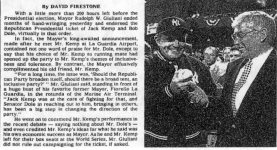

PARTIES PRESSING TO RAISE TURNOUT AS ELECTION NEARS

BOTH SIDES FEAR APATHY

If Voters Are Not Drawn by the Presidential Contest, Other Races Could Be Swayed

By ROBIN TONER

The final 10 days of the 1996 campaign are shaping up as a furious struggle by the two parties and their allies to get their supporters to the polls, in the face of widespread indications that sagging voter interest may well diminish turnout.

Strategists say that fears on both sides are legitimate after a lopsided and largely static Presidential campaign. Democrats worry that President Clinton's comfortable lead in the polls will cause many would-be supporters to think he no longer needs their votes; Republicans fear that Bob Dole's troubled campaign will so dispirit many of the party faithful that they will simply stay home. In either case, it is the struggle for control of the House of Representatives that could be most affected, many analysts say.

Mary Crawford, press secretary for the Republican National Committee, said, "It's totally fair to say that the party, on a national and state level, will be donating unprecedented resources to turning out our voters this year."

Democrats make similar vows. "We saw in 1994 the results of low turnout," said David Eichenbaum, the Democratic National Committee's director of communications. "We lost a number of races by very close margins that had everything to do with turnout and resulted in a Republican Congress that tried to gut a lot of important priorities."

The final drives by the parties and their allied interest groups are well under way, often based on extensive research to identify probable supporters and find the appeals most likely to get them to the polls. This weekend, Democrats are holding rallies and distributing leaflets directed at women from the soccer fields of suburban Baltimore to the Wal-Marts of Georgia. The A.F.L.-C.I.O. has sent 1,000 fresh troops into the field to help unions coordinate the endgame of their effort to oust the Republican House; labor volunteers distributed 100,000 pieces of literature to union members on a single day last week in Washington State.

On the conservative side, the Christian Coalition is distributing 45 million voter guides through 120,000 churches, as well as running get-out-the-vote commercials on Christian radio outlets and getting in touch with more than three million voters

Continued on Page 28, Column 2

Prosecutors Declare Guard Isn't Suspect In Atlanta Bombing

By KEVIN SACK

ATLANTA, Oct. 26 — Clearing away the suspicions that had turned a security guard from hero to pariah, the Justice Department today declared that Richard A. Jewell was no longer a suspect in the July 27 bombing at Centennial Olympic Park.

"Barring any newly discovered evidence, this status will not change," said the long anticipated letter, which was written by Kent B. Alexander, the United States Attorney here, to Jack Martin, one of Mr. Jewell's lawyers.

Mr. Jewell became the subject of almost frenzied media attention after The Atlanta Journal reported on July 30 that, after being widely praised as the guard who first noticed the knapsack containing the bomb, he had become a focus of the intensive Federal investigation into the attack. The newspaper did not cite its sources for the information.

Mr. Jewell maintained his innocence and later passed a polygraph test commissioned by his lawyers.

The pipe bomb filled with nails and metal detonated at 1:20 A.M. as Olympic revelers watched a concert. One woman was killed in the blast, a Turkish cameraman died of a heart attack while covering the bombing,

By the Way, Giuliani Backs Kemp (and Dole)

By DAVID FIRESTONE

With a little more than 200 hours left before the Presidential election, Mayor Rudolph W. Giuliani ended months of hand-wringing yesterday and endorsed the Republican Presidential ticket of Jack Kemp and Bob Dole, virtually in that order.

In fact, the Mayor's long-awaited announcement, made after he met Mr. Kemp at La Guardia Airport, contained not one word of praise for Mr. Dole, except to say that his choice of Mr. Kemp as running mate had opened up the party to Mr. Kemp's themes of inclusiveness and tolerance. By contrast, the Mayor effusively complimented his old friend, Mr. Kemp.

"For a long time, the issue was, 'Should the Republican Party broaden itself, should there be a broad tent, an inclusive party?' " Mr. Giuliani said, standing in front of a huge bust of his favorite former Mayor, Fiorello La Guardia, in the rotunda of the Marine Air Terminal. "Jack Kemp was at the core of fighting for that, and Senator Dole in reaching out to him, bringing in others, has been a big step in changing the direction of the party."

He went on to commend Mr. Kemp's performance in the recent debate — saying nothing about Mr. Dole's — and even credited Mr. Kemp's ideas for what he said was his own economic success as Mayor. As he and Mr. Kemp left for their box seats at the World Series, Mr. Giuliani did not rule out campaigning for the ticket, if asked.

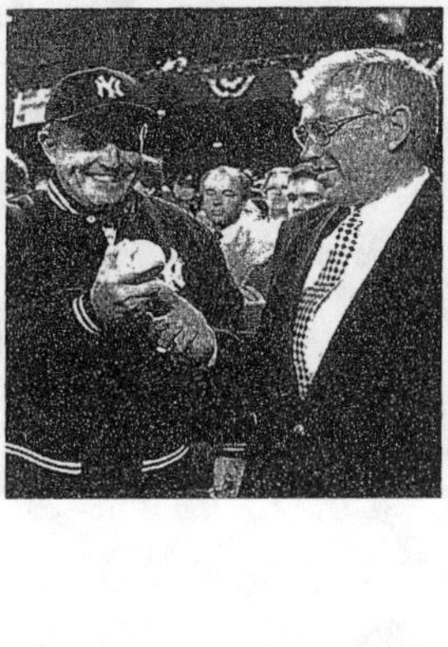

INSIDE

Death of an Afghan Village
Another village in Afghanistan was destroyed last week, one of the thousands razed in the civil war, but this time the destroyers were troops who had vowed to bring peace. Page 12.

Paving Paradise
Several states and environmental groups are challenging the quick permit program the Army Corps of Engineers uses to allow development of wetlands. Page 22.

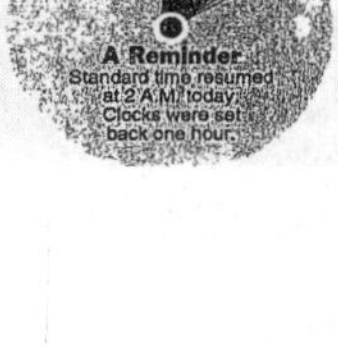
1
2
A Reminder
Standard time resumed at 2 A.M. today. Clocks were set back one hour.

THE EARLY YEARS

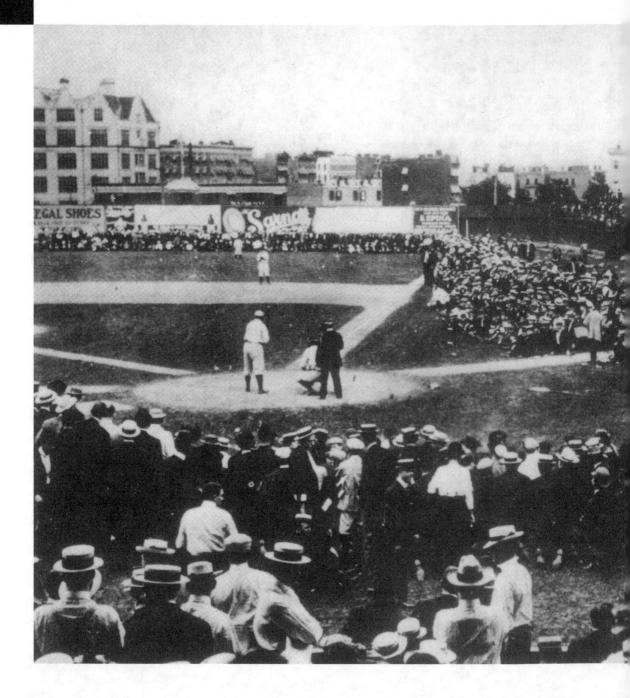

In the beginning, the Yankees were seldom a good team. Then again, they weren't the Yankees. They were known as the Highlanders because they played at Hilltop Park, a hastily erected wooden skeleton at Broadway and 168th Street in upper Manhattan overlooking the Harlem River to the east, where the original Yankee Stadium would open in the Bronx in 1923.

Until 1903, baseball in New York mostly meant the Giants and the Brooklyn team of the established National League; but for the young American League's third season, it had expanded into America's fastest-growing city. With hundreds of immigrants arriving almost daily at Ellis Island, New York's five-borough population had surpassed 3.5 million. However, this was a New York without much to take its citizens' minds off how to pay the rent in the brownstones or tenements.

The swells had their 42nd Street theaters along with golf and tennis, but baseball was about all anybody else had. Horse racing and boxing existed now and then, but baseball was by far the most popular sport. Football was for Ivy League collegians. Basketball had been invented in a Springfield, Massachusetts, YMCA gymnasium only a decade earlier. Ice hockey was played by British troops in Canada. Running and jumping in the Olympics was a new European idea.

There were hardly any telephones, hardly any automobiles. The subway was under construction but wouldn't be completed until 1904, and then only from downtown to 145th Street in Manhattan. To travel more than a few blocks, you climbed onto a trolley, an electric streetcar that clanged along tracks; and when you got off, you weaved your way past horse-drawn wagons.

Radio stations, much less play-by-play announcers, were decades away, and television channels were fifty years in the future. But more than a dozen New York newspapers flourished. Readers in 1903 learned that New York had a new baseball team to rival the Giants, who played at the Polo Grounds on 155th Street and Eighth Avenue below what was known as Coogan's Bluff. For the Highlanders' home opener on April 30, 1903, at Hilltop Park, its field still rocky and uneven, 16,293 spectators arrived by trolley and horse-drawn wagons or trudged there on foot to welcome New York's new team, its roster spliced together mostly with players from the ⟫⟫⟫

★ ★ ★

The New York Highlanders playing at Hilltop Park in upper Manhattan around 1910.

‹‹‹ disbanded 1902 Baltimore Orioles. The Highlanders defeated the Washington Senators, 6–2.

At the time, surely nobody realized how Baltimore's loss of that team might have affected Yankees and baseball history. Less than a year before the Highlanders were formed, on June 13, 1902, an eight-year-old truant who grew up in his father's boisterous bar near the Baltimore waterfront was committed to St. Mary's Industrial School for Boys, where he would develop into quite a left-handed pitcher and hitter. The boy's name was George Herman Ruth, later known as Babe, a baseball player unlike any other. But had the American League team remained in Baltimore, might that Baltimore prospect eventually have signed with it and played there, rather than join the minor league Orioles on his way to the Boston Red Sox and, in 1920, the Yankees?

We'll never know. But what we do know is that in outgrowing their Highlanders' nickname, the Yankees seldom threatened to win the pennant. Over their 17 seasons before Babe Ruth arrived, they finished as high as second only three times, notably in a final-day showdown at Hilltop Park in 1904 with the Boston Puritans, later the Red Sox, that turned on a wild pitch by right-hander Jack Chesbro, a 41-game winner that year, in the tenth inning of the first game of a doubleheader.

Had the Highlanders won that game, they would have trailed by one-half game. Instead, the Puritans led two and a half games to clinch first place. The Giants had won the National League pennant, but there was no World Series that year because the Giants' owner, John T. Brush, refused to play the American League upstarts. In 1906 the Yankees finished three games behind the Chicago White Sox (nicknamed the Hitless Wonders).

In 1910 the Yankees trailed Connie Mack's Philadelphia Athletics by fourteen and one-half games during an era that had a dark side: constant whispers that Hal Chase,

their star first baseman, was throwing games. That rare player who threw left-handed and batted right-handed, Chase was a dazzling fielder who hit .323 with 193 hits in 1906. But in the seasons that followed, some of his teammates didn't trust him. Neither did George Stallings, the manager in 1910; but late that season, Chase convinced the front office to dismiss Stallings and let him manage. The Yankees finished on a 9–2 spurt, but in 1911, despite Chase's .311 average, they skidded to sixth place. Although replaced as manager by Harry Wolverton, he stayed at first base as the Yankees dropped into last place. In 1912, this supposedly classic gloveman made 36 errors. After the 1913 season, when he batted .212, he was traded to the White Sox, jumped to the Federal League, then ended his shady career with the Cincinnati Reds and the Giants.

As a franchise, the Yankees didn't turn upward until the new owners—Colonel Jacob Ruppert, a millionaire brewer, and Captain Tillinghast L'Hommedieu Huston—took charge before the 1915 season. The next year the team climbed into the first division, and by 1919, Miller Huggins's second season as manager, they finished third with a respectable 80–59 record, only seven and one-half games behind the White Sox, eight of whose players would be indicted for having accepted bribes to throw that year's World Series with the Reds. Those eight players, later banned from baseball for life, changed the name of the 1919 Chicago team to the Black Sox. But that little boy in Baltimore two decades earlier, the left-handed pitcher and slugger now known as Babe Ruth, soon would be on his way to New York.

★ ★ ★

The 1903 New York Highlanders team posing for a group photo at South Side Park in Chicago.

Sept 7, 1902

AMERICAN LEAGUE HERE

Another Baseball Team Proposed for New York Next Season.

AS THE PRESENT BASEBALL SEASON draws to a close interest is turned from the pennant race to the war between the National and American Leagues. In the National League Pittsburg has already won the championship for the second time. In all probability the Brooklyns will finish second. A short time ago it was a fierce fight between Chicago and Brooklyn for the next place to Pittsburg, but now Boston leads the Western club in the percentage column.

There never was a baseball horizon so full of promise as it is to-day. This rosy hue of affairs obtains particularly with the players. The merry war now being so fiercely waged between the National and American Leagues is the lever which is lifting the players' salaries as they have never been lifted before.

When a ball player's services are valued at $8,000 for a season's work, there is certainly rich financial reward for the man who can field and bat. That is the salary paid by the Cleveland Club to Lajoie. And every other player who naturally thinks himself able to play as good a game as the French Canadian considers that he, too, is worth a like princely price.

Had it not been for the American League and its persistent bids for the best men, Lajoie would not have received such a salary.

The American League is still offering big money for star players and its rivals of the National Association are no way behind in the bidding.

All this has created a boom in salaries. It has kept the men alive to the value of their services, and every player of the first rank is holding out for bids and will not sign contracts for next season until he had received the last offer.

Christy Mathewson, the New York's pitcher, is a case in point. He has been told that he ⟩⟩⟩

might write his own contract, but persistently delays to sign.

In this battle between the rival forces among the club owners such men as these and Flick and Delehanty and other stars of a like magnitude are wanted at almost any price by the rivals, and they will certainly hold out to the highest bidder. There seems unlimited money in both organizations, and it will be freely spent.

There were rumors afloat that a compromise might be affected between the American and National Leagues, but those in authority are very reticent and nothing definite can be learned. But from the outlook at present, it looks as if the war would be fought all through next season.

One thing is certain, that out of this intense rivalry will grow a revival of baseball such as the country has never seen. And it is highly probable that New York will have a better team than it has had in many years. ◆

January 11, 1903

AGREEMENT IN BASEBALL

Keeler, Griffith, Tannehill, and Chesbro Will Play with New York American League Team.

CINCINNATI, Jan. 10.—THE BASEBALL WAR which has been waging for the last two years between the American and National Leagues virtually ended to-night when the Peace Commission of both Leagues adjourned after coming to an agreement.

According to this agreement an American League team is to be established in New York, and among the players who will represent it on the field are William Keeler, the Captain of the Brooklyn National League team of last year; Clark Griffith, the Chicago pitcher, and the Pittsburg pitchers, Chesbro and J. Tannehill. A number of other strong players complete the make up of the team.

The contract claims of each of the clubs were carefully considered by the Peace Committee, and a list was drawn up of the players awarded to each club. All the players who have received advance money from any other club than that to which they are assigned, are directed to return this money, and will not be permitted to play until this is done.

The agreement of the committee, as given out, was as follows:

"CINCINNATI, Ohio, Jan. 10.—At a prior date the National League and American Association of Professional Baseball Clubs, having appointed a committee, and the American League of Professional Baseball Clubs having appointed a committee, the object and purpose being for said committees to meet, discuss and agree upon a policy to end any and all differences now existing between the said two leagues, and consisting of Harry C. Pulliam, August Herrmann, James A. Hart, and Frank De Haas Robinson, and the said committee of the said American League, consisting of Ben B. Johnson, Charles A. Comiskey, Charles W. Somers, and H. J. Killilea, and said committees having met at the St. Nicholas Hotel, in Cincinnati on Jan 9, 1903, and having continued in session until this 10th day of January, 1903, and after having fairly and fully discussed all complaints and matters of grievances and abuses growing out of the present baseball conditions, and having in mind the future welfare and preservation of the National game, have unanimously agreed as follows:

"First—Each and every contract hereafter entered into by the clubs of either League with players, managers, or umpires shall be considered valid and binding.

"Second—A reserve rule shall be recognized, by which each and every club may reserve play-

The 1904 New York Highlanders Baseball Team. Clark Griffith is second from right, Willie Keeler is fourth from right, and Jack Chesbro is eighth from right.

ers under contract, and that a uniform contract for the use of each League shall be adopted.

"Third—After a full consideration of all contract claims by each and every club, it is agreed that the list hereto attached, marked exhibits 'A' and 'B,' is the correct list of the players legally awarded to each club. Exhibit 'A' being the list of American League players and Exhibit 'B' being the list of National League players.

"Fourth—it is agreed that any and all sums of money received by any player from any other than the club to which he is awarded by the exhibits hereto attached, shall be returned forthwith to the club so advancing said sums, and until all said sums of money so advanced are returned said player shall not be permitted to play with any club in either league.

"Fifth—The circuits of each league shall consist of the following cities:

"American League—Boston, New York, Philadelphia, Washington, Cleveland, Detroit, Chicago, and St. Louis.

"National League—Boston, New York, Brooklyn, Philadelphia, Pittsburg, Chicago, St. Louis, and Cincinnati.

"Neither circuit shall be changed without the consent of the majority of the clubs of each league.

"It is further provided that there shall be no consolidation in any city where two clubs exist, nor shall any club transfer or release its players for the purpose of injuring or weakening the league of which it is a member.

"Sixth—On or before the 1st day of February of each year the President of each league shall appoint a schedule committee of three, who shall be authorized to prepare a schedule of the games to be played during the championship season by each club in each league. This schedule shall be submitted by the committee within three weeks after its appointment to each league for adoption and ratification. This committee shall be authorized, if it deems the same advisable, to provide for a series of championship games between all of the clubs in both leagues.

"Seventh—On or before the first day of February of each year the President of each League shall appoint a Committee on Rules of three each, who shall be authorized to prepare uniform playing rules. These rules shall be submitted by the committee within three weeks after their appointment to each League for their ratification and adoption.

"Eighth—It is further agreed that the said two leagues hereinbefore mentioned shall enter into a National agreement embodying the agreements and conditions hereinbefore set forth: and it is further agreed that Presidents Ban B. Johnson and Harry C. Pulliam be, and they are hereby appointed, each a committee of one from each league for the purpose of making, preparing, and ⟫⟫

≪≪≪ formulating such National agreement: and it is further agreed that they invite President P. T. Powers of the National Association of Professional Baseball League to confer and advise with them in the formulating and said National agreements.

"Ninth—It is hereby agreed that each member hereby binds himself and his respective league by signing this agreement this 10th day of January, 1903.

"HARRY PULLIAM.
"AUG. HERRMANN.
"JAMES A. HART.
"FRANK DEHASS ROBINSON.
"B. B. JOHNSON.
"CHARLES A. COMISKEY.
"CHARLES W. SOMERS.
"H. J. KILLILEA."... ◆

April 23, 1903

New York Team Plays in Washington and Loses to the Local Nine—Score, 3 to 1.

Special to The New York Times.

WASHINGTON, April 22.—THE NEW YORK baseball team of the American League inaugurated the League season here to-day by meeting the Washington team. New York lost by 3 to 1 through inability to bat safely at opportune times. The game proved one of the most enjoyable ever witnessed by local cranks. It was closely contested at every point.

The game proved to be a pitchers' battle, and was won by Washington on the merits of a timely fusillade of safe hits in the fifth inning.

New York was first to score, through a rare piece of base running by Willie Keeler. Keeler got his base on balls, and started for second, when Fultz singled to Delehanty. Delehanty immediately returned the ball to Coughlin, who jabbed at Keeler as the little wonder dropped to the ground and made an exceptionally long slide safely into third base, amid the applause of the multitude that occupied every available seat and completely surrounded the outfield. ◆

American League Park, New York.

April 30, 1903

BIG DAY FOR BASEBALL

New York American League Team Will Open New Grounds To-day.

THIS WILL BE A GALA DAY for baseball in Manhattan, and all roads will lead to the new grounds, which from now on will be known as American League Park, on Washington Heights. The American Baseball League has bent all its energies during the last twelve months to locate a playing club in this city, and this afternoon will see the realization of President Ban Johnson's oft-repeated promises. The Greater New York Baseball Club will celebrate the opening of its new park to-day with a band concert and the initial game of the local American League season.

When attendance swelled at Hilltop Park, fans would stand on the field behind home plate, along the foul lines, and around the perimeter of the outfield, as was the practice of the day.

President Gordon and Manager Clark Griffith will match their team of baseball experts against the Washington team, that "broke even" with them in the opening series last week. The club management has been generous in extending invitations for this event, and it is expected that an army of "cranks," "fans," and "rooters" who talk baseball all the year round will be on hand for the "opening."

The work of blasting rock, filling in and leveling the grounds has been going on day and night for several weeks, and while the great undertaking is not nearly completed, enough progress has been made to enable the games being played. The grand stand is roofless, but the chairs are all in their places, while two large open stands have been constructed hurriedly, so there will be a seating capacity of 16,000 to-day and standing room for as many more. The diamond has been sodded and rolled until it looks as level as a newly covered billiard table, but the outfield is in a rough and rugged condition.

There is a good deal of filling in to be done in right field, and ground rules will be arranged in regard to the value of hits made in that »»

《《《 direction. Only six games have been scheduled for this and the following playing days, and then the team will go over the circuit. It is hoped that by the time the players return from this Western trip everything, to the merest detail, will be completed and that the new club and its team will have a successful season in every respect.

President Ban Johnson will throw the ball to the umpire immediately before the game, which will be started promptly at 3:30 o'clock. The gates will be opened at 1 o'clock, and the Sixty-ninth Regiment Band, under the direction of Bandmaster Bayne, will enliven the proceedings during the afternoon.

The New York Americans won the final game of the series with the Athletics in Philadelphia yesterday, and if they succeed in getting their eyes on the ball while handling the willow to-day, there should be nothing wanting to make the inauguration of the new park a complete success. ◆

May 1, 1903

BASEBALL'S BIG CROWD

Auspicious Opening of American League Grounds in This City.

PRESIDENT BAN JOHNSON'S long-threatened invasion of New York baseball territory became an accomplished fact yesterday afternoon, when the Greater New York Club of the American League opened its new baseball grounds, American League Park, on the loftiest point of Washington Heights. According to the automatic checkers in the revolving turnstiles, 16,243 persons passed in through the several entrances to see the first American League game on Manhattan Island, and yet there was plenty of room for nearly as many more within the spacious inclosure.

Although the stands have not yet been completed, the occupants of the half-finished structures seemed to be perfectly satisfied with the seating arrangements. While the big gathering was not overdemonstrative, the absence of fault finding was in itself an assurance to the management that the patrons fully appreciated the difficulties which beset the new club, and due credit was given to the almost Herculean efforts of the officials who had accomplished so much in such a brief time.

The diamond, newly sodded and rolled to perfection, was the only spot in the big field which could not be improved. The outfield was very rough and uneven and the eastern side of the grounds, known as right field, has yet to be filled in before the work of batters and fielders can be judged with any degree of accuracy. Ground rules governed the long hits made in the opening contest, and these precluded any three-base or home-run hits being made, except the ball were driven out of the grounds.

NEW YORK.	R	1B	PO	A	E
Davis, lf....	1	1	0	0	2
Keeler, rf...	3	2	1	0	0
McF'd, cf...	1	0	0	0	0
Will'ms, 2b.	0	2	2	3	0
Ganzel, 1b..	0	0	12	1	0
Conroy, 3b..	1	2	5	1	0
C'tney, ss...	0	1	2	1	1
O'Connor, c.	0	1	4	1	0
Chesbro, p..	0	0	1	5	0
Total....	6	9	27	12	3

WASHINGTON.	R	1B	PO	A	E
Rob'n, ss...	0	2	2	2	0
Selbach, rf..	1	0	0	0	0
Delh'ty, lf..	0	3	0	0	0
Ryan, cf....	0	2	3	1	0
Carey, 1b...	0	0	8	0	0
C'ghlin, 3b..	1	2	2	1	1
Demont, 2b.	0	1	0	3	0
Drill, c.....	0	0	5	1	0
T'nsend, p..	0	0	1	2	0
*Holmes ...	0	0	0	0	0
Total....	2	7	24	10	1

*Batted for Townsend in ninth inning.

New York..............1 1 0 0 2 0 2 0 .—6
Washington ....0 0 0 0 0 0 1 1 0—2

Earned runs—New York, 2. Two-base hits—Keeler, (2,) Williams, (2,) Conroy, (2,) Coughlin, and Robinson. Sacrifice hits—McFarland and Courtney. Stolen base—O'Connor. Double play—Ryan and Drill. Left on bases—New York, 7; Washington, 9. First base on balls—Off Chesbro, 1; off Townsend, 3. First base on errors—New York, 1; Washington, 3. Hit by pitched ball—By Townsend, 2. Struck out—By Chesbro, 1; by Townsend, 4. Time of game—One hour and thirty minutes. Umpires—Messrs. Connolly and Caruthers.

Ropes were stretched along the back part of the outfield, and a ball batted beyond these was good only for two bases. When the field is leveled off and these rules revoked a ball hit to deep right, left, or centre should be worth a home run, and it will require the efforts of the most husky batsman to drive a ball over the high fence on the north and east sides of the big field.

The weather yesterday was ideal, and the big crowd of men and women seemed not alone to enjoy the outing, but they generally entered into the spirit of the occasion and were quick to applaud every brilliant play, and equally as quick to observe the slightest mistake.

At 8 o'clock both teams formed in line on the northern side of the field. The Greater New Yorks were resplendent in their new white uniforms and caps of white flannel and black facings, topped off with natty maroon-colored coats, while the opposing team from Washington wore their combination suits of white shirts and blue pants.

Headed by Bayne's Sixty-ninth Regiment Band, the parade was begun to the strains of "The Washington Post March," an appropriate compliment to the visiting club. As the men marched across the diamond the occupants of the stands and bleachers arose en masse, each one waving a tiny American flag, and the scene was both picturesque and inspiring.

When the band arrived within a few feet of the grand stand it played "The Star-Spangled Banner." All hats were raised, and the cheering which followed echoed and re-echoed from the Heights across the Hudson to the New Jersey Palisades and back again, and drowned the strains of "Yankee Doodle" as the players broke ranks and began their preliminary practice.

Then the spectators sat down again to watch the different plays and feast their eyes on the movements of the metropolitan representatives, some of whom were comparative strangers to most of the local patrons. "Willie" Keeler, of course, was the most popular member of the new team, while Chesbro and O'Connor were almost as well known as the former Captain of the Brooklyn team. Gabzel Long, Davis, Williams, McFarland, Conroy, and Courtney were in turn pointed out by the "fans" to the uninitiated, while the army of "cranks" and "rooters" leaned back in their seats and passed favorable and unfavorable comments on every little move of the men.

The contest, while one-sided all the way through, was interesting at every stage. Chesbro was in great form and the visitors could not make much headway with his delivery. Delehanty was at the bat five times, but even he could not make a safe hit, neither could Selbach, while the New York team individually and collectively played winning baseball from start to finish. ◆

Oct 11, 1904

BOSTONS WIN AMERICAN LEAGUE CHAMPIONSHIP

New Yorks Lose by the Errors of Williams and Chesbro.

IN THE PRESENCE OF MORE THAN 28,000 persons and amid the wildest enthusiasm the Bostons defeated the Greater New Yorks in the first game of a double-header at American League Park yesterday by a score of 3 to 2, and retained the championship of the American League. It was essentially a pitchers' contest between Chesbro and Dineen, and had the local man received the proper kind of support the result would have been different. In the second game, with Puttmann, the left-hander, and Winter intrusted with the pitching, the New Yorks won by scoring the only run in the tenth inning on a bad throw by Lachance to third base. For its length it was one of the quickest played games of the season, occupying but one hour and ten minutes.

Probably no such interest ever was taken in a baseball event in this city as was manifested in the double-header of yesterday. Some 200 Boston "rooters," accompanied by Dockstader's Band of this city, had the extreme left end of the grand stand to themselves, and with the aid of the band, megaphones, and tin horns kept up a continual din throughout the nine innings. But with all the noise and enthusiasm of the Boston "rooters," it was weak compared to that of the supporters of the home team. In the third inning, when Chesbro batted to the exit gate at right field for three bases the spectators arose from their seats, waved hats, handkerchiefs, and canes madly, and this was continued for some time. But gloom came over the entire assemblage when Williams made a bad throw to the plate which gave Boston two runs and tied the score.

Boston scored the winning run in the ninth on a base hit by Criger, Dineen's sacrifice, Selbach's out, and Chesbro's wild pitch.

After Ganzel had struck out in the ninth inning Conroy reached first on called balls, and Kleinow was second man out on a fly to Ferris. McGuire, who batted for Chesbro, also got to first on four bad balls, and then Fultz ran for him. Dougherty, however, was not equal to the occasion, and for the second time of the game struck out. ◆

April 21, 1907

'YANKEES" START WITH A VICTORY

Hard Hitting Brings In Three Runs and Lands the Opening Game.

Special to The New York Times.

WASHINGTON, April 11.—THE LARGEST CROWD that ever witnessed an athletic event in this city saw New York win the opening game of the American League season here to-day by the score of 3 to 2. There were 12,902 paid admissions. Although both pitchers were hit rather freely, the game resolved itself into a battle between Al Orth and Tom Hughes.

Although the weather was hardly as cold as was expected last night, the conditions were still unfavorable and the players were unable to do their best work because of a stiff wind which blew across the field. The particular features of the game were catches by Keeler and Conroy, a one-handed stop by Perrine, and the rare feat performed by Hughes of striking out Willie Keeler. ◆

July 1, 1908

NO HITS FOR YANKEES OFF VETERAN YOUNG

Veteran Boston Pitcher's Remarkable Performance in Hilltop Game.

DID YOU HEAR ABOUT WHAT old Young did up at the American League Park yesterday? He didn't exactly beggar description, but he came mighty nigh it. He beggared the Elberfeld aggregation so far as runs were concerned, and he made hitless Yankees out of the whole outfit, and he smashed out singles thisaway and thataway, and he scored people that he likes, and he scored people that we don't know whether he cares much about or not, and he was the jolly old plot of the piece, and there wasn't an inning that you could lose track of him.

Even aside from his pitching proclivities, this gay old blade was the life of the party. He galloped around the bases like he was out for the Swift Stakes, and an observant clocker whose occupation at the track is o'er now that they're insisting that somebody pay some attention to the law, gave it out honest and official when he said to the stand generally:

"They must have gave that old skate the electric battery; watch um sail past them bags—why, he's fast as a ghost, I tell you."

The score, which is an entirely immaterial consideration, was 8. That's all, just 8.

The good old man Young had his eye and his hand on the ball yesterday. In the third inning he pounded one over to right and faraway, and on this substantial encouragement Unglaub and Wagner scored. And again, by one of those curious quick repetitions of history that sometimes happen on the ball field, Uncle Cy does exactly the same thing in the ninth. That is, his slam is to left.

W. W. AULICK. ◆

Legendary right-handed pitcher Cy Young.

September 4, 1908

HAL CHASE QUITS YANKEES IN HUFF

First Baseman Declares He Was Unfairly Criticised by Management.

HAL CHASE, THE YANKEES' first baseman, has deserted the Yankees and is now on his way to his home in San Jose, Cal. Chase left the team without any particular warning, although rumors had been circulated during the last few weeks that Chase was dissatisfied with the conditions as they exist in the Greater New York baseball club. It was stated that Chase, after the release of Clark Griffith, had managerial aspirations, and was very much disappointed when Norman Elberfeld was selected to succeed Griffith. This Chase denied yesterday and said he was willing to work under Elberfeld until stories detrimental to his character and honesty were circulated. These stories, he said, were circulated by the club management.

There has been trouble between Chase and Elberfeld extending over a year. But when Elberfeld was appointed manager it broke out anew, and because he was continually harassed, Chase said he could not give his best services. He admits that on the recent disastrous trip of the Yankees he was unable to do his best because of illness. At times he came out to play when he should have been in bed.

No intimation was received as to Chase's intention, and when he failed to appear at first base yesterday all kinds of rumors went into circulation. The management, however, admitted that the star first baseman had quit. He appeared for morning practice, but after it was over he packed all his belongings and left. He afterward took his trunks and left for the West. Before he went away he gave out the following statement:

I am not satisfied to play under a management that sees fit to give out a story detrimental to my character and questions my integrity and honesty. Such a story appeared in a New York Sunday paper, Aug. 23. I feel that I could not do myself justice under such conditions, and therefore I have decided to quit. I never had managerial ideas.

Chase's charges came as a surprise to President Frank Farrell of the Yankees, who denies that any statement reflecting on Chase's ability or integrity was given out by any person connected with the club, and further that nothing that appeared in any local paper on Aug. 23 could be traced to the club management.

The action of Chase in quitting the Yankees so unceremoniously is almost unprecedented in the history of the National sport. He was treated with the greatest consideration by his club, and, according to President Farrell, his excuse for leaving the team is only a subterfuge to escape criticism.

Hal Chase came to New York four years ago and soon worked himself into the good graces of the fans. His first base play is a revelation. Indeed when in condition Chase is the greatest fielding first baseman that ever played professional baseball. There never was a first sacker that was faster on bunt hits or who ever covered as much territory as Chase.

In 1906 he held out for the highest salary ever paid to a ball player outside of a pitcher in recent years. He was receiving $4,100, but demanded an increase, and it is said that Frank Farrell compromised by giving him a contract calling for $6,000. ◆

September 21, 1910

Hal Chase Must Go or Stallings Will

Special to the New York Times.

CHICAGO, Sept. 20. – MANAGER GEORGE STALLING, of the New York Yankees will leave to-morrow morning for New York to issue an ultimatum to Frank Farrell, President of the club. Stallings will demand that Hal Chase be released from the team and will resign as manager unless this request is granted.

The Yankees' manager's decision is the result of a feud between him and the star first baseman that has been on since mid-season. It is said that Chase, acting with the idea that he would succeed Stallings next season, has been "laying down" and not giving his team his best effort. This is Stallings's idea of it. Chase denies that he knows anything about Mr. Farrell's plans, and also denies that he has not played the best ball of which he was capable.

When the Yankees were in Detroit on their second trip West Chase left them and went home, pleading illness. Some of his team mates and New York Baseball writers allege that he played with Andy Coakley's semi-professional team under an assumed name. When he rejoined the club the battle between him and Stallings grew warmer. Most of the players stuck to their manager and Chase became unpopular with his team mates.

The trouble reached its climax in St. Louis when Stallings, it is said, openly accused Chase of trying to throw a game. Hal resented this, and the pair almost came to blows. Members of the New York team prevented a scrap, but some of them went after Chase when the Yankees were beaten here Monday.

Stallings will tell his story to Mr. Farrell, and unless he changes his mind will resign immediately unless Hal is disciplined. This problem may prove a hard one for Mr. Farrell to solve, as Chase is considered at least as good as any first baseman in the big leagues and is a great drawing card. Men in touch with the team say that he had been selected to manage the Yankees next season, so Stallings's visit with his boss may result in Chase's being appointed at once. ◆

"Prince Hal" Chase, left, of the New York Highlanders and with legendary New York Giants manager John McGraw, 1910.

Feb 23, 1910

WILLIE KEELER LAYS DOWN BAT AND BALL

Famous Baseball Player Voluntarily Retires from New York Americans.

WILLIAM KEELER, THE RIGHT FIELDER of the New York Americans, and one of the best-known players in baseball, has been unconditionally released, at his own request. This is considered a high tribute to a player. Several major league clubs would be glad to get the clever little batsman, and two American League teams made good offers for him, but President Frank Farrell, appreciating Keeler's faithful and valuable service to the club in the past, listened to his request and gave him his release. It is not likely that Keeler will sign up with another club unless it is in the capacity of manager.

Keeler had been with the New York team of

The New York Highlanders on the bench in 1906. Hall of Fame players include Wee Willie Keeler, sixth from right, and Jack Chesbro, fourth from right.

the American League since its establishment in this city in 1903, and has played every season since that time. During his whole baseball career he was one of the most proficient batsmen the game ever saw, having a batting average of over .300 for more than thirteen years. Keeler to-day holds the record for the greatest number of base hits in one season, for no player has ever equaled the remarkable performance the little outfielder made with the Baltimore Orioles in 1897, when he batted out 243 safe hits.

Without question "Willie" Keeler, as he is known to every baseball fan, was the most scientific of batsmen, and his faultless style, as he stood at the plate has often been imitated but never equaled.

Keeler was with the Baltimore team that won three championships—in 1894-5-6—and later went back to Brooklyn, playing with that club in 1899-1900, when it won two championships. In 1903 Keeler left the Brooklyn club and joined the Yankees. In his long and successful career he played with only three clubs. Keeler has a remarkable batting record, his averages since 1894 bring: 1894, .367; 1895, .384; 1896, .392; 1897, .432; 1898, .379; 1899, .376; 1900, .366; 1901, .355; 1902, .342; 1903, .318; 1904, .343; 1905, .302, and 1906, .304. ◆

September 22, 1910

Chase to Manage New York Yankees

Special to The New York Times

CHICAGO, Sept. 21.—HAL CHASE will be manager of the New York American League Club next season. His contract as leader of the Yankees already has been signed and approved and is in the hands of Owner Frank Farrell. Chase gave out this news to-day. It was not exactly news at that, for the events of the last week or two all pointed to just such a condition. But it was the first time a positive announcement of any kind has been made. Hal probably would have maintained silence if Manager George Stallings had remained here, but the latter was on his way to New York to confer with Owner Farrell.

Stallings will meet his employer tomorrow morning and the tidings will be broken to him then. However he won't be surprised, either, for his perfectly good eyes have enabled him to read the handwriting on the wall, the bench, and everywhere else. The present manager's contract does not expire until the end of this season, but there is a possibility that he will be paid off and given a permanent vacation. In that event, Chase will continue the job of managing, which he started to-day.

Chase doesn't believe he is "in wrong" with his team mates. He said to-day they knew as well as he did that he was to manage them in 1911 and that none of them had acted as if displeased by the knowledge. Mr. Farrell will hear Stallings's side of the long argument with Chase at the meeting in New York to-morrow, but nothing George can tell him will make any differences with the owner's plans, which already are laid.

Chase, of course, will continue to play first base and will direct the team from the field. It is understood that his added duties will bring him a fat increase in pay. It remains to be seen whether or not there is truth in the stories that the other players are "sore" at him and will not give their best services under his leadership. ◆

April 30, 1911

SCIENTIFIC BASEBALL HAS CHANGED THE OLD GAME

Quick Thinking, Clever Guessing, Faultless Team Work and Intelligent Signaling Necessary for a Pennant Winner To-day—Teams Made Up of Specialists.

SCIENTIFIC BASEBALL OF TO-DAY—"inside ball" they call it—consists in making the opposing team think you are going to make a play one way, then shift suddenly and do it another.

The modern game has developed quick thinkers and resourceful players such as the pioneers of the game never dreamed of. There are few of what were known as "good all-around" players nowadays. The inside game has developed teams made up of baseball specialists. They excel in one position, are trained with that object in view, and are never called on to play in any other position.

The offensive part of the game has not been developed as the defensive has. Nearly every means of attack in the game to-day was used by ball players years ago, but players of the present day have plotted and schemed until they have devised plays, and tricks for meeting almost every play.

A defense has been evolved by pennant winners that baffles every tangible move of attack. The squeeze play, the hit-and-run play, the delayed steal, the pitch out; all these are made useless when the opposing team is shrewd enough to anticipate what is going to happen and is waiting for them. Guessing, indeed, plays an important part.

If a team detects that its signal has been solved by its opponents, it must shift the play quickly. Then here is where the craftiness of the enemy is seen, for sometimes this second shift is detected, and the tactics of the defense are all changed in an instant to meet the new situation.

Nearly every play in the modern game is signaled to every player on the team. This involves a most intricate set of signs and wigwags which must be changed constantly.

Manager McGraw of the Giants is considered one of the best strategists of the game. In a close game, he is always squatted on the third base line, signaling with his hands, the position of his body, or an occasional remark. McGraw can rattle a pitcher at a critical moment. He often delays the game, or makes a protest to take the pitcher's mind off the batsman.

McGraw, probably more than any other manager, changes the line-up of his offensive at critical moments. With one run needed to win in the ninth inning of a game, the shrewd little manager substitutes a fast runner for a slow one, and sends in a pinch hitter when the man he takes out is just as good with the ash as the man he sends in. But it often wins games for the Giants. This constant changing sometimes rattles the pitcher so badly that he has to be taken out at the climax of a game. McGraw is tricky, always, and never rests during a game.

Another hard working manager is Jennings of Detroit. His code signal is spectacular and original. Hopping up and down on the base line he whoops his famous "E-yah" yell and plucks blades of grass from the sod. Often when he yells "Over the fence, Tyrus," Cobb will bunt; the next time he yells the same thing, Cobb will hit it out.

Many baseball critics believe that inside baseball is overdone. They say it is eliminating the individual player and makes a machine of the men. One man doing all the thinking makes the men mechanical, ready to act only on the suggestion of others. He is afraid to take the initiative.

Inside baseball, like the old-fashioned game, may become stereotyped and get into a rut unless it is constantly changed. The tricks and plays used by a pennant winning team are tried by baseball teams all over the country, just as soon as they are solved. In the minor leagues, teams get the inside ball fever, and every play in the present-day collection of scientific baseball tricks is in constant use from Maine to Texas.

It is the unexpected that counts in baseball. The ability to think quickly enough to anticipate what the other team is planning, and execute some unlooked-for play, is where the science comes in. The day of the conventional cut-and-dried style of play has passed. The team that plays in a rut nowadays doesn't get anywhere.

An excellent example of a mechanical style of play was the Cleveland team a few seasons ago. This organization had enough individual players to develop a pennant winning team, and yet the Naps never threatened the top. At times their playing was brilliant, but in the long run the team played in the same old rut. The resource and the trickery of a McGraw or a Chance were lacking.

Pitching has reached a higher state of scientific development than any other department of the game. In its highest forms it is at times a revelation. Not only the curving of the ball, but the study of the batsmen, their weaknesses and peculiarities, the strength and weaknesses of certain spots in the infield and outfield— all these things the pitcher must know.

The pitcher who throws the ball with terrific speed, a straight, fast ball is scarce. The leader to-day in fast ball pitching is Walter Johnson of the Washington Club. His speed is terrific, and few catchers can receive his service. He has marvelous control of this straight ball, which takes a straight and slightly downward course, and the batsman is invariably late in swinging at it.

Another development of later-day pitching is the moist ball. This curve has the sharpest "break" of any ball that is pitched. Russell Ford of the New York Americans and Ed Walsh of the Chicago White Sox have brought it to its highest scientific stage.

A small spot between the seams of the ball ⟫⟫⟫

Christy Mathewson, right, and John McGraw, Hall of Fame pitcher and manager respectively for the New York Giants, on the dugout steps in the Polo Grounds circa 1908.

《《《 is covered with saliva. The pressure on one side of the ball is increased while the fingers slip easily off the wet spot. This gives the ball an unnatural revolution, and when thrown with speed it takes a sharp break, being almost impossible to hit.

The moist ball and the drop ball are wearing on a pitcher's arm and have ruined many pitchers, but these highly developed curves have also ruined the batting averages on many hard hitters.

In speaking of his fadeaway, Mathewson says: "When mastered, there is no more successful ball than the drop ball. It can be made to break very abruptly or a gradual break can be put on it. When it breaks quickly, the batter invariably hits over it, and misses it entirely. It is the ball I usually rely on when there is a man on third base and no one out.

In the old days, a baseball team had one star pitcher and two or three poor ones. The first pitcher was overworked, but was able to keep up the terrific pace with remarkable vigor.

Radbourne of Providence pitched thirty-seven successive games in 1883, and won twenty-eight of them. Mathewson says that such a great amount of tissue is broken down in the pitching arm during a game that it takes a long time to rebuild it, and no pitcher should be required to pitch in more than two games a week.

The pitcher must have brains. Many a ball player hasn't made good because he had a $10,000 arm and a 10-cent head. Take Pat Flaherty of Boston for instance. He is endowed with nothing great in the line of curves or speed, and yet he can fool the craftiest of batsmen by exerting a marvelous control. He can put the ball just where he wants to. Cy Young had this same faculty. Pitchers of this sort can execute more damage with a straight ball by cutting the corners of the plate, by shooting low or shooting high, than a player with phenomenal curves which he cannot put in the right place.

One of the most remarkable features of modern baseball is the tight defense that has been developed in the infield. There is a vast amount of ground for each man in the inner defense to cover.

Of the present-day players none of the first basemen exhibit the remarkable mechanical execution shown by Hal Chase of the New York Americans. He, too, is one of the quickest thinkers in the game. He can accomplish more than other men in this position, not only because he is endowed with natural baseball sense, but the ease and grace of his physical accomplishments on the field enable him to execute a new and surprising play, to meet an unlooked-for situation with promptness.

The batting of the modern ball player has entirely changed in the past few years. The sluggers of the game's early days are no more. Batting has become a scientific operation. The long, crushing sweep has given way to a short, choppy swing. There are not as many "fence breakers."

High batting averages are not sought for by managers any more. They want a batsman who can hit safely to advance runners on the bases and drive in runs. Willie Keeler developed the short choppy batting stroke and the bunt to a high state of perfection.

The modern batsman can do little guessing. His eye must be on the ball from the minute it leaves the pitcher's hand, and his swing must be timed perfectly.

Base stealing is one of the game's most spectacular features. It gives the player a chance to use his wits and show his intuition. Some of the present-day players disregard the signals and steal anyway. Cobb of Detroit is one of these, and he often goes from first to third on a bunt. Stealing home is another of his pastimes.

Modern baseball has the players thinking and scheming all the time for new plays. The new and unexpected thing wins, for when all the teams are trying to work the same trick it fails. But baseball of the future will improve just as the present-day game is more interesting than the old conventional game. New brains are coming into it every day. The quickest thinkers will always be closest to the pennant. ◆

January 23, 1913

YANKEES WILL PLAY ON POLO GROUNDS

PRESIDENT HARRY N. HEMPSTEAD of the Giants and President Frank J. Farrell of the Yankees signed an agreement yesterday whereby the New York American League Club will play all its championship games on the Polo Grounds next season. The negotiations have been under way for some time and there has been absolutely no friction between the two clubs but the hitches have come in legal technicalities and in a possible conflict of dates.

The last legal obstacle was removed Tuesday when the Yankees were incorporated under a new name, the American League Baseball Club of Manhattan, under the laws of the State of New York. Only the names of Mr. Farrell's legal representatives appear in the papers. The league schedule committee at the recent meeting at Aiken, S. C., arranged the schedule so that there could possibly be no conflict in the dates of the two teams here. Mr. Hempstead and Mr. Farrell met yesterday afternoon at the offices of the Giants and affixed their signatures to a souvenir agreement which gives the Yankees the use of the park for one year.

The situation is a unique one between the major leagues and a few years ago the rivalry was so strong that such an arrangement would have been impossible. The clubs of both leagues have used each other's grounds in one or two major league cities for a short time, but never have National and American League clubs played on the same field in any city during the whole season. The New York American League Club expects that during the next year the park at 225th Street and Broadway will be completed and that the Yankees will play there during the season of 1914.

The present arrangement between the two local league teams has been planned so that there will be no open dates at the Polo Grounds from the opening of the season, April 10, to the close on Oct. 5. The schedule-makers have so dovetailed the schedules of the Giants and the Yankees that the playing dates of the two clubs adjust themselves to each other perfectly. ◆

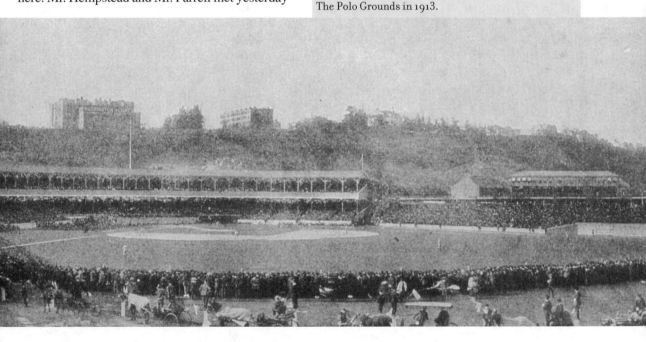

The Polo Grounds in 1913.

January 1, 1915

RUPPERT AND HUSTON BUY THE YANKEES

Farrell Sells New York Baseball Club for $500,000—Donovan Manager.

THE NEW YORK BASEBALL CLUB of the American League was sold yesterday by Frank J. Farrell and associates to Col. Jacob Ruppert, Jr., and Capt. T. L. Huston of Havana. The price is said to have been $500,000, which is a record figure for a franchise which does not include a baseball park and a manager. It is reported that Ruppert and Huston gave $412,000 and the American League made up the difference in the purchase price. Bill Donovan, the former Detroit pitcher, and for the past two seasons manager of the Providence club of the International League, was appointed manager.

Jacob Ruppert will be the President of the club and Capt. Huston will be secretary and treasurer. In a few days the new owners will appoint a business manager, who will probably be some experienced baseball man. Several candidates are already in the field, but the new owners announced last night that they had not yet picked the man for the place.

Mr. Farrell did not sell the club without a pang of regret. He has had the club since the league invaded New York in 1903, and twice came within an ace of winning a pennant. In 1904 he really had a pennant won, but a wild pitch in the last game of the series by the great Jack Chesbro spoiled the Yankees' chances and gave the pennant to Boston. Farrell has tried hard to turn out a winner, but encountered the hardest kind of luck at every turn. There has been constant trouble with managers and internal dissension in the players' ranks.

Col. Ruppert and Capt. Huston are not entering baseball blindly. They know that they have a difficult task before them to build up a new ball club, and Capt. Huston stated last night that too much is not to be expected in the first season or two. In three years, however, the new owners believe that Donovan will be able to turn out a first division club. The Yankees will play at the Polo Grounds next season, but the Giants are anxious for the Yankees to have a park of their own.

Col. Ruppert and Capt. Huston are now considering three sites for the new park. Farrell's grounds at 225th Street and Broadway are under consideration and two sites on property owned by Col. Ruppert. One of these is at 145th Street and Lenox Avenue, which is too small, and the other is in the Bronx. President Johnson stated yesterday that work on the new park would be commenced very soon. ◆

Feb 21, 1915

YANKEES WANT JACKSON.

Ruppert and Huston Willing to Pay Big Price for "Slugger."

WHEN THE AMERICAN LEAGUE assembles here tomorrow, it is expected that an announcement will be made in relation to an important trade to be accomplished with a view of strengthening the Yankees. President Ban Johnson said yesterday that more than one big trade was in view, and he had strong hopes that some of them would go through in order to give the new owners of the club here a better team with which to start the season.

President Johnson refused to divulge the plans the local club's manager, Bill Donovan, had in mind, but it is known that Donovan has been recalled from the South in order to be here tomorrow to take part in the negotiations for new players.

When Manager Donovan visited Cleveland a few weeks ago to sign Roger Peckinpaugh, it is said he had a long conference with the Cleveland club officials in regard to a big trade whereby Outfielder Joe Jackson would come into the possession of the New York club. It is understood that the new owners are willing to pay a high price for the Cleveland star. Donovan wants a hitter of Jackson's caliber for his outfield, as his pitching staff is a good one, and his infield should come up to form this season.

A hard-hitting outfield would go a long way toward making the Yankees a very formidable club, and it is expected that a strong effort will be made to land Jackson. The Yankee officials yesterday refused to discuss what players they would try to land during the meeting tomorrow. ◆

Feb 16, 1916

YANKS BUY HOME RUN BAKER FOR $25,000

Famous Batsman Signs Contract for Three Years

JOHN FRANKLIN BAKER OF HOME RUN FAME, the player who on two occasions crushed the world's championship aspirations of the Giants at the Polo Grounds and in Philadelphia with home-run hits, was purchased yesterday by the New York American League club, and will play third base on the team next season. Baker signed a contract for 1916, 1917, and 1918.

The deal was consummated at a four-hour conference at Ruppert's brewery yesterday between Colonel Jacob Ruppert, Captain T. L. Huston, and Manager Connie Mack of the Athletics. The price paid for the player has not been announced, but it is stated that the New York club paid $25,000 for the player and his contract calls for $8,000 a year.

Before the opening of the playing season last Spring Baker demanded a larger salary than that called for under his contract with the Athletics, which had another year to run. Mack refused to grant the increase and Baker retired to his home at Trappe, Md., remaining out of professional baseball all season. Mack was quoted during the season as saying that he would refuse to sell Baker until his contract expired.

Baker has a record in the American League that was unusual. Never a brilliant third baseman, he was very valuable as a batsman, and drove in more runs than any player in the league for five successive years. From 1909 to 1914 Baker drove in more than 100 runs a year. His hitting has always been timely, and if he comes up to his past prowess with the bat during the coming season, the Yankees should be one of the best clubs in the American League. »»

《《《 The tale of how Baker acquired his home-run fame has not yet been forgotten by New York baseball fans. In the world's series of 1911, after Mathewson, by his great pitching, had beaten the Athletics in the opening game. Baker pounded the ball over the fence in Philadelphia in the sixth inning of the second game and the Giants were beaten. It was in the third game of the series, with Mathewson again pitching, and after he had held the Athletics scoreless for eight innings, that Baker again swung his mighty bat and hit the ball into the right field stands at the Polo Grounds and tied the score, the Athletics winning in the eleventh inning.

Baker is the type of batsman known as the clean-up hitter, and his drives on home and foreign fields have caused him to be feared by all clubs, and when he comes to bat, the outfielders back up to the limit. For several years he led the American League in home-run drives, and the records show that he has driven in more runs than any man in the Johnson organization. Baker is one inch short of six feet, and weighs, in playing condition, 175 pounds. ◆

April 25, 1917

NO-HIT GAME IS PITCHED BY MOGRIDGE AGAINST WORLD'S CHAMPION RED SOX

Special to The New York Times.

BOSTON, April 24.—GEORGE MOGRIDGE, Wild Bill Donovan's young left-handed pitcher, took life membership in the no-hit club this afternoon, flinging the Yankees to a 2 to 1 victory over the Red Sox. The champions scored on the combination of two passes, an error, and a sacrifice fly, but all afternoon they made nothing

Oct 26, 1917

HUGGINS SIGNED AS MANAGER OF YANKS

MILLER J. HUGGINS, WHO FOR THE past five years has managed the St. Louis Cardinals, yesterday was signed as manager of the Yankees to succeed Bill Donovan, who has piloted the New York club for the past three seasons. Huggins's appointment did not come as a surprise, as his name has been associated with the position since he had several conferences last Summer with Jacob Ruppert, President of the Yankees, and Ban Johnson, President of the American League. Huggins's contract is for two years.

The new Yankee leader is considered one of the smartest managers in the game and was able to lift the Cardinals from their lowly position to a place in the sunny first division. Huggins knows the game thoroughly and was rated one of the

that looked the least bit like a safe hit, Mogridge having a great mixture of slow and fast service, which was continually effective.

Dutch Leonard, who held the box against the Yankees, held them scoreless for five innings and then was hit for a run, finally losing the game in the ninth, when McNally and Cady did some weird throwing which materially aided the High-landers in clinching the victory. On the merits of Mogridge's work, however, they surely were en-titled to the game. So effective was the pitching of the New Yorker that the champions only four times drove the ball beyond the limits of the infield, and sure-handedness on easy chances was about all that was called for in the way of infielding.

Usually in no-hit games the boxman's support has been an important factor; not so today, for in spite of three fielding miscues back of him, Mogridge made the other chances easy, declin-ing to become rattled. His pitching of to-day will go down into the history of the game as a really remarkable individual effort.

Fumbles by Peckinpaugh and Maisel, with one pass, allowed three of the Red Sox to reach first base. The only other Bostonian to get on the paths was Barry, who was passed in the seventh inning. Then the champions got their lone run on Maisel's low throw to Peckinpaugh while trying for a forceout, an intentional pass to Walker and a sacrifice boost to Gilhooley by pinch hitter Jimmy Walsh. Otherwise Mogridge had the champions standing on their heads all the afternoon. ◆

brainiest second basemen of baseball when he played with Cincinnati and St. Louis. He said yesterday, after signing his contract, that his playing days were over, as his throwing arm has not been right for the past few seasons.

Huggins is the ninth in the long list of Yan-kee managers. First there was Clark Griffith, and in succession came Norman Elberfeld, George Stallings, Hal Chase, Harry Wolverton, Frank Chance, Roger Peckinpaugh, and Bill Donovan. Elberfeld and Peckinpaugh were only managers pro tem and filled in a few weeks when other managers were dropped.

Huggins's wide knowledge of the manage-rial end of the game and his skill at developing young players should be a big factor in steering the Yankees to success next season. Huggins is a successful disciplinarian and has the faculty of getting the best work out of his players. He has a strong personality, and there is no reason to be-lieve that he will not be an excellent choice as the leader of the Yankees. ◆

Miller Huggins, Yankees manager from 1918-1929.

Feb 5, 1918

HUGGINS COMPILES DON'TS FOR YANKS

Training Rules to be Rigidly Enforced by New Manager of Local Club.

MANAGER MILLER HUGGINS of the Yankees will curb the cigarette habit among his players this season. He stated yesterday that he will prohibit smoking at the baseball park and in and about the clubhouse, and means to have the rule enforced. Away from the park the players' smoking habits will not be curtailed, but it will go hard with the athlete who attempts to take a puff while he is at the park. Huggins believes that it is detrimental instead of beneficial to enforce a rule forbidding smoking entirely.

It is the constant smoking up to the time he goes out on the playing field that affects the players' wind, and by not smoking for a couple of hours before playing time Huggins figures that the bad effects are not especially injurious. The new Yankee manager will also insist on a reasonable hour for retiring, and will get the players up reasonably early in the morning. He is not going to tolerate any late rising, which necessitates a quick breakfast and a hurried trip to get to the baseball park on time for the afternoon game.

Judging from the way the new Yankee leader talks, the days of lax discipline in the club are over. With Huggins baseball is a serious business, and the main object of that business is to win. Any rules which will be laid down by the new manager will be executed with that one object in view. There will be no "iron fist" system of discipline, for Huggins is not a driving manager. He attains his purpose with his players by impressing upon them that it is to their own advantage to play the best and hardest when they are on the ball field.

There will probably be more morning practice with the Yankees this year than ever before. While Huggins has no set plan about this matter, he will have morning practice if the club does not play up to the standard he expects. If the new Yankee pilot sees that the players do their best in the championship games, there will be little morning practice, but if there is any sign of indifference, it will mean that the players will have to buckle down and hustle until this spirit disappears. ◆

September 28, 1919

RUTH WALLOPS OUT HIS 28TH HOME RUN

Terrific Crash Over the Polo Grounds Stands Sets New World's Record.

A new world's batting record was made up at the Polo Grounds yesterday, when Babe Ruth, Boston's superlative slugger, boosted his twenty-eighth home run of the season high over the right field grand stand into Manhattan Field, which adjoins the Brush Stadium. This smashes the thirty-five-year-old record made by Ed Williamson of Chicago, who was credited with twenty-seven homers in 1884.

Ruth's glorious smash yesterday was the longest drive ever made at the Polo Grounds. It came in the ninth inning of the second game of a double-header with the Yankees and tied the score at 1 to 1. Bob Shawkey was doing the pitching and he heaved over a slow curve, hoping to fool Ruth as he has done before.

Ruth stood firmly on his sturdy legs like the Colossus of Rhodes, and, taking a mighty swing at the second ball pitched to him, catapulted the pill for a new altitude and distance record. Several seasons ago Joe Jackson hit a home run over the top of the right field stand but the ball landed on the roof. Ruth's bang yesterday cleared the stand by many yards and went over into the weeds in the next lot.

The Boston mauler not long ago made his twenty-sixth home run at the Polo Grounds, smashing the modern home run record made by Buck Freeman. Then it was discovered in the dusty archives of the game that Williamson had made twenty-seven in one season. Ruth's mark now surpasses all home run achievements, ancient or modern. Ruth got a great reception from the crowd of 5,000 or more fans, and throughout the afternoon he was hailed with cheers every time he came up to bat.

The menace of Ruth's mighty bat was always a shadow in Shawkey's path. In the sixth inning Ruth shot a mighty blow to right centre field for three bases. It looked like a home run, but Ruth in his anxiety to break the record cut second base by a few feet and was declared out by the watchful umpire Tommy Connolly.

Again in the twelfth inning, Ruth brought the crowd to its feet by thumping a tremendous slam to deep right centre which for a moment looked as if it were going to clear the centre field bleachers. Young Chick Fewster then covered himself with glory by romping back at top speed to snare the ball just as it was getting away. ◆

Babe Ruth in a Boston Red Sox uniform in 1919 before he was sold to the Yankees.

2 THE RUTH-GEHRIG ERA

Babe Ruth and Lou Gehrig defined the Yankees and baseball itself in America's best of times, the Roaring Twenties, and in its worst of times, the Great Depression.

The Babe hit 60 home runs in 1927, a record that endured for more than three decades. He hit a career total of 714, a monument for nearly four decades. With him in the batting order from 1920 through 1934, the Yankees won seven American League pennants and four World Series. Nearly a century after George Herman Ruth's arrival in 1914 as a rookie with the Red Sox, he reigns as the most complete player in baseball history. Before he hit all those homers as an outfielder, he was the best left-handed pitcher in the American League, with a 23–12 record and a 1.75 ERA in 1916 and a 24–13 record with a 2.01 ERA in 1917. Nobody else has ever put up the numbers he did as both a slugger and a pitcher.

Gehrig, the muscular first baseman known as the Iron Horse, contributed to seven American League pennants and six World Series titles from 1926 through 1938 before the disease named for him ended his record 2,130 consecutive-game streak in 1939. He hit 493 home runs. He had a .340 career average and a .652 slugging average. He drove in 100 or more runs in 14 seasons, with a high of 184 in 1931—still the American League record. He had 200 or more hits eight times, with a high of 220 in 1936. He hit 30 or more homers 10 times, with a high of 49 in 1936. He had 30 or more doubles 12 times, with a high of 52 in 1927. He had 400 or more total bases five times; the Babe did that only twice, Hank Aaron only once.

The Babe was always himself. When he shook hands with President Warren G. Harding on a brutally hot day in Washington, he said, "Hot as hell, ain't it, Prez?"

In an era of only afternoon games, he was a legendary carouser. His roommate Ping Bodie said, "I don't room with the Babe. I room with his suitcase." But when the Babe was young and lean at 6'2" and 190 pounds, he occasionally could be, shall we say, cantankerous. After

★ ★ ★

Babe Ruth and Lou Gehrig in Yankee Stadium before a game with the St. Louis Browns, on July 12, 1929. The Babe and Lou would combine that season for a total of 81 home runs, 248 runs scored, and 280 runs batted in.

his first World Series with the Yankees in 1921, he defied Commissioner Kenesaw Mountain Landis's rule against barnstorming; he was fined his Series share of $5,265 and suspended for the first six weeks of the 1922 season. On his return, he was suspended for barging into the stands after a fan who loudly criticized his .093 average at the time. Reformed in 1923 for the opening of the original Yankee Stadium, "The House that Ruth Built," he batted .393 with 41 homers and the Yankees finally won the Series.

With his wife Helen about to leave him in 1925, he also was grumbling about Miller Huggins, the manager. When he arrived late at the ballpark in St. Louis after a long night, Huggins fined him $5,000 and suspended him indefinitely. The Babe appealed to Ruppert, but the owner backed Huggins, who let him stew for a week until he apologized. That season was a disaster, the Yankees tumbling to seventh as he batted .290 with 25 homers.

Humbled, the Babe changed. For the rest of his career, he was mostly on his best behavior, at least publicly, and the Yankees flourished.

With the young Gehrig at first base and batting cleanup, they won three consecutive pennants, losing the 1926 Series to the St. Louis Cardinals but sweeping the Pirates and the Cardinals the next two years. More than eight decades later, the 1927 Yankees are still thought of as perhaps the best team ever. They had a 110–44 record, a .304 team batting average, and a 3.20 team ERA. The Babe hit .356 with 164 RBI, but those numbers faded into the shadow of his record 60 homers.

The Babe still had headlines in him, notably his "called" home run in his last Yankees pennant-winner's 1932 Series sweep of the Chicago Cubs. But for all the fun of that homer, the Babe wasn't happy. He resented the Yankees' hiring of Joe McCarthy as manager in 1931: he had wanted the job. After batting .288 with 22 homers in 1934, the Yankees released him so he could join the Braves in Boston, whence he came. He would never manage a major league team. Then again, he had not always managed himself.

Lou Gehrig, in contrast, was the ideal teammate—always in the lineup, never in a dispute. He was also a Yankees rarity: a New Yorker. Born there, grew up there, went to college there, played there, and died there a beloved victim of an incurable disease. As if ⟫⟫

≪≪≪   destined for the Yankees, Henry Louis Gehrig, the son of German immigrants Heinrich and Christina, was born on Second Avenue in Manhattan on June 19, 1903, the Highlanders' first year. On the Columbia University varsity, he hit several long home runs that so impressed scout Paul Krichell, the Yankees signed him for a $2,000 bonus and $1,500 for the rest of the 1923 season at their Hartford farm team. After making the Yankees' opening-day roster in 1925, he pinch-hit for shortstop Pee-Wee Wanninger on June 1st. The next day Huggins decided to rest Wally Pipp, the aging first baseman. Gehrig was in the lineup, to stay. And what a stay it was, until its tragic end. His strength and timing gone, his consecutive-game streak ended on May 2, 1939. He never played again. Two months later, on Lou Gehrig Appreciation Day at Yankee Stadium, he described himself as "the luckiest man on the face of the earth." Two years later, on June 2, 1941, he died at age 37. As baseball mourned, Mayor Fiorello LaGuardia ordered city flags flown at half-staff.

January 6, 1920

RUTH BOUGHT BY NEW YORK AMERICANS FOR $125,000, HIGHEST PRICE IN BASEBALL ANNALS

YANKS BUY BABE RUTH FOR $125,000

Highest Purchase Price in Baseball History Paid for Game's Greatest Slugger.

BABE RUTH OF THE BOSTON RED SOX, baseball's super-slugger, was purchased by the Yankees yesterday for the largest cash sum ever paid for a player. The New York Club paid Harry Frazee of Boston $125,000 for the sensational batsman who last season caused such a furore in the national game by batting out twenty-nine home runs, a record in long-distance clouting.

Colonel Ruppert, President of the Yanks, said that he had taken over Ruth's Boston contract, which has two years more to run. This contract calls for a salary of $10,000 a year. Ruth recently announced that he would refuse to play for $10,000 next season, although the Boston Club has received no request for a raise in salary.

Manager Miller Huggins is now in Los Angeles negotiating with Ruth. It is believed that the Yankee manager will offer him a new contract which will be satisfactory to the Colossus of the bat.

President Ruppert said yesterday that Ruth would probably play right field for the Yankees. He played in left field for the Red Sox last season, and had the highest fielding average among the outfielders, making only two errors during the season.

HOME RUN RECORD IN DANGER.
The acquisition of Ruth strengthens the Yankee club in its weakest department. With the added hitting power of Ruth, Bob Shawkey, one of the Yankee pitchers, said yesterday the New York

club should be a pennant winner next season. For several seasons the Yankees have been experimenting with outfielders, but never have been able to land a consistent hitter. The short right field wall at the Polo Grounds should prove an easy target for Ruth next season and, playing seventy-seven games at home, it would not be surprising if Ruth surpassed his home-run record of twenty-nine circuit clouts next Summer.

Ruth was such a sensation last season that he supplanted the great Ty Cobb as baseball's greatest attraction, and in obtaining the services of Ruth for next season the New York club made a ten-strike which will be received with the greatest enthusiasm by Manhattan baseball fans.

Ruth's crowning batting accomplishment came at the Polo Grounds last Fall when he hammered one of the longest hits ever seen in Harlem over the right field grandstand for his twenty-eighth home run, smashing the home record of twenty-seven, made by Ed Williamson way back in 1884. The more modern home-run record, up to last season, had been held by Buck Freeman, who made twenty-five home runs when a member of the Washington club in 1899.

Ruth's home-run drives were distributed all over the circuit, and he is the one player known to the game who hit a home run on every park on the circuit in the same season.

SPECIALIZES IN LONG HITS.

Ruth's batting feats last season will stand for many years to come, unless he betters the record himself with the aid of the short right field under Coogan's Bluff. The record he made last season was a masterpiece of slugging. He went up to the bat 432 times in 130 games and produced 139 hits. Of these hits 75 were for extra bases. Not only did he make 29 home runs, but he also made 34 two-baggers and 12 three-baggers.

Ruth scored the greatest number of runs in the American League last season, crossing the plate 103 times. Cobb scored only 97 runs last year. Ruth was so dangerous that the American League pitchers were generous with their passes and the superlative hitter walked 101 times, many of these passes being intentional. Ruth also struck out more than any other batsman in the league, fanning 58 times. He also made three sacrifice hits and he stole seven bases.

Ruth is a native of Baltimore and is 26 years old, just in his prime as a baseball player. He was discovered by Jack Dunn, owner of the Baltimore Club, while playing with the baseball team of Mount St. Joseph's, a school which Ruth attended in that city, in 1913. In 1914 Ruth played with the Baltimore team and up to that time little attention had been paid to his batting. It was as a pitcher that he attracted attention in Baltimore. Boston bought Ruth along with Ernie Shore and some other players in 1914. The price paid for Ruth was said to have been $2,700.

HOLDS WORLD'S SERIES RECORD

Ruth was a big success in the major league from the start. In 1916, when the Red Sox won the pennant, he led the American League pitchers in effectiveness and in the world's series of 1916 and 1918. Ruth hung up a new world's series pitching record for shut out innings. He pitched twenty-eight consecutive scoreless innings, which beat the record of twenty-seven scoreless innings made in world's series games by Christy Mathewson of the Giants.

For the past few seasons Ruth's ambition has been to play regularly. While he was doing only pitching duty with Boston he was a sensational pinch hitter and when he played regularly in the outfield last season he blossomed forth as the most sensational batsman the game has ever known. He was also a great success as a fielder and last season he made only two errors and had 230 putouts. He also had twenty-six assists, more than any outfielder in the American League. This was because of his phenomenal throwing arm. His fielding average last season was .992. Ruth didn't do much pitching last season. He pitched thirteen games and won eight and lost five.

Manager Huggins is expected back in New York at the end of next week with Ruth's contract in his inside pocket.

The new contract which the Yankees have offered Ruth is said to be almost double the ⟫⟫⟫

Boston figure of $10,000 a year. While he is out on the coast interviewing Ruth, Huggins is also getting into line, not only Duffy Lewis, but also Bob Meusel, the sensational young slugger of the Pacific Coast League, who is regarded by baseball scouts as the minor league find of the year.

THE PERFECT HITTER.

Ruth's principle of batting is much the same as the principle of the golfer. He comes back slowly, keeps his eye on the ball and follows through. His very position at the bat is intimidating to the pitcher. He places his feet in perfect position. He simply cannot step away from the pitch if he wants to. He can step only one way—in. The weight of Ruth's body when he bats is on his left leg. The forward leg is bent slightly at the knee. As he stands facing the pitcher more of his hips and back are seen by the pitcher than his chest or side. When he starts to swing his back is half turned toward the pitcher. He goes as far back as he can reach, never for an instant taking his eye off the ball as it leaves the pitcher's hand.

The greatest power in his terrific swing comes when the bat is directly in front of his body, just half way in the swing. He hits the ball with terrific impact and there is no player in the game whose swing is such a masterpiece of batting technique. ◆

RUTH NOT SURPRISED.

Home-Run King Expected Red Sox Would Sell Him.

LOS ANGELES, CAL., JAN. 5.—Babe Ruth, champion home-run hitter, tonight said he had had no information regarding his reported sale by the Boston Americans to the New York American club until told by The Associated Press that Colonel Ruppert, President of the Yankees, had announced the deal.

"I am not surprised, however," he added. "When I made my demand on the Red Sox for $20,000 a year, I had an idea they would choose to sell me rather than pay the increase, and I knew the Yankees were the most probable purchasers in that event." ◆

YANKEES ARE 1921 LEAGUE CHAMPIONS

Defeat Athletics in First Game of Double-Header and Clinch Pennant.

THE LONG FIGHT OF THE YANKEES for the pennant symbolizing the championship of the American League was ended and won yesterday afternoon at the Polo Grounds when Elmer Miller, pelting with all his speed after Clarence Galloway's crash to deep left centre, snared the ball in extended hands for the final out of the first game. The score of the tussle whose outcome settled the abiding place of the cherished gonfalon for the Summer of 1922 was 5 to 3.

Cheers and other outcries, varying from basso profundo to falsetto, but all indicating a single sentiment—joy that the game quest of many years had been rewarded at last—blended into a tumult in the stands. Down below in the press box the two Colonels, Jacob Ruppert and T. L. Huston, owners of the Yankees, were compelled to submit, willy-nilly, to a congratulatory reception from their crowding friends. The triumphant blare of a band situated half way up the incline in the centre of the grandstand became as a drop of melody in a sea of sound. The Yankees had captured their first pennant and the world's series of 1921 would have only one stage.

After the excitement had died down and the triumphant athletes, as well as their foemen, the Athletics had had a few minutes in which to rest, the second affray was an eleven-act comedy that wound up the happy afternoon, with Babe Ruth as their comedian, and the newly crowned sovereigns of the younger big league finally won the verdict by the score of 7 to 6. ◆

The New York Yankees pose for their team portrait in 1921. In the middle row Babe Ruth sits fourth from right and Waite Hoyt second from right, while manager Miller Huggins is in the front row, center.

GIANTS WIN SERIES; NEHF BEATS HOYT, 1-0

Peck's Error in First Gives Nationals Only Run—Ruth Leads Lost Cause in Ninth.

ONE LONE RUN, conceived of a pass and reared to its fullest growth without the aid of anything resembling a base hit, was the difference between two fighting ball clubs at the Polo Grounds yesterday. That same lone run, which literally dropped into the lap of the Giants in the first inning, settled the eighth game of the world's series between Giants and Yankees in favor of the National League pennant winners and brought to John McGraw's 1921 machine the baseball championship of the world. The 1-0 victory of the Giants was the fifth for the McGrawmen in the eight games played.

The deciding battle, which was in itself a fitting finale to one of the hardest fought series ever played, had a climax of its own that was perhaps the most thrilling finish in world's series' history. Three Giants played perfect parts in a performance that killed off two Yankees when the least slip might have carried the American Leaguers to a tie score, with the chance of victory.

In a cloud of dust at third base Aaron Ward lunged for the bag, carrying with him the last hope of American League success. Frank Frisch, stalwart guardian of the final turn for the McGraw forces, took a throw from George Kelly and hurled himself into the path of the flying Yankee. With both players sprawled on the ground Frisch raised his hand to show a glistening white ball, Umpire Ernie Quigley snapped his right arm skyward to denote that the runner was out, and the 1921 world's series became history.

The Yankees' half of the ninth had previously given the game a touch of the dramatic such as few world's series crowds have been per-   ⟫⟫⟫

The Yankees playing at the Polo Grounds in 1921.

<<< mitted to gaze upon. From the start of the game Babe Ruth, forced by injury to retire from the series, had been moving back and forth between the third base coaching box and the Yankee dugout to play what seemed to be the only part left for him in the fight of the Yankees. Babe was bundled up in a gray sweater, which added somewhat to his waist line, and the belief was general that Ruth was to be no more than an onlooker and exhorter in this particular game.

When the Yankees went to their dugout to start the closing half of the ninth, Charley O'Leary, who had been coaching at first base, moved over to third and Devormer, substitute catcher, went to the box near first. Then came the thrill that turned a big part of the crowd into a frenzy. Ruth, with left elbow encased in a heavy bandage, moved plateward to take a swing in place of Pipp, who is not very successful against southpaws, though he had made one of the four hits off Nehf earlier in the game.

Every fan in that stand, whether a Giant or a Yankee partisan, knew the ordeal through which Ruth had gone since the series opened, knew the fight that he made, even at the expense of health, that he might aid his team in its battle for a world's championship. Every one knew about the long incision, the draining tube, the bruised knee, the charley horse and the doctors' orders that Ruth should not play. That he could not swing a bat without pain was an open secret but Babe was on his way out to swing in spite of pain and there arose from stands and bleachers one of the most rousing outbursts of applause that any player ever drew. Partisan was cast to the winds in the tribute to as game an athlete as ever wore spikes. Yankee followers welcomed him with the hope that he would prevail against the one-run lead of the Mc-Graw men. Giant followers applauded him for his courage and then hoped that Art Nehf would prove his master at this trying time.

Nehf won the battle. Babe fouled off one, missed a hard swing at another, let a ball glide by and then swung again, bounding to Kelly for an unassisted play at first base.

As he came back to the bench, with head bowed in disappointment or perhaps to hide the twinges of a new pain that had developed from his three swings, Ruth again was singled out by the fans for a remarkable demonstration. It was admiration for effort and a tribute to grit which would not be stilled even by failure. ◆

October 1, 1922

YANKEES PREVAIL IN PENNANT RACE

Clinch Their Second American League Flag by Trouncing Red Sox, 3 to 1.

THE YANKEES ARE "IN." They defeated the Boston Red Sox yesterday, 3 to 1, and brought to a close one of the hardest fought campaigns in the history of the American League. Nothing can beat them now. The Browns also won yesterday, and they may win again today for all that New York cares. Yesterday St. Louis was a dangerous menace; this morning it is merely a city on the Mississippi River.

New York spent an anxious day waiting for the news from Boston. The tickers were watched by thousands. Newspaper offices got hundreds of anxious requests over the telephone wires. At the Polo Grounds, where the Giants were practicing with the Braves for their part of the world's series, the crowd cheered wildly as every inning went up on the scoreboard. When the local game was over and the Yankees still had an inning to go, hundreds of the fans surrounded the press box and had the ninth inning read to them play by play. There was a great roar as the game ended, and the news spread around the park like wildfire.

Over in the Yankee offices, where Business Manager Ed Barrow was almost completely surrounded by clerks and ticket applications, the atmosphere was chill and dark in the early afternoon. Officials of the club were frankly worried over the situation. Lacking a news ticker, Barrow had the news from Boston brought in by telephone, and it was fifteen minutes after the first inning score was received in this city before the Yankee business manager knew the glad tidings.

"You can say for me that that was the sweetest music I ever heard," he said after the game. "Now we can go ahead and rush these world's series tickets out in the mails. Probably the tickets will not be mailed before Monday, and they will be in the hands of purchasers by Tuesday at the latest. I'm glad those Yankees didn't delay another day."

In many respects the American League race this year was the most sensational since 1908, when three clubs fought it out down the stretch run. By midseason the Browns and Yankees had virtually eliminated the six other teams. Throughout late July and all of August the two leaders battled for position. Never more than two and a half games separated them, and as the race swung into September St. Louis, with a pennant looming up as the brightest of possibilities, became a baseball-crazed city.

It was not hard to understand the feel- »»

◀◀◀ ings of the Mound City. Its last pennant had been won away back in 1888, thirty-four years ago. Popular interest was at fever heat. The Browns, back from a successful Eastern trip were dined and fêted.

Then came, in mid-September, the Yankees-Browns series at Sportsman's Park, St. Louis, in many respects the most sensational set of games in baseball annals. It was agreed beforehand that the pennant was at stake; the team which won two games would have not only a substantial lead, but also a moral advantage.

The Yankees beat Urban Shocker in the first game, but that wasn't all of sunny sands of California. But it is a nice question whether the interest will be as great, now that New York has won four pennants in two consecutive years. Students of the game are looking for a reaction from the Manhattan monopoly, and they expect it this year.

To judge by the advance ticket sale the 1922 series will be no weakling. Officials of both Yankees and Giants reported their office forces literally overwhelmed by ticket applications, money orders and certified checks. Letters have been received from all parts of the country and from many foreign countries. The Giants yesterday were nearly at the end of their reserved seat supply; the Yankees, retarded by the lateness of their team in clinching the pennant, were not so far advanced. Both clubs have exhausted their slim supply of box seats.

However, much still remains for the common, or garden, variety of fan. Ten thousand upper grand tickets, all of which tier is unreserved, and 12,000 bleacher seats will be placed on sale at the Polo Grounds each day at 10 A.M., when the gates are opened. The purchasers of these tickets will be required to enter the park at once in order to forestall ticket scalpers.

Following world's series tradition, no fans will be allowed on the playing field. Standing room will be available in the rear of the ground stand. The only concession made by the two clubs will be to raise the green screen in centre field, making room for a few thousand more persons at the cost of spoiling the batters' background.

Police arrangements were completed yesterday afternoon at a conference between police officials and the two baseball clubs. Under the general command of Inspector Joseph Sweeney, a force of 200 officers will keep order outside the grounds. Inside the gates private policemen employed by the clubs will be on duty.

Police officials said yesterday that a less rigid system than last year will be set up in Eighth Avenue and on the Speedway. No deadlines will be established for automobiles and the fans will be allowed to approach as close to the grounds as conditions permit. Those who have tickets will be hustled along by the turnstiles, and those who want to buy tickets will be formed in line.

What of George Herman Ruth? This is one of the biggest questions. The Babe promises to supply most of the national interest in the series. From Kennebunkport to Santa Fé fans will be watching Ruth. He has been injured and suspended and fined. He had to retire early last October, taking his injured arm with him. It looks offhand as if this series will be the Babe's big chance, and the whole nation will be watching for his doings.

This country-wide curiosity will be satisfied by a comprehensive press system. Newspaper men will be present from practically every State. At press headquarters in the Hotel Commodore preparations are being made for more than three hundred writers, and the two clubs will join in caring for the reporters. A special press section has been installed at the Polo Grounds directly behind the centre of the diamond and dozens of extra telegraph wires will be looped up to handle the story of the series. ◆

October 6, 1922

FANS IN UPROAR AS TIE GAME IS CALLED; RECEIPTS TO CHARITY

Thousands in a Riotous Protest After Umpire Halts Play

He Defies Hecklers and Calls Them "Cowards"

INFURIATED BECAUSE THE SECOND GAME of the world's series between the Yankees and Giants was called at 4:45 o'clock yesterday afternoon on account of darkness at the end of the tenth inning with the score tied at 3-3, five thousand fans surrounded the field box of Kenesaw Mountain Landis and hurled jeers and insults at the high commissioner of baseball.

After attempting to pacify the crowd, Mr. and Mrs. Landis had to be escorted from the Polo Grounds under the protection of a cordon of police. Newspapers were thrown at him as he crossed the field, and hundreds of fans took up the cry of "Crook! Robber!" Others shouted that the stopping of the game was a trick by the club owners to get more money from the series.

Commissioner Landis answered this charge in a formal statement issued last night from »»»

Babe Ruth at bat as Joe Dugan leads off first with Giants pitcher Art Nehf on the mound at the Polo Grounds.

«« his headquarters at the Hotel Commodore. After conferring with the players and club owners he announced that the two teams had decided to turn the entire receipts for yesterday's game-- $120,554—over to a fund for disabled soldiers, and to other New York charities. This means that nobody in baseball will benefit financially by the addition of another game to the series.

But the fans at the Polo Grounds thought otherwise. "Baseball's a crooked game," they shouted to the man who left the Federal bench to make baseball clean. "How about Phil Douglas?" a fan shouted, referring to the Giant pitcher who was barred from baseball this Summer. "Where are the Chicago White Sox?" yelled another within hearing of the chief executive of baseball.

HILDEBRAND CALLS GAME.

It was the most dramatic ending that any world's series game ever had. Just a few minutes before the crowd had been in a state of high anticipation. The score was tied, the pitchers were engaged in a great battle, and it looked like either team's game. It was a sort of paradise for the fan, but the paradise was not to last long.

The Yankees were the last to bat in the tenth inning. The great Babe Ruth came up and lifted a high foul to Frank Snyder. Pipp rolled an easy grounder to Kelly. Bob Meusel hit a high foul fly and Snyder ran back to the screen to make the catch.

As soon as the ball settled into his glove, the Yankee players ran out on the field, ready to resume play. But George Hildebrand, the umpire-in-chief behind the plate, wheeled around, held up his hand and announced in a voice which few persons heard that the game was called on account of darkness.

Bewildered at first, the crowd was slow in acting. Most of the record-breaking throng of 37,020 grumbled to itself for a moment, squinted appraisingly at the sky to see how much daylight there really was left and then began filing slowly to the exits. Others started at once for Mr. Landis's box, which was near the Yankee dugout on the first base side.

Before the ex-Judge knew what was going on hundreds had surrounded his box, where Mrs.

Landis also sat.

Some of the fans demanded to know why the game had been called. Other fans began jeering, and the chorus behind took up the refrain.

"Let the game go on," they shouted. "Play another inning, or give us our money back."

"Barnum was right, and we're the suckers," shouted a red-faced individual as he shook his fist at Judge Landis. "The game was called to give those fakers another chance at our money," yelled another.

Catcalls and boos floated through the air. A voice spoke up to ask the Judge if he got $100,000 a year for this. Other fans began shouting "Fight, fight!" and special park policemen rushed to the scene.

LANDIS TRIES TO CALM CROWD.

Before they got there Mr. Landis stood up in his box, hatless, his white hair shaking like a mane, and held up his hand for silence. But he got nothing more than a fresh outburst of jeers. He attempted to talk to the mob, but his voice was lost in the uproar. Mrs. Landis stood at her husband's side and smiled bravely as the fans swirled and eddied around the front of the box.

The police arrived and wanted to escort Commissioner Landis from the park, but he waved them aside with a gesture and said: "Get away from me; I'm not afraid of any crowd in New York. I'll make my own way from the field."

Waving his cane in the air and his eyes flashing in deep anger, the Commissioner pushed the crowd away with his elbow and slowly made his way down to the field. Mrs. Landis, still smiling, went with him. The crowd surrounded the pair in such deep mass that the police were cut off from their charges. More taunts were hurled, and as Mr. Landis neared the right field bleachers, hundreds of persons, leaning over the edge, jeered him and threw folded newspapers in his direction.

Waving his black hat in his hand, the Commissioner walked slowly across the field. Once he turned back on the crowd which was dogging his footsteps and shook his fist at them.

"You cowards!" he cried. He hurled other retorts at the howling fans, and his face was quivering with anger.

After passing through the exit gate to beneath the bleachers, the Judge found other fans blocking his way to the street. Finding this path impassable, the escorting police tacked to the right, forced a wedge through the crowd and led Judge Landis to the club offices. Later he walked, unescorted, to his automobile.

No attempt was made to strike a blow at the Commissioner. He minimized the incident at first and said, "That happens to people every day, doesn't it?"

"I know baseball fans," he said, "and I was never for a moment in fear of physical harm. In fact, I asked the police not to try to pick a path for me across the field. I was perfectly able to make my own way without assistance."

Judge Landis's statement was borne out by the actual situation as he made his way across the field to the clubhouse, surrounded by thousands of booing and jeering fans.

After Mr. Landis had left the field, the furious fans swirled around the press box and informed the newspaper men that they—the fans—had seen their last game of ball. Hundreds of others swarmed out to the club houses of the teams and waited there for the players to come out.

Babe Ruth heard the commotion outside and emerged in trousers and undershirt. When told that the fans were jeering Landis, the Babe remarked, "Well, I don't blame them."

The Yankee players were enraged over the umpires' action. They became suspicious over the fact that the Giants started at once from the field, as if they knew beforehand that the tenth would be the last inning. Some of the players declared that it was a trick by McGraw.

Miller Huggins ordered the door barred to everybody.

"I don't want to see any one," he shouted.

CALL ATTACK A DISGRACE.

Baseball men who are more or less neutral in the matter said last night that the demonstration against Commissioner Landis was unfair and disgraceful.

The Judge had no more authority after the game had started than you or I had," one man declared. "The umpires were in absolute authority and Landis had nothing to say. Furthermore, in my opinion the umpires were justified. Looking out from the stand there seemed to be plenty of light. But if any of those fans got out on the field and had to face the high grandstand, with its tricky shadows, they would change their tune. Lee King misjudged a fly in the ninth inning because of the bad light."

George Hildebrand, who officiated as umpire-in-chief, declared that he called the game at the end of the tenth inning because it would have been dangerous for the players to continue playing.

"Several of the Yankees complained to Barry McCormick and me that the light was so bad that they were unable to see the ball," Hildebrand said. "They said that the players were running a risk of being injured if the game continued beyond the tenth inning. I agreed with them and decided that the best course was to call the game."

Bill Klem, veteran National League umpire, who officiated at third base yesterday, declared after the game that he concurred with Hildebrand's decision.

It was decided to call the game in the tenth at the conference between Umpires Hildebrand and Klem along the third base line in the previous inning. Both umpires confirmed this after the game, and Hildebrand said that the umpires had taken the action on their own initiative.

It was the third tie game in world's series history. In 1907 the Chicago Nationals and the Detroit Americans batted twelve innings with the score the same as yesterday—3 to 3. In 1912 the Giants and Boston Americans played eleven innings to a 6-6 tie. ◆

Apr 1, 1923

YANKS' STADIUM BIG ENGINEERING TASK

About 116,000 Square Feet of Sod and 45,000 Cubic Yards of Earth Used.

2,500 TONS OF STEEL

2,000,000 Board Feet of Lumber for Bleachers, 600,000 Lineal Feet for Grand Stand.

THE TASK OF CONVERTING ten acres of unused land into the largest baseball park in the country is an undertaking that few persons can appreciate until brought in contact with figures on the work involved. Even then it is difficult to realize what a stupendous task has been involved and what had to be expended in labor and material. Major T. H. Birmingham, engineer for the New York American League club, who is in charge of the construction of the Yankees' new stadium, gave out a few figures yesterday on the amount of work and material required.

Before any of the concrete work could be done it was necessary to fill and grade the field. A total of 48,000 cubic yards of earth was used to bring the playing field up to the required grade. About 116,000 square feet of sod was transported from Long Island to cover the diamond and the outfield, a special type of sod having been selected as the best obtainable for a ball field.

The excavation of 25,000 cubic yards of earth was required for the foundations of the big grandstand and bleachers. Before the work of putting the field in order was completed a modern drainage system, consisting of eleven large pipes around the outfield, a network of pipes under the infield and a concrete gutter in front of the grandstand, was installed.

Some of the figures on the material required for the Yankees Stadium are as follows:

Concrete—30,000 yards. This is made up from 45,000 barrels of cement, 30,000 yards of gravel and 15,000 yards of sand.

Structural steel—2,500 tons.

Reinforcing steel—1,000 tons.

Lumber for bleachers and concrete forms—2,000,000 board feet.

Piping for rails in boxes, reserved seats and bleachers—about four miles.

Iron in seats—500 tons.

Time spent in construction—eleven months.

Workmen employed—Up to a maximum of 500.

Other figures on the plant: besides those involving material in construction, tend further to impress one with the magnitude of the work. The plot takes in about ten acres and from extreme points on either side it measures about 700 feet. The distance around the outer edge of stand and bleachers figures 2,501 feet, or about fifty feet less than a half mile. Between the playing field and stands is a running track, twenty-four feet wide and 400 yards in length, with a straightaway of 120 yards in front of the third base wing of the grandstand: This track has been measured by officials of the Amateur Athletic Union and pronounced O. K., so any records made there will be official.

The front of the big grandstand, from the right field bleacher to the bleacher front in left centre, measures 1,176 feet. The lower deck, deepest of the three tiers, is 127 feet from front to rear. The runways in the rear of the stands measure twenty feet in width, the most commodious of any ball park ever built. Wide aisles, wide seats and plenty of space between rows of seats are other features which will be appreciated by the fans. There are sixteen toilet rooms within the park, eight for men and eight for women.

There are no stairs between the decks. All are reached by ramps which are so concentrated near the entrances as to give the fan a minimum amount of climbing. At the main entrance there are two duplex, or scissors ramps, which really constitute four ramps—two to the mezzanine and upper grand stand and two to the lower stand. They are so arranged that all can feed any one particular deck or all decks at the same time.

At the entrance at 157th Street and River Avenue, is one duplex ramp, while at 161st Street and Doughty Street the exit which can be converted into an entrance is also a duplex ramp. The capacity of the combined ramps is estimated at a minimum of 3,000 persons per minute.

Every major league park in the country was inspected, the style of each was studied, so that the Yankee Stadium would combine the best features of each and all. ◆

Yankee Stadium in 1923.

Apr 19, 1923

74,200 SEE YANKEES OPEN NEW STADIUM; RUTH HITS HOME RUN

Record Baseball Crowd Cheers as Slugger's Drive Beats Red Sox, 4 to 1.

25,000 ARE TURNED AWAY

Gates to $2,500,000 Arena Are Closed Half an Hour Before Start of Game.

GOVERNORS, GENERALS, COLONELS, politicians and baseball officials gathered together solemnly yesterday to dedicate the biggest stadium in baseball, but it was a ball player who did the real dedicating. In the third inning, with two team mates on the base lines, Babe Ruth smashed a savage home run into the right field bleachers, and that was the real baptism of the new Yankee Stadium. That also won the game for the Yankees, and all the ceremony which had gone before was only a trifling preliminary.

The greatest crowd that ever saw a baseball game sat and stood in this biggest of all baseball stadia. Inside the grounds, by official count, were 74,200 people. Outside the park, flattened against the doors that had long since closed, were 25,000 more fans, who finally turned around and went home, convinced that baseball parks are not nearly as large as they should be.

The dream of a 100,000 crowd at a baseball game could easily have been realized yesterday if the Yankee Colonels had only piled more concrete on concrete, more steel on steel, and thus provided the necessary space for the overflow. In the face of this tremendous outpouring all baseball attendance records went down with a dull thud. Back in 1916, at a world's series game

in Boston, some 42,000 were present, and wise men marveled. But there were that many people in the Yankee Stadium by 2 o'clock yesterday, and when the gates were finally closed to all but ticket holders at 3 o'clock the Boston record had been exceeded by more than 30,000.

SHAWKEY PITCHES FINE GAME.

It was an opening game without a flaw. The Yankees easily defeated the Boston Red Sox, 4 to 1. Bob Shawkey, war veteran and oldest Yankee player in point of service, pitched the finest game of his career, letting the Boston batters down with three scattered hits. The Yankees raised their American League championship emblem to the top of the flagpole—the chief feature of an opening-day program that went off perfectly. Governor "Al" Smith, throwing out the first ball of the season, tossed it straight into Wally Schang's glove, thus setting another record. The weather was favorable and the big crowd was handled flawlessly.

Only one more thing was in demand, and Babe Ruth supplied that. The big slugger is a keen student of the dramatic, in addition to being the greatest home run hitter. He was playing a new role yesterday—not the accustomed one of a re-

The score:

NEW YORK (A.)	Ab	R	H	Po	A
Witt,cf	3	1	1	3	0
Dugan,3b	4	1	1	1	1
Ruth,rf	2	1	1	3	0
Pipp,1b	3	0	0	12	0
Meusel,lf	4	0	1	0	0
Schang,c	4	0	0	4	2
Ward,2b	3	0	1	3	5
Scott,ss	2	0	1	1	4
Shawkey,p	3	1	1	0	0
Total....	28	4	7	27	12

BOSTON (A.)	Ab	R	H	Po	A
Fewster,ss	3	0	0	2	6
Collins,rf	4	0	0	2	1
Skinner,cf	4	0	0	0	0
Harris,lf	4	0	0	0	0
Burns,1b	3	1	1	9	2
McMillan,2b	2	0	1	2	0
Shanks,3b	3	0	0	3	0
Devormer,c	3	0	0	6	2
Ehmke,p	2	0	1	0	4
aMenosky	1	0	0	0	0
Fullerton,p	0	0	0	0	0
Total....	29	1	3	24	15

aBatted for Ehmke in eighth.

New York...............0 0 4 0 0 0 0 0.—4
Boston ....0 0 0 0 0 0 1 0 0—1

Two-base hits—Meusel, Scott. Three-base hit—McMillan. Home run—Ruth. Sacrifice—Scott. Double play—Scott, Ward and Pipp. Left on bases—New York 5, Boston 4. Bases on balls—Off Shawkey 2, Ehmke 3; Fullerton 1. Struck out—By Shawkey 5, Ehmke 4, Fullerton 1. Hits—Off Ehmke 7 in 7 innings, Fullerton none in 1. Hit by pitcher—By Shawkey (Fewster). Losing pitcher—Ehmke. Umpires—Connolly, Evans, and Holmes. Time of game—2:05.

nowned slugger, but that of a penitent, trying to "come back" after a poor season and a poorer world's series. Before the game he said that he would give a year of his life if he could hit a home run in his first game in the new stadium.

The Babe was on trial, and he knew it better than anybody else. He could hardly have picked a better time and place for the drive that he hammered into the bleachers in the third inning. The Yankees had just broken a scoreless tie by pushing Shawkey over the plate with one run. Witt was on third base, Dugan on first, when Ruth appeared at the plate to face Howard Ehmke, the Boston pitcher. Ruth worked the count to two and two, and then Ehmke tried to fool him with one of those slow balls that the Giants used successfully in the last world's series.

The ball came in slowly, but it went out quite rapidly, rising on a line and then dipping suddenly from the force behind it. It struck well inside the foul line, eight or ten rows above the low railing in front of the bleachers, and as Ruth circled the bases he received probably the greatest ovation of his career. The biggest crowd in baseball history rose to its feet and let loose the biggest shout in baseball history. Ruth, jogging over the home plate, grinned broadly, lifted his cap at arm's length and waved it at the multitude.

HOME RUN SETTLES OUTCOME.

That homer was useful as well as dramatic and decorative. It drove three runs across the plate, and those runs, as later events proved, were the margin by which the Yankees won.

But the game, after all, was only an incident of a busy afternoon. The stadium was the thing. For the Yankee owners it was the realization of a dream long cherished. For the fans it was something which they had never seen before in baseball. It cost about $2,500,000 to build, and eleven months were spent in the construction work. It is the most costly stadium in baseball, as well as the biggest.

First impressions—and also last impressions—are of the vastness of the arena. The stadium is big. It towers high in the air, three tiers piled one on the other. It is a skyscraper among baseball parks. Seen from the vantage point of the nearby subway structure, the mere height of the grandstand is tremendous. Baseball fans who sat in the last row of the steeply sloping third tier may well boast that they broke all altitude records short of those attained in an airplane.

Once inside the grounds, the sweep of the big stand strikes the eye most forcibly. It throws its arms far out to each side, the grandstand ending away over where the bleachers begin. In the centre of the cast pile of steel and concrete was the green spread of grass and diamond, and fewer ball fields are greener than that on which the teams played yesterday.

The Yankees' new home, besides being beautiful and majestic, is practical. It was emptied yesterday of its 74,000 in quicker time than the Polo Grounds ever was. Double ramps from top to bottom carried the stream of people steadily and rapidly to the lower exits, which are many and well situated. Fans from the bleachers and far ends of the grand stand poured out onto the field and were swept through the gates in left field. The grandstand crowd passed through exits opening on both Doughty Avenue and 157th Street, which lies along the south side of the stadium.

THRONG HANDLED WITHOUT CONFUSION.

The record-breaking throng was handled with almost no confusion at all. Transportation facilities were strained before the game because of the big flow of people from downtown points, but the subway, elevated and surface lines handled heavy traffic without a break after the game. There was little congestion in the 161st Street station of the Lexington Avenue subway, much of the crowd walking to nearby elevated and surface lines.

The fans were slow in coming to the stadium. When the gates were thrown open at noon only about 500 persons were in line before the ticket windows. But by 1 o'clock the guardians of law and order in front of the main entrance began finding their hands full. The supply of 50,000 unreserved grand stand and bleacher seats began dwindling rapidly, and by 2 o'clock the huge grand stand was beginning to bulge ⟫⟫⟫

‹‹‹ at the sides. Ten minutes later the gates to the main stand were ordered closed, and patrons who arrived more than an hour before game time were greeted with the "Standing Room Only" sign and the gentle announcement that bleacher seats only were available. When 3 o'clock came around even the bleachers were packed solidly with humanity, and after that there was nothing to do but close the gates and padlock them.

Inspector Thomas Riley, in charge of police arrangements outside the grounds, estimated that 25,000 fans were turned away, and officials of the club agreed with this estimate.

Kenesaw M. Landis, High Commissioner of Baseball, traveled to the scene in democratic style. He disembarked from an Interborough train shortly before 2 and was caught up in the swirl before the main entrance, being rescued finally by the police and escorted inside the stadium.

Preceding him by an hour was the Seventh Regiment Band, which arrived at 1 o'clock and immediately launched on a musical program. Just about the same time the Yankees and Red Sox deployed on the scene, the champions looking neat and natty in new home uniforms of white. The Bostonians were a symphony in red—red sweaters, red-peaked caps, red striped stockings.

GOVERNOR GREETED WARMLY.

Then at 3 o'clock the spotlight shifted from the players to the celebrities of opening day. Governor Smith moved down to his box, accompanied by Mrs. Smith, and got a rousing greeting. Judge Landis, in gray overcoat, doffing his wide brimmed hat in greeting, came on to the field and immediately strode out to centre field, where the American League flag was waiting. The Seventh Regiment Band assembled near the Yankee bench on the third base side, and John Philip Sousa, in bandmaster's uniform, took his baton in hand and moved to the head of the musicians. The two teams clustered into platoon formation and the parade began.

Once out at the flagpole, the ole traditional ritual of opening day began. While the band played "The Star Spangled Banner," the Stars and Stripes were pulled slowly to the peak of the flagpole. After it fluttered the red, white and blue American League pen-

Fans down the first base line cheer as Yankee Stadium is officially opened on April 18 of 1923 in New York City.

nant, and as the last note of the national anthem died away and the halyards were made fast, the big crowd let loose a roar that floated across the Harlem and far beyond.

That wasn't the end of it, by any means. Back to the home plate came the band and the players and the notables. In the front line of march were the Yankee Colonels, Ruppert and Huston, side by side and beaming broadly: Judge Landis, Mrs. Smith, the Governor and Harry Frazee, the Boston club owner. It was noticed for the first time that Mayor Hylan was absent, and club officials explained that the city's chief executive was unable to attend because of illness. Byron Bancroft Johnson, President of the American League, was also missing because of a sudden attack of influenza.

BABE RUTH RECEIVES GIFT.

Then the teams converged around the plate again, and Babe Ruth was presented with a case containing a big bat—a delicate hint to the slugger, possibly. After Babe had blushingly mumbled his thanks, Governor Smith stood up in his box, took a shiny white ball between thumb and first finger and threw it carefully at Wally Schang.

Now here was the first deviation from a decent and proper opening day program. Tradition demands that the thrower miss the objective by several feet. But the Governor, unwinding the official arm, hit Schang's glove as well as Bob Shawkey ever did. Old-time baseball men considered it a distinct social error.

After that there was nothing to do but to play the game. Frank Chance walked out on the coaching line. The Yankees scattered briskly to their positions, Everett Scott going to shortstop as a signal to the world that the record of 986 consecutive games would not be broken yet. Umpire Tommy Connolly, dean of the American League staff, who unexpectedly appeared to take charge of the game, mumbled something to the effect that the contest might begin, and Shawkey, twirling his red sleeved arms, pitched "Ball One" to the first batter, Chick Fewster, who used to play with the Yankees. The season was started. ◆

Lou Gehrig in his first season on the Columbia University baseball team, 1923.

June 12, 1923

YANKS SIGN GEHRIG, COLUMBIA SLUGGER

LOU GEHRIG, COLUMBIA PITCHER, first baseman and outfielder, called by Coach Carris of Pennsylvania and other critics the "best college player since George Sisler," has signed a contract with the Yankees. He practiced at first base in the fielding workout at the Yankee Stadium yesterday, and the announcement of his signing was made after the game with the Indians.

Gehrig's work in fast company will be watched closely. He is easily the longest hitter that ever played at Columbia, and his soubriquet is "the Babe Ruth of the colleges." He holds all long distance records for South Field, having hit one ball over the centre field fence and against the Journalism Building at the corner of 116th Street and into the open space before the library.

As a pitcher Gehrig has won six games and lost three. His latest batting average was .440 and he has hit seven home runs. He is 23, 5 feet 10½ inches and weighs 210. Gehrig is only a sophomore at Columbia, meaning that he has sacrificed two years of academic study to join the Yankees. ◆

October 16, 1923

YANKS WIN TITLE; 6-4 VICTORY ENDS $1,063,815 SERIES

Eighth-Inning Rally Dashes McGraw's Last Hope of Three Straight Championships.

THE YANKEES ARE THE CHAMPIONS. In the greatest game of the greatest world's series they beat the Giants yesterday at the Polo Grounds, 6 to 4, winning in the eighth inning when Arthur Nehf collapsed and Bob Meusel drove a single to centre field with the bases full.

Dreams came true in the eighth inning. The Yankees reached the journey's end, and a world's championship flag will fly in the Yankee Stadium next year. Dreams also went up in a puff of smoke, for when Meusel made that hit and the Giants went crashing down, the life-long hope of John J. McGraw for three consecutive world's championships went down with them.

This dramatic eighth inning finish was a fitting climax for the great three-year battle that had been waged by the two New York teams. Twice McGraw's baseball machine had emerged the winners and only as late as last Friday it seemed invincible. Then the Yankees with their backs to the wall staged one of the most remarkable fights in the history of sport and swept everything before them for three consecutive victories and the championship. Twice the Giants had taken the lead and twice the Yankees had overhauled them before Miller Huggins's team, with a determination that would not be denied, swept on to a complete triumph and its first world's championship.

Great as was this series in the tenseness of the games played and in the varying fortunes of the combatants, it was probably most remarkable of all for the great interest it stirred in fandom. Large new grounds, just completed, and built with an eye to the future, proved inadequate to accommodate the thousands who rushed the gates to be spectators at this gigantic struggle. Scores of thousands were turned away, but 301,430 did get in to witness the six games played, for which they paid the sum of $1,063,815, both figures eclipsing all former records for baseball.

THE BETTER TEAM WON.

The better team won, and, moreover, it was a game team. When the eighth inning opened the Yankees apparently were soundly thrashed. Nehf, the last hope of the old guard, had allowed only two hits in seven frames and only one run, a homer by Babe Ruth in the first inning. With two more chances, the Yanks were three runs behind, and, although they had fought bravely in this series, hardly a person in the big crowd paid them the tribute of believing that they would come through this crisis.

Nehf had been too powerful for them. With terrific speed and a side-breaking curve, with gameness and grim determination back of every pitch, the stocky left-hander had made the Yankee sluggers look like schoolboys. Two hits in the first two innings, and then a row of blanks. From the third to the eighth the Yanks went hitless, and in five innings they went out in one-two-three order.

Nor was the start of the eighth any better. Aaron Ward lifted a feeble fly which George Kelly caught, making the eighteenth batter who had faced Nehf without hitting. The goal was almost in sight for Nehf, but on the very next pitch fate tripped him up. The ball was high and at Schang's ear. Trying to escape it, Schang's bat hit the ball a glancing blow and drove it over third base for a single. Everett Scott followed up this "break" of the game by smashing a single sharply past Kelly. Schang dashed for third and made it, and then Miller Huggins rushed Freddy Hofmann to the plate to bat for Herb Pennock, the Yankee pitcher.

Nehf, his face literally as white as a sheet, was in the tightest hole of his life. After the contest the Yankee players accused him of lack of gameness, but it is a question if the stoutest heart in the world wouldn't have quelled and the steadfast hand trembled in this situation. On what he did in the next few minutes rested all the Giants' hopes for keeping their championship. Nehf, while probably nervous and fearful, was not a coward.

Something snapped inside him. Something gave way, and with it went every vestige of the superb control that had marked his pitching up to that time. In the twinkling of an eye he went down, conquered by something, perhaps by Yankee gameness, or by physical weakness after only a days' rest, or by the enormity of the burden that had been put on his shoulders.

While 34,172 looked on he gave Hoffman four straight balls and filled the bases. He gave Joe Bush, batting for Witt, four more balls, and forced Schang over with a run that made the score 4 to 2. Then Nehf went out, with his head down, his shoulders bent, the most tragic figure

that had appeared in this world's series.

Bill Ryan came in to salvage what he could from the wreckage. Even to hold the Yankees to one more run would have been enough, for the Giants could have won in that case. Ryan gave them that one run by also throwing four balls without a strike to Dugan, and after Scott had been forced over the plate Babe Ruth came up to face his greatest opportunity of the series. The 34,172 rose in their seats and pleaded for a home run, a triple, even a single—and then the Babe struck out!

It didn't check the Yankees, but it did make Ruth again the big failure of the series. With all his home runs and his fielding and his batting that had made McGraw's pitchers pass him, Ruth failed pitifully in the biggest crisis of all. Of all the Yankee players he figured slightest in the final victory that brought the title.

Now Ryan seemed almost out of the woods. He curved a strike over on Bob Meusel that made the Giant partisans howl with joy. But the next ball Meusel hit squarely. It went slightly to the right of ⟩⟩⟩

A view of game one of the 1923 World Series at the Polo Grounds showing the New York Yankees playing the New York Giants in their home.

<<< Ryan on the bound, and it seemed that the pitcher might have tried to break it down, as McGraw himself pointed out after the game. Instead, he turned away from the hit and let it roll out to centre field. There Cunningham stopped it and threw desperately to the only base open to him—third base—whither Dugan was flying like the wind. The ball was straight at Groh, but it hopped badly as Heinie jumped for it and went rolling on to the edge of the stand.

Hinkey Haines, running for Hofmann, scored from third. Johnson, running for Bush, scampered in from second. Dugan did his own running and came all the way from first to the plate, while Meusel slid safely into third. Three runs on one hit, five for the inning, and the world's series was nearly over.

That eighth-inning rally put the stamp of gameness on the Yankee team. For the last time will some critic raise his voice to observe that the Yankees are a great team, but lack the courage to come from behind. Besides winning the championship, the Yankees removed with a single stroke the only blot that still marred their escutcheon in the minds of many, and Colonel Jacob Ruppert, in a little speech he made after the battle, seemed as delighted by the Yankees' gameness as by the fact that they had finally won a world's title.

The Giants had finally been beaten. In three years of championship play they had never before met their match. With uncanny, almost superhuman, ability they had risen to meet every crisis fairly, and they could make the boast of every champion that they had never felt defeat. This series put before them their hardest test; could they break all baseball tradition and win three world's titles in a row? They could not, and so yesterday a great team finally went down.

At the same time another great team came up. Perhaps the Yanks next year will make it four pennants in as many years and equal the record of the old Chicago White Stockings made before the birth of the National League. Certainly the Hugmen are the most powerful team in baseball. With pitching, with batting, with team spirit and with Ruth the Yanks stand out as real champions. ◆

Apr 29, 1925

Ruth's Playing Days Not Over; May Return About the Middle of June, Says Physician

HOW LONG IT WILL BE before Babe Ruth will rejoin the Yankees remains a question of some doubt, but he will play baseball again, according to a statement yesterday by his physician, Dr. Edward King. Reports and rumors have been whispered about the country that the Yankees' master hitter never again would be able to swing a bat, that his baseball days were over and that the true nature of his illnesses was being kept secret, but Dr. King said yesterday that these reports were absolutely without foundation and that nothing had been hidden.

August 30, 1925

RUTH FINED $5,000; COSTLY STAR BANNED FOR ACTS OFF FIELD

Manager Huggins of Yankees Imposes Penalty at St. Louis for "Misconduct."

ST. LOUIS, AUG. 29 (AP).—George Herman (Babe) Ruth, baseball's premier slugger, today was fined $5,000 and suspended indefinitely by Manager Miller Huggins of the Yankees for "general misconduct." Ruth made no comment when Huggins told him to pack up and leave St. Louis for New York. The home-run king checked out of his hotel immediately, ostensibly to follow Huggins's orders.

Later Huggins said Ruth had been penalized for "misconduct off the field."

"I absolutely refuse to discuss the circumstances which led to the fine and suspension except to

"Ruth suffered from influenza, brought on by a general rundown condition," said Dr. King yesterday, after having been questioned concerning the true nature of the star's condition. "After that an abscess formed and an operation was necessary. The combination of these ailments, naturally, have left him in a weakened condition, but as to anything so serious as to prevent him from playing baseball again having developed there is no foundation for the statements.

"Ruth probably will be in the hospital two or perhaps three weeks more. After that it will be a question of time before he will be able to play baseball. Some persons recover more quickly than others, and it depends on how soon he gains his strength, which may be a month. The patient is making satisfactory progress at the present time and I see no reason for any complications to retard his recovery. Nothing that I know of could cause Ruth to retire from baseball or to stop playing the game."

This statement, made in no uncertain terms, should put to rest the rumors of the Babe's condition, and it now seems likely that he will be back in uniform about the middle of June. Ruth has been at St. Vincent's Hospital ever since he arrived here from the Southern training trip three weeks ago tomorrow. He was unconscious when he reached New York and was carried to the hospital in an ambulance. Since then no one has been allowed to see him except Mrs. Ruth, his daughter, Dorothy, Edward Barrow, Secretary of the Yankees, and the regular hospital attendants. The only statements that have been forthcoming regarding his health have been reports of "satisfactory progress."

The same report was made from the hospital yesterday. ◆

---

say that Ruth was guilty of misconduct off the field," Huggins stated, and refused to add to this.

"Does this mean that Ruth is out of the game for the remainder of the season?" Huggins was asked.

"That's entirely up to me, and I will decide that when the time comes," he replied.

"Was Ruth's misconduct what is generally known as breaking the training rules?"

"I have refused to answer that question. The misconduct was off the field of play."

"Does 'misconduct off the field' mean drinking?" Huggins was asked.

"Of course, it means drinking," said Huggins, "and it means a lot of other things besides. There are various kinds of misconduct. Patience has ceased to be a virtue. I have tried to overlook Ruth's behavior for a while, but I have decided to take summary action to bring the big fellow to his senses.

"I am disciplining him for general misconduct off the ball field, detrimental to the best interests of the club during this present road trip. I am not saying anything about his actions on the ball field.

"Every one knows he had been having an off year and his weak batting has been excused on account of his illness this Spring.

"When he started playing the first of June he was on probation more or less, bound to take care of himself physically and live up to the rules of club discipline.

"He has forgotten all about these restrictions on this trip, hence the fine and suspension." »»

Babe Ruth, Miller Huggins and Lou Gehrig during batting practice at League Park in Cleveland in 1927.

《《《 Late tonight it was learned that Ruth had exchanged his railroad ticket for one on the Pennsylvania Railroad leaving here about noon tomorrow.

DID NOT CONSULT RUPPERT.

Manager Huggins said tonight he had penalized Babe Ruth without consulting Colonel Jacob Ruppert, the owner of the Yankees, or Secretary Edward F. Barrow of the club. He acted on his own responsibility entirely, he said.

First news that there had been trouble came this afternoon when the Yankees took the field for the game against the Browns, and Ruth was absent from the line-up. Inquirers were informed that Ruth had deserted the club and gone to New York, but when Huggins was confronted with the report he admitted the fine and suspension, and that he had ordered the slugger to New York.

Employees at the Buckingham Hotel declared that Ruth was smiling and seemingly not worried by the turn of events. They said he left with his suitcases without giving any forwarding address. It was learned at Union Station here that Ruth had canceled reservations, previously arranged, on the 6 P.M. New York train.

At an early hour tonight Ruth could not be reached for a statement. He was said to have appeared at a residence in the West End, but left a few minutes before newspaper men arrived, saying that he intended catching a 6 o'clock train for New York. Ruth was not on the train, however, and had not appeared at the station when it departed.

This is only one of the numerous escapades of

September 1, 1925

RUPPERT DECLARES HUGGINS WILL STAY

Says Ruth Must Make Peace With Manager If He Is to Play With Yanks Again.

BABE RUTH, MAKER OF HOME RUNS, may have played his last game as a Yankee. Unless he can make his peace with Miller J. Huggins, manager of the club, there is very little chance that the man who reigned as the idol of America's youth can ever again don a Yankee uniform.

This was made clear yesterday when Colonel Jacob Ruppert, owner of the Yankees, made the statement that whatever action was to be taken in Ruth's case rested solely with Huggins. And in view of the fact that Ruth has declared that he will not again play with the Yankees so long as Huggins is the manager it is taken for granted that the ultimatum will leave baseball's most fa-mous man out in the cold.

Colonel Ruppert yesterday declared that he still was firm in his stand for Huggins. Though on record as backing Huggins to the limit, it was not until yesterday that it was learned that the owner of the Yankees had taken the stand that as between Ruth and Huggins there was only one choice and that choice was Huggins.

Ruth is due in New York this morning on the Twentieth Century Limited. He may seek an immediate interview with Manager Huggins, who returned last night on the Empire State Express with the Yankee team from St. Louis. The outcome of this interview will be momentous, at least for Ruth.

HUGGINS SAYS BAN STANDS.

When Huggins got in with the Yankee squad last night he was reluctant to say much about the Ruth incident. Huggins alighted from the train at 125th Street and departed immediately for his home, not far from the Yankee Stadium.

"The suspension of Ruth stands, so far as I am concerned," said Huggins. "I did not take any hasty action, but I don't care to go into the

the New York star, who in addition to being proclaimed baseball's most valuable player in 1922 is the highest salaried player in history and probably was the greatest drawing card of all time.

During the Fall of 1921 Ruth violated the rules of organized baseball prohibiting "barnstorming" tours by members of pennant-winning teams. For that incident Ruth was suspended without pay for the first thirty days of the 1922 season. On other occasions Ruth's temperament similarly exhibited itself, resulting in disputes with umpires.

No Comment by Officials Here.

No official comment on the Ruth case could be obtained last night from Yankee executives. Efforts to reach Colonel Jacob Ruppert, the club President, and Ed Barrow, Yankee business manager, were unsuccessful. At Colonel Ruppert's home it was said he was spending the day in the country and was not expected back until late at night. Barrow was out of town for the week-end.

This is a record fine in baseball for a minor or major league player. No other such penalty has been levied. Considering that Ruth is paid a salary that is believed to be $52,000 a year, and under the rules of baseball his salary will cease during the term of his suspension, it is likely that the present difficulty will cost Ruth a greater sum than many star players receive for an entire year's services. It has been calculated that Ruth receives $298 a day during the playing season. ◆

---

details just now. I wish to see Colonel Ruppert before I say anything, and if any statements are necessary Colonel Ruppert can make them."

Ruth has declared that he will not play so long as Huggins is manager of the Yankees. Colonel Ruppert yesterday declared that Huggins could remain as the manager of the Yankees so long as he wished. The only inference to be taken is that Huggins is in command of the situation.

In fact, when questioned yesterday, Business Manager Barrow declared that whatever peace terms might eventuate would have to originate with Huggins and Ruth and that the owner, Colonel Ruppert, would not interfere with Huggins's program.

The possibilities of a Ruth sale or a deal in which he might be traded were talked of with considerable animation in baseball circles yesterday. From an authoritative source it was learned that the possibility of trading or selling Ruth was not the most remote thing in the world. However, there is a string on any such deal, in fact, more than one string.

To begin with, Ruth's salary of $52,000 is a big stumbling block in itself. There is hardly a club in organized baseball that would care to assume such a contract. In the second place, Ruth is signed to a contract that does not expire until the end of the 1926 season. In the third place, it is no certainty that Babe has outlived his usefulness, and it is very probable that if he were offered for sale at this time the asking price would be stupendous, despite his present predicament.

Nevertheless, in view of Colonel Ruppert's flat statement backing Huggins, Ruth's declaration that he would not play with the Yankees if Huggins remains, and Ruppert's rebuttal that Ruth could quit if he desired, there was no doubt but that, if all conditions were right, Ruth would be traded or sold.

Drastic action of this kind, however, was felt to be only such as would be taken as a last resort and baseball men yesterday figured that in the end Ruth would capitulate and once more make his peace with Huggins and Colonel Ruppert. But how easy it will be for Ruth to regain his place in the estimation of his manager remains to be seen. ◆

September 7, 1925

Ruth Is Reinstated, but $5,000 Fine Stands; Leaves With Yanks to Play in Boston Today

BABE RUTH HAS BEEN REINSTATED. This means, according to an announcement made by the Yankee management at the Stadium yesterday afternoon, that Ruth, who has been spending an enforced vacation since one week ago Saturday, will see action in the double header against the Red Sox in Boston this afternoon. The Babe left at midnight with the Yankee party for Boston.

Shortly before game time yesterday Miller Huggins, manager of the Yankees, sent for Ruth, and the Babe was careful to be within calling distance.

"Well, Hug," he explained after a mild reception, "I'm here."

"Yes," Huggins replied, "so I see. I have decided to accept your apology and to lift the suspension. You will not play today, but you can accompany the team to Boston. The $5,000 fine stands."

"All right, Hug, I'll be there," smiled the Babe as he departed. ◆

March 5, 1927

RUTH RIGHT-HANDED SIGNING FOR $210,000

Closes Three-Year Contract With Yankees at Brief Session in Ruppert's Brewery.

BABE RUTH SIGNED his three-year contract with the Yankees yesterday and thereby committed himself to accept the sum of $70,000 for the next three years. The Babe attached his signature to the contract without a struggle and Colonel Jake Ruppert added his without seeming to be in any agony. Edward Grant Barrow then signed his name as a witness, and in just twenty minutes the entire ceremony was completed. The scene of this momentous affair was Colonel Ruppert's Brewery and the witnesses were numerous baseball writers who had gathered just to make sure that George Herman Ruth did not slip up on the formal signing proceedings.

This evening Babe will depart for St. Petersburg, Fla., and on Monday morning he will attire himself in a Yankee uniform and disport himself upon the field at Crescent Lake Park.

The signing was not a very exciting occasion. The Babe and Colonel Ruppert, of course, were early upon the job, and so was Business Manager Barrow. Babe very casually took Colonel Ruppert's fountain pen in hand and the assembled witnesses received a shock as Babe carefully signed the $210,000 contract with his right hand.

RIGHT-HANDED SIGNING AMAZES.

Close observers who had seen the Babe pole out many of his homers and had watched him toss the ball from right field with deadly aim, stood aghast. This was indeed something new. Imagine a left hander whose very fame rested upon his left-handed home runs and his left-handed throws from right field, signing so important a document as a three-year contract calling for $210,000 with his right hand!

But that is just what Babe did.

"How is it that you sign with the right and slug with the left?" some one asked.

"Well," said Babe, "if I tried to hit the old apple with a right-handed swing you know what would happen. So, with such an important thing as signing a contract, you can appreciate that I wouldn't shift my signing style. I am a right-handed signer but a left-handed hitter, and that's all there is to it." ◆

July 12, 1927

BUSTER TIES BABE IN HOME-RUN DASH

Gehrig Bats Out 29th Circuit Blow While Yankees Tame Tigers at Detroit, 8-5.

By RICHARDS VIDMER.
Special to The New York Times.

DETROIT, JULY 11.—The Buster and the Babe are neck and neck once more in the Great American Home-Run Handicap of 1927.

Except for the fact that Buster Gehrig hit his twenty-ninth home run of the season, putting him again on even terms with Babe Ruth, it hardly seems worth while mentioning the little game of baseball between the Yanks and the Tigers here today.

Of course, the Yanks won, 8 to 5. That might be an item of some interest. It also might be mentioned, casually, that Waite Hoyt and Bob Shawkey made the wild and ferocious Tigers appear strangely like house cats. But these factors are merely incidental to the main bit of gossip.

Having done nothing more devastating than to bang out a few singles, doubles, and triples since Independence Day, Lou decided it was about time to get back into the race where hits are really worth while. He warmed up with a double off Lil Stoner in the sixth inning, which started a five-run rally that overcame a slight Detroit lead and he took up the main business of the afternoon as a starter to the seventh.

GEHRIG BREAKS THROUGH.

Stoner, through a little oversight on the part of George Moriarty, was still on the pitching premises. Nobody was on base and the Yankees were far enough ahead to make a run or two of small concern to any one. But Buster had his own personal affairs to think of and took no pity on any one, least of all the ball.

He belted it on a line into the bleachers that nestle between right and centre field and then trotted around the bases as though he hit 'em like that every day. Well, he does—almost. ◆

October 1, 1927

Ruth Crashes 60th to Set New Record

BABE RUTH SCALED the hitherto unattained heights yesterday. Home run 60, a terrific smash off the southpaw pitching of Zachary, nestled in the Babe's favorite spot in the right field bleachers, and before the roar had ceased it was found that this drive not only made home run record history but also was the winning margin in a 4 to 2 victory over the Senators. This also was the Yanks' 109th triumph of the season. Their last league game of the year will be played today.

When the Babe stepped to the plate in that momentous eighth inning the score was deadlocked, Koenig was on third base, the result of a triple, one man was out and all was tense. It was the Babe's fourth trip to the plate during the afternoon, a base on balls and two singles resulting on his other visits plateward.   »»

The Babe hits his 60th home run of the season against Washington Senators' pitcher Tom Zachary, setting a record that would last 34 years.

≪≪   The first Zachary offering was a fast one, which sailed over for a called strike. The next was high. The Babe took a vicious swing at the third pitched ball and the bat connected with a crash that was audible in all parts of the stand. It was not necessary to follow the course of the ball. The boys in the bleachers indicated the route of the record homer. It dropped about half way to the top. Boys, No. 60 was some homer, a fitting wallop to top the Babe's record of 59 in 1921.

While the crowd cheered and the Yankee players roared their greetings the Babe made his triumphant, almost regal tour of the paths. He jogged around slowly, touched each bag firmly and carefully and when he imbedded his spikes in the rubber disk to record officially Homer 60 hats were tossed in the air, papers were torn up and tossed liberally and the spirit of celebration permeated the place.

The Babe's stroll out to his position was the signal for a handkerchief salute in which all the bleacherites, to the last man, participated. Jovial Babe entered in to the carnival spirit and punctuated his Ringly strides with a succession of snappy military salutes. Ruth's homer was a fitting climax to a game. which will go down as the Babe's personal triumph.

The ball, which became Homer 60, was caught by Joe Forner of 1937 First Avenue, Manhattan. He is about 40 years old and has been following baseball for thirty-five years, according to his own admission. He was far from modest and as soon as the game was over rushed to the dressing room to let the Babe know who had the ball. ◆

October 2, 1927

SPORTS OF THE TIMES

By JOHN KIERAN.
Copyright, 1927, by the New York Times Company.

SOME FOUR MONTHS AGO or more there was printed in this column a verified query: "Was there ever a guy like Ruth?" From time to time Yankee rooters suggested the reprinting of the query, and now that Babe Ruth has answered it a recital of the old question may be in order. Here it is:

A QUERY.

You may sing your song of the good old days till
    the phantom cows come home;
You may dig up glorious deeds of yore from
    many a dusty tome;
You may rise to tell of Rube Waddell and the
    way he buzzed them through,
And top it all with the great fast ball that Rosie's
    rooters knew.
You may rant of Brouthers, Keefe and Ward and
    half a dozen more;
You may quote by rote from the record book in a
    way that I deplore;
You may rave, I say, till the break of day, but the
    truth remains the truth:
From "One Old Cat" to the last "At Bat," was
    there ever a guy like Ruth?

He can start and go, he can catch and throw, he
    can field with the very best.
He's the Prince of Ash and the King of Crash,
    and that's not an idle jest.
He can hit that ball o'er the garden wall, high up
    and far away.
Beyond the uttermost picket lines where the
    fleetfoot fielders stray.
He's the Bogey Man of the pitching clan and he
    clubs 'em soon and late;
He has manned his guns and hit home runs from
    here to the Golden Gate;
With vim and verve he has walloped the curve
    from Texas to Duluth,

Which is no small task, and I beg to ask: Was there ever a guy like Ruth?

NO ANSWER NEEDED.

As a matter of fact, there was never even a good imitation of the Playboy of Baseball. What this big, good-natured, uproarious lad has done is little short of a miracle of sport. There is a common axiom: They never come back. But Babe Ruth came back twice. Just like him. He would.

It takes quite a bit of remembering to recall that the great home-run hitter was once the best left-handed pitcher in baseball. When he was a member of the Boston Red Sox team he set a record of pitching twenty-nine scoreless innings in world's series competition.

Then he started to slip and everybody said the usual thing: "Good-bye Forever!" (copyright by Tosti).

Babe gathered in all the "Good-byes" and said: "Hello, everybody! I'm a heavy-hitting outfielder." And he was. He set a league record of twenty-nine home runs in 1919 and then he came to New York and took the cover off the siege gun.

THE HEAVY FIRING.

That was Ruth's first come-back. A mild one. Others had done that, and the Babe yearned to be distinguished even from a chosen few. He wanted to be the One and Only. He nearly knocked the American League apart with fifty-four home runs in 1920, and in 1921 he set the record at fifty-nine circuit clouts for the season.

"It will stay there forever," prophesied the conservatives.

For five years the record was safe enough. In his bland and childlike way the Babe fell afoul of disciplinary and dietary laws, with the result that he was barred from the diamond for lengthy stretches on orders from Judge Landis, Miller Huggins and the Ruth family physician.

He set the record of fifty-nine home runs when he was 27 years old. In the following years he failed to come within hailing distance of his high-water mark, and once again everybody said: "Good-bye Forever!" (copyright by Tosti).

A CHANGE IN TUNE.

The Babe's answer was: "Say au revoir, but not good-bye!" And G. Herman Ruth was as right as rain. It was "Au revoir" for five seasons, and in the sixth season the big boy came back with a bang!

Supposedly "over the hill," slipping down the steps of Time, stumbling toward the discard, six years past his peak, Babe Ruth stepped out and hung up a new home-run record at which all the sport world may stand and wonder. What Big Bill Tilden couldn't do on the tennis court, Babe Ruth has done on the diamond. What Dempsey couldn't do with his fists, Ruth has done with his bat. He came back.

Put it in the book in letters of gold. It will be a long time before any one else betters that home-run mark, and a still longer time before any aging athlete makes such a gallant and glorious charge over the come-back trail.

AND IN CONCLUSION.

You may rise and sing till the rafters ring that sad and sorrowful strain:
"They strive and fail—it's the old, old tale; they never come back again."
Yes, it's in the dope, when they hit the slope they're off for the shadowed vale,
But the great, big Bam with the circuit slam came back on the uphill trail;
Came back with cheers from the drifted years where the best of them go down;
Came back once more with a record score to wear a brighter crown.
My voice may be loud above the crowd and my words just a bit uncouth.
But I'll stand and shout till the last man's out: There was never a guy like Ruth! ◆

October 9, 1927

YANKS SWEEP SERIES, WILD PITCH BEATING PIRATES, 4-3, IN NINTH

Miljus Delivers Wide Toss After Fanning Gehrig and Meusel, Combs Scoring.

RUTH'S HOMER SCORES TWO

By JAMES R. HARRISON.

THERE WERE THREE ON and two were out, the score was tied and it was the ninth inning of the big game. Now, in such a setting Ralph Henry Barbour would have had the modest hero step up and slam one over the fence while 60,000 roared their acclaim of the great man.

Or if Frank Merriwell had been pitching he would have sent over a snaky curve and fanned the batter and then would have won the game himself with a hit in the next inning.

But reality is not always as glamourous as fiction and sometimes falls short. For in just such a situation at the Yankee Stadium yesterday the pitcher wound up and tossed one where no catcher has ever stopped the ball. The little white pill slithered off the glove and rolled to the stand; a runner raced in from third and the world's series was over—with the Yankees new champions in four straight victories.

No resounding slap over the fence and far away. No sapient drive to the place "where they ain't." Not even a long sacrifice fly. Just a wild pitch and a rolling ball—and curtain for the Pittsburgh Pirates.

FOURTH TEAM WITHOUT DEFEAT.

The Yankees won by 4 to 3—the fourth team in twenty-four world's series to take the championship with four straight victories. Sixty thousand sat in at the finish and saw the hardest fought game of the series. Let it be recorded, to the eternal credit of the Pirates, that they went down fighting like men.

It would have made a prettier story if the home run that George Herman Ruth hit into the right-field stand in the fifth had won the game. It would have been nicer if Gehrig or Meusel or Lazzeri could have produced a ringing blow with the bases full and nobody out in the throbbing ninth.

But the bald, raw truth is that John Miljus, after striking out the larruping Gehrig and the dangerous Meusel in the ninth, slipped and fell.

John Miljus went to his task like a lion-hearted veteran. A minor leaguer a year ago, a curve-ball pitcher who failed in Brooklyn and has kicked his way around the "bushes," he pitched like a Mathewson or a Bender in this dire moment.

Miljus had risen to brilliant heights and the tone of the cheering changed now. Before the nerve-wracked spectators had clamored for a Yankee hit; now they were with John Miljus to the last man, woman and child—acclaiming the courageous stand of an obscure hero.

And now here was Tony Lazzeri crouched at the plate—the Yanks' last hope. On a certain clammy day last October he had faced Grover Cleveland Alexander with the bases full and the world's title at stake, and he had struck out.

Tony went after the first one and whipped a long, high foul into the grandstand. Strike one. "Go on, you Miljus," screamed a wild-eyed rooter in the mezzanine deck.

Once again Long John pulled back his arm and swung it around his head and slowly brought his

The American League champion Yankees in an official team photograph. Hall of Fame players on the team include Waite Hoyt, top row, fifth from right, Miller Huggins. middle row sixth from right, Herb Pennock, top row, second from left, Lou Gehrig, top row, far left, Tony Lazzeri, top row, third from left, Earle Combs, second row, third from left, and Babe Ruth, top row, fifth from left.

right hand down. The ball leaped forth and winged to the plate, but there was a gasp of dismay as the little white horsehide sailed high and wide. Gooch jumped upward and sideways and pushed his big glove out with a desperate lunge, but the ball glanced off and dribbled swiftly toward the box where sat Kenesaw Mountain Landis.

For one second Combs hesitated and then he dug his spikes into the dirt and surged across the plate. The world's series was over.

The Yankees showed, in this world's series, a crisp attack, an airtight defense, great pitching and a sprightly spirit. These are generally considered to be four important items in the noble pastime of baseball.

On his own account George Herman Ruth demonstrated again that he is the superman of the game. If there was any hero of this series it was George, with his three singles in the first game, his homer in the second and his fine hitting yesterday. As Uncle Wilbert Robinson so aptly put it, climbing out of the press box yesterday. "That guy ought to be allowed to play only every other day."

To our mind Ruth was the outstanding figure, but the Yanks brimmed over with heroes. The entire infield was magnificent. Gehrig, Lazzeri, Combs and Koenig were trenchant hitters. Dugan was great at third, as were Lazzeri at second, Koenig at short and Gehrig at first.

Pennock's one game was a thing of beauty, and George William Pipgras and Wilcy Moore deserve any laurel wreaths that are being handed out.

If you seek heroes just call the roll of the Yanks. From big Ruth to little Benough, from Forbes Field to the Harlem River, they ruled their domain. No team ever deserved more the proud title of champions. ◆

October 10, 1928

YANKEES WIN SERIES, TAKING FINAL, 7 TO 3; RUTH HITS 3 HOMERS

BOTTLES THROWN AT RUTH

St. Louis Fans Angry After His Second Homer—Makes Great Catch to End Game.

By JAMES R. HARRISON.
Special to The New York Times.

ST. LOUIS, OCT. 9.—Establishing records that will live as long as the game itself, scaling a baseball Matterhorn where no other foot had ever trod before, the Yankees made it four in a row over the Cardinals today, 7 to 3, as Babe Ruth, for the second time in his incredible career, hit three homers in one world's series game.

For the second successive year this super team of supermen defeated its National League rivals in four straight games to build for itself a monument that still will be standing when the names of Ruth and Gehrig and Huggins are mellow memories out of the distant past.

And to climax his marvelous career, to reach the greatest heights ever attained by any ball player, George Herman Ruth did again today what no other man had done even once. Three times he drove the ball over the right field bleachers. He finished with the highest world's series batting average on record .625, while his co-partner and protégé, Lou Gehrig, hit one homer to set a new series record for runs driven in—nine.

GAME IS UNPARALLELED.

This was a game unparalleled in baseball history, not merely because, for the first time in that history, a team had won its second world's series in four straight games. Not merely because Ruth hit three homers for the second time in his career or because Gehrig drove in his ninth run. Not

merely because the Yankees hammered out five homers in one game and set a new mark.

No, it was unparalleled mainly because it saw the Yankees rising triumphantly to overcome the greatest obstacles that might face a world's series team. Because it saw George H. Ruth and the badly crippled New Yorkers reach the very climax of their greatness to do deeds that will be remembered as long as the game lives. If there was any lingering doubt, if anywhere in this broad land there were misguided souls who believed that Babe Ruth was not the greatest living ball player, they should have seen him today.

They should have seen him hooted and hissed, come to the plate three times, twice against Wee Willie Sherdel and once against the great Pete Alexander, and send three mighty drives whistling over that right-field pavilion.

They should have seen him swaggering and waving a friendly fist at the world as he romped out to left field—the play boy of baseball—to be greeted by a barrage of pop bottles thrown by a few sportsmen who thought that the Babe had been struck out in the seventh, a moment before he clouted his second homer to tie the score. Misguided sportsmen who could not appreciate the incredible feats of this incredible man.

TRY TO SPOIL CATCH.

They should have seen him at the very end of the game as he drove an injured knee forward at top speed, dashing down the foul line and past the field boxes to make a one-hand catch while St. Louis partisans threw paper and programs at him to blind his vision.

They should have seen him, that great catch completed, continue to run in, holding the ball aloft in his gloved right hand—the picture of triumph and glee and kindly defiance of the whole world.

It was thus that the world's series of 1928 passed into history—with Ruth triumphant, with Ruth rampant on a field of green, with Ruth again stranger than fiction and mightier than even his most fervent admirers had dreamed he would be.

"The king is not dead, long live the king!" they might have shouted as this amusing play boy, this boisterous soul, in the great hour of his ca-

1928 New York Yankees infielders (l to r) Lou Gehrig, Tony Lazzeri, Pat Collins, Joe Dugan, Gene Robertson, Mark Koeing and Leo Durocher.

reer, added new records to a list already stretching ten years back into baseball history.

PATH STREWN WITH FLOWERS.

They threw bottles and programs and newspapers at him today, did a few small-souled St. Louis fans, but as he ran from the field his path was strewn with the invisible flowers of invisible persons who know real baseball greatness when they see it.

Overshadowed by Ruth were even the other heroes of this Yankee ball team which started the series as the under dog and ended it as the greatest world's series team of all time.

Overshadowed was Henry Louis Gehrig— Gehrig who today tied Ruth's record of four homers in one series and set a new mark for runs driven in. Overshadowed was little Miller Huggins, who now is tied with John McGraw and Connie Mack in number of world's championships—three. Overshadowed was Waite Hoyt, who won his second game from the Cardinals, and Tony Lazzeri and all the other soldiers of this immortal battalion.

No, this game was the Ruth and nothing but the Ruth. So was the series, in which, besides his home run feats, he established a new record for runs scored in one series with nine and for homers in his nine series with thirteen and tied Joe Harris's mark of twenty-two total bases in one series. Except that Ruth hit his in four games and Harris in seven.

The seventh inning was one of the greatest in world's series annals. Hoyt, thanks to two errors in the fourth inning, was on the short end of a 2-1 score when that inning dawned. Wee Willie Sherdel, though roughly handled by the Yanks, had escaped extinction so far.

The only run off him had been Ruth's first homer in the fourth round. The game little southpaw threw a curve a half foot inside the ⟩⟩⟩

«« plate. It was not a ball to swing at, but Ruth isn't human. He smacked it clear over the right-field bleachers without even touching that structure.

At the outset of the seventh Koenig popped to Maranville. Then Sherdel planted two strikes across the plate and had G. H. Ruth in a bad way. Immediately after the second strike Sherdel tried a quick return, tried to sneak the ball over while Ruth, his head turned, was exchanging quips and bright repartee with Catcher Earl Smith.

The sneak delivery was right across there, but Umpire Charley Pfirman refused to call it. He ruled that such a delivery was illegal in a world's series and was upheld by the three other umpires, who pointed out to the Cards that such a ruling had been agreed upon before the series and that both teams had been notified.

Though the Cardinals howled and the crowd joined in, the umpire's verdict stood. It was still two and nothing on the Babe. The next was a ball outside. Ball two was also off the plate. Then Sherdel wound up again and threw a slow curve outside.

With no perceptible effort, the Bambino met the ball and knocked it toward the right-field bleachers. The crowd gasped and then groaned as the ball, flying high and never losing momentum, cleared the roof of the pavilion. Through a narrow aperture at the back you could see a white speck fall and then disappear into the great open spaces of Grand Boulevard.

As he went around the bases Ruth was triumph itself. Mockingly he waved his hand at the crowd. As he passed second base he sent a salute to his friendly enemies in the left-field bleachers. He turned toward home still waving a mocking and derisive hand at a crowd too stunned to give this feat the ovation it deserved.

TRIED TO CATCH KING ASLEEP.

So they had tried to sneak a third strike over on Ruth, eh! They tried to catch the king asleep, did they? Must have been afraid to throw it when he was looking, for see what happened when he was.

And then, in the wake of Babe Ruth came the Yankee attack, the New York shock troops,

fierce and dauntless, fast moving and hard hitting. Look out, the Yanks are coming!

On the second ball pitched by Willie Sherdel, Gehrig came back with that big bat of his and hammered a homer to the roof of the right-field stand, close to the foul line. Ruth had tied the score. Gehrig had put his team ahead. What a pair! What men! Between them they had made this world's series a shamble, a source of humiliation and sorrow for the National League, which in eight straight games against this unbelievable Yankee team had met nothing but one-sided defeat.

This team has something that every great person has—whether a great athlete or a great actor, or a great lawyer, or a great business man. It has a certain intangible something, a confidence, almost cockiness, that it is the best team on earth. It has poise, aplomb, insouciance—a calm, sure faith in itself that shines forth and is radiated to the other team and the enemy crowd.

Anyway, what the Yanks have done in their last two world's series has been incredible and superhuman. They can't be weighed and measured by ordinary standards as long as they have two friends in human form like G. Herman Ruth and H. Louis Gehrig, by far the two greatest ball players ever on one team.

Always we will remember Babe Ruth today—as he ran around the bases after those three homers, as he picked up pop bottles in left field and kidded with the crowd before turning his back on that menacing throng. But particularly we shall remember him as he looked when he charged along the foul line and in front of the field boxes—230 pounds of the best ball player that ever lived—swerving in toward the wooden railing, his gloved right hand outstretched and his legs pounding while fans stood up and pelted paper missives at him.

Then we shall remember how he caught that baseball incredibly and held it up for the world to see in his right hand. Of all our baseball memories that shall be the clearest-etched and most unforgettable. Ruth, indomitable, unconquerable, triumphant. An amazing man, this George Herman Ruth. ◆

January 23, 1929

YANKEES TO WEAR NUMBERS

Plan of World's Champions Will Be an Innovation in the Major Leagues.

HAVING SET THE PACE in championships and home runs, the Yankees are going in for a little pioneering this year. Secretary Ed Barrow announced yesterday that each and every player on the club would bear a large and easily perceived numeral on his brawny back. The score cards will list the players and numbers assigned to them.

It will be a real innovation in the major leagues. Barrow declares that the system of numbering the players has been tried with success in minor leagues and he thinks that the scheme will readily find favor with Yankee Stadium patrons.

Barrow said that the players would probably be numbered in accordance with their place in the batting order, in which case Earle Combs will be decorated with "No. 1." The Babe then would bear "No. 3."

It was suggested to Barrow that Manager Miller Huggins could use a little deception on rival clubs, jumbling up the numbers to leave the opposition in doubt as to just who was batting.

"Yeah," was Barrow's rejoinder. "I suppose we can give the Babe's number to Robertson or Durocher and give one of their numbers to the Babe. Then the other side won't know when the Babe comes to bat." ◆

September 26, 1929

MILLER HUGGINS DIES; MANY PAY TRIBUTE

Manager of Yankees' Baseball Team for 12 Seasons Is a Victim of Blood Poisoning.

MILLER J. HUGGINS, for twelve seasons manager of the New York Yankees and one of the most noted figures in baseball, died yesterday afternoon at 8:15 o'clock in St. Vincent's Hospital. The man who had won fame with the Yankees, which under his guidance captured six pennants and three world's championships, was a victim of blood poisoning brought on by an infection beneath his left eye.

Huggins, who was 50 years old, became unconscious early yesterday morning, and the battle which he had waged since last Friday was virtually over, for Dr. Edward H. King, his physician, said then that his patient had only hours to live.

Toward the end Huggins was able to fight his illness with courage alone, for the once wiry strength that he had combined with remarkable skill to make himself into one of the brilliant second basemen of a decade or more ago had long since left him.

SORROW IS WIDESPREAD.

Sorrow was felt all over the baseball world when news of his death became known. Colonel Jacob Ruppert, owner of the Yankees, who looked upon his manager more as a son than an employee, was grief-stricken. So was Ed Barrow, business manager of the club, who had fought beside Huggins through the many years that the latter was constructing what came to be known as one of the great teams of all times.

Today all games in the American League are called off by order of President Ernest Barnard. Tomorrow the Yankee players will pay a »»

<<< final tribute to their departed leader. The Yankee-Washington game at Washington will be postponed and the players brought on to New York to attend the funeral services. The simple services will be held at the Little Church Around the Corner at 2 o'clock tomorrow afternoon. Dr. J. E. Price of the Washington Heights Methodist Episcopal Church, a life-long friend, will officiate.

The services will be brief and two hours later the body will be placed upon a Pennsylvania Railroad train bound for Cincinnati, where Huggins will be buried beside his mother and his father.

DEATH CAME QUICKLY.

The death of Huggins came with shocking swiftness. A week ago today he was suffering apparently only from a slight infection beneath his eye. On that day he made an engagement with a friend among the baseball writers to play a round of golf last Sunday, but on Sunday he was fighting the fight of his life, and although he gained on that day and blood transfusions helped temporarily, the poison spread throughout his system. Desperate efforts were made by Dr. King and more blood transfusions were given. Monday he rallied somewhat, but apparently he knew his own fate better than those friends who gathered about his bedside, for he called in his pastor and his lawyer.

Shortly afterward he lapsed into unconsciousness, never again to revive completely, although he muttered the names of friends and dear ones. Yesterday morning, after a night that saw his temperature rise slowly to the danger point, he slipped off into a coma from which he never emerged.

BARN IN CINCINNATI.

Miller Huggins was born in the famous old Fourth Ward of Cincinnati, then known as one of the roughest in the Ohio city, on April 19, 1879, according to the family records, though the baseball records give the date as March 27, 1880. Huggins grew up in a neighborhood where he had to learn to fight his own battles. And this he always did. He was handicapped by his size—he was 5 feet 4 inches tall and never weighed more than 145 pounds. Yet despite that he took his place alongside of big men and held his own as a player and almost performed miracles as a manager.

Yankees owner Jacob Ruppert (left) and manager Miller Huggins stand together in 1927.

With the advent of Babe Ruth in 1920 as one of his players more troubles piled upon his frail frame. Ruth was hard to manage in those days and in the years that followed when Huggins was forced to discipline Ruth by heavy fines and suspensions, Huggins lost the backing of the fans. But only for a time.

When the disciplined Ruth burst forth as a still greater star and when youngsters schooled by Huggins began to blossom forth as stars and when the first pennant came to Huggins in 1921 things began to change and the criticism that had been directed at him subsided. It became apparent that New York had a real manager. In time that belief became complete and permanent. Huggins won pennants in 1921, 1922, and 1923, and in the latter year his first world's championship, cementing his hold on the New York public, which continued to stand by him in 1924 and 1925 when the team failed, finishing second in 1924 and seventh in 1925. In 1926 Huggins came back to win his fourth pennant. This was followed with pennants in 1927 and 1928. In those last two years he won two world's championships, beating the Pirates four straight games in 1927 and the Cardinals four in a row last year, which set a record never before approached.

This year luck was against him. Ruth was ill for a long while in the early part of the season and other ill and injured players hampered the progress of the club. Huggins's worry regarding the collapse of his one-time world's champions preyed on his mind and, it is believed, hastened his end. This worry added to the illness that had followed him for years—a series of misfortunes which culminated in an attack of influenza a year ago last Spring and kept him in bed for three weeks at another—and left him in weak physical condition.

For years he had been a highly nervous man, his condition aggravated by bad teeth, a poor digestion and an inability to rest. ◆

October 15, 1930

McCARTHY IS SIGNED AS YANKEE MANAGER

Contract Is for Two Years at Salary Reported to Be More Than $30,000 Annually.

PILOTED CUBS FIVE YEARS

By WILLIAM E. BRANDT.

JOSEPH VINCENT MCCARTHY, for the past five seasons manager of the Chicago Cubs, yesterday signed a two-year contract to manage the New York Yankees.

The financial terms of the document were not made public, but McCarthy stated without hesitation that "it is the best contract I have ever received in baseball." It probably is more than $30,000 a year.

The contract signing was dramatized in the Yankee offices on West Forty-second Street with Colonel Ruppert and the new manager exchanging felicitations and a fountain pen with which each in turn affixed his signature to the paper which made McCarthy successor to Bob Shawkey, manager of the Yanks for the current year.

Movie-tone cameras and sound machines, still cameras and newspapermen were present at the ceremony. Colonel Ruppert took the opportunity to record on the movie-tone film a eulogy of Bob Shawkey, the outgoing manager.

"I have the highest regard for Shawkey," he said. "He was one of the first players we purchased after I became interested in the club. I think he did very well this year. He was in a tough spot and I doubt if any manager could have done better.

SEES FUTURE FOR SHAWKEY.

"I am going to try to help him get a place as a manager somewhere in the minor leagues. »»

◀◀◀ I believe that with a little more experience he will make a great manager. I may some time be sorry for making the change we are making at this time, but we want McCarthy because he has proved his exceptional managerial ability, and he has had ripe experience.

"McCarthy will be absolute boss of the Yankees. Everything is up to him. All we ask is that he give us a winner, bring New York back into the world's series and the world's championship. I hope next time it will be a five-year contract he signs with us."

McCarthy, in his acceptance speech, said:

"I am very happy to take this position and to come into the American League under such fine conditions. I want to thank Colonel Ruppert for the confidence he places in me, and I will do all in my power to give New York fans what they want."

Asked about his plans, McCarthy said:

"We intend to set about reinforcing the club's playing personnel where we think it is needed. I expect to have Jimmie Burke, who has been my assistant for the past few years, as one of my coaches, though I have not yet spoken to him about it. I want Arthur Fletcher to retain his position with the club. I'll be glad to have Fletch if he wants the job."

Yesterday's official announcement of McCarthy's appointment fulfilled the anticipation of baseball men who have considered McCarthy in line for the position ever since he resigned the Chicago managership in favor of Rogers Hornsby in the closing week of the National League season.

The new Yankee chief enjoys the distinction of having become one of baseball's most highly esteemed managers without having attained major league rank during his playing days.

In 1914 he played with Buffalo, then went with the Federal League. When the Federal League disbanded McCarthy joined the Louisville team of the American Association and stayed ten years, first as second baseman, then, in 1919, he became player-manager, and in 1920 he gave up the playing side of the game to devote all of his efforts to managing. He managed the Colonels to two pennants, and his proudest boast is that they were always "in the money" as long as he was manager.

With the Cubs, after taking charge in the Fall of 1925, he built up the team by judicious selection of minor league players and two major deals which brought Cuyler and Hornsby to Chicago's North Side. The winning of the 1929 pennant climaxed his Chicago career, although the Cubs were defeated four games to one, by the Athletics in the world's series. ◆

Joe McCarthy in 1931

March 17, 1932

Ruth's Bat Has Yielded Nearly $1,000,000; Salary Equals That of President of U. S.

Special to The New York Times.

ST. PETERSBURG, FLA., MARCH 16.—Babe Ruth's new contract, the seventh he has signed as a Yankee player, at the termination of its requirements will have advanced his lifetime total of baseball salaries to close to the $800,000 mark.

If his world's series shares are added and his income from newspaper syndicate articles, royalties on trade uses of his name and perquisites such as movie appearances, his lifetime earnings since becoming a professional baseball player in 1914 approach the $1,000,000 mark.

Ruth's salary for the 1932 campaign—$75,000—equals that paid to the President of the United States.

Ruth signed for $600 when he first broke into the game as a professional. That was in 1914 when he joined the Baltimore club. Later in the year he went to the Red Sox, where he drew an additional $1,300.

In 1922 his salary, to the astonishment of the baseball world, rose to $52,000, an unheard-of figure for a player. He then was with the Yankees. He reached the crest in 1930, however, when he signed with the Yanks for $80,000, which pay he also received last year.

The tabulation of Ruth's baseball salaries, as checked by the Babe himself today, follows:

Year.	Club.	Salary.
1914	Baltimore	$600
1914	Boston	$1,300
1915	Boston	$3,500
1916	Boston	$3,500
1917	Boston	$5,000
1918	Boston	$7,000
1919	Boston	$10,000
1920	New York	$20,000
1921	New York	$30,000
1922	New York	$52,000
1923	New York	$52,000
1924	New York	$52,000
1925	New York	$52,000
1926	New York	$52,000
1927	New York	$70,000
1928	New York	$70,000
1929	New York	$70,000
1930	New York	$80,000
1931	New York	$80,000
1932	New York	$75,000
Total		**$785,900** ◆

June 2, 1932

Gehrig Ties Record of Four Circuit Drives in One Game

He Connects in First Four Times at Bat and Nearly Makes Fifth in Ninth.

By WILLIAM E. BRANDT.
Special to The New York Times.

PHILADELPHIA, JUNE 3.—Henry Louis Gehrig's name today took rank in baseball's archives along with Bobby Lowe and Ed Delahanty, the only other sluggers who, in more than half a century of recorded diamond battles, ever hit four home runs in one major league game.

Largely because of Gehrig's quartet of tremendous smashes the Yankees outstripped ⟩⟩⟩

≪≪ the Athletics in a run-making marathon, winning, 20 to 13, after twice losing the lead because of determined rallies by the American League champions.

Homers by Combs, Lazzeri and Ruth, the latter the Babe's fifteenth of the season, enabled the Yankees to tie the all-time record of seven homers by one club in one game, performed three times before 1900, by Detroit, New York and Pittsburgh, of the old National League, and once in modern times, by the Athletics on June 3, 1921.

YANKEES SET TEAM MARK.

The Yanks, with their twenty-three hits, also set a new modern club-batting record for total bases, with fifty, which eclipsed the previous modern major league mark of forty-six and the American League's best total of forty-four. This achievement fell short by only five bases of the all-time record, set by Cincinnati in 1923. Both clubs' total of seventy-seven bases also set an American League mark.

Gehrig in his first four times at bat hammered the ball outside the playing area. In the first and fifth innings he sailed balls into the stands in left centre. In the fourth and seventh he fired over the right-field wall.

The outcome of the game evened the series, two to two, but the crowd of 5,000 seemed to concentrate on encouraging Gehrig to hit a fifth homer and thus surpass a brilliant record in baseball's books.

Lou had two chances. He grounded out in the eighth, but in the ninth he pointed a terrific drive which Simmons captured only a few steps from the furthest corner of the park. A little variance to either side of its actual line of flight would have sent the ball over the fence or into the stands.

As it was, Lou's four homers tied the all-time record of Lowe in hitting for the circuit in four successive times at bat in 1894. Only three of Delahanty's were in successive times at bat. Both Lowe and Delahanty had a single in the same game with their four homers, so that Gehrig fell one short of tying their record for total bases.

Lazzeri's homer with the bases filled was his fifth hit of the game. He and Gehrig each drove in six runs.

◆

June 26, 1932

GEHRIG'S 19TH HOMER HELPS YANKS WIN, 7-4

Plays in 1,104th Successive Game, a League Record, and Celebrates Fittingly.

By WILLIAM E. BRANDT.

LOU GEHRIG, BY DRIVING HOME the first two Yankee runs with his nineteenth homer of the season and by breaking a 4-4 tie with a seventh-inning single, played the major role in the 7-to-4 victory over the Philadelphia Athletics before 20,000 fans at the Yankee Stadium yesterday.

Merely by being in the line-up Gehrig set a new major league record for successive games played as a member of one team. The contest was his 1,104th since becoming the regular first baseman June 1, 1925, surpassing the 1,103 consecutive league games played by Joe Sewell with Cleveland.

In the realm of baseball endurance records, only Everett Scott's string of 1,307 games remains for Gehrig to shoot at and Scott divided his allegiance between the Boston Red Sox and the Yankees in the course of his uninterrupted competition. ◆

July 10, 1932

DICKEY OF YANKEES DRAWS $1,000 FINE

Suspended for Attack on Reynolds.

RUPPERT FILES PROTEST

By THE ASSOCIATED PRESS.

CHICAGO, JULY 9.—Catcher Bill Dickey of the New York Yankees was suspended until Aug. 4 and fined $1,000 for striking Carl Reynolds, Washington outfielder.

The penalty, one of the heaviest ever assessed a major league player for fighting, was announced today by President Will Harridge of the American League after several days' study of the assault, which occurred in the first game of the Washington-New York double-header July 4. The month's suspension went into effect after the battle.

Dickey, one of the big cogs in the Yankee machine, was infuriated when Reynolds scored standing up on a squeeze play. As the Washington outfielder went to pass the plate Dickey struck him on the jaw. The lower part of the jaw was broken in two places and Reynolds has been unable to eat solid food since. He will be out of the game for at least another month, President Harridge was advised.

DICKEY NOTIFIED BY TELEGRAM.

Notification of the fine and suspension of Dickey came in the form of a telegram to the player from President Harridge in Chicago who characterized the attack as "malicious and unwarranted."

Both Colonel Jacob Ruppert, owner of the Yankees, and Manager Joe McCarthy denounced the league's action as unduly excessive, and following an exchange of telegrams between Colonel Ruppert and President Harridge, the latter granted the Yankees' request for an immediate hearing on an appeal from the decision. ◆

Bill Dickey in 1932.

August 14, 1932

HOMER BY RUFFING WINS FOR YANKS, 1-0
Pitching Ace Fans 12 and Gives only 3 Hits in 10-inning Victory Over Senators

By WILLIAM E. BRANDT

WASHINGTON, Aug 18.–Having blanked the Washington Senators with three hits for nine innings and finding himself no better than even the enemy at that stage, Charlie Ruffing stepped to bat today with two out in the tenth inning and whaled a liner into the left field bleachers for a home run and a 1-to-0 decision.

Ruffing achieved the first shutout credited to the Yankee staff since June 19, the staff's ninth of the season and the third which he featured Ruffing as the server. He blanked Cleveland May 15 and Washington May 21 with four and five hits respectively.

Today Ruffing allowed three safe-ties and hung up the first extra-inning whitewashing credited to the Yankee men-at-arms this season. Alphonse Thomas, by holding the Yanks scoreless for nine innings, was the first to take them that far without a score in an American League game.

Ruffing made three out of the seven hits Thomas allowed, thus going to considerable length to attach his fourteenth victory against five defeats.

The big Indianan fanned an even dozen in the course of his mound masterpiece, ten of them in the first nine innings, advancing his season's strike-out standard for the major leagues to date to 161, a lead over seventeen for Lefty Gomez. ◆

October 1, 1932

YANKEES BEAT CUBS FOR 3D in ROW, 7-5, AS 51,000 LOOK ON

Ruth and Gehrig, Each With 2 Homers, Set Pace as New York Nears Series Title.

BABE'S FIRST TALLIES 3

His Second Brings Wild Acclaim—Hartnett and Cuyler Also Deliver Circuit Drives.

PENNOCK STARS ON MOUND

Veteran Relieves Pipgras in Ninth and Halts Chicago Rally—Governor Roosevelt in Crowd.

By JOHN DREBINGER.

CHICAGO, Oct. 1—Four home runs, two by the master hitter of them all, Babe Ruth, and the other pair by his almost equally proficient colleague, Columbia Lou Gehrig, advanced the New York Yankees to within one game of their third World's Series sweep today.

The American League champions once again overpowered the Cubs to win their third straight game of the current classic.

Those four blows made the final score 7 to 5. They crushed not only the National League standard-bearers, but a gathering of 51,000 which jammed Wrigley Field to the limits of its capacity and packed two wooden temporary bleachers outside the park. Included in the gathering was Governor Roosevelt of New York, the Democratic

The American League New York Yankees and the Chicago Cubs carry an oversized American flag into Wrigley Field before a game of the World Series, Chicago, Illinois, 1932.

Presidential candidate.

Thus, with three victories tucked away against no defeats, the Yankees, now skillfully piloted by Joe McCarthy, who bossed these same Cubs only two years ago, have advanced to a point where they need only one more game to clinch the world's championship. In addition they have a chance to add still further to their remarkable world's series record. They have now competed in eleven straight series encounters without suffering a single reversal.

It was a warm day, clear and sunny, though rather windy. There was a gay, holiday spirit in the air that never forsook the gathering, for Chicago puts a great deal more fervor in its baseball than does New York. It seemed as though the fans of this mid-Western metropolis simply would not believe how severely and decisively their champions had been manhandled by the mighty Yankees in the first two games in the East.

RUTH'S DRIVE AWES THRONG.

They roared their approval of every good play made by the Cubs. They playfully tossed bright yellow lemons at Babe Ruth and booed him thoroughly as the great man carried on a pantomime act while standing at the plate.

Then they sat back, awed and spellbound, as the Babe, casting aside his buffoonery, smashed one of the longest home runs ever seen at Wrigley Field.

It was an amazing demonstration by baseball's outstanding figures, who a few weeks ago was ill and confined to his bed. It confounded the crowd, which in paid attendance numbered 49,986.

The Cubs took the field with their hopes resting upon the stout right arm of Charlie Root, but Charlie was unequal to the task. He failed to survive five rounds, retiring immediately after Ruth and Gehrig had blasted their second two homers. These came in succession in the fifth like a flash of lightning and a clap of thunder.

The Babe's two homers were his first of the current series, but they sent his all-time world's series record for home runs to fifteen. For Gehrig, his two gave him a total of three for the series and an all-time record of seven.

Fittingly enough, the Babe was the first to touch off the explosion and his opening smash sent the Yanks away to a three-run lead in the very first inning. There was a sharp wind blowing across the playing field toward the right-field bleachers that threatened to raise havoc with the players, and it did very shortly.

Root pitched cautiously, fearful of what would happen if he allowed the Babe to shoot one high in the air with that brisk breeze behind it. His first two offerings went wide of the plate. Then he put one over, and away the ball went. It was a lofty shot that soared on and on until it dropped deep in the temporary stands. Thus, the Cubs, who had planned to fight so desperately ⟫⟫

«< for this game, already were three runs to the bad.

In the fourth the Cubs drew even amid the most violent vocal demonstration of the afternoon. Jurges, eager to make amends for his earlier miscue, slapped a low liner to left, and the crowd howled with glee as Ruth failed in a heroic attempt to make a shoe-string catch of the ball. Jurges gained two bases on the hit. Good naturedly, the Babe doffed his cap in acknowledgment to the adverse plaudits of the fans and the play went on. But it seems decidedly unhealthy for any one to taunt the great man Ruth too much and very soon the crowd was to learn its lesson. A single lemon rolled out to the plate as Ruth came up in the fifth and in no mistaken motions the Babe notified the crowd that the nature of his retaliation would be a wallop right out the confines of the park.

Root pitched two balls and two strikes, while Ruth signaled with his fingers after each pitch to let the spectators know exactly how the situation stood. Then the mightiest blow of all fell.

It was a tremendous smash that bore straight down the centre of the field in an enormous arc, came down alongside the flagpole and disappeared behind the corner formed by the scoreboard and the end of the right-field bleachers.

It was Ruth's fifteenth homer in world's series competition and easily one of his most gorgeous. The crowd, suddenly unmindful of everything save that it had just witnessed an epic feat, hailed the Babe with a salvo of applause.

Root, badly shaken, now faced Gehrig and his feelings well can be imagined. The crowd was still too much excited over the Ruth incident to realize what was happening when Columbia Lou lifted an enormous fly high in the air. As it sailed on the wings of the lake breeze the ball just cleared the high flagpole and dropped in the temporary stand.

Grimm, the player-manager of the Cubs, called time. Consolingly he invited Root to retire to the less turbulent confines of the clubhouse. ◆

June 20, 1933

Ruth Benched for First Time As Yankees Divide With Tigers

Babe Fails to Start Second Game, Walker Replacing Him in Left.

By JAMES P. DAWSON.
Special to The New York Times.

DETROIT, JUNE 25.—The experience of being a bench warmer for a reason other than illness or accident overtook Babe Ruth today for the first time since he became a big league star.

In the second game of the drawn-out doubleheader with the Tigers, which the Yanks won, 3-0, after losing the opener, 6-5, Ruth was benched. He gave way to Dixie Walker in left field.

The fact that the Babe has been in a hitting slump gave rise to speculation regarding his failure to start the game.

Since he got his sixteenth home run of the season at St. Louis last Friday he has made two hits in seventeen times at bat. Manager Joe McCarthy explained, however, that Ruth merely was getting a rest for which he applied.

"The heat is terrific and Babe just asked for a little respite," said the Yankee pilot, when asked to explain Ruth's absence from the line-up.

A Bronx boy of giant stature supplied the winning wallop for the Tigers in the opener. His name is Hank Greenberg, and he attended James Monroe High School. His contribution was a sharp single to centre with two on in the twelfth which scored Gehringer with the winning run after Frankie Crosetti had booted Gehringer's grounder to give him a life. ◆

Babe Ruth scoring his two-run homer at the first All-Star Game at Comiskey Park in Chicago. Lou Gehrig and the White Sox bat boy greet him.

July 6, 1933

AMERICAN LEAGUE BEATS RIVALS, 4-2

49,000 See Ruth's Homer as Nationals Are Toppled.

By JOHN DREBINGER.
Special to THE NEW YORK TIMES.

CHICAGO, JULY 6.—The National League is still trying to catch up with Babe Ruth, but apparently with no more success than in recent world's series conflicts.

Today, in the presence of a capacity throng of 49,000 in Comiskey Park, the great man of baseball fittingly whaled a home run into the right-field pavilion that gave the American League's all-star cast the necessary margin to bring down the pick of the National League in the "game of the century."

That smash, propelled off Willie Hallahan, star left-handed pitcher of the Cardinals, and with a runner on base, gave the team piloted by the venerable Connie Mack the victory by a score of 4 to 2. There was nothing the equally sagacious John J. McGraw could do about it.

McGraw, coming out of retirement for this singular event, the first of its kind in the history of the two major leagues, threw practically all his available manpower into the fray.

But there seemed to be no way whatever of effacing the effect of that Ruthian wallop, even though the National Leaguers later staged a mild uprising of their own with Frankie Frisch, banging a homer into the stands.

Mack and McGraw, matching wits for the first time since their last world series clash in 1913, each sent three hurlers to the mound, but to Mack went the honors because the greater power was to be found in the mighty bludgeons of the American Leaguers. ◆

September 30, 1933

LOU GEHRIG WEDS IN NEW ROCHELLE

Mayor Otto Marries Yankees' First Baseman to Miss Eleanor Twitchell.

Special to The New York Times.

NEW ROCHELLE, N. Y., SEPT. 29.—Henry Lou Gehrig Jr., first baseman of the New York Yankees, was married this morning at his home, 5 Meadow Lane, this city, to Miss Eleanor Grace Twitchell of Chicago, daughter of Frank Bradford Twitchell, retired Chicago restaurant operator.

The ceremony was performed by Mayor Walter G. C. Otto. News of the ceremony was kept a secret until 3 o'clock this afternoon so that the first announcement of the marriage could be made at the New York and Washington ball game.

The couple will live here at 5 Circuit Road. The ball player gave his age as 30 and the bride, 27.

Miss Twitchell, a baseball enthusiast, was said to have met Gehrig on one of his trips West in 1926. She is a graduate of the University of Wisconsin. ◆

Lou Gehrig, first baseman for the Yankees, with his fiancee, Eleanor Twitchell, at Comiskey Park in Chicago on June 19, 1933

September 2, 1934

BABE RUTH YIELDS TO TIME, THE UMPIRE

About to Leave the Diamond, He Tells Of His Big Thrills In Baseball

THE KING OF DIAMONDS is about to abdicate. His crown has been a flannel cap and his scepter a hardwood bat. His dominions have been ball parks and his loyal subjects cheering "fans." The sphere which other monarchs have grasped tightly in their hands he has rapped with mighty swings.

His prowess caught the imagination of the nation. To ragamuffin as well as scholar, to rotund business man as well as social debutante, Babe Ruth became a hero. Candy and clothes were named for him; articles signed by him were printed throughout the country; hard wallops in other sports were described by his name, and his round face with its broad nose and heavy lips became as well known as the blue bell on a telephone sign. No tale of ancient monarch has more romance attached to it than Babe Ruth's saga, which opens in a parochial school in Baltimore.

I waited for him the other day by appointment in front of the Yankee Stadium, the huge amphitheatre which is known as the "House That Ruth Built." As he drove up in his little roadster the policeman with whom I was talking nudged me and with awe in his voice whispered, "Here comes the Babe." Suddenly, apparently from nowhere, appeared half a hundred youngsters, who surrounded the big man as he alighted from his car. The day was warm and he wore neither hat nor coat. His white silk shirt had half-length sleeves and was open at the throat, disclosing the powerful muscles of his neck and forearms. Striped slacks clothed legs which seemed slight for his massive torso.

Using the back of the car as a desk, this left-handed ball player began signing in pencil, with his right hand, copy books which were eagerly held up to him.

"Babe, please sign this," the youngsters shouted. Without saying a word he began to do so. It was evident this was a daily procedure.

Presently a sheet of rumpled paper was handed to him.

"That's out!" he roared. His voice is deep and husky. "I've told you over and over again I'll only sign books and pictures. Sheets of paper don't go."

Then he saw the boy who was holding it—a tiny lad, thin and undernourished, who could not hold back his tears of disappointment. Six foot three looked down on three foot six and noticed moisture in large blue eyes.

"Well, I guess I'll have to make an exception," he said as he took the thumb-marked sheet and wrote "'Babe' Ruth" on it.

At last he was finished and entered the building and made his way through a maze of underground passages. A steady barrage of "Hello, Babe!" met him. He acknowledged the greetings with a grunt and a salute of his left hand. The response was always the same until a huge colored cook, bending over a great range, turned and hailed him as the others had done.

"It's nuts to you," responded the Babe as he entered the Yankee dressing room.

It was in this room, filled with green lockers, stools, low divans, sun lamps and fifteen or twenty chattering men getting into their uniforms, that the Babe posed and talked. At times the conversation was interrupted; at times the crowd made drawing difficult.

The Babe sat on a low three-legged stool, looking very self-conscious. It was not until the proceedings had lost some of their novelty and the spectators had dispersed that he relaxed and became easy in his manner.

It was then that he spoke about his early days in Baltimore and how he happened to go to St. Mary's Industrial School in that city. He was playing in the streets when a man in clerical garb, whom he mistook for a priest but who was

Babe Ruth in Yankee Stadium with two rookies, Red Rolfe, left and Don Heffner before a 1934 game.

really a brother, came up to him and offered him a good home and also the chance to learn a trade.

"They started out to teach me to be a shirt-maker, and I'll bet you if I hadn't become a ball-player I would have been a darned good one," he said.

The school had a ball team and it was not long before the newcomer was spotted by the boys as good material. George Herman Ruth became a regular member. At first he played any position but his mastery over drop-balls and curves resulted in his being put in the pitcher's box whenever a game was played with a visiting team.

The school coach was Brother Gilbert, and it was he who was responsible for Ruth becoming a professional ball-player. Noticing Ruth's ability, he spoke about him to Jack Dunn, owner of the Baltimore Orioles.

"Dunn was a chap who was always willing to try out new players," Ruth said. "So when Brother Gilbert talked to him about me he came down to watch me play. After the game he told me to come and see him. As I was leaving his office one of the older players said, 'Here comes another one of Dunn's babies!' I was a big fellow then, although I was only 18, and I guess calling a guy my size 'baby' struck the bunch as funny. They all started calling me 'Babe,' and that's been my name ever since. I am so used to it that any time some one calls me George I have to pinch myself to let myself know that I am being talked to." »»

«««   It was twenty-two years ago that Ruth became a professional. By the time he was 21 he had developed into a first-class pitcher who had made a record of twenty-nine consecutive scoreless innings for the Boston Red Sox. But Ed Barrow, manager of that team, noticed that the young pitcher had a terrific wallop when he hit the ball. It was he who made Ruth an outfielder, so that he could use the Babe's hitting powers every day.

"The ideas about baseball were changing just about that time," the Babe said. "Socking the apple became more popular than twirling it.

"I was tickled at the change for another reason. I liked pitching, and I was good at it, if I say so myself. The trouble with pitching is that you don't play every day. An outfielder does. So it was all right by me when they took me out of the box and put me in the field.

"You know," he continued, "a fellow who hits the onion gets more credit than the fellow who tries to prevent him. I suppose that's human nature. The shouting is all for the fellow who does something, not for those who prevent something from being done.

"A lot of folks think that when a man gets up to bat all he has to do is wait until the right kind of ball comes along and then hit it. There's something more to the game than just that. I learned a good lesson when I was pitching one of my first games. I had done pretty well up to that time, but we were up against a team we had never played before, and somehow or other I could not fool the batters. Every time I pitched a curve, they stood still; every time I sent one over the plate, they connected with it.

"After the game was over an old-timer came to me and said: 'Say, kid, how do you ever expect to pitch? You stick your tongue out whenever you are going to send over a curve. What are you trying to do, let the batter know in advance what to expect?'

"I study the pitchers. I learn to know them and try to get a line on how they think, so that I have an idea of what they are likely to do, even if they don't stick out their tongues. When you get to know a fellow well enough, you can sort of know beforehand what his next move will be."

He rubbed his chin with his brawny hand when I asked him what he thought were the high spots in his career.

"That's a hard one to answer," he said. "I felt pretty good the first time I played in a world series game. I got a kick when I struck out the three strongest hitters of the Detroit team in one inning. One of them was Ty Cobb, who, I think, was the best all-around player I came across in my whole career. Those twenty-nine scoreless innings meant something in my young life, too. So did the catch which decided the world series with the Cardinals. I don't mean maybe when I tell you that I felt pretty good making a record of sixty home runs in one season. But I think the proudest moment of my life was that day, a bunch of years ago, when I first walked out on a baseball field as a 'pro' wearing the uniform of the old Orioles.

"I was in a daze. Here I was being paid for doing what I wanted to do. I was to get $600 and that seemed an awful lot of money to a kid who never had any and whose one ambition was to own a bicycle."

There is something of the boy still about Ruth. He is generous, easy-going and in some ways ingenuous. One can understand what happened to the gawky, spindly-legged youth, who never had had more than a dollar or two to his name, when such a salary loomed before him. Within a few months his pay was raised. At the end of the first year he was sold to the Red Sox and he received another rise. Yearly he found his income increasing—and he found ways of spending it. The Bambino became the bad boy of baseball. He defied authority, he gambled and he caroused.

Yet his popularity increased and he was the greatest drawing card in the game. This was for two reasons. First, he could be depended upon to hit the ball when a run was necessary. Second, there is a picturesque quality in everything he does.

He visited sick children whom he did not know. He forgot to keep an appointment with Queen Mary. He showed Marshal Foch how to swing a bat. And day after day, while he was doing such things, he was pounding balls into the bleachers.

In 1922 Colonel Ruppert, owner of the Yan-

Babe Ruth relaxes at home with wife Claire (right) and daughter Dorothy in February 1934 after recovering from the flu.

kees, signed him to a four-year contract at the unheard-of figure of $52,000 a year. Within two years it began to look as though that contract had been a mistake. The Babe seemed incorrigible. Brother Gilbert had been called in and Ruth had promised to be good. James J. Walker, at that time a State Senator, had delivered a speech telling him that he was the idol of the younger generation and as such should be an example, and the big, good-hearted ball-player gulped hard and said he would reform. But nothing happened except that his waistline began to grow larger and his batting percentage smaller. The wise-acres saw him on the downgrade, going fast.

The opening of the 1925 season found him a physical wreck; he was not able to get into a uniform until June. But even a serious illness had no effect upon this exuberant player. Huggins, the little manager of the Yankees, felt that something drastic in the way of punishment was needed. A $5,000 fine and a suspension were imposed for misconduct off the ball field.

Then Ruth changed. In his own words, he "woke up to what a fool he had been." He reformed his ways, began living a regular life and saving money. The old-time sting returned to his hits.

When his old contract expired he signed a new one at $80,000 a year. More money piled in— from syndicated newspaper articles, from the use of his name in connection with merchandise and from half a dozen other sources.

This year, although his hitting and his salary are well below his best, he is still an important factor in the Yankee line-up. He has passed the 700 mark for home runs in his major league career, a record no one else has approached. And he still makes a strong appeal to the public. Yet he has announced his intention of retiring.

I asked him his reason.

"I am getting too old for the game," he replied, "and know it, even if the folks in the grand stand don't. The trouble with most players is that they don't get on to the fact until long after the guys in the bleachers are beginning to turn their thumbs down. There's nothing sadder than to see a fellow trotting around the diamond and hear his legs creaking for want of oil. If I kept on playing much longer I'd be tripping over my whiskers or putting on a pair of specs to see the ball.

"In my day I've seen too many players trying to look frisky on the field when they ought to be home dandling their grandchildren on their knees. That's when the crowd begins to feel sorry for them. I don't want to become one of that kind. I know enough to stop running when my legs begin to feel tired.

"Thank goodness, I woke up to myself soon enough to salt away some dough. My family is looked after and I have enough to worry along on. I am going to take things easy. Play a game of contract if I feel like it or go out and shoot some golf. I can also hunt and fish. And then, if I find that things are sort of boring, there are always enough vacant lots around that I can go out and have a game of ball with a bunch of kids." ◆

January 20, 1935

YANKEES ACQUIRE TWO MORE CLUBS

Oakland and Joplin Bring the Total to Seven.

By JOHN DREBINGER.

APPARENTLY CONVINCED THAT "chain store" base-ball offers the best means known for the devel-opment of talent, the Yankees yesterday virtually placed themselves on a par with the world's cham-pion Cardinals as outstanding exponents of this system by announcing that they had just increased their minor league holdings by two more clubs.

The two new Yankee farms, Secretary Ed Bar-row revealed, are the Oakland Club of the Pacific Coast League and Joplin of the Western Associa-tion, which now bring Colonel Ruppert's minor league affiliations to a total of seven clubs. Still another club of lower classification is to be ac-quired later.

The acquisition of Oakland also gives the Yan-kees their second Class AA holding, their other being the Newark Bears in the International League. Joplin operates in a Class C circuit to give the Yanks their second club in this minor league group, the other being Wheeling in the Middle Atlantic League.

OTHER CLUBS IN FOLD.

The other clubs now in the Yankee fold, which operate under the general supervision of George Weiss, are Binghamton in the New York-Penn-sylvania League, a Class A loop; Norfolk in the Piedmont League, a Class B circuit, and Wash-ington, Pa., of the Pennsylvania State Associa-tion, which has a Class D rating.

Thus in the short space of about five years the Yankees have constructed for themselves an elaborate labyrinth of minor league connections which, like that perfected by the Cardinals, in-cludes one or more farm clubs in each of the five divisions of minor league baseball.

Although entering into "working agreements" with and buying into minor league clubs have been practiced in major league baseball for many years, "chain store" baseball, as it first was popularly or, rather, unpopularly called, is generally conceded to have been the product of the fertile baseball mind of Branch Rickey, vice president of the Cards.

At first the idea encountered considerable oppo-sition from numerous quarters, not the least of these being Commissioner K. M. Landis, who openly voiced his disapproval of the practice as savoring too much of "syndicate baseball."

In time, however, as the Cards continued to ex-ploit the system with success and with no unfavor-able reactions otherwise, the opposition lessened and finally disappeared altogether when, during the years of depression, it was shown that numer-ous minor leagues were weathering the storm chiefly because of their major league backing.

Commissioner Landis himself gave his si-lent consent with the adoption of stringent rules stipulating that no major league club can hold more than one franchise in the same league, that all such affiliations must be openly recorded and that all player transactions among affiliat-ed clubs must observe the same restrictions as among unaffiliated clubs. ◆

Feb 27, 1935

RUTH LEAVES YANKS TO JOIN THE BRAVES

Gets 3-Year Contract as Vice President, Assistant Manager and Active Player.

By JAMES P. DAWSON

BABE RUTH TERMINATED his fifteen year career with the Yankees yesterday to become an executive of the Boston Braves as well as assistant manager and an active player.

The home run monarch closed the deal, by which he leaves the American League to join the National League, with Judge Emil Fuchs, president of the Boston club. A three-year contract has been agreed upon.

Under the terms Ruth receives a straight salary, the amount of which was not divulged. But, according to Judge Fuchs Ruth's earnings under the new contract will be greater than his income from the Yankees last year, when he received $35,000.

Colonel Jacob Ruppert, owner of the Yankees, presented Ruth with his unconditional release and was instrumental in inducing American League club owners to waive on the Babe, making possible his transfer from the American League to the National.

Actual signing of the contract will take place tomorrow, it is expected, in Boston. Ruth will leave tomorrow to be the guest of honor at a testimonial dinner in the Copley Plaza Hotel.

His work with the Braves commences at once. The Babe said he plans to leave Sunday afternoon for St. Petersburg, Fla., to join Manager Bill McKechnie and the Braves assembled there. If he is going back to familiar scenes and surroundings when he returns to Boston as a player-manager, Ruth will be back at an old stamping ground when he goes to St. Petersburg.

Perhaps not more than a mile will separate the burly figure, who will be clad in a foreign uniform, from the Miller Huggins Field training ground of his old cronies, the Yankees, in St. Petersburg. The Braves train across town from the Yankee site, at Waterfront Park.

LETTER OUTLINES THE PLAN.

A letter outlining his plan was sent by Judge Fuchs to Colonel Ruppert under date of Monday. Yesterday, when the announcement was made officially, copies of the letters were made public, together with a letter from Ruth to Judge Fuchs. In this the Bambino acknowledged the generosity of Colonel Ruppert in permitting him to transfer his baseball activities from a 154-game player to part-time player, advisor and executive; expressed the pleasure he felt in his long association with Colonel Ruppert and the Yankees and pledged himself to work unstintingly for success in Boston.

When plans were finally worked out, Colonel Ruppert summoned newspaper men to his office for the official announcement.

"I am going to tell you something that may surprise you," he began, while Judge Fuchs, Ruth and Barrow listened as attentively as the newspaper men. "Last September Ruth told me he would not sign another player contract, that he would sign only as a player-manager. Shortly after he left for Japan and I did not see him again until today.

"Reports were circulated regarding Ruth's future, but of these I knew nothing officially. All I knew was that Ruth was determined to sign only as a player-manager, and in this capacity our lists were closed to him.

"Last Sunday Ruth phoned me and told me he had been talking with Judge Fuchs and that there might be something doing in Boston if I would consent. The judge phoned me Monday and outlined his plan. After hearing it I felt it my duty to aid Ruth in every way toward attaining the goal he had set himself in baseball. ≫≫

◀◀◀   TELLS OF GREAT OPPORTUNITY.

"It would have been unsportsmanlike of me if I didn't grant Ruth's request. Opportunity knocks but once at the door of any man, and I saw here the greatest opportunity Ruth ever had. It would not have been fair to stand in his way.

"We have been together for fifteen years and our relations have always been cordial. We always got along well. We have had our little battles, but none of them was serious and all were easily ironed out.

On opening day of Boston Braves training camp, Babe Ruth shakes hands with Manager Bill McKechnie in St. Petersberg, Florida, March 5, 1935.

"Today I hand Ruth his unconditional release. The American League clubs have all waived on him. He goes back to Boston, the city in which his major league career started. There are no strings on the release I give him. I get not a penny in return, not a promise, nothing. Ruth is a free man.

"Ruth has always been a credit to baseball, and it has always been a pleasure to have had him with us. We regret that our long association is ending. We will miss him, but his future is of paramount importance. Baseball needs Ruth, just as Ruth needs baseball, and in giving him his release I offer him my heartfelt congratulations and hope sincerely he will continue the success that has been his for so long a time."

Ruth pledged his every effort in the interests of Braves success in a short speech.

"I am glad and thankful for the opportunity Colonel Ruppert made possible with his unselfish aid," said Babe. "We have always been friends, and we will continue to be friends. He has always been wonderful to me. Our little arguments never did last long, and never really meant much.

"I am pleased to be going to Boston, back where I started in baseball, and I promise that I will work to the limit of my strength to deliver. I'll play as many games as my legs will permit, and I'll be glad to understudy my friend, Bill McKechnie."

Unquestionably, Ruth's engagement by the Braves paves the way for him eventually to move into a position of supreme command as manager. McKechnie, Judge Fuchs said, is engaged under a year-to-year contract. When, and if, Ruth succeeds to the Braves management, it is expected McKechnie will be promoted to an executive berth with the club. ◆

June 6, 1936

Mayor Fiorello LaGuardia presents Lou Gehrig with a scroll in honor of Gehrig's 1700th consecutive game.

GEHRIG'S HOME RUN HELPS YANKS SCORE

Playing 1,700th Game in Row, Lou Smashes No. 9 in 4-3 Victory Over Indians.

By JAMES P. DAWSON

LOU GEHRIG CELEBRATED his 1,700th consecutive game in a matchless career yesterday at the Stadium as the Yankees opened a three-game series against the Indians.

Lefty Gomez celebrated his first pitching assignment since May 26, when he went into temporary retirement claiming a sore flipper.

And the Yanks celebrated the return of their guests from the banks of Lake Erie by slapping their sixth defeat in an unbroken string against Cleveland to maintain their position two and a half games ahead of the Red Sox. The score was 4 to 3.

Gehrig celebrated in typical fashion. He clouted No. 9 in his season's collection of home runs, but he did it the hard way. This latest four-master was a drive inside the park to left field by a deadly consistent right-field hitter.

The blow came in the sixth inning, a slap that for any one except Gehrig would have been just a single. But Steve O'Neill, quite naturally, had his outfielders playing Battering Lou the way they used to play Babe Ruth, with the swing decidedly to the right.

Before the Indians could recover from their amazement, or Joe Vosmik could recover the ball as it careened crazily in this strange pasture, the Iron Horse had galloped around the four-cornered route, completing his charge with a noble dive, face forward, in the dust at the plate. ◆

January 27, 1937

Babe Ruth Discusses Gehrig, Dean, The 1937 Pennant Races—And Golf

Believes Lou's 'Iron Man Stuff' Will Shorten Great Career

GEORGE HERMAN RUTH, promising New York left-handed golfer, spread his 240 pounds over a new Christmas chair yesterday and cheerfully discussed Lou Gehrig, baseball, the future, the past and the sad state of his putting.

A former ball player himself, now happily retired, Ruth dropped these remarks for The Associated Press:

Gehrig: "I think Lou's making one of the worst mistakes a ball player can make by trying to keep up that 'iron man' stuff....He's already cut three years off his baseball life with it.... He oughta learn to sit on the bench and rest.... They're not gonna pay off on how many games he's played in a row....

"The next two years will tell Gehrig's fate. When his legs go, they'll go in a hurry. The average ball fan doesn't realize the affect a single charley horse can have on your legs. If Lou stays out there every day and never rests his legs, one bad charley horse may start him downhill."

NO MORE $80,000 SALARIES

Note to prospective holdouts: "A ball player's worth whatever he can get, and believe me whatever he gets he's worth. I don't think salaries will ever get to the $80,000 a year stage again.... Dizzy Dean says he won't sign for less than $50,000....He'd be worth that in New York, but he won't get it in St. Louis....The Cards don't take in much more than that in profits."

The 1937 pennant races: "The Yanks should run away with the American. The Cards oughta win the National....I see McCarthy wants a couple of starting pitchers. If he gets 'em, the race will be over in the middle of the Summer.... Cleveland should be tough....I think they probably got the best of that St. Louis deal."

Future: "I'm not interested in any business. I've had all sorts of offers. One week in an office and I'd be dead. I've had a chance to go into the front office of a major league club, but I'm not interested. I need fresh air. If I can't get a major league manager's job, I'll just take it easy. The minors are out."

PLANS RADIO PROGRAM

"I guess I've made over $900,000 out of baseball alone. I didn't take very good care of it at first, but I started soon enough. Right now I'm making enough out of side lines to pay all my expenses. I made $1,500 for a five-minute broadcast the other night, and I've got a thirteen-week's program on the fire now."

Golf: "If it wasn't for golf, I'd really miss baseball. I play 240 days out of the 365 now. I've got my handicap down to three, but my putting's bad. I used to be a good putter, too. I'm not gonna cut down to the fourteen-club limit. I need sixteen. The weather's been so good, I may not spend so much time down South this Winter. I'll be in New York for my forty-second birthday on Feb. 6 and for the baseball writers' dinner the next day; then I'm going to Bermuda for a golf tournament on Feb. 15."

Whereupon the Babe looked down from his Riverside Drive apartment to the sun on the Hudson and moved from the Christmas chair toward the St. Albans golf course. ◆

March 4, 1937

Gehrig Signs for Movies, Bars Tarzan Role

By THE ASSOCIATED PRESS.

HOLLYWOOD, CALIF., MARCH 3.—Husky Lou Gehrig, a first-base fugitive from the New York Yankees, became a rookie movie actor tonight with a one-picture film contract "signed, sealed and delivered."

"And I won't go for that 'Tarzan' stuff, either," snapped the iron man of the Yankee infield after President Sol Lesser of Principal Productions announced Gehrig had been signed to make a picture after the baseball season was over.

Lesser, who made the announcement at a luncheon which followed Gehrig's arrival, said immediate tests will be made to determine "the type of character Lou will portray." Whatever the success of that first picture, it will not interfere with Gehrig's baseball career, the unsigned Yankee said.

Financial details were not disclosed.

That 'Tarzen stuff' harked back to the time last Winter when Gehrig, posing scantily clad and whirling a bludgeon, was being advanced as a possible successor to Johnny Weissmuller, the screen's swimming Tarzan.

"I hope to do something for the screen," said Lou, meditating on his esthetic nature as he caressed an overnight growth of beard. "Maybe they can do something for me too."

Gehrig will return to New York Saturday to renew salary negotiations with his baseball boss, Colonel Jacob Ruppert. The negotiations involve between $31,000 and $50,000, but Gehrig was reluctant to delve into details.

"All I can say is that I have no idea of giving up baseball," he declared.

Asked when he would join his playing mates at the Yankee training camp in Florida, Gehrig hedged:

"I won't know about that until I talk with the Colonel." ◆

January 14, 1938

Ruppert, Owner of Yankees and Leading Brewer, Dies

BOUGHT YANKEES IN 1915

With Huston He Paid $450,000 for Club Now Valued in the Millions

COLONEL JACOB RUPPERT was born in New York on Aug. 5, 1867. He was the son of Jacob Ruppert, owner of the Ruppert brewing concern, and Anna Gillig Ruppert. His paternal grandfather was a brewer in Bavaria, his native country, and afterward in New York, where he became owner of the old Turtle Bay Brewery in 1851, >>>

Yankees owner Jacob Ruppert watches from a knoll at the team's spring training facilities in St. Petersburg, Florida in March of 1937.

≪≪≪ establishing the nucleus of the latter-day institution. Jacob Ruppert Sr. entered the business the year the Colonel was born, and under his administration it became prosperous.

Young Jacob went to the Columbia Grammar School and afterward passed an examination to enter the School of Mines of Columbia University. At his father's request, however, he did not matriculate but entered the brewing business. He began by washing barrels and afterward served his time in the various departments of the brewery, eventually moving into the office to learn from his father the administrative details.

When the Colonel was 23 years old the elder Ruppert went away on an extended trip and young Jacob was placed in charge as general superintendent. He did so well that, in 1890, the position was made permanent. A few years afterward he was made general manager and later became vice president. Under his direction the brewery grew from an output of 350,000 barrels a year in 1892 to 1,300,000 barrels shortly before the adoption of the Eighteenth Amendment and the passage of the Volstead act in 1920. He was regarded as a special authority on all questions affecting the brewing industry.

JOINED NATIONAL GUARD IN 1886.

In 1886 Colonel Ruppert joined the Seventh Regiment, National Guard, serving as a private until 1889. He was appointed a Colonel on the staff of Governor David B. Hill that year, serving as aide de camp. In the administration of Governor Roswell P. Flower he continued as senior aide. For the rest of his life he retained his interest in military affairs and kept in continuous touch with the National Guard organization.

In 1899 Colonel Ruppert, named as a Tammany candidate, was elected to Congress from the Fifteenth district. Although the district was Republican at that time by a majority of 4,500, the Colonel won by a majority of 10,000, largely, it was said, because of his personal popularity. He served in the Fifty-sixth, Fifty-seventh,

Fifty-eighth and Fifty-ninth Congresses, retiring in 1907 to devote himself entirely to his business interests. During his service in Washington he observed strict party regularity.

In 1911 Colonel Ruppert was elected president of the United States Brewers Association, a position he held until 1914 and again after repeal. The organization represented an enormous capitalization. It saw the approaching shadow of a prohibitory amendment and waged a losing fight. Colonel Ruppert argued that thoughtful regulation of the liquor traffic was the solution of the drink problem. He declared that wherever prohibition had been adopted a state of disorder had followed and that the consumption of spirituous liquors and drugs had increased.

Colonel Ruppert maintained that beer was a liquid food, a healthful beverage and in no wise injurious to the human system. He never believed that the country would continue to endure the evils he saw arise as a result of prohibition and, in 1922, he announced that his brewing company would increase its capitalization, foreseeing a modification of the Volstead act and the legalizing of the sale of light wines and beer.

His anticipations realized, first by the return of legal beer and later by repeal of the prohibition amendment, Colonel Ruppert pushed his expansion plans. In 1932 he built a $500,000 warehouse at Third Avenue and Ninety-first Street, with a storage capacity of 500,000 barrels of beer. On May 25, 1933, he obtained from the Alcoholic Beverage Control Board the first license to manufacture beer in New York State. Two years later he bought the old Ehret brewery, adjoining his own plant on the north. The assessed valuation of the Ehret building was $1,500,000.

Since then the Ruppert brewery has reached an all-time production peak of more than 1,500,000 barrels annually. Colonel Ruppert maintained the active direction of its affairs until a short time before his death. He had been head of the business for 42 years, his father, who died in 1915, having retired in 1896.

Colonel Ruppert became interested in baseball in seeking investment outlets for his wealth, accumulated in the brewery business. Real estate and the stock market were other outlets, but none appealed to him over the years as did baseball. The game was a hobby with him also, like his interest in race horses, horse shows and his kennel of St. Bernard dogs, with which he won prizes for years, but it far overshadowed them, too. At the end it was his chief interest in life.

ENTERED BASEBALL IN 1915

The colonel's advent in baseball in 1915, when he and the late Colonel T. L. Huston jointly paid $450,000 for the then decrepit Yankees, marked the beginning of a team that has been distinguished for record-breaking performances in the national game.

Including 1921, when the first American League flag came to the Ruppert forces, the Yankees have won ten pennants and seven world series, both new records. Three times they took three pennants in a row, another unmatched achievement.

Colonel Ruppert's interest in his players was personal and profound. He knew them all and was as well posted on their capabilities and performances as any consistent baseball follower. He expected big things of his boys, as evidenced by his remark to Pitcher Vernon Gomez when the latter signed in 1937.

"Now," said the colonel, "go out and win thirty games."

Colonel Ruppert never married. His home was a twelve-room apartment at 1120 Fifth Avenue, where, alone, he directed a staff of servants consisting of a butler, maid, valet, cook and laundress. He was distinctly of the masculine type, and this was reflected in his business office, which was paneled in dark wood. There were no curtains. The only ornaments were two bronzes of American Indians, a bronze of an American eagle and a gold-fish aquarium. They all stood on marble pedestals. ◆

October 10, 1938

Letters to the Sports Editor.

MUCH ADO ABOUT LOU

Gehrig's 'Iron Man' Record Is Subject of Close Scrutiny

TO SPORTS EDITOR OF THE NEW YORK TIMES:

It was indeed refreshing to read the letter in your column last Saturday relative to "Iron Man" Gehrig. I believe that it echoes the sentiments of many baseball fans.

To my mind, Gehrig is the greatest first baseman ever, and I take my hat off to him for that. But this consecutive game drivel is a bit annoying because the streak is synthetic for several reasons.

As far as this fan is concerned, Gehrig's streak ended in June, 1932 (if memory does not fail) when, after having been seriously hurt by a pitched ball the previous day, he was the first man up for the Yankees in a game at Philadelphia in ⟫⟫⟫

Lou Gehrig poses on the dugout steps of Yankee Stadium shortly before he plays in his 2000th consecutive game.

which the batting order was scrambled for his benefit.

That incident was a travesty which should have been treated as such by the writers at the time. And just this week Gehrig's name appeared in a Yankee game with an unbroken string of zeros beside it—not even an "at bat" credited to him. Another silly procedure.

Furthermore, I don't think there ever has been a ball player who gets away with so much murder in the matter of "sassing" umpires. I have seen Gehrig on several occasions rant and rave to such an extent that he would have been thrown out and suspended were he some other player.

As one fan remarked recently while Gehrig was gesticulating wildly at the umpires, "I wonder what fine would be imposed on the umpire who dared to throw Gehrig out of a game, especially if it happened to be the first game of a double-header?"

So, all hail to Gehrig as the game's greatest first baseman! But as for the 2,000-odd consecutive game record, let's forget it. Unlike Gehrig, the ball player, the record is just "phoney."

Harold A. Reynolds.
New York, Oct. 3, 1938.

ABSENCES ARE INFREQUENT
To Sports Editor of the New York Times:

I am writing in reply to a letter concerning Lou Gehrig which appeared in last Saturday's edition of The Times.

I will admit that Gehrig at times has played only portions of games but that does not occur very often. As a rule he is on the field giving his all for the full nine innings. Therefore, I do not think that these occasional absences detract from his remarkable feat.

"A Reader" seems to have forgotten that the Yankee first baseman has compiled many enviable records of an entirely different nature from the consecutive-game record.

Upon examining the books, one will discover that he has a lifetime batting average well over .300. Besides that, he holds the records for runs batted in any one season and always is among the leaders in this department.

If Joe McCarthy were not satisfied with the performance of Gehrig, he would have benched him long ago. No manager will jeopardize his team's pennant chances by using an incapable player when he can secure some one else who is superior.

W. F. F.
New York, Oct. 3, 1938.

SEVEN MANAGERS AGREE
To Sports Editor of The New York Times:

Last Saturday I read a brilliant letter in The Times from "A Reader" who stated very forcibly that he was sick of seeing Lou Gehrig's name in the box scores.

Thinking there might be something to his argument, I wrote to seven managers of teams in the American League and all agreed that they were sick of seeing Gehrig in there, too.

I couldn't get a definite statement from Gabby Hartnett, but he admitted he would feel better if Gehrig's name were not in the box score during the world series.

On the other hand, Joe McCarthy states that he has seen Gehrig's name in the box scores so often that he might get sick if it were not included.

William Zupnik.
Hillside, N. J., Oct. 3, 1938.

EDITORIAL NOTE: There is no doubt that there is a strongly "synthetic" taint on Gehrig's streak of 2,122 consecutive games. At the same time, it must be admitted in all fairness that, in by far the greater number of those games, he has been a valuable cog in the Yankee machine. ◆

Barrow Is Elected President of Yanks After George Ruppert Declines Post

Weiss is Named Secretary

By JAMES P. DAWSON

EDWARD GRANT BARROW, who since 1920 has been business manager and secretary of the organization, yesterday was unanimously elected president of the American League Baseball Club of New York, the official title of the world champion Yankees, to fill the vacancy caused by the recent death of Colonel Jacob Ruppert.

The election was held in the home of the late owner of the Yankees and took place following a reading of that part of Colonel Ruppert's will which involved disposition of his baseball properties. Mr. Barrow's status as business manager is unchanged.

George M. Weiss, vice president of the Yankee organization's minor league clubs in Newark and Kansas City and general manager of the extensive farm-club system the late owner organized on the recommendation of Mr. Weiss, was elected secretary of the Yankees. This office he will occupy in addition to carrying on his duties in connection with the Yankees' minor league affairs.

REMAINS AS VICE PRESIDENT

Mr. Barrow's election as president was effected when George E. Ruppert, brother of the late colonel and titular head of the Ruppert family, declined the post because of the increased responsibilities he now faces in connection with the varied activities in which Colonel Ruppert was interested. George Ruppert remains vice president of the Yanks.

Fundamentally the business of the baseball club will experience little or no change under the reorganization. The affairs of the club, to all intents and purposes, will be conducted as they have been in past years when Mr. Barrow, as advisor to Colonel Ruppert, was the guiding influence in all of the late owner's decisions. ◆

Gehrig Voluntarily Ends Streak at 2,130 Straight Games

RETURN OF ACE INDEFINITE

By JAMES P. DAWSON
Special to The New York Times.

DETROIT, MAY 2.—Lou Gehrig's matchless record of uninterrupted play in American League championship games, stretched over fifteen years and through 2,130 straight contests, came to an end today.

The mighty iron man, who at his peak had hit forty-nine home runs in a single season five years ago, took himself out of action before the Yanks marched on Briggs Stadium for their first game against the Tigers this year.

With the consent of Manager Joe McCarthy, Gehrig removed himself because he, better than anybody else, perhaps, recognized his competitive decline and was frankly aware of the fact he was doing the Yankees no good defensively or on the attack. He last played Sunday in New York against the Senators.

When Gehrig will start another game is undetermined. He will not be used as a pinch-hitter.

DAHLGREN GETS CHANCE

Meanwhile Ellsworth (Babe) Dahlgren, until today baseball's greatest figure of frustration, will continue at first base. Manager McCarthy said he had no present intention of transferring Tommy Henrich, the youthful outfielder whom he tried at first base at the Florida training camp. Dahlgran had been awaiting the summons for three years.

It was coincidental that Gehrig's string was broken almost in the presence of the man he succeeded as Yankee first baseman. At that time Wally Pipp, now a business man of Grand Rapids, Mich., was benched by the late Miller ⟩⟩⟩

«« Huggins to make room for the strapping youth fresh from the Hartford Eastern League club to which the Yankees had farmed him for two seasons, following his departure from Columbia University. Pipp was in the lobby of the Book Cadillac Hotel at noon when the withdrawal of Gehrig was effected.

"I don't feel equal to getting back in there," Pipp said on June 2, 1925, the day Lou replaced him at first. Lou had started his phenomenal streak the day before as a pinch-hitter for Peewee Wanninger, then the Yankee shortstop.

This latest momentous development in baseball was not unexpected. There had been signs for the past two years that Gehrig was slowing up. Even when a sick man, however, he gamely stuck to his chores, not particularly in pursuit of his all-time record of consecutive play, although that was a big consideration, but out of a driving desire to help the Yankees, always his first consideration.

TREATED FOR AILMENT
What Lou had thought was lumbago last year when he suffered pains in the back that more than once forced his early withdrawal from games he had started was diagnosed later as a gall bladder condition

The Iron Man first baseman looks out at Tiger Stadium after requesting not to play on May 2, 1939, ending his record 2,130 consecutive-game streak.

for which Gehrig underwent treatment all last Winter, after rejecting a recommendation that he submit to an operation.

The signs of his approaching fadeout were unmistakable this Spring at St. Petersburg, Fla., yet the announcement from Manager McCarthy was something of a shock. It came at the end of a conference Gehrig arranged immediately after McCarthy's arrival by plane from his native Buffalo.

"Lou just told me he felt it would be best for the club if he took himself out of the line-up," McCarthy said following their private talk. "I asked him if he really felt that way. He told me he was serious. He feels blue. He is dejected.

"I told him it would be as he wished. Like everybody else I'm sorry to see it happen. I told him not to worry. Maybe the warm weather will bring him around.

"He's been a great ball player. Fellows like him come along once in a hundred years. I told him that. More than that, he's been a vital part of the Yankee club since he started with it. He's always been a perfect gentleman, a credit to baseball.

"We'll miss him. You can't escape that fact. But I think he's doing the proper thing."

LOU EXPLAINS DECISION

Gehrig, visibly affected, explained his decision quite frankly.

"I decided last Sunday night on this move," said Lou. "I haven't been a bit of good to the team since the season started. It would not be fair to the boys, to Joe or to the baseball public for me to try going on. In fact, it would not be fair to myself, and I'm the last consideration.

"It's tough to see your mates on base, have a chance to win a ball game, and not be able to do anything about it. McCarthy has been swell about it all the time. He'd let me go until the cows came home, he is that considerate of my feelings, but I knew in Sunday's game that I should get out of there.

"I went up there four times with men on base. Once there were two there. A hit would have won the ball game for the Yankees, but I missed, leaving five stranded as the Yankees lost. Maybe a rest will do me some good. Maybe it won't. Who knows? Who can tell? I'm just hoping."

Gehrig's withdrawal from today's game does not necessarily mean the end of his playing career, although that seems not far distant. When that day comes Gehrig can sit back and enjoy the fortune he has accumulated as a ball player. He is estimated to have saved $200,000 from his earnings, which touched a high in 1938, when he collected $39,000 as Yankee salary.

When Gehrig performed his duties as Yankee captain today, appearing at the plate to give the bat-ting order, announcement was made through the amplifiers of his voluntary withdrawal and it was suggested he get "a big hand." A deafening cheer resounded as Lou walked to the dugout, doffed his cap and disappeared in a corner of the bench.

Open expressions of regret came from the Yankees and the Tigers. Lefty Vernon Gomez expressed the Yankees' feelings when he said:

"It's tough to see this thing happen, even though you know it must come to us all. Lou's a great guy and he's always been a great baseball figure. I hope he'll be back in there."

Hank Greenberg, who might have been playing first for the Yanks instead of the Tigers but for Gehrig, said: "Lou's doing the right thing. He's got to use his head now instead of his legs. Maybe that Yankee dynasty is beginning to crumble."

With only one run batted in this year and a batting average of .143 representing four singles in twenty-eight times at bat, Lou has fallen far below his record achievements of previous seasons, during five of which he led the league in runs driven home.

Some of his more important records follow:

Most consecutive games—2,130.

Most consecutive years, 100 games or more—14.

Most years, 150 games or more—12.

Most years, 100 runs or more—13.

Most consecutive years, 100 runs or more—13.

Most home runs with bases full—23.

Most years, 300 or more total bases—13.

Most years, 100 runs or more driven in—13.

Most games by first baseman in one season—157.

Most home runs in one game—4 (modern record).

Most runs batted in, one season—184 (American League). ◆

June 22, 1939

Infantile Paralysis Terminates Gehrig's Playing Career

Mayo Clinic Report Bars Lou From Playing— He Takes Verdict Philosophically

By ARTHUR J. DALEY

LOU GEHRIG, THE ROBUST IRON HORSE whose baseball endurance record of 2,130 consecutive games may never be broken, is suffering from a mild attack of infantile paralysis, it was disclosed yesterday upon the return of the Yankee captain from a week-long examination at the Mayo Clinic.

This shocking news was revealed by President Edward Grant Barrow of the Yankees just before yesterday's game at the Stadium. As a result, the spectacular career of the big first basemen is at an end.

It was on May 2 of this year that Gehrig, aware that his continued presence in the line-up was a detriment to the team, voluntarily withdrew to complete his unbroken string at 2,130 games. Last year he had started to slip and this season his downhill descent was alarming. When he quit he was batting only .143.

TEXT OF THE REPORT

With his health worrying him he visited the Mayo Clinic at Rochester, Minn., for a thorough examination. Tuesday night he returned to New York by airplane and on his arrival at the Stadium yesterday presented Mr. Barrow with the following report from the Mayo Clinic:

To whom it may concern:

This is to certify that Mr. Lou Genrig has been under examination at the Mayo Clinic from June 13 to June 19, 1939, inclusive.

After a careful and complete examination, it was found that he is suffering from amyotrophic lateral sclerosis. This type illness involves the motor pathways and cells of the central nervous system and in lay terms is known as a form of chronic poliomyelitis (infantile paralysis).

The nature of this trouble makes it such that Mr. Gehrig will be unable to continue his active participation as a baseball player inasmuch as it is advisable that he conserve his muscular energy. He could, however, continue in some executive capacity.

(Signed) H. C. HABEIN, M. D.

BARROW RECEIVES DATA

Along with this formal statement Gehrig had with him a complete set of charts, X-rays and all manner of detailed reports. He presented them to President Barrow and the two, along with Manager Joe McCarthy, were closeted for about ten minutes.

Then Barrow summoned the baseball writers. Holding the statement in his hand he said:

"Gentlemen, we have bad news. Gehrig has infantile paralysis."

The writers stared at him in disbelief. It seemed inconceivable that the broad-shouldered iron man could be laid low in such fashion.

As for Gehrig, he merely grinned. "I guess I have to accept the bitter with the sweet," he said. "If this is my finish, I'll take it."

Neither he nor Barrow could venture to guess what Gehrig's future would be. "We'll keep him on the active player list at full salary for this year at least," declared Barrow. That full salary, by the way, is said to be $35,000.

When Gehrig walked into the Yankee dressing room he found his team-mates waiting for him uneasily. As the door opened some one started to cheer and then the rafters rocked with the acclaim he received from his fellows. They wanted to show him that they still were with him to the man.

The big captain dressed and sat on the bench with his fellow Yankees clustered around him as he described all the tests he had had out at the Mayo Clinic, telling his story with a ready laugh and ever-present grin. They tried to look unconcerned and as if nothing had happened. It was a brave attempt, but it failed. Bill Dickey, Gehrig's room-mate, sat on the steps, his chin on a bat, staring morosely at Lou and never saying a word.

When he stepped up to the plate before the game to hand the batting order to the umpires in his role as captain, the crowd gave Lou a rousing cheer, most of the fans in total ignorance of what had happened.

But Lou Gehrig, the player, has come to the end of the trail, thus ending one of the most amazing careers in baseball.

No accurate picture can be given of his earnings in his fifteen seasons with the Yankees, but the general impression is that he has received $361,500. Together with his world series shares, his total income has been around $400,000.

SALARY TOTAL $361,500

When Lou Gehrig receives his full salary for this season he will have been paid $361,500 by the Yankees for his services as a regular on the club if the first baseman has drawn the salaries generally reported to have been paid him.

In 1925, when he became a Yankee regular, he received only $3,750, but last year he was reported to have been paid $39,000, or more than ten times the amount which he drew in his initial full season with the club.

A compilation of his salary year by year does not include his share in seven world series, so his total baseball earnings have been approximately $400,000.

The salary tabulation follows:

1925	$3,750
1926	$6,500
1927	$7,500
1928	$25,000
1929	$25,000
1930	$25,000
1931	$25,000
1932	$25,000
1933	$28,000
1934	$23,000
1935	$31,000
1936	$31,000
1937	$36,750
1938	$39,000
1939	$35,000
Total	$361,500 ◆

July 5, 1939

61,808 FANS ROAR TRIBUTE TO GEHRIG

Captain of Yankees Honored at Stadium—Calls Himself 'Luckiest Man Alive'

By JOHN DREBINGER

IN PERHAPS AS COLORFUL AND DRAMATIC a pageant as ever was enacted on a baseball field, 61,808 fans thundered a hail and farewell to Henry Lou Gehrig at the Yankee Stadium yesterday.

To be sure, it was a holiday and there would have been a big crowd and plenty of roaring in any event. For the Yankees, after getting nosed out, 3 to 2, in the opening game of the doubleheader, despite a ninth-inning home run by George Selkirk, came right back in typical fashion to crush the Senators, 11 to 1, in the nightcap. Twinkletoes Selkirk embellished this contest with another home run.

But it was the spectacle staged between the games which doubtless never will be forgotten by those who saw it. For more than forty minutes there paraded in review two mighty championship hosts—the Yankees of 1927 and the current edition of Yanks who definitely are winging their way to a fourth straight pennant and a chance for another world title.

OLD MATES REASSEMBLE

From far and wide the 1927 stalwarts came to reassemble for Lou Gehrig Appreciation Day and to pay their own tribute to their former comrade-in-arms who had carried on beyond all of them only to have his own brilliant career come to a tragic close when it was revealed that he had fallen victim to a form of infantile paralysis.

In conclusion, the vast gathering, sitting in absolute silence for a longer period than perhaps any baseball crowd in history, heard Geh- >>>

◀◀◀ rig himself deliver as amazing a valedictory as ever came from a ball player.

So shaken with emotion that at first it appeared he would not be able to talk at all, the mighty Iron Horse, with a rare display of that indomitable will power that had carried him through 2,130 consecutive games, moved to the microphone at home plate to express his own appreciation.

And for the final fadeout, there stood the still burly and hearty Babe Ruth alongside of Gehrig, their arms about each other's shoulders, facing a battery of camera men.

All through the long exercises Gehrig had tried in vain to smile, but with the irrepressible Bambino beside him he finally made it. The Babe whispered something to him and Lou chuckled. Then they both chuckled and the crowd roared and roared.

LATE RALLY FALLS

The ceremonies began directly after the debris of the first game had been cleared away. Then, from out of a box alongside the Yankee dugout there spryly hopped more than a dozen elderly gentlemen, some gray, some shockingly baldish, but all happy to be on hand. The crowd recognized them at once, for they were the Yanks of 1927, not the first Yankee world championship team, but the first, with Gehrig an important cog in the machine, to win a world series in four straight games.

Down the field, behind Captain Sutherland's Seventh Regiment Band, they marched—Ruth, Bob Meusel, who had come all the way from California; Waite Hoyt, alone still maintaining his boyish countenance; Wally Schang, Benny Bengough, Tony Lazzeri, Mark Koenig, Jumping Joe Dugan, Bob Shawkey, Herb Pennock, Deacon Everett Scott, whose endurance record Gehrig eventually surpassed; Wally Pipp, who faded out as the Yankee first sacker the day Columbia Lou took over the job away back in 1925, and George Pipgras, now an umpire and, in fact, actually officiating in the day's games.

At the flagpole, these old Yanks raised the world series pennant they had won so magnificently from the Pirates in 1927 and, as they paraded back, another familiar figure streaked out of the dugout, the only one still wearing a Yankee uniform. It was the silver-haired Earle Combs, now a coach.

OLD-TIMERS FACE PLATE

Arriving at the infield, the old-timers strung out, facing the plate. The players of both Yankee and Senator squads also emerged from their dugouts to form a rectangle, and the first real ovation followed as Gehrig moved out to the plate to greet his colleagues, past and present.

Gifts of all sorts followed. The Yankees presented their stricken comrade with a silver trophy measuring more than a foot and a half in height, their thoughts expressed in verse inscribed upon the base.

Manager Joe McCarthy, almost as visibly affected as Gehrig himself, made this presentation and hurried back to fall in line with his players. But every few minutes, when he saw that the once stalwart figure they called the Iron Horse was swaying on shaky legs, Marse Joe would come forward to give Lou an assuring word of cheer.

Mayor La Guardia officially extended the city's appreciation of the services Columbia Lou had given his home town.

"You are the greatest prototype of good sportsmanship and citizenship," said the Mayor, concluding with "Lou, we're proud of you."

Postmaster General Farley also was on hand, closing his remarks with "for generations to come, boys who play baseball will point with pride to your record."

When time came for Gehrig to address the gathering it looked as if he simply would never make it. He gulped and fought to keep back the tears as he kept his eyes fastened on the ground.

But Marse Joe came forward again, said something that might have been "come on, Lou, just rap out another," and somehow those magical words had the same effect as in all the past fifteen years when the gallant Iron Horse would step up to the plate to "rap out another."

Lou Gehrig at the microphone during Lou Gehrig Appreciation Day, a farewell to the slugger, at Yankee Stadium on July 4, 1939.

GEHRIG SPEAKS SLOWLY

He spoke slowly and evenly, and stressed the appreciation that he felt for all that was being done for him. He spoke of the men with whom he had been associated in his long career with the Yankees—the late Colonel Jacob Ruppert, the late Miller Huggins, his first manager, who gave him his start in New York; Edward G. Barrow, the present head of baseball's most powerful organization; the Yanks of old who now stood silently in front of him, as well as the players of today.

"What young man wouldn't give anything to mingle with such men for a single day as I have for all these years?" he asked.

The gifts included a silver service set from the New York club, a fruit bowl and two candlesticks from the Giants, a silver pitcher from the Stevens Associates, two silver platters from the Stevens employes, a fishing rod and tackle from the Stadium employes and ushers, a silver cup ⟫⟫⟫

◄◄◄ from the Yankee office staff, a scroll from the Old Timers Association of Denver that was presented by John Kieran, a scroll from Washington fans, a tobacco stand from the New York Chapter of the Baseball Writers Association of America, and the silver trophy from his teammates.

The last-named present, about eighteen inches tall with a wooden base, supported by six silver bats with an eagle atop a silver ball, made Gehrig weep. President Barrow walked out to put his arms about Lou in an effort to steady him when this presentation was made. It appeared for an instant that Gehrig was near collapse.

On one side of the trophy were the names of all his present fellow-players. On the other was the following touching inscription:

TO LOU GEHRIG

We've been to the wars together,
We took our foes as they came,
And always you were the leader
And ever you played the game.

Idol of cheering millions,
Records are yours by the sheaves,
Iron of frame they hailed you.
Decked you with laurel leaves.

But higher than that we hold you,
We who have known you best,
Knowing the way you came through
Every human test.

Let this be a silent token
Of lasting friendship's gleam,
And all that we've left unspoken,
Your pals of the Yankee team.

As Gehrig finished his talk, Ruth, robust, round and sun-tanned, was nudged toward the microphone and, in his own inimitable, blustering style, snapped the tears away. He gave it as his unqualified opinion that the Yanks of 1927 were greater than the Yanks of today, and seemed even anxious to prove it right there.

"Anyway," he added, "that's my opinion and while Lazzeri here pointed out to me that there are only about thirteen or fourteen of us here, my answer is, shucks, we only need nine to beat 'em."

Then, as the famous home-run slugger, who also has faded into baseball retirement, stood with his arms entwined around Gehrig's shoulders, the band played "I Love You Truly," while the crowd took up the chant: "We love you, Lou."

ALL TRIBUTES SPONTANEOUS

All given spontaneously, it was without doubt one of the most touching scenes ever witnessed on a ball field and one that made even case-hardened ball players and chroniclers of the game swallow hard.

When Gehrig arrived in the Yankee dressing rooms he was so close to a complete collapse it was feared that the strain upon him had been too great and Dr. Robert E. Walsh, the Yankees' attending physician, hurried to his assistance. But after some refreshment, he recovered quickly and faithful to his one remaining task, that of being the inactive captain of his team, he stuck to his post in the dugout throughout the second game.

Long after the tumult and shouting had died and the last of the crowd had filed out, Lou trudged across the field for his familiar hike to his favorite exit gate. With him walked his bosom pal and team-mate, Bill Dickey, with whom he always rooms when the Yanks are on the road.

Lou walks with a slight hitch in his gait now, but there was supreme confidence in his voice as he said to his friend:

"Bill, I'm going to remember this day for a long time."

So, doubtless, will all the others who helped make this an unforgettable day in baseball. ◆

Yanks Never to Use Gehrig's 'No. 4' Again

THE BIG NUMERAL "4," which ever since the numbering of players was introduced at the Stadium by the Yankees has adorned the broad back of Lou Gehrig, will never be worn by another Yankee ball player.

This was announced yesterday by President Ed Barrow, who also revealed for the first time what the future relations will be between the world champions and their famous first-sacker, whose brilliant career came to a close early last season when he fell victim of a form of paralysis.

Though Gehrig will never be able to play again, Larrupin' Lou, who recently took up his duties as Commissioner on the Municipal Parole Board and is waging a heroic fight against his malady, will not receive his unconditional release from the Yankees. Instead, his name will be placed on the club's voluntarily retired list.

In addition to retiring his No. 4 permanently, Barrow disclosed that Gehrig's old locker in the Stadium—the one over in the corner of the club-house by the window—will never be used by any other player. Lou's name will remain over the door and the locker will be reserved for his personal use.

"We always want Lou to feel he is still one of us," said Barrow, "and that he always will be welcome to use his locker whenever he wants to."

The gesture of retiring Gehrig's number, reminiscent of the University of Illinois's action years ago in perpetuating Red Grange's famous "77" jersey in its trophy room, is a tribute which, so far as is known, has never before been conferred upon a ball player by a major league club.

Even when the glamorous and spectacular Babe Ruth retired from the Yankees no one thought to put his familiar No. 3 out of circulation. The number was given to George Selkirk the following Spring and Twinkletoes has been wearing it ever since.

But there will never be another No. 4 on a Yankee scorecard or scoreboard or stitched to the back of another Yankee uniform except the one worn by Lou Gehrig. ◆

GEHRIG, 'IRON MAN' OF BASEBALL, DIES AT THE AGE OF 37

Rare Disease Forced Famous Batter to Retire in 1939—Played 2,130 Games in Row

LOU GEHRIG, FORMER FIRST BASEMAN of the New York Yankees and one of the outstanding batsmen baseball has known, died at his home, 5204 Delafield Avenue, in the Fieldston section of the Bronx, last night. Death came to the erstwhile "Iron Man" at 10:10 o'clock. He would have been 38 years old on June 19.

Regarded by some observers as the greatest player ever to grace the diamond, Gehrig, after playing in 2,130 consecutive championship contests, was forced to end his career in 1939 when an ailment that had been hindering his efforts was diagnosed as a form of paralysis.

The disease was chronic, and for the last month Gehrig had been confined to his home. He lost weight steadily during the final weeks and was reported twenty-five pounds under weight shortly before he died.

MEMBER OF PAROLE BOARD

Until his illness became more serious Gehrig went to his office regularly to perform his duties as a member of the New York City Parole Commission, a post he had held for a year and a half following his retirement from baseball. »»»

≪ Ever hopeful that he would be able to conquer the rare disease—amyotrophic lateral sclerosis, a hardening of the spinal cord—although the ailment was considered incurable by many, Gehrig stopped going to his desk about a month ago to conserve his strength.

Two weeks ago he was confined to his bed, and from that time until his death his condition grew steadily worse. He was conscious until just before the end. At the bedside when he died were his wife, the former Eleanor Twitchell of Chicago; his parents, Mr. and Mrs. Henry Gehrig; his wife's mother, Mrs. Nellie Twitchell, and Dr. Caldwell B. Esselstyn.

It was said last night that funeral services would be private and would be held tomorrow morning at 10 o'clock in the Christ Episcopal Church in Riverdale. The Rev. Gerald V. Barry will officiate.

The body was taken this morning to the E. Willis Scott Funeral Parlor at 4 West Seventy-sixth Street. ◆

July 26, 1941

IT'S LOU GEHRIG PLAZA

Signs Placed in 161st St., the Bronx

THE LOU GEHRIG PLAZA came into being yesterday afternoon with the erection of two blue and white enameled signs placed atop eight foot poles on the island in the middle of 161st Street, one sign at Walton Avenue and the other at the Grand Concourse, the Bronx. There was no ceremony.

About 100 persons, mostly children, along with Borough President James J. Lyons, Councilman Joseph E. Kinsley and three members of the New York Yankees, Joe McCarthy, manager; Bill Dickey and Vernon (Lefty) Gomex, were present when the signs were placed in position. ◆

July 16, 1942

'Pride of the Yankees,' a Film Biography of Lou Gehrig, With Gary Cooper and Teresa Wright, on View at Astor

By BOSLEY CROWTHER

SO MANY HUNDREDS OF PERSONS loved Lou Gehrig with a devotion that few men know and literally thousands of others held him in such true regard that the film biographers of the modest and valiant ball player assumed an obligation too ticklish for casual approach. But no one can say that Samuel Goldwyn has not been respectful of its due. In a simple, tender, meticulous and explicitly narrative film, Mr. Goldwyn and his associates have told the story of Buster Lou with sincere and lingering affection, in face of which dramatic punch has been subdued. It is called "The Pride of the Yankees," and it opened at the Astor last night—and also, for a single performance, in forty neighborhood theatres hereabout.

For months Mr. Goldwyn had seen to it that the word generally got around that this was not to be so much the story of Lou Gehrig, the great ball player, as of Lou Gehrig, a fine and humble man. That advice was absolutely on the level. For "The Pride of the Yankees" is primarily a review of the life of a shy and earnest young fellow who loved his mother, worked hard to get ahead, incidentally became a ball player for two reasons—because he loved the game and also needed the cash—enjoyed a clumsy romance which eventually enriched his life and then, at the height of his glory, was touched by the finger of death.

It is, without being pretentious, a real saga of American life—homely, humorous, sentimental and composed in patient detail. But, by the very nature of its subject, it lacks conflict till well on toward its end. And that is its principal weakness as a dramatic film. For the youth and early manhood of Lou Gehrig, according to this account, were picturesque without being too difficult, beset by shyness more than anything else. And the same was true of his ripe years and his romance—at least, in this film. It is not until illness leads the "Iron Man" into the valley of the shadow that this story of his life becomes dramatic. Illness and death are the only adversaries faced by Lou.

In view of the fact that a good three-quarters of this more than two-hour long film is devoted to genial details, it inclines to monotony. This is further aggravated by the fact that the details are repetitious in themselves. Lou shows his mother that he loves her, not once but many times, and his coy and playful frisking with his wife becomes redundant after awhile.

Furthermore, sports fans will protest, with reason on their side, that a picture about a baseball player should have a little more baseball in it. Quite true, this one has considerable footage showing stands and diamonds of the American League with Lou at bat, running bases and playing the initial bag. What is shown is accurate. But it is only shown in glimpses or montage sequences, without catching much of the flavor or tingling excitement of a tight baseball game. Fans like to know what's the inning, how many are on and how many out. At least, the score.

This underemphasis of Gehrig's profession is partially excused by the fact that Gary Cooper, who plays the great hero, doesn't look too good slamming or scooping 'em up. Mr. Cooper is perfectly able when it comes to playing the diffident, home-spun man, and his performance in the touching final sequence—the presentation of the Gehrig tribute—is excellent. He even bears a slight resemblance to the "Iron Man," especially about the eyes. But when he's in there snagging the hot ones, he isn't likely to be mistaken for the real Lou.

The cast is superb, however, and does handsomely under Sam Wood's direction. Elsa Janssen and Ludwig Stossel are delightful humans as Ma and Pop Gehrig, and Teresa Wright has a lovely, gracious quality as Mrs. Lou. Walter

Gary Cooper as Lou Gehrig in film "The Pride of the Yankees."

Brennan, Dan Duryea and Ernie Adams are a credit to Hollywood in lesser roles, and Babe Ruth—the real old Babe—roars and wrangles titanically in a couple of scenes playing himself. A few other old-time Yankees—Bill Dickey, Mark Koenig and Bob Meusel—are in the background as local scenery, and Dickey gets a chance to slug a guy.

As a baseball picture—in which Veloz and Yolanda, for some reason, dance—"The Pride of the Yankees" is not anything to raise the blood-pressure. But as a simple, moving story with an ironic heart-tug at the end, it serves as a fitting memorial to the real Lou, who called himself the "luckiest man alive."

Preceding the feature on the program—and made at Mr. Goldwyn's request—is a deliciously confused Disney cartoon, a goofy burlesque called "How to Play Baseball." ◆

YANKEES APPROVE BABE RUTH PLAQUE

THE CLAY MODEL for the bronze plaque that is to be erected in the Yankee Stadium in memory of Babe Ruth has been approved, it was announced yesterday by the New York Yankees. A cast will now be made and the memorial will be ready for dedication on April 19, when the Yankees open their home season against Washington.

The plaque, an original sculpture by Vincent Carano, will present a head-and-shoulders portrait of the great slugger and carry an inscription composed by members of the New York Chapter of the Baseball Writers' Association of America, which reads as follows:

George Herman (Babe) Ruth
1895-1948
A Great Ball Player
A Great Man
A Great American
Erected By
The Yankees
And
The New York Baseball Writers
April 19, 1949.

It is planned to erect the plaque on a monument near the Stadium's center field flagpole, where memorials to Lou Gehrig, Miller Huggins, and Col. Jake Ruppert now stand. ◆

Babe Ruth, Baseball Idol, Dies At 53 After Lingering Illness

Famous Diamond Star Fought Losing Battle Against Cancer for 2 Years

BABE RUTH DIED LAST NIGHT. The 58-year-old baseball idol succumbed to cancer of the throat at Memorial Hospital at 8 o'clock, less than two hours after a special bulletin had announced he was "sinking rapidly."

The home-run king's death came five days after he had been placed on the critical list. It end-

Ruth's Pay by Seasons During Baseball Career

Babe Ruth's salary by seasons for his professional baseball career follows:

Year.	Team.	Salary.
1914	Baltimore (I. L.)	$600
*1914	Boston (A. L.)	1,300
1915	Boston (A. L.)	3,500
1916	Boston (A. L.)	3,500
1917	Boston (A. L.)	5,000
1918	Boston (A. L.)	7,000
1919	Boston (A. L.)	10,000
1920	New York (A. L.)	20,000
1921	New York (A. L.)	30,000
1922	New York (A. L.)	52,000
1923	New York (A. L.)	52,000
1924	New York (A. L.)	52,000
1925	New York (A. L.)	52,000
1926	New York (A. L.)	52,000
1927	New York (A. L.)	70,000
1928	New York (A. L.)	70,000
1929	New York (A. L.)	70,000
1930	New York (A. L.)	80,000
1931	New York (A. L.)	80,000
1932	New York (A. L.)	75,000
1933	New York (A. L.)	50,000
1934	New York (A. L.)	35,000
1935	Boston (N. L.)	40,000
1938	Brooklyn (N. L.)	15,000

Total $925,900

*Bought by Red Sox from Baltimore and farmed to Providence (I. L.).

ed nearly two years of fighting against a disease that had sent him repeatedly to hospitals.

About a half hour before his death the famous Yankee slugger said a prayer. Last rites of the Roman Catholic Church had been administered on July 21.

After his death, the Rev. Thomas H. Kaufman of Providence College, Providence, R. I., who had blessed him shortly before death, said: "The Babe died a beautiful death. He said his prayers and lapsed into a sleep. He died in his sleep."

At the deathbed, besides the priest, were the Babe's wife, Claire, his two adopted daughters, Mrs. Daniel Sullivan and Mrs. Richard Flanders; his sister, Mrs. Wilbur Moberly; his doctor, his lawyer, and a few of his closest friends.

There was a hush around the hospital when the end came. The groups of youngsters who had gathered about the red-brick hospital since Wednesday when the name of George Herman Ruth first appeared on the critical list, were home having dinner.

In the marble lobby, where late last week groups of boys had occasionally tarried, sometimes leaving flowers for the great right fielder, there were just a handful of adults, all of them waiting to see other patients.

On the ninth floor, where the Babe had spent his final illness, nurses and doctors talked in whispers. Those who had seen him had been shocked at the change since the days of his baseball prime.

The powerful six-footer who had once electrified Americans with sixty homers in a season, had wasted away. The famous round face had become so hollowed that his snub nose looked long. The once black hair so often seen when the Babe doffed his cap rounding the bases, was almost white. ≫≫

Baseball great Babe Ruth, in uniform, addressing crowd and press during final appearance at Yankee Stadium.

««   Deeply moved, Father Kaufman said little as he left after having been with the Babe most of the day. Others in the party were just as uncommunicative and hastened past the dozens of youngsters who quickly gathered in East Sixty-eighth Street outside the hospital.

The Babe's death brought tributes from men equally famous in other fields. Among those who sent messages were President Truman and former President Herbert Hoover. Included in the many tributes from baseball figures were those from Will Harridge, president of the American League, and Ford Frick, head of the National League.

Members of the Ruth family said that although funeral plans had not yet been completed, it had been arranged tentatively that a mass would be sung in St. Patrick's Cathedral at 11 A.M. Thursday. Meanwhile the body was to be taken to the Universal Funeral Chapel, 595 Lexington Avenue. ◆

June 24, 1949

Ruth and Gehrig Lockers Will Go to Hall of Fame

THE LOCKERS USED BY Babe Ruth and Lou Gehrig will be presented to the Baseball Hall of Fame in a home plate ceremony at Yankee Stadium Monday night, before the start of the Mayor William O'Dwyer sandlot benefit game between the Yankees and Giants.

When the Yankees retired the uniforms of their two great sluggers—No. 3 for Ruth and No. 4 for Gehrig—they also put permanently aside the lockers used by these diamond immortals. Bob Quinn of Cooperstown, N. Y., will accept the gift on behalf of the Hall of Fame, with President Dan Topping of the Yankees making the presentation. ◆

August 12, 1973

Baseball's Queen Widow

by DAVE ANDERSON

ABOUT TWO DOZEN LETTERS, the latest batch, were on a brown chair in the living room of the Riverside Drive Apartment.

"The mail is always heavy," Mrs. Claire Ruth said, "but this year it's been 10 times as heavy. People remember."

They remember because Thursday will be the 25th anniversary of Babe Ruth's death and because Henry Aaron won't let them forget. Below the closed venetian blinds were the trees of Riverside Park and the yachts in the 79th Street marina of the Hudson River. The view hasn't changed much since the man who hit 714 home runs lived in the 11-room apartment that is now a private museum for his widow. She belongs in the old orange brick building. She would be out of place in a high-rise glass apartment. She lived there when she's not visiting her two daughters or when she's not traveling. She was at the Hall of Frame induction in Cooperstown, N.Y., last Monday and yesterday she attended the annual Yankees' Old Timers celebration. Tomorrow she will go to Monroe, N.C. for a Babe Ruth League tournament. She is baseball's queen widow.

"Don't you think that's kind of cute?" she said, smiling. "How I keep getting plaques."

She's thin, but with the petite features of a beauty in her day. She's snappy and alert.

"I started to look for another apartment a few years ago, but I couldn't find one I liked, " she was saying in the living room with its green walls, yellow ceiling and parquet floor. "Everything here is just the way Babe left it. Most of Babe's things are at Cooperstown; they went out of here by the truckload. But many of the personal things are here. That likeness of him in Japanese needlepoint. And the three Japanese jade urns. They gave out four of them one year. He won his three for home runs, extra-base hits and batting average. Babe said the only reason he didn't win the fourth was that he wasn't pitching."

In a small room, framed photos adorn the walls. One shows the Babe with Lou Gehrig, each immense.

"And to think," Claire Ruth said, "that they both weighed less than 100 pounds when they died."

In a foyer, a baseball, brown and stiff with age, is mounted, but without identification.

"I don't know what that ball's for, there's no writing on it," she said. "I don't even have an autographed ball. You don't ask your husband for an autographed ball. He'd probably think you were nuts or something."

She had returned to the living room now, sitting on a soft-green couch near a humming portable air-conditioner.

"Babe was just a wonderful man. He had a wonderful disposition. If he lived to be 100, he still would've been a kid. He never raised his voice. Not to me. Not to my mother, who lived with us. Not to his two daughters. But you knew when he wanted things done. He liked an immaculate house. Our oldest daughter, Julia, once said, 'No wonder Babe can hit home runs. He can see a speck of dust over behind the piano.'"

They were married in 1929 at St. Gregory's Church, only a few blocks from this apartment.

"The mass was about 6 o'clock in the morning. We had it then to maintain some privacy, but there were about 100 people there anyway. That was opening day, but the game was rained out. The next day, Babe hit a home run the first time up. After that, when the Yankees went on the road, I made every trip. He wanted me to go. To tell the truth, Babe needed somebody along. Babe didn't like to be alone. We always had a big suite."

In those years, the Babe's milestone home runs received routine attention.

"When he hit his 700th, he knew he was supposed to do it and he did it. There was no commotion about it. I remember the 500th happened in Cleveland, but he thought nothing about it until that night at the hotel when James Kilgallen, the writer, called to ask Babe about it. The conversation only lasted a few minutes. Babe told me later, 'He asked me what kind of ball I hit and I said low and inside and hung up.' Babe didn't think it was important. James Kilgallen told me later that was the greatest story he ever wrote from three words."

But these days Henry Aaron is an invisible intruder in Claire Ruth's private museum.

"I don't think Babe would pay any more attention to what Aaron is doing than I am," she said. "Hank Greenberg, Jimmie Foxx, Hack Wilson, when they had a chance to break his record of 60 homers in a season, he was sure they'd get it, but they didn't. Now it's Aaron's show and he should have it to himself."

Somehow, despite all her baseball travels, she has never met the man who is approaching Babe Ruth's career total.

"I don't know when I will meet him," baseball's queen widow said. "In the next few weeks, I'll be traveling for the Babe Ruth League and then I'll be pretty well worn out. But no matter what happens, there's only one Babe, he stands alone and he always will. Roger Maris hit 61 home runs, but who writes about him today?" ◆

June 2, 1991

Ruth and Gehrig: Forced Smiles

By RAY ROBINSON

WHEN LOU GEHRIG DIED 50 years ago today, on June 2, 1941, 17 days before his 38th birthday, he had already won his place among baseball's demigods.

But one question lingers today among his legion of admirers, which includes a surprising number of young people searching for heroes. These fans are eager to learn what Gehrig's true relationship was with his Yankee brother-in-arms, Babe Ruth. For after all, these two sluggers formed the marrow of the Yankees' omnipotent ball club from 1925, when Gehrig became a regular, through 1934, when Ruth's Yankee career ended, as complementary as ham and eggs. 》》》

Babe Ruth, right, embracing Lou Gehrig, who was almost too moved to speak to the vast throng at his farewell at Yankee Stadium on July 4, 1939.

«« At first the two dissimilar men formed a mutual admiration society, despite the fact that Ruth was an outrageously undisciplined man in every facet of his life except home-run hitting, while the modest, insecure Gehrig was never much taken with flamboyance or empty boasting. The larger-than-life Ruth was "a runaway personality," remarked Eleanor Gehrig, who married Lou in 1933. Lou, on the other hand, took his role as loyal son and team player quite seriously.

THE IRRITATION OF PROXIMITY

Sharing confidences, eating, traveling and barnstorming together, playing cards, swapping batting tips, fishing and golfing together, Ruth and Gehrig should have grown closer with the passing years. Instead, they pulled apart, their sharp differences of personality and character souring their relationship.

It was common that sportswriters of that day emphasized that Gehrig seemed content to live in Ruth's substantial shadow. But as time went on, one could not be certain that Lou willingly accepted his role as second banana. With each act of hell-raising and carousing, Ruth won laughs and widespread tolerance, while Gehrig, "unvarying and ongoing as a railroad track," in the words of baseball historian Donald Honig, received only condescending applause for his commitment to duty.

Much stage-managing always accompanied Ruth's yearly contract-signing. Few, however, paid much notice as Gehrig quietly signed on with the Yankees' owner, Col. Jacob Ruppert. The Babe made $80,000 during the height of the Great Depression, Gehrig less than half that amount.

It is difficult to pinpoint precisely when the relationship turned frigid, as it did. But Gehrig increasingly objected to Ruth's public declamations against Yankee Manager Joe McCarthy, a man Gehrig almost revered as a second father. To Gehrig, such loose talk was just not permissible.

AN UNPLEASANT VISIT
A petty incident curtailed further civility between Gehrig and Ruth. Dorothy, the 12-year-old daughter of Babe's first wife, went to visit Lou's mother one weekend in the early 30's dressed like a shabby tomboy. In the eyes of Mrs. Gehrig, who was domineering and opinionated, this was an insult.

"Why doesn't Claire dress her as properly as she does Julia?" Mrs. Gehrig said, angrily. (Julia was Claire Ruth's daughter by her first marriage.)

The remark quickly reached Claire's ears, then Babe's. Ruth barked: "Why doesn't Mom Gehrig mind her own damned business!"

Fiercely attached to his mother, Gehrig could never tolerate such a crude verbal assault on his mother's integrity. As a result, Babe and Lou rarely spoke to each other off the field. They shook hands at home plate in the traditional ritual after home runs and managed to be accommodating when photographers asked them to pose together. But Lou was forced to play-act his familiar grin in the presence of Ruth.

ONE BRIEF GESTURE
The last straw came when Ruth spoke disparagingly of Gehrig's cherished consecutive game streak. He said he regarded it as little more than a boring statistic. "This Iron Horse stuff is just a lot of baloney," Ruth growled. "I think he's making one of the worst mistakes a player can make. He ought to learn to sit on the bench and rest. They're not going to pay off on how many games he's played in a row."

The rift never healed. For a moment, when the Babe dramatically flung his arms around Lou at the Yankee Stadium ceremony on July 4, 1939 at which Gehrig delivered his famous farewell speech, it appeared that the disaffection between them may have eased. But in the last two years of Lou's life, Ruth paid little heed to his dying ex-teammate.

When Lou's body was being viewed in the Bronx at a Riverdale funeral parlor, Ruth finally did show up, but his unruly behavior only served to underline what had previously gone wrong between them.

"Lou's father and mother were there when we came to the house," wrote songwriter Fred Fisher, a good friend of the Gehrigs, to a doctor who had cared for Lou during his last fight against amyotrophic lateral sclerosis.

"There were a lot of friends there, too. Eleanor was very composed, having been prepared for the shock. But she became very angry when Ruth and his wife came in very intoxicated. He certainly wasn't wanted by the Gehrigs, as there was friction between them for years." ◆

3 THE DiMAGGIO ERA

When Babe Ruth hit 60 home runs in 1927, he shouted, "Sixty, count 'em, sixty! Let's see some other son of a bitch match that!" But in 1961, Roger Maris hit 61. When Lou Gehrig's consecutive-game streak ended at 2,130 in 1939, virtually everybody in baseball assumed that nobody would ever match that record. But in 1995, Cal Ripken Jr. shattered it—then extended it to 2,632 games.

Records are made to be broken, as the Babe, the Iron Horse, and the baseball public learned. But of all the records in baseball, if not in any sport, the least likely to be broken is Joe DiMaggio's 56-game hitting streak that transfixed the nation in 1941. Nobody else has come close. Only Pete Rose's 44-game streak for the Cincinnati Reds in 1978, the modern (since 1900) National League record, has even approached it. Back in 1897 Willie Keeler also hit safely in 44 consecutive games for the Baltimore Orioles, then in the National League. For all of DiMaggio's accomplishments with the Yankees—nine World Series rings, ten American League pennants, three Most Valuable Player awards, his Hall of Fame induction—his 56-game hitting streak almost became part of his name. More than any other Yankees icon, Joseph Paul DiMaggio endured as the symbol of the franchise.

The Babe was around as a slugger and the first Old-Timers' Day honoree for 28 years; the Iron Horse, for 16 years. But until the Yankee Clipper's death in 1998, after having been around for 62 years, it was as if he never took off his uniform. Joe DiMaggio threw out the ceremonial first pitch on opening day of the World Series. At Old-Timers' Day, he was always the last to be introduced, always to the loudest ovation.

Everybody always knew Joe DiMaggio. Not long after he arrived for spring training in 1936 among the palm trees of St. Petersburg, Florida, the now retired Babe visited the clubhouse. Over the years, the Babe had never been good with names, even some of his teammates' names. Instead, he would say, "Hiya, kid," which he usually pronounced as "keed." And as he renewed his friendship with some former teammates, he was heard

★ ★ ★

Legendary Yankee Joe DiMaggio, also known as "Joltin' Joe" and "The Yankee Clipper," in 1939.

to say, "Hiya, keed ... Hiya, keed." Now he stopped at the rookie's locker: "Hiya, Joe," he said.

Even the Babe knew this rookie's name. Three years earlier, at age 18, DiMaggio had torn apart the Pacific Coast League, batting .340 with 169 RBI and 28 homers for his hometown San Francisco Seals while hitting safely in 61 consecutive games. When he tore cartilage in his left knee during the 1934 season, some major league teams shied away—but the Yankees didn't. They purchased him for $25,000, five players, and the promise that he remain with the Seals in 1935 when he batted .398 with 154 RBI and 34 homers. No wonder the Babe knew his name.

Ever since, just about every baseball fan knew his name and nicknames: the Yankee Clipper, Joe D., Joltin' Joe, the Jolter. Despite missing three seasons while in the United States Army Air Force during World War II, his career average over 13 seasons was .325 with 361 homers and 1,573 RBI. He seldom swung and missed, striking out only 369 times in 1,736 games and only 13 times in 1941, the year of the hitting streak. He has lived on in literature and song: In The Old Man and the Sea, Ernest Hemingway writes that the Cuban fisherman "would like to take the great DiMaggio fishing. They say his father was a fisherman." DiMaggio's father, Giuseppe, was a fisherman off of Palermo, Sicily, before docking his boat at San Francisco's Fisherman's Wharf.

As a rookie, DiMaggio blended easily into the Yankees lineup, batting third ahead of Gehrig while hitting .328 with 206 hits, 125 RBI, and 29 homers. His quiet manner earned him immediate acceptance and support from Gehrig during an incident early in the season involving the plate umpire George Moriarty. After the crusty umpire called a strike on a high pitch DiMaggio thought was a ball, he glanced back at Moriarty, who growled, "Turn around." In other words: Don't question my call, rookie. But from the on-deck circle, Gehrig said firmly, "Leave the kid alone, George. If you call 'em right, he won't have to turn around." Two seasons later, while making $25,000 after a contentious holdout, that kid was batting cleanup. And in 1949, as baseball's first $100,000 player, he missed the first two months of the season with a bone spur on his right heel before a theatrical return: in a three-game sweep at Fenway Park, he demolished ▸▸▸

<<< the Red Sox with four homers, nine RBI, and five runs scored.

After the 1951 season, with his skills eroding at age 37, he announced that he was retiring. "I no longer have it," he said. But as an icon, he still had it. He married Marilyn Monroe, his second wife, in 1954. They soon divorced, but after her death, he arranged for fresh flowers to be placed on her grave twice a week for years. He never talked about her and never did a book, because "that's all a publisher wanted me for." But a story endures of their honeymoon in Japan, when she made a quick visit to U.S. Army troops in South Korea.

"Joe, you never heard such cheering," she said.

"Yes, I have," he said. And, of course, he had.

November 22, 1934

Yankees Obtain DiMaggio, Coast League Batting Star

By THE ASSOCIATED PRESS.

LOUISVILLE, KY., Nov. 21.—The Chicago Cubs tonight sent Pitchers Bud Tinning and Dick Ward and cash to the St. Louis Cardinals for Tex Carleton, right-handed pitcher.

News of this trade, made public during the minor league meetings here, followed an announcement that the Yankees had acquired Joe DiMaggio, San Francisco outfielder, who established a Pacific Coast record in 1933 by hitting safely in sixty-one consecutive games. Under present arrangements, DiMaggio will report to the Yanks next Fall.

There was a hitch in this transaction, however, as the Yanks wanted to make certain that Joe was not slowed down permanently by a knee injury last season. Under the terms the New York club is to send five players to San Francisco next Fall, two on option and three outright.

The Yankees were advised that DiMaggio not only was physically fit but that he was even a better prospect than Paul Waner was when he came from the Pacific Coast League to the Pirates. While names of the players who are to be sent to the Seals were not disclosed, unofficial reports indicated that Pitcher Floyd Newkick and Pitcher Nosbert would be among them. ◆

Joe DiMaggio in 1934 in his San Francisco Seals uniform.

March 15, 1936

DiMaggio Assured of Outfield Berth With the Yankees, McCarthy Announces

By JAMES P. DAWSON
Special to The New York Times.

ST. PETERSBURG, FLA., MARCH 14.—Torrential rain today washed out the scheduled first Spring exhibition game of the Yankees with the Boston Bees and marooned Manager Joe McCarthy's athletes in the lobby of the Hotel Suwanee.

The Yankee leader is looking forward eagerly to the start of the series with the Bees tomorrow for the opportunity it will afford to inspect his talent. He said today without qualification that Joe DiMaggio, Coast sensation, is assured of an outfield berth. Whether it will be center or left, however, remains to be decided. Indications now are that DiMaggio will patrol the left garden, because, in McCarthy's opinion, that is the easiest berth in any ball park.

If the outfield holds two left-hand hitters, either Roy Johnson or Red Rolfe will be the lead-off man in the batting order. Two right-hand hitters in the outfield will find Frankie Crosetti back at the top of the batting order. With two left-hand hitters in the outfield, there is no provision for Chapman, as the premise that DiMaggio is an assured regular. But Manager McCarthy made no mention of a trade.

Tomorrow the Yankee pilot will start the line-up he announced for today's game. Uhalt will lead off with Rolfe, DiMaggio, Gehrig, Selkirk, Lazzeri and Crosetti following. Glenn and Hershberger are to be the catchers, while Pat Malone, Ted Kleinhans and Steve Sundra will do the pitching. ◆

May 25, 1936

YANKS OVERWHELM ATHLETICS, 25 TO 2

LAZZARI CONNECTS FOR 3 HOMERS

Two Come With Bases Filled, New Mark for the Majors

By JAMES P. DAWSON
Special to The New York Times.

PHILADELPHIA, MAY 24.—Tony Lazzeri hammered his way to baseball fame today with an exhibition of batting unparalleled in American League history as he set the pace in the Yankees' crushing 25-2 victory over the Athletics at Shibe Park.

The 33-year-old veteran of the New York infield blasted three home runs, two of them with the bases loaded, two of them in successive times at bat. He missed a fourth by a matter of inches and had to be content with a triple. With his three-bagger in the eighth with two on Lazzeri erased the American League record for runs batted in by a player in a single game. His homers with the bases filled came in the second and fifth. His third started the seventh.

Tony's hitting today gave him the distinction of driving in eleven runs. The best previous mark was that of Jimmie Foxx, who drove home nine in Cleveland with a double, a triple and a home run in 1933. The National League record is twelve, set by Jim Bottomley in 1924.

RUTH NEXT IN LINE

Lazzeri's two homers with the bases filled in a single game created a new major league record. Babe Ruth comes closest to this distinction. He hit homers with the bases loaded in two consecutive games, accomplishing the feat twice, once in 1927 and again in 1929. ⟩⟩⟩

‹‹‹ Lazzeri also set another major league mark with six homers in three consecutive games. He walloped three in yesterday's doubleheader and three today. In addition, he smashed seven in four consecutive games, still another major league record.

Frankie Crosetti hit two homers in successive times at bat with no one on and Joe DiMaggio also smashed one. In addition, Joe had a double and a single.

FIFTY-TWO RUNS IN THREE GAMES

In the three games of the series the Yanks have clouted thirteen homers, Lazzeri showing the way with his six, five of them in two games. The squad has hit for a total of 107 bases, made 52 runs, 40 in two games, and collected 49 hits.

The New Yorkers established a new major league standard for most homers by one club in two consecutive games. They hit five in yesterday's nightcap and six today for a total of eleven. The Pirates set the old record of ten in 1925. The previous American League mark of nine was made by the Yankees in 1930. ◆

Tony Lazzeri in the 1930s.

October 7, 1936

YANKS CRUSH GIANTS, 18-4, A WORLD SERIES RECORD

Fans Cheer Roosevelt and Remain Till He Leaves at End.

By JOHN DREBINGER

WITH PRESIDENT ROOSEVELT casting a keen, critical and, beyond question, an appreciative eye on the thoroughness of the spectacle, Marse Joe McCarthy's Yankee juggernaut rolled out on the hard, smooth terrain of the Polo Grounds yesterday and put on the most amazing exhibition of devastating power in all world series history.

For with no Carl Hubbell or slippery underfooting to distract and derail them, the American League champions emptied broadside after broadside into the riddled defenses of Colonel Bill Terry's Giants and, in a final shower of records, individual and collective, bagged the second engagement of the Fall classic by the overwhelming score of 18 to 4.

It was the most decisive, humiliating defeat ever suffered by a contender in the thirty-one years of world series warfare and left a crowd of 45,000 stunned and awed at the finish, while the President and James A. Farley exchanged significant glances. For they had observed a truly remarkable steamroller in action.

ITALIAN TRIUMVIRATE SHINES

Behind the somewhat erratic pitching of their Castillian comrade, Lefty Vernon Gomez, the Italian battalion of the Yankees swung magnificently into action as first Tony Lazzeri, then Frankie Crosetti and finally Joe DiMaggio ripped and slashed five hapless Giant hurlers to ribbons.

Tony, providing the high spot of a fearful seven-run explosion in the third inning, cracked a homer with the bases full, subsequently pushed another run across the plate and with this equaled a series record for runs batted in, a total of five.

Crosetti, blazing a trail with three singles and a pass, carried four runs across that severely dented plate to tie another mark.

And DiMaggio, the latest addition to this singular array of Latins from far off Telegraph Hill in San Francisco, touched off two singles and a double, then brought the uneven struggle to a dramatic close by making a spectacular catch of a towering shot directly in front of the Eddie Grant Memorial tablet in center field.

BEWILDERED BY CATCH

Hank Leiber had stroked that blow with an effort born of despair and wound up standing on second base in utter bewilderment, unable to comprehend why all the other players were rushing past him to the clubhouse.

The crowd arrived early and seemed bent on enjoying itself, although it again failed to touch the capacity mark, which had been set at 52,500. The paid attendance totaled only 43,543, with the re- »»

Tony Lazzeri crossing the plate after hitting a home run in Game 2 of the 1936 World Series at the Polo Grounds. The Giants catcher is Gus Mancuso.

<<< ceipts $184,962, and the baseball people last night were shaking their heads and wondering. For there seems to be something radically wrong with the present manner of selling world series tickets.

The clock atop the center-field clubhouse had passed 1 by a few minutes when the center-field portals swung open and, amid a great scurrying of police and Secret Service agents, who seemed to view with suspicion Yanks and Giants alike, four large, shiny automobiles rolled onto the field.

The crowd rose and cheered—all but Henry Fabian, venerable ground custodian of the Polo Grounds, who just rose and glared. Old Hennery wasn't disrespectful, but his greatest concern is for his velvety grass, and those mammoth machines were putting some terrible ruts in that outfield. It would have pained him less had they ridden over his feet.

In the first one, an open touring car, sat the President, who presently removed his large tan fedora to flash the famous Roosevelt smile. Senator Robert F. Wagner and Mr. Farley accompanied the Chief Executive. On the running board clung the ever-watchful Secret Service agents, looking more like somebody who just hopped on to get a lift down to the next corner.

ROOSEVELT NEAR GIANTS

With the President and his retinue safely and comfortably lodged in the boxes alongside the Giant dugout, the scene moved on to its closing number.

October 7, 1936

Yanks Win Series, Routing Giants With 7 Runs in Last Inning, 13-5

Take Title, 4 Games to 2, After Losers Miss Big Chance to Tie

By JOHN DREBINGER

THE OVERPOWERING FORCE behind the Yankee bludgeons, which crushed the entire American League this year, reigns supreme in the baseball universe today.

There was no checking it, and the end to the 1936 world series came under a gray and murky sky that hung over the Polo Grounds yesterday as the Joe McCarthy juggernaut battered Colonel Bill Terry's Giants into submission in the sixth and final game by a score of 13 to 5. That clinched the classic by a margin of four games to two.

Seven of those thirteen runs came hurtling over the plate in the ninth after the last desperate but gallant stand of the Giants had failed by one of bringing about a tie, and sent a crowd of 38,427 on its way convinced there had been miscarriage of justice.

It was the second world championship to fall to the Yankees under the leadership of the square-jawed but affable enough Joseph V. McCarthy, who never played a game of ball in the major leagues in his life, and the fifth title to come to roost under the Ruppert banner.

The crowd, the smallest of the series, nevertheless brought the aggregate to 302,924, a record for six games and the second highest figure ever attained in world series history. The receipts for the day, $169,213, brought the grand total to $1,204,399, which also sets a six-game record and falls short by only a few thousand dollars of the all-time mark of $1,207,864.

That record was set in the seven-game series between the Yankees and Cardinals in 1926, when the paid attendance totaled 328,051.

That year the Yankees lost, but it was to be their

The President, scarcely discernible from above amid the battery of cameras which flanked him on all sides, rose with a white ball in his hand, and with Managers Terry and McCarthy standing before him, he tossed it for a perfect wild pitch well over the heads of the perspiring, jostling photographers.

Then he shook hands with the rival pilots and also insisted that McCarthy and Terry likewise exchange greetings to make it look like a real happy family all around. Little, however, did the unsuspecting Colonel Bill realize at that moment what terrible intent was in the usually affable Marsa Joe's heart.

DiMaggio alone retired three Giants in the ninth, the job being interrupted only for a mo-ment while Bartell inserted his double. The fi-nal lift, by Leiber, sent Joe clear out to the cen-ter field clubhouse. First he misjudged it, then he readjusted his sights and caught it. Then he stopped in his tracks. The announcer previously had requested the crowd to remain where it was until the Presidential party had retired.

Modest Joe considered himself one of the crowd and decided not to move. He was almost knocked down a couple of times by the return-ing automobiles and finally was induced to join the other players in the exodus to the clubhouse. The Yanks looked eminently satisfied. The Gi-ants appeared in a trance. ◆

---

last defeat for baseball's highest honors, though they appeared in four classics since. They even entered the clash just ended with the amazing record of three series triumphs scored in twelve straight games without a single reversal.

The American Leaguers simply had proved themselves too powerful. Flawless play and super-pitching could stop them for a time; but when the hurling became just ordinary, they fair-ly murdered it. In the second game they set an all-time series record with eighteen runs.

When the bars were let down again at the fin-ish yesterday they sent seven more tallies pour-ing over the plate. Marse Joe had merely rolled the juggernaut on the field. Ground-keeper Henry Fabian need hardly roll it again to make it ready for the football season. The jubilant Yanks had left the Polo Grounds and the Giants flatter than a golf green. A most remarkable baseball season had come to a close. ◆

October 7, 1937

61,000 SEE YANKS CRUSH GIANTS, 8-1, IN SERIES OPENER

Hubbell Routed in Sixth as Gomez Pitches Superbly

By JOHN DREBINGER

BURSTING OUT OF THE MISTY HAZE like an envel-oping flame such as a man might encounter on locating that leak in a gas pipe with the aid of a match, the Yankee juggernaut exploded only once at the Stadium yesterday, but that once sufficed to blow the opening clash of the 1937 world series virtually into atoms.

It came with cyclonic effect in the sixth in-ning, toppled Carl Hubbell like a reed in a high gale, tossed Colonel Bill Terry and his Giants into such confusion that they even nominated a relief pitcher who was sitting awed and spell-bound in the dugout, and went on to hurtle seven runs across the plate. »»

‹‹‹ Two rounds later the venerable Anthony Lazzeri wafted a towering home run into the stands and the sum total of all this was a smashing victory for Marse Joe McCarthy's amazing American League champions behind their own left-hander, Vernon Gomez. The final score, 8 to 1, left a crowd of 61,000 almost as stunned and bewildered by it all as were the crestfallen National Leaguers.

CLINGS TENACIOUSLY TO LEAD

For five innings, Hubbell, ace pitcher of his circuit, strove heroically to repeat his notable triumph in the series opener of 1936. In four of these rounds, in fact, the work of the famous screwball maestro was absolutely flawless as he clung tenaciously to a one-run margin he had gained over his left-handed adversary.

But in this, perhaps, he made a mistake, for it is a matter of scientific knowledge that at times it is extremely dangerous to keep a highly volatile explosive too tightly bottled up. Something simply had to give and in the sixth it was ol' Hub himself.

Confronted by the inviting set-up of the bases full and nobody out but a few less hardy Giant rooters who doubtless already felt what was coming, Joe DiMaggio, he whom they call the wonder player of his time, crashed a single to center field to start the avalanche of Yankee runs pouring across the plate.

MORE SHELLS ARE FIRED

Presently the bases again filled. In fact, those Yankees seemed to keep the bases filled for an almost interminable period while Bill Dickey and George Selkirk fired more shells into the gaunt frame of ol' Hub, who was unmistakably going down with all his comrades on board.

Finally, with the seven big tallies tucked away, the Yankees storm subsided, leaving only Gomez to move serenely on to his fourth victory in world series warfare.

The singular Castillian, who once made the classic remark that he would rather be lucky than good, now reveled in the picture of combining both of these rare qualities so vital to success in any venture.

For not only had fortune smiled on him to the extent of having runs poured in for him in a carload lot, but he was undeniably superb as well. He pitched smoothly and easily, held the straining National League standard bearers to six blows, only two of which did any damage at all, and all in all was a far cry from the Gomez who stumbled badly to two victories last Fall behind a similar withering barrage. ◆

Lefty Gomez, one of the best World Series pitchers in history, hurls the Yankees to an 8–1 victory over the Giants in the 1937 opener.

DIMAGGIO DEMAND STILL OVER $25,000

Joe Loses $162 for Missing Opener, but Can Be Ready in 'From 5 Days to a Week'

SAN FRANCISCO, APRIL 18 (AP).—Joe DiMaggio, hold-out outfielder of the Yankees, stood pat today on his demand for more than $25,000 while his club was taking an opening-day beating from the Red Sox.

Of the Yankees' defeat, he said: "That's too bad." It cost DiMaggio $162 in salary to be absent for the season's opener, but he gave no indication of concern about it.

The long-legged youth, busy with the operation of his restaurant, tossed an optimistic note into the discussion of the Yankees' defeat. He pointed out that the club had lost the opener in 1937, but had won the pennant in a walkaway.

"We'll do it again this year," he said enthusiastically, momentarily forgetting he was a hold-out.

If and when he signs, Joe said he thought he could get into playing condition in "from five days to a week. My weight is perfect—198 pounds. Last year I weighed 204 pounds during the season. It looks like I'll have to eat my way back into shape."

DiMaggio said he had not heard from headquarters. ◆

BROWNS BID FOR DIMAGGIO

But Yankees Refuse $150,000 for Hold-Out

ST. LOUIS, APRIL 18 (AP).—The Browns offered the Yankees about $150,000 for Joe DiMaggio but failed to swing the deal, it was learned tonight.

Colonel Jacob Ruppert, owner of the world champions, was quoted by The Globe-Democrat as saying in a telephone conversation that his star outfielder "is not for sale at any price."

President Don Barnes of the Browns admitted he had made an "offer in six figures." It was learned from a reliable source the offer was approximately $150,000 cash.

Barnes said he was "mighty sorry" Colonel Ruppert's stand was so determined, but "the deal isn't dead as far as the Browns are concerned. I would certainly like to get DiMaggio for the Browns."

"I don't know whether our price was wrong," he added, "or whether Colonel Ruppert wouldn't consider losing DiMaggio." ◆

April 21, 1938

DIMAGGIO AGREES TO $25,000 TERM

Ruppert Wins Salary Battle—Pay Starts When Joe Shows He is Ready to Play

STAR DUE HERE SATURDAY

'Can't Get Back Quick Enough' He Declares Preparatory to Leaving Coast Home

JOE DIMAGGIO'S HOLD-OUT siege against the Yankees terminated abruptly and without much dramatics yesterday, when it was announced that the American League home-run champion and so-called "wonder player" had notified Colonel Jacob Ruppert from his home in San Francisco that he has accepted terms.

The terms, Business Manager Ed Barrow, who made the announcement, hastily explained, are those laid down by the Yankees. This means that the young Coast star, who has been a sensation with the world champions the past two years, will accept a one-year contract at $25,000, less the time he has lost in reporting.

What is more, his salary will not start with his arrival in New York, but only when he is pronounced ready to play. Manager Joe McCarthy is to be sole judge of this.

WILL DON UNIFORM

According to Barrow, DiMaggio, who ever since Jan. 21 has stoutly insisted he would not don a uniform this year unless the Yankees met his demand for $40,000, left San Francisco at 3:40 P.M., Pacific Coast time, yesterday. He is due to arrive in the city at 7:30 Saturday morning and will be in uniform when the Yankees face the Senators in the afternoon at the Stadium.

The ultimatum to DiMaggio that he must get ready at his own expense is similar to that which was meted out to Charlie Ruffing last year, but if Manager McCarthy follows precedent in that case, DiMaggio's salary is likely to start as soon as he arrives.

McCarthy did this in the Ruffing case, explaining that was the more satisfactory way to handle the matter.

"I don't want to be unfair to a player," he said then, "and I don't want him hustling too fast to get in shape. He may tell me he is ready before he actually is and only harm may result."

At his brewery offices Colonel Ruppert, winner in the salary battle, expressed himself as satisfied his difficulty with his young star had come to an end, though it was not without a touch of irony that he added,

"I hope the young man has learned his lesson. His pay will be $25,000, no more, no less, and it won't start until McCarthy says it should."

A THIRD-YEAR MAN

The salary dispute ends with DiMaggio one of the highest-salaried players in organized baseball and indisputably the highest-paid third-year man in the game's history. Before coming to the Yankees in 1936, DiMaggio was under a six-months' contract in the Pacific Coast League for $1,800. He received $8,000 as salary from the Yankees in 1936, in addition to a cut of the victors' share in the world series. Last year DiMaggio's salary was $15,000, plus a world series cut which amounted to about $8,000.

Only Lou Gehrig, with his $39,000 contract, tops DiMaggio in Yankee salaries. The 23-year-old Coast player, on a $25,000 basis, outranks even the great Carl Hubbell, Giant pitching ace, whose salary is $22,500.

DiMaggio last year hit .346. He hammered out forty-six homers, batted in 167 runs, second only to Hank Greenberg, and got 215 hits for 418 total bases in 151 of the 157 contests in which the Yanks engaged. All this earned him recognition through the Winter as the player of the year, a distinction accorded him through the award of plaques by the New York Chapter of the Baseball Writers Association and the Philadelphia Sports Writers Association.

JOE APPEARS RELIEVED

SAN FRANCISCO, April 20 (AP).—Obviously relieved by termination of his holdout campaign, Joe DiMaggio said today he was "all excited about getting back there and rapping the ball again."

Confirming he had accepted the Yankees' terms, Joe declared he was going to try to get in such a good season that "there won't be any chance of an argument over salary next year. Naturally, I thought I was worth more this year. But I'd rather play ball than hold out. I can't get back quick enough now and I'm rarin' to go."

While completing packing DiMaggio ventured the prediction the Yankees would walk off with the pennant again, "not because I'm through holding out, though. It is a championship club anyhow. My team-mates are a swell bunch of fellows and I'd rather play with the Yanks than any other team in baseball." ◆

April 27, 1938

Ladies' Day Set for Stadium

NEW YORK'S WOMEN BASEBALL FANS will have their innings Friday, when the Yankees have their first ladies' day. Every Friday thereafter when the world champions are playing at home women will be admitted to the Stadium free. This Friday's game will find the Red Sox as opponents of the McCarthymen. ◆

August 6, 1938

62,753 See Feller Beaten, 6-1, As Yanks Take 3½-Game Lead

By JOHN DREBINGER
Special to The New York Times.

CLEVELAND, AUG. 5.—Urged on by the ear-splitting exhortations of an all-time record ladies' day crowd that numbered 62,753 and converted Cleveland's huge stadium into a riot of noise and color, Oscar Vitt's Indians made a desperate attempt to nudge themselves back into the American League pennant fight today.

But with that touch of irony which so often manifests itself in these vastly interesting sporting events it was the Tribe's own pride and joy, the youthful Bob Feller, that nudged them right out of it.

For though young Bob held the Yankees to only three hits, he walked eleven of them to first base, let them run hog-wild after that and the result of it all was that the McCarthymen, by simply rolling along behind the smooth hurling of their own Bump Hadley, made off with the opening contest of the three-game series, 6 to 1.

A DISCOURAGING TURN

That tightened the grip of the world champions on first place to the extent of three and a half games, and over the Forest City tonight hangs a feeling that all up to now has been in vain.

Certain it is the pitching of the Iowa prodigy was a most excruciating and futile piece of business today. Even Joe Gordon's fifteenth home run of the season with one aboard in the seventh was hardly needed to bag this game. For by that time the Yanks already had been prodded into a 4-1 lead, and this, behind Hadley's steady five-hit hurling, proved sufficient to carry the day. »»

《《《   In all, the Yanks, who entered the struggle with some misgivings because they had to
leave the injured Bill Dickey sitting on the bench,
collected only four hits. They got their fourth off
the left-handed Al Milnar, who pitched the final
two frames.

But they scarcely needed any hits at all, what
with Feller literally showering them with those
eleven passes, hitting one batsman and permitting five stolen bases while his frantic colleagues
almost turned gray-haired.

Although the paid attendance was only 22,220,
the women guests of the management numbered
40,533. ◆

October 10, 1938

YANKS WIN SERIES FROM CUBS BY 4-0; SCORE, 8-3, IN FINAL

Club First to Take 3 World Titles in a Row—McCarthy, Pilot, Shares Record

RUFFING AGAIN TRIUMPHS

Hurls 2d Victory as Losers Send Six to Box—Henrich, O'Dea Drive Home Runs

By JOHN DREBINGER

BASEBALL HISTORY WAS MADE yesterday as the
Yankees again conquered the Cubs, 8 to 3, and
captured the 1938 world series by 4 games to 0.

The triumph gave the New Yorkers the distinction of being the first club ever to annex three
successive world championships. In addition,
the Yankees' manager, Joseph V. McCarthy,
who never played a game of major-league ball,
became the first to direct a team which accomplished this magnificent feat.

What had happened to Bill Terry's Giants in
1936 and 1937 had come to pass again, with
these latest National League champions as victims, and the final battle at the Stadium yesterday, viewed by 59,847 onlookers, seemed merely

a repetition of what had gone before, only there
was more emphasis to it.

AGAIN HURLS COMMENDABLY

Burly Red Ruffing, victor in the series opener
in Chicago last Wednesday, came back to spin
another commendable performance on the
mound, and behind him there again was that
steady drumfire of long-range blows that tossed
the Cubs into hopeless confusion whenever they
made the slightest mistake. Perhaps their greatest mistake was in showing up at all.

Frankie Crosetti, concluding a brilliant stretch
of four games with a grand flourish, drove in
four of the Yankee runs, the first two with a triple
in the second inning, which saw the Yanks score
three times after a grievous misplay, with two
out, had given them the necessary opening.

In the sixth Tommy Henrich sent a booming
home run into the right-field stands and when, in
the eighth, the Cubs had the temerity to whittle the
score down to 4 to 3 on the wings of a homer by
Kenneth O'Dea, the Yanks immediately lashed back
in the same inning with a cluster of four. Crosetti
fetched home the final pair with a double off Dizzy
Dean, the celebrated hollow shell whom Frankie already had punctured once before in this series.

In desperation, a fighting Gabby Hartnett jug-
gled his meager man power in every conceivable
combination. He even benched himself, but un-
happily he could not bench enough. The rules of
the game still require that nine men must appear
on the field at any given time.

He hurled no fewer than six pitchers into the
futile struggle, which in itself constitutes another
world series record.

And so Marse Joe, the square-jawed, affable

manager whom only those behind the scenes ever see wielding an active hand, has achieved a feat which up to now had eluded the greatest of baseball leaders. The immortal John McGraw had his chance in 1923, but that Fall a Yankee team, which his Giants had walloped in 1921 and 1922, turned on the Little Napoleon. And in 1931 Connie Mack, after his Athletics had crushed the Cubs in 1929 and the Cardinals in 1930, missed his bid for a third straight world title when the Cards surged back to upset him.

The victory yesterday also marked the seventh world championship banner to be hauled in by these amazing Bronx Bombers, the fourth under McCarthy, who bagged his first in 1932.

It was also the fourth time the Yanks had recorded a grand slam of four straight. They first achieved this feat in 1927 at the expense of the Pirates, repeated the stunt with the Cardinals in 1928, and in 1932, their next world series appearance, bowled over the Cubs without losing a game. This, incidentally, gives the Chicagoans the unenviable record of having lost eight straight to the Yanks in world series warfare.

All told, over a span of twelve campaigns, this astounding New York club has brought to the American League six world championships by winning twenty-four games and losing only three. The Yanks dropped two in hammering the Giants into submission in 1936 and lost only one to the Terryman last Fall.

It was, in truth, as one-sided a struggle as any series has ever provided despite the fact that until this last game the Cubs managed to keep the scores close. For from the very beginning there was ever present the feeling of Yankee superiority which would manifest itself whenever the pressure was on. And in this the Yanks never failed.

The one exciting battle of the entire set was that second game which the wraith of a once great Dean almost won. But two devastating blows by Crosetti and DiMaggio had wrecked that, and after that, no matter what happened, one always felt that more such blows were in waiting should exigencies demand their appearance.

And so the Yanks still top the baseball world, their position more impregnable than ever. Three years running they have stamped all competition out of their own American League and in three successive tries the National League certainly has shown it has nothing to match this remarkable machine which many contend is the mightiest ball club of all time. At all events, if there are still any disbelievers, it is quite certain they are keeping in hiding today. ◆

The crowd exits Yankee Stadium after Game 3 of the World Series between the Cubs and the Yankees on October 8, 1938

May 26, 1939

RUFFING ANNEXES 200TH VICTORY, 5-2

Becomes Fifth Hurler Still in Majors to Attain Mark as Yankees Stop Tigers

By JAMES P. DAWSON

Pitcher Charles 'Red' Ruffing at Yankee Stadium.

AN UNUSUAL RECORD WAS ATTAINED by Charley (Red) Ruffing yesterday at the Stadium as the Yankees resumed their winning ways at the expense of Del Baker's Tigers and stretched their lead in the American League flag race to five and one-half games.

Turning back the Detroiters, 5 to 2, for his seventh straight victory in a clean record this year, Ruffing became the fifth pitcher still active in baseball to hang up his 200th triumph, and the second right-hander to crash into a select circle which includes Robert Moses Grove of the Red Sox, Carl Hubbell, the Giants' kingpin; Earl Whitehill of the Cubs, and Ted Lyons, White Sox right-hander.

In his tenth year with the Yankees, his sixteenth in the major leagues and his seventeenth in organized baseball, this distinction came to the redhead from Nokomis, Ill., who came up with the Danville club of the Three-Eye League back in 1923.

In his ten seasons with the Yanks, Ruffing, 35 years old, has clicked off 161 victories. In 1930, after losing five games, he came to New York from the Red Sox in a trade for Cedric Durst. ◆

July 12, 1939

62,892 See American League Beat National for 5-2 Lead in All-Star Games

HOMER BY DIMAGGIO MARKS 3-1 VICTORY

By JOHN DREBINGER

RIDING HIGH ON THE WINGS of a Joe DiMaggio home run and finishing with a blinding burst of speed on the part of its foremost pitching wizard, Bobby Feller, the American League reasserted its superiority over the National League at the Yankee Stadium yesterday by winning the seventh annual All-Star game, 3 to 1.

The victory, cheered impartially by a vast gathering of 62,892 onlookers, who paid $75,701 to see the show, completely reversed the order of a year ago in Cincinnati, when the National forces had finished on top, and marked the fifth triumph for the American League in the seven games played starting in 1933.

It was not, perhaps, the most dramatic game ever played between the keen and sometimes bitter rivals of baseball's two major leagues. But it had its moments when the crowd, basking in the sunlight of a perfect Summer afternoon, reared up and roared its approval.

And at the finish there was occasion once again to acclaim Marse Joe McCarthy, head man of the world champion Yankees, who skillfully piloted the American League troops to victory over gay Gabby Hartnett, the florid boss of the Cubs, who directed the battle lines of the vanquished.

UNDERDOGS DRAW CHEERS

There was the tug for the underdog, so inherent a characteristic of New York crowds, when the National Leaguers, 2-to-1 long shots in the betting, made off with a 1-0 lead in the first three innings.

Paul Derringer, ace right-hander of the National League's front running Reds, slightly out-pitched burly Charlie (Red) Ruffing of the Yanks in that opening brush to gain the one-run margin, and the crowd magnanimously conceded the point. It even applauded vociferously when Linus Frey, one of five of Bill McKechnie's Cincinnatians in the starting line-up, rammed that tally home with a rousing two-base smash.

But in the fourth the American Leaguers, doubtless fired to action by the presence of no fewer than six world champion Yankees in their battlefront, surged irresistibly in the fore with a pair of runs wrenched from big Bill Lee, strapping right-hander of the Cubs.

George Selkirk of the Yanks banged in one of these with a single. A momentary crack-up in the

Joe DiMaggio in 1939.

Nationals' usually airtight defenses, a fumble by Arky Vaughan, Pirate shortstop, let in the other.

An inning later the matchless DiMaggio, hailed as the wonder player of his time, stepped majestically into the picture all by himself. With nobody on the base-paths and practically nothing at all going on at the time, Jolting Joe leaned into one of Lee's most ardent deliveries and sent the ball sailing high through the clear blue sky into the left wing of the lower grandstand. ◆

October 9, 1939

DiMaggio's Base Running Is Praised as Yanks Celebrate

VICTORY SONGFEST LED BY M'CARTHY

Yanks' Pilot 'Tickled Beyond Words'—Plaudits for Keller, Dickey, DiMaggio, Murphy

From a Staff Correspondent

CINCINNATI, OCT. 8—There was hoopla on all sides as the victorious Yankees trooped into their quarters today after their series sweep over the Reds.

"East Side, West Side," rang out in strident tones. "Roll Out the Barrel" followed, with Marse Joe McCarthy leading in a throaty bari-tone. Coaches Art Fletcher, Earle Combs and Johnny Schulte, slightly off key, lent lusty aid, for all that, and the players to a man joined in while shaking hands, slapping backs, playfully punching each other and generally giving themselves over to a wild celebration.

Everybody was glad the series was over. Everybody was tickled it had ended in four straight with a 10-inning 7-4 victory.

NOISE TOO MUCH FOR HARRIDGE

President Will Harridge of the American League was drowned out by the shouting and singing. So were Warren Giles, Reds' general manager, and the crushed Paul Derringer, Cincinnati pitcher, who came in to present their felicitations.

The retired Lou Gehrig, missing active participation in a Yankee triumph for the first time in his long association with the club, joined in the hullabaloo and smilingly declared it "the greatest finish I have ever seen."

The plaudits were for the hammering Charley Keller, the quiet-spoken Bill Dickey with the noisy bat, the alert Joe DiMaggio for as fancy a

bit of heads-up base running as has been seen in years, and for old reliable Johnny Murphy, the club's fireman, who has been putting out enemy flare-ups for so long he is entitled to enjoy the distinction of his first world series victory.

Manager McCarthy congratulated his boys. Keller was so enthusiastic he twice congratulated Mac, until the Yankee skipper said, "That's the second time you did that. Now I guess you want me to kiss you."

PILOT PRAISES DECISION

"Don't forget it's nine straight world series victories, boys," yelled McCarthy to assembled writers. "And another thing, that decision by Pinelli in the tenth was one of the greatest I have ever seen. He called it right, exactly as it happened, on DiMaggio, in a tight situation. I guess it will be McCarthy pitching tomorrow. I'm tickled beyond words. It's great to have a ball club like this one winning the way it does. They proved themselves today, every one of them. Any time you beat Derringer and Walters in one day you've done something."

Coach Fletcher took time out from singing and shouting to praise DiMaggio. "I told him nothing but watch the ball," said Fletcher. "And boy, he watched it. He gave us one of the greatest pieces of sliding I've ever seen. He had to slide over Lombardi's hand and then dig down and touch the plate, and he did it to perfection. Lombardi found out you can't sit down with those Yankees on the base paths, hey?"

DiMaggio was tickled and proudly showed his scars of battle. His legs and hips are covered with sliding bruises.

Keller and Dickey congratulated each other on their homers and Keller wise-cracked: "It's great to hit to homer in a world series, until Dickey comes up and hits one fifty feet farther." ◆

Joe DiMaggio slides into home plate while Ernie Lombardi, catcher for the Cincinatti Reds tries unsuccessfully to stop him from scoring during Game 4 of the World Series, at Crosley Field, October 8, 1939.

February 5, 1941

Rizzuto to Be Honored Tonight

FRIENDS AND ADMIRERS of Phil Rizzuto, Glendale youth, who is expected to be in the Yankees' infield when the American League baseball season opens, will give him a testimonial dinner tonight at the Rhineland Garden in the Ridgewood section of Brooklyn. Among the invited guests will be Marius Russo, Yankee pitcher, who lives in Ozone Park. ◆

June 9, 1941

DIMAGGIO CONNECTS FOR CIRCUIT THRICE

Drives Two Homers in Opener, One in 7-Inning Nightcap, as Browns Bow, 9-3, 8-3

By JAMES P. DAWSON
Special to The New York Times.

ST. LOUIS, JUNE 8—The Yankees fired a home-run barrage today to take two games from the Browns, sweep the series at Sportsman's Park and vault into a tie for third place with the White Sox in the American League race.

A crowd of 10,546 saw the McCarthymen hit seven drives for the circuit, to bag the first game, 9 to 3, and the second, 8 to 3. The nightcap was called after the completion of the seventh inning when storm clouds brought darkness to the field. Four homers came in the opener, touching a new season's high for the Yanks.

Joe DiMaggio led the home run derby with three round-trippers. He struck two in succession in the first encounter to tide Charley Ruffing over the rough spots and give Red the decision over Elden Auker.

In the nightcap DiMaggio smote his eleventh round-tripper of the year after Charley Keller had exploded No. 9 and Joe Gordon No. ⟫⟫

⫸ 8. These blows erased a homer by Chet Laabs which helped to chase Marius Russo in the third inning, and clinched the victory for Marv Breuer, who finished the game falteringly.

DRIVE TALLIES 3 RUNS

DiMaggio's first circuit smash sank into the left-field bleachers in the third inning of the opener after Auker had walked Rolfe and Henrich. When Joe drove his second into the center-field pavilion opening the sixth the result was clinched.

DiMaggio's home-run blasts stretched to twenty-four the number of games in which he has hit consecutively. ◆

June 18, 1941

DIMAGGIO'S STREAK REACHES 30 GAMES

Joe's Lucky Hit Sets All-Time Mark for Yanks, Who Lose to White Sox, 8-7

By LOUIS EFFRAT

JOLTING JOE DIMAGGIO was lucky, but the same couldn't be said of his Yankee mates at the Stadium yesterday. A ground ball that was labeled an easy out in the seventh suddenly took a bad hop, hit Luke Appling on the shoulder and DiMaggio's hitting streak zoomed to thirty consecutive games, an all-time Yankee record. But a more important streak, collected by the McCarthymen in eight straight victories, ceased to exist.

Despite some heavy cannonading in the seventh and eighth, when the Yankees erased a 5-run deficit and pulled even, the decision went to the White Sox, 8 to 7. When the local club had the tying and winning runs on the basepaths and one out in the ninth, only to strand both runners, the 10,442 fans voiced their disappointment, to put it mildly.

DiMaggio's record surpassed the Yankee mark shared by Roger Peckinpaugh and Earle Combs. The former hit in twenty-nine straight games in 1919, the latter in 1931.

In the eighth, prior to Keller's homer, DiMaggio sent a screaming liner to right. It looked like the jackpot, but Taft Wright made a leaping, one-handed stab and pulled the ball down, just as it was about to clear the barrier. ◆

June 21, 1941

M'CARTHYMEN WIN WITH 17 HITS, 14-4

DiMaggio Gets Four, Running Two-Game String to Seven—Yanks Near Homer Mark

By ARTHUR DALEY

APPARENTLY THE YANKEES never heard the bell signal the end of batting practice. They kept flailing away at Bobo Newsom and Archie McKain for seventeen hits that totaled twenty-nine bases at the Stadium yesterday and rolled right over the Tigers, 14 to 4. The fast-moving Bombers reduced the Cleveland lead to two games.

This spectacle was greatly enjoyed by a ladies' day gathering of 14,055. The fans saw action from the first inning on. In the first Johnny Sturm singled and Tommy Henrich hit his eleventh home run. This performance was duplicated a few moments later when Joe DiMaggio lashed the first of his four hits and Charlie Keller cracked his fourteenth circuit shot into the bleachers.

CAN'T GET HIM OUT

Though he struck no homers, DiMaggio extended his consecutive hits record to seven for two games with his four blows yesterday.

Of much more importance to Jolting Joe is that he has hit safely in thirty-three consecutive games. The American League targets immediately ahead of him are George McQuinn's thirty-four, Ty Cobb's forty and George Sisler's forty-one.

DiMaggio, the perfect ball player, made an error in the first when he slipped while fielding Paddy Mullin's hit and the runners each took an extra base.

York sent DiMaggio to the center-field bleach-ers, 450 feet from the plate, to pull down his clout. The Great Man collared it with ease and nonchalance. ◆

Outfielders Joe DiMaggio, Charlie Keller and Tom Henrich pose before a 1941 game at Yankee Stadium.

June 30, 1941

YANKEES CONQUER SENATORS, 9-4, 7-5

DiMaggio, Getting Hit in Each Contest, Beats Modern Mark— Keeler Record 44 Games

31,000 HAIL BATTING ACE

Henrich, Gordon, Keller Keep Homer Streak Intact— Lead Over Indians 1½ Lengths

By JAMES P. DAWSON
Special to The New York Times.

WASHINGTON, JUNE 29—Joe DiMaggio scaled new heights today.

In a Yankee sweep of a double-header with the Senators that attracted 31,000 fans to the seething cauldron that was Griffith Stadium, the New Yorkers' batting marvel set a modern record for hitting in consecutive games.

With his only hit of the first encounter, a rousing double that rolled to the 422-foot sign on the bleacher wall, in the sixth inning, DiMaggio tied the modern record, hitting safely in forty-one successive contests, set by George Sisler.

This mark had withstood the assault of major league players since 1932.

In the nightcap DiMaggio was turned back three times before he connected. Finally, in the seventh inning Joe sent a screaming single to left that boosted his string to forty-two consecutive games and sent him in quest of the all-time major league record, forty-four games, made in 1897 by Willie Keeler, who "hit them where they ain't."

CROWD FORGETS HEAT

The fact that the thermometer hovered around 98 was forgotten in the excitement of this epochal clubbing by one of the greatest players baseball ever has known. The fans roared thunderous acclaim to the record-maker, first as he tore madly for second on his double in the opener, then as he loped to first on his single in the nightcap.

DiMaggio's teammates, to a man, were as excited as schoolboys over his feat. That the Yankees stretched their home-run record to forty in their last twenty-five games by hitting for the circuit in each struggle was an anti-climax. That they swept two games by scores of 9 to 4 and 7 to 5 was incidental, even though the McCarthymen thus took a lead of a game and a half over the second-place Indians in the American League.

DiMaggio was jubilant, albeit slightly embarrassed over the fuss.

"Sure, I'm tickled. Who wouldn't be?" he said, in the clubhouse between games as he donned a fresh suit, after a shower. "It's a great thing. I've realized an ambition. But I don't deserve the credit all alone.

"You have to give Mr. McCarthy some of it. I got many a break by being allowed to hit that '3 and 0' pitch. It brought me many a good ball to swing at. You know, he's got to give you the signal on '3 and 0' pitches and he was right with me all the time.

GLAD STRAIN IS OVER

"I'm glad the strain is over. Now I'm going after that forty-four-game mark and I'll keep right on swinging and hitting as long as I can."

DiMaggio explained he hit a low, fast ball to tie the record." I never really was concerned about the mark until around the thirty-third game," he said. "Yester-

DiMaggio's Streak

Date.	Hits.	Pitcher.	Club.
May 15	1	Smith	White Sox
May 16	2	Lee	White Sox
May 17	1	Rigney	White Sox
May 18	3	Harris (2)	Browns
		Niggeling (1)	Browns
May 19	1	Galehouse	Browns
May 20	1	Auker	Browns
May 21	2	Rowe (1)	Tigers
		Benton (1)	Tigers
May 22	1	McKain	Tigers
May 23	1	Newsome	Red Sox
May 24	1	Johnson	Red Sox
May 25	1	Grove	Red Sox
May 27	4	Chase (1)	Senators
		Carrasquel (1)	Senators
		Anderson (2)	Senators
May 28	1	Hudson	Senators
May 29	1	Sundra	Senators
May 30	1	Johnson	Red Sox
May 30	1	Harris	Red Sox
June 1	1	Milnar	Indians
June 1	1	Harder	Indians
June 2	2	Feller	Indians
June 3	1	Trout	Tigers
June 5	1	Newhouser	Tigers
June 7	3	Muncrief (1)	Browns
		Allen (1)	Browns
		Caster (1)	Browns
June 8	2	Auker	Browns
June 8	2	Caster (1)	Browns
		Kramer (1)	Browns
June 10	1	Rigney	White Sox
June 12	2	Lee	White Sox
June 14	1	Feller	Indians
June 15	1	Bagby	Indians
June 16	1	Milnar	Indians
June 17	1	Rigney	White Sox
June 18	1	Lee	White Sox
June 19	3	Smith (1)	White Sox
		Ross (2)	White Sox
June 20	4	Newsom (2)	Tigers
		McKain (2)	Tigers
June 21	1	Trout	Tigers
June 22	2	Newhouser (1)	Tigers
		Newsom (1)	Tigers
June 24	1	Muncrief	Browns
June 25	1	Galehouse	Browns
June 26	1	Auker	Browns
June 27	2	Dean	Athletics
June 28	2	Babich (1)	Athletics
		Harris (1)	Athletics
June 29	1	Leonard	Senators
June 29	1	Anderson	Senators

In the nightcap Arnold Anderson almost knocked DiMaggio down with a pitch in the seventh inning, but Joe swung at the next one and hammered a clean single to left. The cheers grew in volume when DiMaggio tore over the plate on Charley Keller's triple with the seventh Yankee run.

DiMaggio was mobbed even before the games. Fans interfered with his batting practice to get his autograph. He took it all good naturedly.

DiMaggio's favorite bat disappeared between games. A fan, discovered with the bat in the stand, refused to return it.

It became known today that DiMaggio, after the game yesterday in Philadelphia, visited a sick boy, 10-year-old Tony Morell, at Jefferson Hospital. Lefty Gomez, DiMag's roomie, accompanied him.

When the visit came to light today DiMaggio pleaded that it be given no publicity. ◆

day, in Philadelphia, I think, was the first time I was really nervous. I was tense out there today, too."

DiMaggio made his record-equaling hit off Dutch Leonard, adding a new pitching victim to his list. He swung at the first pitch, looked at a ball, then banged his double.

July 2, 1941

YANKEE STAR HITS 44TH GAME IN ROW

DiMaggio Bats Safely in Two Contests to Equal Keeler's All-Time Major Mark

By ARTHUR DALEY

THE GREATEST OF THE PRESENT-DAY ball players drew even with one of the legendary figures of the past yesterday when Joe DiMaggio equaled Wes Willie Keeler's all-time major league record of hitting safely in forty-four consecutive games.

A double-header at the Stadium with the Red Sox gave Jolting Joe the opportunity of overhauling the old Oriole batting artist. And a vast crowd of 52,832, a record for the Stadium this season, wheeled through the turnstiles to see him do it.

This was the Great Man's personal show. No one seemed to care who won the games. The spectators merely wanted to see DiMaggio hit.

OVATION GREETS SOLID HIT

Twice in the first fray he went out while a pall settled over the stands. In the third trip he scratched a hit that half in the crowd suspected was an error. So when he lined a ringing single to left in his next try roars of delight filled the humid air.

With those hits DiMaggio boosted his modern mark to forty-three straight games. But could he equal Keeler's record of 1897? That was the question uppermost in every one's mind during the intermission.

The crowd did not have long to wait. On his first trip Jolting Joe lined a screaming single to center. He had done it.

Oh, yes. The double-header. The Yankees won both ends with a tremendous display of batting power, cracking out twenty-five hits for 7-to-2 and 9-to-2 victories. ◆

July 3, 1941

HOME RUN IN FIFTH TOPS KEELER MARK

DiMaggio's Wallop Stretches His Hitting Streak to 45 Games—Old Record 44

YANKS HALT RED SOX, 8-4

Win Sixth Straight to Extend First-Place Margin Over Indians to 3 Contests

By JOHN DREBINGER

SWEEPING MAJESTICALLY onward with a thunderous smash that soared deep into the left-field stands, Joe DiMaggio yesterday rocketed his current hitting streak beyond the all-time major league record.

For with that home-run clout, boisterously acclaimed by 8,682 sweltering fans in the sun-baked Yankee Stadium, DiMaggio the Magnificent extended his astounding string to forty-five consecutive games in which he has connected safely.

This surpasses by one the major league mark of 44 games set forty-four years ago by that famous mite of an Oriole, Wee Willie Keeler, who gained renown for his skill in "hitting them where they ain't." Yesterday DiMaggio shattered that mark by the simpler expedient of hitting one where they just couldn't get it.

CLEAN SWEEP OF SERIES

Jolting Joe's record-smashing blow was struck off Heber Newsome, freshman right-hander, in the fifth inning of a game which also saw the Yankees flatten the Red Sox, 8 to 4. That gave the Bronx Bombers a clean sweep of the three-game series, extended a new winning streak to six in a row and bolstered their hold on first place to three full games over the Indians.

But all this provided merely incidental music, for the crowd's attention remained riveted on the tall, dark-haired Yankee Clipper who, despite a warm and genial personality, seems to move so coldly aloof on a ball field.

The modern record of 41 games, set by George Sisler of the Browns in 1922, had already fallen by the wayside in last Sunday's double-header in Washington. Actually, there was no comparison between this new DiMaggio mark and the old record of Keeler's, for different rules prevailed in Wee Willie's day back in 1897. There was no foul strike rule hampering the hitter then so that DiMaggio, when he equaled the 44-game Keeler record on Tuesday, already seemed to have achieved a greater feat.

MAKES LEAPING CATCH

But, in order to preclude all further argument, Joe yesterday decided to smash the last remaining record and he certainly did it in the most emphatic manner possible. He almost broke the mark the first time up when he shot a sharp liner to right center which Stanley Spence for a moment misjudged. But the Boston right fielder righted his course just in time to make a leaping catch.

A snappy pick-up and throw by Third Baseman Jim Tabor on a difficult bounding ball checked DiMaggio again in the third, but there was no stopping him in the fifth as he clubbed the ball into the left-field stand with Red Rolfe on base.

The shot came in the midst of a six-run rally which routed Newsome and enabled DiMaggio's bosom pal and roommate, Lefty Gomez, to chalk up his sixth mound victory of the year de-

spite the fact that the heat forced Lefty to vacate in the next inning.

The DiMaggio clout was his eighteenth homer of the year, his thirteenth of the batting streak and his 100th hit of the season.

A souvenir hunter almost got away with a grand coup at the close of the game when he snatched DiMaggio's cap off his head and started dashing for the nearest exit like one of football's greatest open-field runners. But the Stadium's vigilant secondary defense of special guards finally nailed the culprit some twenty yards from his goal. ◆

The box score:

BOSTON (A.)	ab.	r.	h.	po.	a.	e.
D. DiMag., cf	5	1	0	1	0	0
Finney, 1b	5	1	2	10	1	0
Williams, lf	3	1	1	1	0	0
Cronin, ss	2	1	1	0	1	1
L. N'some, ss	0	0	0	1	1	0
Spence, rf	4	0	1	4	0	0
Tabor, 3b	4	0	2	1	2	0
Doerr, 2b	4	0	0	1	4	0
Pytlak, c	4	0	0	5	1	0
H. N'some, p	2	0	1	0	0	0
Wilson, p	0	0	0	0	0	0
Potter, p	1	0	0	0	0	0
aFoxx	1	0	1	0	0	0
Total	35	4	9	24	10	1

NEW YORK (A.)	ab.	r.	h.	po.	a.	e.
Sturm, 1b	4	1	0	9	0	0
Rolfe, 3b	3	2	2	0	4	0
Henrich, rf	5	0	3	3	0	0
J. DiMag., cf	5	1	1	3	0	0
Keller, lf	4	2	2	4	0	0
Dickey, c	3	1	0	3	0	0
Gordon, 2b	5	1	0	2	3	0
Rizzuto, ss	4	0	2	3	4	1
Gomez, p	3	0	1	0	1	0
Murphy, p	1	0	0	0	0	0
Total	37	8	11	27	12	1

aBatted for Potter in ninth.

Boston	0 0 0	0 0 3	1 0 0—4
New York	0 1 1	0 6 0	0 0 .—8

Runs batted in—Keller, J. DiMaggio 3, Rolfe, Gomez 2, Spence 2, Tabor, Cronin. Two-base hits—Rizzuto, Rolfe. Home runs—Keller, J. DiMaggio. Stolen base—Sturm. Double plays—Gomez. Rizzuto and Sturm; Rolfe, Gordon and Sturm. Left on bases—New York 11, Boston 7. Bases on balls—Off Gomez 2, H. Newsome 3, Wilson 1, Murphy 1, Potter 2. Struck out—By Gomez 2, H. Newsome 2, Wilson 1, Murphy 1, Potter 1. Hits—Off H. Newsome 6 in 4 1-3 innings. Wilson 1 in 2-3, Potter 4 in 3, Gomez 5 in 5 1-3, Murphy 4 in 3 2-3. Wild pitch—Gomez. Passed balls—Pytlak 2. Winning pitcher—Gomez. Losing pitcher—H. Newsome. Umpires—Rommell, Stewart, Summers and Rue. Time of game—2:22. Attendance—8,682.

July 13, 1941

DIMAGGIO, THE UNRUFFLED

Portrait of a ballplayer who just keeps hitting 'em

By RUSSELL OWEN

WHEN, A FEW YEARS AGO, a much-touted youngster named Joe DiMaggio came from the Pacific Coast to join the Yankees, Ed Barrow, president of the club, thought the publicity DiMaggio received might turn his head. So he called the new member in and gave him fatherly advice about keeping his shirt on and not letting advance praise spoil his playing.

"Don't worry, Mr. Barrow," said young Joe. "I never get excited."

Joe never does. He didn't get excited the other day when he broke Wee Willie Keeler's forty-four-year-old record of hitting safely in forty-four consecutive games. Before Joe drove a homer into the left-field stands for the hit of the forty-fifth consecutive game he was as nonchalant as duck on ice.

"Of course," he said in the locker room, "it is kinda hard to keep from pressing. I didn't think much about the record until I got within three games of it, and then I realized it was worth trying for. The last few games have been a little hard. I know I mustn't press, for if you do you can't hit successfully, and yet I want to. And just holding back and trying to be natural is a bit of a strain."

Well, this was the big day. He had already equaled Keeler's record, and he wanted to smash it if he could. But one would never have known it while talking to DiMaggio. He was sitting beside his locker, and an attendant brought him over a cup of hot coffee. Then Joe lit a cigarette in a manner most composed. His long legs stretched out in front of him and, as he had on little more than a shirt, it was obvious that he is a powerfully built man. His thighs are tremendous, his arms long and well muscled, and the veins stood out on them this hot day. Keep in condition?

"Oh, I don't pay much attention to it. I eat about everything I want to, but I suppose in another year or two I'll have to think about that. Now my weight doesn't change much." He stands 6 feet 2 and weighs 200 pounds.

He sat on a bench beside the lockers. His locker is No. 5, the same number he wears on the field. Next to it is the empty locker with the name Lou Gehrig on it, a silent memorial in the clubhouse to one of the greatest of all players. It will always be empty, and there will never be another No. 4.

"It doesn't pay to get excited in this game, although some fellows naturally are more tense than others," said Joe. "They can't help it, and just now I can understand why. But after today, whether I break that record or not, there will just be a lot of ball games. It's my job. I do the best I can."

This has been DiMaggio's best year, because until recently he was always getting hurt. Where? In his legs. Something was always going wrong. Perhaps there might have been a little bit more to it than that, but Joe is married now, and his wife will have a baby this Fall, and life is a little more serious. He is 27, which is not young as ball players go; he has settled down now, and is going about the business of baseball with deadly seriousness. He is buying an annuity and has a nice restaurant business out in San Francisco, which his family runs.

San Francisco is Joe's home town. There his father built up a fish business after coming to this country from Italy with his young wife and a few children. When Joe got big enough he began to play baseball for a boy's club, and then he played on his high-school team. And in between he played football and basketball and softball, and nearly every other game that came his way. He even determined for a short time to be a tennis champion.

Joe DiMaggio pays the price of idolatry as enthusiastic fans run at him from all sides after last out at Yankee Stadium. Joe extended his hitting streak to 48 consecutive games.

His brother Vince was an outfielder for the San Francisco Seals when it became time for Joe to go to work. Joe went with an orange juice company—for one day—and while he was looking for another job he managed to make the Seals. Before he quit that team the year before he came to New York he had hung up a record of hitting in sixty-one consecutive games and getting a lot of home runs. And just to show how "nervous" he is—in his first game with the Yankees in 1936 he got a triple and two singles. The Yankees now pay him $35,000 a year.

It has been said that he is shy and inarticulate. He may have been once, but he had plenty of poise this day. He is a good-looking chap, with black curly hair, sparkling eyes, and a rather long nose, which gives him a sort of Cyrano de Bergerac profile. One can imagine that, had he lived long ago, Joe might have been quite a boy with the rapier. He is usually quiet, but smiles easily, if a smile can be called a slight brightening of the features and a bit of light behind the eyes. Altogether a likable fellow.

What makes a good batter?

"I don't know," said DiMaggio. "Probably it is good eyesight, a sense of timing, and balance. And a good use of the wrists. We use our wrists a lot in this, you know."

He held his out. They were surprisingly small for so large a man; well-proportioned, but slender and tough looking. So were those of Lefty Gomez, the pitcher, who came over and sat down and contemplated the spikes on the bottom of a shoe. The two players compared wrists, and wondered why they had never noticed that their thumb and 〉〉〉

◀◀◀ forefinger went around with a bit to spare.

"I like a top-heavy bat," said DiMaggio. "A bat kinda thick out at the end, with most of the weight there. It keeps me from swinging too fast, and when I do connect, the ball travels."

It certainly does. During the game later it was interesting to try and follow that bat. The eye wasn't fast enough. DiMaggio has a stance that would make most ball players shudder. He stands with his feet far apart, and the bat in a sort of "port arms" position. The way some of the old photographs show ball players standing in the days when Keeler was making his record.

"That's the only way I can bat," said Joe. "It is

Yankee Clipper Joe DiMaggio's hands gripping his bat.

natural for me. I don't think I shift my left foot more than three inches when I swing."

How far away is the ball when he decides what to do with it? DiMaggio pointed to a spot about ten feet away and said he thought it was about that far. How could he work so fast? He didn't know; instinct, probably. It has to be instinct and good eyes. Also, he thinks that by not moving his feet very much, by having them wide apart before his swing, he minimizes the shifting of his eyes in relation to the ball's line of flight and the dropping of his shoulders.

Jack London once wrote a story about an Alaskan he-man named Burning Daylight. He couldn't be licked in a scrap. He saved his energy for that fraction of a second when he exploded every ounce of vitality in him and overwhelmed his opponent. Well, DiMaggio is like that. At bat he has a dead pan; he stands as if frozen, with his bat in the funny "port arms" position. You try to follow the ball toward him, until bat and ball meet, and try to see what happens. It can't be done. That bat must come back a little before it starts its swing but Joe simply seems to explode.

Up in Mr. Barrow's box, which is a good place to observe the unpredictable phenomena of a baseball field, it was interesting to watch this characteristic break into action. The first time DiMaggio was up on his record-breaking day he sent a powerful drive to right center—it would have been a safe hit as a rule, but it was pulled down by a splendid effort. The next time up he drove the ball down the third-base line, and the third baseman nailed it with another remarkable stop. The third time he fouled into the stand, and then he banged a home run only a few feet from where the foul had landed.

In every one of these swings there was the same instantaneous output of every bit of energy in DiMaggio's body. After the last there was a tribute from the crowd.

DiMaggio doesn't pay much attention to the crowds. He knows that they are with you when you are good and boo you when you fall down,

and he has no illusions about popularity.

"This is the way I make my living," he said to me before the game. "I like to be popular, who doesn't? But I don't pay much attention to the fans. While I give them all I have, and I hope I can make good for them, primarily I am out there playing ball for the club—and for myself. You have got to do the best you can while you last in this game, and I want to make what I can while I last."

While we were talking Tom Connolly, who has charge of the umpires in the American League, came along and grabbed Joe's hand for a moment. He has an Irish brogue that is a delight, and he used to know Willie Keeler, whose record DiMaggio was about to break.

"B'y," said he, "I hope you do it, and if you do you're breaking the record of the foinest little fellow who ever walked and who never said a mean thing about any one in his life. Good luck to ye."

Barrow recalled that Keeler batted very differently from DiMaggio. Keeler was only 5 feet 4 and weighed 138 pounds. He "choked" his bat, holding it far up the handle, and the bat was short and fat, "like a paddle." "But he came as close as any man I ever knew to placing his hits where he wanted them, in any part of the field. 'Hit 'em where they ain't' was his motto," Barrow grinned.

Down in the dugout before the game DiMaggio had come in for a razzing that recalled Keeler's famous line. The photographers had him polishing his bat with a beef bone—a way batters have of keeping their bats smooth so that they will not splinter, for a pet bat is a precious thing and must not be spoiled. And, while he polished, Joe was subjected to a running fire of kidding, which affected him not at all. He just smiled and kept on polishing, and then rubbed his neck with a towel at the photographers' direction.

"Hey, Joe," said a fellow Yank beside him. "How do you make a record? Hit 'em where they ain't?" And other players went by and made some caustic remark, or yelled, "Hey, grandpop," to an old friend and life was very free and easy. And Joe just kept on rubbing his bat or saying a quiet word or two to somebody >>>

≪≪≪ near him. Nerves? Self-consciousness? He hasn't any.

"He's a good ball player because he knows he's good," said Lefty Gomez when DiMaggio walked away for a few minutes. "I don't mean he is conceited. He isn't. But he is confident. He knows what he can do and that is why he is relaxed. He's always relaxed."

He doesn't care much what they serve him, incidentally. What does he like?

"A nice straight one down the center," he said with a grin. Who wouldn't? "But I go after anything I think I can hit, and a change of pace doesn't bother me. You don't think much about anything at bat, except to try to outguess the pitcher, just as he is trying to outguess you. They don't serve the same ball to me twice."

DiMaggio seems just as indifferent in the outfield, playing center, the position his two brothers also play on other teams.

"There is a little trick about that," said DiMaggio. "I'm pretty much on my toes, even if it doesn't seem so. I know that when I run these long legs of mine make me look as if I were just loping along, but I can travel fairly well. I'm not as fast as some men, by a long shot. But there is a little trick of leaning in the direction you know the batter is apt to hit the ball, and, when he hits, you are already on your way. That helps a lot."

He got up and showed how he stood and leaned. The big locker room was filled with players, some of them stripped to the waist, big, powerful fellows. Only their arms and faces and necks were brown. Most of them had skin of pure white, untouched by sun. They get enough sun on the field. Beyond was the shower room, and near by a drying cabinet for wet shirts peeled from dripping bodies.

Gomez came back and sat on the edge of a table and again examined his spikes. He was fidgety compared with the tranquil DiMaggio, with whom he rooms while on the road. He and Gomez used to drop paper bags full of water out of hotel windows, but this doesn't happen any more. "We go out to the movies in the evening, or perhaps play a little hearts or rummy," said Gomez. "Nothing very exciting. Generally in bed by 12. Up by 8? Nothing doing. About 9:30, and then a little breakfast. And how that feller can sleep," he said, nodding at Joe.

"Well, you don't do so badly," said DiMaggio, addressing Gomez. And then to me: "He's quite a joker, too. Once down at Miami he gave me a suitcase to carry back to the hotel. I thought it would take my arm off, it was so heavy. I ached for a week. Thought his shoes must be in it. Look at those feet. And what do you think it was? A log of wood. That log would have burned for four days. Nice joke."

Did DiMaggio read much? No, he used to, but decided that it hurt his eyes. His wife reads a lot. He likes to listen to the radio. Sometimes he and Lefty go fishing, and Lefty is trying to get him to go hunting and hiking during the Winter season to keep in condition.

"He's the reader," said Joe, looking at Lefty. "I never saw a feller read so much. The tabloids. He's always reading newspapers. We like the funnies, too."

"Know what he reads?" asked Lefty, with an impish look. "We go into a hotel, and get to the newsstand, and he whispers to me, 'Hey, there's a new Superman. Get it for me.' He doesn't dare buy it himself, they all know him, you know. So he gets me to buy it for him. Superman and the Bat Man. That's his favorite reading."

And DiMaggio just looked mildly embarrassed.

"I like Westerns, too," he said. ◆

July 7, 1941

DiMaggio Hits 56th Game in Row And Yanks Crush Cleveland, 10-3

Joe Slams Two Singles and a Double While Bombers Extend Lead to Six Games With Donald in Box—Keller Drives No. 20

By JOHN DREBINGER
Special to The New York Times.

CLEVELAND, JULY 16—There again was no stopping the Yankees today as, with Joe DiMaggio still the spearhead of their spectacular drive, they ripped through the Indians with such combined speed and force that the Tribe scarcely had time to figure what was coming off.

Jolting Joe, tearing into the combined left-handed hurling of Al Milnar and Joe Krakauskas for two singles and a double, extended his sensational hitting streak to fifty-six consecutive games.

Along the way, Charlie Keller exploded his twentieth home run and a four-run demonstration, sparked by doubles by Buddy Rosar and Phil Rizzuto, finished Milnar's efforts for the day in the fifth. At the close of a harrowing >>>

Joe DiMaggio drives a pitch up the middle to establish a new, and still standing, record, hitting in 56 straight games at Cleveland on July 16, 1941.

afternoon for 15,000 helpless onlookers the final reading showed the flying New Yorkers in front, 10 to 3.

AMAZING STREAK CONTINUES

The victory, opening a three-game series, was the Bronx Bombers' sixteenth in their last seventeen games, their twentieth in twenty-two and thirtieth in thirty-five, a maze of statistics that seemed to prostrate the Tribe completely. At all events, the Yanks' supposedly most formidable rivals are now six full lengths in the rear and that in itself is enough to prostrate any formidable rival.

DiMaggio clicked off game No. 56 in record time for any course. He lashed the first pitch Milnar served him in the first inning through the box, over second and out to center for a single.

The game was played in old League Park, but for tomorrow's night conflict hostilities will shift to the Municipal Stadium. Lefty Gomez and Al Smith are slated to make it a left-handed duel. ◆

The Box Score

NEW YORK (A.)							CLEVELAND (A.)						
	ab.	r.	h.	po.	a.	e.		ab.	r.	h.	po.	a.	e.
Sturm, 1b	5	0	0	8	1	0	Boudreau, ss	4	1	1	2	1	0
Rolfe, 3b	4	0	0	2	2	0	Keltner, 3b	4	0	1	0	3	0
Henrich, rf	4	1	0	2	1	0	Weatherly, cf	3	0	0	2	0	0
DiMa'gio, cf	3	3	3	0	0	0	Heath, rf	4	1	2	5	0	0
Gordon, 2b	4	2	2	2	3	0	Trosky, 1b	3	0	1	7	1	1
Rosar, c	5	1	3	5	1	0	Campbell, lf	4	0	0	2	0	0
Keller, lf	3	3	2	4	0	0	Mack, 2b	3	1	1	3	3	0
Rizzuto, ss	5	0	1	0	2	0	aBell	1	0	0	0	0	0
Donald, p	4	0	0	1	0	0	Desautels, c	3	0	0	6	0	0
							bWalker	1	0	1	0	0	0
Total	38	10	11	27	10	0	Milnar, p	2	0	1	0	1	0
							Krak'skas, p	1	0	0	0	0	0
							cRosenthal	0	0	0	0	0	0
							Total	33	3	8	27	9	1

aBatted for Mack in ninth.
bBatted for Desautels in ninth.
cBatted for Kraksuskas in ninth.

New York ....2 0 0 1 4 0 0 1 2—10
Cleveland ....1 1 0 0 0 1 0 0 0— 3

Runs batted in—Gordon, Rosar 5, Rizzuto, 2, Keller, Trosky, Milnar, Heath.
Two-base hits—Mack, Rosar 2, Rizzuto, DiMaggio, Walker. Three-base hit—Keller. Home runs—Keller, Heath. Double play—Rosar and Rolfe. Left on bases—New York 8, Cleveland 7. Bases on balls—Off Donald 4, Milnar 4, Krakauskas 3. Struck out—By Donald 5, Milnar 3, Krakauskas 3. Hits—Off Milnar 8 in 5 innings, Krakauskas 3 in 4. Losing pitcher—Milnar. Umpires—Stewart, Summers and Rue. Time of game—2:17. Attendance—15,000.

SMITH AND BAGBY STOP YANKEE STAR

DiMaggio, Up for Last Time in Eighth, Hits Into a Double Play With Bases Full

M'CARTHYMEN WIN BY 4-3

Stretch Lead Over Indians to 7 Lengths Before Biggest Crowd for Night Game

By JOHN DREBINGER
Special to The New York Times.

CLEVELAND, JULY 17—In a brilliant setting of lights and before 67,468 fans, the largest crowd ever to see a game of night baseball in the major leagues, the Yankees tonight vanquished the Indians, 4 to 3, but the famous hitting streak of Joe DiMaggio finally came to an end.

Officially it will go into the records as fifty-six consecutive games, the total he reached yesterday. Tonight in Cleveland's municipal stadium the great DiMag was held hitless for the first time in more than two months.

Al Smith, veteran Cleveland left-hander and a Giant cast-off, and Jim Bagby, a young right-hander, collaborated in bringing the DiMaggio string to a close.

Jolting Joe faced Smith three times. Twice he smashed the ball down the third-base line, but each time Ken Keltner, Tribe third sacker, collared the ball and hurled it across the diamond for a put-out at first. In between these two tries, DiMaggio drew a pass from Smith.

Then, in the eighth, amid a deafening uproar, the streak dramatically ended, though the Yanks routed Smith with a flurry of four hits and two runs that eventually won the game.

With the bases full and only one out Bagby faced DiMaggio and, with the count at one ball and one strike, induced the renowned slugger to crash into a double play. It was a grounder to the shortstop, and as the ball flitted from Lou Boudreau to Ray Mack to Oscar Grimes, who played first base for the Tribe, the crowd knew the streak was over.

STARTED MAY 15

It was on May 15 against the White Sox at the Yankee Stadium that DiMaggio began his string, which in time was to gain nationwide attention. As the great DiMag kept clicking in game after game, going into the twenties, then the thirties, he became the central figure of the baseball world.

On June 29, in a double-header with the Senators in Washington, he tied, then surpassed the American League and modern record of forty-one games set by George Sisler of the Browns in 1922. The next target was the all-time major league high of forty-four contests set by Willie Keeler, famous Oriole star, forty-four years ago under conditions much easier then for a batsman than they are today. Then there was no foul-strike rule hampering the batter.

But nothing hampered DiMaggio as he kept getting his daily hits, and on July 1 he tied the Keeler mark. The following day he soared past it for game No. 45, and he kept on soaring until tonight. In seeking his fifty-seventh game, he finally was brought to a halt.

Actually, DiMaggio hit in fifty-seven consecutive games, for on July 8 he connected safely in the All-Star game in Detroit. But that contest did not count in the official league records.

DiMaggio's mark ends five short of his own Pacific Coast League record of sixty-one consecutive games, which he set while with San Francisco in 1933. The all-time minor league high is sixty-seven, set by Joe Wilhoit of Wichita in the Western League in 1919. ◆

August 4, 1941

37,829 SEE BROWNS TRIUMPH BY 6-2, 5-0

DiMaggio Hitless in 2 Games After Batting Safely in 16 Straight for Yankees

RUFFING STREAK SNAPPED

Ends Following 9 Victories in Row—Keller Slams No. 27—Harris Has 2-Hit Shutout

By JOHN DREBINGER

WITH THE YANKS, apparently, everything must be done in the grand manner. So it happened that before the astonished gaze of 37,829 onlookers at the Stadium yesterday the mighty Bronx Bombers, who for a month and more had been grinding the American League to a pulp, blew both ends of a double-header to—of all people—the lowly Browns.

Behind the skillful four-hit pitching of Johnny Niggeling, Luke Sewell's St. Louisans bagged the opener, 6 to 2, and that, despite Charlie Keller's twenty-seventh homer, snapped a number of Yankee streaks.

It brought an end to the Bombers' latest string of four straight victories, crushed Charlie Ruffing's bid for his tenth mound triumph in a row and even Joe DiMaggio's latest hitting skein came to grief. After connecting safely in sixteen consecutive games, Jolting Joe failed to get a safe blow in four tries, thus ending a string of sixteen games which had begun the day after the Indians checked his major streak at fifty-six on July 17.

Then just to show this was no mere flash-in-the-pan performance, Bob Harris came on the scene not only to handcuff the great DiMag >>>

<<< for the second time but virtually the other Yanks as well in spinning a brilliant two-hit shutout victory for the Browns. The score of this one was 5 to 0.

It marked the first time the Bombers lost a double-header since that ill-fated afternoon of Sept. 15 last year when the same Browns smeared Joe McCarthy's juggernaut in a twin bill that wrecked their spectacular bid for a fifth straight pennant.

But nothing quite so serious is apt to develop from this double setback. The Yanks still lead the second-place Indians by eleven and a half lengths and have dropped only six of their last thirty-six games.

DiMaggio saw still another streak snapped, that first encounter marking the first time in eighty-four games that he failed to get on base at least once. He went through four hitless trips to the plate in the afterpiece. ◆

October 6, 1941

YANKS WIN IN 9TH, FINAL 'OUT' TURNS INTO 4-RUN RALLY

Game-Ending Third Strike Gets Away From Dodger Catcher, Leading to 7-4 Victory.

By JOHN DREBINGER

IT COULDN'T, PERHAPS, have happened anywhere else on earth. But it did happen yesterday in Brooklyn, where in the short space of twenty-one minutes a dazed gathering of 33,813 at Ebbets Field saw a world series game miraculously flash two finishes before its eyes.

The first came at 4:35 of a sweltering afternoon, when, with two out and nobody aboard the bases in the top half of the ninth inning, Hugh Casey saw Tommy Henrich miss a sharp-breaking curve for a third strike that for a fleeting moment had the Dodgers defeating the Yankees, 4 to 3, in the fourth game of the current classic.

But before the first full-throated roar had a chance to acclaim this brilliant achievement there occurred one of those harrowing events that doubtless will live through all the ages of baseball like the Fred Snodgrass muff and the failure of Fred Merkle to touch second.

MAKES FRANTIC DASH

Mickey Owen, topflight catcher of the Dodgers, let the ball slip away from him and, before he could retrieve it in a frantic dash in front of his own dugout, Henrich had safely crossed first base.

It was all the opening Joe McCarthy's mighty Bronx Bombers, shackled by this same Casey ever since the fifth inning, needed to turn defeat for themselves into an amazing victory which left a stunned foe crushed.

For in the wake of that excruciating error came a blazing single by Joe DiMaggio, a two-base smash against the right-field barrier by Charley Keller, a pass to Bill Dickey by the now thoroughly befuddled Casey and another two-base clout by the irrepressible Joe Gordon.

FLATBUSH'S DARKEST HOUR

Four runs hurtled over the plate and, though the meteorological records may still contend that this was the brightest, sunniest and warmest day in world series history, it was easily the darkest hour that Flatbush ever has known.

For this astounding outburst gave the Yankees the game, 7 to 4, and with this victory McCarthy's miraculous maulers moved to within a single stride of another world championship. Their lead, as the series enters the fifth encounter at Ebbets Field today, now stands at three games to one, and the Bombers need to touch off only one more explosion to bring this epic interborough struggle to a close.

Casey replaced a wavering Johnny Allen in the fifth inning to repulse the Yanks with the bases full and he kept repelling them right on and up through the ninth until Owen's crowning misfortune turned the battle and the arena upside down.

Johnny Sturm, Yankee lead-off man, had opened that last-ditch stand in the ninth by grounding out to Pete Coscarart, who again was at second base for Brooklyn in place of the injured Billy Herman. Red Rolfe proved an even easier out. He bounced the ball squarely into Casey's hands and was tossed out at first with yards to spare.

Two were out, nobody was on, the Yanks looked throttled for the second time in the series and the Brooklyn horde scarcely could contain itself as it prepared to hail the feat with a tumultuous outburst of pent-up enthusiasm.

A Swing and a Miss

Casey worked carefully on Henrich and ran the count to three balls and two strikes. Then he snapped over a low, sharp-breaking curve. Henrich swung and missed. A great Flatbush triumph appeared clinched. But in the twinkling of an eye the victory was to become an even greater illusion.

As the ball skidded out of Owen's mitt and rolled toward the Dodger bench with Mickey in mad pursuit, police guards also came rushing out of the dugout to hold back the crowd which at the same moment was preparing to dash madly out on the field.

Owen retrieved the ball just in front of the steps, but Henrich, who the moment before had been at the point of throwing his bat away in great disgust, now was tearing like wild for first and he made the bag without a play.

The Yanks, of course, had not yet won the game. They were still a run behind and, though they had a man on first, Casey needed to collect only one more out to retain his margin.

But there was an ominous ring to the manner in which DiMaggio bashed a line-drive single to left that sent Henrich to second. A moment later Keller belted the ball high against the screening on top of the right-field fence. It just missed being a home run.

It was recovered in time to hold the doughty King Kong on second for a double, but both Henrich and DiMaggio streaked around the bases and over the plate. The dreaded Yanks were ahead, 5-4. To make matters even more excruciating, Casey had had a count of two strikes and no balls on Keller when King Kong pasted that one.

Down in the Brooklyn bullpen Curt Davis was warming up with great fury, but the Dodger board of strategy appeared paralyzed by the cataclysm and Manager Leo Durocher did nothing.

Casey pitched to Dickey and walked him. Again the Yanks had two on base. Casey stuck two strikes over on Gordon, then again grooved the next one. Ironically, Joe the Flash smacked the ball into left field, where Wasdell, who might have been one of the heroes, was left to chase it while Keller and Dickey raced for home with two more runs to make it four for the round.

This was enough, more than enough. Few clubs in major league history have ever had an almost certain victory snatched from them under more harrowing circumstances.

Snuffing out the final three Dodgers in the last half of the ninth was almost child's play for the relief hurler whom the Yanks affectionately call Grandma Murphy. Indeed, the kindly Grandma appeared motivated by only the most humane feelings as he put those battered Dodgers out of their misery.

Like Casey in the top half of that ninth, Murphy had to face the head of the batting order. But at that moment the Dodgers didn't know whether they were standing on their heads or their heels. Peewee Reese fouled out to Dickey and Walker and Reiser ended the game by never getting the ball out of the infield.

The Flock, then, indeed is in a mighty tight spot, and all because it had a pitcher yesterday who threw such a curve it not only fooled the batter but his catcher as well. ◆

October 7, 1941

PUNCHES, TOWELS FLY IN PROFUSION

World Champions' Celebration Looks and Sounds Like a Free-for-All Fight

By JAMES P. DAWSON

"YI-P-P-E-E-E-E!"

The shriek, shrill and penetrating, echoed in the catacombs under the Ebbets Field stand yesterday and heralded the approach of the conquering Yankees as they came trooping into their dressing room.

Leading the way were Twinkle-toes George Selkirk, piping-voiced Frankie Crosetti and old reliable Bill Dickey, who was still wearing his catcher's protector and shinguards.

A contrast was provided by this farewell march of the rival clubs. The beaten Dodgers, quiet and saddened, came out of the runway first. But the Yanks, instead of following right on the heels of their rivals, came after a brief lapse of time, as if the teams deliberately had been separated to avoid an ugly aftermath to a fifth-inning flare-up in which Joe DiMaggio and Whitlow Wyatt almost came to blows.

The piercing shriek came from the gray-haired Coach Earle Combs. It sent the warriors tumbling pell-mell into the clubhouse, where Tiny Bonham, the 6-foot 2-inch 220-pounder, was belabored by his joyous team-mates, where Tommy Henrich was given a good-natured cuff-

Joe DiMaggio has just caught the final out of the 1941 World Series. Left to right are: Phil Rizzuto (almost hidden), Red Rolfe, Johnny Sturm and Joe Gordon.

ing, where everybody hammered, thumped and pushed everybody else.

It looked like a free-for-all fight. Punches were flying, bodies were swaying, trunks were being banged around, benches were pushed out of place, towels flew through the air. And the noise was terrific.

The Yankees were celebrating, as only the Yankees can, in the old-fashioned Yankee way.

Fletcher jumped up on a trunk. He didn't yell for order. He made no signal for assembly. Everybody knew what that meant. Song. Strident, certainly not harmonious, but loud song. "East Side, West Side." The words were hardly distinguishable. Two choruses of it. Then, enthusiasm mounting, Fletcher led the gang in "Roll Out the Barrel."

Joe DiMaggio and Lefty Gomez, room-mates, were on the fringe of the crowd, but as jubilant as the rest. Said DiMag: "I didn't like how close a couple of pitches came at my head in the fifth inning, and when I was crossing the field I reminded Wyatt the series wasn't over yet. He came back with a remark that made me go for him, and he came for me. I was just waiting for him to throw the first punch, but I don't recall that he did."

DiMaggio, guarding the last ball he caught to end the game on Jimmy Wasdell's fly, presented it to Bonham as a souvenir. ◆

September 12, 1942

RIZZUTO RECEIVES ORDERS

NORFOLK, VA., SEPT. 11 (AP)—Shortstop Phil Rizzuto of the New York Yankees has been ordered to report at the Norfolk Naval Training Station Oct. 10 for recruit training, the Fifth Naval District announced today. Rizzuto was sworn in as a seaman first class earlier this week at the Naval recruiting station here.

After completing recruit training Rizzuto will report to the commanding officer of the Norfolk Station for "such duty as the commandant of the Fifth Naval District may assign," the Fifth District public relations office announced. ◆

October 6, 1942

CARDS DOWN YANKS WITH HOMER BY 4-2; WIN WORLD SERIES

BEAZLEY DEFEATS RUFFING

By JOHN DREBINGER

IN THE NINTH INNING of yesterday's fifth game of the 1942 world series, with a crowd of 69,052 looking on while two fine hurlers, old Red Ruffing and young Johnny Beazley, were locked in a 2-all tie, George (Whitey) Kurowski, a youngster just one year out of the minors, bashed a home run into the densely packed stands of the Yankee Stadium.

It streaked through the mist of a leaden gray afternoon and, on the wings of that shot, which came with a runner on the base paths, there came to an end one of the most remarkable world series dynasties baseball has ever known. »»»

《《《   For with that blow the St. Louis Cardinals brought down Joe McCarthy's mighty Yankees, 4 to 2, to win their fourth straight encounter. It bagged the world championship for Billy Southworth's National League champions, four games to one, and completed the most amazing upset in series history since 1914, when the miracle Braves bowled over Connie Mack's heavily favored Athletics.

A YOUTHFUL BAND

And so astride the baseball universe there soars today a band of youthful Redbirds. They had come from nowhere to eliminate the swashbuckling, boastful Dodgers in their own league. They were still looked upon as 2-to-1 underdogs as they squared away against the powerful Yanks, who hadn't been vanquished in world series conflict in sixteen years.

Yet there they were last night, dashing gaily into the West and victors in a great wartime classic which, as baseball's concluding act of the year, had contributed heavily to the nation's war chest. The receipts yesterday were $266,858, to bring the total for five games to $1,105,249, out of which sum the USO received a substantial slice. ◆

January 5, 1943

Ruffing in Army Today

LONG BEACH, CALIF., JAN. 4 (U.P.)—Charles (Red) Ruffing, former ace hurler of the New York Yankees, reports tomorrow morning at near-by Fort MacArthur for processing into the United States Army. Ruffing has been on a seven-day furlough, granted all Army inductees, during the past week. ◆

January 12, 1943

Yanks Select Asbury Park for Training Camp

M'CARTHYMEN PICK JERSEY SHORE SITE

By JAMES P. DAWSON

THE YANKEES WILL DO their Spring training at Asbury Park, N. J., starting March 15, it was announced yesterday by President Edward G. Barrow.

Decision to pitch camp at the New Jersey shore resort came following an inspection of near-by sites last Saturday by Manager Joe McCarthy and Paul Krichell, chief of the Yankee scouting system.

First of New York's three major league clubs to make a decision in this respect since being ousted from Florida, the Yankees are the eighth major league club to complete arrangements in compliance with the wishes of Joseph B. Eastman, Office of Defense Transportation director. The two Chicago clubs, the two Philadelphia clubs, the Red Sox, Senators and Tigers already have adjusted their Spring training plans to wartime conditions.

Most of the other major league organizations are expected to make definite plans before the end of the week. The Giants today are to meet a civic delegation from Lakewood, N.J., to resume negotiations for a site in the "land of the pines." The Dodgers are awaiting word from Yale whether the Army is to take over the Coxe Memorial Cage there. ◆

YANKS' STAR GETS 'ACTION' ON COAST

Frisco Draft Board Complies With DiMaggio's Desire to Join Army Immediately

By THE ASSOCIATED PRESS.

SAN FRANCISCO, FEB. 16—Joltin' Joe DiMaggio trades a $35,000 or better baseball job tomorrow for the $50 monthly pay of a buck private.

The 28-year-old Yankee star reported today he had received permission from his draft board to become a voluntary inductee. The usual procedure is to assign San Francisco inductees to Monterey before sending them to training camps.

With a smile breaking his usual dead-pan expression, DiMaggio said he had no idea which branch of the service he would join.

"All I know is I'm to report for physical examination tomorrow morning at 7:30," he said.

For the past few weeks, DiMaggio had vacationed in Hollywood with his wife. She will reside there permanently, Joe said, with their infant son, Joe Jr.

As a married man with a child, DiMaggio had a draft status of 3-A. Under voluntary induction, tantamount to enlistment, he was reclassified 1-A.

DiMaggio expressed the hope baseball would be allowed to continue to function, "if war conditions permit, I think everybody wants it to go on," he said. ◆

BRITONS CONFUSED BY WORLD SERIES

'Never Heard of It,' Bartender Tells U.S. Troops Who Want the Radio Turned On

LONDON, OCT. 6 (AP)—Britons who were beginning to think they understood American ways today are shaking their heads and wondering.

"World series? Sorry, I never heard of it," said a bartender as American soldiers cajoled him and offered bribes to get him to turn on the radio for the 15-minute summary of the series carried by the British Broadcasting Corporation.

British telephone operators at some Red Cross clubs were polite enough, but were confused by "inquiries on these Yankees and Cardinals. Who are they?"

Things weren't the same at American Army camps and bomber bases either. Here less money was put up in dice and black jack games. It went into pools—all kinds of pools on the series winner, game winner, hits, errors.

American soldiers in Britain are hungry for world series news, but only the lucky ones at some camps can get on the American Army Forces network where a limited number of special sets in each base receive the broadcasts.

BBC is giving a 15-minute nightly summary which is helping to satisfy, somewhat, the appetite of the baseball fans.

But the Americans were annoyed over the handling of the opening game. They think Commissioner Kenesaw M. Landis and the rival managers, Joe McCarthy and Billy Southworth, are good enough guys, but with a limited time for broadcast they want baseball straight, and no speeches.

There is nothing on the series in the British newspapers, and hundreds of calls are being handled by Stars and Stripes, the official U. S. Army newspaper in the European Theater of Operations. ◆

October 12, 1943

YANKS WIN SERIES, BEATING CARDS, 2-0, ON DICKEY'S HOMER

SHUT-OUT FOR CHANDLER

By JOHN DREBINGER
Special to The New York Times.

ST. LOUIS, OCT. 11—Joe McCarthy and his Yankees once more reign as the baseball champions of the universe.

Making complete atonement for their humiliating defeat of a year ago, the American League champions vanquished Billy Southworth's Cardinals in the fifth game today, 2 to 0, and with this victory clinched the 1943 world series title, four games to one. With these same figures the Cards had tripped the McCarthy forces exactly a year ago.

The end, to all intents and purposes, came in the sixth inning. Then, with Charlie Keller on base, Bill Dickey, catching in his eighth fall classic, hammered a home run over the right-field stand.

That stroke decided a mound duel between Spud Chandler and Mort Cooper and gave to the Yankees' 34-year-old right-hander his second triumph of the series. In the opener he had conquered Max Lanier, and today, before 33,872 keenly disap-

pointed onlookers, he turned back Cooper, who in the dramatic second game had pitched the National League champions to their only victory.

So to this amazingly successful baseball organization there comes another world championship, the tenth in the history of the club, which captured its first title in 1923 under the late Miller Huggins and from there has gone on to an all-time high.

For McCarthy it is his seventh triumph, a record that places him far ahead of any other manager in world series accomplishments. Connie Mack's Athletics, over a span of three decades, won five, while the late John J. McGraw, though he appeared in nine interleague classics with the Giants, won only three. ◆

January 23, 1944

KELLER ENTERS SERVICE

Yankee Star Dons Maritime Uniform

ST. PETERSBURG, FLA., JAN. 22 (AP)—The New York Yankees' Charley (King Kong) Keller traded uniforms today and wished for big league baseball "a good season this year."

The former outfielder donned the maritime uniform with the rank of ensign at the St. Petersburg Maritime Service Base's athletic training department.

Preceding him into service were the two other members of the "Big Three" Yankee outfield, Joe DiMaggio of the Army and Tommy Henrich of the Coast Guard. ◆

March 16, 1944

Dickey, Catching Star of Yankees, Is Inducted Into the Navy

Yanks Are Left With Serious Catching Problem

By LOUIS EFFRAT
Special to The New York Times.

ATLANTIC CITY, N. J., March 15—News of Bill Dickey's induction into the Navy reached the Yankees today after they had enjoyed their initial outdoor workout. The report from Little Rock, where Bill passed his examination, disclosing that he had made Uncle Sam's team, came as a jolt, what with a gas station attendant with no big league aspirations the only backstop in camp at the moment.

"What is there for me to say?" Manager Joe McCarthy countered when informed of Dickey's status. "I guess it's only the beginning. Uncle Sam wants him and that's all there is to it. I wish Bill the best of luck. We'll all miss him. He was a great catcher, great hitter and a great man to have on a ball club. The records prove Dickey was the greatest catcher of all time."

Precisely how much the loss of Dickey will affect the Yankees remains to be seen, but opinion here among the newspaper men is that this must rank with the biggest, comparable to the loss of Joe DiMaggio, Charley Keller, Tommy Henrich and Charley Ruffing, all of whom are in the service. Apparently, the Yankee front office saw the handwriting on the wall and purchased the veteran, Joe Glenn, from Kansas City a few days ago. ◆

Game three of the 1943 World Series at Yankee Stadium.

January 27, 1945

SPORTS OF THE TIMES
A Baseball Empire Changes Hands

By ARTHUR DALEY

Larry MacPhail in the early 1940s.

THE NEW YORK YAN-KEES, mightiest of all baseball empires, have a new emperor —or emperors. Col. Larry MacPhail, Capt. Dan Topping and Del Webb have purchased the richest franchise in either league from the heirs of the late Col. Jacob Ruppert. This undoubtedly is the most momentous happening sports has had in decades.

For one thing it changes the entire complexion of the erstwhile Bronx Bombers. Ruppert was a conservative and he had that arch-conservative, Edward Grant Barrow, running the show for him. Cousin Ed probably is the soundest man in the national game. But he frowned on such things as night baseball, as well as all the other colorful and flashy innovations which MacPhail was to introduce in Cincinnati and later in Brooklyn.

This is a new and different challenge to MacPhail. He moved into Cincinnati in 1933 when the Reds were chronic cellar-dwellers and hung up a sign which read: "1938 is the year." He was just one season too fast for himself even though he had switched from Cincinnati to Brooklyn before the Reds won the pennant in both 1939 and 1940. They won, by the way, with the ball players Laughing Larry had left behind him.

He did an even quicker job with the frowsy Brooklyn franchise. Spending money lavishly, he saw the Brooks come surging up to beat out the Cardinals for the pennant in 1941. It cost more than $880,000 to buy the stars he wanted, but before he was finished he had not only refurbished Ebbets Field but the franchise too. Furthermore, he paid off more than a million dollars in debts.

For the first time though, this bundle of dynamite is placed in charge of a going concern, the most efficient and businesslike baseball organization in the game. It even transmits its efficiency and businesslike qualities to its diamond heroes. You don't find any swaggering, colorful operatives on the Yankees. They have been chosen for character almost as much as for anything else. Possibly Ed Barrow is responsible for that. Or maybe it's Joe McCarthy. Perhaps it's both.

Mention of Marse Joe instantly brings to mind the fact that McCarthy and MacPhail are as different as night and day. They may even be as insoluble as oil and water. Time alone can answer that question. But it's impossible to visualize the tempestuous redhead firing McCarthy as constantly as he fired Leo Durocher in the old days. With Marse Joe that first battle probably would be the last. And McCarthy never would stand for the slightest bit of front-office interference.

That was the beauty of Joe's relationship with Barrow. Cousin Ed never came near the dressing room and his hands-off policy never once was altered. If he disagreed with a McCarthy move he kept his opinions to himself. MacPhail could no more do that than a live volcano could refuse to erupt.

It will be interesting to see what effect MacPhail will have on the Yankees. Most probably the Stadium will have lights for after-dark play the instant priorities can be obtained. There will be plenty of changes made, because the mercurial Larry is ever on the move, a stirrer-upper in the old John McGraw tradition.

If MacPhail could build something out of nothing as he did in Cincinnati and Brooklyn, it almost scares you to think what he'll do with the Yankees in the post-war era. Probably have every pennant clinched by the Fourth of July. ◆

January 27, 1945

Yankee Club Sold for $2,800,000 To MacPhail-Topping Syndicate

By JOHN DREBINGER

THE NEW YORK YANKEES, baseball's wealthiest and most powerful organization, changed ownership yesterday when a syndicate comprised of Col. Larry S. MacPhail, former president of the Dodgers and about to retire from the Army; Capt. Daniel R. Topping, wealthy tin plate magnate and professional football promoter, and Del E. Webb, millionaire head of an oil construction company in Phoenix, Ariz., bought 96.88 per cent of the club's stock held by the heirs of the late Col. Jacob Ruppert and Edward G. Barrow.

The purchase price was announced at an estimated $2,800,000 and includes all of the Yankee property holdings in addition to the club's vast minor league empire that had Newark, Kansas City, Binghamton and Norfolk as its major links. The Yankee-owned Newark and Kansas City arenas also are included as well as the ornate stadium in the Bronx—"the house that Ruth built"—and title to an estimated total of 400 ball players.

Announcement of the transaction which, though rumored for months, closed with startling swiftness, was made in one of the upper floors of the 21 Club on West Fifty-second Street when Colonel MacPhail, Webb and Barrow who for a quarter of a century, first as general manager and then as president, guided the great baseball enterprise, faced a battery of baseball scribes and press photographers.

Captain Topping, now serving with the Marines, was not present. He had been in town the past week, presumably while negotiations were being completed, but then had to return for duty in the Pacific.

In the new set-up Colonel MacPhail, now on furlough from the Army until his retirement on Feb. 10, becomes the new president and general manager. Barrow, though he too disposed of his stock in the club, will remain with the organization as chairman of the board of directors and for the present will continue to run things until such time as MacPhail is ready to take over.

"Mr. Barrow and I," said Colonel MacPhail, "are in full accord on the policy of the club and he will continue to direct affairs until such time as I can permanently take over my new duties."

In taking over the Yanks the new syndicate literally bought the vast empire lock, stock and barrel. The 88.88 per cent share of the stock owned by the three principal heirs of the late Colonel Ruppert—these being his two nieces, Mrs. Joseph Halloran and Mrs. J. Basil McGuire, and Miss Helen Winthrop Wayant—was purchased through the Manufacturers Trust Company, which was appointed administrator of the Ruppert estate in 1941.

The cost of this block of stock was placed by MacPhail at a definite cash figure of $2,500,000. No exact amount was given for Barrow's 10 per cent, but MacPhail said it approximately would reach about $300,000. The remaining unsold 3.12 per cent of stock is still held by George Ruppert, brother of the late colonel; Ruppert Schalk, a nephew, and Mrs. Anna Dunn, a niece. ◆

NEGROES PICKET STADIUM

Hit 'Jim Crowism in Baseball'

ABOUT TWENTY NEGROES, carrying signs which said that "If We Can Pay, Why Can't We Play" and "If We Can Stop Bullets, Why Not Balls," marched around the Yankee Stadium yesterday as the crowd entered for the opening game with the Red Sox.

The pickets were led by two officers of the League for Equality in Sports and Amusements.

James E. Pemberton, Democratic leader of the Fourteenth Assembly District, Harlem, president of the League for Equality, said that the picketing was a protest against "Jim Crowism in baseball," and that he intended to have 500 pickets on hand for Sunday's game at the Polo Grounds.

Also among the pickets was Col. Hubert Fauntleroy Julian, "The Black Eagle" of Harlem, secretary of the league, which has its headquarters at 115 West 116th Street.

Criticizing Col. L. S. (Larry) MacPhail, president of the Yankees, as "a czar," Julian said he had conferred with Colonel MacPhail yesterday morning, pointing out that although 25 per cent of the Yankees' attendance comprises Negroes, there are no Negro employees at the Stadium, either as players or as service personnel.

The picketing resulted from the conference, said Julian, who declared, "The Negro is entitled to equal rights in sports. If we can fight together, we can play together." ◆

YANKEES CONTRACT FOR STADIUM LIGHTS

Arcs for Night Baseball and Football by April 1 Head $500,000 Improvements

By JOHN DREBINGER

ILLUMINATION OF THE YANKEE Stadium to provide night baseball, and very likely night football, bruited about these many weeks, will become an actuality next spring.

It received its official blessing yesterday when President Larry MacPhail of the Yankees, in announcing that the club's directors had approved an outlay of $500,000 for improvements to the "House that Ruth Built," revealed that contracts had been let for the installation of lights at a cost of about $250,000.

The towers will be erected by the Blaw-Knox Construction Company. Reflectors will be installed by General Electric. Work will commence on Jan. 1 and should be completed by April 1.

Thus Colonel MacPhail, trail blazer of the nocturnal game and first to introduce night ball in the major leagues, embarks upon his fourth lighting venture. He installed lights in Columbus in the American Association in 1932. In 1935 he lit up Crosley Field in Cincinnati.

LIGHTS ON FOR DODGERS IN 1938

He brought the arcs to Ebbets Field in 1938 when the Brooklyn inaugural was embellished by the second of Johnny Vander Meer's two successive no-hitters. And in 1946 he will turn on the lights in the huge stadium which so long had held out exclusively for daytime baseball.

MacPhail declined to commit himself on whether he would book seven or fourteen home night games for the Yankees next summer, saying he would be guided in this by whatever action might be taken at the major league meetings in Chicago next month.

The announcement came in his first official press conference in the club's sumptuous quarters on the twenty-ninth floor of the Squibb Tower.

Continuing a moment longer on baseball, MacPhail disclosed that elaborate changes were being made in the Yankees' vast farming empire, the most important of these having to do with the duties of George M. Weiss.

Hitherto confined solely to the club's minor league activities, Weiss has been placed in command of all the players in the Yankee organization, both on the parent club as well as in the minors. He will have sole charge of signing the players to their contracts in the spring and full authority to make any trades he may consider beneficial to the Yankees. ◆

May 14, 1946

YANKEES' PLANE IS IN ST. LOUIS

ST. LOUIS, MAY 13 (AP)—The "Yankee Mainliner," a four-engined DC-4, carrying thirty members of the Yankees and Manager Joe McCarthy, landed at Lambert-St. Louis Airport at 6:47 o'clock (CDT) tonight, inaugurating the first arrangement by a major league team to use chartered planes to complete a baseball schedule. The plane, with a total of forty-four passengers, took off from New York at 3:15 P. M. (EDT).

Air travel was "old stuff" to most of the Yankees, who had flown to Panama and to a couple of Southern cities during the spring training season and several members of the Bronx team had flying experience in the service.

McCarthy, a veteran air passenger, said the team planned to use planes on all the Yankees' Western trips.

"The advantage is that players will be able to get places quickly and will be able to have a full night's sleep," he added. ◆

May 25, 1946

M'CARTHY RESIGNS; DICKEY YANK PILOT

Illness Forces Out Manager Who Won 8 Flags, 7 World Series in 15 Seasons

By JAMES P. DAWSON
Special to The New York Times.

BOSTON, MAY 24—The career of Joseph Vincent McCarthy as manager of the Yankees ended today. In his sixteenth year at the helm of baseball's richest property, McCarthy tendered his resignation in a wire from his farm at Tonawanda, N. Y., to President Larry MacPhail.

Illness was given as the reason for McCarthy's resignation, closing the most brilliant chapter in Yankee baseball history. Under McCarthy's leadership the Yankees won eight American League pennants and seven world series.

MacPhail announced acceptance of McCarthy's resignation tonight at a meeting with the press here.

At the same time MacPhail revealed that Bill Dickey had been engaged to succeed McCarthy. A new form of player-manager contract will be drawn up for Dickey, who assumed the management immediately. »»

《《《   An increase in salary for the veteran catcher was agreed upon, although MacPhail would not reveal the financial terms of the new contract. Dickey's contract, revised for the remainder of this season, also will cover 1947.

TEXTS OF THE TELEGRAMS

McCarthy's resignation was contained in the following telegram to MacPhail:

It is with extreme regret that I must request that you accept my resignation as manager of the Yankee Baseball Club, effective immediately. My doctor advises that my health would be seriously jeopardized if I continued.

This is the sole reason for my decision which, as you know, is entirely voluntary upon my part. I have enjoyed our pleasant relationship and I was hoping it would continue until we won a championship. I am going to miss the team very much and I am sure that they are going to continue on to win the pennant and the world championship.

(Signed) JOE McCARTHY

MacPhail's telegram of acceptance to McCarthy follows:

As you know I have been extremely reluctant to accept your resignation, even though I understood the reasons why you feel you should not continue. I am glad to know your services are available to me personally and to the club in an advisory capacity and I hope you will feel able to act in that capacity in a very short time. I think I speak for every member of the club as well as myself when I tell you how much we regret you are not going to continue and how much we will miss you.

(Signed) LARRY MacPhail

Record of Yankee Clubs Managed by McCarthy

Year	Finish	W.	L.	PC.
1931	Second	94	59	.614
1932	First	107	47	.695
1933	Second	91	59	.607
1934	Second	94	60	.610
1935	Second	89	60	.597
1936	First	102	51	.667
1937	First	102	52	.662
1938	First	99	53	.651
1939	First	106	45	.702
1940	Third	88	66	.571
1941	First	101	53	.656
1942	First	103	51	.669
1943	First	98	56	.636
1944	Third	83	71	.539
1945	Fourth	81	71	.533

WORLD CHAMPIONS

Year	Opponent	Games Won Yanks	Opponent
1932	Cubs	4	0
1936	Giants	4	2
1937	Giants	4	1
1938	Cubs	4	0
1939	Reds	4	0
1941	Dodgers	4	1
1943	Cardinals	4	1

MacPhail said McCarthy would remain in the organization in an advisory capacity. The Yankee executive emphasized there was no friction between him and McCarthy. Speaking in glowing terms of McCarthy's managerial ability, he added, without reservation, "McCarthy was the most cooperative manager with whom I have ever been associated in baseball."

While announcement of McCarthy's resignation came with surprising suddenness it was not altogether unexpected. As far back as a year ago it was known McCarthy's days with the club depended entirely upon his physical condition.

Indeed, when MacPhail and his associates

bought the Yankees from the late Col. Jacob Ruppert's heirs it was understood then that McCarthy would not go with the purchase. It will be recalled McCarthy left the Yankees in mid-season last year, when only the strongest representations from MacPhail induced the manager to reconsider his plan to retire.

McCarthy became ill on the first swing of the Yankees through the West, which ended in Detroit yesterday. He missed the last game at Cleveland and was absent from both games in Detroit. Coach Johnny Neun led the club through those three games.

Confined to Hotel in Detroit

Recurrence of a gall bladder condition from which he has suffered for several years confined McCarthy to hotel quarters during this siege until yesterday morning. He flew from Detroit to his Tonawanda farm at 9:50 A. M. yesterday.

This illness in Cleveland immediately revived speculation concerning McCarthy's retirement. Nothing developed, however, until McCarthy reached his home. Apparently, after examination by his physician, McCarthy reached his final decision.

All the players expressed joy over the selection of Dickey, indicating that they would give the same unity and cooperation to Bill that McCarthy always insisted upon and received.

Dickey, oldest Yankee player in point of service, refused the job as Newark manager on his return from the Navy. He received $20,000 a year as a player.

McCarthy's 2-year contract at $37,500 annually ends this season. MacPhail wanted to pay him for the rest of the season, but McCarthy declined, saying he would not accept any money for which he did not work. ◆

May 26, 1946

SPORTS OF THE TIMES
Exit for Marse Joe

By ARTHUR DALEY

IT HAD TO HAPPEN sooner or later. When Larry MacPhail moved in as the head of the Yankee baseball empire, Joe McCarthy figuratively began to pack his bag and move toward the exits. It was remarked then in this space that MacPhail and McCarthy were as insoluble as oil and water. That wasn't clairvoyance. It was a mere statement of an obvious fact.

Both men like fiercely to win. But there their similarity ends. Marse Joe is an ultra-conservative man who hates change, emotionalism, gloss or glitter. Larry is a radical who relishes change, flash, color, excitement and argument. Temperamentally they are as far apart as the poles. That they'd some day come to a parting of the ways was absolutely inevitable.

Last July McCarthy offered a verbal resignation but MacPhail, sticking his pride in his pocket, shuffled off to Buffalo for a personal plea to his manager. That step seemed to unruffle Joe's ruffled feelings and he consented to remain on the job. There seems to be some slight dispute now as to exactly what category the departure of the Yankee skipper touches. It's one of those did-he-fall-or-was-he-pushed things. No matter. Denials will be formally made that the split was anything but amicable. Maybe it was half and half.

For one thing McCarthy always insisted that he was the boss. That's the way Ed Barrow ran the team in the past but that's hardly the way MacPhail was used to running his organization. Marse Joe is an extremely sensitive man and he has not the rhinoceros hide of Leo Durocher whom the impetuous redhead used to fire every hour on the hour when at the Dodger controls.

Leo the Lip, suave and a politician born, could take in stride the transfer from MacPhail to that MacPhailian antithesis, Branch Rickey. In fact, they joshingly say of him that he promptly became the Mahatma's favorite reclamation ⟩⟩⟩

project. It's worked out well, too, and will undoubtedly continue to do so.

SELF-TORMENT

But Marse Joe wasn't gaited that way. Furthermore, he writhed inwardly as the war destroyed that awesomely efficient Yankee machine he'd built so carefully, leaving him with a dreadful collection of ersatz ball players. It's true that he showed his managerial genius to greater advantage than ever before when he drove one group of misfits to a world championship in 1943 and didn't miss by much a year later.

However, he was unhappy, so unhappy and upset that he became physically ill. On top of that he had all the money he'd ever need as well as a rural retreat near Buffalo where he could escape from all the worry, grief and turmoil of a tempestuous baseball life. That beckoned him with more and more urgent appeal.

And now he's gone from the Yankee empire he helped create. The blow is softened somewhat by the appointment of Bill Dickey as the new manager. The quiet-spoken Arkansas Traveler, popular and personable, is an ideal choice, one of the last links between the old Miller Huggins era of Ruth, Gehrig, Meusel et al and the present. Unquestionably he'll have the solid support of both the team and the fans.

It's almost ironic how fate functions. Years ago Babe Ruth was offered the job of managing

Joe McCarthy, the manager of the Yankees from 1931–1946.

Newark, the Yankee farm team, but demanded, instead, that Col. Jacob Ruppert choose between him and McCarthy as head man of the Yankees. The colonel stubbornly stuck to Marse Joe. This year MacPhail also offered Dickey the Newark post. Bill politely declined. And now he has baseball's top job. More power to him, too.

But those are mighty large shoes he's stepping into. Any sound baseball man can attend to the mechanical chores of directing a team's play. Except for Durocher, a gambler by nature, they all follow the same routine of sticking to percentages. The difference between a successful and an unsuccessful manager is the way he handles men. In that, McCarthy had few equals.

THE YANKEE TYPE

He demanded that they fall into the pattern he often described as "the Yankee kind of ball player." He quickly rid himself of the malcontents, the rowdies, the individualists, the clubhouse lawyers and the like. Any athlete who lingered long with the Bronx Bombers was accepted as more than just a star. It meant also that he qualified under the stringent McCarthy rules of personal conduct.

In addition, he brought them all along so cagily. Often he'd take an embryo stellar performer and judiciously drop him into his line-up. But as soon as that athlete began to feel the pressure too intensely, he'd yank him to the bench, permit him to drink deeply at his side from the font of baseball wisdom and then return him to the field of play. He did it with most of them, Charlie Keller, Tommy Henrich, Phil Rizzuto, Joe Gordon, Snuffy Stirnweiss and others of his present troupe. And countless others before them, too. Gosh, but that paid off richly.

It's no wonder that his players idolized him. However, the baseball writers assigned to the Yankees found Marse Joe a tough customer to shave. He was always singularly uncommunicative. "Let me worry about that," he'd say crossly to a simple question. If he grew expansive, it was with tales of his days at Wilkes-Barre or Louisville, never with the Yankees. He wouldn't talk about Lou Gehrig or Joe DiMaggio. He'd tell tales of Jay Kirke and other odd characters from his minor league experiences.

After a while you began to realize what was behind it all. Barrow detested managers who popped off. So did McCarthy. So, in his conservative way, he never took a chance on speaking out of turn. He trusted no one except a very few intimates among the Gentlemen of the Fourth Estate, and he didn't trust them too much for fear of a distorted statement. He had a dread that something he'd say about one of his players would be construed as a criticism.

Joe never criticized them—in public, anyway. Instead, he'd always wait until the next day, summon them into his office and talk to them in father-and-son fashion. In retrospect, that seems to be an admirable quality, and Joe had so many of them. Yet he could slay his hired hands with a glance or a word—such as the time his scathing: "So you're Yankees, huh?" sent a group of joyous, singing youngsters slinking ashamedly out of a hotel lobby.

The McCarthy stamp was indelibly imprinted on his team, HIS Yankees. This grim-visaged man was in a class by himself. With Bill Dickey, one of his model pupils, now taking over, it's likely to remain that same way. But you can't improve on perfection. Joseph Vincent McCarthy was exactly that. ◆

September 14, 1946

NEUN TO RUN CLUB UNTIL SEASON ENDS

Coach Succeeds Dickey

By JOHN DREBINGER
Special to The New York Times.

DETROIT, SEPT. 13—Making his second startling move in little more than twenty-four hours, William Malcolm Dickey today peremptorily removed himself as manager of the Yankees.

Following a long evening's chat with Bucky Harris, engaged a few days ago to serve the club in an executive capacity, Dickey this morning telephoned his resignation to Larry MacPhail, club president, in New York, and within a few minutes MacPhail was back on the phone with the announcement appointing Johnny Neun as Dickey's successor. Dickey then left immediately for his home in Little Rock, Ark.

Neun, 46 years old and long in the Yankee organization as minor league manager and coach of the club the past three seasons, has been named only to complete the current campaign. No references have been made to MacPhail's 1947 managerial plans.

Thus the Yankees, who for many years had only two pilots, Miller Huggins and Joe McCarthy, ex-cept for a brief one-year interlude by Bob Shawkey, have now come up with three managers within one season—McCarthy, Dickey, who took over on May 24 last, and now Neun, and with a fourth almost certain to follow before winter's snow flies. Rumors persist in focusing on Billy Herman, brilliant National League second baseman, as the eventual 1947 skipper should MacPhail fail to entice Leo Durocher away from Brooklyn and Branch Rickey.

SWIFTLY MOVING EVENTS

Dickey's resignation came as the climax to a series of swiftly moving events that began on Monday when MacPhail, in announcing the engagement of Harris, dropped the significant remark that his 1947 managerial set-up "had not been decided yet."

And so rings down the curtain on another brilliant Yankee who for so long played a prominent part in that club's amazing successes. He came to the Yanks from Little Rock in 1928 under Huggins and by 1929 already had attained stardom, catching 130 games.

In the years to follow he was to become one of the great catchers of all time, playing in all the games the Yanks played in eight world series under Joe McCarthy.

He interrupted his career in 1944 to enlist in the Navy, in which he served as an officer. He returned as a player this spring but found that his age and his two years of inactivity had taken their toll, and appeared only briefly behind the plate. ◆

September 20, 1946

YANKEES RECALL FOUR

Brown, Berra, Colman, Raschi Are to Return From Newark

Newark having been eliminated from the International League play-offs, the parent Yankee organization yesterday recalled four Bears— Bobby Brown, shortstop; Larry Berra, catcher; Frank Colman, outfielder, and Victor Raschi, right-handed pitcher. Brown, owned by the Yankees, was recalled, while the contracts of the other three have been purchased from Newark.

Brown, who batted .344 and was runner-up to Jackie Robinson of Montreal for the league hitting crown, is a flashy infielder, of whom much is expected. Berra batted .315 and Colman .301. Raschi, who did most of his pitching for Binghamton in the Eastern League, struck out 160 in 168 innings, while winning ten and losing ten. Reporting late to Newark, he won two and lost one with the Bears. ◆

November 6, 1946

DRESSEN TOP AIDE TO BOMBERS' PILOT

With Yanks Since September, Harris Accedes to MacPhail Request He Manage Club

EX-SENATOR 'BOY WONDER'

Bucky Also Guided Phils and Red Sox—Signing of Former Dodger Coach Defended

By JOHN DREBINGER

THE VEIL OF MYSTERY has finally lifted on the identity of the Yankee manager for 1947. It will be Stanley Raymond (Bucky) Harris and while the announcement scarcely bowled over anyone with surprise, it cannot be said that Impressario Larry MacPhail failed to extract all the dramatics the situation had to offer.

The Yankee prexy made the disclosure yesterday in the club's Squibb Tower offices to a roomful of scribes, radio broadcasters and press photographers. He announced that Harris, who had come to the Yanks in a somewhat undefined capacity as "assistant to the president" last September, had signed a two-year managerial contract. Salary terms were not disclosed but it is understood that Bucky, one-time "boy manager" of the Senators but reaching fifty next Friday, will receive a yearly stipend of $35,000.

At the same time MacPhail also revealed that Charles (Chuck) Dressen, who likewise had been engaged for an "undetermined job" when he re-signed as coach from the Dodgers a couple of weeks ago, will serve as top aide to Manager Harris at a salary believed to be $15,000. This, too, occasioned no startling surprise, inasmuch as the moment Dressen severed connections in Brooklyn it had been generally accepted he would serve in a similar capacity under Harris who, despite repeated denials, had been reported as the next Yankee manager as far back as the world series.

DICKEY SUCCEEDED MCCARTHY

Thus the Yanks, who for more than a quarter of a century got along under the aegis of three skippers, Miller Huggins, Bob Shawkey and Joe McCarthy, round out a year in which they have had no fewer than four pilots. When McCarthy resigned in May he was succeeded by the veteran catcher, Bill Dickey, who in turn quit in September to let Johnny Neun, then head coach, take over. Neun stepped out with the close of the season to become manager of the Reds.

With Harris and Dressen both present to substantiate his remarks, MacPhail spent considerable time yesterday defending the manner in which he had made the selections. He denied that he had purposely delayed announcement of the Harris appointment and was equally emphatic in declaring he had no apologies to offer to the Dodgers for signing Dressen, who, he said, had received a pay slash in 1943 from $10,500 to $6,500 and was not restored to his former salary until this year.

"I admit that the Harris appointment could have been announced a week ago," he said, "but I had to withhold it for a purely personal reason. However, I want to assure you, and Bucky will corroborate me on this, that Harris was not my original choice for manager. He told me when he joined us in September he was not interested in the job and wanted to work in the front office.

"With the close of the season we considered many candidates. I finally decided I could make no better choice than Harris and only then per-suaded Bucky to take the job."

MacPhail flatly denied he at any time approached Leo Durocher, the Dodger manager who frequently had been mentioned as a possible Yankee choice.

DUROCHER WAS INTERESTED

"Durocher did send word over to me that he was interested in the Yankee job," said MacPhail. "I replied that if Leo were free to act, he could come and see me. He never came."

MacPhail also took exception to frequent inferences that he makes a practice of firing managers.

"Harris actually is the first manager I have named for the Yankees," he pointed out. "I was satisfied with the manager we had when I took over the Yankees and when McCarthy resigned I felt I had to pick a veteran player in the organization. When he quit I let the head coach finish the season.

"In Cincinnati I had only one manager, Dressen, and only one in Brooklyn, Durocher. Durocher still is there and Dressen would still be in Cincinnati had I not left the Reds."

Regarding Dressen's acquisition, MacPhail denied he did any tampering with Brooklyn property despite accusations by Branch Rickey that his coach had agreed to accept a contract to remain with the Dodgers two more years.

DRESSEN IMMEDIATELY SIGNED

"When Dressen came to me," said MacPhail, "he told me that he had resigned from the Dodgers, so I signed him at once. What is more if anyone else wants to resign from Brooklyn and tells me he wants a job—and if I think he is qualified—he will get it."

Returning to Durocher he then added that "I don't think Durocher would be a logical choice for the Yankee job. I want to make it clear, though, that I think he is a first-rate manager. He did a great job for me in Brooklyn and he has continued to do great work there. But there are angles to the job here that change the picture." ◆

January 9, 1947

Barrow, 79, Retires After Building Yanks Into Baseball's Top Empire

In Sport 51 Years, He Managed Wagner and Ruth Before Masterminding New York to 14 Flags and 10 World Titles

By JOHN DREBINGER

EDWARD GRANT BARROW, rugged individualist who master-minded the Yankees into fourteen American League pennants and ten world championships, finally has severed all contact with the organization he helped weld into the greatest baseball empire the game has known.

Announcement of his retirement as chairman of the board of directors was made by Barrow yesterday and confirmed by the Yankees. The resignation took effect last Dec. 31.

Although his contract, which he had held under the new Larry MacPhail regime since 1945, still had three years to run, Barrow revealed inclusion of a clause permitting cancellation after two years with the payment of one year's salary. This was followed, Barrow said, adding: "We are parting on very friendly terms."

RESIGNATION ACCEPTED DEC. 1

The Yankees revealed that Barrow had tendered his resignation as far back as Nov. 21 and that it had been accepted with regret on Dec. 1 at the annual meeting of the board of directors.

To this Colonel MacPhail added a personal letter, also disclosed yesterday, in which the Yankee president thanked his predecessor for services rendered in his advisory capacity and expressed deep regret at his retirement. MacPhail conclud-

ed with this assurance: "There will always be a box at the Yankee Stadium available to you, your family and friends and we hope to see you often."

Barrow, 79 years old and in baseball for more than a half century, was uncertain of future plans. "I had a few things in mind," he said, "but when a man gets to be as old as I am, well, I'm afraid he's getting pretty old."

This was much the same stand taken by Cousin Ed several years ago when, on the death of Baseball Commissioner Kenesaw M. Landis, friends and club owners sought to induce him to step into the vacancy. The post doubtless could have been his, but he declined on the plea that his health and years would not permit him to accept.

WAGNER A BARROW DISCOVERY

Although never a player, Barrow became one of baseball's greatest executives. He launched his career fifty-one years ago. In 1895 he managed Wheeling to a minor league pennant and then moved on to Paterson. A player he developed there was later to become one of the game's immortals—John Honus Wagner, greatest of all shortstops.

In succeeding years he managed Indianapolis, Detroit, Toronto, Montreal and the Red Sox, whom he led to a pennant and world championship in 1918. It was with the Sox, too, that he launched Babe Ruth on the path to baseball immortality by converting the Bambino from a left-handed pitcher into an outfielder who became the greatest home-run clouter of all time.

Barrow joined the Yankees Dec. 31, 1920, and under the then dual ownership of Colonels T. L. Huston and Jacob Ruppert served as general manager. He engaged managers, signed players, made all the deals. In time he made the Yanks the most successful club in baseball history.

Upon the death of Colonel Ruppert, Barrow was elected president of the club, a post he held until early 1945, when the Ruppert heirs sold the vast baseball empire to the Larry MacPhail-Del Webb-Dan Topping syndicate. He remained associated with the club as chairman of the board.

◆

April 8, 1947

BOMBERS OVERCOME HASSETT TARS, 19-5

Berra Drives Across 6 Runs With Homer, Double, Single

By JOHN DREBINGER
Special to The New York Times.

NORFOLK, VA., APRIL 7—Looks as though something will have to be done about this Yogi Berra and very soon the burden of the task will rest with the seven other clubs in the American League.

For today this amazing little fellow, whom Bucky Harris on a starry night in Caracas converted from a chunky catcher into a chunky outfielder of even more extraordinary proportions, again grabbed all the spotlight as the Yankees belted Buddy Hassett's Norfolk farm hands into submission, 19 to 5.

With a homer, a single with the bases full and sundry other accomplishments, Yogi, who alone seems totally unaware of the commotion he is stirring all around him, hammered in six tallies for the Bombers who were making this their next to the last stop on their journey home.

THIRD 4-BAGGER IN TWO DAYS

Berra seemed determined to stop at nothing. His homer, a tremendous clout with two aboard in the first inning, was his third in two days and fourth of the training campaign. His single in the second with the bases full drove in two more tallies. Actually it cleared the sacks, for the shot also went through the opposing rightfielder, so terrifying are the blows that zoom off the Yogi bludgeon these days. Later on he rattled a two-bagger off the rightfield fence.

Playing here was like a homecoming for a number of Yanks who got their start with the Tars. Members of the Norfolk alumni now with the parent club include Berra, Frank Shea, Bill Johnson, Aaron Robinson, Jack Phillips and, of

Yogi Berra in 1948.

course, Lil' Phil Rizzuto, one of the most popular players ever to come out of the Piedmont circuit.

The Berra homer, incidentally, was one of the longest shots ever seen in this park. It cleared a high barrier in almost dead center, 450 feet from home plate.

The shot drew tremendous applause from every quarter but the Yankee bench, where Yogi's team-mates continue to rib him by greeting his every outstanding achievement with a stony silence. ◆

September 29, 1947

Three Local Television Stations Will Take Turns Covering World Series

By JACK GOULD

FINAL ARRANGEMENTS for televising the world series baseball games have been worked out. Under a system agreed upon by all interested parties the three television stations operating in the New York area will take turns in bringing the contests between the Yankees and the Dodgers to owners of television sets.

This year's series will be the first ever televised. As previously announced the television broadcasts will be co-sponsored by the Ford Motor Company and the Gillette Safety Razor Company.

The technical schedule worked out by the broadcasters calls for tomorrow's opening game at the Yankee Stadium to be picked up by WNBT, Channel 4, and the second by WABD, Channel 5. WCBS-TV, Channel 2, will handle the third and fourth games from Ebbets Field. The fifth game again will be covered by WNBT and the sixth and seventh, if played, will be WABD presentations.

The television play-by-play coverage also will be shared by the regular sportcasters of the three stations: Bob Edge for WCBS-TV, Bob Stanton for WNBT and Bill Slater for WABD. Each will handle the play-by-play when his station makes the technical pick-up. ◆

October 4, 1947

DODGERS' ONLY HIT BEATS YANKEES, 3-2, WITH 2 OUT IN NINTH

Lavagetto's Pinch Double Bats in 2 Runs, Evens Series and Spoils Bevens' No-Hitter

By JOHN DREBINGER

WITH THE FIRST NO-HITTER in world series history in the making at Ebbets Field yesterday, Cookie Lavagetto rewrote the script with two out in the ninth inning to establish the Dodgers as the first club in baseball's autumnal classic ever to win a game on just one hit.

In his familiar role of pinch hitter, the veteran Lavagetto slammed a two-bagger off the right-field wall against Floyd (Bill) Bevens that drove in two runners put on by walks. That floored the Yankees on the spot for a 3-to-2 Brooklyn triumph, tied the series at two victories apiece, stunned about half the crowd of 33,443 and sent the other half—the faithful of Flatbush—screaming hysterically on to the field in an endeavor to lay fond hands on their hero.

Bevens, stalwart right-hander, was within one short stride of baseball immortality until he lost all in the twinkling of an eye to Burt Shotton's unpredictable Dodgers.

For eight and two-thirds innings of this nerve-tingling fourth game Bevens, a strong, silent man from Salem, Ore., held the bats of Brooklyn's Bums even more silent than a tomb. No series pitcher ever had gone that far without allowing a hit.

On the way, Bevens established another world

series mark, though he will never reflect upon that one in his later years with any feeling of gratifications. He gave ten bases on balls, one more than Colby Jack Coombs of the Athletics permitted in 1910.

Two of those passes helped the Dodgers to their first run in the fifth inning to whittle away one of two tallies the Yanks had counted earlier. And the final two were indirectly to cause his defeat, though the last one was not wholly of his choosing. It was ordered by Manager Bucky Harris, who by that decision left himself open to sharp criticism. Most observers seemed to feel the usually astute Yankee skipper had pulled something of a strategic "rock."

As the final half of the ninth opened, with the Bombers leading, 2 to 1, Bruce Edwards went out when Johnny Lindell hauled down his lofty shot in front of the left-field stand with a leaping catch. But Carl Furillo walked for Bevens' ninth pass before Shotton fairly sprayed the summery afternoon with a maze of masterminding.

JORGENSEN FOULS OUT

After Spider Jorgensen had fouled out to George McQuinn back of first, Shotton sent Al Gionfriddo, rookie outfielder, to run for Furillo. Only one more batter need be retired then to clinch the victory for Bevens as well as that world series no-hit goal which has eluded some of baseball's greatest hurlers since 1903.

The batter was Pete Reiser, whom Shotton sent up for Hugh Casey, relief ace who had entered the contest in the top half of the ninth with the bases full and one out to end the inning on one pitch. Pistol Pete, limping painfully on a swollen ankle which he had sprained the previous day, had sat this one out up to that moment.

Shotton's strategy flashed again with one strike and two balls on Reiser as Gionfriddo streaked for second and stole the bag on an eyelash play. That pitch, too, was wide, making the count three and one.

There Harris made his questionable move. He ordered Bevens to toss the next one wide, thereby walking the lame Reiser. It seemed a direct violation of one of baseball's fundamental precepts which dictates against putting the "winning run" on base in such a situation.

Shotton followed with two more moves on the field, which seemed suddenly converted into a chessboard. He sent Eddie Miksis in to run for Reiser, an obvious shift, and then called on Lavagetto to bat for Ed Stanky.

The swarthy-complexioned veteran, a right-handed batter, swung viciously at the first pitch and missed. Then he swung again and connected, the ball sailing toward the right-field wall.

Over raced Tommy Henrich. The previous inning the brilliant Yankee gardener had made a glittering leaping catch of a similar fly ball to rob Gene Hermanski of a blow and keep the no-hitter alive.

There was nothing Tommy could do about this one, though. It soared over his head and struck the wall. Desperately he tried to clutch the ball as it caromed off the boards in order to get it home as quickly as possible, but that sloping wall is a tricky barrier and as the ball bounced to the ground more precious moments were lost.

Finally Henrich hurried the ball on its way. McQuinn caught it and relayed it to the plate, but all too late. Gionfriddo and Miksis already were over the plate while in the center of the diamond Dodger players and fans were all but mobbing Lavagetto in their elation.

While that was going on Bevens, the silent man from the northwest, was walking silently from the field. In a matter of seconds a priceless no-hit victory had been wrenched from his grasp and converted into a galling one-hit defeat. Only two other pitchers had tossed world series one-hitters before with both, of course, winning. They were Ed Reulbach of the Cubs in 1906 and Claude Passeau, a later day Cub, in 1945. ◆

October 6, 1947

DODGERS SET BACK YANKEES BY 8 TO 6 FOR 3-3 SERIES TIE

Rout Page With Four in Sixth to Win Before 74,065, New Crowd Mark for Classic

38 PLAYERS IN THE GAME

Gionfriddo's Catch of DiMaggio's Drive Prevents Losers From Tying Score

By JOHN DREBINGER

INCREDIBLE AS IT MAY SEEM to a bewildered world at large, the 1947 world series is still with us, and so are the Dodgers.

For in one of the most extraordinary games ever played, one that left a record series crowd of 74,065 limp and exhausted, Burt Shotton's unpredictable Flock fought the Yankees in a last-ditch stand at the Stadium yesterday and defeated them, 8 to 6.

As a consequence, the classic, which in this same park last Tuesday had started as a soft touch for Bucky Harris' American League champions, now stands tied at three victories apiece. The seventh and deciding game will be played at the Stadium today.

The game also was marked by one of the greatest catches in series history—Al Gionfriddo's collaring of Joe

DiMaggio's 415-foot drive in the sixth inning.

The fans saw the aroused Dodgers fighting to keep the series alive, rout Allie Reynolds inside of three rounds, getting two runs in the first and two in the third. It saw the Bombers roar back in the lower half of the third to blast Vic Lombardi from the

The 1947 World Series at Yankee Stadium.

mound with a four-run demonstration.

The Yanks added one more tally off Ralph Branca in the fourth to take a 5-4 lead, while the Bums screamed to the high heavens that the umpires were blind in calling Yogi Berra's single down the right-field foul line a fair ball.

In the lower half of the sixth round the crowd was to witness the Bombers come within an eyelash of tying the score again. With two on, DiMaggio sent a tremendous smash in the direction of the left-field bullpen only to see Gionfriddo, a rookie outfielder, rob Jolting Joe of his greatest moment.

Dashing almost blindly to the spot where he thought the ball would land and turning around at the last moment, the 25-year-old gardener, who had been merely tossed as an "extra" into the deal that shipped Kirby Higbe to the Pirates earlier this year, leaned far over the bullpen railing and, with his gloved hand, collared the ball.

It was a breathtaking catch for the third out of the inning. It stunned the proud Bombers and jarred even the usually imperturbable DiMaggio. Taking his position in center field with the start of the next inning, he was still walking inconsolably in circles, doubtless wondering whether he could believe his senses. ◆

October 6, 1947

Brooks Agree DiMaggio's Drive, Snared by Gionfriddo, Was Headed for the Bullpen

By ROSCOE McGOWEN

LITTLE AL GIONFRIDDO, the 5-foot 6-inch outfielder, who was tossed into the $300,000 Dodger deal with the Pirates on last Derby Day, may have been forgotten last Friday but nobody overlooked him yesterday.

When the Dodgers came romping into their clubhouse after evening the series at three-all in the lengthiest world series game ever played, Gionfriddo was the Dodger every photographer and every writer wanted to see.

Everybody knows what happened, but only Gionfriddo and Bobby Bragan, another hero of the game, can tell how it happened. There were two Yankees on base, with the great Joe DiMaggio at bat and lefty Joe Hatten pitching.

When DiMag' belted a towering drive that perhaps would have cleared the left field roof in Ebbets Field, Gionfriddo, who can run like a striped ape, raced back toward the low gate that leads to the visitors' bullpen.

"The ball hit my glove," said Al, "and a split second later I hit the gate. I knew I had it but I certainly couldn't have said I was going to get it—because how could any guy say he was on the ball all the way on one like that?

"It certainly would have gone into the bullpen alley for a home run if I hadn't got it," the little fellow continued. Bragan, so recently a denizen of the bullpen, was quick to verify that.. ◆

October 7, 1947

YANKS WIN SERIES, PAGE TAKING FINAL FROM DODGERS, 5-2

Relief Pitcher Hero as 11th Title Goes to American Leaguers Before 71,548

By JOHN DREBINGER

THE YANKEES HAD A TRUMP CARD after all, and as a consequence the Bronx Bombers are back once more in a long-familiar role as baseball champions of the universe.

They brought the 1947 world series to a close at the Stadium yesterday in almost perfunctory fashion as they downed the Dodgers in the seventh and deciding game by a score of 5 to 2.

And the ace in the deck who nailed down the final trick before a gathering of 71,548 was the fellow whom Bucky Harris had toasted all summer with the quaint line: "Gentlemen, Joe Page."

The 30-year-old southpaw from Cherry Valley, Pa., in another of his inimitable relief jobs, stepped into the breach immediately after the Yanks had grabbed a 3-2 lead in the fourth-inning on hits by Phil Rizzuto, Bobby Brown and the old reliable Tommy Henrich, and he never allowed Burt Shotton's Flock to come up for air again in the first $2,000,000 world series ever played.

A STARTLING RESIGNATION

Thus to the Yanks, most successful baseball organization in all history, came another world's title, the eleventh since it bagged the first, in 1923, and the first under the aegis of Larry MacPhail who, curiously, chose this dramatic moment to announce his retirement as president of the club.

The fiery redhead made the announcement at the very moment his players came thundering into their dressing room to celebrate the final triumph. It startled everyone but in no way interrupted the celebration that started with congratulations being showered upon the popular Manager Harris, who, after twenty-three long years, is once more riding a world champion.

Back in 1924, as the "boy manager," Bucky piloted the Washington Senators to the title in his first year as pilot. Now at 51 he is on top again as first-year manager of the Yanks, and only the third to lead the Bombers to their many titles.

The late Miller Huggins brought them their first championships in 1923, 1927, and 1928. Then Joe McCarthy, most successful of all, skippered the series winners in 1932, '36, '37, '38, '39, '41 and '43.

American Leaguers also were rejoicing, for this marked the twenty-seventh victory for the junior loop against sixteen for the National.

It was the second time that the Yanks had toppled the Dodgers, who have failed to win the world championship in four tries. They bowed to the Red Sox in 1916, the Indians in 1920 and the Yanks in 1941.

The only consolation the Dodgers had last night was the fact that this time they had come closer to their goal than any of their predecessors. But when it came down to the final test with all the blue chips in the middle, they simple didn't have it; and the fellow who convinced them of that was the one they were toasting in the Yankee clubhouse, Joe Page.

Only the previous afternoon Page had taken a heavy battering from the Bums from Flatbush for a victory that kept their series hopes alive for another twenty-four hours. But yesterday the southpaw simply smothered the Brooklyn boys in this final "struggle of the bullpens."

In an amazing come-back, Page faced only fifteen batters in his five innings on the mound. Not until one had been retired in the ninth could a Dodger get on base. He was Eddie Miksis, who singled. A moment later Bruce Edwards banged into a double play and the classic was over. ◆

Joe DiMaggio, Joe Page and Larry MacPhail celebrate winning the 1947 World Series against the Brooklyn Dodgers.

October 8, 1947

WEISS APPOINTED GENERAL MANAGER

Former Farm Chief to Direct Yankees, Although Topping Becomes New President

DISPUTES PRECEDE SHIFTS

Partners Accept Resignation of MacPhail After Buying His One-Third Interest

By JOHN DREBINGER

AT A PRESS CONFERENCE that lasted less than twenty minutes, a record in itself for the Yankee organization of recent years, Del Webb and Dan Topping yesterday read Larry MacPhail right out of the party.

They announced that they had accepted MacPhail's resignation as president, general manager, treasurer and director of the Yankees and that they had purchased the fiery redhead's one-third share of stock in the organization.

Topping, the remaining two owners disclosed in a joint statement, was elected president of the corporation by the board of directors, and also secretary. George Weiss, long associated with the Yankees as director of the far-flung farm system and a vice president under the MacPhailian regime, became general manager.

Webb, Western contractor, considered the key man in the three-man syndicate that purchased the Yankee baseball empire from the estate of the late Col. Jacob Ruppert in 1945, remained vice president. The office of treasurer is to be filled later.

The announcement, made in a suite in the Waldorf-Astoria, developed shortly after MacPhail, from another part of the town, had announced to news services his resignation as head of the Yankees and the sale of his share "for $2,000,000."

Neither Topping nor Webb would confirm or deny the figure. Asked what MacPhail had received, Topping said, "Well, you can figure that out for yourself."

DECISION MADE BEFORE SERIES

He then disclosed that the decision to buy out MacPhail had come before the world series and at a time when MacPhail had offered to sell a one-half interest of the Yankees, less 100 shares, for $3,000,000 to a group of bankers, who were then going to conduct a public sale.

"MacPhail asked Webb and me," said Topping, "to pool our third interests with his one-third and then sell half the club to that group of bankers for $3,000,000. We turned it down and told him instead we would buy him out."

As that would place the present value of the club at $6,000,000, MacPhail's one-third share therefore would be worth $2,000,000. However, on Topping's admission, MacPhail did not own outright a one-third share when the syndicate was first formed, and it is thought likely considerable deductions were made. A conservative estimate, some observers believed, would place what MacPhail realized from the entire transaction at considerably less than $2,000,000. It is probable, though, that MacPhail cleared $1,000,000 from his three-year association with the Yanks.

As president, under a contract that was to have served until 1950, MacPhail was receiving $50,000 a year, although a public Federal income tax report recently showed that with salary and other commitments MacPhail received in excess of $110,000 last year.

Topping declared that though they had bought out MacPhail, neither he nor Webb had an idea that MacPhail also planned a resignation until Larry's explosive announcement in the Yankee dressing rooms directly after the Bombers had clinched the final game from the Dodgers on Monday.

"That was the first inkling I had of it," said Topping, "but so long as he asked for it we decided to let him have it." He then read a scrawled note, signed by MacPhail, in which the turbulent proxy abdicated his throne and automatically abrogated his contract.

The Topping-Webb press conference closed twenty-four tempestuous hours which had begun with MacPhail announcing to the press he was quitting, and continued with an all-night victory celebration in the Biltmore from which emanated tales of brawls and fist fights, during which MacPhail was alleged to have struck John MacDonald, a former aide in the days when the two were with the Dodgers, and various exchanges of sharp words between MacPhail and the two men he had taken into the Yankee empire. MacPhail was not present at the Topping-Webb conference.

In announcing he had taken over the presidency, Topping made it clear that he planned no serious active hand in the baseball operations of the Yankees, but would confine most of his activities to his favorite sport of football.

"There's the guy who will have the headaches in baseball," said Topping, pointing to Weiss, who up to that moment had stood quietly and almost unobserved in a corner of the room while reporters were grouped around Topping and Webb.

It was a familiar pose for Weiss, long regarded the "strong silent man" of the Yankee organization, the fellow who for years has been digging up the young talent that has resulted in so many pennants and world titles for the Bombers.

Weiss accepted congratulations with his usual modesty and said he expected things to go along as usual. Bucky Harris, with another year to go on his contract, was sure to remain as manager, said Weiss. ◆

Harris Is Dropped as Manager of Yankees

Rift Between Harris and Weiss, Yankees' General Manager, Rumored for Six Weeks

By LOUIS EFFRAT

STANLEY RAYMOND HARRIS, better and more familiarity known as Bucky, yesterday was dropped by the Yankees. After managing the club to a pennant and world championship in his first year, and piloting an overaged outfit—alive and in the running for the flag as late as last Saturday—to third place in his second, Harris found himself without a job after two seasons as head field-man of the New Yorkers.

Shortly before 6 o'clock last night the club broke the news, not entirely unexpected in view of persistent rumors of the past five or six weeks.

"After a conference this afternoon among Dan Topping, president; George M. Weiss, general manager, and Bucky Harris, it was decided that by mutual agreement Harris' contract would not be renewed. The name of the new manager will be announced at some future date. Several candidates, not including any player active with the Yankees in 1948, are being considered for the post."

POPULAR WITH THE PLAYERS

The aforegoing bulletin, issued by the Yankees, would have startled the diamond world if it had been flashed six weeks ago. At the moment, however, it came as no surprise. In fact, numerous "I told you so's" preceded expressions of regret among those who were close to the situation. Harris, undeniably popular with the players, press and public, was sort of living on »»»

<<< borrowed time, so far as his connection with the Bombers was concerned.

Even as the Yankees were fighting for the American League pennant, reports of a "rift" between Harris and Weiss continued to be heard. There were denials from all sides—from Harris, from Weiss, from Topping and from Del Webb, co-owner of the club. At no time, however, did Bucky receive a clear-cut, convincing vote of confidence. Hence the conviction among the experts that Harris' days were numbered.

Among those in town, the big question was: "Was he pushed?" Put directly to Harris, the deposed pilot answered: "I left on friendly terms and have no further comment." Bucky added that he had nothing definite in mind; parried a query about the possibility of hooking on with the Tigers and said he would go to Boston to witness the world series—a series in which he might have been managing one of the contestants if he had been favored with more luck and better pitching than he had throughout 1948. ◆

June 29, 1949

JOE IN FIRST START AS BOMBERS SCORE

Red Sox Are Set Back by 5-4, Yankees' DiMaggio Hitting Home Run and a Single

By LOUIS EFFRAT
Special to The New York Times.

BOSTON, JUNE 28—Joe DiMaggio became a Yankee in good standing tonight. Too long was that wait for his official return and there were probably times during the sixty-five games he missed because of an ailing right heel that all concerned wondered if the Clipper ever would make it. But make it he did for the first time this season tonight—and how!

Before the season's biggest turnout and the largest after-dark attendance in Fenway Park history, 36,228 fans, DiMaggio started to earn the $90,000 or $100,000 he is being paid. Like the DiMaggio of old, he made the enemy cringe, as he carried his team to a thrilling 5-4 victory over the red-hot Red Sox.

Carried is the word, too. For Joltin' Joe, directly and indirectly, had his hand in the scoring of all the New York runs. In his first time at bat, DiMag-gio opened the second inning with a solid single to left center. The next two Yankees were fanned by Southpaw Maurice McDermott, so that if Joe had not hit, the visitors would have been retired.

DRIVES INTO THE SCREEN

Given this life by DiMaggio, the Bombers remained alive and, after Johnny Lindell walked, Hank Bauer hit his third homer of the campaign, giving the New Yorkers a 3-0 bulge. Nor did DiMaggio stop there. In the third, with Phil Rizzuto aboard via a single, DiMaggio came through with his first homer, a dynamic clout into the screen above the high left-field wall and it was 5-0.

Idle so long, in need of batting practice and facing a brilliant, 20-year-old lefthander with a fair strike-out record, the Yankee Clipper was hitting 1.000 after his first two trips to the plate. In two other attempts, Joe grounded to the pitcher and walked, but he had provided the big punches that enabled his team to stave off Boston's strong closing bid.

Wearing a special shoe on his right foot—no spikes under the heel—DiMaggio patrolled center field flawlessly. He captured six flies and fielded three ground singles that came his way with his old-time grace. In the eighth, when Joe walked, Yogi Berra grounded to Bobby Doerr. DiMaggio was an easy force-out at second, but his take-out slide prevented Vern Stephens from completing a double play. In short, it was a tremendous night for the returning hero. ◆

October 6, 1950

Yanks Beat Phils, 2-1, in 10th On a Home Run by DiMaggio

Reynolds Hurls Bombers Into 2-0 Lead in Games, Missing Shutout on Bad Hop—Series Shifts to Stadium Today

By JOHN DREBINGER
Special to The New York Times.

PHILADELPHIA, OCT. 5—For nine innings today under a cloudless sky, Ed Sawyer's Whiz Kids matched the mighty Yankees move for move and for a time it looked as if they did have all the world series answers. But in an unguarded moment they overlooked the Bombers' mightiest weapon.

With the score deadlocked at 1–all, Joe DiMaggio, first up in the tenth inning and still seeking his first hit in the classic, leaned into a pitch delivered by Robin Roberts.

The ball streaked on a line into the upper deck of the densely packed left-field pavilion at Shibe Park and on the wings of that shot Casey Stengel's American League champions, behind fast-balling Allie Reynolds, brought down the Phillies in the second encounter of the series, 2 to 1.

It was a jolt that plunged the majority in a crowd of 32,660 deep in grief since it gave the vaunted Bombers a 2-to-0 lead in games as the series now swings to New York, where tomorrow at Yankee Stadium the third engagement will be played.

It was, though again a low scoring mound duel, a far more rugged contest than yesterday's 1-0 opener. For where Vic Raschi had held the Phils virtually helpless with his two-hitter, they gave Reynolds a far more robust battle.

They clipped the Chief for seven hits, including a triple and three doubles, and several times appeared on the verge of breaking through. But the deeply tanned Oklahoman, a part Creek Indian, stoically held on to the end to nail down the victory and he even would have accomplished it in nine innings except for a crazily bounding ball that helped the Phils to their run.

A year ago Reynolds had tossed that sparkling two-hitter at the Dodgers to win the opener. Though not quite that sparkling, the Chief pitched perhaps an even more important triumph. For with two games in the sack, the New Yorkers are now halfway to the goal line and need only two more to stalk off with their thirteenth world series title.

Roberts, handsome dark-haired youth who last Sunday had pitched the Phils to the National League pennant over the Dodgers, did a stout job, too. The 24-year-old bonus righthander yielded ten blows, but none really hurt until the Clipper, with the count at two balls and one strike, rifled that shot into the stands with the deadly accuracy of a billiard expert banging the winning ball into a side pocket. ◆

March 4, 1951

DiMaggio Plan to Quit After '51 Stuns Yankee Players, Officials

By JAMES P. DAWSON
Special to The New York Times.

PHOENIX, ARIZ., MARCH 3—The Yankee training camp was stunned today by Joe DiMaggio's announcement last night that he planned to make this his last season in baseball.

Overnight reaction found some of the players unbelieving, a few doubtful, the entire squad regretful.

Club executives were surprised also, but hopeful, according to a statement issued by General Manager George M. Weiss, as follows:

"Joe DiMaggio has not discussed this angle with any club official. We regret to hear anything like this and we hope we will have the sort of season which will cause him to change his mind."

In his typical volcanic style, Manager Casey Stengel said:

"I haven't heard anything about it, but, if that's the way he feels, that's his prerogative. I can't hold a gun at his head and say 'You've got to play ball.' Of course, I'd hate to see it happen. But, that's a decision the player makes himself."

Stengel said he had no set plan to meet such a contingency and would cross the bridge when he came to it.

DiMaggio had nothing to add to his announcement. "What I said yesterday goes," he said, carefully pointing out he did not make the announcement "emphatic." He added: "I still feel this may be my last year."

Those who commented on the situation stressed what DiMaggio's absence would mean to Yankee fortunes. There was no attempt to minimize this.

Coaches Bill Dickey and Frankie Crosetti, who were close to the last days of the late Babe Ruth and Lou Gehrig, agreed the passing of DiMaggio would mean the end of another baseball era.

"It's always sad when a great ball player moves out of the picture," said Dickey, who is numbered among the game's greatest catchers. "It's sad not only for his own club but for baseball generally. You know it's got to happen, but, somehow, it's hard to take when the time comes."

Crosetti echoed this sentiment, but refuses to believe that DiMaggio has reached the end of his playing days.

"He's young yet," said Frankie. "He has plenty of good baseball left. When his time does come the effect will be felt by every player, like when Ruth bowed out. The Babe kept those salaries up there and Joe has done the same thing, so that every player has benefited from his presence."

Jerry Coleman said such a development would be almost a calamity. "All my life DiMaggio and the Yankees have been one and the same," he added. ◆

October 9, 1951

YANKS BEAT GIANTS' BY 6-2, TIE SERIES; HOMER BY DIMAGGIO

Reynolds Pitches Bombers to Their 2d Victory—Maglie Loser Before 49,010

DARK DRIVES 3 DOUBLES

But Four Double Plays Spoil National Leaguers' Attack— Mays Hits Into Three

By JOHN DREBINGER

Joe DiMaggio congratulated by teammates during Game 4 of the 1951 World Series.

AS JOE DIMAGGIO GOES, so go the Yankees!

The aging Clipper, thought by many to have slipped deep into the shadows, came back with a resounding wallop yesterday. He exploded a two-run homer midway in the fourth game of the world series at the Polo Grounds and that shot gave Casey Stengel's Bombers all the inspirational lift they needed to bring down the Giants, 6 to 2. That squared the series at two victories apiece before a crowd of 49,010. »»»

《《《 Three games in a row the 37-year-old Jolter had gone hitless in the series. His swan song had been written and they were ready to run it off the presses. More feeble than ever he seemed in the first inning when Sal Maglie, squaring off for his mound duel with Allie Reynolds, struck him out. The Barber shaved a corner with a called third strike.

In the third the Clipper produced a brief flashback of the Clipper of old as he plunked a single into left field with two out and the bases empty. It was his first hit of the classic after having gone "twelve for oh" in the parlance of the dugouts. The gathering cheered enthusiastically.

But the noise here wasn't a patch to the din that went up two innings later, the fifth to be exact, when the Great DiMag, with Yogi Berra on first base and Reynolds holding a slim 2-1 edge over Maglie, blasted the ball deep into the upper deck of the left field stand.

There wasn't a shadow of a doubt where that white pill was going from the moment it left the Clipper's bat, and for the first time in the entire series the American Leaguers let out a deafening roar, and down to the last die-hard in the rival camp there must have been the conviction that for this engagement at least this was the decisive blow. ◆

December 12, 1951

DiMaggio Retires

No Ambition to Manage

Decision Made Last Spring, Laid to Age and Injuries— Mantle Due for Post

By JOHN DREBINGER

THE YANKEE CLIPPER has made his last graceful catch and taken his last cut at the ball.

Amid a fanfare without precedent in the retirement of a player, Joe DiMaggio yesterday told the Bombers and the world that he was retiring as an active performer and that nothing could ever persuade him to play again.

As newsreel cameras clicked, light bulbs flashed and photographers and reporters jammed every inch of the Yankees' Fifth Avenue suite in the Squibb Tower, the son of an Italian immigrant, who rose from the wharves of San Francisco to a position of eminence and an accumulation of more than $700,000 in baseball earnings quietly revealed that he alone had made the decision.

It was prompted, he said, by advancing years–he was 37 on Nov. 25–physical injuries and the conviction that as a player "I no longer have it." He said also night baseball was partly to blame and was convinced it had shortened his career by at least two years. DiMaggio started his major league career in 1936, and was with the Yankees for thirteen seasons, with three years out for Army service.

Dan Topping, who was present with his co-owner Del Webb and Manager Casey Stengel, said that up to the last he had hoped to persuade DiMaggio to change his mind. But the Clipper's mind had been made up long ago.

DiMaggio said he knew last spring this would be his last year. The Clipper said he regretted having hinted at his retirement then, for he realized later his remarks had been ill-timed.

"But I knew my mind was made up, although I never mentioned it again until after the world series and then only to Topping," said DiMaggio. "He asked me to think it over a while longer and in fairness to him I decided this was the only thing to do. I never mentioned it to another soul and not even my brother Dominic knew what my decision would be today."

'WHAT IS THERE TO SAY?'
The usually loquacious Stengel had little to say.

"What is there to say?" said Casey, "I just gave the Big Guy's glove away and it is going to the Hall of Fame, where Joe himself is certain to go. He was the greatest player I ever managed and right now I still say there isn't another center-fielder in baseball his equal."

Concerning a replacement, Stengel said the job would be "wide open," with Mickey Mantle, rookie star of the past season receiving first call, closely followed by Jackie Jensen.

As the appointed hour of 2 P.M. arrived Arthur (Red) Patterson, in charge of the ceremonies and striving to keep reporters from choking on sandwiches and stumbling over newsreel wires,

Joe DiMaggio with Manager Casey Stengel, left, and Yankee co-owner Del Webb during his retirement announcement.

issued a typed statement for DiMaggio.

"I told you fellows last spring," the statement read, "I thought this would be my last year. I only wish I could have had a better year, but even if I had hit .350, this would have been the last year for me.

"You all know I have had more than my share of physical injuries and setbacks during my career. In recent years these have been much too frequent to laugh off. When baseball is no longer fun, it's no longer a game.

"And so, I've played my last game of ball.

"Since coming to New York I've made a lot of friends and picked up a lot of advisers, but I would like to make one point clear–no one has influenced me in making this decision. It has been my problem and my decision to make.

"I feel that I have reached the stage where I can no longer produce for my ball club, my manager, my team-mates and my fans the sort of baseball their loyalty to me deserves.

"In closing, I would like to say that I feel I have been unusually privileged to play all my major league baseball for the New York Yankees.

"But it has been an even greater privilege to play baseball at all. It has added much to my life. What I will remember most in days to come will be the great loyalty of the fans. They have been very good to me."

After fulfilling his obligations to the photographers and radio commentators, the Clipper drifted back to the press room, where he answered a barrage of questions.

When did he first realize he was slipping?
About three years ago.

What ailments bothered him most?
"My right knee," he replied. "It kept buckling under me every little while. Also both shoulders. These have bothered me for a long time and finally retarded my swing so much I simply couldn't hit in front of the plate as I used to. Right now, though, I feel fine, and have no intention of going near a doctor. But I know I couldn't do it again on the ball field."

What were his biggest thrills in his major >>>

<<< *league career?*

"Well, I guess the fifty-six game hitting streak in 1941," he said. "And then there was that series up in Boston in 1949 when, after missing the first sixty-five games because of my heel operation, I belted a couple of home runs."

In that series, the Clipper exploded four home runs in the three games, drove in nine runs and virtually wrecked the Red Sox for the rest of the campaign.

Who was the toughest pitcher he ever faced?

"When I first came up, Mel Harder. But last season," he added with a chuckle, "they all were pretty tough."

What was his greatest fielding play?

"I guess that one I made off Hank Greenberg back in 1938 or 1939 out by the flagpole in the Stadium just in front of the 461-foot mark. Don't know yet how I made it. Just stuck my glove up at the last money and there was the ball."

Few rookies ever had to respond to so great a ballyhoo as accompanied DiMaggio eastward in the spring of 1936. But his place in stardom was established almost from the start. Manager Joe McCarthy needed only one look to realize he had the player of a generation.

And with the rise of DiMaggio, the Yanks rode to great triumphs. In his first four years, from 1936 through 1939, the Yanks won four pennants and world titles. In all, DiMaggio played in ten world series and nine times was with the winner. And in his final game last October, he ran his total of series games to fifty-one, one above the previous record held by Frankie Frisch.

Starting with $8,000 in his first season and continuing until his salary reached $100,000 for each of the last three, DiMaggio received an estimated $646,250 in pay from the Yankees. World series shares raised this by $58,519.17 for an over-all total of $704,769.71. To this must be added about $250,000 received for radio and television appearances and for endorsements of products.

Despite this income, DiMaggio, when asked if he would like to loaf for a year, replied with a grim smile:

"Yes, I would like to loaf, but I'm afraid I'm not that well fixed." ◆

January 15, 1954

Joe DiMaggio Weds Marilyn Monroe

Special to The New York Times.

SAN FRANCISCO, JAN. 14—Marilyn Monroe, the motion-picture actress, and Joe DiMaggio, former outfielder of the New York Yankees baseball club, were married here today at the City Hall.

Municipal Court Judge Charles S. Peery performed the ceremony in his chambers after clearing the room of reporters and photographers who had awaited the couple's arrival. The bride had telephoned her studio in Hollywood that the wedding would take place at 1:30 P. M.

Reno Barsocchini, Mr. DiMaggio's partner in his Fishermen's Wharf Restaurant, served as best man and Mrs. Barsocchini was matron of honor. The bride wore a dark brown broadcloth suit with an ermine collar.

Marilyn Monroe and Joe DiMaggio.

The couple answered questions and posed for pictures before the ceremony. The picture-taking was resumed after the wedding, when Judge Peery had the doors unlocked.

Mr. DiMaggio retired from baseball in 1951 and now stars on a television show produced for children. The bride said she would continue her movie career.

This was the second marriage for both. Mr. DiMaggio was divorced in 1944 from the former Dorothy Arnold, an actress. Miss Arnold has custody of their son, Joe, Jr. Miss Monroe was married at 16 to a merchant seaman. The marriage lasted two years. ◆

January 27, 1955

Joe DiMaggio Elected to Baseball's Hall of Fame

By JOHN DREBINGER

JOSEPH PAUL DIMAGGIO, son of a humble San Francisco fisherman, swept into baseball's Hall of Fame yesterday.

With the renowned Yankee Clipper, who retired as an active player after the 1951 season, went three others. They were Ted Lyons, pitching star of the Chicago White Sox between the years 1923 and 1946; Dazzy Vance, fireballing right-hander of the Dodgers and strike-out king of the National League in the Twenties, and Gabby Hartnett, slugging catcher of the Chicago Cubs between 1923 and 1941.

The announcement of the result of the election, conducted by the members of the Baseball Writers Association of America, came after a day-long counting of the ballots in Commissioner Ford C. Frick's office. With only writers of ten or more years of service eligible to vote, a total of 251 ballots was cast. A three-fourths vote, or 189, was necessary for election.

DiMaggio, a brilliant outfielder for the Bombers starting in 1936, had fallen short in two previous elections since his retirement. He made it this time with a decisive count of 223 votes. Lyons was next with 217, followed by Vance with 205 and Hartnett with 195.

After spending the week-end in Boston, Joe was driving to New York when, stopping for a traffic light, he was recognized by a truck driver, who called to him "congratulations, Joe." DiMaggio then turned on his car radio and got the news in detail.

On arriving here the Clipper exclaimed, "I'm thrilled to death. I played in Cooperstown once in an exhibition game. But this time when I go there it will be something special and you can bet I won't miss it."

DiMaggio was referring to the annual Hall of Fame day held in July when the newly chosen are officially inducted and their plaques hung alongside those of the other immortals.

Joseph Paul DiMaggio, a native of San Francisco, appeared headed for stardom virtually from his first game with the Yankees. That was on May 3, 1936. He hit a triple and two singles that day.

From then until he retired at the close of the 1951 campaign Joe was the "big guy" of the Bombers. He put in thirteen seasons with the Yanks, exclusive of three years of military service in World War II.

Joe appeared in ten world series, only one of which the Yankees lost, and he played in eleven All-Star games for the American League. His fifty-one world series games stand as a record.

He compiled a lifetime batting mark of .325 and poled 361 home runs. He was voted the American League's most valuable player three times—1939, 1941 and 1947. Twice he carried off the league batting crown, in 1939 with a mark of .389 and in 1940 with .352. He also led twice in homers, 1937 with forty-six, and 1948 with thirty-nine.

But perhaps his greatest achievement ▶▶▶

<<< came in 1941, when he set a major league record of hitting safely in fifty-six consecutive games. The streak began on May 15 and did not end until July 17 in a night game in Cleveland.

Although plagued with injuries throughout his career, the Clipper nevertheless rose to defensive heights that matched his batting prowess. A perfectionist in the field, his flawless style gave him rank as one of the game's greatest center fielders.

Joe was 37 when he retired. Injuries hastened his decision. ◆

January 6, 1957

Prophetic 1937 All-Star Picture Stirs DiMaggio Memories

By LOUIS EFFRAT

HOW PROPHETIC WAS the photographer who, nearly twenty years ago, snapped the accompanying picture? Even the casual baseball fan, if he is in his thirties, will recognize all the principals immediately and agree that the lensman batted 1.000.

Was it mere coincidence that the late Tommy Sande, an Associated Press photographer, requested Lou Gehrig, Joe Cronin, Bill Dickey, Joe DiMaggio, Charley Gehringer, Jimmie Foxx and Hank Greenberg to pose before the 1937 All-Star game at Griffith Stadium, Washington?

Or had Sande, on the morning of July 7, 1937, peered into a crystal ball and been tipped off that all seven would one day be in the baseball Hall of Fame?

Gehrig, who died in 1941, was the first of the seven to be admitted to the Cooperstown, N.Y., shrine. He was voted in in 1939. Gehringer's year was 1949, Foxx's 1951. Dickey, in 1954, and DiMaggio, in 1955, preceded Cronin and Greenberg, who entered the Hall of Fame last summer. It took two decades, but all seven "made" it.

This is the photo that Joe DiMaggio found in a dresser drawer. From left: Lou Gehrig, Joe Cronin, Bill Dickey, DiMaggio, Charley Gehringer, Jimmie Foxx and Hank Greenberg.

One picture, it has been said, is worth a thousand words. To what height does the value soar when both the picture and the words are supplied by DiMaggio? The former Yankee Clipper is the strong, silent type. But he was persuaded to tell this story.

A CHRISTMAS GIFT

It was the week before last Christmas and Joe was looking through a drawer in his Madison Hotel apartment. He ran across all sorts of old pictures, but this one caught and held his eyes. At a glance DiMaggio knew that this was extraordinary—seven Hall of Famers in a group, long before any of them had "made" it.

"This is a wonderful picture," DiMaggio mused. "I'll have copies made, matted and framed and I'll send one to each of the fellows still living. I know they'll get as big a kick out of seeing it as I did."

Within a couple of days DiMaggio had mailed a picture and a letter to Cronin at Boston, Dickey at Little Rock, Ark.; Gehringer at Detroit, Foxx at Miami, and Greenberg at Cleveland. The other set went to Mrs. Eleanor Gehrig, Lou's widow, in New York.

DiMaggio is not a millionaire. He only lives like one—often because it is necessary. He was able to ride the subway only during his first year with the Yankees.

After that, because of his fame and his easily recognizable features, Joe was in danger of being mauled by fans and admirers in the subway. So, except for one day during a taxi strike seven years ago, he has not been in the subway in twenty years. He is the cabbies' best customer.

That requires money. In recent years DiMaggio has enjoyed moderate success in the stock market. Now he is about to venture into real estate. Numerous television appearances and various endorsements help to fatten the kitty enough so that Joe is not under pressure to accept "any sort of job."

Five years after his retirement from baseball DiMaggio remains a "big" man. Not, however, so "big" that he has forgotten the game of baseball or the men he played with and against.

His finding of the picture and what he did with it prove that. ◆

January 14, 1978

Joe McCarthy, Yanks' Ex-Manager, Dies at 90

By JOSEPH DURSO

JOSEPH V. McCARTHY, the Hall of Fame baseball manager who led the New York Yankees to eight American League pennants, died yesterday evening in Millard Fillmore Hospital in Buffalo. He was 90 years old.

Mr. McCarthy died of pneumonia, a hospital nurse said. He had entered the hospital in November for treatment of the lung disease.

He was either "a pushbutton manager," in the words of Jimmy Dykes, or "the greatest manager who ever lived," in the words of Edward G. Barrow, who hired him for the New York Yankees in 1931.

But whatever he was, Joe Vincent McCarthy became the most successful baseball manager of his time and formed the middle link in the chain of Yankee achievements during the last half-century.

A CONSERVATIVE MANAGER

He was a stocky, 5-foot-8-inch Philadelphian with a strong Irish face, an inexpressive manner, a conservative outlook—the master of the noncommittal reply and the devotee of the "set" lineup. He had neither the quiet desperation of Miller Huggins, who preceded him as the Yankee empire-builder, nor the loud flamboyance of Casey Stengel.

But like them, he called the signals for some of the most celebrated players in history, from Babe Ruth to Joe DiMaggio. And, like them, he produced winners so relentlessly that the cry "Break up the Yankees" became an inside joke that was applied to monolithic teams in all professional sports.

Mr. McCarthy, who never played an inning in the major leagues, joined the Yankees after they had won six American League pennants under Mr. Huggins in the 1920's. He led them for 15 full seasons, winning seven World Series titles in his eight appearances. »»»

«« Later, during the Stengel era through the 1950's, the Yankees won 10 more pennants. And by the time the empire plunged into decline after the 1964 season, the Yankees had taken 29 pennants and 20 world titles in 45 years.

The middle years in this remarkable stretch fell to Mr. McCarthy, who had spent 20 seasons as player and manager in the minor leagues before becoming manager of William Wrigley's Chicago Cubs of 1926. Three years later, they won the National League pennant, and two years after that, Mr. McCarthy switched to the rival league and the Yankees. He finally left them in 1946, sat out one season, then managed the Boston Red Sox in 1948 and 1949 before retiring in June, 1950.

A Good Teacher

By then, he had become the first manager in baseball to win pennants in both major leagues and the first to win four straight World Series titles, which the Yankees did from 1936 through 1939. They missed the pennant by two games in 1940, but then won three more and two world titles during World War II.

"John McGraw won four straight pennants with dictatorial pugnacity," Arthur Daley wrote in The New York Times. "Connie Mack did the same through sheer paternalism. McCarthy did it with phlegmatic unobtrusiveness."

"Never a day went by," Joe DiMaggio recalled, "that you didn't learn something from McCarthy."

"I hated his guts," said Joe Page, the relief pitcher, "but there was never a better manager."

Mr. McCarthy's whole career was spiced by extremes despite the Yankees' consistency. He was taunted as a "busher" even after rising to the majors. He was the obscure manager trying to handle the famous and tempestuous, like Grover Cleveland Alexander, Rogers Hornsby and Mr. Ruth. He was faintly praised when his teams won and blamed when they lost. And finally, after the glory years in New York, he suffered the gall of losing two consecutive pennants in Boston—one in a playoff game in 1948, the other to the Yankees on the final day of 1949.

Mr. McCarthy was born in the Germantown section of Philadelphia on April 21, 1887, broke his kneecap while playing sandlot ball and never had a real shot at a big-league career.

He attended Niagara University for a while, then turned pro with the Wilmington (Del.) club of the Tri-State League in 1907—a year when Honus Wagner and Ty Cobb led the majors in hitting, each with a .350 average. Mr. McCarthy played until 1921 with a succession of teams between the boondocks and the highest minor leagues: Franklin, Toledo, Indianapolis, Wilkes-Barre, Buffalo and Louisville.

The nearest he came to the big time was in 1916 when the rebel Federal League tried to rival the established big leagues. Mr. McCarthy, then with Buffalo of the International League, signed with the Federal franchise in Brooklyn. But the league collapsed before the season began, and he jumped back to the Louisville Colonels of the American Association.

However, he had added something to his portfolio three years earlier when he was named manager of Wilkes-Barre in the New York State League. And, although he hit .325 that season while doubling as a player, his "other" hat soon became the big one. After jumping back to Louisville in 1916, he was named player-manager in 1919 and finally left the field for the dugout in 1921.

The switch came, he remembered later, after he had criticized a player named Jay Kirke for a wild throw in the infield and Mr. Kirke replied:

"Who are you to be telling a .380 hitter how to play ball? Why don't you go home and take a look at yourself."

"I did take a look at myself that night in the clubhouse," Mr. McCarthy said, "and I agreed with him that I was through as a player. The next day, I was just the manager."

Mr. McCarthy was still a minor-league manager in 1926, though he had two pennants and had finished out of the first division only once. Then he was hired by the Chicago Cubs, who had finished last in the National League. Overnight, he had arrived.

Overnight, he also encountered the "star" system for the first time. He was conducting a clubhouse briefing that first spring when Mr. Alexander strolled in just as Mr. McCarthy was saying, "Now, suppose we get a man on second base—." Mr. Alexander, one of the great pitchers and great individualists in the business, lighted a cigarette and commented:

"You don't have to worry about that, Mr. McCarthy. This club will never get a man that far."

A month later, Mr. McCarthy sold Mr. Alexander to the St. Louis Cardinals and amid the catcalls, got a telegram from Mr. Wrigley that read:

"Congratulations. For years I've been looking for a manager who had the nerve to do that."

The Cubs, meanwhile, finished fourth in an eight-team league in 1926 and 1927, then edged into third place and won the pennant in 1929. But they lost the World Series to Mack's Philadelphia Athletics, who added insult to injury by scoring 10 runs in the seventh inning of the fifth game when the Cubs were in front, 8-0.

Neither the Chicago fans nor Mr. Wrigley ever quite forgave Mr. McCarthy for that, and in September of 1930, he was replaced by Mr. Hornsby.

But Mr. McCarthy landed on his feet with a vengeance. He was signed by the Yankees, who had finished second under Bob Shawkey and who were suffering against Mr. Mack's rampaging Philadelphia team. The contact was Mr. Barrow, who had been president of the International League during Mr. McCarthy's days there and who now was running the Yankees for Col. Jacob Ruppert and his partner, Col. Tillinghast l'Hommedieu Huston.

Mr. McCarthy, perhaps bracing for his first collision with the rough, rowdy Yankees, stumbled verbally over the threshold as he joined them. Acknowledging his new contract before a swarm of writers and officials, he nodded toward Mr. Ruppert and said: "Thank you, Colonel Huston."

To which Mr. Ruppert replied: "Maybe McCarthy will stay around long enough to know my name."

THE COMING OF JOE D.

He did, too. He stayed 15 years and became the man in the New York dugout during many of the most dramatic moments in sports history. But before he did, he had to solve the problem of Babe Ruth: the home-run hitter supreme, the demigod leader of a rousing bunch of baseball heroes, a law unto himself.

Mr. McCarthy met that challenge by avoiding any direct clash with the Bambino, even though the strategy involved a bending of his usual policy that all players were to be treated alike. He pretty much let Mr. Ruth do as he pleased, and in return the Babe stayed more or less in line and kept hitting home runs.

In 1931, the Yankees finished second but in 1932 they made it to the top. And their rival in the Series in 1932 was the Cubs.

These were the Yankees of Mr. Ruth, Lou Gehrig and Tony Lazzeri, the only regular holdovers from the Huggins era, and of new stars like Frank Crosetti, Bill Dickey, Lefty Gomez and Red Ruffing. In four games, they not only outshouted the Cubs in the dugout repartee but flattened them for the title while Mr. Ruth "called" his legendary shot before hitting a titanic home run off Charlie Root.

After three seasons in second place, the Yankees, with Mr. Ruth gone and a 21-year-old San Franciscan named Joe DiMaggio in center field, struck in 1936. They overpowered their rivals for four straight years as an endless stream of talent was moved upward by George M. Weiss from farm teams like the Newark Bears and Kansas City Blues.

In 1936, they won 102 games; in 1937, it was 102; in 1938 it was 99; and finally in 1939, 106.

"Sure," Mr. McCarthy said when people questioned his role in all this maurauding, "I »»»

≪≪ spend every summer in Atlantic City and only come back to get ready for the World Series."

After pausing in 1940, the juggernaut rolled again for three more years. In 1943, with Mr. DiMaggio and many of the others in service, Mr. McCarthy put together his last winner. In the Series the Yankees beat the Cardinals in five games for Mr. McCarthy's seventh world title in eight tries.

HUNTING, FISHING AND BASEBALL

Mr. McCarthy was still the same stolid sort of man who enjoyed few hobbies except hunting and fishing. He rarely read books, he never fraternized with his players, he was making $40,000 a year and he smoked big black cigars.

In 1946, beset by a stomach ailment and by the free-wheeling flair of Larry MacPhail, the Yankees' new president, "Marse Joe" called it quits. He was succeeded by Bill Dickey, then by Bucky Harris, sat out a year and then returned as manager of the Boston Red Sox. But after two seasons there, during which he lost photo-finish pennants to the Indians and Yankees, he retired for good in June of 1950.

He retreated to his 61-acre farm outside Buffalo with his wife, Elizabeth (Babe) McCave, who died Oct. 18, 1971. He was elected to baseball's Hall of Fame in 1957, but lived quietly in his colonial house far from the clamorous scenes of the Yankee heyday. ◆

JOE DIMAGGIO: 1914-1999; Today's Yankees Mourn a Timeless Hero

By BUSTER OLNEY

TAMPA, FLA, MARCH 8—They began paying tribute to Joe DiMaggio here early this morning, fans old and young visiting the pinstriped plaque erected in his name outside Legends Field, many of them wearing Yankees caps. A few brought flowers, others took pictures, some prayed.

The Yankee players, too, honored the man introduced as "the greatest living ballplayer" at Yankee Stadium every year. Before tonight's exhibition game with Philadelphia, they emerged from their dugout, hats off, for a moment of silence, DiMaggio's No. 5 sewn onto each uniform's left sleeve. Rob Cucuzza, the equipment manager, had brought 300 of the emblems to Florida, just in case; he had hoped he would not have to use them.

When a highlight reel was shown on the video scoreboard, the fans all stood before anybody asked them to. "It's a sad day here," David Cone said.

Derek Jeter said, "There was a mystique about him, the way he played."

George Steinbrenner said, "It was the class and dignity with which he led his life that made him a part of us."

Many Americans shared that sentiment. President Clinton, in Managua, Nicaragua, said: "Today, America lost one of the century's beloved heroes, Joe DiMaggio. This son of Italian immigrants gave every American something to believe in. He became the very symbol of American grace, power and skill."

Jeter learned of DiMaggio's death when the news crawled across the bottom of his television screen. To Jeter and to most other Yanks, DiMaggio was royalty who passed through the clubhouse once or twice a year: you never initiated conversation with him. You could joke and laugh and swap stories with Whitey Ford and Reggie Jackson and other Yankee greats; with DiMaggio, most of the Yankees remained silent until he spoke to them. Jeter, Darryl Strawberry, Cone and others mentioned how they never had the intestinal fortitude to ask DiMaggio for an autograph; you heard stories, Andy Pettitte said, about how he refused autograph requests. Cone, in fact, bought a dozen balls autographed by DiMaggio, rather than ask.

But DiMaggio repeatedly surprised them. Someone apparently mentioned to DiMaggio that right fielder Paul O'Neill had a collection of autographed bats, and before an Old-Timers' Day game, DiMaggio approached O'Neill and asked, "You have that bat for me to sign?" That bat, O'Neill said, is encased in his basement, "and always will be."

DiMaggio came face-to-face with Cone once, told him he had seen him pitch on many occasions. "Sometimes you look unhittable," DiMaggio said, "and sometimes you look very hittable." Cone laughed today, recalling the exchange. "I didn't know what to make of it," Cone said. "I walked away with my tail between my legs."

Andy and Laura Pettitte attended a team dinner following the 1996 World Series victory and DiMaggio happened by, looking for a place to sit. He took the chair next to the pitcher and chatted amiably during the meal. "He really was very nice," Pettitte said. DiMaggio once paused to compliment Bernie Williams, the latest heir in the Yankees' long line of superlative center fielders. The praise stunned Williams.

David Wells, traded to Toronto this spring, may have had the most extensive contact with DiMaggio. Before DiMaggio was honored before the final game of last season, on Joe DiMaggio Day, he congratulated Wells for his perfect game. Wells was so fidgety during the game that Manager Joe Torre facetiously suggested that he go bother DiMaggio -- and Wells did, taking the elevator to Steinbrenner's office.

Wells joined DiMaggio, Phil Rizzuto and Steinbrenner, gabbing and laughing. Wells asked DiMaggio -- "Mr. DiMaggio," Wells called him -- for an autograph and the Yankee legend obliged. "When he showed up at the Stadium,

George treated him like a king," Wells said today.

Some of the hundreds of fans who stopped at DiMaggio's plaque today mentioned DiMaggio's grace, his dominating presence on the field. Approaching DiMaggio's plaque, Pete Mastrobono, 86, removed his blue Yankees cap and covered his heart, silent words moving his lips. Now of Zephyr Hills, Fla., Mastrobono grew up in Westchester County and went to Yankee Stadium on Sundays with his friends, to watch DiMaggio. Mastrobono remembered, in his mind's eye, how DiMaggio slammed home runs, the way he slowed gracefully after rounding first base once he knew the ball had cleared the fence.

Mastrobono backed away from DiMaggio's plaque before removing his Yankees cap. His aged eyes bright, Mastrobono smiled and said, "I just said hi to old Joe." ◆

Joe DiMaggio in 1947.

4 THE STENGEL YEARS

When the Yankees hired Casey Stengel, people laughed—at him. In his nine seasons as a major league manager with the Brooklyn Dodgers and Boston Braves, his teams never finished higher than fifth. In his twelve seasons as a minor league manager in Worcester, Toledo, Milwaukee, Kansas City, and Oakland, only two of his teams won a pennant, twenty years apart. As an outfielder with a .284 career average for the Dodgers, Pirates, Phillies, Giants, and Braves, he was a class clown, once tipping his cap to a crowd's boos as a sparrow flew out of it. When he was introduced at the "21" Club as the Yankees manager for the 1949 season, he prompted more laughs when he said, "I want, first of all, to thank Mr. Bob Topping for this opportunity."

Oops! Dan Topping was the Yankees' co-owner, not his brother Bob.

And throughout Charles Dillon Stengel's twelve seasons speaking "Stengelese" to "my writers" covering the Yankees, people laughed too—with him. His Yankees teams won ten pennants and seven World Series, including a record five in a row in his first five years as manager. As he liked to say, you can look it up.

"He's not a clown," his wife, Edna, has said. "He's one of the smartest men in baseball, in business, in anything he'd try."

He was a vice president of a Glendale, California, bank. He owned Texas oil wells. And he knew baseball. George Weiss realized that. Years before, Weiss was the front-office boss of the New Haven, Connecticut, club in the Eastern League when Stengel was managing the Worcester, Massachusetts, team. He knew that Stengel, throughout his managerial travels, had never had a roster with much talent. But as the Yankees' general manager, Weiss knew he could provide Stengel with gifted players. After the Yankees skidded to third place under Bucky Harris in 1948, Weiss hired his old pal from the Eastern League.

"This is a big job, fellows," Stengel said, "and I barely have had time to study it."

He was a quick study. He managed Joe DiMaggio at the end, and he managed Mickey Mantle and Whitey Ford

★ ★ ★

Casey Stengel, nicknamed "The Ol' Perfessor," the manager of the Yankees from 1949 to 1960.

at the beginning. He consulted Yogi Berra, calling him "my assistant manager." He popularized the platoon system, using right-handed-hitting outfielder Hank Bauer against left-handed pitchers and left-handed-hitting outfielder Gene Woodling against right-handers. He persuaded the front office to purchase the fiery second baseman Billy Martin, whom he had managed at Oakland in the Pacific Coast League. He molded the Yankees' first African-American player, catcher Elston Howard, into a 12-time All-Star. He eased the departure of Vic Raschi, Allie Reynolds, and Eddie Lopat into the arrival of Bob Turley, Don Larsen, and Ryne Duren. He oversaw the transition from shortstop Phil Rizzuto and second baseman Jerry Coleman to Tony Kubek and Bobby Richardson. He used Gil McDougald at second base, third base, and shortstop. He installed Moose Skowron at first base. He presided over the arrival of Roger Maris.

Day after day, season after season, he preached his philosophy of baseball, and of life, to anybody who happened to be listening—players, writers, fans, politicians, even Washington lawmakers.

After instructing Mantle, then a rookie, on how to play a ball's ricochet off an outfield wall that he, as an outfielder himself, had coped with a quarter of a century earlier, Stengel said, "He thinks that I was born at the age of 62 and started managing immediately."

He once rambled on before a Senate antitrust committee headed by Senator Estes Kefauver.

"Mr. Stengel," Kefauver said, "I am not sure that I made my question clear."

"Well, that is all right," Stengel replied. "I'm not sure I am going to answer yours perfectly either."

In the World Series he played no favorites: His Yankees beat the Dodgers four times, lost once; beat the Braves once, lost once; beat the Giants once; beat the Phillies once; lost to the Pirates once on Bill Mazeroski's ninth-inning home run off Ralph Terry at Forbes Field in the decisive seventh game. The Yankees had outscored the Pirates, 55 runs to 27, but the Yankees front office thought that Stengel, at 70, was no longer sharp enough to continue as a day-to-day manager.

Two years earlier, in recalling his departure from other teams for the Senate committee, Stengel

»»»

〈〈〈 acknowledged that he had been discharged. "We call it discharged," he said, "because there is no question I had to leave."

His friend George Weiss also had to leave as general manager at the same time for the same reason: The Yankees owners considered each to be too old, too out of touch. Both soon resurfaced in New York with the Mets, the 1962 National League expansion team that replaced the departed Brooklyn Dodgers and New York Giants after they relocated to California following the 1957 season. As the Mets' general manager, Weiss hired—who else?—Stengel as manager. He was introduced to the news media in the same ballroom where the Yankees had discharged him: Le Salon Bleu of the Savoy Hilton Hotel.

"My health," he said, "my health is good enough above the shoulders, and I didn't say I'd stay fifty years or five years. Most people are dead at my age, and you could look it up."

You also could look up that the 1962 Mets, playing in the decrepit but freshly painted Polo Grounds, had a decrepit 40–120 record, 60 and a half games out of first place—but to their manager, they were "my amazing Mets." They lost 111 the next season, then 109, and were on their way to 112 losses in 1965 when, on July 25, five days before his 75th birthday, Stengel was hospitalized with a broken left hip. He had slipped in the washroom of Toots Shor's restaurant after an Old-Timers' Day dinner. He would never manage again.

In telling his Mets players good-bye at Shea Stadium, he said, "If you keep on, you can be here four or ten years." As always, with the Yankees or the Mets, he left them laughing—with him.

October 13, 1948

STENGEL SIGNS AS YANKS' MANAGER WITH 2-YEAR CONTRACT

'Big Job' Confronts Pilot of Bombers

By JOHN DREBINGER

MEET THE NEW MANAGER of the Yankees: Charles Dillon (Casey) Stengel, one-time hard hitting outfielder, manager of both major and minor league clubs, sage, wit and gifted raconteur as glib with the wisecrack as the late Jimmy Walker.

Stengel's appointment, rumored for more than a week while the baseball people were engrossed in their world series, became official yesterday when the Yankee co-owners, Dan Topping and Del Webb, made the announcement at the 21 Club amid a terrific turmoil as press photographers, television operators and radio commentators strove to put the momentous event over with a crash. Stengel signed a two-year contract for an undisclosed salary.

In time, a bewildered Casey got in a word with his old pals, the baseball writers, many of whom he had known for more than a quarter of a century. He said, "This is a big job, fellows, and I barely have had time to study it. In fact, I scarcely know where I am at." In the circumstances that's understandable.

CASEY JOINS OLD FOES

Thus, twenty-five years to the day after he had played a prominent role in the fortunes of the Yankees he was back to direct the club he once defeated almost single-handedly in a world series game. For it was on Oct. 12, 1923, at the Stadium that Stengel, then playing for John McGraw's Giants, hit a home run off Sad Sam Jones in the seventh inning to produce the tally that beat the Yankees, 1 to 0.

Two days previously he had hit a homer to beat the Yankees, 5 to 4. Those circuit clouts provided the Giants' only victories in a series won by the Yanks, four games to two.

The 57-year-old Stengel succeeds Bucky Harris who, engaged by Larry MacPhail before the 1947 campaign, won a pennant and world championship in his first year with the Yanks and this year kept what generally was regarded a badly outmatched club in the race until next to the last day, only to be dismissed for a reason as yet not explained by anyone.

In the light of this, most observers, always kindly disposed toward the engaging Stengel, were viewing his forthcoming assignment with some misgivings. But the ever-ready Casey made it clear he was not likely to become overawed by his prospects.

No Upheaval in Prospect

"There'll likely be some changes," said the new skipper, "but it's a good club and I think we'll do all right. We'll go slow because you can tear a club down a lot quicker than you can build it up."

Born in Kansas City, Mo., with the initials K. C. providing the origin of his nickname, Casey launched his professional career with Kankakee, Ill. He went to Brooklyn in 1912, and then subsequently beat a trail that was to see him play for the Pirates, Phillies, Giants and Braves.

Casey's rows with umpires stand as classics, one of his most brilliant performances having occurred one day when he strode to the plate, bowed to the arbiter and doffed his cap, from which a sparrow escaped. Just what he plans to spring out of his cap for the Yankees next spring is a matter which gives much food for speculation. ◆

October 3, 1949

YANKS WHIP RED SOX IN SEASON FINALE TO WIN 16TH AMERICAN LEAGUE PENNANT

By JOHN DREBINGER

PERHAPS IT WAS DESTINED from the very beginning that Casey Stengel and his amazing Yankees were to win this 1949 American League pennant.

At all events, this is what happened amid the thunderous roars of 68,055 frenzied fans at the Stadium yesterday as the battered Bombers, behind the stout hearted hurling of their big right-hander, Vic Raschi, brought down Joe McCarthy's Red Sox, 5 to 3, in the final game of the campaign.

The victory, the second achieved in two 〉〉〉

Red Sox shortstop Vern Stephens and second baseman Bobby Doerr watch a ball thrown by Stephens' as Yogi Berra slides during the final game of the 1949 season.

◀◀◀ successive afternoons over Boston's power-laden cast, snapped the first-place deadlock with which the two clubs had begun the day and brought to the Yankees their sixteenth league championship.

It was a breath-taking battle, of a sort scarcely reflected in the cold figures of the final score, that was waged by those astonishingly inspired Bombers, whose chances had looked so forlorn on Saturday as they squared off with the mighty Bosox, a full game behind.

For eight innings, Raschi, behind a one-run lead which a triple by Li'l Phil Rizzuto had given him in the opening round, blanked Boston's formidable array on two hits in a tense mound duel with Ellis Kinder, who was gunning for his twenty-fourth victory of the year.

Then, in the last of the eighth, came a swirl of action that was to close out the spectacle in a blazing climax. With Kinder stepping aside for a pinch-hitter, a desperate McCarthy called on Mel Parnell, his 25-game winning southpaw, to hold the Bombers for one more round until his own clouters could have their final chance.

But Tommy Henrich, the indomitable Old Reliable, crashed a home run into the right-field stands and when, a few moments later, Tex Hughson replaced Parnell, the Bombers, in the manner of a true thoroughbred heading straight for the wire, closed with an exploding burst.

They filled the bases and in the twinkling of an eye they were emptied as Jerry Coleman, 25-year-old rookie second baseman, cleared the sacks with a pop fly two-bagger into short right field.

That final four-run outburst was to carry the day, for in the top half of the ninth the aroused Bosox lashed back with a deal of pent-up fury. With another world series chance slipping through their fingers for the second successive year, they ripped into Raschi for three runs.

The first pair rode home on the wings of a triple, which Bobby Doerr walloped over the head of a Joe DiMaggio, who was now running on shaky legs. At this point the Clipper called time and dramatically took himself out of the game.

He received a great ovation as he jogged into the Yankee dugout, for the fans understood well enough why he was leaving. He had been a sick man these past three weeks, fighting off a virus infection, and he was still far from recovered. It was, therefore, a move of excellent foresight on the part of the famed Clipper who, with victory almost within grasp, wasn't going to let it slip away through any physical shortcomings of his own.

Hastily Stengel re-formed his picket line, something he had been doing all year with his injury-riddled Bombers, and when play was resumed a Bosox single drove in another tally. Three were in and the tying run was at the plate.

But Raschi never allowed it to get any farther. Birdie Tebbetts lifted a high pop foul which Henrich caught just back of first base and so Vic finished on his own power with his twenty-first victory of the year.

VICTOR IN FIRST YEAR

Thus 60-year-old Charles Dillon Stengel in his first year in the American League becomes the fourth manager to bring home a pennant to the most amazingly successful baseball organization of modern times. The sixteenth pennant not only added one more to the American League record which the Bombers already have held, but it enabled the Yanks to tie the all-time major league high of sixteen held by Chicago's National League club which won its first flag in 1876. ◆

Yankee Pennant Winners

Year.	Manager.	W.	L.	PC.
1921	Miller J. Huggins	98	55	.641
1922	Miller J. Huggins	94	60	.610
•1923	Miller J Huggins	98	54	.645
1926	Miller J. Huggins	91	63	.591
•1927	Miller J Huggins	110	44	.714
•1928	Miller J. Huggins	101	53	.656
•1932	Joseph V. McCarthy	107	47	.695
•1936	Joseph V. McCarthy	102	51	.667
•1937	Joseph V. McCarthy	102	52	.662
•1938	Joseph V. McCarthy	99	53	.651
•1939	Joseph V. McCarthy	106	45	.702
•1941	Joseph V. McCarthy	101	53	.656
1942	Joseph V. McCarthy	103	51	.669
•1943	Joseph V. McCarthy	98	56	.636
•1947	Stanley R Harris	97	57	.630
1949	Charles D. Stengel	97	57	.630

•World series winner

October 10, 1949

YANKS WIN SERIES, BEATING DODGERS IN FIFTH GAME, 10-6

JOE PAGE IS HERO AGAIN

By JOHN DREBINGER

CASEY STENGEL AND HIS YANKEES, who took off last spring on a forlorn hope only to wing their way to the American League pennant, brought a year of remarkable achievement to a triumphant close yesterday as they crushed the Dodgers in the fifth and final game of the 1949 world series.

Battering six of Burt Shotton's hurlers for a total of eleven hits, which included an eye-filling home run by the still ailing Joe DiMaggio, the Bombers vanquished their National League rivals by a score of 10 to 6.

The result, witnessed by a crowd of 33,711, including Governor Dewey and Mayor O'Dwyer, gave the classic to the American Leaguers by a margin of four games to one. It was their twelfth world championship, a record without parallel in baseball history.

For the first time in a world series the great

batteries of electric lights atop the stands were turned on in the ninth inning to safeguard against the possibility that encroaching darkness might interfere with a definite decision. But the additional illumination, which cast an eerie light in the autumn dusk, was scarcely needed to reveal the disparity between the two teams.

For though the Dodgers, trailing at one stage, 10 to 1, fought valiantly enough, bringing heart to their Flatbush legions with a stirring four-run rally in the seventh that routed the Yanks' starting ace, Vic Raschi, three of the tallies riding in on a circuit blow by Gil Hodges, they then crashed head-on into a stone wall. »»

Yankees celebrate their 1949 World Series win over the Dodgers: Left to right: Phil Rizzuto, Cliff Mapes, Casey Stengel, Charlie Silvera (partially hidden by Joe Page-foreground), Gus Niarhos, and Fred Sanford.

<<<

The incomparable Joe Page, making his third appearance of the series, took over with two out in the seventh and from that moment to the end they might just as well have plunged the entire arena into total darkness.

In sharp contrast with the earlier games—the first two contests were decided by 1-0 margins—this one was a slam-bang affair in which each side struck eleven blows. But the Yankees, capitalizing on the early wildness of Shotton's starting hurler, Rex Barney, did the more effective slamming and they did it first.

Bobby Brown, a thorn in the side of the Dodgers just as he was in 1947 with his three pinch hits, touched off a triple and two singles. Gene Woodling contributed three hits, two of them doubles. The youngster, Jerry Coleman, finished Barney in the third with a two-run single with the bases full. And so it went, on down the line.

But it was the DiMaggio homer, struck off Banta with the bases empty in the fourth, that struck the most responsive chord among the jubilant American Leaguers in the crowd.

Earlier in the day there had been a report that DiMaggio, suffering from a recurrence of a virus infection, had been taken to a hospital with a fever of 103. This was found to be untrue.

But the Clipper was still far from being a well man. In the four previous games he had come up with just one skimpy infield hit and he admitted he was some eighteen pounds below his normal weight.

He was determined to go through with the show to the end. He drove in the first Yankee run with a tremendous fly and the homer, the sixth of his career in world series competition, capped the day for the Yankee star. The ultimate victory gave the Clipper the added distinction of having actively participated with a world series winner for the seventh time, matching the series records of Babe Ruth and Bill Dickey.

By far the most dazzling achievement of all was that turned in by Charles Dillon Stengel, 60-year-old grizzled campaigner, wit and philosopher and regarded by many up to this year as mostly clown. For to the popular Casey now comes his first world title in his first year in the American League.

Back in 1923 as a Giant, Stengel as a player had beaten the Yankees in two games of a world series, but the Yanks eventually went on to win the prize. Perhaps it was then Casey set himself to the ancient formula, "If you can't beat a racket, get in with it." ◆

January 20, 1950

Page Chosen Outstanding '49 Series Player

By JOHN DREBINGER

SEEMS THERE IS NO END to the laurels showered on the Yankees. Joe Page moved into the spotlight yesterday as the latest in line for signal honors.

The New York Chapter of the Baseball Writers Association of America announced that it has named the Bombers' matchless relief hurler for the Babe Ruth Memorial Award as the outstanding player of the 1949 world series.

The Ruth award will become an annual fixture and in deciding to limit it to world series competition the scribes felt that in no other form could they pay greater tribute to the memory of the immortal Bambino. For it was in the autumn classics that the Babe set nineteen world series records, seventeen of these as a batter, two as a pitcher.

Page easily was the standout of the 1949 Yankees' triumph over the Dodgers. He appeared in three of the five games and received credit for winning the third encounter when he hurled the last five and one-third innings to bring the Bombers home in front, 4 to 3. In all he pitched a total of nine innings, allowing six hits, two runs, fanning eight and walking three. ◆

February 5, 1950

SPORTS OF THE TIMES
The Scooter and the Ol' Perfessor

By ARTHUR DALEY

IT HAPPENED thirteen years ago. The Brooklyn Dodgers were holding tryouts at Ebbets Field under the searching gaze of their manager, Casey Stengel.

"Go peddle your papers, little boy," said Stengel to one undersized tyro. "You're too small ever to become a major leaguer."

Phil Rizzuto gulped hard, fighting back the tears. He was only a kid of 18 and hope was fading much too rapidly for him. Pancho Snyder hadn't even given him a second glance when little Phil had reported to him at the Polo Grounds in a valiant effort to become a Giant—in name anyway. Now the Ol' Perfessor also was giving him the gate.

Only the Yankees were left for the boy from Richmond Hill High School and he knew full well that the Yanks would never keep what Giants and Dodgers had discarded so summarily. But he was a determined little cuss. He'd at least make the effort. What had he to lose?

So Rizzuto became just another number among scores of oddly assorted ball players on tryout day. The usual procedure is to weed out the culls as rapidly as possible, discarding the fellows who are too slow, too weak of arm or too small. If it hadn't been for the Yankee eagle scout, Paul Krichell, the chances are that little Phil would have been whisked into oblivion quickly.

REFLEXES OF A CAT
Even today Krich can't explain why he held the Scooter for a second look. "I still don't know what I saw in him," he has since confessed, "unless it was that he had quick hands and the reflexes of a cat. What probably sold me on him was that Phil hit one ball into the stands. That was the convincer."

Paul Pettit received $100,000 last week for

Casey Stengel talks with shortstop Phil Rizzuto (10) in the early 1950s.

signing with the Pirates. Rizzuto received as his "bonus" the munificent reward of one container of milk and a couple of sandwiches. Once the inner man had been thus appeased, Krich slyly offered Rizzuto a fountain pen and contract. The Scooter practically broke an arm in his eagerness to sign.

One day in the closing stages of last season's pennant race the mischievous Rizzuto strolled into Stengel's office. He scuffed the carpet in feigned embarrassment and grew so suddenly formal that the Ol' Perfesser became alarmed.

RHETORICAL QUESTION
"Mister Stengel, sir," he said, a deadpan expression masking his face. "Do you still think I'm too small to become a major leaguer?"

Casey chased him right out the door with a baseball bat. Only when the two had met in St. Petersburg last March did either recall the occasion of their first meeting at Ebbets Field so »» many years before. But a sense of delicacy prevented each from mentioning the subject until Phil gave it back to Ol' Case with both barrels.

The two will meet once more tonight as the twin honored guests of the New York Chapter of the Baseball Writers Association at the Waldorf-Astoria. Stengel will receive a plaque for honorable service to the sport over a period of years. Rizzuto will receive a plaque as the athlete of the year. It's quite possible that neither of them would be there if it hadn't been for the other.

Each of them will appreciate his plaque to the full, but laughter bubbles out of their hearts so richly and spontaneously that neither will be at all impressed with his own importance. That isn't the way either is built.

As a matter of fact, there never was a more significant line spoken than the one the Ol' Perfesser uttered a couple of months ago. He had been named as the "Manager of the Year" for 1949. It just so happened that he encountered Billy Meyer of the Pirates, the "Manager of the Year" in 1948. Meyer, as you will recall, had had a most disappointing season last year, his Pirates finishing a dismal sixth.

A RAPID SWITCH

"Hiya, Bill," said Stengel in greeting, an amused glint in his eyes. "Didn't I get bright quick and didn't you get dumb?"

Casey has been around much too long to think that only his personal genius was responsible for the winning of a world championship. For all of his previous baseball life he'd been connected with chronic second division misfits.

"I won't fail," he kept repeating at St. Pete, almost like a man trying to convince himself of something he doesn't believe. "I never had so many good ball players before."

The most reliable of these, of course, was Rizzuto, who missed hardly a game and was the cement which held together the patched-up Yankee organization. Without him the Yanks would have become unstuck—and good.

It's nice that they are being honored together. They deserve it. ◆

October 8, 1950

BOMBERS' HEROES MOBBED BY MATES

Ford, Berra and DiMaggio Are Besieged in the Clubhouse After Series Triumph

By JAMES P. DAWSON

IT WAS AN OLD STORY with the Yankees, a familiar tune in the victory strain inside the clubhouse of the noisy band which yesterday trooped off the Stadium field with the 5-to-2 victory over the Phillies for a clean sweep of the four world series games against the National League champions.

The place was a scene of noisy celebration. Headed by Coach Frankie Crosetti, Pitcher Ed Lopat, Manager Casey Stengel and Coach Bill Dickey, this smiling, happy band came trooping into the clubhouse yelling and stamping and smacking each other on the back or playfully roughing each other up. The racket that started with the stamp and scrape of spiked feet and swelled gradually, in an amazingly brief period, to roaring volume as, spontaneously, the clubhouse presented a mob scene.

Here was the club that had just won its fourth straight series game for a sweep, the squad which had achieved this enviable distinction no fewer than six times, a club happily celebrating its thirteenth world series triumph. Its members, veterans of the campaigns and the rookies in the squad, were making the most of it.

The rookie pitcher, Whitey Ford, who missed finishing the first world series game of his career because of a last enemy threat; Yogi Berra, the

Whitey Ford, left, celebrates the 1950 World Series win manager Casey Stengel.

clubber who festooned this finale with an authoritative home run; Allie Reynolds, the husky right-hander who throttled the Phillies' uprising before it assumed damaging proportions; Joe DiMaggio, the slugger who hit the only other homer of a series many expected would hold more of these round-trippers, these were the besieged.

These, and a weary, gray-haired leader, Casey Stengel, who was full of praise for his players, lavish with compliments for his beaten rivals, who modestly deflected the compliments aimed at him—and who was uncertain of the future, who was talking as though he seriously was considering retiring.

Here was an amazing development, to be sure. The man whose exploits as player and manager in the major leagues were legendary before he went back down to the minors, the popular figure who came back from the minors to pilot baseball's most valuable property into two successive American League pennants and as many world series triumphs, was talking of giving it all up and enjoying the ease all seek with advancing years.

Listeners were taken by surprise when the announcement came. It was in response to Casey's plans for the winter.

"Of only one thing am I sure for the winter,"

said Stengel. "I am going to duck the banquet circuit. I'm going to try and conserve my strength and protect my health by taking it easy. I don't know whether I'm coming back next year. My contract's up this year. It has three months to run. I never said this before, but I get twelve checks a year, not six.

"I'm 60 years old now. I'm too old for that banquet stuff. You get no rest. And, if you don't get rest now how can you keep coming back for such a hard struggle as we've had this year. I was sick in the spring; if I feel all right next year, I'll be back. I don't expect to have any trouble over contract matters with my bosses if I decide to come back. I never have had any trouble on contracts with anybody. I've never had a contract I couldn't get out of, either. I imagine they'll want me back again, but it will depend upon my health. If you don't feel right you can't take over a job like this without going batty. And, nobody wants to do that."

The blond-haired rookie, Ford, was surrounded in the melee, but smiled gallantly through his first such ordeal. He had no complaint at being "lifted" in that threatening ninth inning.

"When Casey came out after Woodling lost Seminick's drive, I was afraid he was going to take me out and I didn't want to leave," said the youth. "If he had it would have been all right. He hasn't made a mistake yet. But I wanted to stay and he let me. To me it was like pitching any other game. I felt all right. When Goliat hit that single, I figured I was losing my stuff and when Casey came out I was ready to go. He said 'I'm going to bring in a strong-armed guy to finish this thing.' And he did. Reynolds did exactly that. I would have liked to finish, of course, but I'm not too disappointed. The club won. That's the big thing."

Manager Stengel felt the impact of the boos which rang from the stands when he yanked Ford in the ninth, with the tying run at the plate, but he forgot about this in a few moments when Reynolds strong-armed pinch-hitter Stan Lopata into striking out to end the game.

"Ford pitched a great game, and maybe I shouldn't have taken him out," said Stengel. "But, I had to protect the lead. It was baseball. >>>

<<< They weren't hitting the kid hard. That one Goliat shot between third and short wasn't a hard-hit ball. The hardest hit ball was the one Woodling dropped. When you're in a spot like that you throw the ball over the plate and let them hit it. You don't walk a man. Ford was doing all right. But, self-protection dictated I call in a fresh, strong arm.

"I had Ferrick and Reynolds warmed up in the bull pen and I knew either could finish it quickly. This was the time to do it. I can understand the sentiment of the crowd. It was a tough spot. But, I had to do it and then it was over." ◆

October 27, 1950

RIZZUTO OF YANKS IS MOST VALUABLE

By JOSEPH M. SHEEHAN

TO THE UNBOUNDED DELIGHT of Yankee adherents, who had screamed to the high heavens when he was passed over in favor of Ted Williams a year ago, Phil Rizzuto yesterday officially was proclaimed the American League's most valuable player of 1950.

The dashing little shortstop, widely hailed as the "indispensable man" of the world champion Bombers, won in a landslide. He polled 284 points of a possible 322 and was top choice of sixteen of the twenty-three voting members of the Baseball Writers Association of America.

Billy Goodman, Red Sox utility star who captured the league batting title, and Catcher Larry Berra, a Yankee team-mate, divided the first-place votes that were denied to Rizzuto. Goodman, runner-up with 180 points, was on top in four ballots. Berra, third with 146 points, was favored by three writers.

With five other players besides Rizzuto and Berra receiving mention, the Yankees, befitting their status as league champions and world series winners, dominated the list. Vic Raschi finished seventh, Joe DiMaggio ninth and Johnny Mize tied for seventeenth. Whitey Ford and Ed Lopat also were remembered.

Selection of Rizzuto marked the ninth time in the twenty-nine-year history of the official voting for this award that a Yankee finished on top. Babe Ruth was named in 1923, Lou Gehrig in 1927 and 1936, DiMaggio in 1939, 1941 and 1947, Joe Gordon in 1942 and Spud Chandler in 1943. ◆

American League President Will Harridge, right, presents Phil Rizzuto with the Most Valuable Player award for 1950.

July 13, 1951

Reynolds No-Hits Indians

By JOHN DREBINGER
Special to The New York Times.

CLEVELAND, JULY 12—Allie Reynolds, ace righthander of the Yankees, tonight became the third major league hurler and second in the American circuit to spin a no-hitter this year as he hurled the Bombers to a 1-0 triumph over the Indians in the opener of a three-game series before 39,195 fans.

The victim of Reynold's sterling performance was Bob Feller, who on July 1 had turned in the third no-hitter of his career on this same field.

Rapid Robert kept pace with Reynolds for five and one-third innings but Mickey Mantle cracked him for a double with one out in the sixth.

Then, in the seventh, Feller gave up another blow and that one was to decide the battle. For it was a home run clout by Gene Woodling that cleared the right-field barrier at the 365-foot mark. In all, Feller gave up four blows as he went down to his third defeat against twelve victories.

Reynolds gave a masterful demonstration of his skill as he made this the first no-hitter of his career and the first to be turned in by a Yankee hurler since Monte Pearson flashed one against another tribe of Indians in 1938 at the Yankee Stadium.

Four Indians managed to get to first base, three on passes, one on a first-inning error by Phil Rizzuto. Only one member of Al Lopez' Tribe got as far as third, however. ◆

September 29, 1951

YANKS CLINCH FLAG, AIDED BY REYNOLDS' NO-HITTER

By JOHN DREBINGER

IN A BRILLIANT DISPLAY of all-around skill that included a nerve tingling no-hitter in one encounter and a seven-run explosion in the other, the Yankees yesterday clinched the 1951 American League pennant. It was their third flag in a row and eighteenth in thirty years.

With Allie Reynolds tossing his second no-hitter of the year—a feat previously achieved by only one other hurler in history—the Bombers vanquished the Red Sox in the opener of the double-header at the Stadium, 8 to 0.

Then, behind big Vic Raschi, the Stengeleers crushed the already eliminated Bosox, 11 to 3, to the cheers of 39,038 fans. Joe DiMaggio further embellished the triumph with a three-run homer as another flag was nailed to the Yankee masthead.

In yesterday's smashing Yankee triumph, Reynolds' masterful performance provided most of the thrills, making even the clinching of the pennant somewhat anti-climatic.

Those who sat in on the show are not likely to forget those last tense moments when Reynolds, who had walked four batters during the game, had to collect "twenty-eight outs" before reaching his goal.

With two out in the ninth and the still fearsome Ted Williams at bat, a high foul was struck back of home plate. Yogi Berra, usually sure on these, scampered under it but in the next agonizing moment the ball squirmed out of his glove as the Yanks chunky backstop went sprawling on his face.

It meant Williams would have to be pitched to some more. But Reynolds, an amazingly good-natured competitor under the most trying circumstances, patted Berra consolingly on the back and said, "Don't worry, Yogi, we'll get him again."

And, sure enough, up went another high, ⟫⟫

‹‹‹ twisting foul off to the right side of the plate. It looked tougher than the first one. But Yogi meant to catch this one if it burst a girth rope and as he finally froze the ball directly in front of the Yankee dugout, Reynolds first, and virtually all the other Yanks jubilantly piled on top of him. For a moment it looked as if Berra, not Reynolds was the hero of the occasion.

Only one other major league hurler has ever fired two no-hitters in one season, and none ever in the American League. In 1938, Johnny Vander Meer, Cincinnati southpaw, turned in two on successive mound appearances, holding the Braves hitless on June 11 and repeating the trick on June 15 against the Dodgers in the first night game played in Ebbets Field. ◆

October 11, 1951

YANKS WIN SERIES AS BAUER'S TRIPLE TOPS GIANTS, 4 TO 3

American League Team Takes Third World Title in Row, by Four Games to Two

By JOHN DREBINGER

THE YANKEES TURNED BACK a fighting band of Giants in the sixth game of the 1951 world series at the Stadium yesterday, 4 to 3, and with that

rang down the curtain on one of the most thrill-packed baseball campaigns on record.

For with this triumph, achieved before 61,711 onlookers, the famed Bombers, on the wings of a base-clearing triple by Hank Bauer, hauled down the winners' share, four games to two, for their third world championship in a row and fourteenth in eighteen chances.

Also, it gave to 61-year-old Charles Dillon (Casey) Stengel the distinction of becoming the first manager ever to win three world titles in a row in his first three years in a league, not to mention adding still another victory to the overwhelming total the American League has piled up over its older rival.

For this marked the American circuit's thirty-first triumph in world series play against only seventeen for the National.

Durocher's last hope, Dave Koslo, was battling big Vic Raschi in a one-all tie when Bauer, coming up with the bases full in the sixth inning, swept the sacks with a three-bagger that sailed over the head of Monte Irvin in left field. That shot put the Bombers in front, 4 to 1.

But those extraordinary Giants, who had overcome a similar deficit in their electrifying play-off finish with the Dodgers, almost did it again.

Then, in the top of the ninth, they finally broke through to fill the bases on three successive hits. At this point Stengel, who somehow always seems to have the right card at his disposal, called on his southpaw relief star Bob Kuzava for perhaps as deep and mystifying a piece of managerial strategy as any world series has seen.

Eddie Stanky had singled to left, Alvin Dark had outgalloped a bunt and Lockman had pounded another single into right to fill the bases when the left-handed Kuzava came in to face Irvin, who already had eleven hits to his credit in the first five games and was seeking his twelfth to tie a series record.

The Negro star blasted a tremendous fly into deep left center. Gene Woodling caught it, but Stanky scored. The other two moved up to second and third.

Next came Bobby Thomson, who had so spectacularly blasted the Dodgers out of the series with his epic three-run homer in the ninth of the play-off final last Wednesday. The setting, in fact, was identical, with first base open, the Scot at the plate.

Now the Strategy Works

And here, for the benefit of the game's outstanding academic minds, it might be pointed out that Stengel pursued the same strategy as had Chuck Dressen.

He too had his hurler pitch deliberately to Thomson. But where the move had spelled complete disaster for the Dodger skipper, it worked well enough for Ol' Case.

Thomson hit a towering fly in deep left center that Woodling also caught, and though, like the Irvin effort, it scored a runner as Dark came easing in from third, the Giants were still one short and down to their last out, the tying run still at second.

In this dire extremity, Durocher, woefully short of pinch-hitting material throughout the series, called on his third string catcher. Sal Yvars who, like Thomson and Irvin, swings from the right side Sal smacked the first pitch on a line toward right and for a moment it appeared that the Giants had extricated themselves again.

But Bauer, a determined fellow, wasn't going to let this great victory, gained largely by his own efforts, slip away. He dashed directly in front of the drive, caught it while tumbling to the turf for the final out and the Giants breathed their last.

Stengel had called on a left handed pitcher to stop three long ball hitting right-handed batsmen and, disdaining to give up a single intentional pass, had got away with it. ◆

The players line up before the start of 1951 World Series between the New York Yankees and the New York Giants.

Ebbets Field during 1952 World Series.

October 8, 1952

YANKS DEFEAT DODGERS

Stengel Ties Managerial Mark as Team Gains Fourth Title in Row, 4 Games to 3

By JOHN DREBINGER

AS THE BIG CLOCK atop of the scoreboard in Ebbets Field turned 3:55 yesterday afternoon a dramatic baseball season came to a close with a grizzled 62-year-old campaigner cheering himself hoarse at the very moment an entire borough found itself plunged deep in gloom.

For as the Yankees, perennial champions of the American League, conquered Chuck Dressen's Dodgers in the seventh and deciding game, 4 to 2, to win the 1952 world series, 4 games to 3, Charles Dillon (Casey) Stengel became the second manager in history to bag four such titles in a row.

The feat, viewed with mingled feelings by a crowd of 33,195, tied the four-straight record notched by Joseph V. McCarthy with another team of Yankees from 1936 through 1939.

For Brooklyn, though, the result closed another year on a note of frustration. It marked the sixth time since 1916 a Dodger club had striven to win a world championship only to meet with failure.

Three times those determined Dodgers had stormed into the lead by taking the first, third and fifth games. Each time the Bombers caught them and then when it came to that last odd numbered battle, which the Stengeleers couldn't afford to lose, the Yanks simply made off with it to capture their fifteenth world title, a record without parallel.

The victory was achieved, too, in a whirlwind struggle that left the fans exhausted as the Bombers scored their runs singly from the fourth through the seventh inning. The first came on a blazing single by mighty Johnny Mize. The next two on a pair of eye-filling homers that Gene Woodling and Mickey Mantle exploded in the fifth and sixth rounds, while for an encore the precocious Mickey slammed home the fourth in the seventh with a single.

And when this heroic bid was threatened with failure, since Eddie Lopat had crashed in the fourth and a tired Raschi was stumbling badly in a brief appearance in the seventh, the Ol' Perfessor came up with perhaps his most astounding move of the entire series.

He called on a tall, blond left-hander who had

seen little service in the closing weeks of the pennant race, but whom world series observers had occasion to remember. For he was Bob Kuzava, the same lefty who last October had come out of the shadows of the bullpen to slam the door on the Giants.

Yesterday the tall Michigander made it a repeat performance as he stepped to the rubber in that sizzling seventh with the bases full and only one out and turned back the redoubtable Duke Snider and Jackie Robinson on the end of a pair of pop flies.

At that the Robinson pop-up came within a whisker of producing the most amazing thriller of all. It looked simple enough as Billy Martin, Yank second sacker, stalked in for it. But the ball seemed to get caught in a wind eddy that sent it back toward the plate, and Martin, now racing at top speed, since no one else could interfere in such a ticklish spot, just about made it with a head-long dive.

Since there already were two out, all three base runners were in full flight and doubtless all three would have scored had that ball fallen safely.

After that play Kuzava, who last October had turned back Monte Irvin, Bobby Thomson and Sal Yvars to snuff out the Giants' last grasp at the Polo Grounds, never gave the Brooks another chance, although credit for the victory went to Reynolds, who worked three innings.

It was the Chief's second triumph of the series and brought his victory total in world championship competition to six, the highest of any of today's active pitchers. ◆

December 18, 1952

CAUTIONED ON BIAS, ROBINSON ADMITS

JACKIE ROBINSON said yesterday that he had talked with Commissioner Ford Frick concerning a television interview in which the Brooklyn infielder had accused the Yankees of discriminating against Negro players.

Robinson added, however, he had not been "silenced" by the commissioner but simply had been asked to avoid such issues in the future.

"Frick called," the Dodger second baseman told The Associated Press, "and asked for a transcript of the interview. I told him exactly what had taken place at the studio. The question was brought to me, 'do you think the Yankee management is prejudiced against Negro ball players?' I answered 'yes.' That's all I said. I didn't elaborate except to add that as far as the Yankee ball players were concerned, they were some of the finest I've ever met. I merely said what I honestly felt. Whether it's true I do not know, but that's the way I felt.

"Frick asked me to avoid the issue in the future if I could do so and I said 'certainly.' But I also told him while I was not looking for any arguments with Yankees or anybody else, I would give the same answer if I were ever asked the same question again.

"As I told the commissioner, I'm not looking for any arguments with anybody but I have to live honestly with myself. That's the way I felt about it then and that's the way I feel about it now. There are thousands upon thousands of people in Harlem who feel the same way. Maybe we're wrong. But that's the way I feel. I've at least tried to be honest as in everything I've done. I've made mistakes before but they were honest ones. I hope I'm mistaken in this too.

"Please remember this. I didn't bring it up. I was just asked a question and I merely answered it simply and honestly. But why all the fuss? Nothing more would have been said about it if the Yankees hadn't blown it up. I've been asked that same question a number of times before and I've always given the same answer. Nobody ever made much of it before." ◆

July 26, 1953

Philosophy of C. Stengel

The sage skipper of the New York Yankees expounds on the fickle fates of baseball.

By ARTHUR DALEY

WHEN CASEY STENGEL WAS managing the Brooklyn Dodgers many years ago, his maladroit and hapless heroes had just lost a double-header to the Cincinnati Reds in typically preposterous

Casey Stengel in the Yankee dugout during Game 6 of the 1952 World Series.

fashion, thereby extending their long losing streak to heaven knows what. After the second game, Stengel dropped into a barber shop and ordered a shave. "But don't bother to cut my throat," he said dispiritedly. "I might want to do it myself later on."

However, this same Charles Dillon Stengel never dreamed for an instant of slicing his gullet when his New York Yankees recently plunged into a nine-game losing streak, a failing which was all the more dispiriting because it had followed immediately on the heels of an eighteen-game winning streak. "Why should I?" said the Ol' Perfessor the other day, a challenging ring in his voice. "I got me a good ball club. When I was with the Dodgers and with the Braves, I didn't have nuthin'. I specialized in losin' streaks."

He shook his head slowly in obvious puzzlement. "Maybe I'm too dumb to learn from experience," he continued. "But a slump and how to get outa one is a complete mystery to me. It ain't like a gallstone or a busted appendix that you can diagnose with X-rays. I can't explain a losin' streak any better than I can a winnin' streak. And I just had both."

He winked suggestively. The wink is the Ol' Perfessor's favorite punctuation mark, often his only one. He frequently launches into monologues which lack subjects or predicates or conjunctions or coherence. This private version of the English language is known as "Stengelese" and normally contains double negatives, slurred final consonants, an utter lack of identification for persons mentioned and fascinating non sequiturs. Yet he can be as grammatical as a Shakespearean scholar when he so elects.

"Like I wuz sayin'," he resumed. "No one can explain winnin' or losin' streaks. When you're winnin', you're doin' everything right. You get every break imaginable. Even the baseball itself seems to cooperate, bouncin' away from their fielders in favor of your hitters or bouncin' into your fielders' gloves to stop their hitters. Then all of a sudden the slump comes. You seem to be doin' everything the same way, livin' right and drinkin' your orange juice. But something has happened and you can't find the handle to it.

"The only thing I know about a winnin' streak is that all four departments are workin' for you. You're getting' the pitchin', the hittin', the field-in' and the spirit of your ball club is tree-men-dous. The ball players feel better and keep impr-ovin'. Nothin' can hop up a pitchin' staff faster than to have a pitcher win every time he pitches. The batters seem to bat better and field better.

"But when we lost those nine straight, every-thing fell apart at once. Our battin' wuz bad, our fieldin' wuz bad, our pitchin' wuz bad and our managin' wuz bad. And judgin' by what I read in the newspapers, the Yankee writers wuz in a slump, too. They didn't do so good, either."

The Ol' Perfessor winked slyly. "Fans mailed me in all sorts of good luck charms to help break our slump," he said. "I knew they wouldn't help none and I'll tell you why. I discovered in my last year as a player with the Giants that nuthin' helped my hittin' more than for me to step on second base as I ran in from the outfield to take my turn at bat. I musta been hittin' something like .330. But then John McGraw recklessly tossed away his chance to win his fifth straight pennant—ahem!—by tradin' me to Boston. I still faithfully stepped on second base in comin' in from the outfield, but I had a real bad year. It cured me of bein' superstitious.

"When you're goin' bad, nuthin' works. Even the manager keeps havin' one bad day after another. I couldn't make a mistake when we were rippin' off those eighteen victories in a row. I'd send up a pinch hitter and he'd belt one. I'd make a sub-stitution and he'd come through for me. My strat-egy clicked a hunnert per cent. But in the losin' streak, I couldn't behave like a genius at all. I'd order a hit-and-run, never realizin' that the feller at bat ain't hittin'. That makes it a dangerous play, a stupid play. Maybe I see that my pitcher's gonna need three or four runs. I decide to go for the big innin' with three or four runs, we come up with no runs at all. That ain't smart managin'."

Ol' Case crinkled his weather-beaten features. "The law of averages. Yep, I guess there's no way of beatin' it. That's what I gotta battle in tryin' to win the fifth straight pennant. You see, I got no-where to turn for advice on that 'cause nobody ever done it before. The end has gotta come. But when?

"Funny thing about that winnin' streak," he went on. "It sorter set up the losin' streak. Ev-eryone else in the league ganged up on us. They sorter merged ideas. A pitcher on one team would ask the pitcher on another team, 'How do you pitch to that guy? I can't get him out.' Then the first feller tells the second feller what he does, but asks the same question about some other guy which has been givin' him trouble. They study you more. I figger we'll have a lot more trouble in the second half of the season.

"But there are no systems for curing team slumps the way there are for individual slumps, and those don't always work. When I was a coach on the Dodgers, we had a young outfielder—never mind his name' cause he didn't last long. The first time he faced Wild Bill Hallahan he hit him as though he owned him. He did the same with Hubbell.

"So he comes to me and sez, 'Are these the best pitchers in the league?' I sez, 'They are, son. You won't have no trouble with your hittin'. Just polish up your fieldin'.'

"Well, sir, he then goes for twenty-five at bats without a hit while I'm workin' to get him outa his slump. He makes a hit. 'Now you're off again,' I sez to him. But he wasn't. He then went twenty-seven at bats without a hit. So he comes to me again.

"'Case,' he sez, 'I just figgered why I ain't hittin'.'

"'Good,' I sez, wonderin' if he's discovered his stance was wrong, his swing was wrong or what.

"'Case,' he sez, 'I've finally solved it. Them pitchers are mad at me.'"

The Ol' Perfessor paused dramatically for ef-fect, winked and grinned.

"I'm beginning to think he was right," he said. "The other teams are gettin' mad at us." ◆

October 6, 1953

YANKS TAKE 5TH SERIES IN ROW, A RECORD

Martin's Hit in 9th Beats Dodgers, 4 to 3

By JOHN DREBINGER

IN A WHIRLWIND, breath-taking finish that doubtless will be remembered as long as baseball is played, Casey Stengel's Yankees yesterday became the first club in history to win five world series championships in a row.

The extraordinary feat was achieved at the Stadium before a crowd of 62,370 roaring fans. They saw the American League's amazing Bombers vanquish a fighting band of Dodgers, 4 to 3, to clinch the 1953 classic by a margin of four games to two.

For one throbbing moment in a thrill-packed ninth inning, Chuck Dressen's Flatbush Flock stood even. This came when Carl Furillo blasted a two-run homer off Allie Reynolds. It deadlocked the score at 3-all.

Minutes later, in the last half of the ninth, amazing Bill Martin, doubtless cast from the start to fill the hero's role, slammed a single into center field off relief hurler Clem Labine. That shot, which gave Billy a series record of twelve hits, sent Hank Bauer racing over the plate with the decisive tally.

SIXTEEN IN THIRTY YEARS

And so to 63-year-old Charles Dillon Stengel, who in some forty-odd years has just about touched all the bases in an astounding career, now goes the distinction of becoming the first manager to match five straight pennants with five successive world titles. He did it, too, in his first five years in the American League. For prior to 1949 the Ol' Perfessor, as the gravel-voiced philosopher, sage and wit of the diamond is fondly known, had never so much as played, coached or managed a single inning in the junior circuit.

As a fitting climax to the classic's fiftieth an-

Billy Martin (fourth right, without cap) mobbed by teammates after the Yankees won the final game of the 1953 World Series.

niversary, the Yankees chalked up their sixteenth world championship against only four defeats. This achievement is all the more remarkable in that all sixteen triumphs were gained in a span of thirty years.

Actually, all that final drama began with the eighth inning. It was then that Stengel, in a move as startling as any in his brilliant managerial career, withdrew Ford. The bull-pen gates opened to reveal the confidently striding figure of Reynolds. The redoubtable Chief, who had started the opener for the Yanks, had strained a muscle in his back in that game. He came back to stop the Flock in its tracks in the ninth inning of the fifth game in Brooklyn Sunday. Now he was being called upon to lock up the clincher.

Ford, in his seven innings had given up only six hits. He was leading 3 to 1, and there seemed to be no particular reason for making a change. Still, the Ol' Perfessor often makes alterations that defy analysis by baseball's outstanding academic minds.

Anyway, little did anyone suspect that Reynolds, now entering the game simply to save it for the youthful Ford, would wind up the winner himself, for it was his seventh world series mound triumph, tying the record of another Yankee stalwart of another period, Red Ruffing.

But the Yanks were still two in front and they were still that way when Gil Hodges, first Dodger up in the ninth, flied out. But Duke Snider, whom Ford had fanned three times earlier in the battle, now worked Reynolds for a pass after running the count to three and two.

Then came Furillo. He, too, worked it to three and two. Then he lashed one on a line into the lower right field stand and the Flatbush host was beside itself. The score was deadlocked and one could see Reynolds felt keenly disappointed.

The Chief fairly burned the ball across the plate as he next struck out Billy Cox and Labine to end the inning. But the score was tied.

Now the grand finale. Bauer, first up in the last of the ninth, walked. Yogi Berra, flied out but Mickey Mantle topped a ball to the left of the diamond which skipped off Cox's glove and went for a hit. This set up the break in the game.

For up came that incredible 25-year-old star, Martin, a .257 hitter through the regular season who was now emerging as the grand hero. His base clearing first inning triple had sent the Yanks off to a flying start at the outset of the series. He later was to hit two homers and up to this moment he had made eleven hits, tops for the series.

ONE SMACK TO GLORY

Labine worked carefully, got the count to one and one. Then Billy smacked it. Right over second base it went and that was all.

It was the twelfth hit of the series for the peppery Californian who once played for Stengel when the latter managed Oakland in the Coast League before coming to the Yanks. In fact, it was largely on the insistence of Casey that Martin came to the Yanks at all. They never did think too much of him. Now he can name his own price. Those twelve hits gave Martin the record for a six-game series and tied the mark of a dozen blows made in a seven-game classic. ◆

March 5, 1954

Martin Leaves Yanks for Army

By JOHN DREBINGER
Special to The New York Times.

ST. PETERSBURG, FLA., MARCH 4—They all but shed tears today as Billy Martin, spunky, scrappy second baseman of the Yankees, packed his belongings and headed west to finish his stint in the Army.

Tagged yesterday to report to the San Francisco Army Induction Center on Monday morning, the 25-year-old surprise hero of the 1953 world series, had his final workout with the Bombers this morning. Then the Californian boarded a plane to complete his service with the Army in which he had seen duty for five and a half months in 1950-51.

All hands were sorry to see Billy go.

Rough, gruff Casey Stengel was perhaps most deeply affected.

"Miss him?" asked Casey in the perfect rasping voice of a top sergeant. "Certainly, I'm going to miss him. Why, the kid's been terrific. Sure, he told off the owners. Also let George Weiss have it, and had me seeing red.

"But he made us like it because he proved he could do everything we thought he couldn't do on that ball field. He hit fifteen home runs, drove in seventy-five runs, played a tremendous game at second base and they haven't recovered yet from what he did to them in Brooklyn last October. I think he would have had his greatest year this season."

Most touching scene of all came when Billy and Jerry Coleman posed for the photographers with a battered old glove around which could be woven quite a story. Two years ago the glove belonged to Coleman, then the star second sacker of the Yanks.

Then Jerry, who had served brilliantly as a Marine bomber pilot in World War II, was recalled to duty. The day he left he tossed the glove to Martin, saying, "Here, kid, take over."

Martin did. Today he tossed the glove back to Coleman while the cameras clicked. Jerry took one look at the leather, which Martin had worn pretty thin the past two years. Coleman shook his head and said, "I'm afraid I wouldn't do much of a job filling Billy's shoes with that old thing." ◆

November 19, 1954

YANKS CONFIRM ACQUISITION OF TURLEY, LARSEN

Yankees Count on Stronger Staff of Pitchers in Bid to Recapture Pennant

By JOHN DREBINGER

THE YANKEES YESTERDAY confirmed their deal with the Baltimore Orioles, one of the biggest in major league baseball history.

The trade involved sixteen players, representing in current market values close to a million dollars. Nine players were named in the trade yesterday. Seven more, mostly minor leaguers will be announced later.

The Yankees acquired two ace pitchers, Bob Turley and Don Larsen, to bolster a faltering mound staff, and a shortstop, Billy Hunter, who is to replace aging Phil Rizzuto.

The Orioles got two pitchers, Harry Byrd and Jim McDonald; a seasoned outfielder in Gene Woodling, one of the few active players remaining who helped the Bombers win their five world championships; Willie Miranda, the brilliant fielding but light hitting shortstop, and two rookie catchers, Gus Triandos and Hal Smith.

The Orioles are to receive three more players, while four more are to come to New York. Their identities, said General Manager George M. Weiss, who made the announcement for the Yankees, will not be revealed until after next week's major league draft sessions.

"When we got Turley and Larsen," said Weiss, "we plugged the major weakness of the Yankee club—pitching. They are two of the finest and fastest young right-handers in the game. Both figure to get better and they are young. Turley is only 24, Larsen 25.

"Hunter is the best available shortstop for whom we could deal," added Weiss, thereby tacitly conceding that efforts on the part of the Yanks to wheedle Chico Carrasquel from the White Sox had drawn a blank.

The shortstop position, admittedly, had become a serious problem with the Bombers, what with the once brilliant Rizzuto showing unmistakable signs during the 1954 season of being near the end of his career. ◆

April 1, 1955

SPORTS OF THE TIMES
What About Elston Howard?

By ARTHUR DALEY

ST. PETERSBURG, FLA., MARCH 31—The charge has been leveled against the New York Yankees that they have been prejudiced against Negroes. It has been made mostly by irresponsible persons who point to the fact that the Bombers have never had one on their squad. It also has been made by the sensitive and crusading Jackie Robinson. This tourist has never believed a word of it.

The men in the Yankee front office have stubbornly refused to be panicked into hiring a Negro just because he was a Negro. They've waited for one to come along who answers the description of "the Yankee type."

It's quite possible that their search has ended. Elston Howard would seem to have qualified for the team, both as a ballplayer and as a person. There's nothing official about this as yet. But he has been a mighty impressive performer thus far.

What does Casey Stengel think of him? You may listen to one of the Ol' Perfessor's admirably lucid expositions and then decide for yourself.

As Clear as Mud

"Howard's a good boy," began Professor Stengel. "But I can't make up my mind where he's best at, even though I've had him hittin' clean-up which I don't do except with a real good hitter which he is. He's a three-way man, right field, left field and catch, which I caught him some games and he came down on some bad pitches, blockin' them good.

"He hit pretty good and gotta stance similar to DiMaggio, although a lotta ballplayers look like DiMaggio but ain't good hitters like him which this feller is. Last year they said he couldn't catch which he did for Toronto and they win the pennant so he couldn't have hurt much.

"He also played the outfield when he didn't catch and became the most valuable player in the International League. This winter, if you ask him, he played the outfield.

"They say you got Berra to catch and ain't that awful. What's awful about it? He blocks balls 150 per cent better.

Fly in the Ointment

"The outfield he hasn't mastered and can't fly like Mays. A beautiful arm wasted. But Skowron didn't get the jump on the ball and so I put him on first. Or you can take that little Johnny Cooney which I had was a great fielder but couldn't run fast."

The conversation is getting a little fuzzy but don't let it bother you.

"He needs a course in outfielding," continued Stengel, unexpectedly getting back to the point. "I'm not pickin' him apart but he done well. Yet as soon as I bring out my good outfielders that's common sense. He looks good but I can't say he's made the team but I don't see why he won't stay, right, left or catch."

And there you have it. If you had been wondering precisely where Howard fits into Stengel's plans, you need wonder no longer—or should you?

Howard doesn't carry a chip on his shoulder the way the aggressive Robinson does. Nor is he a hearty, hail-fellow-well-met the way the popular Roy Campanella is. Elston is a nice, quiet lad of 25 whose reserved, gentlemanly demeanor has won him complete acceptance from every Yankee.

Volunteering an Answer

The big fellow—he's 6 feet 2 inches and 190 pounds—was asked whether he thought there was or had been any prejudice among the Yankees. As a preliminary to that, however, »»

Elston Howard, the first black player to wear a Yankee uniform, at his debut, in Yankee Stadium, April 11, 1955.

《《《 he was told that it wasn't to be deemed a loaded question. If he didn't want to answer, the query would be considered unasked.

"I don't think there's ever been any prejudice," he said slowly. Then he brightened. "The way I've been treated—well, you couldn't beat it. Everyone's been so nice to me. I couldn't ask for better treatment or consideration."

Long before he entered Vashon High in St. Louis, Howard aspired to be a doctor. But by the time he was playing for the Kansas City Monarchs after he'd been graduated at the age of 17, medicine had begun to fade from his mind. He became baseball-crazy and his hopes soared in 1950 when Tom Greenwade, the same scout who had discovered Mickey Mantle, signed him for the Yankees. Howard played a year at Muskegon and then had two years in the Army.

The Yanks brought him to their preliminary school down here in 1953 and decided to make him a catcher. But he played most of that season in the outfield for the Kansas City farm. However, he was mostly a catcher for Toronto last campaign, hitting .331 and winning the most valuable player distinction.

The chances are that he's a better catcher than outfielder by now. Blocking his way, though, is the durable Yogi Berra, who happens to be the best in the league. But Howard hits too well and throws too well to be kept out of the line-up long. He seems certain to be the first Negro to make the Yankees. ◆

May 6, 1955

Theatre: The Devil Tempts a Slugger

'Damn Yankees' Tells Tale of Witchery

By LEWIS FUNKE

AS SHINY AS A NEW BASEBALL and almost as smooth, a new musical glorifying the national pastime slid into the Forty-sixth Street Theatre last night. As far as this umpire is concerned you can count it among the healthy clouts of the campaign.

It is called "Damn Yankees" and it tells about how Casey Stengel's stalwarts are brought down to defeat by the Washington Senators in the final game of the season with the American League bunting the prize. But even the most ardent supporters of Mr. Stengel's minions should have a good time. And, as for that Dodger crowd, well you can just imagine.

Heading the board of strategy for this outfit is that shrewd manipulator of talent, George Abbott. He acts as general manager of the proceedings on the stage in addition to having collaborated on the book with Douglass Wallop, from whose novel. "The Year the Yankees Lost the Pennant," this merry romp was taken.

To be sure, like any other manager in the course of a long season. Mr. Abbott has not been able to iron out all the kinks in his combination. In spite of his emphasis on speed afoot and timing there is a tendency every now and then for things to settle down a bit flatly on the ground. But the story of how Joe Boyd leases his soul to the Devil in order to become Joe Hardy, champion home-run hitter and inspiration of the Washington Senators, succeeds in being a sufficiently satisfactory vehicle on which to hang some highly amusing antics and utilize some splendid performers.

There is for instance that enchantress, Gwen Verdon, who socked a home-run two years ago in "Can-Can." Miss Verdon is the devil's handmaiden called upon to aid in sealing the fate of Joe Hardy's soul. It is difficult to understand how Joe was able to hold out for so long. For Miss Verdon is just about as alluring a she-witch as was ever bred in the nether regions. Vivacious, as sleek as a car on the showroom floor, and as nice to look at, she gives brilliance and sparkle to the evening with her exuberant dancing, her wicked, glistening eyes and her sheer delight in the foolery.

For the Devil there is the impeccable Ray Walston, a suave and sinister fellow who knows how to be disdainful of the good in man, whose pleasure, as you might expect, is to make humans squirm. Authoritative and persuasive, he does not overdo a role that easily could become irritating in less expert hands. Stephen Douglass, as Joe Hardy, is a completely believable athlete, clean-cut and earnest about his work. And, although it is impossible to spread the full credits to a large and vigorous cast, mention must be made of the effective contributions by Jean Stapleton as an autograph hound, Nathaniel Frey and Jimmy Komack as a couple of ball hawks, and Rae Allen as a nervy feminine sports writer. ◆

October 5, 1955

DODGERS CAPTURE 1ST WORLD SERIES; PADRES WINS, 2-0

By JOHN DREBINGER

BROOKLYN'S LONG CHERISHED dream finally has come true. The Dodgers have won their first world series championship.

The end of the trail came at the Stadium yesterday. Smokey Alston's Brooks, with Johnny Podres tossing a brilliant shut-out, turned back Casey Stengel's Yankees, 2 to 0, in the seventh and deciding game of the 1955 baseball classic.

This gave the National League champions the series, 4 games to 3. As the jubilant victors almost smothered their 28-year-old left-handed pitcher from Witherbee, N. Y., a roaring crowd of 62,465 joined in sounding off a thunderous ovation. Not even the staunchest American League die-hard could begrudge Brooklyn its finest hour.

Seven times in the past had the Dodgers ⟩⟩⟩

Brooklyn Dodgers pitcher Johnny Podres is mobbed by teammates and fans at Yankee Stadium after the last out of the 1955 World Series.

◄◄◄ been thwarted in their efforts to capture baseball's most sought prize—the last five times by these same Bombers.

When the goal finally was achieved the lid blew off in Brooklyn, while experts, poring into the records, agreed nothing quite so spectacular had been accomplished before. For this was the first time a team had won a seven-game world series after losing the first two games.

VICTOR IN THIRD GAME

And Podres, who had vanquished the Yankees in the third game as the series moved to Ebbets Field last Friday, became the first Brooklyn pitcher to win two games in one series.

Tommy Byrne, a seasoned campaigner who was the Yanks' "comeback hero of the year," carried the Bombers' hopes in this dramatic struggle in which victory would have given them their seventeenth series title. But Byrne, whose southpaw slants had turned back the Dodgers in the second encounter, could not quite cope with the youngster pitted against him.

In the fourth inning a two-bagger by Roy Campanella and a single by Gil Hodges gave the Brooks their first run.

In the sixth a costly Yankee error helped fill the bases. It forced the withdrawal of Byrne, though in all he had given only three hits.

Stengel called on his right-handed relief hurler, Bob Grim.

Bob did well enough. But he couldn't prevent Hodges from lifting a long sacrifice fly to center that drove in Pee Wee Reese with the Brooks' second run of the day.

Fortified with this additional tally, Podres then blazed the way through a succession of thrills while a grim band of Dodgers fought with the tenacity of inspired men to hold the advantage to the end.

Fittingly, the final out was a grounder by Elston Howard to Reese, the 36-year-old shortstop and captain of the Flock. Ever since 1941

had the Little Colonel from Kentucky been fighting those Yankees. Five times had he been forced to accept the loser's share.

Many a heart in the vast arena doubtless skipped a beat as Pee Wee scooped up the ball and fired it to first. It was a bit low and wide. But Hodges, the first sacker, reached out and grabbed it inches off the ground. Gil would have stretched halfway across the Bronx for that one.

Thus to the 43-year-old Walter E. Alston of Darrtown, Ohio, goes the distinction of piloting a Dodger team to its first world title. As a player, Smokey had appeared in the majors only long enough to receive one time at bat with the Cardinals. What is more, he ruefully recalls, he struck out.

Dropped back to the minors soon after that, Alston didn't appear in the majors again until he was named manager of the Brooks in 1954.

Yet, in his second year he not only led the Dodgers to an overwhelming triumph for the National League pennant but also attained a prize that had eluded such managerial greats as the late Uncle Wilbert Robinson, Leo Durocher, Burt Shotton and Chuck Dressen.

The Dodgers made their first world series appearance in 1916. They lost to the Boston Red Sox. In 1920 they bowed to the Cleveland Indians. Then in 1941, '47, '49, '52 and '53 they went down before the mighty Bombers.

As for the Yanks, the defeat brought to an end a string of world series successes without parallel. Victors in sixteen classics, they suffered only their fifth setback. It was their first defeat under Charles Dillon Stengel, who bagged five in a row from 1949 through 1953.

And now the Dodgers are the world champions after as extraordinary a series as has been played. For six days the home team won. The Yanks won the first two games with their left-handed pitchers, Whitey Ford and Byrne, at the Stadium. Then the Brooks tore off three in a row in Brooklyn.

But when Stengel tried to make it again with

his two lefties, he slipped up. Ford came through to win a second time on Monday to square it at 3-all. But in this final test, Byrne, a tower of strength to the Yanks in their stirring pennant fight, wasn't up to taking the youthful Podres.

Johnny, recovering from a sore arm, which had plagued him in midseason, more than took up the slack caused by the loss of Don Newcombe's services.

Far into the night rang shouts of revelry in Flatbush. Brooklyn at long last has won a world series and now let someone suggest moving the Dodgers elsewhere!

National Leaguers, too, were rejoicing. For, coming after the Giants' triumph over the Indians last October, this marks the first time since 1933 and 1934 that the senior loop has been able to put together two successive series winners. In 1933 and 1934 the Giants and Cardinals did it. ◆

August 26, 1956

Yanks Drop Rizzuto

PHIL RIZZUTO's long and brilliant career with the Yankees came to a close yesterday. The 38-year-old shortstop received his unconditional release, presumably to devote full time to radio and television broadcasting.

Personable, articulate, and a close student of baseball, Rizzuto has a definite future in radio and television work if he does not choose to continue actively in baseball.

He has been mentioned as a possible substitute for Frank Frisch, who conducted a postgame interview show from the Polo Grounds before his recent heart attack. Phil also has been auditioned for a job as a play-by-play announcer for the Baltimore Orioles. ◆

October 9, 1956

LARSEN BEATS DODGERS IN PERFECT GAME; YANKS LEAD, 3-2, ON FIRST SERIES NO-HITTER

Mantle's Home Run and Bauer's Single Send Maglie to 2-0 Loss

By JOHN DREBINGER

DON LARSEN is a footloose fellow of whom Casey Stengel once said, "He can be one of baseball's great pitchers any time he puts his mind to it." Larsen had his mind on his work yesterday.

He pitched the first no-hit game in world series history. Not only that, but he also fired the first perfect game—no batter reaching first base—to be posted in the major leagues in thirty-four years.

This nerve-tingling performance, embellished with a Mickey Mantle home run, gained a 2-0 triumph for the Yankees over the Dodgers and Sal Maglie at the Stadium. It enabled Casey Stengel's Bombers to post their third straight victory for a 3-2 lead in the series. The Bombers are within one game of clinching the series as it moves back to Ebbets Field Today.

CROWD ROARS TRIBUTE

With every fan in a gathering of 64,519 hanging breathlessly on every pitch, Larsen, a 27-year-old right-hander, slipped over a third strike on Dale Mitchell to end the game.

Dale, a pinch hitter, was the twenty-seventh batter to face Larsen. As he went down for the final out, the gathering set up a deafening roar, while jubilant Yankees fairly mobbed the big pitcher as he struggled to make his way to the dugout.

The unpredictable Larsen had triumphed at a time when the Bombers needed it most with one of the most spectacular achievements ⟫⟫

Yogi Berra (8) embraces Don Larsen his perfect game in Game 5 of the 1956 World Series.

‹‹‹ in diamond history. Last spring the tall, handsome Hoosier, who now makes his home in San Diego, Calif., had caused considerable to-do in the Yankees' St. Petersburg training camp. In an early dawn escapade, Don wrapped his automobile around a telephone pole. He later explained he had fallen asleep at the wheel.

Yesterday big Don remained wide-awake through every moment of the nine innings as he wrapped his long fingers around a baseball to make it do tricks never seen before in world series play.

He did it, too, with a most revolutionary delivery, which might account for his sudden rise to fame. Don takes no wind-up at all. Each pitch is served from a standing delivery that he adopted only a little over a month ago.

In the history of baseball this was only the seventh perfect game ever hurled in the major leagues and only the fifth in baseball's modern era, which dates back to the beginning of the present century. A perfect game is one in which a pitcher faces exactly twenty-seven men with not one reaching first base through a hit, base on balls, error or any other means.

The last perfect game in the majors was achieved by Charlie Robertson of the Chicago

White Sox on April 30, 1922, when he vanquished the Detroit Tigers, 2-0.

So amazing was Larsen's feat that only four batted balls had a chance of being rated hits. One was a foul by inches. Three drives were converted into outs by miraculous Yankee fielding plays.

In the second inning, Jackie Robinson banged a vicious grounder off Andy Carey's glove at third base for what momentarily appeared a certain hit. But Gil McDougald, the alert Yankee shortstop, recovered the ball in time to fire it for the put-out on Jackie at first base.

In the fifth, minutes after Mantle had put the Yanks ahead, 1-0, with his blast into the right field stand, Gil Hodges tagged a ball that streaked into deep left center, seemingly headed for extra bases.

But Mantle, whose fielding in the series has at times been a trifle spotty, more than made amends. He tore across the turf to make an extraordinary catch.

On the next play, Sandy Amoros leaned into a pitch and rocketed a towering drive toward the right field stand. This drive promised to tie the score, but at the last moment the ball curved foul.

And then, in the eighth, Hodges once again was victimized by a thrilling Yankee fielding play. Gil drove a tricky, low liner to the left of Carey. The Yankee third sacker lunged for the ball and caught it inches off the ground.

For a moment it was hard to say whether he had caught the ball or scooped it up. Andy, just to make certain, fired the ball to first in time to make the putout doubly sure. Officially, it was scored as a caught ball.

So accurate was Larsen's control that of the twenty-seven batters to face him, only one managed to run the count to three balls. That was Pee Wee Reese, the doughty Dodger captain and shortstop, in the first inning. Pee Wee then took a third strike. In all, Larsen fanned six.

One could have heard a dollar bill drop in the huge arena as Carl Furillo got up as the first Dodger batter in the ninth. Carl lifted a fly to Bauer in right and one roar went up. Roy Campanella slapped a grounder at Martin for out No. 2 and the second roar followed.

Then only Mitchell, batting for Maglie, remained between Larsen and everlasting diamond fame. The former American League outfielder, for years a sure-fire pinch hitter with the Cleveland Indians, ran the count to one ball and two strikes.

Mitchell fouled off the next pitch and as the following one zoomed over the plate Umpire Babe Pinelli called it strike three. At this point the Stadium was in an uproar.

Mitchell whirled around to protest the call and later he said it was a fast ball that was outside the strike zone. But Dale was in no spot to gain any listener. The Yanks were pummeling Larsen and the umpires were hustling off the field. ◆

October 9, 1956

Perfectionist of Sorts
Don Larsen

"SEE THAT BIG FELLER out there: He can throw, he can hit, he can field, he can run. He can be one of baseball's great pitchers any time he puts his mind to it."

The speaker was Casey Stengel, off and running on one of the penetratingly obser- »»»

The Yankee Stadium scoreboard after Don Larsen's perfect game.

<<< vant non-stop monologues with which he regales visitors to the Yankee dugout every day of any baseball season. The unidentified subject—Casey never identifies his subjects—was Don Larsen, yesterday's architect of the first perfect game in world series annals.

There couldn't have been a more succinct analysis of Larsen as a baseball player. A lean 220 pounds, 6 feet 4 inches, strong-armed, agile and well coordinated, Don has a world of natural athletic ability.

The implications in Stengel's qualifying additional observation also hit the target. The 27-year-old right-hander has not always undividedly had his mind on his work. Despite some recent evidence of reform, Don probably never will qualify as a wholly dedicated athlete.

On a Yankee squad that includes a liberal share of bon vivants, Larsen has had the reputation of being one of the gayest blades. His casual regard for training rules has put him in hot water with the Bombers on a couple of occasions.

NEW TROUBLE LOOMS

A bachelor so far as it was generally known previously, it now also has just come to light that Don is involved in marital difficulties that have resulted in court action against him.

It was to harden his resolution to capitalize more fully on his great talents, as much as for a sore arm, that the Yankees shipped Larsen to Denver for a spell last season.

The disciplinary sojourn in the minors worked. On his recall to the Stadium on July 31 Don reeled off eight victories, while losing only once, to pace the Yankees' late drive to the 1955 pennant.

Although he was quickly shelled to cover by the Dodgers at Ebbets Field in the fourth game of the 1955 series, Larsen's impressive work at St. Petersburg, Fla., this spring tabbed him as a key man in Stengel's pitching plans for 1956.

Casey was particularly delighted with Larsen's "new attitude." Even when Don fell asleep at the wheel and ran his new convertible into a pole at 5 A.M. returning to his hotel after a late date, the Yankee manager did not fine him. Stengel has a "live and let live" policy as long as ball players produce.

Although he received plenty of chances, Don did not produce early in the season. Apparently, however, he stayed reasonably close to the line off the field, for Stengel turned back to him toward the end of the campaign. Again Larsen proved a tower of strength.

His strong finish earned Larsen the starting assignment in the second game of this series at Ebbets Field last Friday. It proved to be a debacle. Sent off to a 6-0 lead, Larsen turned wild in the second inning, had to be removed and the Dodgers went on to win.

But Casey now says "I still believed in him." So Don was back yesterday, with historic results.

AN EASY-GOING MAN

Fun-loving but hardly volatile, Larsen was as moved as a man of his easy-going nature could be after his perfect game. Under the ninety-minute brain-washing he good-humoredly endured from press and radio inquisitors afterward, he admitted that his knees had nearly buckled during the ninth inning.

However, when asked whether he had taken any special pains to be ready for the great occasion (Tom Sturdivant, the Yankee hero of the day before, admitted taking a sleeping pill for the first time in his life and turning in at 9 P.M. to rest for his Sunday start), Don patiently replied:

"Why, no. I did just like I always do. Had a few beers and went to bed around midnight or so."

Born in Michigan City, Ind., the blue-eyed, brown-haired Larsen now makes his home with his parents in San Diego, Calif. At Point Loma High School there, he showed enough ability as a pitcher to be spotted by Art Swartz, a scout for the defunct St. Louis Browns. He was signed to a minor league contract in 1947 and worked his way up through the Browns' farm system.

STARTED WITH BROWNS

Following a two-year interlude of Army service Larsen crashed the majors in 1953 with the

Johnny Kucks (third from left), celebrates with Yankee teammates and batboys after winning the 1956 World Series.

Browns and went with them to Baltimore when the St. Louis franchise was shifted. With Baltimore in 1954, he had the dubious distinction of leading the American League in defeats, losing twenty-one of twenty-four decisions.

The Yankees acquired Don Nov. 18, 1954, in a package deal with the Orioles that involved eighteen players.

Despite his unimposing record, Don was as much a target in that deal for Stengel as the more celebrated Bob Turley.

For, as Casey observes as often as he can find a listener, "That big feller can be one of the greatest, if he wants to be." The rest, it would seem, is up to Larsen. He could not be faulted on any score yesterday. ◆

October 11, 1956

YANKS CHAMPIONS; KUCKS' 3-HITTER TOPS DODGERS, 9-0

By JOHN DREBINGER

AFTER A SOLID WEEK OF THRILLS, the 1956 world series ended yesterday in an old and familiar pattern.

The Yankees, whose virtual monopoly of the world championship had been interrupted last October, roared back to reclaim their laurels in a welter of superlative performances.

Casey Stengel's Bombers crushed the Dodgers in the seventh and deciding game at Ebbets Field, 9 to 0, before a gathering of 33,782. »»»

‹‹‹ It was a loud and emphatic vindication. It violently reversed last October's struggle, when Walter Alston's Brooks bagged the seventh game to capture Brooklyns' first series title.

Four home runs, the last a grand slam, fired behind the brilliant three-hit pitching of 23-year-old Johnny Kucks, wrapped up this one. The amazing American League champions gained their seventeenth world series title and sixth under the leadership of Charles Dillon Stengel.

Eighth Setback for Dodgers

For the Dodgers, the setback was their eighth in nine series. Today the Brooks hop off for San Francisco and then across the Pacific on a tour of the Orient. But so far as the Flatbush faithful are concerned, the Brooks would be no less obliging if they jumped into the Atlantic.

The incomparable Yogi Berra exploded the first two Yankee homers, each with a runner aboard. The first was hit in the first inning, the second in the third.

In the fourth, Elston Howard, making his first appearance in the series, sailed one out of the arena. That shot routed Don Newcombe, the Dodgers' twenty-seven-game winner. Newcombe, making his second start of the series, was shelled out for the second time.

Brooks Use Five Hurlers

The final and most bruising blow of all was clouted in the seventh, when Bill Skowron unloaded a base-clearing shot into the left-field stand. Roger Craig, a young right-hander, was the victim of that smack.

In desperation, Alston tossed five hurlers into the fray, but it did him no good. The Bombers were out to avenge last year's series reverse in a shower of records.

Their four homers made their total twelve for the series. That is a new high, replacing the former mark of ten set by a Yankee team in 1952.

Berra, by driving in four runs, wound up with ten runs batted in for the series. That topped by one the record the late Lou Gehrig had set with the Yanks in 1928.

When Skowron cleared the sacks in the seventh, it marked the first time two grand slams had been hit in one series. Berra had hit a four-run homer in the second game. Only six have been hit in series history.

The most dejected figure after all was over was easily the luckless Newcombe. He had entered the series as the Dodgers' big wheel, a twenty-seven-game winner in the regular season. But he was belted for six runs inside of two innings in the second game.

Luckily for Newcombe, the Dodgers had stormed back to retrieve that game. There was no saving him yesterday, when the Yanks again put him to rout with five runs. A quiet, soft-spoken fellow named Kucks took care of that. ◆

Mickey Mantle, Billy Martin, Hank Bauer and Bauer's wife Charlene (l. to r.) leaving the district attorney's office after a grand jury declined to indict Bauer on charges of assaulting a delicatessen owner.

May 17, 1957

YANKEE IS LINKED TO FIGHT IN CAFÉ

But Hank Bauer Denies That He Took a Swing at Fan in Copacabana 'Incident'

By McCANDLISH PHILLIPS

A 200-POUND NEW YORK YANKEE fan assertedly was struck by a 190-pound New York Yankee at the Copacabana night club, at 2:30 A.M. yesterday.

The ball player, Hank Bauer, a right fielder now batting a perilous .203, is reported to have blinked in innocence and said:

"Hit him? Why, I haven't hit anybody all year."

The injured man, a Bronx delicatessen owner, said:

"I love the guy, anyway."

The injured man's lawyer, who envisions a $250,000 civil suit against Mr. Bauer and the Copacabana, told his client:

"Well, don't let your love of the Yankees run away with you."

Edward Jones, 40 years old, of 600 West 188th Street, does not specifically remember having been hit by Mr. Bauer.

MARTIN'S BIRTHDAY MARKED

Mr. Jones' brother, Leonard, of 562 West 186th Street, sketched these details for the police:

The Jones party, numbering seventeen persons, entered the night club—it is at 10 East Sixtieth Street—at about 10:30 P.M. Wednesday and was shown to two tables on the right-hand side of the downstairs room. It was celebrating the end of the bowling season.

Shortly thereafter, five or six members of the Yankees came in to mark the twenty-ninth birthday of Billy Martin, Yankee infielder. The players were seated near the Jones party.

At about 2:30, Mr. Jones, a Yankee fan from way back, went over to the players' table to extend his compliments. He was accompanied by friends. An argument developed and Copacabana employees stepped between the contending factions.

Mr. Jones was taken to Roosevelt Hospital. Attendants there said that he had suffered an "undisplaced fracture of the nose" and a possible fracture of the jaw.

Mr. Jones' physician reported finding a brain concussion, a fractured jaw and various skull bruises.

Lieut. Thomas >>>

<<< Cavanagh, chief of the detective squad at the East Fifty-first Street Precinct, said that, as yet, there was no evidence of felonious assault.

Lieutenant Cavanagh said that employees of the Copacabana were to be questioned last night. He added that Mr. Bauer had denied striking anyone.

Casey Stengel, Yankee manager, seized upon the incident as an opportunity to scramble his line-up, which is one of his favorite pastimes.

Ford Is Withdrawn

He withdrew Whitey Ford, scheduled to pitch last night against the Kansas City Athletics at Yankee Stadium, in favor of Bob Turley.

Mr. Ford, along with Yogi Berra, Mr. Martin, Mickey Mantle and Johnny Kucks, was said to have been among the birthday celebrants.

Mr. Bauer, a long ball hitter, was dropped to eighth in the Yankee batting order. Mr. Berra was withdrawn from the line-up altogether, while Mr. Mantle trotted out to his regular place in center field.

"We have twenty-five birthdays on this ball club, not to mention wedding anniversarys," Mr. Stengel said, implying that no ball club could long survive rigorous observances of its members' personal milestones.

George Weiss, the Yankees' general manager, issued the following statement last night:

"The Yankees have made a preliminary examination of the facts surrounding Billy Martin's birthday party, which was attended by certain players, all with their wives with the exception of Martin, and are convinced that neither Hank Bauer nor any Yankee player struck anyone. Mr. Bauer has engaged counsel of his own and the legal aspects of this matter are in the hands of said counsel." ◆

June 16, 1957

Kansas City Obtains Martin From Yanks

Special to The New York Times

KANSAS CITY, June 15—Billy Martin and Harry Simpson were the key figures in an eleventh-hour, seven-player deal between the Yankees and the Athletics tonight.

Ryne Duren, a right-handed pitcher, and Jim Pisoni, an outfielder—both of whom played against the champions tonight—became Yankees in the deal, but not for long. They were sent outright to the Yankees' American Association farm club at Denver.

Trade No Surprise

That Martin would not survive the trading deadline had been rumored since the fight at the Copacabana on May 16, while his birthday was being celebrated. Martin, Mickey Mantle, Hank Bauer, Yogi Berra and Whitey Ford were fined $1,000 by the Yanks for their role in the brawl. Johnny Kucks was assessed $500.

The 29-year-old infielder has been involved in a number of scrapes, including fights with Jim Piersall of the Red Sox and Clint Courtney of the Orioles. It had been whispered that the Yankee front office did not look kindly upon the influence Martin was said to exercise over Mantle.

In Simpson, who is 31, the Yankees obtained a long-ball hitter who last year drove in 105 runs for the Athletics. Harry, nicknamed Suitcase, broke into the majors with the Cleveland Indians. He was sold to the A's in 1955. ◆

October 11, 1957

Burdette Hurls 7-Hit Shutout in 7th Game for His 3d Victory

By JOHN DREBINGER

MILWAUKEE, which less than five years' ago didn't even boast a major league club, bestrides the baseball universe today.

Manager Fred Haney's Braves, playing inspired ball behind another brilliant pitched effort by their tireless Lew Burdette, smothered the supposedly invincible Yankees, 5 to 0, in the seventh and deciding world series game at the Stadium yesterday.

The victory, generously cheered by a gathering of 61,207 as Burdette gained his third mound triumph of the classic, gave the National Leaguers the series, 4 games to 3. It brought to Milwaukee a world championship in its first crack at the title.

Inversely, it wound up a damaging campaign for New York. In more than a month Old Gotham had lost two ball clubs, the Dodger and Giants. Yesterday it was shorn of the world series crown it had held, with one or another of its three entries, since 1949.

TAKES IT FROM BOTH SIDES

One sharp, decisive four-run thrust in the third inning yesterday gave the Milwaukeans a stranglehold they never relinquished. There just wasn't anything the inexhaustible baseball brain of Casey Stengel could do about it.

Haney, a one-time pint-sized infielder who was appearing in a world series for the first time, had Stengel licked from the start of the game.

A costly error by Tony Kubek, rookie star of the Bombers during the earlier stages of the series, opened the gates for the Braves in the third. Before the inning was over, Don Larsen, Casey's starting pitcher, had been put to rout.

Eddie Mathews unloaded a two-run two-bagger. Bobby Shantz replaced Larsen, but the Braves rolled on. Hank Aaron and Wes Covington singled. Before the little Yankee southpaw could stem the tide, four runs were in and the American Leaguers were about out on their feet.

For good measure and by way of giving his team additional security, Del Crandall, Burdette's catcher, dropped a home run in the eighth. But that shot was not needed.

For by then one Selva Lewis Burdette Jr., 30-year-old right-hander and one-time farm worker in the Yankee chain, was putting the finishing touches to one of the most astounding exhibitions of sustained pitching mastery in more than a half-century of world series competition.

Burdette vanquished the Yankees in the second game, 4 to 2, last Thursday in New York. Last Monday in Milwaukee he shut them out, 1 to 0, in the fifth game to put the Braves in front. Yesterday, with his second dazzling shutout after only two days of rest, he completed a stretch of twenty-four scoreless innings. In the twenty-seven innings of his three complete games he allowed only two runs.

Only one hurler, perhaps the greatest of all, topped this. In 1905 the immortal Christy Mathewson rolled up twenty-seven innings of scoreless hurling to win three shutouts for the Giants.

SEVEN 3-GAME WINNERS

Burdette yesterday became the seventh pitcher to gain three victories in a world series. The last was Harry Brecheen in 1946. But the Cardinal southpaw gained one in a relief role.

Four, besides Burdette, posted three complete-game victories. They were Mathewson, Jack Coombs of the Philadelphia Athletics in 1910, Babe Adams of the Pittsburg Pirates in 1909 and Stanley Coveleski of the Cleveland Indians in 1920.

The only other pitcher to win three games was Urban Faber of the Chicago White Sox in 1917. But in one of his triumphs he was removed for a relief hurler.

Back in 1914 another Braves' team made history. That was when the "Miracle Braves" came out of the National League cellar on July 4 to win the pennant and then down the then formidable Athletics four straight in the world series. But that was out of Boston. Thirty-nine years later Boston was to give up on the Braves.

Now Milwaukee rules the roost. It will be many a year before they'll forget the pitching of Lew Burdette. ◆

June 16, 1958

Yanks Arrange Record TV Pact

By ROSCOE McGOWEN

THE NEW YORK YANKEES yesterday wrapped up a television package worth considerably more than a million dollars. The Bombers will telecast all of their seventy-seven home games and at least sixty-three road games this year on WPIX, Channel 11.

How much the local American League club—the only baseball club left in New York—will gain from the deal was left to conjecture. Lee MacPhail, the Bombers' assistant general manager, would release no figures.

"But I can say that it is a very satisfactory package," MacPhail said in the Yankee offices at 745 Fifth Avenue at 12:30 P.M. yesterday.

SPONSORS REMAIN THE SAME

MacPhail made the announcement along with Leonard B. Faupel, advertising manager of P. Ballantine & Sons, which company will share the sponsorship with the R. J. Reynolds Tobacco Company, as it has done in the past.

Ed Fisher, the promotion manager for the brewing company, is the authority for the size of the package.

"Anybody who guesses it was a million dollars," said Fisher, "is going to be away off—on the low side."

The decision to "televise this unprecedented number of games" was reached "following a careful evaluation of the local TV set-up brought about by the departure of the New York Giants and the Brooklyn Dodgers for California."

"Both the people at Ballantine's and the New York Yankees," said MacPhail, "felt that the millions of baseball fans in the New York area both desired and deserved the largest TV schedule that could be put together by our club." ◆

October 10, 1958

YANKS BEAT BRAVES, 6-2, AND WIN SERIES; TURLEY, IN RELIEF, OUTPITCHES BURDETTE

By JOHN DREBINGER
Special to The New York Times.

MILWAUKEE, OCT. 9—Whatever else may be topsy-turvy in the world today, baseball at least is back to normal. The Yankees rule the roost again.

Completing a thrilling, uphill three-game sweep, Casey Stengel's Bombers today crushed Milwaukee's Braves, 6 to 2, in the seventh and deciding encounter of the 1958 world series. This gave the honors to the American League's perennial standard bearers by a margin of four games to three.

The Yanks, in avenging last year's defeat at the hands of Fred Haney's National League champions, gained their eighteenth world championship and their seventh under the ten-year aegis of the 68-year-old Stengel.

An explosive four-run eighth inning, which saw Bill Skowron propel the last three tallies across with a towering homer into the left-field bleachers, settled this one before a stunned gathering of 46,367.

The blow came off Lew Burdette, who had turned back the Bombers three times last October, and it crowned a new world series mound star—the Yankees' Bullet Bob Turley.

The burly right-hander, who has added a baffling curve ball to his fast one, entered the struggle in the third inning. The Yanks were leading, 2-1, but their starter, Don Larsen, was in trouble.

Turley saved the situation, retiring the Braves without a run. He lost his grip momentarily in the sixth when a homer by Del Crandall tied the score. But he never let go again, in this, his third straight appearance of the series.

Nor were Turley and Skowron the only Bomber heroes in this final drive that capped one of the most spectacular pull-ups in series history. There was Gil McDougald, who again performed pro-

Bob Turley and Whitey Ford during the 1958 World Series.

digiously in the field. Also, there was Elston Howard, who contributed another steady job in a tricky left field and who also singled home the tie-breaking run in the eighth.

At one stage in the series the Bombers had trailed, three games to one. The surge began with the fifth game for New York last Monday, which Turley won with a five-hit shutout. The next victory came in ten innings here yesterday, with Turley pitching the final out after great relief hurling by Art Ditmar and Ryne Duren had held the Milwaukeeans at bay for seven innings.

Only once before had a club come from behind to win the last three games in a seven-game series. That was in 1925 when the Pirates defeated the Senators. In 1903 the Red Sox vanquished the Pirates by winning the last three encounters, but that was in a five-of-nine-game series.

As in yesterday's game, when he gambled by opening with Whitey Ford, Casey had taken another flier when he started with Larsen today. The big right-hander, who had helped in the shutout that produced the first Yankee victory in the third game of the series last Saturday, but since then had been plagued by pains in his right elbow, failed to survive three rounds.

However, when he did start to falter, Stengel wasted no time hauling him out.

Off Turley the bewildered Braves collected only two hits, Crandall's homer and a pinch single by Joe Adcock in the ninth. That performance gave Bullet Bob his second victory of the series and also won him the Sport Magazine annual award, a Chevrolet Corvette as the outstanding performer of the series.

It was quite a climax for a fellow who had survived only one-third of an inning in the second game. ◆

October 14, 1960

PIRATES WIN, 10-9, CAPTURING SERIES ON HOMER IN 9th

Mazeroski Hit Beats Yanks, Lifts Pittsburgh to First World Title in 35 Years

By JOHN DREBINGER
Special to The New York Times.

PITTSBURGH, Oct. 13—The Pirates today brought Pittsburgh its first world series baseball championship in thirty-five years when Bill Mazeroski slammed a ninth-inning home run high over the left-field wall of historic Forbes Field.

With that shot, Danny Murtaugh's astounding Bucs brought down Casey Stengel's Yankees, 10 to 9, in a titanic struggle that gave the National League champions the series, four games to three.

Minutes later a crowd of 36,683 touched off a celebration that tonight is sweeping through the city like a vast conflagration. For with this stunning victory, which also had required a five-run Pirate eighth, the dauntless Bucs avenged the four-straight rout inflicted by another Yankee team in 1927.

FIRST TITLE SINCE 1925

The Steel City thus had its first world title since 1925, when the Corsairs of Bill McKechnie conquered the Washington Senators.

As for the 70-year-old Stengel, if this is to be his exit—his retirement has been repeatedly rumored—the Ol' Professor scarcely could have desired a more fitting setting short of a victory.

For this was a terrific, nerve-tingling struggle that saw a dazzling parade of heroes who followed on the heels of one another in bewildering profusion.

It saw the Bucs dash off to a four-run lead in the first two innings as they clobbered Bob Turley and Bill Stafford. The first two runs scored in the first inning on a homer by Rocky Nelson.

BERRA HITS 3-RUN HOMER

But in the sixth the Bombers suddenly opened fire on their two arch tormentors of the series, Vernon Law and the Bucs' ace reliever, ElRoy Face. Law, with the help of Face, was seeking his third victory over the Bombers, but the Yanks scored four times in this round, three riding in on a homer by the incomparable Yogi Berra.

These four tallies, along with one which they had picked up in the fifth on a Bill Skowron homer, had the Yanks in front, 5 to 4. When they added two off Face in the eighth for a 7-4 lead, Stengel appeared to have his eighth world series title wrapped up, along with the Bombers' nineteenth autumn triumph.

But in the eighth the Corsairs suddenly erupted for five runs, the final three scampering across on an electrifying homer by Hal Smith. That had the Bucs two in front, but still the conflict raged.

In the ninth the embattled Yanks counted twice as once again they routed Bob Friend. Then left-handed Harvey Haddix, winner of the pivotal fifth game, brought them to a halt.

In the last of the ninth, it was the clout by Mazeroski, first up, that ended it. Ralph Terry, the fifth Yankee hurler, was the victim. It made him the losing pitcher and Haddix the winner.

So, instead of the Bombers winning the nineteenth title, they had to accept their seventh world series defeat. As for Stengel, he remains tied with Joe McCarthy, a former Yankee manager, with seven series triumphs. The setback was his third. McCarthy lost two, one with the Yanks and one with the Chicago Cubs. ◆

Casey Stengel celebrating his 70th birthday in Yankee Stadium on July 30th, 1960.

October 19, 1960

STENGEL, 70, IS LET GO BY YANKEES

Manager Who Won Ten Pennants Will Receive $160,000

By JOHN DREBINGER

CASEY STENGEL, who in the last twelve years brought ten American League pennants and seven world series championships to New York, was let go yesterday as manager of the Yankees.

Ostensibly his contract was not renewed because of an age-limit program which the co-owners of the Yankees, Dan Topping and Del Webb, have decided to put into effect. Stengel was 70 last July 30.

But Stengel, addressing a roomful of writers and photographers at the Savoy-Hilton Hotel, where announcement of his retirement was made, left no doubt that the owners gave him no chance to remain.

"I was told that my services no longer ⟩⟩⟩

⫷ were desired," said a grim-faced Stengel, who appeared in a role totally unlike the one of flamboyant, wise-cracking half-clown and half-philosopher the baseball world has known these many years.

Topping said in a prepared statement that, under a Yankee profit-sharing plan, "Casey will have on Oct. 31 an amount exceeding $160,000 to his credit to do with as he pleases." Stengel's salary is understood to have been $80,000 a season.

Stengel made it clear he would have stayed as manager had the owners agreed to certain demands. These, he said, would have continued to give him sole authority over player personnel, such as had been granted to him in the last twelve years.

But the chance to present these demands, Stengel said, was never given to him.

In his remarks he even eliminated his double-talk, which in the past has made him almost as famous as his managerial manipulations on the field. Stengel strove to keep bitterness out of his voice, but he gave the unmistakable impression that he did not like what had happened.

"Yes, sir," he said, "Mr. Topping and Mr. Webb paid me off in full and told me my services were no longer desired because they want to put in a youth program as an advance way of keeping the club going. That was their excuse—the best they've got.

"When I heard their demands, about this new program they said they were trying to build, I told them, 'If that's your program, gentlemen, don't worry about Mr. Stengel. He can take care of himself.'"

No successor to Stengel has been named. However, there is to be another news conference tomorrow. A new manager may be named then, or there may be a disclosure of other changes in the club's set-up.

There have been reports that George M. Weiss will step out as the general manager. If the 65-year-old Weiss, a force in the Yankee dynasty for more than twenty-five years, leaves his job, it is believed he will be succeeded by his present assistant, Roy Hamey.

HOUK HEADS POSSIBILITIES

The leading possibility as the team's next field manager is Ralph Houk, who has been a coach under Stengel the past three seasons.

No details on further changes were mentioned yesterday. "We've decided to let this be Casey's day," Topping said, adding that matters of reorganization would be disclosed later.

Stengel implied, however, that sweeping changes were contemplated. He even cited these as among the reasons he was being retired.

Topping opened the conference by reading his statement explaining why Stengel was being dropped.

He said that two years ago Stengel "quite reluctantly signed a new two-year contract with the understanding that after the first year he could retire if he desired to do so. Keeping in mind his possible retirement, the Yankees set out to develop a program for the eventual replacement of Casey."

Of the two owners, only Topping was present. The absence of Webb led to speculation that differences involving Stengel and the future conduct of the club were arising between the partners.

Topping concluded his statement with the hope that Casey would be elected speedily to the baseball Hall of Fame. Under Hall of Fame rules, no player or manager is eligible for consideration until five years after his retirement from the game.

When Topping was done, Stengel took over. Appearing more serious than anyone could remember, he said:

"If I had been offered a new contract I would have wanted certain changes made. I would have wanted to have known who was the boss. When Weiss was the boss and I wanted a player, he would go get him for me."

END OF 'THE OLD WAY'

Stengel then revealed that the first he had known he was through was three days ago, when he conferred with the two owners.

"They say they need a new manager for a new system and a new organization," Stengel said. "They don't want the old way. Mr. Webb is letting Mr. Topping run the ball club. I don't want to return to an organization where I don't have the authority.

"I want to run the players on the field. I want to discharge the players and tell them who to get rid of. I want to play the players I want and not the players they want.

"That is the way it has been with me the past twelve years and I never intend to be a yes-man for anybody. If I manage, I must manage with full authority."

Stengel was asked whether there ever had been any front-office interference with his handling or disposing of players.

Casey replied, "Just once. They got rid of one player but they got him back for me." Stengel declined to identify the player.

It could have been Ralph Terry, a young right-handed pitcher the Yankees traded to the Kansas City Athletics in 1957, then reacquired in another deal in 1959.

Stengel refused to discuss his plans, but left the impression that he had no intention of permanently retiring from baseball.

Asked whether he thought a man of 70 was too old to manage, he replied:

"It depends on what you can instill into a ball club and how you run the club. The results—a pennant in 1960—prove it."

Stengel is under contract to manage the Yankees until Nov. 1 and cannot associate himself with another club until after that date. But he did say: "I never will return to the Yankees."

Not until someone asked him whether his wife, Edna, wanted him to step out of baseball, did Stengel's familiar impish grin emerge.

"Well, now," said Casey, who, even in this tense moment could not resist getting in a laugh, "naturally Mrs. Stengel is my wife and she'd like to see me make some money somewhere."

He has been making money for years. His salary of $80,000 is believed to be the highest for a manager. There is also the $160,000 he is receiving from the Yankee profit-sharing plan. In addition, he is known to have made wise investments.

He was his usual fiery self yesterday as he made what certainly must be his baseball farewell to New York.

"No, I'm not leaving under a cloud," he retorted to a question on whether he resented the manner in which he was stepping out. "I'm leaving on friendly relations. The owners have an idea in mind and I'm not going to stand in their way."

Casey then concluded by expressing his thanks and paying tribute to all his players, past and present. He spoke most warmly of the 1960 team, which won the pennant with a fifteen-game winning streak, only to lose the world series to the Pirates in seven games.

And so ends, as far as the Yankees are concerned, the career of a manager whose record was unparalleled in major league history.

As a player Stengel bounced from one club to another. As a Dodger he played in the world series in 1916. As a McGraw Giant he played against the Yankees in 1923 and hit two home runs.

He managed in the minor leagues before his tenures with the Dodgers and Braves. In 1949 he went to the Yanks and won pennants in his first five seasons, with world series titles to match. He wound up with his tenth and last pennant this year.

It had been Stengel's intention to leave for his home in Glendale, Calif., at once. However, the New York baseball writers prevailed on the Ol' Perfessor to stay until tonight, when he will be their guest at a dinner in the Waldorf-Astoria. ◆

October 21, 1960

HOUK, 41, SUCCEEDS STENGEL

Houk, Yankees' New Pilot, Assured of 'Free Hand' at Helm by Topping

By JOHN DREBINGER

RALPH HOUK, who never rose higher than a third-string catcher but who apparently was tabbed for one of baseball's top jobs two years ago, yesterday was named the new manager of the New York Yankees.

In a setting similar to the one where Casey Stengel made his dramatic exit in the Savoy-Hilton Hotel last Tuesday, the 41-year-old Houk was inducted as the skipper of the fabulously successful Bombers under a one-year contract.

Ralph Houk, manager of the Yankees from 1961 to 1963, and then from 1966 to 1973.

The terms were not revealed, but it is understood he signed for $35,000. That is believed to be a little higher than the salary Stengel received in his first Yankee contract in 1949. In winning ten pennants in twelve years, Casey increased it to $80,000.

TOPPING AGAIN PRESIDES

"The signing of Houk for only one year was made at his own request," said Dan Topping, the Yankee co-owner, who, as he did Tuesday, presided at a news conference at which the details were announced. "He'll explain to you why."

"I also want to make it plain that there will be no interference from the front office. He will receive an absolutely free hand to run the club on the ball field."

With that Topping left Houk to face a battery of microphones and a room jammed with photographers and reporters.

At the end of his ordeal of almost three hours, it was conceded that the solidly built Kansan, who entered the Army in World War II as a private and rose to the rank of major, had undergone the examination with extraordinary poise.

"I asked for a one-year contract because at the end of the year I want the Yankees to feel free to do what they want if they don't think I did a good job," Houk said.

ASSURED OF FULL AUTHORITY

"In no shape or form am I going to be a yes-man," Houk added, alluding to comment made by Stengel that, had he remained as manager, he felt he would no longer have the full authority that had been his in the past.

"I don't think I was hired for the purpose of being a yes-man," said Houk. "I have been assured by the owners I am to receive a free hand. Certainly, I'll work with the front office regarding player deals and things like that. But at no time is anyone going to tell me how to run the club on the field."

The new field manager is the sixteenth in Yankee history. He is the eighth since 1921, when the Bombers began their amazing collection of twenty-five pennants.

Houk, who smiles easily and smokes cigars, but never puffs at them nervously, answered all questions in crisp military fashion.

"I realize," he said, "that there will be great pressure on me in following behind a great manager like Casey Stengel. I know I'll be the prime target for second-guessers.

"But I don't fear it because this is a goal I've been shooting for all my life. I've been around Casey a long time and I feel I've learned a great deal from him. After all, there's only one Casey Stengel; I'm Ralph Houk."

Houk, who entered the Yankee farm system in 1939, made the parent club in 1947, following his war years. Although he never revealed the talent to take the place of Yogi Berra as a catcher, he apparently did make an impression on the owners when he managed the Denver club farm from 1955 through 1957.

When he returned to the Yanks as a coach in 1958, the owners apparently already had him tabbed as their manager when the day came for Stengel's retirement. That also explains why Houk several times during the past two years turned down managerial offers from other major league clubs.

CHOICE TERMED 'EXCELLENT'

Stengel confirmed yesterday that he always felt Houk would be his eventual successor. At the same time, Casey, still receiving friends and messages of goodwill, paid glowing tribute to Houk.

"I think his selection is an excellent one," said Casey. "He's been in the organization as long as I have. As coach with us and manager in Denver, he knows the players, many of whom he helped develop. He's taking over a good club and he should do well."

In outlining his plans for 1961, Houk said he was confident the players would come through for him and win another pennant.

"They are all pros and I'm sure we have the nucleus of a good ball club," he said. "I don't anticipate making any changes. When you win a pennant you usually don't make many.

"I have long been familiar with our players and I had many of them with me at Denver, such as Bobby Richardson, Tony Kubek, John Blanchard, Ryne Duren and Ralph Terry. I definitely don't agree with those who are saying the Yankees have a 'dead team'."

So far as the Yankee players are concerned, it is generally believed Houk's appointment will strike a happy chord. They have given frequent evidence that they respect his baseball knowledge, his physical prowess and his ability to make snap decisions.

An incident shedding light on Houk's character was recalled yesterday. On a train ride back to New York following a pennant-clinching celebration, Houk became involved in a brief flurry with Duren, who playfully tried to flatten a cigar in Ralph's face.

Houk settled the matter in less than a minute. Despite efforts later to blow up the matter to a king-sized row, the major just laughed it off. He and Duren have always been the best of friends.

◆

August 8, 1970

Stengel's No. 37 Joins Retired Yank Uniforms

CASEY STENGEL, 80 years old, did a merry jig on the way to his position of honor yesterday as the feature attraction of Old-Timers Day at Yankee Stadium.

The energetic, mystic baseball genius who piloted the Yankees to 10 American League pennants and seven world championships during the years he ran the Bombers—1949-1960—was surprised to learn that his No. 37 was being retired by the club.

Only Babe Ruth (3), Lou Gehrig (4), Joe DiMaggio (5) and Mickey Mantle (7) had previously received the honor of having their numbers forever removed from active service.

After being presented with the uniform by Whitey Ford and Yogi Berra, two of his most reliable players, Stengel confessed:

"Now that I've finally got one [a retired uniform], I think I'll die in it."

Stengel then retired to his customary spot in the home team dugout and attempted to mastermind a team of his star former Yankees over a team made up of some of the Yankees' star opponents.

The ebullient master of baseball lore, who enjoys telling people that "most people my age are now dead at the present time," slightly abridged his comments on the retirement of his number after retreating to the dugout.

"I'm very impressed," he said. "I hope they bury me in it." ◆

Casey Stengel (left) is presented with his number 37 retired uniform from Whitey Ford (center) and Yogi Berra.

October 1, 1975

Stengel's Death At 85 Widely Mourned

By JOSEPH DURSO

CASEY STENGEL, who died Monday night in California at the age of 85, was mourned yesterday by a public that had marveled for more than 60 years at his antics and achievements as a baseball player, manager, and nonstop showman.

Tributes poured in during the hours after "the Ol' Professor" died in Glendale Memorial Hospital from around the country—from public officials like Governor Carey and Mayor Beame, who recalled that he had worked for all four of New York's major league teams in this century, to former players like Yogi Berra who remembered him as "a great man."

Mr. Stengel died at 10:58 P.M., Pacific Time, only a few hours after a family spokesman disclosed that he was suffering from cancer of the lymph glands. He had entered the hospital two weeks earlier for tests, not far from the home he had shared for half a century with his wife, Edna, who was in a nursing home nearby.

The legends that he had created continued long after his retirement 10 years ago, and as recently as June, he enlivened the Mets' annual old-timers' reunion by riding into Shea Stadium in a Roman chariot dressed in a toga and gladiator's helmet.

Casey Stengel will be ranked in the history of baseball with such great managers as John McGraw, Connie Mack and Joe McCarthy. And New Yorkers will always hold him in their hearts, with warm memory, because he is the only baseball figure who wore the uniforms of the Dodgers, Giants, Yankees and Mets.

He made a unique contribution, too, to American letters with his inimitable 'Stengelese,' a language for which he invented his own prose and syntax. He was a joy in more ways than anyone in public life. We shall not see his like again.

The man behind the legend—Charles Dillon Stengel of Kansas City, the man from K.C.—owned oil wells in Texas, was vice president of a bank in California and controlled real estate that made him a millionaire. But for all his status, he was best known as a baseball man with a wrinkled expressive face and a guttural voice.

He was transported to his early baseball games as a boy in Missouri in horse-drawn surreys and wound up flying coast to coast in jetliners. He reached the major leagues in 1912 when William Howard Taft was President and retired in 1965 during the Administration of Lyndon B. Johnson.

He was a player, coach or manager on 17 professional teams. He was traded four times as a left-handed outfielder in the major leagues. He was dropped or relieved three times as a manager in the big leagues. He was even paid twice for not managing.

From 1910 to 1931, he played on four teams in the minors, then five in the majors and finally two more in the minors. Then, as a manager, he lived through 25 years of frustration at both levels, finishing no higher than fifth in an eight-team league during one decade.

Then he suddenly graduated to the New York Yankees in 1948 as the 15th manager in their 46-year history of dominating the sport and won 10 pennants and 7 world championships in 12 years.

Finally, at the age of 72, he wound up as the first manager of the New York Mets where he had started—at the bottom of the ladder.

Through it all, he was one of the busiest characters on the American scene—and one of the most theatrical. His pantomime, monologues and storytelling defied description, until he was accused (with some reason) of carrying on to distract the public from the less effectual performances of his teams.

He spoke in a nonstop style that came to be known as Stengelese—a kind of circuitous doubletalk laced with ambiguous antecedents, dangling participles, a lack of proper names and a liberal use of adjectives like "amazing" and "terrific."

He drew on baseball lore back to the days of John J. McGraw, his idol as a manager, and would clinch points in rhetoric by saying ⟫⟫⟫

‹‹‹ with finality: "You could look it up." When a listener's attention waned, he would recapture it by suddenly exclaiming, "Now, let me ask you," and would be off and running again.

The perpetrator of this commotion was born in Kansas City, Mo., on July 30, 1890. His father had emigrated from Germany in 1851 and had settled in the farm country across the Mississippi River from Davenport, Iowa. A first child Louise, was born in 1886; a son, Grant, in 1887, and Charles three years later.

Charles became an all-around athlete at Kansas City Central High School and pitched (and won) against Joplin for the state championship in 1909. He turned professional the following year with the Kansas City Blues, who farmed him out to Kankakee, Ill., in the Northern Association.

Baseball was a means to an end: Stengel was working his way through the Western Dental College in Kansas City. But two things swerved him from his course. He was left-handed, which raised some problems for his instructors. And left-handed dentists had a less riotous future than left-handed baseball players.

For whatever reasons, he became a fulltime ballplayer and was discovered by Larry Sutton, a scout for the Brooklyn Dodgers. In September of 1912, the Dodgers—then known as the Trolley Dodgers and Superbas—called him up from Birmingham, and he was in the big leagues.

For the next 14 seasons, Stengel played the outfield in the National League—with Brooklyn until 1917, Pittsburgh until 1920, Philadelphia until the middle of 1921, New York until 1924 and Boston until 1925.

He batted .284 and hit 60 home runs in 1,277 games. His best year was 1922, when he hit .368 in 84 games with McGraw's Giants. His best moments came in the World Series of 1923, when he hit two home runs and won two games—only to be upstaged by the young Babe Ruth, who hit three home runs as the Yankees won the Series.

After the 1923 Series, Stengel was traded to the Boston Braves and two years later began his career as a manager with Boston's farm club at Worcester, Mass.

He already had gained a sizable reputation as a brawler and clown, and promptly increased it when the Boston club installed him as a one-man triumvirate at Worcester—president, manager and right fielder.

Casey fretted until the final day of the season, then hatched a monumental triple play to escape. As manager, he released Stengel the player; as president, he dismissed Stengel the manager; and as Stengel, he resigned as president.

The owner of the Boston team, Judge Emil Fuchs, was outraged by this impertinence, but nobody was too surprised. After all, Stengel had long since become famous as "the king of the grumblers," a locker-room clique whose chief talent was trouble.

He had been the bane of umpires and of managers like Wilbert Robinson of Brooklyn, who became the butt of one Stengel prank at Daytona Beach, Fla., in the spring of 1915. On that occasion, Casey was inspired by the recent feat of Gabby Street, who had caught a baseball dropped from the Washington Monument. The question now became: Could a man catch a baseball dropped from an airplane?

The airplane was supplied by Ruth Law, the pioneer woman flier, and the baseball was supplied by C. D. Stengel, except that somehow it became a grapefruit by the time it was dropped.

"Uncle Robbie," Stengel recalled, "was warming up this pitcher on the sidelines—we didn't have six coaches in those days. And this aviatorix—it was the first one they had—she flew over and dropped it. And Uncle Robbie saw it coming and waved everybody away like an outfielder and said, "I've got it, I've got it.""

"Robbie got under this grapefruit, thinking it was a baseball, which hit him right on this pitcher's glove he put on and the insides of it flew all over, seeds on his face and uniform, and flipped him right over on his back. Everybody came running up and commenced laughing, all except Robbie."

In one of his most fabled escapades, Stengel returned to Ebbets Field in 1918 with the Pittsburgh Pirates, who had just acquired him from Brooklyn. He was greeted by a rousing round of

Stengel's Yankee teams won a record five consecutive World Series, but didn't win in 1954.

catcalls from the fans. In reply, he marched to home plate, bowed with courtliness to the grandstand, doffed his cap—and out flew a sparrow. He had given them the bird.

On another occasion, he went to right field, found a drainage hole and simply disappeared from sight. A moment later he rose majestically, the manhole cover under his arm, just in time to catch a fly ball.

Later, when he became a manager, Stengel looked back on his wayward years and said:

"Now that I am a manager, I see the error of my youthful ways. If any player ever pulled that stuff on me now, I would probably fine his ears off."

Stengel's success as a manager, meanwhile, was lean. In seven years in the minor leagues from 1925 to 1931, his teams won only one pennant. But he was developing skills that became his trademark in later years: He was thriving as a buffoon who could draw attention away from inept players to himself, and he was learning the business side of baseball—buying players low, selling them high and converting farm clubs into pools of talent for the major leagues.

He also was branching out in his personal life. In 1924 he had married Edna Lawson, a tall, lively brunette from California who once had acted in silent films with Hoot Gibson and who later was an accountant with a shrewd business sense.

They settled in a two-story house at the foothills of the Sierras in Glendale, Calif. And ⟫⟫

≪≪ for the next 40 years it was their base as both roamed the country on Casey's travels.

They had no children, but had hordes of relatives who lived nearby, plus young ballplayers who often stayed with them. They also had interests in real estate, established the Valley National Bank with Mrs. Stengel's family, and literally struck oil in Texas on a chance investment Casey had made with some baseball friends.

With all this going for him, Stengel was hardly considered the type of man who would flower late in life into a baseball manager of renown— not even when he was called to the Brooklyn Dodgers as a coach in 1932 and became manager two years later.

From 1934 until 1943, his teams at Brooklyn and Boston never finished higher than fifth in an eight-team league. Then in 1943, when he was struck by a taxi in Boston and suffered a broken leg, it appeared that his career was finally ended.

However, the following year he agreed to leave his swimming pool and patio in Glendale to take over the Milwaukee club in the American Association. He did it as a favor for a friend, but it proved to be a turning point. After one season as manager at Milwaukee and another at Kansas City, he spent three at Oakland in the Pacific Coast League, won 321 games and suddenly at the age of 58 was offered the job as manager of the lordly Yankees.

His selection as the replacement for Bucky Harris evoked surprise. It was widely thought

Casey Stengel signs autographs after a Mets game in 1963.

that the Yankees had hired "Professor" Stengel to throw a screen of hilarity around the club for a season or two while rebuilding. But the "interim" manager, who had never spent a day in the American League, stayed 12 years and the Yankees reached spectacular heights.

In 1949, his first season, the Yankees suffered 72 injuries. Joe DiMaggio even missed half the season. But Stengel kept juggling lineups and the Yankees defeated the Boston Red Sox in the last two games, won the pennant and defeated the Dodgers in the World Series.

A year later they won again and they kept on winning until they had taken five straight pennants and world championships. It was a record streak for a team and a manager. In a rash moment Stengel remarked that if the Yankees didn't make it six in a row in 1954, the manager should be dismissed. They didn't, but he wasn't.

In 1955, they won the pennant again and also took it in 1956, 1957, 1958 and 1960. But they won only two World Series during that time, and in 1959 even slipped to third place.

Stengel was earning $85,000 a year by now and was the foremost manager in baseball. He was surrounded by stars like Yogi Berra, Whitey Ford, Phil Rizzuto, Mickey Mantle and Roger Maris. But the second half of his administration was a somewhat troubled time, and he grew increasingly arbitrary with players and bitter to suggestions that he was "too old."

His bitterness reached a peak on Oct. 18, 1960, five days after the Yankees had lost the series to Pittsburgh.

In an acrimonious press conference at the Savoy Hilton Hotel, the Yankee brass—led by Dan Topping—announced that Stengel had "retired." A short time later George M. Weiss, Stengel's friend and sponsor, was released as general manager.

"I was fired," Casey commented.

After a year in the California sunshine, though, he was hired again—by Weiss, who now was organizing the Mets, the successors to the Giants and the Dodgers, who had left New York in 1957 for the West Coast.

So, at the age of 72, Stengel began a new career, one that crystallized all his talents for teaching, acting and enchanting the public. The Mets needed such talents, too, since they lost 452 games while winning 194 during the next four years, finishing dead last each time.

They were as downtrodden as the Yankees had been exalted. But they were cast in the image of the stumpy, waddling old man who directed them, a team whose sins were pardoned by an adoring public, whose life was surrounded by legend, whose bank account grew with the legend.

In 1965, Stengel's last year in a baseball suit, 1,768,389 persons paid up to $3.50 each to watch the Old Man and his celebrated Youth of America in their new Shea Stadium on Flushing Bay, and 1,075,431 paid to see them on the road.

The partnership began to fold on July 25, 1965, when Stengel fractured his left hip—somewhere between an old-timers' party at Toot Shor's restaurant, where he slipped and fell, and a house in Queens, where he slipped and fell again while getting out of an automobile.

In any event, he was in Roosevelt Hospital that afternoon while 39,288 persons celebrated his 75th birthday at Shea Stadium. Two days later he underwent an operation on his hip and one month later he retired to the side of his swimming pool as titular vice president of the Mets.

One year later, however, leaning on a crooked black cane, he limped into baseball's Hall of Fame at Cooperstown, N.Y., alongside Ted Williams. Stengel, the 104th person inducted into the shrine, told the crowd in valedictorian Stengelese:

"I want to thank my parents for letting me play baseball, and I'm thankful I had baseball knuckles and couldn't become a dentist....I got $2,100 a year when I started in the big league, and they get more money now....I chased the balls that Babe Ruth hit." ◆

October 2, 1975

A Plaque for Stengel

CASEY STENGEL, who died Monday night in California, will be memorialized in a plaque that will be installed in Yankee Stadium, where he managed the New York Yankees to 10 pennants and seven world championships in 12 years.

The Yankees announced yesterday that they would honor their former manager when the stadium reopened next April after two years of modernization and rebuilding.

Stengel, who led the Yankees through their greatest years from 1949 through 1960, died of cancer at the age of 85. His funeral will be held Monday in Glendale, Calif., where he lived for 51 years. ◆

August 14, 2007

Phil Rizzuto, Yankees Shortstop, Dies At 89

By RICHARD SANDOMIR

PHIL RIZZUTO, the sure-handed Hall of Fame Yankees shortstop nicknamed The Scooter, who extended his Yankee life as a popular and even beloved broadcaster, punctuating his game-calling with birthday wishes to fans and exclamations of "Holy cow!", died late Monday night. He was 89.

The cause was pneumonia, his daughter Patricia said. Rizzuto, who had been in declining health for several years, died at a residential facility in West Orange, N.J. He had lived in Hillside, N.J., since 1945.

Rizzuto played for the Yankees from 1941 to 1956. His departure was abrupt. No longer willing to carry an aging, seldom-used infielder, the team cut him on Old-Timers' Day. Soon after, he began calling Yankee games for WPIX-TV/ Channel 11 and remained in that job until 1996.

Rizzuto played an integral role on the dynastic Yankees before and after World War II. He was a masterly bunter and defensive specialist for teams that steamrolled to 10 American League pennants and nine World Series championships. He was one of 12 Yankees on teams that swept to five consecutive World Series triumphs, from 1949 to 1953.

He was a 5-foot-6-inch, 150-pound sparkplug who did the little things right, from turning the pivot on a double play to laying down a perfect sacrifice bunt. He left the slugging to powerful teammates like Joe DiMaggio, Mickey Mantle, Tommy Henrich, Charlie Keller and Yogi Berra.

"I hustled and got on base and made the double play," he said. "That's all the Yankees needed in those days."

His career statistics were not spectacular: a batting average of .273, 38 home runs and 562 runs batted in. But he played in five All-Star games, and in his best season, 1950, he hit a career-high .324, drove in 66 runs and won the American League's Most Valuable Player award.

Rizzuto was frequently compared to other shortstops of his era, like Pee Wee Reese of the Brooklyn Dodgers and Marty Marion of the St. Louis Cardinals. But to DiMaggio, his teammate for eight seasons — each man lost three seasons to military service during World War II — Rizzuto was the best.

"The little guy in front of me, he made my job easy," said DiMaggio, one of the game's great centerfielders. "I didn't have to pick up so many ground balls."

A major league career was not foreordained. One of five children of Rose and Fiore Rizzuto, a construction foreman and trolley motorman, Philip Francis Rizzuto grew up in Brooklyn and moved to Glendale, Queens, when he was 12.

While attending Richmond Hill High School, he tried out for the Dodgers, but the manager, Casey Stengel, told him he was too small. The New York Giants told him to get lost. But Stengel's rejection — "Go get a shoeshine box," the manager told him — was the most vivid.

"When he became the Yankee manager in 1949, I reminded him of that, but he pretended he didn't remember," Rizzuto said of Stengel. "By '49, I didn't need a shoebox, anyway. The clubhouse boy at the Stadium shined my Yankee spikes every day."

The Yankees signed him in 1937 and sent him to their Class D minor league team in Bassett, Va.

Stopping for a meal in Richmond, Rizzuto was served grits for the first time.

"I didn't know what to do with them, so I put them in my pocket," he said.

A mistreated left leg injury during his stint in Virginia — he had stepped in a gopher hole — nearly led to amputation. Or maybe it didn't, depending on how Rizzuto told the tale. "They had to cut part of the muscle out of my leg because it was infested with gangrene," he said, "and actually that was a break for me because I used to be so fast when I was a kid, I'd run by the ground balls, and this slowed me just enough so that I could make the ball."

In 1941, his appearance at spring training with the Yankees made the pitcher Lefty Gomez wonder why the team had summoned a "Lilliputian," but Rizzuto soon established himself, replacing the veteran Frank Crosetti, and hit .307 in his rookie season.

Rizzuto became a bulwark of the Yankees' infield, forming superior double-play combinations with second basemen Gerry Priddy, Joe Gordon and Jerry Coleman (who in the 1960s would join Rizzuto in the broadcast booth). He also developed into an eccentric — funny, superstitious, afraid of thunder and the target of pranks. When the tradition was for fielders to leave their gloves in the field when they came in to bat, Rizzuto would often return to the field to find a mouse, a snake or a rat wedged in the glove fingers. »»»

The Yankee Stadium videoboard shows the late Phil Rizzuto during a moment of silence before the game on August 14, 2007

Phil Rizzuto, here at Yankee Stadium in 1994, played for shortstop for 13 seasons, and was a Yankee broadcaster for 40.

《《《   Two plays in 1951 were emblems of Rizzuto's career.

In the first, Rizzuto was at bat (he was right-handed) against Bob Lemon of the Cleveland Indians. It was the bottom of the ninth inning, in the middle of a pennant chase. The score was tied at 1. DiMaggio was on third base. Rizzuto took Lemon's first pitch, a called strike, and argued the call with the umpire. That gave him time to grab his bat from both ends, the sign to DiMaggio that a squeeze play was on for the next pitch. But DiMaggio broke early, surprising Rizzuto. Lemon, seeing what was happening, threw high, to avoid a bunt, aiming behind Rizzuto. But with Joltin' Joe bearing down on him, Rizzuto got his bat up in time to lay down a bunt.

"If I didn't bunt, the pitch would've hit me right in the head," Rizzuto said. "I bunted it with both feet off the ground, but I got it off toward first base."

DiMaggio scored the winning run. Stengel called it "the greatest play I ever saw."

Later that year, Game 3 of the World Series against the New York Giants provided Rizzuto with an enemy he would fulminate about for the rest of his life.

With one out in the fifth inning, the Giants' Eddie Stanky drew a walk against the Yankees' pitcher Vic Raschi. The next batter was Alvin Dark, and the Yankees intercepted a hit-and-run sign to him. Berra, the catcher, signaled a pitchout, and his throw to Rizzuto at second base beat Stanky by 10 feet. But as Rizzuto waited with the ball in his glove, Stanky slid and kicked the ball into center field with his right foot. He ran to third. Rizzuto was charged with an error, and the Giants scored five unearned runs.

"I was nonchalanting it," Rizzuto admitted sheepishly. "I was looking at the TV camera."

Rizzuto was shocked when the Yankees released him in 1956 to sign the outfielder Enos Slaughter. But he soon accepted a job in the Yankee radio and TV booth with Mel Allen and Red Barber, two towering figures in sportscasting. "You'll never last," Howard Cosell, then a radio sportscaster, told him. "You look like George Burns and you sound like Groucho Marx."

Three days into his new career, Rizzuto told his wife, Cora, that he wanted to quit — but he stayed, despite occasional threats to resign, until 1996. To those who heard him exclaim "Holy cow!" for a play (or a cannoli) that excited him, or chide a player as a "huckleberry" for committing an error, Rizzuto was an endearing, idiosyncratic voice despite his lack of professional credentials.

Rizzuto met Cora Ellenborg in 1942 after substituting for DiMaggio as a speaker at a communion breakfast in Newark. He had been invited to her home afterward for coffee and cake by her father, a Newark fire chief. "I fell in love so hard I didn't go home," Rizzuto recalled. He rented a nearby hotel room for a month to be near her.

Besides his daughter Patricia, his wife also

survives him, as do their daughters Cynthia and Penny; a son, Philip Jr., and two grandchildren.

Over four decades in the Yankee announcing booth, Rizzuto transformed himself from a conventional announcer with a distinctly New York voice into an often comic presence. And he became well known beyond New York. The comedian Billy Crystal parodied him, and Meat Loaf used Rizzuto's broadcast voice in his 1978 hit song "Paradise by the Dashboard Light."

As for his trademark expression, "Holy cow," he said he had adopted it in high school, at his baseball coach's suggestion, to replace profanity. When the Yankees celebrated Rizzuto with a day in his honor in 1985, retiring his uniform No. 10, the team presented him with a cow, which promptly stepped on his foot and knocked him over.

Rizzuto often diverged from actual game-calling, pausing to extend birthday, anniversary and confirmation congratulations. He never used the first names of his partners at WPIX-TV — they were "Coleman," "Murcer," "White," "Messer," "Seaver," or "Cerone," never Jerry, Bobby, Bill, Frank, Tom or Rick. Listeners heard about his wife (he called her "my bride"), an employment appeal for his son, Scooter Jr., reports about his golf game, or exultations about a new Italian dish.

Rizzuto's ramblings and pro-Yankee sentiments maddened detractors. But his fans adored Rizzuto as they would a delightful uncle, and colleagues were fond of recalling his scorecard notation of "W.W.," for "Wasn't Watching."

Rizzuto often left a game at Yankee Stadium before its conclusion to beat the traffic over the George Washington Bridge. As one game headed into extra innings, he asked Messer, "Want a cup of coffee?" Messer nodded. But Rizzuto was gone, to his home in New Jersey. As he entered the broadcast booth the next day, Rizzuto tapped Messer on the shoulder and said, "Here's your coffee."

After many years of failing to be elected to the Hall of Fame in Cooperstown, N.Y., he was voted in in 1994 by the Hall's Veterans Committee, which reconsiders candidates rejected by sports writers. Friends like Yogi Berra, Bill White and Pee Wee Reese sat on the committee.

Rizzuto resigned from Channel 11 abruptly in August 1995, distraught that he had remained to broadcast a game at Fenway Park rather than join former teammates at Mickey Mantle's funeral in Dallas. He watched the services on television from the booth. "I took it hard and knew I made a big mistake," he said later. "I got more upset as the game went on and left in the fifth. They tried to drag me back, but I wouldn't."

But he returned in 1996 for a final season, persuaded by fans, Mantle's sons and George M. Steinbrenner III, the principal owner of the Yankees. The pull of his cherished team was too strong. He was, after all, someone who practically saw the world filtered through Yankee pinstripes.

When the news came in 1978 that Pope Paul VI had died, Rizzuto said on the air, "Well, that kind of puts the damper on even a Yankee win."

TASTE OF SCOOTER IN THE BOOTH

In 1993, Tom Peyer and Hart Seely edited Phil Rizzuto's actual broadcast commentary into verse for a book called "O Holy Cow! The Selected Verse of Phil Rizzuto." Here is an excerpt.

What kind is it?
Ohhhhh!
Pepperoni!
Holy cow!
What happened?
Base hit!
A little disconcerting,
Smelling that pizza,
And trying
To do a ballgame. ◆

THE MANTLE-MARIS ERA

Mickey Mantle and Roger Maris were all about home runs. The Mick hit 536, many attached to a tape measure—373 swinging left-handed, 163 right-handed. He also hit a record 18 in the World Series. Roger Maris hit 203 homers for the Yan-kees, including one briefly attached to an asterisk. But for all they accomplished individually, in 1961 they reigned together on a pedestal: most home runs, two teammates, one season—115.

Maris hit a record 61 that year, the Mick hit 54. They surpassed the Ruth–Gehrig total of 107 in 1927, when the Babe hit 60 and the Iron Horse hit 47. Third best at the time was a total of 93 by Jimmie Foxx (58) and Al Simmons (35) for the Philadelphia Athletics in 1932. More recently, even the twosomes with suspected steroid enhancement, Barry Bonds and Mark McGwire, couldn't exceed the Maris–Mantle total. Bonds (73) and San Francisco Giants shortstop Rich Aurilia (37) combined for 110 in 2001. McGwire (70) and St. Louis Cardinals outfielder Ray Lankford (31) had 101 in 1998.

Mantle was also all about winning. Over his first fourteen seasons, the three-time most valuable player would help the Yankees win seven World Series and twelve American League pennants in streaks of three, four, and five years. Maris, a two-time MVP, contributed to five consecutive pennants and two Series titles with Mantle as a teammate. Oddly, the Yankees put together Mantle and Maris the same way they put together the Babe and Gehrig—a can't-miss prospect developed in their farm system with a slugger acquired from a major league franchise considered a Yankees "farm." Maris batted third, as the Babe did. Mantle was the cleanup hitter, as Gehrig was.

Mantle and Gehrig were prospects 25 years apart: one as fast afoot as he was powerful out of the Commerce, Oklahoma, mining area, where scout Tom Greenwade found him; the other a college muscleman at Columbia, where scout Paul Krichell spotted him. Maris and the Babe arrived 40 years apart: one from the Kansas City Athletics, a frequent trade partner at the time; the other from the Boston Red Sox, about to become a frequent trade partner at the time.

Mickey Charles Mantle (he was named for Mickey Cochrane, a Hall of Fame catcher in the 1930s) was five years old when his father, Elvin (Mutt) Mantle, taught him how to switch-hit. In 1949, at age 17, he signed ⟩⟩⟩

★ ★ ★

Mickey Mantle (7) and Roger Maris (9) during the 1961 season.

<<< for a $1,500 bonus and $140 a month with the Yankees Class D team in Independence, Kansas, as a shortstop. The next year he batted .383 at Joplin, Missouri, in Class C, then dazzled the Yankees brass with his power at their 1951 spring training base.

"You're not a shortstop anymore," Casey Stengel told the rookie, who had made 43 errors at Independence. "You're an outfielder now."

With Joe DiMaggio in center field for what would be his final season, the Mick played right field. After a slow start, he went to the Kansas City farm in the American Association then returned in late August. For his rookie season he batted .267 with 13 homers. In the 1951 World Series, he tripped on a sprinkler head in Yankee Stadium's right field and seriously sprained his left knee, his first of several leg injuries. He would never quite regain the sprinter's speed of his teens, but he still ran faster than most across the vast pasture in the original stadium's center field.

Year by year, those injuries and an admittedly crude lifestyle diminished the Mick's power but added to his mystique. When he retired after the 1968 season, he joined the Babe, Lou Gehrig, and Joe DiMaggio as the most beloved Yankees.

In contrast, Roger Eugene Maris, out of Fargo, North Dakota, arrived in the big leagues with Cleveland in 1957, but early the next season he was traded to Kansas City, where he hit 19 homers for a total of 28 that year. He swatted only 16 in 1959, but the Yankees saw a lethal left-handed uppercut stroke that fit the stadium's right-field stands. To get Maris, they traded the aging outfielder Hank Bauer, the no-longer-perfect-game right-hander Don Larsen, outfielder Norm Siebern, and young first baseman Marv Throneberry (later a Mets symbol of futility).

Maris erupted in 1960, hitting 39 homers and driving in 112 runs for his first Most Valuable Player Award, then made history in 1961 with 61 homers, breaking the Babe's record in the season finale at the stadium, when he lofted a pitch from Red Sox right-hander Tracy Stallard into the lower right-field stands. In earning another MVP Award, he had 142 RBI with a .269 average. Under constant questioning from the news media during the last few weeks of the season, he lost some hair and some sleep but never lost that lethal left-handed stroke.

For whatever reason, Maris never approached those numbers again. In 1963 he had 33 homers—a respectable total—and 100 RBI, but skidded to 23 and 53 in 1963, to 26 and 71 in 1964, to 8 and 27 in only 46 games in 1965, and to 13 and 43 in 1966. Traded to the Cardinals, he helped them win the 1967 World Series and the 1968 National League pennant. His seven pennants in the sixties were the most for any one major leaguer.

For more than a decade Maris seemed to be forgotten by the Yankees, until he was invited to the 1978 Opening Day ceremonies. His plaque in Monument Park was dedicated in 1984. Yankees fans argue whether Maris, if only because he broke the Babe's record, should be in the Baseball Hall of Fame in Cooperstown, New York, but his career numbers are not that compelling: 275 homers, 851 RBI, .260 average. The fans' consolation is that for all the homers hit by suspected steroid-enhanced sluggers, his 61 in 1961 remain the pure home run record for one season.

February 24, 1951

MANTLE IN OUTFIELD SHIFT

Stengel Plans to Experiment With Rookie in Center

By JAMES P. DAWSON
Special to The New York Times.

PHOENIX, ARIZ., FEB. 23—Mickey Mantle, rookie from Commerce, Okla., will be the subject of an extensive experiment in the Yankee training campaign. No less an authority than Manager Casey Stengel revealed this information today, one of those rare days when rain dampened activities in the Valley of the Sun.

Stengel said he would work the 20-year-old Mantle in center field and immediately speculation arose over whether the Yanks regarded the rookie as the eventual successor to the great Joe DiMaggio.

That Mantle will "stay up" this year is a possibility, although not exactly a probability. Despite his spectacular record with Joplin, Mantle faces the tradition that few rookies ever have gone from Class C to the majors in one leap.

Nevertheless, Mantle's ability as a switch hitter, his success in belting a long ball, reflected in his sixty-eight extra-base hits at Joplin, and the general agreement that he is the most promising rookie in camp, are factors in his favor.

Stengel pointed out that Mantle has the speed to range far and wide and has a throwing arm more suited to the outfield than to third base. ◆

May 2, 1951

Mantle Leads Yanks Over White Sox

ROOKIE HITS HOMER IN 8-TO-3 TRIUMPH

By JAMES P. DAWSON
Special to The New York Times.

CHICAGO, MAY 1—Joe DiMaggio was a casualty today as the Yankees paid their first visit of the season to Comiskey Park, but Mickey Mantle took over in approved manner, as the Bombers defeated the White Sox, 8-3.

A neck ailment put DiMaggio out of action and led Manager Casey Stengel into starting the rookie sensation in the outfield, with Jackie Jensen in center and Mantle in right.

DiMaggio was X-rayed at Mercy Hospital and the examination showed a muscular spasm, which should dissolve with massage and manipulation.

In a defensive move, the Yankee skipper sent Cliff Mapes in as a seventh-inning replacement for Mantle. But by that time the Oklahoman had virtually assured Vic Raschi of his third victory.

Mantle was the big factor in the successful start of the Bombers' first western swing. He belted his first major league homer, a two-run blast from the left side of the plate off the right-handed Randy Gumpert in the sixth. He hammered in another run with a long fly. He shot a hopper through Orestes Minoso's legs that went for an error in the second inning, letting in two Yankee runs. ◆

June 3, 1951

Case History of a Rookie

Young Mickey Mantle finds baseball is more than ball-swatting.

By GILBERT MILLSTEIN

MICKEY CHARLES MANTLE, the new 19-year-old right fielder for the New York Yankees, is, in the opinion of most sports writers, the most promising young man to enter big-league baseball since the ascension of Joe DiMaggio, who thinks, without any editorial equivocation at all, that Mantle is the greatest rookie he has ever seen. "Greatest" is a word used sparingly by DiMaggio and then only in its veritable, or non-show business sense. The morning after the Yankees arrived in New York to open the season

with the Boston Red Sox, Dan Parker wrote that "if the inking device on the Fordham University seismograph didn't trace a design like a cross-section of Mount Everest set in the middle of the American prairies it's a fraud because Mickey Mantle, the rookie of the aeons, hit New York like fifteen simultaneous earthquakes.

The day after the opening game, which the Yankees won and in which Mantle made one hit, Jimmy Cannon, declining the cataclysmic gambit for the emotional-exhaustion approach,

Mickey Mantle follows the ball with his eyes during a road game in the 1950s. Yogi Berra watches the action from the on deck circle.

declared: "I'm all out of breath hollering it up for this kid." Casey Stengel, the manager of the Yankees and a notoriously cautious man who is inclined to save his wind when discussing the future of his charges, said to an inquirer: "I'll tell you this—I got sense enough to play him."

Having become a legend before he came of age and a commercial product of considerable speculative value in less than six months, Mantle has been subjected to a series of pressures, both on and off the baseball field, for which nothing in his life, either professionally or privately, had prepared him. In addition to having to learn to become an outfielder, instead of a shortstop, which he used to be, he has been interviewed and photographed almost daily, invited out to dinner every night, asked to appear on radio and television programs (which he has done in moderation), questioned closely about the state of his health (he was recently classed in 4-F by the Army because of a chronic osteomyelitis or bone infection in his left ankle), and approached even more closely by promoters of one kind or another seeking to make money for him and only incidentally for themselves, they all said.

To some extent this is experienced by every young baseball player, but Mantle is younger than most and, up to this point, has shown more talent than any of his immediate contemporaries. He was graduated from high school in his home town of Commerce, Okla.—the population of which is 2,500—only two years ago. He has played professional baseball for only two seasons: in 1949, with the Class D Independence, Kan., club of the K. O. M. League, and in 1950 with the Class C Joplin, Mo., team of the Western Association. His earnings in those two seasons were between $175 and $250 a month. As recently as last winter he was working for $40 a week as an electrician's assistant in a lead mine

in Commerce. When the Yankees signed him in 1949, for future use, he was paid a little over $1,000, or roughly $24,000 less and five players fewer than the Yankees gave for DiMaggio, or $99,000 less than the Pittsburgh Pirates paid last year as a bonus to a pitcher named Paul Pettit. Mantle's wage with the Yankees this year will be about $7,500, or just $2,500 more than the minimum which must be paid to a big-league player.

For a "green-pea kid," as rookies are known in the baseball business, Mantle has handled himself with considerable aplomb on the field and with becoming diffidence, not unmarked by an understandable confusion, off it. His physical appearance serves to evoke the image, traditional and dear to Americans, of the clean-living country boy grappling, at great odds but ultimately in triumph, with the big city and its perils. He is five feet eleven inches tall and weighs 185 pounds, all of them symmetrically distributed. His shoulders are extremely broad and his ⟫⟫⟫

The young Mickey Mantle.

<<< forearms, wrists and neck unusually heavy even for an athlete. His hair is a dark blond and he cuts it fairly short. His eyes are blue and set far apart over a blunt nose. His mouth is big and sensitive and his teeth are big and white. When he smiles, even on request, as photographers are continually asking him to do, he looks a good deal younger than 19 and just as vulnerable.

It is possible that this image was on Stengel's mind a couple of weeks ago when he discussed Mantle with an acquaintance, although at the time Mantle was batting .316, had hit four home runs, two of them right-handed and two left-handed, and was leading the American League in runs batted in with 26.

"This publicity," Stengel said, "isn't too much good for him. He's bothered by it. Any kid just coming up would be. Here he is with all those interviews, trying to enlighten other people about himself rather than tending to baseball business. I don't think it's hurt him. I don't think it will, but if he reads all those press notices he'll ruin his eyesight. And then people want him to do this and do that, outside work, things that are not a baseball issue. A ball park is a player's home. He ought to stay home and use it."

Among the things that are not strictly baseball issues are the financial rewards for endorsements, testimonials and personal appearances, and perquisites of one kind or another that a baseball player may pick up outside the home Stengel likes his men to live in. Their size is limited only by the popular appeal of the player, his ability to bargain or that of the people he permits to bargain for him. This is clearly recognized by the Yankee organization. In a booklet called "Play Ball With the Yankees," which the club has its scouts distribute to likely prospects, it is noted that "Headlines in New York pay off richly in paid testimonials from products using baseball as a means of advertising."

This was pointed out to Mantle, not merely in the booklet but by George Weiss, the general manager of the Yankees, who recalled recently that during spring training he took Mantle aside informally, as he has done other talented young men before, and talked to him in these terms: "Mickey, we like to have our boys protected off the field as well as on. You'll get all kinds of propositions advanced to you. I would suggest that you avoid getting tied up with anybody. The club is at your service without cost." From that point on Mantle's experiences may be said to have been enlightening and they probably will prove profitable eventually, financially as well as intellectually.

By comparison with what has happened to him since he came to the big leagues, Mantle's life previously might be called bucolic or at least calm. He was born on Oct. 20, 1931, in Spavinaw, Okla., a town of 255 persons. Shortly thereafter, the family moved to Commerce. The boy was named Mickey Charles Mantle by his father, Elvin C. (Mutt) Mantle, now a ground foreman for a lead and zinc mining company. The Charles was for his grandfather, a left-handed pitcher for a semi-professional baseball team, who is now dead, and the Mickey for Mickey Cochrane, the outstanding catcher for the Philadelphia Athletics, whose real name is Gordon Stanley Cochrane. Mantle has a half-brother, Theodore (his mother had been married before), who was wounded while fighting with the Army in Korea and is in a hospital in Japan; twin brothers, Roy and Ray, 15; another brother, Larry, 10, and a sister, Barbara, 13.

"I always admired Cochrane," the senior Mantle has said, "and I wanted to make Mickey into a ball player ever since he was born, I guess. I put a glove on his hand when he was just a little bitty kid." In addition to this, the father, a right-hander, and the grandfather, a left-hander, pitched to the boy and taught him to bat from either side of the plate, a talent not often developed in ballplayers, and which has since earned young Mantle a typically alternative sportswriter's identification: "The Sweet Switcher."

At Commerce High School, Mantle played baseball, football and basketball. It was there that he met Merlyn Johnson, the girl he will probably marry when the season is over. The osteomyelitis that kept him out of the Army developed in 1946 when he was kicked above the left ankle in a football game. In high school baseball, he alternately played shortstop and pitched. His marks in school stayed satisfactorily between B and C.

Young Mantle was playing in a kid league in 1949 when an umpire suggested that he have a talk with Johnny Sturm, an old Yankee player who was then managing Joplin. Sturm got in touch with the Yankee office and a scout, or ivory-hunter, named Tom Greenwade saw Mantle play, paid him a shade more than $1,000 to bind him to a Yankee contract and sent him to Independence, where he batted .322 in 87 games. Last year, he came up to Joplin and led the Western Association with .383. In spring training with the Yankees this year, he outran everybody, batted .402, hit nine home runs and knocked in another thirty-one runs, whereupon the Yankees decided to season him neither at Binghamton nor Kansas City, but to bring him right up.

The job of converting Mantle into an outfielder was turned over to, among others, Tommy Henrich, the Yankees' great right fielder and first baseman, who is now a coach, and Joe DiMaggio, who has literally directed Mantle's steps in the field. "If he's a good ballplayer, and I think he is," Henrich said not long ago, "you won't know him in five years. The piece of business he is is there. The sculptor goes to work on him and there he is, a masterpiece."

Another thought crossed Henrich's mind and he stopped for a moment. "You know, in this great big city," he continued, "just base hits won't do the job. Heck, baseball is a form of education. Look at Joe—he got a better education out of baseball than out of college. It's probably the most important thing about the game. Mickey'll acquire a lot of culture out of baseball. An over-all polish."

Among other things, Mantle has acquired an apartment in midtown Manhattan, which he shares with Hank Bauer and Johnny Hopp, and some new clothes. During the Yankees' first home stand he bought two suits, two sport jackets, two pairs of slacks, two pairs of shoes and a half dozen pairs of argyle socks. "This is a lot better living, you know," he told a friend one day while sitting in the Yankee dressing room. "Look around," he said, and pointed at the floor of the lounge, which is covered with an expensive broadloom carpet. "When I first saw this," he went on, "I couldn't believe guys would walk around in spikes on rugs like that there."

Like other minor-league players, Mantle had been accustomed to traveling in buses, dressing out of rusty iron lockers on splintered wooden floors; to cold showers, playing mostly night games under poor lights, and eating on a $2.25 daily meal allowance which was never enough. He never saw a club doctor, a trainer or a diathermy machine until he came up to the Yankees, to say nothing of three changes of uniform at home and three on the road; unlimited meal allowances, roomettes and compartments on trains, accommodations in the best hotels, and fan mail. A couple of weeks ago he received some lyrics which hymned him thus:

DiMaggio recognized his ability for the game
And predicted he'd make the Hall of Fame.
At 19, talented and very able,
Mickey's skill is not a fable.
His arm is strong, his feet swift;
To watch him play gives one a lift.

"When you get up here," he said, reasonably enough, after discussing his new advantages, "you're bound to feel good about it, and you want to keep getting better and better so you can stay there. Maybe it bothered me a little bit at first, talking to all those people, but when they quit bothering you is when you start worrying."

◆

July 16, 1951

Mantle, Yankees' Prize Rookie, Shipped Back To Kansas City

Special to The New York Times.

DETROIT, July 15—Art Schallock, the 26-year-old lefthanded pitcher recently obtained from Hollywood, reported today and with his arrival, the Yankees immediately had another startling announcement.

For, in order to keep within the player limit, the Yanks had to lop off somebody and the fellow who drew the unlucky straw was Mickey Mantle, the highly touted youngster the Bombers had confidently expected to win the rookie-of-the-year accolade.

For Manager Casey Stengel the decision wasn't an easy one. For Casey is still very high on Mantle, who now goes to Kansas City on option, subject to recall on twenty-four hours' notice. But, as Stengel explained, he felt that in the end it would prove more beneficial for the 19-year-old infielder-outfielder if he got more minor league experience.

"This boy is good and make no mistake about that," emphasized Casey. "He came up as a shortstop but we converted him into a rightfielder and overnight he showed me he could do everything, run, field, throw, and hit a long ball. They don't come any faster.

"However, he had one weakness in that he struck out too often, but I'm certain he'll overcome that and he'll be back."

So certain is Stengel of this that as Mantle leaves to join the Yankee farm club he goes with the instructions that he is to be played regularly in centerfield, indicating that the Yankee board of strategy is convinced that Mickey will be the eventual replacement for the fading Joe DiMaggio.

In sixty-nine games this season, Mantle compiled a batting mark of .260, hit seven homers, nine doubles, five triples and drove in forty-five runs. ◆

October 6, 1951

Yanks' Joy Is Tempered by Loss of Mantle

By JAMES P. DAWSON

The Yankees were happy yesterday, but not excessively so. They were noisy, but in a restrained way. Casey Stengel was giving out with the big wink as he led his triumphant squad up the dugout runway to the clubhouse. But only the muscles about his eyes moved. There was no smile. Rather, the impression was that the Yankee pilot was more relieved than enthusiastic about this 3-to-1 victory over the Giants which deadlocked the world series at a game apiece.

For the triumph was costly. The Yanks lost the services of the highly publicized high school boy, Mickey Mantle, for the remainder of the series.

Dr. Sidney Gaynor, the Bombers' physician, made this announcement. He diagnosed Mantle's trouble as a sprained muscle on the inside of the right knee, sustained when Mickey crashed in some mysterious manner in the fifth inning under a fly raised by the Giants' Willie Mays.

Carried off the field on a stretcher as Hank Bauer took over in right field, Mantle was ruefully appraising a right leg encased in a splint and bandages when his mates barged into the clubhouse. With difficulty Mantle got into his street clothes, after answering solicitous inquiries. He hobbled, painfully, into Trainer Gus Mauch's room.

Mantle was concerned with his misfortune, sorrowed by an accident he could not explain, which abruptly took him out of his first world series before he really had a chance to shine. ◆

April 18, 1953

MANTLE'S 565-FOOT HOMER

By LOUIS EFFRAT
Special to The New York Times.

Mickey Mantle holds the ball he hit 565 feet and points to the dent in the ball where it hit a house after clearing the left field wall at Griffith Stadium.

WASHINGTON, APRIL 17—Unless and until contrary evidence is presented, recognition for the longest ball ever hit by anyone except Babe Ruth in the history of major league baseball belongs to Mickey Mantle of the Yankees. This amazing 21-year-old athlete today walloped one over the fifty-five-foot high left-field wall at Griffith Stadium. That ball, scuffed in two spots, finally stopped in the backyard of a house, about 565 feet away from home plate.

This remarkable homer, which helped the Yankees register a 7-3 victory over the Senators, was Mickey's first of the season, but he will have to go some, as will anyone else, to match it.

Chuck Stobbs, the Nat southpaw, had just walked Yogi Berra after two out in the fifth, when Mantle strode to the plate. Batting right-handed, Mickey blasted the ball toward left center, where the base of the front bleachers wall is 391 feet from the plate. The distance to the back of the wall is sixty-nine feet more and then the back wall is fifty feet high.

BOUNCES OUT OF SIGHT

Atop that wall is a football scoreboard. The ball struck about five feet above the end of the wall, caromed off the right and flew out of sight. There was no telling how much farther it would have flown had the football board not been there.

Before Mantle, who had cleared the right-field roof while batting left-handed in an exhibition game at Pittsburgh last week (only Babe Ruth and Ted Beard had ever done that) had completed running out the two-run homer, Arthur Patterson of the Yankees' front-office staff was on his way to investigate the measure.

Patterson returned with the following news:

A 10-year-old lad had picked up the ball. He directed Patterson to the backyard of 434 Oakdale Street and pointed to the place where he had found it, across the street from the park. The boy, Donald Dunaway of 343 Elm Street N.W., accepted an undisclosed sum of money for the prize, which was turned over to Mantle. The Yankee was to send a substitute ball, suitably autographed to the boy.

Until today, when Mantle made it more or less easy for Lefty Ed Lopat, who worked eight innings, to gain his first triumph, no other batter had cleared the left-field wall here. Some years ago, Joe DiMaggio bounced a ball over, but Mickey's accomplishment was on the fly.

Later in the contest, Mickey dragged a bunt that landed in front of second base and he outsped it for a single. Thus, in the same afternoon, it would appear, the young man from Commerce, Okla., fashioned one of the longest homers and the longest bunt on record. ◆

June 22, 1956

What a Change Mantle Hath Wrought in Fans

By LOUIS EFFRAT
Special to The New York Times.

CHICAGO, JUNE 21—A remarkable change seems to have come over baseball fans. Those who used to jeer the all-conquering Yankees now are cheering Casey Stengel's Bombers.

But what about the new popularity of the Yankees? One man is responsible—Mickey Mantle. Everywhere the Bombers go the Oklahoma Kid is acclaimed by the fans.

The demonstration at Briggs Stadium last night, following Mickey's twenty-seventh home run, was an amazing one. After the contest, which lifted the team's winning streak to seven, the outfield sprinkling system had to be turned on to save Mantle from being mobbed.

Mickey, who is eighteen games ahead of Babe Ruth's 1927 record pace, leads the majors in virtually every department. He is sizzling and spectators everywhere appear to be pulling for the switch-hitting slugger to better Ruth's mark of sixty homers in a season.

Most of the applause has been for Mantle, but some of the friendliness has rubbed off on other Yankees. Andy Carey, outstanding during the past month; Gil McDougald, sparkling at shortstop—a position that was foreign to him prior to this season—and Yogi Berra, enjoying his best campaign, are sharing in the popularity contest.

Mantle, setting a torrid pace with a .380 average and sixty-four runs batted in, has connected safely in his last eight contests. He has hit homers in every park in the league except Baltimore's Memorial Stadium and Boston's Fenway Park. Carey has hit in eleven consecutive games.

Beyond a doubt Mantle is the most talked-about player in the land. Currently, two national magazines are carrying Mickey's picture on the front cover. He appears to be enjoying the limelight and he is taking it in stride. ◆

June 22, 1956

MANTLE BEATS KANSAS CITY SHIFT IN 9-TO-3 TRIUMPH BY BOMBERS

Mickey Gets 4 Hits, 2 Against Trick Set-Up—Yanks Pole 4 Homers, 2 by Siebern

By LOUIS EFFRAT
Special to The New York Times.

KANSAS CITY, JUNE 25—Norm Siebern hit two homers, Hank Bauer and Joe Collins slugged one apiece and the Yankees snapped their four-game losing streak with a 9-3 victory over the Athletics tonight.

But even on a night when Mickey Mantle did not get a homer—he came close with a 421-foot triple—the Oklahoma kid "made" the news. It was not so much what Mantle did (4-for-5) but how he did it that excited the 24,642 fans at Municipal Stadium.

Mickey beat the "Mantle shift"—beat it twice, once by bunting, the next time by sheer power and speed.

On the last visit of the Athletics to the Yankee Stadium, Lou Boudreau, the Kansas City pilot, introduced a new shift against Mantle. He moved all his players, except the pitcher and catcher, to unorthodox positions whenever Mickey batted left-handed with no one on base,

ZERNIAL MOVES IN

Four times in the series Mantle was stymied by the special maneuver, devised by the man who previously had created the "Williams shift."

It is Boudreau's theory that there is safety in conceding a single to Mantle. So when Mickey came up in the third, facing Troy Herriage, a right-hander, and batting from the left side of the plate, the Athletics went into their act.

Gus Zernial, the left fielder, moved to third base and the others moved to deep positions, all protecting the right side. Mantle waited until the count had reached 3-and-2. Then, as Zernial moved toward a deep shortstop post, Mickey bunted his way to first base.

A similar situation developed in the fifth. This time Mantle, with Jose Santiago on the mound, overpowered the shift. He slashed a 2-and-2 delivery through the right side. It was a single, but Mickey had to hustle. He was almost thrown out at first by Cletis Boyer, the second baseman, who was stationed in short right field.

The next two times Mantle batted it was against Bobby Shantz and Jack McMahon, left-handers, so there was no shift. He singled against Shantz and flied to left against McMahon. In the first inning, Mantle had tripled to center against Herriage.

FOUR RUNS IN FIRST

The Yankees needed this victory to remain ahead of the idle Chicago White Sox. They got off in the right direction with a four-run outburst in the first. Billy Martin singled, Mantle tripled and Yogi Berra hit a sacrifice fly, scoring Mantle.

Following an error by Herriage on a grounder by Collins, Siebern hit the first of his two opposite-field homers over the left-field wall.

The Athletics put together singles by Joe De-Maestri, Enos Slaughter, Harry Simpson and Tim Thompson to score twice in the same frame, but Johnny Kucks had no trouble posting his tenth victory of the season. Siebern got his second round-tripper in the fourth. In the fifth Bauer and Collins put the Bombers out of reach with their homers.

Berra, fighting to emerge from one of the worst slumps of his career, doubled in the ninth. It was his first safety in twenty-four trips to the plate. To those who had suggested a rest for Berra, he said: "I have to stay in there and keep swinging. No one ever broke a slump sitting on the bench."

◆

October 1, 1956

MANTLE HEADS BOTH LEAGUES IN HOMERS, RUNS BATTED IN AND BATTING

By WILLIAM J. BRIORDY

MICKEY MANTLE YESTERDAY became the fourth player to win the major league triple batting crown.

The switch-hitting centerfielder of the Yankees closed the 1956 season with a batting percentage of .353, fifty-two homers and 130 runs batted in. Mantle drove in one run as the American League's champion Yankees ended their regular campaign by bowing to the Boston Red Sox, 7 to 4, in ten innings at the Stadium. ⟫⟫⟫

Mickey Mantle at Yankee stadium in 1956.

《《《 Since the Cleveland Indians lost to the Detroit Tigers, the Bombers completed their 154-game schedule nine games in front of the pack.

The fact that the Red Sox pushed three runs over the plate in the top of the tenth to beat the Yankees was secondary. Mantle commanded the news as he became the first Yankee to perform the batting feat for both leagues since Lou Gehrig turned the trick in 1934.

The last player to take the three championships in the majors was Ted Williams of Boston. He headed both leagues in 1942. Williams also led the American League in the three divisions in 1947.

Rogers Hornsby, with the Cards in 1925, was the first to win honors in both leagues.

Mantle, who will be 25 on Oct. 20, had already clinched the laurels in the home run department. On Saturday he had virtually sewed up the batting honors in his fight with Williams.

The only man who had a chance to beat the Oklahoman for the runs-batted-in title was Detroit's Al Kaline. Kaline batted two runs across yesterday to finish with 128.

Mantle had every intention to start yesterday's game, but Manager Casey Stengel saw it otherwise. Mickey, bothered by a pulled groin muscle, was kept on the bench until the ninth inning.

Stengel and the tenants of the Stadium press box had been receiving up-to-the-minute reports on Kaline's progress. The Ol' Perfessor said earlier in the day that in the event Mantle's runs-batted-in title was in jeopardy, he planned to send the Oklahoman in as a pinch-hitter.

Casey did just that. Mantle hit for Jim Coastes, a rookie right-hander, in the ninth. With Jerry Lumpe stationed at third base, Mantle's grounder to third brought in the run that tied the score, at 4-4. ◆

December 12, 1959

Yanks Trade Bauer, Larsen and Get Maris

By JOHN DREBINGER

THE YANKEES FINALLY BROKE the trading barrier yesterday. And no one need more than a single guess to name the party of the second part. Those obliging Kansas City Athletics have come through again this time in a seven-player transaction.

Balked at every turn in their efforts to deal elsewhere, the Bombers obtained Roger Maris, potentially an outfield star of major magnitude; Joe DeMaestri, a 31-year-old infielder, and Kent Hadley, a rookie first baseman.

The A's received Norm Siebern, a "potentially great" outfielder who, with the Yankees, never quite made it; Hank Bauer, a Yankee outfielder since 1948; Don Larsen, who in 1956 tossed the only perfect game in world series history, and Marv Throneberry, a husky young first baseman.

Fifteen deals, involving fifty-nine players, now have been made between the Yanks and the A's since 1955, when the Athletics moved their franchise from Philadelphia to Kansas City.

"I hated to see so fine a competitor as Bauer go," said Weiss, "and we'll always feel indebted to Larsen for his perfect game performance. However, in Maris we have a young outfielder who should develop into a fine player at the Stadium.

The 25-year-old Maris definitely was the key man of the deal so far as the Yankees were concerned. A left-handed batter, Roger made his major-league debut with Cleveland in 1957 and was traded to the A's in June of 1958 in a multi-player deal that sent Vic Power to the Indians. Roger hit twenty-eight home runs that year.

Maris started the 1959 season with a great splurge and was leading the league with a .344 average when, shortly before the first All-Star game, he was stricken with appendicitis. Though he recovered quickly, he never regained his former stride and finished the season with a .273 average, sixteen homers and seventy-two runs batted in. ◆

March 12, 1960

MANTLE ACCEPTS $7,000 PAY SLASH

Mantle Reports to Yanks in Fine Trim but Will Miss Cardinal Game Today

By JOHN DREBINGER
Special to The New York Times.

ST. PETERSBURG, FLA., MARCH 11—In no more than it takes him to scoot from home plate to first base, Mickey Mantle brought his holdout siege to a close today.

The Yankees' 28-year-old outfielder star, who had flown in from Dallas to make a surprise appearance here late last night, went into a huddle with George Weiss, the Yankee general manager, this morning. Minutes later the pair emerged with the announcement that Mickey had signed his 1960 contract after missing nine days of training.

It is understood that Mantle signed for $65,000. This represents a $7,000 slash from the $72,000 he received last year. The contract that the club originally sent to him in January, which he immediately rejected, called for $55,000.

Directly after the signing, Mantle was whisked out to Miller Huggins Field, where Casey Stengel and his Bombers already were working out in preparation for their first exhibition game with the Cardinals tomorrow at Al Lang Field.

PLAYERS SEEK SHELTER

Not even the fact that a heavy shower came down minutes after Mantle took the field dampened the enthusiasm with which the players greeted the husky Oklahoman. As all hands scurried for shelter in the spacious new field house, there was an air of jubilation such as is rarely seen except after an important victory.

A few of the first-year rookies, who never had seen Mantle before, gaped open-mouthed. From the older hands came back-slapping and the usual clubhouse banter. Whitey Ford, one of Mickey's closest friends, quipped with a dead pan: "I thought I hadn't seen you around of late. What kept you?" Everyone seemed relieved that the tension was over.

Mantle also appeared relaxed; he was all smiles even when he ruefully admitted, "They gave me a pretty stiff cut." Asked whether the figure he accepted was a compromise, Mickey shrugged and said: "Compromise?" and let it go at that. Incidentally, this was his first pay slash since joining the Yankees in 1951.

Asked what had brought about this change of heart after he repeatedly had said that he would not report until his differences were settled, Mantle said that he had acted on the advice of friends.

In explaining his side of it, Weiss said he had felt all along that the "money difference" would be no problem.

"To me it was a question of attitude," said Weiss. "And I wanted him here to tell him why he had to take a cut. I pointed out that in the last five years his salary had been steadily increased from $11,000 to—well, make it seventy-odd thousand.

"I then explained that when a player with that money fell off the way he did last year, he had to expect a cut of something more than just $1,000. And that's all there was to that. It's all there for him to get back, and more, if he has the kind of season I fully believe he can have." ◆

November 10, 1960

MARIS EDGES MANTLE FOR M.V.P.

BOSTON, Nov. 9 (AP)—Roger Maris today was named the American League's most valuable player for 1960. The slugging outfielder edged his New York Yankee team-mate, Mickey Mantle, by three votes on the balloting.

The prize trade acquisition from the Kansas City Athletics collected 225 points in his first season with the league champions to Mantle's 222.

The results of the balloting announced by Hy Hurwitz, secretary of the Baseball Writers Association of America, were the second closest in the history or the award. In 1947, Joe DiMaggio beat Ted Williams for the honor, 202-201.

Mantle received the honor in 1956 and 1957. In 1957, he received 233 points to 209 for Williams, who at the age of 39, batted .388. Williams lost out by being named ninth on one ballot and tenth on another.

Maris is a 26-year-old, Minnesota-born athlete. He led the American League in runs batted in (112) and slugging percentage (.581) while hitting .283. His thirty-nine home runs put him one behind Mantle's title-winning 40.

Maris apparently won the hairline decision on the basis of a great first-half campaign and some timely September slugging. He missed three weeks of the race after midseason because of bruised ribs suffered while trying to break up a double play sliding into second base. Thereafter he could not match his early pace.

"I thought it was possible, but I wasn't expecting to win it," Maris said when notified at his Raytown, Mo., home that he had received the honor. "This is a happy feeling." ◆

Roger Maris won the 1960 Most Valuable Player award by three votes.

March 22, 1961

Yankees Shift Training Camp to Fort Lauderdale

By JOHN DREBINGER
Special to The New York Times.

WEST PALM BEACH, FLA., MARCH 21—The Yankees today confirmed that they would switch their spring training camp from St. Petersburg to Fort Lauderdale in 1962.

Simultaneously, city officials in St. Petersburg announced that New York's new National League club, which begins operations next year, would replace the Bombers in the Sunshine City, long the training base of the Yankees.

Some such move as this had to be taken before the Yankees could complete arrangements to switch to Fort Lauderdale in 1962 because the Bombers were under contract to train in St. Pete next spring.

However, E. C. Robison, chairman of the St. Petersburg Baseball Committee, released the Yankees from this obligation when he closed with the new National League entry.

The National League club, of which George M. Weiss, the former Yankee general manager, is president, signed a five-year contract, with a five-year option, to train in St. Petersburg as co-tenant of the St. Louis Cardinals. ◆

July 18, 1961

Ruth's Record Can Be Broken Only in 154 Games, Frick Rules

FORD FRICK THREW a protective screen around Babe Ruth's season record of sixty home runs yesterday. The baseball commissioner ruled that no batter would be credited with breaking the record unless he did it in 154 games.

The ruling was prompted by the home run feats this season of Roger Maris and Mickey Mantle of the Yankees. Maris had hit thirty-five homers before last night's double-header with the Orioles and Mantle had clouted thirty-two.

Maris is nineteen games ahead of the pace Ruth set in 1927 when he established the mark with the Yankees. Mantle is eight games ahead of Ruth's schedule.

TEN TEAMS PLAY NOW
The prospects of the record being broken are further enhanced by the expanded schedule in the American League. With ten teams in the league, the Americans are playing 162 games.

The National League will add Houston and New York next year and also will expand to 162 games.

However, Frick said that any player who hit more than sixty homers after the 154th game would get a distinctive mark in the record book to show it was compiled under a 162-game schedule.

Frick's ruling:

"Any player who may hit more than sixty home runs during his club's first 154 games would be recognized as having established a new record. However, if the player does not hit more than sixty until after his club has played 154 games, there would have to be some distinctive mark in the record books to show that Babe Ruth's record was set under a 154-game schedule and the total of more than sixty was compiled while a 162-game schedule was in effect.

"We also would apply the same reasoning if a player should equal Ruth's total of sixty in the first 154 games, he would be recognized as tying Ruth's record. If in more than 154 games, there would be a distinction in the record book." ◆

August 21, 1961

Maris Hits No. 49 and Mantle No. 46

By JOHN DREBINGER
Special to The New York Times.

CLEVELAND, AUG. 20—The Yankees advanced majestically on all fronts today before a gathering of 56,307, the season's largest paid attendance in Cleveland's picturesque lake-front stadium.

Roger Maris and Mickey Mantle finally got around to resuming their assault on the Babe Ruth home run record of sixty. Roger hit his forty-ninth and Mickey his forty-sixth. This precious pair provided all the runs in the Bombers' 6-0 victory over the Indians in the first game of the double-header.

Ralph Terry tossed the shut-out with a glittering four-hitter. It was his tenth mound triumph against one defeat.

Mantle's homer came in the first inning of the opener with two aboard. It was Mickey's first home run since last Sunday in Washington. Mantle, who also had two singles and a walk in the first game, singled, walked twice and grounded out in the second, driving in a total of six runs in the two games.

MARIS, MANTLE AHEAD

Maris' homer, which put him within eleven of the coveted Ruthian goal, came in the third with one aboard and was his first since last Wednesday. It also ended a hitless string of thirteen official times at bat and was, in fact, Roger's only hit of the four-game series here.

However, despite this let-down, both Maris and Mantle are still running well ahead of the record pace of 1927. That year, the Babe did not hit No. 46 until the Yanks' 132d game, on Sept. 6. He hit No. 49 in the 134th game on Sept. 7.

It might be noted that it was on those two days, Sept. 6 and 7, that Ruth piled up a total of five homers. Those, in a large measure, contributed to his whirlwind September spurt of seventeen. Maris, at least, has hurdled this imposing obstacle.

In the Yankees' 162-game schedule, Maris and Mantle have thirty-nine games remaining, although they have only thirty-one if they are to reach their objective within Commissioner Ford Frick's 154-game limit.

Mantle, who seldom takes batting practice before a double-header, was relaxing in front of his locker before the opener when he was asked, "What's the big idea of taking batting practice in the first game?"

"Why not," said the switcher. "You always belt one or two in batting practice that don't count, so why not take it when it counts." Mickey then proved his point by clouting No. 46 his first time up. ◆

September 11, 1961

Mantle Hits No. 53; Maris Is Stopped

By JOHN DREBINGER

MICKEY MANTLE EDGED BACK into the home run derby at the Stadium yesterday with his fifty-third homer of the year but Roger Maris, the pace-setter in the joint assault on Babe Ruth's record of sixty, remained stalled at fifty-six.

Added to this, the Yankees again thrashed the Indians, taking both ends of a double-header by scores of 7-6 and 9-3. That gave Ralph Houk's Bombers a sweep of the five-game series and extended their winning streak to twelve.

Any combination of eight Yankee victories and Detroit defeats will mathematically clinch the pennant for New York, an amazing turn of events considering that barely ten days ago the Yanks held a lead of no more than a game and a half.

MANTLE BEHIND RUTH

Mantle, trailing Maris by three as the thrilling home run derby moves into its final stages, is now two games behind the Ruthian pace of 1927. Maris, though held to two singles, one in each game yesterday, is still four games ahead of Ruth's timetable.

Yesterday's second game was the 144th for the Yanks. Ruth's fifty-third homer came in his 143d game. His fifty-sixth was hit in his 149th game.

Maris and Mantle now have ten games left if they are to match Ruth's record within the 154-game limit set by Commissioner Ford Frick. Eighteen games remain on the Yanks' full schedule of 162 games.

Mantle's homer gave the M-squad a combined total of 109, which surpasses by two the combined Ruth-Lou Gehrig total of 107 in 1927. ◆

September 13, 1961

Homer? No. Maris Wanted to Bunt

Ace Says Umpire's Bad Calls Spoiled A Squeeze Play

By LOUIS EFFRAT
Special to The New York Times.

CHICAGO, SEPT. 12—Roger Maris is a forthright young man who speaks his piece, lets the chips fall where they may and, possibly, would rather be right than the home run king of the majors.

In the unbearably hot dressing room where the Yankees awaited the official calling-off of tonight's damp doings at Comiskey Park, Maris blamed Hank Soar, the plate umpire, for his failure to hit a homer in four attempts.

Maris, with fifty-six home runs to his credit, lost ground in his race against Babe Ruth's 1927 record of sixty. He now is only three games ahead of Ruth's pace. Mickey Mantle, who, like Maris, got a single in three official times at bat tonight (Maris walked once), is three games behind Ruth.

Maris insisted he was right and Soar was wrong at least three times on strike calls during the abbreviated contest. "I didn't get too many strikes, yet they were being called strikes," Maris complained. "I was swinging in self-defense."

"Soar is usually a good umpire," he went on, "but he was off tonight."

He went on:

"In the second inning, he called a third strike against me, saying I had swung, although I checked my swing. My body moved, but the bat didn't. Then, in the sixth, I was going to bunt, but the pitch was high and unbuntable, but he called that a strike, too."

Maris did not pinpoint the third time he felt Soar had erred. »»»

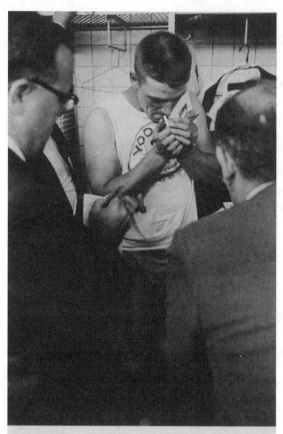

Roger Maris being questioned at his locker after a 1961 game.

«« Why would Maris, who now has only nine games left in which he can, in accordance with Commissioner Ford Frick's ruling, catch or pass Ruth within 154, want to waste a pitch with a bunt?

"Why not bunt?" he countered. "Bobby Richardson was at third, Tony Kubek on first, two were out and the infield was laying back. A successful bunt would have squeezed over an important run."

And how did Maris feel about the rain having cost him at least one more time at bat, at least one more chance to swing for the fences?

"Look, right now winning the pennant is as important to me as breaking that record." ◆

September 18, 1961

Maris, Second Only to Ruth Now, Stirred by the Thrill of the Chase

By LOUIS EFFRAT
Special by The New York Times.

DETROIT, SEPT. 17—What was Roger Maris thinking as he rounded the base paths following his game-winning homer in the twelfth inning at Tiger Stadium today?

"Truthfully," the Yankee slugger said later, "I thought first that these were two runs that would put us ahead of the Tigers. When I stepped on home plate, I thought about having hit my fifty-eighth homer. Now, here in the dressing room a half hour later, I'm thinking about what a great thrill it is to know that I'm second to Babe Ruth."

By that, Maris meant that only the Babe ever hit more home runs than he has. Ruth walloped sixty for the Yankees in 1927, fifty-nine in 1921. Two others, Jimmie Foxx in 1932 and Hank Greenberg in 1938, hit fifty-eight.

The 27-year-old right fielder, who now needs only two homers to tie Ruth's record and three to beat it, was asked to compare his emotions today with those after earlier long-range blasts this season.

"You always feel good when you hit one, but you don't lose your head," he said. "Maybe if I make sixty I'll lose my head then, but up to now I haven't."

HOW MUCH OF A CHANCE?

And how much of a chance did he feel he has to make sixty or more?

"I should be able to do it, based on what I've done so far," Roger said, "but I can't be sure. I might go into a slump and not hit another. Don't forget, except for the last five games at Yankee Stadium, I'll be playing in two big ball parks for a left-handed hitter—Memorial Stadium at Baltimore and Fenway Park at Boston."

(Incidentally, Maris has not connected for an

official homer at Baltimore this year. He hit one in July, but rain washed that game out.)

Throughout the season, Maris has been thinking in terms of 162 games rather than the 154-game deadline set by Commissioner Ford Frick.

"I think Maris will do it within 162 games," Manager Ralph Houk said.

Yogi Berra was more emphatic. "Roger is a cinch to do it in 162 games," he said.

Mickey Mantle, who has been going along with Frick's ruling, repeated what he had said yesterday: "I think Roger has a helluva shot at the record."

The longer Maris sat on a stool answering questions, posing for pictures and sipping a cold drink, the more he seemed to realize the significance of his accomplishment.

He was grateful for the extra two times at bat afforded him when the game went into extra innings, of course. He was appreciative, too, of Tony Kubek's two-out single that made it possible for Maris to come up for the big swing in the twelfth.

Belatedly, the feeling of excitement, the electricity, the drama and the suspense seem to have gripped Maris.

Today he showed he is a man with feelings, not a smooth-swinging automaton. ◆

Roger Maris about to swing against the Tigers at Briggs Stadium in Detroit.

September 21, 1961

Maris Is Resigned to * in the Record Books

* Will Mean Record Was Set After 154 Games

By LOUIS EFFRAT
Special to The New York Times.

BALTIMORE, SEPT. 20—Beads of sweat rolled down his cheeks. Fatigue was written on his face. But his eyes told the story.

Roger Maris described his reactions to hitting homer No. 59 in the Yanks 154th game, but his eyes were more eloquent. They told of happiness, of pride, and of a feeling of relief.

Maris, surrounded and half-pinned to the dressing room wall at Memorial Stadium, even conceded to Commissioner Ford Frick's asterisk.

The commissioner, it will be recalled, had ruled that if Maris was to match or break Babe Ruth's record of sixty homers in a season, he would have to do it within 154 games. Any mark beyond that, Frick insisted, would get an asterisk in the record book.

"I tried hard all night," said Maris, who con-

Mickey Mantle and Roger Maris after a game with the Baltimore Orioles in 1961.

nected for No. 59 against Milt Pappas in the third inning, "but I got only one. (It was a low fast ball, which Maris pulled to right.)

"Now that it's all over, I'm happy with what I got. From now on I'll concentrate on straightening myself out—I was swinging for some bad balls—for the world series."

What about the 162-game season? What if he went on to hit one or more homers?

"Commissioner Frick makes the rules," he said. "If all I will be entitled to will be an asterisk, it will be all right with me."

The 27-year-old Maris now is in line to earn a considerable sum of money because of his long-range clouting, but he had one regret. Twice he had tried to check his swing against the knuckleballing Hoyt Wilhelm in the ninth. The second time the ball tricked meekly to Wilhelm, who made the out.

"I wanted to go out swinging, but I never did get to swing once against Wilhelm," Maris said.

Meanwhile, the other Yankees, led by their freshman manager, Ralph Houk, were celebrating the victory in the pennant race. They poured champagne over one another's heads, and when they ran out of champagne they switched to beer.

Few escaped this ritual. Few wanted to.

Houk, taking time out to review the season, called it a "team effort." He missed hardly anyone when it came to giving credit.

"Twenty-five players did it. Sure, the homers by Maris and Mickey Mantle helped. They were great. But so was the infield. So was Yogi Berra in left field.

"So were the catchers and so were Whitey Ford, Luis Arroyo, Ralph Terry and the others. Everyone lent a hand. This was a team effort.

'Now,' said Houk, "let's all have fun tonight. After that, we'll try to get set for the world series against the National League team. I plan to keep Maris in the line-up and move the others around to keep them in shape for the series." ◆

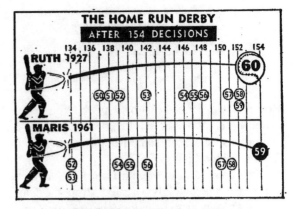

Ruth-Maris Comparison

Comparison tables showing the home-run production of Babe Ruth in 1927 and of Roger Maris this season, both in 154 decisions:

	HR.	Total RH. Pitch.	LH. Pitch.	BB.	SO.	AB.	Avg.
Ruth	60	41	19	138	89	540	.356
Maris	59	47	12	89	77	567	.270

WHERE HOMERS WERE HIT

	Ruth	Maris
Baltimore	..	1
Bloomington, Minn.	..	1
Boston	8	4
Chicago	3	5
Cleveland	4	5
Detroit	4	5
Kansas City	..	4
Los Angeles	..	2
New York	28	28
Philadelphia	5	..
St. Louis	4	..
Washington	4	4
Total	**60**	**59**

TOTALS AGAINST TEAMS

	Ruth	Maris
Baltimore	..	2
Boston	11	6
Chicago	6	13
Cleveland	9	8
Detroit	8	8
Kansas City	..	5
Los Angeles	..	4
Minnesota	..	4
Philadelphia	9	..
St. Louis	9	..
Washington	8	9
Total	**60**	**59**

September 27, 1961

Maris Hits No. 60

By JOHN DREBINGER

ROGER MARIS LAST NIGHT became the first major league baseball player to hit sixty home runs in a championship season since Babe Ruth achieved that record total in 1927.

Maris connected in the third inning of a game the Yankees eventually wrested from the Baltimore Orioles at the Stadium, 3 to 2, before a roaring crowd of 19,401.

Under Commissioner Ford C. Frick's ruling, Maris will not be credited with a tie for the Ruthian record because his No. 60 was not made within the 154-game schedule limit that prevailed in Ruth's day.

The 27-year-old Missourian's feat will be listed in the record book, along with any more homers he may hit in the Yankees' four remaining games of their 1961 schedule, with a notation that all those after No. 59 were made in a 162-game season. Last night's game was the Yanks' 159th, including a tie. The Bombers' season ends Sunday.

With Jack Fisher, a 22-year-old right-hander on the mound, Maris exploded his homer in the third inning with two outs, the bases empty and the count two balls and two strikes.

The Roger stroked a powerful drive that soared into the third deck of the right-field stand some six feet inside the foul pole and crashed into the seats four rows back.

BALL PRESENTED TO MARIS

It struck the back of a seat and bounced back onto the field. Earl Robinson, the Oriole right fielder, picked it up and tossed it to the first-base umpire, Ed Hurley. The umpire flipped it to the Yankee first-base coach, Wally Moses, who rolled it to the Yankee bench seconds after Maris arrived there amid a deafening roar from the crowd.

The jubilant fans kept up their wild cheering until the shy, modest Maris emerged from the dugout, appeared on the top step and waved his cap to them.

The Maris blow landed some forty feet to the right of Babe's No. 60, which landed in the then wooden Stadium bleachers that extended to the right-field foul line.

Mrs. Claire Ruth, the Babe's widow, was present last night and appeared on television on the Red Barber Show after the game. She congratulated Maris on his achievement.

"This is easily the greatest thrill of my life," said Maris. ◆

Roger Maris hits number 61.

October 2, 1961

MARIS HITS 61ST IN FINAL GAME

Yank First to Exceed 60 Home Runs in Major Leagues

By JOHN DREBINGER

ROGER MARIS YESTERDAY became the first major league player in history to hit more than sixty home runs in a season.

The 27-year-old Yankee outfielder hit his sixty-first at the Stadium before a roaring crowd of 23,154 in the Bombers' final game of the regular campaign.

That surpassed by one the sixty that Babe Ruth hit in 1927. Ruth's mark has stood in the record book for thirty-four years.

Artistically enough, Maris' homer also produced the only run of the game as Ralph Houk's 1961 American League champions defeated the Red Sox, 1 to 0, in their final tune-up for the world series, which opens at the Stadium on Wednesday.

Maris hit his fourth-inning homer in his second time at bat. The victim of the blow was Tracy Stallard, a 24-year-old Boston rookie right-hander. Stallard's name, perhaps, »

Maris' 61st homer was caught in the rightfield stands by Sal Durante.

≪≪ will in time gain as much renown as that of Tom Zachary, who delivered the pitch that Ruth slammed into the Stadium's right-field bleachers for No. 60 on the next to the last day of the 1927 season.

Along with Stallard, still another name was bandied about at the Stadium after Maris' drive. Sal Durante, a 19-year-old truck driver from Coney Island, was the fellow who caught the ball as it dropped into the lower right-field stand, some ten rows back and about ten feet to the right of the Yankee bull pen.

For this achievement the young man won a $5,000 award and a round trip to Sacramento, Calif., offered by a Sacramento restaurant proprietor, as well as a round trip to the 1962 World's Fair in Seattle.

Maris was fooled by Stallard on an outside pitch that he stroked to left field for an out in the first inning. He let two pitches go by when he came to bat in the fourth with one out, and the bases empty. The first one was high and outside. The second one was low and appeared to be inside.

WAIST-HIGH FAST BALL

The crowd, interested in only one thing, a home run, greeted both pitches with a chorus of boos. Then came the moment for which fans from coast to coast had been waiting since last Tuesday night, when Maris hit his sixtieth.

Stallard's next pitch was a fast ball that appeared to be about waist high and right down the middle. In a flash, Roger's rhythmic swing, long the envy of left-handed pull hitters, connected with the ball.

Almost at once, the crowd sensed that this was it. An ear-splitting roar went up as Maris, standing spellbound for just an instant at the plate, started his triumphant jog around the bases. As he came down the third-base line, he shook hands joyously with a young fan who had rushed onto the field to congratulate him.

Crossing the plate and arriving at the Yankee dugout, he was met by a solid phalanx of teammates. This time they made certain the modest country lad from Raytown, Mo., acknowledged the crowd's plaudits.

He had been reluctant to do so when he hit No. 60, but this time the Yankee players wouldn't let Roger come down the dugout steps. Smiling broadly, the usually unemotional player lifted his cap from his blond close-cropped thatch and waved it to the cheering fans. Not until he had taken four bows did his colleagues allow him to retire to the bench.

Ruth's record, of course, will not be erased. On July 17, Commissioner Ford C. Frick ruled that Ruth's record would stand unless bettered within a 154-game limit, since that was the schedule in 1927. Maris hit fifty-nine homers in the Yanks' first 154 games to a decision. He hit his sixtieth four games later.

However, Maris will go into the record book as having hit the sixty-first in a 162-game schedule.

Maris finished the season with 590 official times at bat. Ruth, in 1927, had 540 official times at bat. Their total appearances at the plate, however, were nearly identical—698 for Maris and 692 for Ruth.

Though it had taken 162 games (actually, 163, since the Yankees played one tie) a player finally had risen from the ranks to pass Ruth's majestic record. Maris himself missed only two of these games, although he sat out a third without coming to bat when, after playing the first inning in the field, he was bothered by something in his eye.

For thirty-four years the greatest sluggers in baseball had striven to match Ruth's mark. Mickey Mantle fought Maris heroically through most of the season, but in the closing weeks he fell victim to a virus attack and his total stopped at fifty-four.

The two who came closest in the past were Jimmie Foxx and Hank Greenberg. In 1932, Foxx hit fifty-eight. In 1938, Greenberg matched that figure. Indeed, Greenberg had the best chance of all to crack the record. When he hit No. 58, he still had five games to play in a 154-game schedule. ◆

October 10, 1961

Yanks Defeat Reds, Take World Series for 19th Time

Blanchard and Lopez Hit Homers—Jay Routed in 5-Run First Inning

By JOHN DREBINGER
Special to The New York Times.

CINCINNATI, OCT. 9—The Yankees defeated the Cincinnati Reds today, 13 to 5, and won the world series for the nineteenth time in twenty-six attempts.

Eight Cincinnati pitchers gave a total of fifteen hits, including home runs by John Blanchard and Hector Lopez. A five-run first inning started the Yankees to their fourth victory in the five games that this series lasted.

Before a crowd that numbered 32,589 for the third successive day, Ralph Houk's Bombers routed Joey Jay after he had retired only two batters. This was the Jay whose four-hitter in the second game had brought Cincinnati its only victory of the competition.

Three innings later the Yanks staged another five-run drive and sealed the defeat of Fred Hutchinson's National Leaguers. The 41-year-old Houk, who succeeded Casey Stengel last winter, had won a world championship in his first season as manager.

YANKEE STRENGTH DILUTED

The Yanks won this game with several of their stars sidelined or playing only minor roles.

Mickey Mantle, who had appeared in only two series games because of a painful wound in his right hip, played no part in this one. Neither did Yogi Berra. Berra was out with a bruised right shoulder, the result of a slide into third base yesterday.

Roger Maris hit nothing more than a double. It was only the second safe blow of the series for Maris, who had hit sixty-one home runs in the regular season.

Blanchard, who played right field in Houk's revised line-up, hit a homer that started the scoring in the first inning. Later he hit a double.

Lopez, playing left field, hit his homer with two runners on base in the fourth. Lopez drove in five runs in all. Before his homer, he had batted in a run with a triple. After the homer, he pushed over a run with a bunt.

Only once did the Reds raise a threatening hand and it was enough to wreck the afternoon for Ralph Terry, whom Houk had chosen to pitch the series clincher.

Terry had a 6-0 lead after the second inning, but he was removed in the third after a three-run homer for the Reds by Frank Robinson.

Terry was replaced by Bud Daley, a knuckleballing left-hander. Daley yielded a two-run homer to Wally Post in the fifth, but that was to be all for the Reds.

Daley, who had started the season with the Kansas City Athletics, received credit for the victory. He held the mound for six and two-thirds innings and permitted only five hits. ◆

Roger Maris accepts the 1961 Most Valuable Player award from American League President Joe Cronin at Yankee Stadium.

November 16, 1961

Maris Named Again as Most Valuable With Mantle Next

By JOHN DREBINGER

PRIZES CONTINUE TO FALL to Roger Maris and yesterday he picked up the big one.

The Yankee right fielder, whose sixty-one home runs last season were the most ever hit by a major league player in a championship campaign, was voted the American League's most valuable player for 1961.

The 27-year-old Midwesterner, who makes his home just outside Kansas City, bagged the prized award for the second year in a row. And for the second time he made it after a stirring race with his illustrious team-mate, Mickey Mantle. Roger won it by 4 points in the third closest contest in the history of the award.

In the poll of the twenty-man committee of the Baseball Writers Association of America, Maris scored 202 points to Mantle's 198. Mickey had battled Maris in the most thrilling two-man home run derby in history until illness and an infection in the final ten days stalled him at fifty-four homers. In last year's voting Maris topped Mantle, 225 to 222.

ONLY ONE RACE CLOSER

Only one other race was ever closer than these last two. That was in 1947 when Joe DiMaggio of the Yankees outscored Ted Williams of the Red Sox, 202 to 201.

Maris got the news at his home in Raytown, Mo., just before he left to survey some property. He is building a new house outside of Kansas City, a sure indication that he plans to cash in heavily on his big year when he signs for 1962.

Maris is the fifth American Leaguer to win the prize in two successive years since the present system was inaugurated in 1931.

Jimmy Foxx, then with the Philadelphia Athletics, did it in 1932 and 1933. Hal Newhouser, a one-time Detroit pitching star, made it in 1944 and 1945. Another Yankee, Yogi Berra, scored in 1954 and 1955 and Mantle in 1956 and 1957. Berra and DiMaggio are the only ones to have won three times. ◆

December 23, 1961

RECORD OF MARIS HAS NO ASTERISK

Slugging Averages Reflect Cronin's View on Homers

By JOHN DREBINGER

THIS IS THE TIME when the "official averages" hit the sport pages. They have come to be something of a pre-holiday tradition. For the most part they merely put the stamp of authenticity on what fans have known ever since the season ended.

However, every now and then something interesting comes up, such as in the final batch of statistics released by the American League yesterday. These are on the slugging percentage competition which, as was unofficially reported weeks ago, Mickey Mantle won quite decisively. Also, they offer a compilation of the various records broken in the major leagues during 1961.

And here something intriguing comes to light. Among the thirty-five major league marks set, there is this listing:

"Most home runs by player, season, 61, Roger Maris."

The significant point is that there is no star, asterisk or footnote attached to the listing to show the record was set in a 162-game schedule and therefore not to be confused with the Babe Ruth record of sixty, or any other record set when the league played only 154 games.

It simply states that the record for most home runs in a season is 61 and the Yankee slugger set

it. And so, in his customary quiet way, Joe Cronin, president of the American League, seems to have put over a point he maintained last summer while debates raged over Commissioner Ford C. Frick's 154-game ruling.

Frick had ruled that to gain recognition for breaking the Ruth record of sixty, set in 1927, Maris must achieve it within 154 games. On that game Maris had only fifty-nine.

Although he never made an open issue of it. Cronin made no secret of the fact that he never saw eye to eye with that ruling, so far as it applied to any season records.

"Sure," he remarked only recently, "you can put in the record books anything you want. The book is full of all sorts of conditions under which various records were set. But if anyone asks what's the record for most home runs in a season, you have to say sixty-one, by Maris. A season is a season."

As distinguished from a league record, a major league record is one that tops both the National as well as the American League.

Mantle, who trailed Maris in the home run derby with fifty-four, and also was shaded by his teammate for the most valuable player award, got some measure of revenge when he won the slugging title for the third time with a mark of .687.

Slugging percentage is determined by dividing the official times at bat into the total bases on hits, instead of only hits, as is done in determining batting averages.

Mantle, in 514 official times at bat, hit for 353 total bases. In addition to his fifty-four homers, he hit eighty-seven singles, sixteen doubles and six triples. Norm Cash of the Tigers placed second with .662 and Jim Gentile of the Orioles finished third with .646. Maris placed fourth with .620. ◆

January 8, 1962

Maris' Analysis: The Bat Was Live

Yank Says Lightness and 'Whip' Help Modern Hitter

By FRANK M. BLUNK

A BETTER BAT, not a livelier ball, helped Roger Maris to his record total of sixty-one home runs last year.

The 27-year-old Yankee outfielder expressed this belief yesterday while attending the Sporting Goods Fair, in which some 250 manufacturers of equipment, accessories and apparel are participating at the Hotel New Yorker.

"Newspapers and sports magazines devoted many columns last season to discussions of the official major league baseball," said Maris. "They had scientists taking the ball apart and comparing it with the baseballs used in Babe Ruth's time. Some found it livelier; others saw no difference. But no one had much to say about the bats we use.

"There has been a great improvement in bats. The ones we use nowadays are comparatively light, with slender handles. You can 'whip' them with greater facility and speed. They are more neatly in line with the speed of a man's reflexes, enabling him to meet a curving ball squarely or to get a better piece of a jumping fast ball.

"I daresay that if you made a survey of all the power hitters in the major leagues today, you'd find that most of them prefer these lighter, more slender bats.

"As a hitter, I am a natural upper-cutter. That means that I come up under a ball with the bat. In order to get a good piece of the ball, I have to have perfect timing. I do this better with the new bats than I ever did in the early part of my career with heavier, fat-handled bats.

"Last year, quite by accident while on a visit to North Carolina, I met a fellow who had one of the bats used by Ruth, when he was blasting home runs out of American League parks. The

Roger Maris during his record 61 homer season.

Babe had autographed the bat and on it also were some records of what it had done. I was asked to take some swings with it.

"Boy, compared to our present-day bats, this one, surely more than 40 ounces, was like swinging a 4-by-4 piece of timber at an aspirin tablet. Last year with the Yankees, I used a 33-ounce bat. I'll use the same type and weight this year."

Maris was here primarily to inspect the new glove that A. G. Spalding and Bros., Inc., had designed for him. It has a wide slitted web between the thumb and first finger and is a far cry from the thin-webbed, small fingered gloves of earlier years.

"Most of the balls dropped by outfielders," Maris said, "are those that hit the glove squarely in the palm and bounce out. So, with these new gloves, we don't make many errors on catches these days, we'd better not, if we want to stay in the big leagues."

The tensions and pressures that come with fame continue to bother Maris. He is a sensitive young man, and upset by some of the writings and utterances of "old-timers who think any modern baseball player who even aspires to equal or better the records made thirty and forty years ago is a bum."

After a few more years in the limelight, Maris may become hardened to his critics, but at the moment he has an idea that as soon as he has established financial security for himself and his family he will, "by a snap decision," quit the game. ◆

May 20, 1962

Whitey Ford: 27,500 Pitches and Five Worn Fingers

He Has Virtually Erased Whorls in 12-Year Career

By ROBERT L. TEAGUE

DURING THE NATURAL COURSE of his exemplary career as a major league baseball pitcher, Edward Charles (Whitey) Ford has forced his left arm to execute a staggering number of unnatural exercises, so many in fact that their cumulative effect is tantamount to self-torture and mutilation.

Ford has delivered approximately 27,500 pitches to American League batsmen since joining the Yankees in 1950. Few if any human arms were designed with such a pastime in mind.

For that reason, the bellwether of the Yankee mound staff was buttonholed between mound assignments and asked to describe the life, care and hard times of his doughty throwing arm.

"In the first place," he began, "It's almost an inch longer than my other arm. It doesn't feel that way, but I'm reminded of the difference whenever I go to have a suit made."

A TEMPORARY CHANGE

Ford's limbs were as nearly symmetrical as those attached to other 5-foot-10-inch towheads when he entered organized baseball with the Class C Butler (Pa.) Yankees fifteen years ago. Imperceptibly at first, the muscles and ligaments in his busier ⟩⟩⟩

Edward "Whitey" Ford pitched for the Yankees from 1953 to 1967.

≪≪≪ arm became so stretched that they started sneaking closer and closer to Whitey's knee.

Ironically, the left arm becomes noticeably shorter than the right immediately after a stint of six or seven innings in competition. This temporary change—it lasts only a couple of hours—results from contractions of muscles and ligaments that have been exerted to an unusual degree.

An expected peculiarity of the pitching arm is its greater girth and the superior articulation of its muscles. The difference from the right arm can be seen with the naked eye.

"My left shoulder's quite a bit larger than my right, too," Ford said. "Doctors comment on that every time I have a physical examination."

It probably would be extremely difficult to take fingerprints of Ford's left hand. The print areas are quite glazed, the result of countless trips to the resin bag, and they are flat and hard with callouses.

Whitey encourages the growth of these shields. They minimize the damage done by raised stitches in the hide of the ball.

Finally, there is a bony marble-sized lump on the inside edge of his left elbow. "No, I didn't get that in any accident," Ford explained. "That's what happens when you pitch a lot of curves."

In short, the left arm looks rather odd. It is respected and admired around the league, though. It has an uncanny knack for baffling batters, and will thus earn $50,000 for its owner this year. The Yankees undoubtedly would pay a similar sum for another such arm.

A 25-4 Record in 1961

When the 1962 season began, Whitey already had appeared in 317 big league games, winning 158 and losing 63. He had registered 1,209 strikeouts and posted an earned-run average of 2.76. The gaudiest figures in his dossier at the time were his won-lost record of 25—4 for last season.

The 33-year-old southpaw estimates that he averages 120 pitches in each nine innings of work. On that basis, it was determined that Ford had, in his terms, "really exerted the arm" about 3,700 times during his 283 innings on the mound in 1961.

When told that he apparently had thrown hard more than 27,000 times during his first 2,095 innings in the majors, Ford raised both eyebrows and whistled.

"Gee, I didn't realize it was that much," he said thoughtfully, rubbing the left bicep with his glove. He sounded as if he wouldn't have taken the job had he been privy to those figures in advance.

Besides the offerings Whitey serves in league games, there are thousands he delivers annually in spring training and exhibitions. Furthermore, he lets fly about fifty times warming up before innings during a game. And just before play begins, he loosens up for about fifteen minutes, throwing about eighty times.

Gradual Increase in Effort

"Sometimes I warm up even longer if the weather is cool," said the pitcher. "Of course, not all of those throws are real hard. I start out slow and easy and gradually increase the effort to half-speed, three-quarters and then full speed."

The pitch that puts the greatest strain on Ford's arm is his curve.

"You have to twist your wrist and your elbow out like this," he said while demonstrating. "The screwball is hard on the arm, too, because you're twisting your wrist and elbow in the opposite direction, although you don't twist quite so much."

Generally speaking, one of every three Whitey Ford deliveries is a curve.

"There are days, though, when I throw more and other days when I throw fewer curves," he said, "depending on how well my other stuff is working."

His "stuff" does not include the torturing screwball. He relies on the fast ball, slider, change-up and curves of varying speeds and arcs.

"Next to the curve, the slider takes the most out of my arm," said the Yankee star.

"When you throw it, you have to lean over and make a side-arm delivery.

"That means you haven't got your body behind it and your arm has to do all the work of putting speed on the ball. You've always got a good chance of hurting your arm with the slider."

'FREAK' PITCHES SHUNNED

Ford steadfastly has declined to add what he calls "freak pitches" to his repertoire, because the freakish effects—including those of the baffling knuckleball—are gained by doing harmful things to the arm. Men who specialize in such dark arts usually are relief pitchers, expected to work only a few innings at a time.

"If I could get away [with] it—that is, get as many guys out—I'd throw nothing but a fast ball," said Ford. "You throw it with an overhand or three-quarter motion. Sure, you throw real hard, but it doesn't put much of a strain on your arm because the motion is natural for the arm, so you can put all your weight behind it to do a lot of the work.

"I couldn't get away with it, of course, but what I mean to say is those freak pitches can hurt you. You take guys like Warren Spahn [of the Milwaukee Braves] and Early Wynn [of the Chicago White Sox]. They don't fool around with that freak stuff. They're over forty years old, but they seldom have trouble with their arms."

Like those celebrated old pros, Whitey is a regular starter. He works every fourth day of the schedule.

"If I take a shorter rest between starts," he explained, "my arm is too stiff and too weak from the last game. Sometimes when you finish nine innings, your arm feels so heavy you have to look down to see if somebody's hanging from it.

"On the other hand, if I take a longer rest between games, my arm is stronger, but my control not nearly so good. That's the most important thing—control. All the stuff in the world won't help you win a ball game if you can't get the ball over the plate."

Ford's regimen between starts goes like this:

On the first day of his four-day cycle, he throws "real easy" for seven or eight minutes, never harder than three-quarter speed.

"This is just enough throwing to get some of the stiffness out of my arm from pitching the day before," he said. "I do a little running before I throw. Not much. Sometimes I just ⟫⟫⟫

Whitey Ford pitching during the 1962 World Series in San Francisco.

◄◄◄ shag flies with the outfielders. The running takes the stiffness out of my back and legs."

MATES TAKE FIELD FIRST

On the second day, Whitey puts in what he calls "the real good workout." He runs about twenty laps around the ball park and throws hard for about fifteen minutes.

On the third day, he again shags flies, but does little or no throwing, except to return balls to the man with the fungo bat.

On the fourth day, the one on which he works, the pitcher relaxes in the clubhouse long after his team-mates have taken the field. He goes out just in time to take a few swings in the batting cage.

When the scoreboard clock shows 15 minutes to game time, he begins warming up his arm on the sideline. He wears a jacket between innings and during those rare moments when he is on base, to keep it warm.

After the game, he occasionally has the arm massaged by the trainer for about five minutes before going under a hot shower. When he goes to bed that night, he sleeps on his stomach with his pitching arm lying straight along his thigh. He has trained himself to sleep that way the year round in fact, supporting his head with the other arm.

Does he do anything else special to protect the golden flipper?

"Well, I do a lot of bowling in the off-season," said Ford. "I own a bowling alley on Long Island. But I do my bowling right-handed. I've found it's okay to play golf left-handed, though."

Ford doesn't believe in pampering his pitching arm, as some major leaguers do.

"I've seen guys beg off from pitching every time they feel a little twinge in their arms," he said. "They start crying they've got a sore arm. The way I see it, you've got to learn to pitch with those little things. I've started a game many times with a twinge in my arm. But as long as I can do the job, I stay in there, and nine times out of ten the pain works itself out.

"The thing is, a little pain doesn't mean there's anything seriously wrong. When you've got a real sore arm, you can hardly throw the ball. Sometimes the pain is such that it keeps me from using certain pitches. But I still won't leave the mound as long as I can get guys out with the pitches I can use."

HAMMER JOBS BANNED

Off the field, Whitey protects his arm to this extent: He will not lift heavy objects with his left arm and he sidesteps all household projects that require the use of a hammer.

"I learned about the hammer several years ago," he explained. "We were putting a new porch on our house and I spent two or three hours driving nails.

"I had to pitch the next day, but I had to take myself out of the game in the second inning. No, it wasn't my arm; it was a finger blister, under the callous here.

"We use a stone—a pumice stone—to keep the callouses from building up too high. When they get too high, you can develop a bad blister under them just from throwing the ball.

"That's as much babying as my arm gets," the master concluded. "I don't bother it unless it bothers me."

Whitey's eyes darted about nervously as he spoke, somewhat like a man looking over his shoulder to see whether something was gaining on him. At that moment, so far as he knew, his arm was free of bone chips, bone spurs, pulled ligaments, inflamed tendons and various other dreaded disorders.

But who could say what would happen the next time he threw the ball? ◆

October 17, 1962

YANKS BEAT GIANTS, 1-0; WIN WORLD SERIES

By JOHN DREBINGER
Special to The New York Times.

SAN FRANCISCO, Oct. 16—Baseball's longest season ended today with the New York Yankees still the world champions.

Manager Ralph Houk's Bombers, behind the four-hit pitching of their ace right-hander, Ralph Terry, turned back the Giants, 1 to 0, in the seventh and deciding game of the 1962 World Series.

That gave the Yanks the Series, four games to three, and brought to their Stadium in the Bronx their 20th world championship.

Only seven times since 1921 have the Yanks been defeated in a World Series. But they came mighty close to losing another one today.

For in the last of the ninth, as a crowd of 43,948 looked on, the issue hung for a split second on the last play of the game.

With runners on second and third and two out, huge Willie McCovey blasted a line drive that appeared headed for right field. Had it reached its destination, two runs would have scored and folks would be dancing in the streets of San Francisco tonight.

But the ball landed squarely in the glove of the Yankee second baseman, Bobby Richardson. With that, Manager Alvin Dark's spunky Giants, who had performed spectacular feats through the long campaign, breathed their last.

Although the Yankees' tally, scored off Jack Sanford in the fifth inning, was achieved in prosaic fashion, this struggle, fought by both sides against a spanking 35-mile-an-hour wind that blew in from dead center, was perhaps the tensest and most dramatic of the Series.

For Terry and Sanford this was their third meeting. Sanford had won the first one, Terry the second. This was the rubber match that was to decide everything.

And though the home folks at the time refused to believe it, it was settled in the fifth inning when Sanford, suffering a brief letdown, saw the Yanks fill the bases with nobody out on singles by Bill Skowron and Cletis Boyer and a walk to Terry.

A routine double-play ball that Tony Kubek plowed into drove in Skowron with the run that was to settle the issue.

Then came the dramatics in the ninth. Matty Alou, in the role of pinch-hitter, caught the Yankee inner defense flat-footed with a beautifully executed drag bunt to the right of the mound for a hit—the third off Terry.

An expectant roar went up from the crowd, but it turned to groans as Felipe Alou and Chuck Hiller struck out. However, Terry still had to dispose of Willie Mays.

Mays Smacks Double

Willie the Wonder, whose bat had kept the Giants alive time after time during the thrill-packed days of the National League pennant race, came through again. It was his drive that Tresh had caught in left field in the seventh. But this time Willie smashed a double down the right-field line.

Only swift work by Roger Maris in the right-hand corner of the field prevented Matty Alou from scoring the tying run. However, the Giants were still breathing. They had the potential tying and winning runs on third and second, and at the plate was the 6-foot-4-inch McCovey.

Out of the Yankee dugout came Houk for a conference on the mound. Down in the Yankee bull pen Bill Stafford, winner of the third game, and Bud Daley were warming up furiously.

But the one-time Army major decided that he would sink or swim with the fellow still on the hill, McCovey took a swing and hit a tremendous drive that curved foul down the right-field line.

He swung again, and for an instant it looked like the pay-off for San Francisco. But Richardson froze to the ball as it landed in his glove with a thud and in the next instant the jubilant Yanks were smothering and pounding Terry on the back.   >>>

‹‹‹ **TERRY IS TWO-TIME WINNER**

The 28-year-old Oklahoman had gone into this Series with three defeats against no victories in post-season play. To this he added a fourth setback when Sanford beat him in the second game. But now, with his superb four-hitter, he was bowing out of this Series a two-time winner.

Minutes after the game, it was announced that the smiling Westerner had made off with the eighth annual Sport Magazine Corvette Award as the outstanding player of the 1962 Series. ◆

October 3, 1963

STRIKE-OUT MARK IS SET BY KOUFAX; DODGERS 5, YANKS 2

Left-Hander Fans 15 Batters in World Series Opener— Ford Losing Pitcher

By JOHN DREBINGER

THE LOS ANGELES DODGERS defeated the Yankees, 5—2, in the first game of the 1963 World Series yesterday at the Stadium. The man of the day was 27-year-old Sandy Koufax, who set a Series record by striking out 15 batters.

The crowd of 69,000 was there to see a pitching duel between Koufax and Whitey Ford, the left-handed ace of the Yankees. But the Dodgers made it no contest with four runs off Ford in the second inning, Koufax did the rest.

Sandy Koufax of the Los Angeles Dodgers during the opener of the 1963 World Series at Yankee Stadium.

The Brooklyn-born left-hander wiped out the Series record set exactly 10 years ago, on Oct. 2, 1953, by another Dodger pitcher against another Yankee team. The pitcher was Carl Erskine, a right-hander, and he struck out 14 batters at Ebbets Field in the days when the Dodgers called Brooklyn home.

WORKING MARGIN FOR KOUFAX

In his one previous World Series start—against the Chicago White Sox in 1959—Koufax had lost, 1-0. The Dodgers finally got him some Series runs with their second-inning outburst against Ford. Three of the four runs tallied on a homer by Koufax's catcher, John Roseboro.

In the third, the 35-year-old Ford yielded another run and that was all the scoring until the eighth. In that inning, the Yankees broke Koufax's scoreless string on a two-run homer by Tom Tresh.

During the regular season, Koufax had fanned 306 batters for a National League record. Yesterday he struck out Tony Kubek, Bobby Richardson and Tresh in the first inning. In the second he got Mickey Mantle and Roger Maris with his bewildering curves, fast balls and floaters.

Those five consecutive strike-outs tied a Series record set by Mort Cooper of the Cardinals against the Yankees on Oct. 11, 1943.

The bid for a record ended when Elston Howard lifted a short pop foul that Roseboro nailed close to the Yankee dugout.

But this didn't slow Koufax's strike-out operations. He got the top three of the Yankee batting order again in the fourth and Mantle again in the fifth.

That was his last strikeout against Mickey and in this he didn't match Erskine's performance of 1953. On Erskine's big day the Yankee slugger struck out four times. ◆

October 23, 1963

Yankees Make Houk Executive; Yogi Berra Due to Be Manager

By JOSEPH M. SHEEHAN

RALPH HOUK, THE MANAGER who led the Yankees to three baseball pennants and two world championships in three years, has given up the job to move into the front office as general manager.

The general expectation is that Lawrence Peter (Yogi) Berra, the long-time catching star of the Yankees, will be named tomorrow to succeed Houk as field manager of the American League champions. The picturesque Berra was player-coach last season.

In baseball, the field manager selects the daily line-up, dictates the strategy of play and supervises the deportment of his players in and out of uniform, The general manager's chief concern is player procurement and development, with an eye to the club's immediate and long-range interests.

The 44-year-old Houk, a hard-bitten World War II hero, succeeds H. Roy Hamey, who will remain with the Yankees in a less active role.

Houk's promotion to the team's highest command post was announced yesterday by Daniel R. Topping, the co-owner of the Yankees with Del Webb. The announcement was made at a news conference in the Savoy-Hilton Hotel.

Another news conference is scheduled for tomorrow to reveal the identity of the new Yankee manager, who already has been selected. Speculation begins and ends with the name of Berra as the man who will take over baseball's most glamorous managerial assignment.

Both Topping and Houk pointedly dodged questions about Ralph's successor. "You'll find out Thursday," they said. Berra, usually one of the most accessible of baseball men, on and off the field, discreetly made himself unavailable.

But it was considered certain that the ⟫⟫⟫

Yogi Berra tips his cap on being named to succeed Ralph Houk (left) as Yankee manager.

《《《 38-year-old catcher, highly esteemed by Yankee fans and by teammates, would inherit the mantle worn with such distinction by Miller Huggins, Joe McCarthy, Casey Stengel and, most recently, Houk.

A LONG TIME PLANNING

The news of the Yankees' second major administrative shift in three years caught even the local baseball insiders off guard. However, on the word of the principals—Topping, Hamey and Houk—the move had been in the works for more than a year and had been set since last February.

The 61-year-old Hamey had been appointed to succeed George M. Weiss as the Yankee general manager at the end of the 1960 season, shortly after Houk was named to replace Stengel as the field manager. Hamey underwent a serious operation last year and has not been in the best of health. ◆

September 25, 1964

Myth Traces Yankees' Revival To Linz, a Harmonica Rascal

By LEONARD KOPPETT
Special to The New York Times

WASHINGTON, SEPT. 24—When the elements of legend fall into place and the details are fed repeatedly to a public only too eager to believe, nothing can be done to dispel the myth that results. Thus it will be told, over and over, for years to come, how the "dead" Yankees were revived and the 1964 pennant won because Manager Yogi Berra got mad at Phil Linz's harmonica-playing on a bus. If there is any truth at all to such an interpretation of the last few weeks of the American League season, it is only a little bit of peripheral truth. The real reasons for the Yankee turnabout are more complex, less amusing and (to anyone who seriously cares) much more interesting.

Yet the legend will become a part of sports history as soon as this 29th Yankee pennant is officially recorded. The story will be told, with varying degrees of accuracy, of the four straight defeats the Yankees suffered in Chicago Aug. 17 through 20; of the bus ride from Comiskey Park to O'Hare Field, with Linz tooting on his newly purchased instrument and Berra telling him to shut up; of Linz giving one defiant toot too many, and of Berra stalking back, of Linz tossing the harmonica, of strong words exchanged; of the nation-wide fuss that followed and the $200 fine imposed on Linz; and of the Yankees, impressed by Berra's being "boss", shaking off a season-long lethargy and running off with the flag.

A few details will be glossed over, of course. The fact that the Yankees lost the next two games, too, will usually be left out; the fact that the "season-long" lethargy really lasted only one month, co-inciding with the incapacitation of Whitey Ford, will be overlooked. And the real changes that took place won't be mentioned at all.

"Did that incident turn things around for us?" Berra was saying today. "I certainly don't think so, but how can anybody ever really tell? I know that's what a lot of them will say. But I do know this: Three other things happened, before and after, that made a lot of difference to us."

These three things were the arrival of Mel Stottlemyre, the return of Mickey Mantle and the acquisition of Pedro Ramos from the Cleveland Indians. Each had an effect on morale as important as anything that happened on the field.

In mid-August, the Yankees knew that they couldn't make it with the pitching staff they had. Ford and three relief pitchers were hurt. Stottlemyre, straight from Richmond, won his first two starts against Chicago and Baltimore, and at almost the same time Ford's hip healed. Suddenly, the Yankees had a starting rotation they could believe in.

In Baltimore on Aug. 14, Mantle reinjured his knee diving back to first base. He couldn't play in the four games that were lost in Chicago. On Aug. 21, in Boston, he insisted on going back to work even though he had to shift to left field to favor the damaged leg.

The Yankees didn't win another game until Mantle hit a home run, the night of Aug. 22, while Stottlemyre pitched a shutout.

That was the beginning of the comeback. The way Mantle forced himself seemed to make all the other players more determined, perhaps a little ashamed of them- 〉〉〉

Bobby Richardson, Tony Kubek, Pete Mikkelsen (with Elston Howard's arms around him), Phil Linz and Yogi Berra (l. to r.) celebrate at Yankees' 29th pennant with an 8-3 victory over the Cleveland Indians.

‹‹‹ selves; the way he hit restored everyone's confidence and relaxed the other hitters.

Still, on Sept. 4, the Yankees were four games behind, and the bull pen was still a terrible problem. On Sept. 6, Ramos arrived, and the lift in morale was visible even before he threw a pitch. The Yankees knew what Ramos could do; he did it, and the final drive gathered full speed.

Since Stottlemyre came up, the Yankees have won 14 of the 19 games started by him and Ford.

Since Mantle went back to work prematurely, the Yankees have won 24 and lost 9.

Since Ramos arrived, the Yankee record is 15-3.

Meanwhile, the Orioles have been 11-12 in September and the White Sox 10-10. Both simply found their level. Each has 90 victories with eight games to play, and neither team figured to win that many before the season began.

The Yankees figured to win 100, and they'll come close. The harmonica story is a good one, worthy of a place in baseball's anecdotal lore; but it shouldn't be taken too seriously. ◆

October 11, 1964

Mantle's 3d-Tier Drive Off Schultz Provides 2-1 Series Lead

By LEONARD KOPPETT

MICKEY MANTLE'S 16th World Series home run broke a tie, a record and Barney Schultz's heart at Yankee Stadium yesterday. Coming on the first pitch of the last half of the ninth inning, Mantle's drive into the third deck in right field gave the New York Yankees a 2-1 victory over the St. Louis Cardinals and a 2-1 lead in the four-of-seven-game series. The record Mantle broke was one of the most distinguished in baseball's volumes of statistics. Babe Ruth had hit 15 home runs in 41 games in 10 series. Last October Mantle caught up, with a home run off Sandy Koufax in the fourth game. Yesterday Mantle moved ahead in his 61st World Series game.

Only one other player has hit as many as 12 homers in Series competition—Lawrence P. (Yogi) Berra, yesterday's winning manager.

This dramatic ending to a sparkling game, which had a crowd of 67,101 in a state of steadily mounting excitement, snatched attention away from the pitching duel that preceded it.

Jim Bouton, the 25-year-old Yankee right-hander, and Curt Simmons, the 35-year-old Cardinal left-hander, engaged in it. Simmons was tougher, but Bouton was more exciting as he escaped from one threatening situation after another.

But Simmons had to be removed for a pinch-hitter in the ninth because the Cards had a chance to score and, as the visiting team, could not risk passing it up. Bouton stopped them again, however, and Schultz, the 38-year-old knuckleball specialist who had done so much to pitch the Cards to the National League Pennant, took over.

His first pitch, in his own words, "had to be a knuckleball." It was, but not a good one.

According to Mantle, "It didn't quite knuckle."

At any rate, Mickey took one big swing from the left side of the plate—the side from which he doesn't hit so well because of the pressure on his weakened legs. The sound that resulted was more of a "click" than a "crack," but once the ball was airborne, it was clearly a home run. It landed in the third-tier boxes, about 40 feet in from the foul line, about 60 feet above the ground, about 360 feet from home plate.

As Mantle trotted around the bases, a stream of young fans raced across the outfield from the left-field bleachers. As Mantle rounded third, Coach Frank Crosetti joined him and they crossed home plate almost in step. Mick's enthusiastic welcome by teammates was a departure from traditional Yankee calm. ◆

December 9, 1966

Yankees Trade Maris to Cardinals for Smith, a Former Met Third Baseman

By LEONARD KOPPETT

ROGER MARIS, the man who surpassed Babe Ruth's single-season home run record in 1961, was traded yesterday by the New York Yankees to the St. Louis Cardinals for Charlie Smith, a third baseman who spent two seasons with the New York Mets.

It was an even trade, with no money or "players to be named" involved. As such, it represented a staggering devaluation of Maris, who has earned more than $70,000 a year since hitting 61 home runs in his second season as a Yankee.

Ruth had hit 60 in 1927, creating the most glamorous of batting records and establishing a target other sluggers approached with mounting excitement, and eventual disappointment, year after year. When Maris finally achieved the goal controversy developed over the "validity" of his record, because that season the league had expanded to 10 teams and the schedule had increased from 154 to 162 games.

This controversy helped embitter Maris, who became a magnet for jeers and his subsequent performances could not live up to his big year. Leg and wrist injuries limited his effectiveness in the last two seasons, during which he hit a total of only 21 homers and started less than half of the Yankee games. Finally the Yankee management became disenchanted with him, too.

HUGE SALARY A DETERRENT

It was well known, therefore, that the Yankees would try to trade the 32-year-old Maris. What was so surprising was the low value put on him. When the Yankees asked waivers on him at the end of the season, 18 of the other 19 major league clubs passed him by. When they talked trade during the winter meetings last week, they met almost total indifference.

One factor was his salary. Baseball regulations forbid cutting a man's salary more than 25 per cent in any one year. Maris was getting $72,000 as a Yankee, and had not been cut for three years, in recognition of the fact that injuries were not his fault. Nevertheless, this meant that any team acquiring him would have to pay him at least $54,000. The deterrent was not so much the actual amount paid Maris, but its effect on the salary structure of the rest of the team.

Another factor was age. In recent years, rules that limit the number of players any one major league organization can control have been adopted. As a result, clubs are eager to fill their rosters with younger prospects, and don't want to make room for any older player who is for any reason an uncertain quantity, even if he may prove to have three or four good years left.

Smith, then, was the best the Yankees could get for Maris. A right-handed hitter with some power and an adequate fielder at best, Smith is 29 years old.

The Yankees took Smith because they had traded Clete Boyer, their regular third baseman for six years, to Atlanta last week. For Boyer they received Bill Robinson, a 23-year-old ≫

Maris's Record

Year	Club	League	G	HR	RBI	BA
1953	Fargo-M'rhead	North.	114	9	80	.325
1954	Keokuk	I.I.I.	134	32	111	.315
1955	Tulsa	Tex.	25	1	9	.233
1955	Reading	East.	113	19	78	.289
1956	Indianapolis	A.A.	131	17	75	.293
1957	Cleveland	Amer.	116	14	51	.235
1958	Cleveland-K.C.	Amer.	150	28	80	.240
1959	Kansas City	Amer.	122	16	72	.273
1960	New York	Amer.	136	39	112	.283
1961	New York	Amer.	161	61	142	.269
1962	New York	Amer.	157	33	100	.256
1963	New York	Amer.	90	23	53	.269
1964	New York	Amer.	141	26	71	.281
1965	New York	Amer.	46	8	27	.239
1966	New York	Amer.	119	13	43	.233

Major League Totals   1,238   261   755   .260

‹‹‹ right fielder, who will be a rookie this year. With Steve Whitaker, who showed promise as a rookie outfielder for the Yankees last year, also on hand, the Yankees could not both use Maris and develop the youngsters.

"We are committed to making a fresh start with young players," said Lee MacPhail, the Yankee general manager, yesterday. "I think Maris can have three or four more good years, and we hope he does. There doesn't seem to be anything wrong with him physically. But if our new men are going to play, we've got to make room for them."

As a Yankee in 1960, Maris hit 39 home runs, helped win a pennant, and nosed out Mickey Mantle for the league's most valuable player award. The next year, of course, he was most valuable again as he tied Ruth with a home run off Jack Fisher of Baltimore and hit No. 61 in the last game of the season off Tracy Stallard of the Boston Red Sox. He also hit a key home run in the third game of the World Series, which the Yankees won from Cincinnati in five games.

In 1962, his home-run production fell to 33, but he was still a main cog in another pennant winner. In 1963, he was in fine form for the first half of the season but then missed most of the second half because of an infection. In 1964 he played a full season and his September drive was a principal factor in winning a fifth consecutive pennant.

In 1965, he injured a wrist in June, and was unable to play the rest of the year. At first, X-rays showed no bone chip, but finally he needed a delicate operation for its removal (in September). Last year, he was slow working into shape but seemed in full stride when he injured a knee in May, and was not sound again for three months as he kept re-injuring it.

He spoke often of retirement, even right after his big year, but never had any serious disagreement with his employers at contract time. ◆

May 15, 1967

MANTLE HITS 500TH HOMER

By LEONARD KOPPETT

MICKEY MANTLE'S 500TH home run finally arrived yesterday, in style. He hit it off Stu Miller of the Baltimore Orioles with two out in the seventh inning at Yankee Stadium, and it proved to be the winning run in the New York Yankees' 6-5 victory.

The crowd of 18,872 gave Mantle a standing ovation, which continued through Elston Howard's turn at bat and on into the interval between innings. Mantle's blow, with no one on base, made the score 6-4 and seemed important only ceremonially at that time, because a two-run, pinch-hit homer by Joe Pepitone had given the Yankees the lead in the sixth.

But the crowd's response, and the feat itself—only five other men have hit that many major league home runs—made Mantle so nervous that he almost threw the game away in the next half inning.

Mantle's Homer Record

Year	Home Runs
1951	13
1952	23
1953	21
1954	27
1955	37
1956	52
1957	34
1958	42
1959	31
1960	40
1961	54
1962	30
1963	15
1964	35
1965	19
1966	23
1967	4
17 years	**500 home runs**

"It got to me," he said with a smile afterward. He was more grateful that the game had ended in a victory than that the milestone had been passed. "If we'd lost—and I'd have had to face all those reporters—I don't know if I could have done it."

It was the first homer he had ever hit off Miller, an experienced pitcher who specializes in slow-speed delivery. It came on a 3-2 pitch and landed deep in the lower right-field stands, where it was caught by Louis DeFillippo, an 18-year-old high school student from Mount Vernon, N. Y.

De Fillippo presented the ball to Mantle outside the door of the Yankee clubhouse, and received a season pass and some Mantle souvenirs in return. He identified himself as a Yankee fan "all the way" and an amateur center fielder who switched to first base "after Mantle did."

Only Babe Ruth (who hit 714), Willie Mays, Jimmie Foxx, Ted Williams, Mel Ott and Mantle are in the 500 Club, although Eddie Mathews and Hank Aaron will probably join before long.

◆

June 15, 1967

MANTLE BREAKS A GEHRIG RECORD

Plays in 2,165th Game as a Yankee—Downing Gains 7th Victory in Opener

By DEANE McGOWEN
Special to The New York Times

WASHINGTON, JUNE 14—Mickey Mantle broke the late Lou Gehrig's record for games played when he appeared as a pinch-hitter in the eighth inning of the second game of a double-header that the New York Yankees split with the Washington Senators tonight.

The Yankee slugger stepped to the plate amid a tremendous ovation from the 15,158 fans and flied out to right field. It was Mantle's 2,165th game for New York, breaking by one game the mark set by Gehrig. Mantle, hampered by a muscle pull in his left thigh, had missed the Yankees' last four games.

Gehrig, the Iron Horse of the Yankees' Murderers' Row days, played 2,130 of his 2,164 games consecutively in a 14-year span that ended in April, 1939. Mantle is in his 17th season with the Yankees. ◆

Mickey Mantle blasts his 500th home run into the lower right field stands at Yankee Stadium on May 14, 1967.

May 31, 1968

Yanks Triumph on Mantle's 2 Homers

SLUGGER'S 5 HITS CRUSH SENATORS

By LEONARD KOPPETT

MICKEY MANTLE, a fading star flared up to peak luminosity for one game yesterday and made Memorial Day memorable for a crowd of 28,197 at Yankee Stadium.

The 36-year-old first baseman, whose frequently damaged legs forced him out of the outfield two years ago; hit two home runs, a double and two singles as he batted in five runs in the Yankees' 13-4 victory over the Senators in the opener. Never in his 18-year career has he had a more productive game.

Then he sat on the bench during the second game, which Washington won, 6-2. Mantle did get as far as the on-deck circle as a potential pinch-hitter with two out and a man on base in the ninth, but Gene Michael struck out.

Mantle began the day with a .223 batting average. He hit a home run in the first inning off Joe Coleman, who had struck him out four times in a row in Washington last week. That gave Stan Bahnsen, the Yankee pitcher, a 2-0 lead, since Roy White had walked before the homer.

524TH OF HIS CAREER

In the third, Mantle singled and scored on Joe Pepitone's long double, making the score 3-0. He led off the fifth by greeting Bob Humphreys with another homer, his sixth of this season and 524th of his career.

His double, a ground shot past first base in the sixth, drove in the second run of that inning and made the score 7-1. And his single in the eighth, after two walks with one out, sparked a six-run inning that made this New York's highest-scoring game since last August.

Only twice before in his career had Mantle made five hits in one game, a rare feat for anyone. He did it once in 1955 in Washington (no homers) and once in 1956 in Detroit (one homer, four singles, and a walk).

In 1956 he was at the height of his powers—a triple crown winner with a .353 average, 52 home runs and 130 runs batted in. Today, his average is .254, even after a five-hit game.

Also among the statistical fallout was the fact that this was the 45th time Mantle had hit two or more homers in one game. Only Babe Ruth and Jimmy Foxx have done it more often in American League competition. Only Willie Mays and Eddie Mathews among active players are ahead of Mantle in this category. ◆

September 20, 1968

McLain Wins No. 31 Despite Mantle's 535th Career Homer

By JOSEPH DURSO
Special to The New York Times

DETROIT, SEPT. 19—Mickey Mantle and Denny McLain shook some baseball records out of the cool gray sky here this afternoon as the Detroit Tigers defeated the New York Yankees, 6-2.

Mantle hit the 535th home run of his 18-year career and became the third ranking home-run producer in the history of the major leagues. He passed Jimmie Foxx with a line drive into the right-field stands in the eighth inning. And the only men who have hit more are the late Babe Ruth with 714 and Willie Mays with 585.

The pitch was a medium fastball delivered with senatorial courtesy by McLain, who was already far along the path toward becoming the first pitcher in 37 years to win 31 games.

STANDING OVATION FOR MANTLE

McLain was coasting along with a 6-1 lead on a four-hitter when Mantle went to bat with one out in the eighth. It was Mantle's last appearance of the year in Tiger Stadium—perhaps forever, so far as anybody knows—and the crowd of 9,063 gave him a standing ovation.

McLain waited until the cheers had subsided, then threw the 37-year-old switch-hitter two fastballs on the inside corner of the plate for strikes. Then he threw a fastball over the plate at the knees and Mantle, swinging left-handed, lined it just inside the yellow foul screen into the second deck in right field.

It was his 17th home run of the season and his first since he had tied Foxx on Aug. 22 with a pinch-hit homer in Minnesota. And, as he neared home plate to another standing ovation, McLain tossed a salute to the man who had been his boyhood hero.

The ball was retrieved from the upper deck and the game was halted while the first-base umpire, Hank Soar, flipped it to Mantle near the Yankee dugout.

"McLain has made a fan of me for life," Mantle said later.

"I didn't throw it to him," McLain said modestly in the Detroit clubhouse. "It was a good pitch, a fastball low. I wanted to finish the game because I'd gained about 10 pounds from all the celebrating over our pennant the last two days, and I wanted to work it off. But that Mantle—he was my idol."

Mantle's shot was the only redeeming note of the Yankees' three-game visit to Detroit. They arrived in third place with a 10-game winning streak and left in fifth place with a three-game losing streak. ◆

March 2, 1969

MANTLE RETIRES FROM BASEBALL AFTER 18 YEARS;

'I CAN'T HIT ANYMORE' SLUGGER SAYS

By GEORGE VECSEY
Special to The New York Times

FORT LAUDERDALE, FLA., MARCH 1—Mickey Mantle, one of baseball's greatest stars for the last 18 years, announced his retirement today at the spring training base of the New York Yankees.

"I can't hit any more," the 37-year-old Mantle said at a news conference at the Yankee Clipper Motel in a room overlooking the Atlantic Ocean. He also said his business interests were demanding more of his time and he would not be with the Yankees this year in any capacity.

Mantle is baseball's third leading home run hitter with 536, behind Babe Ruth's 714 and Willie Mays' 587. He led the American League in home runs four times and was voted most valuable player three times.

He batted as high as .365 in 1957, but his average slipped in the last four years. He batted only .237 last year and his career average slipped to .298.

Mickey Mantle and Yankee manager Ralph Houk at the news conference announcing his retirement on March 1, 1969.

"I feel bad that I didn't hit .300," he said in an unemotional 15-minute talk. "But there's no way I could go back and get it over .300 again. I can't hit when I need to. I can't go from first to third when I need to. There's no use trying."

The club management expressed sorrow at the retirement of one of the greatest of Yankees.

"He's one of a kind," said the Yankees' president, Michael Burke, who added that Mantle's uniform number, 7, would be retired "of course."

Burke and Manager Ralph Houk also gave strong indication they had not pressured Mantle into playing one more season.

"This is Mickey's future," Burke said, "and he has agonized over this major decision. We want him to do what is right for him."

Mantle had fostered rumors of his retirement last winter in private talks with friends. However, he told the press over and over again that he would not make up his mind until spring training, probably after having worked out for several weeks.

Mantle reported here from his home in Dallas last night, three days after other regulars had reported. He spoke with Houk on the phone last night, he said, and then had a long talk with Burke at breakfast this morning.

"I really hadn't made up my mind," Mantle said, "but I think I was just kidding myself. I told Ralph how I felt and he said if he was me he'd make up his mind as fast as possible. I'm really glad I decided to do it."

In recent years it had seemed the Yankees needed Mantle for his ability and his appeal at the gate as much as he needed his $100,000 salary. But business has improved for both of them.

A victim of several bad investments in his early years, Mantle recently became involved in Mickey Mantle's Country Cookin', a Southern-style restaurant chain based in Dallas, and Mickey Mantle's Clothing Store in Knoxville, Tenn.

"I've got to appear at the opening of each franchise," Mantle said today, "We've opened 45 of them so far and if we sell 100 more this year, that's one every three days."

Things have improved in the Bronx, also. The Yankees finished fifth last year after having been

Mickey Mantle wipes his eyes as 60,096 fans give him an eight-minute ovation on Mickey Mantle Day at Yankee Stadium, June 8, 1969.

out of the first division for three years.

"We've got some good players who had terrible years and should come back," Mantle said, "and we've got some good young players like Roy White and Bill Robinson. It may be another year before the Yankees win the pennant, but I think they'll be back again."

"I don't know how I'll feel not playing ball. I've been playing ball for 20 years and I'll probably miss it like crazy. But Mike told me I have a job with the Yankees any time I want it. I'm not going to say I never want to be a manager, because Ted Williams said that nine years ago and now he's managing.

"I don't know how my four boys feel about it, but my wife has been after me to quit for three years. I know she's happy." ◆

After Decade, Maris Resents Asterisk

By MARTY RALBOVSKY

TEN YEARS AGO TODAY, Roger Maris of the New York Yankees hit his 61st home run to surpass by one baseball's most revered accomplishment—60 homers by Babe Ruth in 1927. Now a beer salesman in Gainesville, Fla., Maris said that his memories of 1961 are punctuated with an asterisk.

"The 61 homers? I don't think much about that anymore," Maris said yesterday in a telephone interview. "It's all in the past, and I'm too busy now anyway. Maybe it'll become important to me when I'm 65 or 70. Maybe then I'll think about it more, and even enjoy it."

On Oct. 1, 1961, Maris hit a 2-and-0 pitch from Tracy Stallard of the Boston Red Sox into the right-field seats at Yankee Stadium and was immediately rewarded with the infamous asterisk. The commissioner of baseball at the time, Ford Frick, said that Maris's record would stand for 162-game seasons and that Ruth's would remain as the record for a 154-game season, the asterisk distinguishing between them.

But since 154-game schedules were already obsolete (expansion spawned eight more games a season), Maris interpreted the maneuver as repayment for his attitude which, at times, contained all the reverence of a man jigging at the bier.

Now, a decade later, the asterisk still superimposes itself on an otherwise uncomplicated life for Roger Maris. He and his brother, Rudy, operate Anheuser-Busch beer distributorships in Gainesville and Ocala in Florida, spending their days in taverns and supermarkets, checking on the Budweiser stock, surveying its placement on shelves, accommodating the orders of retailers. Only occasionally does he think of baseball and, when he does, the asterisk clouds his memories.

"Look, I never made up any schedules," he said. "Do you know any other records that have been broken since the 162-game schedule that have an asterisk? I don't. Frick should have said that all records made during the new schedule would have an asterisk, and he should have said that before the season—if he should have said it at all. But he decided on the asterisk when I had about 50 homers, and it looked like I'd break the record.

"When they say 154 games, what 154 games are they talking about? The first 154, the middle 154, or the last 154? If it's the first 154, then I'd still have tied Ruth because I didn't hit my first homer until the 11th game that year. If it was the middle 154, or the last 154, I'd have broken the record anyway. But I can understand why it all happened: a lot of people didn't want me to break Ruth's record at all, especially older people. They tried to make me into the mold of Babe Ruth, and I don't want to fit anyone's mold. I'm Roger Maris."

Since he retired from baseball three years ago this month at the relatively young age of 34, after two seasons with the St. Louis Cardinals, Maris has added 20 pounds to his blockish frame. He does not participate in old-timers' day ceremonies in New York or in St. Louis, nor is he overwhelmed with nostalgia whenever the New York Yankees are mentioned to him. The Yankees, it seems, rank somewhere near the asterisk in Maris's pecking order.

"They [the Yankees] always favored Mickey [Mantle] to break the record," he said. "I was never the fair-haired boy over there. When I'd get hurt, they thought I could still play. When Mickey or Tom Tresh or someone got hurt, they'd let 'em rest."

Maris said that the physical problems he endured as a player remain with him to this day.

"Every day my body tells me I used to be a baseball player. I can't sleep on my stomach because my ribcage is so tender. It got that way because of how I'd bust up double plays. And my knees hurt if I just brush against them; that's from banging into outfield walls. And I still don't have any feel in the ring finger of my right hand, from when I broke my hand in '65. If I had to do it again, I would have been more careful about my health, not to jeopardize it like I did."

Although his personal life is comparable to those led by Greta Garbo, J. D. Salinger and Howard Hughes (Maris covets privacy and avoids social gatherings), he said that while making his professional rounds in northern Florida he still meets people who would rather remember him for his baseball than his beer.

"My customers used to talk baseball a lot," he said, "but not so much anymore. Now and then they'll ask me how I think the Cardinals will do, or something like that. Myself, I never look at the standings. Not at all; too busy."

Maris and his wife, Patricia, have six children, two of whom—Roger Jr. and Kevin—have played in Gainesville Little Leagues.

"I didn't do anything to encourage them and I didn't do anything to stop them. They didn't ask for my help, and so I didn't do nothin' with either one. Better they played the way they wanted to," Maris said.

As for the 10th anniversary celebration for his 61st home run, Maris said that it would be anything but ribald.

"I'll just go home, and have a beer." ◆

Mantle and Ford Voted Into Hall of Fame

By JOSEPH DURSO

THE NEW YORK YANKEES received a dramatic reminder of their long lost past yesterday when Mickey Mantle and Whitey Ford were voted into baseball's Hall of Fame.

Mantle, who retired five years ago with 536 home runs and two crippled knees, made it the first year he was eligible. Ford, who retired six years ago with 236 victories and a pitching percentage of .690, made it the second time around.

It was the first time in the 35-year history of the Hall of Fame that two players—two roommates, in fact—who had spent their entire careers with one team were elected on the same ballot.

Otherwise they were a study in contrasts: Mantle, the country bumpkin from Oklahoma, and Ford, the city slicker from East 66th Street and Second Avenue in Manhattan. The pitcher made the team in 1950, the switch-hitting outfielder in 1951. And for the next 18 seasons they formed the core of the great clubs that won 13 American League pennants and eight world championships.

Since then, the Yankees have undergone radical changes in fortune and ownership and have won nothing. Their chief consolation has been the occasional echo of the past. So far, 142 persons have been elected to the Hall of Fame and, with the accession of Mantle and Ford, 21 of them have been "old Yankees."

To be elected, a player must be retired at least five years and then must be carried on at least 75 per cent of the ballots. This year, 365 ballots were cast; 272 were needed for election. Mantle got 322 votes, 88 per cent of the total; Ford, who missed by 29 a year ago, drew 284, or 78 per cent.

Mantle thereby became only the seventh big leaguer to make it on the first attempt, a feat >>>

Mickey Mantle and Whitey Ford smile on their election into the Baseball Hall of Fame.

‹‹‹ that eluded even his predecessor in center field, Joe DiMaggio. The others who did make it were Ted Williams, Stan Musial, Jackie Robinson, Bob Feller, Sandy Koufax and Warren Spahn.

"I'm closer to Whitey than to any other man in the world," Mantle said yesterday when he and Ford were reunited at the Americana and later at a private lunch at the 21 Club. "I talk to Billy Martin a lot now that he lives in Dallas, and I talk to Yogi Berra on the phone. But Whitey and I were roommates for 12 years, and it wouldn't have been any fun getting into the Hall of Fame without him."

"I quit in 1967 and the last thing on my mind was the Hall of Fame," Ford said. "I knew you had to wait five years. Suddenly, it sneaked up on me. But I was even thrilled last year when I missed it by 29 votes.

"How good was Mickey? As good as you can get, considering his legs and the big ball park he played in. He hurt all the time. After a game, we'd be sitting around and he'd even have trouble getting up."

"My right knee is only 30 per cent stable now," Mantle reported. "The left knee is better. But I still have to take aspirin some nights to ease the pain to sleep." ◆

December 15, 1985

ROGER MARIS IS DEAD AT 51, SET RECORD HOME RUNS

By JOSEPH DURSO

ROGER MARIS, who held the major league record for the most home runs in a single season, died yesterday at M. D. Anderson Hospital and Tumor Institute in Houston after a two-year bout with cancer, hospital officials said. He was 51 years old.

During the early 1960's when the New York Yankees reigned for five straight pennant-winning seasons, Roger Maris was all things to all people. But baseball history will remember him as the home-run twin to Mickey Mantle, and generations of fans will remember him as the man with the asterisk in the record books: *Hit 61 home runs in 1961 in a 162-game season.

The asterisk was inserted to distinguish Maris's home-run record from the one set in 1927 by the greatest Yankee of them all: Babe Ruth, who hit 60 in the days of the 154-game season.

It was inserted into the record books by Ford C. Frick, the commissioner of baseball, who apparently reflected the traditionalist view of many fans that the Olympian feats of Babe Ruth must be defended against long seasons, short fences and newly arrived sluggers, even one who eventually played in seven World Series and hit 275 home runs in 12 seasons in the big leagues.

On Oct. 1, 1961, asterisk or no asterisk, Roger Maris made history when he hit his 61st home run of the season in his 161st game on the final day of the 162-game season in Yankee Stadium against Tracy Stallard of the Boston Red Sox.

It was the rousing end to a rousing season, and it ended with the Yankees winning the pennant race before roaring sellout crowds and swarms of writers and broadcasters drawn by Mantle and Maris, the power hitters on yet another great Yankee team. Mantle, who was injured in September, still managed to hit 54 home runs, so the "twins" combined for an awesome total of 115. But Maris, an accomplished outfielder with a powerful arm and bat, was besieged as he pursued the memory and the record of Ruth.

And yet, Maris was not universally embraced for his achievement. The Yankees received 3,000 messages a day during the final weeks of the season, many of them cheering him on. But the commissioner, a onetime colleague of Babe Ruth, announced that any record would have to be set in 154 games. And Rogers Hornsby, the Hall of Fame slugger, who also had been a contemporary of Ruth, said in the passion of the day:

"Maris has no right to break Ruth's record."

Maris had no "right" to break Ruth's record ostensibly because he was none of the things that had made Babe Ruth renowned as the Bambino. He was imported to the Yankees from the Kansas City Athletics, a stocky figure with a blond crewcut, and he

was playing only his second season in the celebrated pinstripes. He was considered an upstart in the House That Ruth Built, and the house that Mantle dominated. He was dour, aloof, sometimes arch, and in no way the flamboyant bear portrayed by Babe Ruth.

His manager in 1960, Casey Stengel, once said: "You ask Maris a question, and he stares at you for a week before he answers."

"I was born surly," Maris acknowledged in 1961 when the home-run race had ended, "and I'm going to stay that way. Everything in ⟫

Roger Maris tips his hat to the fans after being introduced before an Old Timers game at Yankee Stadium.

≪≪ life is tough. "Even the Yankee clubhouse attendants think I'm tough to live with. I guess they're right. I'm miffed most of the time, regardless of how I'm doing. But, regardless of my faults, I'll never take abuse from anybody–big or small, important or unimportant–if I think it's undeserved."

After 1964, the Yankees stopped winning pennants after an extraordinary run of 14 in 16 years. Maris, meanwhile, endured several seasons of injuries to his back, hand and legs, and said later that he was outraged by intimations that he had been exaggerating his ailments. On Dec. 8, 1966, he was traded to the St. Louis Cardinals, where he again distinguished himself as a professional with a strong right-handed throwing arm from right field and a strong left-handed swing at the plate.

He played in the World Series of 1967 and 1968 for the Cardinals, and then retired at the close of the 1968 season. His career line, with no asterisk, read: 12 years in the big leagues, 1,463 games, 5,101 times at bat, 1,325 hits, 275 home runs, 826 runs, 851 runs batted in and an average of .260. In seven World Series, he hit six home runs.

For many years, Maris lived in Independence, Mo., with his wife, the former Patricia Carvell, and their six children. After retiring from baseball, he lived in Gainesville, Fla., where he owned a beer distributorship.

For a while, he shunned old-timers' games, because he resented the criticism and controversy from his playing days. But he began to appear at reunions later, and he remained close friends with Mantle, Whitey Ford, Yogi Berra, Tony Kubek and his other teammates from the time when the Yankees ruled the day. ◆

July 20, 1986

REMEMBERING ROGER MARIS

By DAVE ANDERSON

IT'S KNOWN AS "having a year." And no other baseball player ever had a year like Roger Maris did in 1961 in hitting a record 61 home runs. Most of the players on the 1961 World Series champion Yankees returned to the Stadium yesterday for their silver anniversary old-timers' reunion. And as they were squeezing into pinstriped uniforms again, Whitey Ford glanced across the Yankee clubhouse filled with people carrying notebooks and microphones.

"The last month of that season." the Hall of Fame left-hander said, "it looked like this every day."

The last month of that season Maris was trying to break Babe Ruth's record of 60 home runs. Even as the Yankees battled the Detroit Tigers for the pennant, whatever their crew-cut right fielder did or didn't do was more important than anything else that happened. Ford had a 25-4 record as the Yankees won 109 games with a record 240 home runs. Mickey Mantle hit 54, Bill (Moose) Skowron hit 28, Yogi Berra hit 22, Elston Howard and John Blanchard each hit 21. But Maris was always the focus. "I remember a game where Ellie hit a home run in extra innings to win it after Roger had hit one earlier," Bobby Richardson recalled. "After the game the writers went right by Ellie's locker to talk to Roger –that's the way it was."

"My locker was next to Roger's," Blanchard said. "After a game writers would jam into my locker to talk to Roger through the mesh that made it look like a confessional. I'd take my clothes and get dressed down at Hector Lopez's locker."

Sitting in Manager Lou Piniella's office yesterday, Ralph Houk, a rookie manager in 1961, remembered a night in Detroit when Maris went into the Yankee trainer's room to visit with his brother Rudy, who had come over from their Fargo, N.D., hometown. Maris hadn't done much that night, but the writers were waiting for him.

"Go talk," Maris suggested, "to the guy who got the big hit."

The pursuit of the really big hit, the 61st homer, stirred baseball as never before. It also stirred the day-by-day pursuit of Roger Maris's life and times. During that same Detroit series, Maris hit his 58th home run, the one that Tony Kubek remembers best. Now an NBC broadcaster but then the Yankee shortstop, Kubek was on second base when Maris suddenly stepped out of the batter's box.

"Roger looked up at a flock of maybe 250 geese that were flying up behind the right-field roof," Kubek said. "I think Nestor Chylak was the home-plate umpire, and he finally had to tell Roger to get back in the box. I think Terry Fox was the pitcher. The next pitch was about six inches off the ground, but Roger pulled it into the upper deck. He told me later that watching those geese was one of the only times he'd had any peace."

In that year's new 162-game schedule, the Yankees were in Baltimore on Sept. 20 for their 155th game - one more than the Yankees had played in 1927, when the Babe hit 60 - and Maris hit his 59th off Milt Pappas. Four games later, the Yankees played Baltimore at the Stadium. "Going into that game, Roger had 59," Richardson said, "then he hit his 60th off Jack Fisher, and when he got back into the dugout, his teammates pushed him out to acknowledge the crowd."

The final day of that season, Maris hit his 61st homer off Tracy Stallard, a Boston Red Sox right-hander who later pitched for the Mets. But that Sunday afternoon Mickey Mantle was in a midtown hospital for treatment of a cyst.

"I saw Roger's 61st on TV and I got goose bumps," Mantle remembered as he autographed baseballs. "That was the greatest single feat I've ever seen in sports."

Mantle had a better home-run ratio that season -54 in 514 times at bat, in contrast to Maris's 61 in 590 times at bat. During the first 30 games, Mantle had 10 homers. Maris didn't groove his home-run swing until he hit nine during the last two weeks of May, then hit 15 in June. But until Mantle was hounded by injuries that September, he also was ahead of the Babe's record 1927 pace.

"You forget that Ruth hit 17 in September the year he hit 60," Mantle said. "You keep thinking you're ahead of him, but then you've got to hit 17 the last month to stay ahead."

When the Yankees were at home that season, Mantle and Maris, along with another outfielder, Bob Cerv, lived in a Queens apartment not far from what is now Kennedy Airport.

"The airport was called Idlewild then," Mantle said with a smile. "Every so often that year >>>

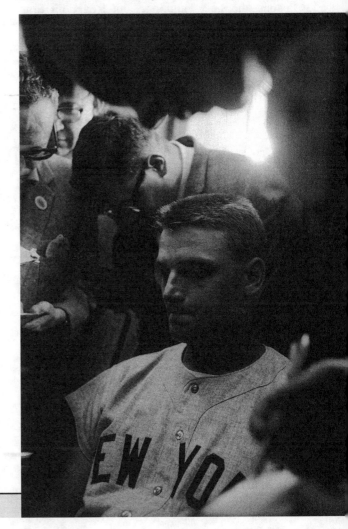

Roger Maris, surrounded by reporters, after a 1961 game.

≪ there'd be a story that Roger and I were fighting over something. I remember one morning Roger went out to get coffee and the papers and he came back to the apartment and said, 'Wake up, Mick, we're fightin' again.'"

As the Yankees' bullpen ace that year, Luis Arroyo had a 15-5 record with 29 saves.

"In the dugout," Arroyo said, "Roger would tell me, 'Just hold 'em a couple of innings and we'll get you some runs.' I think he won six or seven games for me with home runs."

Clete Boyer, the third baseman who hit 11 homers, remembered hitting two in a doubleheader.

"I thought I was going to get my name in the paper," he said, laughing, "but Roger hit four that day."

Those 61 homers always upstaged Maris's skills as an outfielder, base-runner and team player.

"We beat the Reds in the World Series that year," Houk recalled, "but the thing I'll never forget about Roger was the throw in San Francisco he made from down the line that prevented Willie Mays from scoring the tying run in the seventh game of the Series the following year. He could do everything. With a man on second and nobody out, he'd drag the ball to move the runner over. And he was one of the best at breaking up the double play."

But in recent years, Kubek believes, Maris realized that more people had been rooting for him to break Ruth's record than he originally thought when Commisssioner Ford Frick decreed that an asterisk should be attached to those 61 home runs because of the 162-game schedule.

"Roger started drifting back in time," Kubek said. But last year Roger Maris died of cancer at 51. "I went to the funeral," Blanchard remembered, "but I wouldn't look at the casket. I didn't want to remember him that way. I wanted to remember him on the ballfield." ◆

June 11, 1995

Something Always Kept Mantle From His Full Potential

By ROBERT LIPSYTE

MICKEY MANTLE was 19 years old when he burst into our lives, as strong as the heart of the great golden West, a fielder of dreams in a time of infinite promise. It was 1951, the boom-time after a world war won, early summer afternoon in the American Century.

Yesterday, Mantle was transferred out of intensive care after the most invasive of heroic medical procedures. He got his new liver at about the same time the country took heart from the brave rescue of a downed flier in a murky military adventure. Rooting for Mantle's recovery, America may also be rooting for itself in a troubled time of re-evaluation, insecurity and discord.

It has always been easy to make a symbol of the Mick. He arrived all blond and sunny, heralded as the new Joe DiMaggio, if not the next Babe Ruth. His power, his energy, his youth reflected his country; all things were possible when you had infinite resources and the will to win.

And like America in the 50's, he was burdened with a distant sense of doom. For America it was the threat of atomic attack by the Soviet Union. A generation of sports fans grew up with the Mick and with "duck and cover" air-raid drills in school. For Mantle it was the Hodgkin's disease that killed most males in his family before they reached 40. His father, his biggest booster, died after Mickey's rookie season.

The threats to both America and Mantle ultimately proved empty, but they dominated the psyche of the country and the center fielder and gave each an urgency and a poignancy that affected behavior in often destructive ways. America abused itself with the cold war. Mantle had booze.

Nevertheless, the country thrived and so did Mantle. He could run, he could hammer booming drives from either side of the plate, those cannon-ball shoulders rolling under pinstripes could send shivers up the grandstand. Yet something always kept him from totally applying himself, from honing his own talent. He turned surly at criticism, and the Yankee Stadium crowds, reacting to his hype and his attitude, booed him. Osteomyelitis was ravaging Mantle's legs, yet a columnist actually wondered in print how he could play the game when he wasn't healthy enough to fight for his country in Korea. Bleacher bums called him "draft dodger" and "coward," even that ultimate 50's curse, "Commie."

"I got into trouble with the press early because I was scared," said Mantle. "I was young when I came to New York and got misquoted, well, maybe not so much misquoted as it came out not sounding like me talking. I was scared and I didn't really know how to handle it, so if you misquoted me, I just wouldn't talk to anybody, which made the whole joint mad."

But not so mad they wouldn't continue to write about him. The media was building a superstar as much for itself as for the Yankees and baseball. In 1956, he won the Triple Crown—batting .353, hitting 52 homers, driving in 130 runs. It was the first of his three most valuable player awards. And the Yankees beat the Dodgers in the World Series.

But fans and sportswriters considered that golden year a prelude, not a peak, and the pressure to do better increased. It was not until 1961, when it became clear that he would not be the next Babe Ruth, that Mantle began to feel the affection from the stands that he has enjoyed ever since, at card shows, at old-timers' games, at joke-a-stroke golf events, at his fantasy camp, in his Manhattan restaurant. The affection seemed to grow as his vulnerability, his humanity, overtook the myth. There were financial and family failures. One of his four sons was diagnosed with Hodgkin's disease as a teen-ager and died at 36 from a heart attack after years of substance abuse. Last year, after his detoxification at the Betty Ford Center, Mantle was again embraced by his fans.

They were middle-aged now, those duck-and-cover kids, predominately white males who talked about Mantle with a kind of warm awe, of how he played with pain, of how great he might have been if he hadn't been injured so often, if he had taken better care of himself. How much of that emotional feeling was about a great baseball player who somehow never fulfilled the predictions of his cultural or athletic domination, how much about his fans who also sought reasons for never having quite set the records at which they aimed.

And how much of that feeling was about America, still swinging, but no longer so cocksure of leading the league into the next century.

In recent years, Mantle has had an appealing fin-de-siècle sadness of his own; he knows he has lived on press clippings, and he is honest about being no longer sure of what they mean. He once said: "Sometimes I sit in my den at home and read stories about myself. Kids used to save whole scrapbooks on me. They get tired of 'em and mail 'em to me. They might as well be about Musial or DiMaggio. It's like reading about somebody else." ◆

August 14, 1995

MICKEY MANTLE, GREAT YANKEE SLUGGER, DIES AT 63

By JOSEPH DURSO

MICKEY MANTLE, the most powerful switch-hitter in baseball history and the successor to Babe Ruth and Joe DiMaggio as the symbol of the long reign of the New York Yankees, died of cancer yesterday in Dallas. He was 63.

Mantle died at 2:10 A.M. Eastern time at Baylor University Medical Center, succumbing to the disease that had spread from his liver to most of his other vital organs. His wife, Merlyn, and son David were at his bedside.

On June 8, Mantle underwent a transplant operation to replace a liver ravaged by cancer, hepatitis and cirrhosis. At the time, doctors said he would die within two to three weeks if he did not receive a new organ. On July 28, he re-entered Baylor Medical Center for treatment of cancerous spots in his right lung. Recently, he had been suffering from anemia, a side effect of aggressive chemotherapy treatment, and had been receiving blood transfusions. On Aug. 9, the hospital said the cancer had spread to his abdomen.

"This is the most aggressive cancer that anyone on the medical team has ever seen," said Dr. Goran Klintmalm, medical director of transplant services at Baylor. "But the hope in this is that Mickey left behind a legacy. Mickey and his team have already made an enormous impact by increasing the awareness of organ donation. This may become Mickey's ultimate home run."

Mantle, who said he was "bred to play baseball," traveled from the dirt-poor fields of Oklahoma to reach Yankee Stadium in the 1950's and, after his retirement in March 1969, the Baseball Hall of Fame as one of the superstars of the second half of the 20th century.

He commanded the biggest stage in sports as the center fielder for the most successful team in baseball, and he did it at a time when New York was blessed with three great center fielders renowned as "Willie, Mickey and the Duke," home run hitters who captivated the public in the 1950's as the leaders of memorable teams: Willie Mays of the Giants, Mantle of the Yankees and Duke Snider of the Brooklyn Dodgers.

He outlived the family curse of Hodgkin's disease, which had contributed to the death by heart attack of his 36-year-old son Billy, and the early deaths of his father, at 39, his grandfather and two uncles. He was separated from Merlyn, his wife of 43 years, although they remained friendly. He was an alcoholic, which doctors said was at least partly responsible for causing his liver cancer.

Through all the adversity, he exhibited a quiet but shrewd wit that he often unfurled in a down-home Oklahoma drawl. Of his fear of dying early, he once said: "I'll never get a pension. I won't live long enough." And after years of drinking and carousing with Whitey Ford and Billy Martin as his chief running mates, he joked, "If I knew I was going to live this long, I'd have taken better care of myself."

In the end, though, he had a more poignant message. In a news conference on July 11, a remorseful Mantle told the nation, especially its children: "Don't be like me. God gave me a body and the ability to play baseball. I had everything and I just . . ."

But that's not how he was remembered by teammates. "He was not a phony role model, and I think people really identified with that," former teammate Tony Kubek said. "Mick was never a contrived person, he was a genuine person. He brought a lot of Oklahoma with him to New York and never really changed. He showed a certain amount of humility and never let the stardom go to his head."

Said Gene Woodling, who played in the outfield beside Mantle for four seasons: "What can you say about Mickey after you say he was one of the greatest?"

THE POWERFUL SYMBOL OF A YANKEE DYNASTY

He was the storybook star with the storybook name, Mickey, or simply Mick, or Slick to Martin and Ford, who were also known as Slick to one another. He was the blond, muscled switch-hitter who joined the Yankees at 19 in 1951 as DiMaggio was winding down his Hall of Fame career. Wearing No. 7, he led the team through 14 years of the greatest success any baseball team has known before he endured four more years of decline.

He not only hit the ball, he hammered it. He hit often, he hit deep and he did it from both sides of the plate better than anyone else. He could drag a bunt, too, with runaway speed, and he played his role with a kind of all-American sense of destiny. He signed his first contract for $7,500 and his last for $100,000, which seemed princely enough at the time. But he became wildly famous for his strength, his dash, his laconic manner and, somewhat like Joe Namath in football, for his heroic performances on damaged knees.

Long after the cheers faded, so did Mantle, although he revived his image as a kind of fallen hero who carried his afflictions with grace and humor. He acknowledged that some of them were self-inflicted, especially drinking, a habit that had seemed harmless enough when crowds were cheering and he was playing and hitting home runs despite an occasional hangover.

In 1994, while presiding over Mickey Mantle's restaurant in Manhattan as a greeter, he entered the Betty Ford Center in Palm Springs, Calif., to undergo treatment for alcoholism. He came out of the clinic a chastened figure, and his frailty was reinforced by the public decline in his health since June. His transplant revived a debate over whether an alcoholic, even a recovering one, deserves a new liver, and whether his celebrity status had increased his chances of getting one.

Frail, and humbled by the sad events of his later life, Mantle received thousands of letters of support after his transplant operation and discovered that the public could forgive and forget. People chose instead to remember his baseball

feats, unforgettably part of the heroic character he portrayed.

He was the anchor of the team for 18 seasons, first in center field and later, when his knees couldn't take the stress anymore, at first base. He played in 2,401 games and went to bat 8,102 times -- more than any other Yankee -- and delivered 2,415 hits for a .298 batting average. He hit 344 doubles, 72 triples and 536 home runs (373 left-handed, 163 right-handed), and he knocked in 1,509 runs.

He led the American League in home runs four times (in 1955, 1956, 1958 and 1960) and led the league in almost everything in 1956, when he won the triple crown with a .353 batting average, 130 runs batted in and 52 home runs. He was named the league's most valuable player in 1956, 1957 and 1962. He also hit a record total of 18 home runs in 12 World Series, and 2 more in 16 All-Star Games.

He took such an all-out swing at the ball that he struck out regularly and broke the record set two generations earlier by Ruth. It was a record that Mantle put into perspective when he was inducted into the Hall of Fame on Aug. 12, 1974.

"I also broke Babe Ruth's record for strike-outs," Mantle said. "He struck out only 1,500 times. I did it 1,710 times."

With Mantle established in the lineup in 1951, the Yankees won the pennant seven times and the Series five times in the next eight years. And from 1960-64, with the addition of Roger Maris, they won five pennants and two World Series.

Not only that, but in their championship year of 1961, Mantle and Maris provided a season-long drama in their chase of Ruth's home run record; Mantle, sidelined by an abscessed hip, dropped out in mid-September with 54, while Maris finished with a record 61.

EARLY BASEBALL LESSONS
FROM BOTH SIDES OF PLATE

Mickey Charles Mantle was born in Spavinaw, Okla., on Oct. 20, 1931. His father, Elvin, nick-named Mutt, worked in the zinc mines. But he was also a part-time baseball player who >>>

Yankee legends Joe DiMaggio and Mickey Mantle in 1953.

<<< had such a passion for the game that he named his son in honor of Mickey Cochrane, the great catcher for the Philadelphia Athletics and player-manager for the Detroit Tigers. When Mantle was 4 years old, his father would come home from work and teach him how to swing the bat from both sides of the plate while his mother held dinner for them until there was no more daylight.

"When I was a kid," Mantle remembered a few years after he retired, "I used to work in the mines with my dad for $35 a week. Then my dad got me a job cleaning out the area around telephone poles. You see, when you have a prairie fire, if you don't clean out a 10-yard spot around a telephone pole, it will burn the telephone pole out, and it will cost you a lot of money.

"I was still in high school and we were living out near Commerce in 1948, and we didn't have a hell of a lot. My mother made every baseball uniform I ever wore till I signed with the Yankees. I mean, she sewed them right on me. I was 16 years

old then, and my brothers and me would play ball out in the yard or out back in one of the fields.

"I was also playing semipro ball for a team they called the Baxter Springs Whiz Kids, and one night a scout from the Yankees named Tom Greenwade came through Baxter Springs. The ball park was right beside the road, and he was on his way to watch some guy play in another town. But he pulled his car over and stopped and watched us play. And I hit three home runs in that game, two right-handed and one left-handed, and one of them even landed in the river out beyond the outfield.

"When I graduated from high school in 1949, Greenwade showed up again. He even got me out of the commencement exercises so I could play ball because he was thinking of signing me for the Yankees. I think I hit two more home runs that night. When Greenwade came back a week later, he said he'd give me a $1,500 bonus and

$140 a month for the rest of the summer. That's how I signed with the Yankees."

The Yankees started Mantle at Independence, Kan., where they had a Class D minor league club. He hit .313, played shortstop and made 47 errors in 89 games. The next summer, at 18, he played Class C ball in Joplin, Mo., where he hit .383 but made 55 errors in 137 games at shortstop, mostly on wild throws to first base. The team won the pennant by 25 games, and the following spring, he was in Phoenix as a rookie with the Yankees.

Ford, his ally on and off the field for years, remembered how shy and inarticulate the young Mantle seemed when he reported.

"Everything he owned was in a straw suitcase," he said. "No money, none of those $400 suits he got around to buying a couple of years later. Just those two pairs of pastel slacks and that blue sports coat that he wore every place.

"Years later, we were sitting around the dining room at the Yankees' ball park in Fort Lauderdale, and they had this oilcloth on the table, and Mickey said: 'This is what we used to have in our kitchen at home. We didn't even have chairs then; we had boxes instead of chairs, and linoleum on the floor. And when it got cold, the draft would raise the linoleum up at the ends.' "

Mantle was so insecure that he remembered later how he had ducked DiMaggio, even though he was playing his final season in center field and Mantle, who had been converted from shortstop to the outfield, was playing alongside him in right.

"Joe DiMaggio was my hero," Mantle said, "but he couldn't talk to me because I wouldn't even look at him, although he was always nice and polite."

Trip Back to Minors
In First Year in Majors

Two months into the 1951 season, Manager Casey Stengel sent Mantle down to the Yankees' top farm team in Kansas City because he was striking out too much. Against Walt Masterson of the Boston Red Sox he struck out five times in one game. He stayed in the minors for 40 games, returned to New York and closed his rookie season hitting .267 with 13 home runs in 96 games.

"Then in the World Series in 1951," Mantle said, "I tripped on the water-main sprinkler in the outfield while I was holding back so DiMaggio could catch a ball that Willie Mays hit, and I twisted my knee and got torn ligaments. That was the start of my knee operations. I had four.

"Once, they operated on my shoulder and tied the tendons together. I had a cyst cut out of my right knee another time. And down in Baltimore in 1963, Slick was pitching one night and Brooks Robinson hit a home run over the center-field fence. I jumped up and tried to catch it, and got my foot caught in the wire mesh on the fence, and that time I broke my foot about halfway up."

He became one of the damaged demigods of sport, but he played with such natural power that he remained the key figure on a team achieving towering success for the fifth straight decade.

His strength as a hitter became legendary. In 1953, batting right-handed, he hit a ball thrown by Chuck Stobbs of the Washington Senators over the 55-foot-high left-field fence in Griffith Stadium, a drive that was measured at 565 feet from home plate. Three years later, and again in 1963, batting left-handed each time, he smashed a ball into the third deck, within a few feet of the peak of the facade in right field in Yankee Stadium, and no one has come closer to driving a fair ball out of the park.

In 1956, he hit 16 home runs in May. In 1964, he hit two home runs in his final two times at bat on July 4, and two more in his first two times up in the next game the following day. In 1956, he hit three home runs in the World Series, three more in the 1960 Series and three more in the 1964 Series, running his total to 18 and breaking Ruth's record.

"Casey Stengel was like a father to me," Mantle said. "Maybe because I was only 19 years old when I started playing for him, and a couple of years later my own dad was gone. The Old Man really helped me a lot. I guess he even protected me. But I still didn't have it in my head that I was a good major league ballplayer. ≫

Mickey Mantle waves to fans at Old Timers Day at Yankee Stadium in 1982.

≪ "Then Ralph Houk came along and changed my whole idea of thinking about myself. I still didn't have a lot of confidence. Not till Houk came along and told me, 'You are going to be my leader. You're the best we've got.' "

AFTER LEAVING BASEBALL, DAY AND NIGHT DRINKING

The Yankees stopped winning pennants after the 1964 season, and Mantle stopped playing after the 1968 season. He remembered later what it was like: "When I first retired," he wrote in an article in Sports Illustrated in 1994, "it was like Mickey Mantle died. I was nothing. Nobody gave a damn about Mickey Mantle for about five years."

By then, he reported, he was living in a steady haze induced by all-day and all-night drinking.

"When I was drinking," he said, "I thought it was funny -- the life of the party. But as it turned out, nobody could stand to be around me. I was the best man at Martin's wedding in 1988, and I can hardly remember being there." Martin died in a one-vehicle accident on Christmas night 1989. He was legally drunk at the time.

Mantle admitted that drinking had become a way of life even while he was playing. But it finally became a nightmare that undermined his life. And at the request of his son Danny and Pat Summerall, the former football player and current television broadcaster, he checked into the Betty Ford Center in 1994.

He remembered what his doctor told him then: "Your liver is still working, but it has healed itself so many times that before long you're just going to have one big scab for a liver. Eventually, you'll need a new liver. I'm not going to lie to you: The next drink you take may be your last."

There was no next drink, Mantle said. And after leaving the Betty Ford Center, he seemed to be a revived person.

"Everywhere I go," he said, "guys come up and shake hands and say, 'Good job, Mick.' It makes you feel good. It's unbelievable. They give a damn now."

In addition to his wife and son David, he is survived by two other sons, Danny and Mickey Jr.

Funeral services are scheduled for 2 P.M. Tuesday at Lovers Lane United Methodist Church in Dallas. ◆

6 | THE DOWN YEARS

Whenever Yogi Berra, in his first year as the Yankees manager in 1964, came to a fork in the road, he took it—all the way to the American League pennant and the seventh game of the World Series, a disappointing 7–5 loss to the St. Louis Car-

dinals. But days later, strangely, Yogi was fired. Even more strangely, Johnny Keane, who had managed the Cardinals to their Series triumph, was hired as his successor. And two weeks later, when Yankees ownership came to a fork in the road, it took it. All the way to what would turn out to be a dead end until a new owner, a stranger from Cleveland, repaved the road to the World Series.

On November 2, 1964, the Columbia Broadcasting System purchased the Yankees from Dan Topping and Del Webb for $14.4 million. After all the success of the Topping–Webb regime—mostly with Casey Stengel as manager and Joe DiMaggio or Mickey Mantle batting cleanup, and, before that, of the Jake Ruppert reign, when Babe Ruth and Lou Gehrig created the Yankees legend—the franchise suddenly had a corporate owner. CBS was the world's dominant television entertainment and news conglomerate. Its chairman, William S. Paley, had assembled marquee names: Jackie Gleason, Lucille Ball, Bing Crosby, Jack Benny, Red Skelton, George Burns and Gracie Allen, as well as Walter Cronkite, Charles Collingwood, and Eric Sevareid. Its Columbia Records division had signed Johnny Cash, Barbra Streisand, Tony Bennett, Doris Day, and Johnny Mathis.

CBS put Mike Burke in charge. Long a toast of the town, with flashy shoulder-length white hair, flashy suits, and a flashy résumé, Burke had served during World War II in the United States Office of Strategic Services, the forerunner of the Central Intelligence Agency, including time with the French resistance before D-day. As the boss of the Ringling Bros. and Barnum & Bailey Circus, he had put the big top into the big arenas.

Ralph Houk remained the general manager, but Keane was handed an aging roster that in 1965 toppled into sixth place. With no reinforcements from a dried-up farm system, the Yankees thudded into last place in 1966, finishing 26 and a half games out. Halfway through that season, Keane was dismissed and Houk, who had guided the Yankees to four pennants in his first term as manager, returned to the dugout. Lee MacPhail, son of boisterous Larry MacPhail, was installed as general manager in 1967, a ninth- »»»

★ ★ ★

The Yankees invited nuns to be their guests at a 1971 Stadium Game.

≪≪≪ place mess, but the farms were being replenished. Soon the Yankees were respectable. Mel Stottlemyre, the right-hander who had preserved the 1964 pennant, would be a three-time 20-game winner. Roy White would be a dependable switch-hitting outfielder for 14 seasons. Bobby Murcer, unfairly hailed as "the next Mantle," would be a four-time All-Star outfielder who hit .331 in 1971 and 33 homers in 1972. Thurman Munson, a catcher who was the American League rookie of the year in 1969, would grow into a Yankees icon.

After the once woebegone Mets upstaged the Yankees with their 1969 World Series victory, left-hander Fritz Peterson posted a 20–11 record in 1970 as the Yankees climbed into second. When they dipped to fourth the next two seasons, CBS tired of owning a famous franchise no longer famous. During the 1972 season the word was that the Yankees were for sale; and in Cleveland, millionaire shipbuilder George Steinbrenner heard the word. Assembling a group of wealthy Cleveland pals, he had also heard that the price was around $10 million, less than what CBS had paid.

As the deal developed, Steinbrenner had Gabe Paul, a career baseball executive and then the Indians president, meet with Burke to explore the Yankees' finances. On December 19, 1972, Burke ushered Steinbrenner into Paley's inner sanctum high in the CBS offices. Paley accepted Steinbrenner's offer, but stipulated that Burke remain as chief operating officer. Steinbrenner assured Paley that he had a ship company to run, that he wouldn't have "much time" for baseball, and that Burke would remain the face of the franchise. Soon the deal was done. The net price would be $8.7 million, with Steinbrenner holding 10 percent. On January 3, 1973, the Yankees called a press conference at the Stadium Club to announce the sale. Asked about his role, Steinbrenner insisted, "We plan absentee ownership."

Within days, the "absentee" owner installed Gabe Paul, who had resigned from the Indians, as the Yankees' baseball boss and relegated Burke to supervising the $100 million stadium renovation that would begin after the season. On April 25, Burke, fed up with Steinbrenner's deceit, resigned as general partner. The "absentee" owner now was in complete charge, loud and clear and seldom absent. So loud and so clear that after the Yankees finished fourth again, seventeen games out, Houk grew tired of being second-guessed and decided to depart as manager when the 1973 season ended. Across the Triborough Bridge, meanwhile, the Mets upstaged the Yankees again. With manager Yogi Berra, of all people, and an aging Willie Mays in his last season, the Mets were the talk of the town, despite losing the World Series to the Oakland Athletics.

The Yankees played home games at Shea Stadium in 1974, while their big ballpark in the Bronx was being remodeled, and the new manager, Bill Virdon, lifted them to second place. But late that year Steinbrenner suddenly found himself to be an absentee owner after all. He was suspended for two years by Commissioner Bowie Kuhn after having pleaded guilty to making illegal contributions to President Richard Nixon's campaign, and to aiding and abetting the obstruction of an investigation. Officially, at least, he was not the boss when right-hander Jim "Catfish" Hunter, declared a free agent because Oakland Athletics owner Charles O. Finley had breached his contract, agreed to a $3.35 million deal. On Old-Timers' Day in 1975, Steinbrenner's managerial merry-go-round began. Virdon was out and Billy Martin was in.

Hunter's 23–14 record helped the Yankees finish third in 1975, but free agency, as declared by arbitrator Peter Seitz's tie-breaking vote, was about to turn the baseball world, and George Steinbrenner's wallet, upside down.

October 20, 1964

Keane Due to Sign as Yankee Manager

EX-CARD LEADER VISITED BY HOUK

JOHNNY KEANE is due in New York today to sign as manager of the Yankees.

The club has called a news conference for this afternoon at the Savoy Plaza to announce its choice. Ralph Houk, the Yankee general manager, was in Houston yesterday, talking to Keane about the position.

Houk arrived at Keane's home late Sunday night and spoke with the former St. Louis Cardinal manager for two hours. Yesterday, the pair was in seclusion, presumably straightening out such details as length of contract and salary.

Keane had reiterated all weekend long that he would accept the post if it were offered.

His hiring would cap one of the most bizarre weeks in major league history. Keane resigned as the Cards' manager on Friday, one day after his team had won the World Series by upsetting the Yanks. Two hours after Keane resigned, the Yanks dismissed Yogi Berra as manager.

It is believed that Keane will be accompanied here for the news conference by his wife, Lela.

The Keanes spent a hectic weekend, leaving St. Louis Friday afternoon and completing a 900-mile auto trip to Houston early Sunday. ◆

September 9, 1965

YANKEES DEFEAT SENATORS, 6 TO 5

Bombers' Longest Losing Streak in 12 Years Ends

THE NEW YORK YANKEES broke their longest losing streak in 12 years last night when Elston Howard's two-out single in the ninth inning defeated the Washington Senators, 6-5.

Despite their victory, the Yankees were eliminated from the American League pennant race when the Minnesota Twins defeated the Chicago White Sox last night, 3-2.

The Yankees had lost seven straight, the same number as their starting pitcher, Jim Bouton, who worked five innings and stood to be the winning pitcher as late as the top of the ninth.

But Ken McMullen tied the game, 5-5, with a long home run to left field off Steve Hamilton with two down in the Senators' ninth and Bouton was denied his first victory since June 30.

Then, in the home ninth, Roy White led off with his fourth hit in two days in the major leagues, a single to center off Ron Kline. Bobby Richardson bunted him to second, Bobby Murcer flied to left and Tom Tresh was walked intentionally.

That put the issue up to Howard, who settled it by ripping the 2-and-2 pitch through the left side of the infield for a single as White scored the winning run. ◆

January 26, 1966

Kubek of Yankees Is Forced to Retire at 29 by an Injury

By LEONARD KOPPETT

WITHIN A FEW HOURS yesterday, the New York Yankees announced the retirement from baseball of Tony Kubek, a cautiously optimistic report on Mickey Mantle's shoulder operation, and the return of Bobby Richardson.

Kubek's retirement came as a shock to the public, but the Yankees had been aware of the possibility in recent weeks. The 29-year-old shortstop is suffering from damage to a nerve at the top of his spinal column and his reflexes are affected.

This condition, gradually worsening in the last couple of years, is the result of improper healing of a neck injury suffered at an undetermined time. There was some danger in continuing to play, so Kubek decided to retire.

Meanwhile, in Rochester, Minn., two doctors at the Mayo Clinic operated on Mantle's right shoulder. They removed a loose particle from the tendon sheath, reported no complications, and said that Mantle should be available for spring training on March 1, or shortly thereafter.

Mantle will remain in the hospital for three weeks, and then begin a program of therapy.

RETIREMENT IS POSTPONED

Richardson, the second baseman who has been teamed with Kubek for more than a decade, dating back to the minor leagues, spoke to the Yankees shortly after Kubek made his decision. Richardson had been considering retirement for his own reasons, involving interest in a career in church and youth work. But in view of Kubek's unavailability, he decided to continue.

The Kubek story is mysterious and tragic. During the last three seasons, Tony has been on the injured list repeatedly, with an assortment of pains and stiffnesses in the neck, side, shoulder and arm.

After last season, he went to the Mayo Clinic for a thorough test. It developed that at some time several years ago, he had suffered what amounts to a broken neck, without knowing it.

Shortstop Tony Kubek played for the Yankees from 1957 to 1965.

The crack healed, but bone spurs developed.

"I really have no idea how it happened," declared Tony yesterday, doing a good job of acting self-possessed. "It may have happened in a touch football game I played after the 1961 World Series, when I went into the Army—I got racked up and lost a couple of teeth."

DISCOUNTS BAD BOUNCE

"They also say it could have happened when I got hit in the throat by the bad bounce in the 1960 World Series, but I find that hard to believe because I don't remember having any pain in the back of the neck at that time. In fact, even the throat wasn't that painful—I just couldn't talk."

The "bad bounce" occurred in Pittsburgh in the seventh inning of the seventh game of the World Series between the Yankees and the Pirates. The Yankees were leading at the time, but a double-play ball took a bad hop on the hard surface of the Forbes Field infield, and knocked Kubek out. The Pirates went on to take the lead that inning, were tied, but won the World Series in the ninth on a home run by Bill Mazeroski.

Always a line-drive hitter rather than a slugger, Kubek was at his peak in 1961, when he helped the Yankees win the pennant and the World Series in Houk's first year as manager. He went into the Army after that and missed the first half of the 1962 season. When he came back, he reclaimed the shortstop job from Tom Tresh, then a rookie, and finished strong. But in the next three seasons he was never able to hit consistently.

REFLEXES ARE UNRELIABLE

"The doctors seemed surprised I hadn't had more trouble than I did," Tony said. "I feel fine now—but my reflexes are unreliable and erratic. Eventually surgery may be needed; as it is, a sudden jarring movement might even result in paralysis. Away from baseball, if I don't wrestle with my kids too much, and avoid accidents, I should be all right."

Kubek will devote his time to his new position as vice president of a cheese manufacturing company in his hometown of Wausau, Wis. ◆

May 8, 1966

YANKS NAME HOUK TO REPLACE KEANE

Beat Angels on Coast, 3-1— Kauai King Triumphs in Kentucky Derby

THE LAST-PLACE New York Yankees dismissed Johnny Keane as manager last night and replaced him with Ralph Houk, the club's general manager.

The shuffle, expected for some time, returns Houk to a familiar role—he managed the Yanks to pennants from 1961 to 1963 before moving up to the front office.

Keane was named Yankee manager when he suddenly resigned from the St. Louis Cardinals after leading the Cards to the National League pennant and a World Series triumph in 1964. New York finished sixth in the American League last season.

Houk was given a four-year contract and relieved of his duties as general manager, which have been assigned to Dan Topping Jr. Houk returned to uniform last night at Anaheim and the Yankees beat the California Angels, 3-1. ◆

Ralph Houk and Mets manager Casey Stengel.

September 21, 1966

Yankees' New President Says Familiar Voices Will Continue

By VAL ADAMS

MICHAEL BURKE, the new president and chairman of the New York Yankees, said yesterday he had no plans to change the baseball club's broadcasting staff. In recent weeks there had been rumors that one or more of the four announcers on the staff now might not be back next year.

Mr. Burke, a vice president of the Columbia Broadcasting System, which is now the sole owner of the Yankees, became head of the club on Monday when Dan Topping Sr. resigned.

"At the moment I don't have any plan to make changes in the broadcasting staff," Mr. Burke said. "The question is premature. I haven't dealt with the matter in any serious way."

The announcers for the Yankees are Red Barber, Jerry Coleman, Joe Garagiola and Phil Rizzuto. Mr. Garagiola is the junior member of the staff, having been hired after Mel Allen was dropped two years ago.

It was reported yesterday that their future with the Yankees might have taken a turn for the better after the departure of Mr. Topping. In a memorandum sent to each one last May, Mr. Topping referred to their work on the air as "horrible." He accused them of talking about everything except the game in progress.

The memorandum, dated May 27, was addressed to Perry Smith, head of the radio-TV staff. It indicated the Yankees had been receiving many letters of complaint from listeners about the work of the announcers.

"We have by far the best broadcasting crew in baseball," Mr. Topping said. "However, of late all four have been horrible. I would just as soon you relayed this message to them.

"I realize it was a mighty tough job during our losing streak to give an interesting broadcast. But certainly the way the club has been doing recently there is no excuse for all the talk about everything but reporting the game. This should not be directed to any one announcer in particular, because they have all done this at one time or another. As you know, I listen to the games on radio or TV whether I am in the ball park or not. And it has gotten so bad that I am tired of having to answer all the letters of complaint and trying to find excuses.

"I think it simply means this—sticking to reporting the game and current facts, rather than talking about past history and personal things.

"The club is coming out of the slump—tell the four in the [broadcasting] booth to get going, too."

Mr. Smith gave a copy of the memorandum to each announcer without comment. They were said to have been considerably shaken. Mr. Topping never talked to them directly, but all season long they have wondered just where they stood with the head of the club and whether they would be renewed for the next season.

The Yankees are the only major-league club with a four-man announcing staff. The New York Mets have three, but most clubs have only two. ◆

October 1, 1966

YANKEES CLINCH 10TH PLACE

CHICAGO, SEPT. 30 (AP)—John Romano's two-out, run-scoring single in the 11th inning gave the Chicago White Sox a 6-5 victory over the New York Yankees tonight. The loss insured a 10th-place finish for the once-mighty Yankees.

Even if the Yankees win their last two games, at best they will finish one-half game behind the Boston Red Sox in the American League standings. It is the first time the Yankees have finished in the cellar since 1912. There were eight teams in the league at that time.

Wayne Causey led off the 11th with a single and was sacrificed to second. One out later, Romano singled to left field for the winning run and Mel Stottlemyre's 20th defeat. A year ago Stottlemyre won 20 games. Stottlemyre entered the game as a relief pitcher in the 10th. ◆

December 1, 1967

YANKS PURCHASE A SHORTSTOP, 29

Get Michael of Dodgers in Straight Cash Deal

Special to The New York Times

MEXICO CITY, Nov. 30—The New York Yankees finally entered the trading market at baseball's winter meetings today after four days of mourning "the shortstop who got away."

They bought Gene Michael from the Los Angeles Dodgers for an undisclosed amount of cash reported to be $30,000.

Michael is a 29-year-old Ohioan who spent seven years in the minor leagues before the Pittsburgh Pirates brought him up in 1966. He played in 30 games, then was traded last winter to the Dodgers along with Bob Bailey, in exchange for Maury Wills.

That was frustration No. 1 for the Yankees, who had been trying to get Wills themselves. Frustration No. 2 came yesterday when they lost out to the Chicago White Sox in bidding for Luis Aparicio of Baltimore. Now they have acquired Wills's part-time successor at Los Angeles.

In between, the Yankees tried Clete Boyer at shortstop, but he was really a third baseman. Then they bought Ruben Amaro, but he fractured his kneecap. Then they promoted Bobby Murcer, but he was drafted by the Army. Then they came to Mexico City looking for a shortstop or third baseman, and were outbid.

At Los Angeles, Michael played in 97 games, got 45 hits (no home runs) and batted .202. He is a switch hitter, though the Yankees promptly heard jibes about having acquired a switch-no-hitter. ◆

Thurman Munson gets the out at home against the Cleveland Indians during a 1969 game at Yankee Stadium.

March 15, 1969

MUNSON IMPRESSES HOUK

By GEORGE VECSEY
Special to The New York Times

MIAMI, MARCH 14—Thurman Munson is supposed to spend the summer in Syracuse, according to the master plan. But there are days when Ralph Houk can envision Munson in the Bronx, squatting behind home plate, doing things that Yankee catchers haven't done in several years.

Houk has used Munson in all seven exhibitions, including tonight's 5-2 loss, as the Yankees made only two hits against the Orioles.

Munson is a 21-year-old from Kent State. The Yankees drafted him as their top selection last June. He batted .301 at Binghamton in his first professional season and a promotion to Syracuse would seem to be the highest anybody could expect for him.

But Houk was a catcher once himself. Didn't he spend a career watching Yogi Berra and Elston Howard keep him out of the line-up? Thus, there is an appreciation for the finer things in catching and Houk was discussing them before last night's game with the Orioles.

COOL BEHIND THE PLATE

The first sign to Houk was the way the husky 5-foot-11-inch rookie seemed at ease in his first spring camp. Then last Sunday Munson caught the Orioles' pinch-runner, Chico Fernandez, standing flat-footed away from second base. A sudden throw to second made Fernandez an embarrassed and out pinch-runner.

"This guy can throw," Houk said. "He's got a doggone cannon on him."

Then on Wednesday, Munson goes to his right to steer an outside pitch that seemed headed for the screen.

"Most catchers would try to move sideways,"

Houk said, "but Munson just stuck his glove across his body so damned fast that he caught the ball. I'm telling you, this guy is really something. You don't see many like him."

Not in New York you don't. Houk has been doing his best to promote Jake Gibbs and Frank Fernandez for the last couple of years, but Gibbs batted only .213 last year while Fernandez hit only .170 with some power. Fernandez was limited by service obligations and he does have a fine arm, but, even between Gibbs and Fernandez, the Yankees are not strong in catching.

Therefore, Houk watches Munson and he dreams. "I couldn't keep him if he wasn't going to play," Houk muses. "A guy this young should play every day."

Then Houk is asked bluntly if he's considering keeping Munson as his first-string catcher. The question is direct. Houk could duck it or he could degrade it. Instead, he laughs, because he has no evasive plan. Finally, he stops chuckling and he admits out loud, "Well…you'd want to see him a lot more…you don't know what he can do…but, dammit, yeah, you think about it." ◆

November 25, 1970

MUNSON RECEIVES ROOKIE AWARD

By DEANE McGOWEN

THURMAN MUNSON, the New York Yankees' fine catcher, yesterday was named the American League's rookie of the year. He was an almost unanimous choice in the voting by the Baseball Writers Association of America. Munson received 23 of the 24 votes cast, with two writers voting from each city in the league. Roy Foster, the Cleveland outfielder, got the other vote.

The 23-year-old Munson, in becoming the first catcher to earn the American League honor, was interviewed at the Stadium Press Lounge by telephone from his home in Canton, Ohio. After modestly expressing his pleasure in being selected, Munson spoke to Lee MacPhail, the Yankees' general manager.

MacPhail: "I suppose I can expect a request from you for a small raise."

Munson: "Ah, well, Mr. MacPhail, if the team does as well as I think it will next season, I'm sure there will be some raises."

Munson's reply was not what MacPhail had anticipated, but he laughed and said, "You did not say what I thought you would, and I was prepared because I have several witnesses here."

But Munson, despite his youth and comparative lack of major-league experience, was not about to get involved in a public contract discussion with the front office.

Munson, the sixth Yankee to be honored in the 22-year history of the B.B.W.A. award, was the club's first selection in the June, 1968 free-agent draft. He had played only 99 minor-league games before winning the Yankees regular catching job this last season.

OFF TO A POOR START

The catcher did not look as if he would have the job long. He got off to a poor start last April with only one hit in his first 30 plate appearances. But, bolstered by Manager Ralph Houk's confidence in him, Munson shook the slump and hit at a .322 pace for the rest of the season.

He finished with 137 hits and a .302 average, highest of the club. He was also outstanding defensively, throwing out 40 would-be base-stealers in 69 tries.

Munson joins five other Yankee rookie winners—Gil McDougald (1951), Bob Grim (1954), Tony Kubek (1957), Tom Tresh (1962) and Stan Bahnsen (1968). ◆

January 20, 1972

BERRA VOTED INTO HALL OF FAME

By JOSEPH DURSO

SANDY KOUFAX, Yogi Berra and Early Wynn were elected to baseball's Hall of Fame yesterday in the heaviest voting in the 35-year history of the poll.

In a landslide Koufax led the rest with 344 of the 396 votes cast by the Baseball Writers Association of America. It was the highest total ever received by a player and, at the age of 36, the former pitching star of the Brooklyn and Los Angeles Dodgers also became the youngest elected.

He also joined a select group of nine who made it the first year they had become eligible—five years after retirement.

Berra, for 18 seasons a catcher with the Yankees, made it on his second attempt with 339 votes. Wynn, a 300-game winner on the mound with Washington, Cleveland and the Chicago White Sox, made it on his fourth with 301.

March 23, 1972

Yanks Trade for Lyle

By JOSEPH DURSO
Special to The New York Times

ST. PETERSBURG, FLA., MARCH 22—The New York Yankees were held scoreless for the sixth time in 18 games today, and adding insult to injury, it was the Mets who did the shutting out, 3-0.

But help was on the way. Three hours after the annual reunion of the clans, the Yankees traded Danny Cater to the Boston Red Sox for Sparky Lyle, the left-handed relief pitcher they had been coveting all winter.

That is, they gave up a bat for an arm. The reasoning was that Cater, after two seasons of utility work, still did not have a regular position at the age of 32.

He plays third base or first, but the thing he does best is hit: a .279 career average after eight seasons with the Philadelphia Phillies, Chicago White Sox, Oakland Athletics and Yankees.

He batted .301 and .276 for New York, but the Yankees, meanwhile, had a graver problem—their bull pen last summer "saved" only 12 games. They were especially shy a left-hander like Steve Hamilton who could get the big out, and they made no bones of their admiration for Albert W. Lyle, a mod 27-year-old with long hair and a short earned-run average.

"We've been trying to get him for two years," said Lee MacPhail, general manager.

The Yankees will drop off Cater tomorrow at Winter Haven, where they play an exhibition against the Red Sox, and will return with Lyle, a 6-foot-1-inch Pennsylvanian. He has pitched five seasons for Boston with a 2.85 earned-run average and he is absolutely the "short" type of relief man—in 50 appearances last year he pitched only 52 innings. ◆

To be elected, they had to be mentioned on 75 per cent of the ballots, in this case 297. They made it one year after an election in which nobody got enough votes, and will be inducted into the Hall at Cooperstown, N.Y., on Aug. 7.

For Berra, who was named Lawrence Peter after his birth 46 years ago in St. Louis, the voting reversed a disappointment suffered a year ago, when he fell 28 votes short.

"I thought maybe I'd make it this year," he said. "Even a great player like Joe DiMaggio didn't make it in his first year. But whenever you make it, it's a great thrill. I got four or five phone calls from friends this morning, and I had to tell them I didn't know anything yet, even though I did."

During his 20-year career as a player, Berra batted .285, chiefly as the catcher on the great Yankee teams of the 1950's; hit 358 home runs and appeared in 14 All-Star games and 14 World Series.

He also was manager of the Yankees in 1964, was dropped after they lost the Series, switched to the Mets, played briefly with them and has been their first-base coach the last six seasons.

He was short and squat, and became part of the national folklore. But in uniform he was all business. He once went 148 games without an error, handling 950 chances cleanly. He has hit more home runs than any other catcher, and holds 10 Series records. ◆

August 17, 1972

Yanks, City Sign 30-Year Stadium Lease

By EDWARD RANZAL

THE NEW YORK YANKEES will play at Yankee Stadium for the next 30 years under terms of a lease signed yesterday with the city, which will renovate the venerable Bronx ball park into what Mayor Lindsay called "the most modern sports arena in the country."

Work on the Yankee Stadium superstructure, which will result in a cantilevered area with no spectator obstructions, is expected to take two years. Mike Burke, president of the Yankees, said the team would play at Shea Stadium in the 1974 and 1975 seasons under an agreement with the New York Mets.

Mayor Lindsay expressed his appreciation to Mrs. Joan Payson and Donald Grant of the Mets, "whose public-spirited cooperation was crucial to the agreement for the Yankees' two year use of Shea Stadium."

The city has committed $24-million in capital funds for the purchase and renovation of the 49-year-old stadium. Modernization of the structure is expected to cost a little more than $21-million. However, the commitment includes an additional 15 per cent for escalating costs so that the ultimate total cost will probably reach $27-million.

The signing of the lease by Mayor Lindsay and Burke was done at a City Hall news conference. The Mayor described the occasion as "an important day in the history of New York. It is the first step in renovating Yankee Stadium and making the 'house that Ruth Built' an even greater attraction for present and future generations of New Yorkers."

The changes in the stadium's superstructure were designed by the architectural firm of Praeger, Kavanagh and Waterbury, which also designed Shea Stadium and Dodger Stadium in Los Angeles.

John Waterbury, a member of the architectural firm, said there would be no seats with obstructed views of the playing field. Existing pillars will be removed, he said, and the mezzanine and part of the upper level will be cantilevered and supported by a system of structural cables. This will reduce the seats for baseball from 65,010 to 57,500. ◆

January 4, 1973

C.B.S. Sells the Yankees for $10-Million

By JOSEPH DURSO

THE COLUMBIA BROADCASTING SYSTEM said yesterday that it was selling the New York Yankees to a 12-man syndicate headed by Michael Burke, now president of the team, and George M. Steinbrenner 3d of Cleveland.

The price is $10-million in cash, which is $3.2-million less than C.B.S. paid for the franchise in 1964, the last year the Yankees won the American League pennant. Mr. Burke, who has been running the club for C.B.S., will continue to direct it for the self-styled "absentee owners," and the Yankees, he said, will remain in New York.

The paying public probably will not be affected by the change in ownership, both men conceded. But Mayor Lindsay said in a statement that the city welcomed the news "as the landlord of the Yankees" and he promised that the city's $24-million program to buy and modernize Yankee Stadium would "continue in full force."

The only partners in the syndicate who appeared at Yankee Stadium for the announcement were Mr. Burke and Mr. Steinbrenner, 42-year-old chairman of the American Ship Building Company and part-owner of the Chicago Bulls basketball team. No other partners were identified—except as "prominent business executives and sportsmen"—though the Yankees said they would be introduced in person here next week.

The sale itself was no surprise, since Mr. Burke

acknowledged last July that C.B.S. was listening to offers. He even granted the possibility that he might some day be involved in buying the team.

But two aspects of the sale did raise some eyebrows: the price, which was considered a bargain in today's professional sports market, and the fact that C.B.S. sold so far below its original purchase price.

In recent years, during baseball's expansion to 24 big league teams, $10-million has been paid to establish new clubs in Seattle and San Diego—clubs with neither the population nor the tradition of the New York Yankees. The Cleveland Indians, whom Mr. Steinbrenner tried to buy two years ago, finally went for $10.8-million. The Los Angeles Rams football team was sold last year for $19-million.

"It's the best buy in sports today," Steinbrenner conceded, referring to the Yankees. "I think it's a bargain. But they [C.B.S.] feel the chemistry is right—they feel they haven't taken a loss on the team."

Herman Franks, the former manager of the San Francisco Giants, who also had been trying to buy the Yankees, agreed with some surprise that the deal was a good buy. Reached by telephone in Salt Lake City, he said:

"We were talking somewhere between 13 and 14 million. I thought we still had a chance, because my man called me this morning and said he was still talking to people."

ENOUGH BUT TOO LATE

However, despite their high offer, Franks and his associates were five days too late. Burke said he had been introduced to Steinbrenner by a mutual friend and "George and I have been talking for two or three months." On Dec. 19 they made their offer to William S. Paley, chairman of C.B.S., and on Dec. 22 he agreed to accept it.

"We thought it would take until mid-January to get the proper action," Burke said, "but Mr. Paley got the Finance Committee to approve inside three days. We exchanged memorandums of agreement last Friday."

Burke, who will leave the network now, noted that he had advised C.B.S. to buy the Yankees in 1964 when he was vice president in charge of investments. He laughed when asked if he in turn had advised C.B.S. to sell the Yankees in 1972. As for the reasons for selling now, he said:

"C.B.S. substantially broke even on this deal, taking account of investment and depreciation and things like that. Some years were profitable, some were not. The first half of last season was disastrous, but in the second half our attendance doubled.

"I think C.B.S. suffered some small embarrassment in buying a club at its peak and then having it fall from first place in the league to sixth and then to 10th. The bottom fell out. The Yankees no longer fit comfortably into C.B.S.'s plans.

"Last summer people were tripping over themselves to buy the club, but until recently Mr. Paley was not interested in selling it. Lately, he believed the Yankees did not fit into C.B.S.'s plans. He did feel that I should stay on as chief executive officer and the club should be sold to a respectable group. Now there's $10-million on the table—and it's not a dollar down and a dollar a month."

As he spoke before a crowded news conference in the stadium restaurant, Burke was surrounded by huge photographs depicting the Yankees' glory days: 29 pennants and 20 World Series titles in 45 years.

Two stars from past winners were there, too: Elston Howard, now a coach, and Phil Rizzuto, now a broadcaster. So was Lee MacPhail, who signed a three-year contract as general manager last September and who will remain, as will Ralph Houk, who signed a three-year contract as manager at the same time.

Burke, MacPhail and Houk have formed a triumvirate since C.B.S. bought the club in August, 1964, from Dan Topping and Del Webb. But in the eight seasons since then, the Yankees finished no higher than third in the league. Last summer they finished fourth in the Eastern Division after a rousing run for the pennant in July, August and September.

The new ownership of the Yankees in 1973. George Steinbrenner is in the front row, fourth from the left.

»»»

≪≪ However, attendance dipped to 966,328, the first time the Yankees had missed one million since 1945. In Queens, meanwhile, the Mets were finishing third in the National League's East and were drawing 2,134,185 customers to Shea Stadium.

Despite the slump at the gate, the Yankees have been rustling themselves in recent months. They acquired Graig Nettles and Matty Alou, established stars, in trades last month. And after the 1973 season, their 50th anniversary in Yankee Stadium, they will move to Shea for two years while the city modernizes their home park. The football Giants, meanwhile, still are expected to relocate in New Jersey.

Deputy Mayor Edward Hamilton, who stood alongside Burke, denied that the city's project represented a $24-million windfall for an outside syndicate. He termed the plan "an investment" in the Bronx area and said:

"Any landlord is delighted to learn that the tenant is hot property. We are delighted."

"As landlord of the New York Yankees," Mayor Lindsay said in his statement, "the city welcomes today's news. The city has made firm plans and appropriated funds to refurbish completely the stadium and its environs by 1975. These plans, appropriations and all agreements continue in full force and effect. For the Yankees, which are such an integral part of the Bronx and the whole city, we know the best is yet to come."

In its statement C.B.S. said "the $10-million purchase price substantially recoups the original C.B.S. investment of $13.2 million, taking into account consolidated financial results during the period of ownership. The purchase price is well in excess of the value carried on the C.B.S. books."

"We plan absentee ownership as far as running the Yankees is concerned," Steinbrenner said. "We're not going to pretend we're something we aren't. I'll stick to building ships." ◆

January 4, 1973

New Owner Held Yanks in Awe as Boy

By MURRAY CHASS

AS A BOY, George M. Steinbrenner 3d lived in Cleveland so he had to be an Indian fan. But he remembers the Yankees well.

"When the Yankees came to town, it was like Barnum and Bailey coming to town," he said yesterday. "I don't mean that they were like a circus, but it was the excitement. They had these gray uniforms, but there was a blue hue to them. I'll never forget them. Watching them warm up was as exciting as watching the game. Being in Cleveland, you couldn't root for them, but you would boo them in awe."

The 42-year-old chairman and chief executive officer of the American Ship Building Company doesn't have to hold back the cheers any longer. When the Yankees go to Cleveland next May, he can scream and wave Yankee banners all he wants because he'll be one of the team's owners.

Involved in numerous activities, including business, politics, sports, showbusiness and civic and charitable functions, Steinbrenner put together the group that is buying the Yankees from the Columbia Broadcasting System.

"The Yankees are important to New York, but they're also especially important to baseball and to the whole nation," he said in an interview at the Stadium Club in the Yankee ball park.

"The Yankees are baseball. They're as American as apple pie. There are still great things about the past that are worth going back to and grabbing into the present. I think that's so with the Yankees."

Steinbrenner's past is filled with various efforts in sports. Son of a collegiate champion hurdler, he ran in the hurdles at Williams College

Mike Burke, president of the Yankees, with George M. Steinbrenner (right), who was a Cleveland shipping executive at the time.

from 1948 to 1952 (he was good enough to be invited to compete against, and lose to, Harrison Dillard at Madison Square Garden) and was a halfback on the football team in his senior year.

While serving with the Strategic Air Command he set up an athletic program at his base. After being discharged, he became a high school football and basketball coach in Columbus, Ohio.

Then, after a year each as an assistant football coach at Northwestern and Purdue, he quit coaching in 1957 and went into the family business, shipping.

But he couldn't stay away from sports for long, and from 1959 to 1961 he operated the Cleveland Pipers of the National Industrial Basketball League and then of the American Basketball League.

Aside from winning two championships and losing about $250,000, the most notable thing he did with the Pipers was to sign Jerry Lucas to a contract that Lucas never fulfilled.

Despite the losses, Steinbrenner raised enough money to buy the family concern from his father, Henry Steinbrenner, and parlayed the five Great Lakes ore carriers of the Kinsman Marine Transit Company into control of the company he now heads.

American Ship Building was struggling when he assumed command in 1967, but it since has tripled its volume to more than $100-million.

Along the way, Steinbrenner also became part-owner and vice president of the Chicago Bulls of the National Basketball Association, owner of the 860-acre Kinsman Stud Farm in Ocala, Fla., and a general partner in Kinship Stables, whose 2-year-old Kinsman Hope, won the Remsen Stakes at Aqueduct last Nov. 29.

In addition he is in partnership with James Nederlander in a theater outfit that produced >>>

the musical, "Applause," on Broadway and has a new musical, "Seesaw," with Lainie Kazan, scheduled for the spring, and is part-owner of a fleet of New York limousines, in one of which he rode from LaGuardia Airport to the stadium yesterday.

But investing and making money aren't Steinbrenner's only concerns. He's considered one of the most effective fund-raisers for civic and charitable purposes in Cleveland, and, though a Protestant, was named man of the year for 1972 by Cleveland's Israel Bond Organization.

Many of his projects are carried on quietly, such as his efforts toward putting about 75 students through college with his own money or with scholarships he arranged.

The Yankees won't be simply another of his projects, but they won't take precedence over his shipping business, either.

"I won't be active in the day-to-day operations of the club at all," said Steinbrenner, who has four children ranging in age from 4 to 15. "I can't spread myself so thin. I've got enough headaches with my shipping company."

If the team fails to live up to his expectations and provides more headaches, he can always drift back to the past when he watched such favorite Yankees as Joe DiMaggio and Lou Gehrig.

"I hate to think how many times I've watched 'Pride of the Yankees' on television," he said. "I watch it every time it's on."

And now he can watch the Yankees, perhaps still with awe but at least also with fervor.

◆

March 6, 1973

2 Yankees Disclose Family Exchange

Peterson and Kekich Give Details of Arrangement

By MURRAY CHASS
Special to The New York Times

FORT LAUDERDALE, FLA., MARCH 5—Fritz Peterson and Mike Kekich, the Yankees' starting left-handed pitchers, disclosed today details of an exchange of families.

The pitchers, who have been the two closest friends on the team for several years, said they and their wives began discussing last July the possibility of an exchange and that they put it into effect at the end of last season in October.

At this time, Peterson is living with Susanne Kekich and her two daughters, Kristen, 4 years old, and Reagan, 2, and they plan to be married as soon as they can divorce their spouses. That would be next October at the earliest, Peterson said.

Kekich Is 'Dubious'

The other half of the relationship, though, hasn't worked out as well. Kekich lived with Marilyn (Chip) Peterson and her two sons, Gregg, 5, and Eric, 2, for two months last fall and then again briefly during the winter. They've also been together for the last 10 days here. Kekich said he hoped they could return to a good relationship, but "I'm dubious."

Both pitchers, in separate interviews after the Yankees disclosed the basic details, stressed that there was nothing sordid about the situation and it wasn't a matter of wife-swapping.

"It wasn't a wife swap," said Kekich, who married Susanne in 1965. "It was a life swap. We're not saying we're right and everyone else who thinks we're wrong are wrong. It's just the way we felt."

"It wasn't a sex thing," Peterson emphasized. "It was not a cheap swap."

Peterson and his wife, who were married in 1964, are legally separated. Peterson said he and Susanne Kekich planned to file divorces in New Jersey under what he said was that state's no-fault divorce law.

Bitter Feelings

Both said they felt the situation wouldn't affect the Yankees as a team or themselves as pitchers. But it was obvious they had bitter feelings toward each other.

General Manager Lee MacPhail said he considered trading one of them after learning about the situation in January (Peterson said he told MacPhail he thought he should trade him), but he decided not to.

Manager Ralph Houk said he didn't think it could have any effect on the team.

"It doesn't bother me other than what effect it might have on their pitching," Houk said. "Their personal lives are their own business. They live their own lives and they've got a lot of years to live. If you're unhappy, you have to remember

Mike Kekich, left, in the Yankee clubhouse with Fritz Peterson.

you only go through the world once. Why go through it unhappy?"

The other Yankee players know the situation now, but none evidently was aware of the plans of Peterson and Kekich during the last 2 months of last season.

Talk of Double Divorce

The two Yankees and their wives began discussing the possible exchange last July 6, on what the pitchers said was a high plane and amid "a tremendous amount of affection and compatibility." While remaining with their own families, they spent a lot of time together and individually—each player with the other's wife.

There was such harmony, Peterson said, they even thought about having a double divorce and a double marriage, and they discussed the possibility of dividing the children so that the older in each instance would go with the father and the younger with the mother.

Once the season was over, Kekich and Mrs. Peterson lived in the Petersons' rented home in Mahwah, N.J., and Peterson and Mrs. Kekich lived in the Kekiches' rented home in Franklin Lakes, N.J. Peterson said they even switched dogs.

"The only way I could justify giving up my daughters," said Kekich, 27, "was for a love far greater than I had ever known. By American standards, we both had good marriages; we had relative happiness with our families. But we were striving for something greater. Maybe that's too ideal. Now I feel hurt and the thing that hurts me most is I'm losing my children."

Peterson, 31, said Kekich wanted Marilyn because he wanted a wife with more education and zest." He himself, he said, wanted more freedom.

"Susanne is a perfect person for me," said Peterson, who hasn't signed his 1973 contract. "She's what I always wanted in a wife, a person and a mother. Before, we both felt dominated. Now we have free minds."

In relating the story, Kekich and Peterson disagreed on the interpretation of one aspect of the situation, a disagreement that has led to whatever bad feeling exists. »»»

«« Kekich said the four have agreed that if any one of them at any time wanted to call the whole thing off and return to his or her original partner, they would do that. Peterson agreed that that was so until Dec. 14, but not afterward.

He explained that on Dec. 14, after the two pitchers had lived with each other's family for about two months they each turned to their own families for what was to be a period of final decision. The Kekiches were in California, the Petersons in New Jersey. If they wanted to remain that way, that's the way it would be. If they wanted to return to each other's wife, that also would be the path they would take.

On Dec. 14, Peterson said, after he called the Kekiches and said he wanted Susanne, she flew east to New Jersey and Marilyn flew to meet Mike in Portland, Ore. At that point, Peterson said, there was no turning back.

Kekich disagreed, contending Peterson had misled him into thinking Marilyn wanted to make the change at that time. Kekich said he and Marilyn both wanted to remain with their spouses for the time being.

"The morning Chip was going to leave," Peterson explained, "she asked me, 'How can you do this to me?' That was the first inkling I had that she had doubts. The night before she told me how much she wanted Mike."

Kekich said everything was fine until then. But he explained: "All of a sudden Marilyn and I were both left out in the cold and it changed our situation. It affected her because of her upbringing and her family. Her feelings put a great strain on me and a lot of friction was created between us. After a while I left Montana, where we were living, and went to New York.

"I would like it to work out with Marilyn and me, but I'm dubious. I've tried to stay with her throughout this whole thing, but love is funny. It can build fast, but it can wear on you, too."

Peterson said he had nothing to hide and nothing to be ashamed of but he had one regret.

"I never would have left my kids if I knew this was going to happen," he said. "I don't know what happened. I just have regrets for my kids. It's hard for me to think of them without a father and a family. If Mike and Marilyn don't get together, they'll be without a father. That eats me up. But I won't go back. I'll never go back." ◆

April 7, 1973

Blomberg's 'dh' Bat Goes to Hall of Fame

By MURRAY CHASS
Special to The New York Times

BOSTON, APRIL 6—Some day Ron Blomberg will tell his grandchildren how he was the first player to bat as the designated hitter in the major leagues and how his bat wound up in the Hall of Fame to recognize that distinction.

Somewhere, in some encyclopedia of baseball trivia, someone may also record for posterity the fact that in today's opening-day baseball game in wind-whipped Fenway Park, the Yankees and the umpires wore their new uniforms for the first time.

But there really was nothing about the game the Yankees want to remember or ever read in a history book—unless, that is, they should win the remaining 161 games of the season. Then it might be fun to recall how they were bombed by the Boston Red Sox, 15-5, in a game that included more bizarre features than a believe-it-or-not magazine.

"Nobody got hurt, did they?" Manager Ralph Houk asked as he boarded the team bus after the game. "We're going to bring in a helicopter in the morning so we can practice catching fly balls in the wind. That's one thing we forgot to do in spring training." Houk said he never had seen a game so affected by wind and sun.

The brothers Alou sandwiched doubles before and after three straight walks by Luis Tiant in the first inning and the Yankees, in their new double-knit uniforms with white piping outlining the blue numbers and letters, rocketed to a 3-0 lead.

The third walk by Tiant, who was so instrumental in Boston's run at the pennant last season, went to Blomberg with the bases loaded in the first time at bat for a designated hitter in the majors.

The walk immediately raised a question: Should Blomberg be called a dh or a dw—designated walker? It also prompted a comment from one observer as Matty Alou trotted home with a run: "See, it's added offense to the game already."

In his next three designated times at bat, Blomberg singled, lined out and flied out. He broke his bat on the single, which means the first two bats he used today wound up in contrasting places—the first in the Hall of Fame, the second in the trash can. ◆

October 1, 1973

Yankee Stadium Finale Stirs Memories of Days of Glory

By JOHN DREBINGER

THEY RANG DOWN the curtain on historic Yankee Stadium yesterday, and it came down with quite a thud. However, considering what such an occasion might have produced, it was quite an orderly procedure.

For one thing, the crowd was a far cry from the 74,200 fans who stormed the gates on that opening day back in April of 1923. The paid attendance yesterday was 32,328. Not bad at that, all things considered.

Incidentally, the game itself, which supplied most of the incidental music, produced ⟫⟫⟫

Fans walk off with grandstand seats after the last 1973 game at Yankee Stadium.

<<< nothing startling either. The Yankees played it as they had in most of their games in this rather disastrous season. As late as the seventh inning the Yankees were leading the Detroit Tigers, 4-2.

Then, in the eighth, the bottom fell out for Ralph Houk and his suddenly becalmed stalwarts. The Tigers sent six runs hurtling over the plate and from there went on to win, 8-5. John Hiller, in relief, was the winning pitcher. Lindy McDaniel, also in relief, lost for the silenced Bombers.

Thus the Yanks, who at one stage this season looked as if they might recall those good old days by finishing on top, wound up in fourth place of a six-club division, with a record of 80 victories against 82 defeats.

It is, of course, rather misleading to say that this marks the end of the Yanks on the site of the matchless arena that has been their home this last half-century. For only what's inside the present outer walls is to be demolished. This demolishment is to start this morning and is to continue for two years.

However, by 1976, there will be a brand new arena within those outer white walls, which once again is to provide the last word in modern sports arenas.

As for whatever demolishment was expected after yesterday's game, this also failed to materialize. Immediately after the finale, some 20,000 or so fans stormed onto the field, but there was little actual damage. Those cherished plaques in centerfield had been removed several days ago.

The three bases, of course, vanished. One of those was to go to Mrs. Babe Ruth, the other to Mrs. Lou Gehrig. But there was a touch of humor to the saving of home plate. A stalwart uniformed private policeman dashed out to the plate, stood on it and defied one and all to remove him. None did. He even turned down a bribe of $20. His name was Harvey Levene, a postal worker in Long Island City.

April 18, 1923. It seems hardly possible to believe that all of 50 years have elapsed since they raised the curtain on what was to become a landmark in the world of sports. As for this observer, it was to become an entire turnabout in what up to then had been a rather orderly life.

In the 10 years or so prior to this I had been what in those days was politely referred to as a country editor. I had helped to convert the Staten Island Advance from a crummy little weekly into a sparkling afternoon paper. I covered sports, politics, criminal cases and a murder case plumb into the execution chamber in Sing Sing.

And then came a day in March of '23 I decided to try my hand on the Big Time, where there were some dozen dailies flourishing on Manhattan. Naturally, I had even then my eyes set on The New York Times. But I didn't make it that fast. My first job was with the Globe, an evening newspaper.

I was a sort of second-string baseball reporter and it was as such that Walter St. Denis assigned me to help cover the opening of Yankee Stadium. The late Will Wedge wrote the lead while I just filled in, doing, as they called it, "crowd and sidelights."

And in that vast crowd of 74,200 I sat in the right wing of those enormous wooden outfield bleachers—they extended from the right-field foul line to the left—hearing the fans around me chortling in wonder as Howard Ehmke of the Red Sox squared away to pitch against Bob Shawkey.

Came the third inning, when the one and only Babe Ruth hit his first Yankee Stadium home run, with two aboard, into those right-field bleachers. From there the Yanks went on to win, 4-1.

A couple of months later another lucky break came my way. I made The New York Times and began a fascinating career in which I was to meet and, in many cases, become a personal friend of the game's greatest stars.

Needless to say, the mighty Babe blazed the trail as one electrifying feat followed another, capped by the 60-home run peak in 1927.

Presently, a new star moved on the scene as Lou Gehrig began thundering home runs. As a dazzling showman, Lou could never match the Babe. But he did set some mighty records that simply will have to live as long as the game is played. Outstanding is an incredible endurance record, which from June 1, 1923, through April 30, 1939, saw Lou complete a consecutive string of 2,130 games without a break.

Meanwhile other diamond greats came moving in. There was the first of the famed Bombers Murderers' Rows, including such names as Bob Meusel, Joe Dugan, Earle Combs and Tony Lazzeri. Presently, these were to be joined by another star of the very first magnitude—Joe DiMaggio, who in 1941 was to dazzle the world of sport with his 56-game hitting streak.

While all this was going on, an amazing array of managers followed one another to keep the Yanks on top as from 1921 on they set the astounding record of 29 American League pennants and 20 World Series championships. Miller Huggins set the fashion with six.

Then came Joe McCarthy who between 1936 and '43 won seven flags in eight seasons. In '36 Marse Joe spread-eagled the field to win by 19½ games. And following this came the fabulous Casey Stengel, who in 12 campaigns bagged 10 pennants.

In the 1956 World Series Don Larsen tossed the only perfect game in Series history. And there were countless other thrillers, such as Mickey Owen, Dodger catcher, dropping a third strike, which would have squared the 1941 Series at two victories apiece. Instead, behind that slip the Yanks went on to score four runs to win this one and the next day they wrapped up another world title. ◆

October 1, 1973

Houk Out As Yanks' Manager

By SAM GOLDAPER

RALPH HOUK SAID GOOD-BYE yesterday, not only to Yankee Stadium, but to his ballclub.

On the final day of the baseball season, the Yankees' last appearance at the Stadium until at least 1976, Houk quit as Yankee manager, entirely on his own initiative.

Still dressed in his Yankee pinstripes, Houk made the announcement at a news conference after the Detroit Tigers had beaten his team, 8-5. Minutes earlier, with the dressing room closed to all visitors, Houk broke the news to his players. An onlooker described the scene as, "emotional, with Houk in tears."

His voice cracking with emotion as he fought back the tears, Houk told a hastily called news conference, "Sometimes when you've been with somebody as long as I've been here, and when you don't accomplish what you are after, you get the feeling it is better off for the Yankees, who have done so much for me and my family, to resign."

"I believe I'm making the right decision. I decided four or five days ago to resign. This has been a rough year, we really thought we had a winner. A man has to go with his convictions. I blame no one but myself. It will be better for the Yankees to have a new manager."

Houk, who has been with the Yankee organization for 35 years, said he had no immediate plans for the future nor was he considering another managerial job for a while.

"I'm going down to Florida, put out some lines without hooks and just sit there for a while," he said. His home is at Pompano Beach, Fla.

Houk had two years left on a three-year contract, but said, "I'm giving up my contract. I'm doing this for one reason. We've won some pennants here, but it's been a little rough since 1966. You can't work that long in one place with ⟫⟫

≪≪ the feeling you haven't quite got there."

Houk said that Lee McPhail, the general manager; Gabe Paul, an administrative partner; and George Steinbrenner 3d, a general partner all tried to talk him out of leaving.

Steinbrenner, who wasn't present at the news conference, said in a statement, "When Ralph informed us Friday night of his decision to resign, we were shocked and deeply distressed. We had already announced our determination to keep Ralph Houk as Yankee manager. We tried our very best to dissuade him from his decision. But when we realized that he had a firm mind on the subject and expressed himself as disappointed at the team's failures this year and felt that a change would be better for the Yankees and for himself, there was nothing further we could do but express our best wishes to Ralph wherever he may go eventually."

Yankee ownership took a more active role in today's activities of the team than did Mike Burke when he ran the Yankees for the Columbia Broadcasting System.

Houk had won three straight American League pennants for the Yankees and two World Series in his first tour as Yankee manager (1961 through 1963). He returned as manager again in 1966 and the Yankees finished no higher than second in eight seasons. ◆

October 2, 1973

$27-Million Face-Lifting of Yankee Stadium Starts

By MURRAY SCHUMACH

A ROARING BULLDOZER, with Mayor Lindsay in the cab, scooped up grass and dirt in short right field at Yankee Stadium yesterday and the extensive modernization of the ball park had begun.

For the next two years the Yankees will play at Shea Stadium while their stadium, which was opened in 1923, is being renovated from playing field to roof at a cost to the city of more than $27-million.

"Nothing could be more important to the economic vitality of our city than to assure that the house that Ruth built and the New York Yankees remain here in the Bronx for future generations of New Yorkers," said the Mayor. "That commitment has been made and today we not only honor the past, but look with great expectation to the future."

105 PILLARS TO GO

In beautiful World Series weather, the Mayor preceded the groundbreaking, shortly after noon, by presenting mementos of the stadium to the widows of Ruth and Lou Gehrig. Mrs. Clare Ruth received home plate and Mrs. Eleanor Gehrig received first base.

One of the major changes in the stadium will be removal of the 105 bothersome steel pillars that supported the three-tier ball park and so often obstructed the spectator's view of the field.

The dimensions of the renovated park will be only slightly different. The right field foul line will be 310 feet instead of 296; left field will be 313 instead of 301 and deepest center will be 419 instead of 461. Seating capacity will be 52,671 instead of 64,644.

The roof will be removed and the famous frieze, topped with pennant flags, will be placed over a new large scoreboard. Sodium vapor lights will ring the new roof, giving even more illumination than the present clusters of bulbs.

Future Yankee outfielders will have to play ground balls a bit differently. The present field

The original Yankee Stadium was gutted during the 1973–1975 renovation project.

slopes from infield to outfield. The new one, according to John Waterbury, vice president of Madigan-Praeger, designers of the new field, will tilt from outfield to infield.

To help keep the memory of the old Yankee Stadium alive, the Smithsonian Institution will receive the Yankee batrack and the Museum of the City of New York will get a box seat. Mayor Lindsay turned over his box seat to Gracie Mansion.

As the gift chairs were being singled out by workmen, Gabe Paul, administrative partner of the New York Yankees, called out to workmen:

"Make sure nobody steals those chairs."

This was a reference to the bedlam that followed the end of the last game on Sunday when more than 20,000 fans began breaking up and trying to steal seats or anything else they could carry. ◆

April 7, 1974

Yanks Win Shea Debut Amid Spitball Controversy

By MURRAY CHASS

AFTER HAVING LOST their last four season openers in such places as Boston, Baltimore and Yankee Stadium, the Yankees tried a new place yesterday for their 1974 opener, and the move worked as they defeated the Cleveland Indians, 6-1.

However, as new as their home—Shea Stadium—and their manager—Bill Virdon—were, the Yankees took part in one of baseball's oldest and longest running controversies. It involved Gaylord Perry, the Cleveland pitcher, and—what else?—his alleged spitball.

The dispute that arose from Marty Springstead's warning to Perry for throwing what the umpire called an illegal pitch added important overtones to the Yankees' debut at Shea and their warm reception from 20,744 cold but spirited fans.

Mel Stottlemyre pitching the Yankees' first game at Shea Stadium in 1974.

Ignited by Mel Stottlemyre's good pitching and the team's timely hitting, which included a two-run homer by Graig Nettles, the fans chanted, "We're No. 1, we're No. 1, we're No. 1." They also cheered lustily when the Mets' 5-4 loss was posted on the scoreboard, proving they were Yankee fans all the way and not Met enthusiasts who strayed into the park, thinking their heroes were home.

The fans, though, could have been only superficially aware of the controversy that raged between the umpires and the Indians and threatened to lead to legal action by Perry.

Springstead used his judgment to warn Perry on a pitch to Nettles with a runner at second and one out in the sixth inning. The pitch broke down suddenly and sharply as it reached the plate, a characteristic of a spitter.

"It was a spitball," Nettles said matter of factly. "It sank like all his other spitters. But he showed me a lot of guts because he came back on the next pitch and threw another spitter."

Perry and his manager, Ken Aspromonte, contended vehemently that the guilty pitch was a fork ball, but Nettles said, "It was too hard for a fork ball and it had too much spin for a sinker." ◆

September 25, 1974

Yanks Lose Twice, Drop to 2d As Orioles Down Tigers, 5-4

Bow to Red Sox, 4-0, 4-2— Trail by ½-game

By JOSEPH DURSO

THE NEW YORK YANKEES tripped over the supposedly fallen Boston Red Sox last night, dropped both halves of a critical double-header and tumbled out of first place with only six games left in the American League's Eastern free-for-all.

It was a stunning night for the Yankees, who had opened it with a one-game lead over the Baltimore Orioles and eyes fixed on their first prize in 10 years. But then the Red Sox, who had lost 20 of their 28 previous games in a dramatic collapse from first place, got off the floor and dealt two haymakers.

With Luis Tiant pitching a six-hitter and winning his 21st game, the Red Sox scored a 4-0 victory in the opener. Then, with Roger Moret pitching a seven-hitter, they took the second game by 4-2.

The result, with the Orioles beating the Detroit Tigers in Baltimore, was disastrous. The Yankees fell into second place, half a game back with half a dozen remaining.

To add to the Yankees feeling that this was a night to forget, they were watched by their second largest crowd of the season—46,448 persons, many of whom spent the evening in pitched battles with one another and with the Shea Stadium guards.

In mob scenes reminiscent of the Mets' playoff last October, they threw fists, whisky bottles, beer, rubber balls, and firecrackers in outbreaks of fighting and hooligan behavior that kept the crowd howling.

While that was going on the Yankees were suddenly hitting the skids after four straight victories over the weekend. Their pursuit of the division title abruptly came down to this: They have lost one more game than Baltimore, they play their final home game tonight against Boston, then head for three games in Cleveland and two in Milwaukee. ◆

Jim (Catfish) Hunter pitching against the Milwaukee Brewers at County Stadium.

January 1, 1975

Yankees Sign Catfish Hunter In Estimated $3.75-Million Deal

By MURRAY CHASS

JIM (CATFISH) HUNTER signed a five-year contract estimated at $3.75-million with the New York Yankees last night, ending the most celebrated bidding war in American sports history. The total value of the pact sets a record for baseball.

The Yankees, trying to regain the glory that was theirs until the last decade, landed the 28-year-old right-hander, considered by many experts to be baseball's premier pitcher, with an assist from Clyde Kluttz, a club scout, Kluttz signed Hunter to his first professional contract with the Kansas City A's in 1964.

The signing, announced at a New Year's Eve news conference, took place at the Yankee offices in the Parks Administration Building in Flushing, Queens, where intricate negotiations

wound up after Hunter and his lawyers flew here from North Carolina earlier in the day.

Gabe Paul, the Yankee president, refused to disclose monetary terms but it was believed to be a $3.75-million package.

Hunter charged that Charles O. Finley, owner of the Oakland A's, had breached his 1974 contract by not paying $50,000 of his $100,000 salary on a deferred payment basis to an insurance company by the stipulated time.

Before baseball adopted its free-agent draft, major league clubs competed for young prospects and frequently paid upwards of $100,000. But a free agent of Hunter's experience and status was unheard of.

And when it came time for the American League's 1974 Cy Young Award winner to make his choice, he was swayed not by the money but by Kluttz's involvement and the Yankee image.

"Clyde never lied to me then and he never lied to me now," said Hunter, who has won 88 games in the last four seasons while helping pitch the A's to three consecutive World Series championships. "If it hadn't been for him, the Yankees would've had a little more trouble signing me."

The irony of Kluttz's presence is that if he had accepted an offer to join the newly created major league scouting bureau late last season, he wouldn't have been available to help the Yankees with Hunter. Kluttz, who never earned more than $10,000 as a major league catcher, is a hunting companion of the pitcher in the offseason in North Carolina where both live.

Continuing his explanation of why he picked the Yankees, Hunter said, "To be a Yankee is a thought in everyone's head and mine. Just walking into Yankee Stadium chills run through you. I believe there was a higher offer, but no matter how much money offered, if you want to be a Yankee, you don't think about it."

Joseph Flythe, one of the attorneys from Ahoskie, N.C., said six other teams—Pittsburgh, Los Angeles, Montreal, San Diego, Kansas City and Cleveland—remained in the serious bidding until Hunter decided he wanted to join the Yankees.

As Hunter set calmly behind a desk in a blue long-sleeved sport shirt, blue and black checked slacks and a blue Yankee cap, Paul, his new boss, explained that as late as 8 o'clock "there were some areas [in the agreement] that could've killed the whole thing."

Just a year ago, the Yankees went through a devastating experience with another former Finley employee. That was their signing of Dick Williams to manage the club after he resigned as manager of the A's with one year to go on his contract.

In that instance, Finley was successful in foiling the Yankee effort.

Notably absent from the proceedings was George Steinbrenner, the Yankee general partner who is forbidden from participating in Yankee affairs under terms of his two-year suspension from baseball following his conviction for illegal political contributions.

"…when his unfortunate suspension was invoked," Paul said of Steinbrenner, "he told me, 'any time you have an opportunity to buy the contract of a player for cash, I want you to go ahead whenever, in your judgment, it would be advantageous to the Yankees.'"

In obtaining Hunter, the Yankees immeasurably improved their chances for winning their first pennant since 1964. Asked if Hunter's high salary would affect the morale of the other players, Paul said, "The morale of the club is helped when you add a man of Hunter's status. It increases the club's chances of winning a pennant." Nor, Hunter said, would all the money dilute his desire to win. "In the last World Series," he said, "I had a card in my locker that said, 'Winning isn't everything, but wanting to is.' I always want to win." Hunter, a major leaguer for 10 years, tied for the most victories in the majors last season with 25. He lost 12 games and had a 2.49 earned-run average. He won 21 games in each of the previous three seasons while losing only 23, giving him a four-year record of 88 victories and 35 defeats. He also won four times without losing in the World Series. This was the pitcher who was the object of the affections and treasuries of teams that sent a constant stream of representatives to the tiny town of Hertford where Hunter has lived all of his life and the tiny town of Ahoskie where the law firm of Cherry, Cherry and Flythe has its offices. Hertford and Ahoskie had never seen anything like it and now the Yankees hope Hunter will help them see the things they always used to see—pennants. ◆

MARTIN STARTS JOB WITH YANKS

'Brat' of 1950's Now Team's Manager

By JOSEPH DURSO

On a day dedicated to baseball memories, the New York Yankees reached into their rich but remote past yesterday and named Billy Martin as manager in place of Bill Virdon.

The switch marked the climax of a whirlwind week that began with the Yankees losing a double-header to the Boston Red Sox and that ended with an abrupt changing of the guard in Shea Stadium. In between, the Yankees pursued Martin to the trout streams of Colorado and finally signed him as their 20th manager at 1:30 o'clock in the morning just after the team had won its third straight game on the field.

The 47-year-old Californian, the controversial "brat" of Casey Stengel's infields in the nineteen-fifties, flew into New York on Friday evening just 10 days after he had been dismissed by the Texas Rangers. Virdon was dropped officially at 1 A.M. after an evening of rumors. Martin was signed half an hour later, was unveiled ⟫⟫⟫

«« as the new manager at 9:45 in the morning and took charge of the Yankees during their 29th annual Old-Timers reunion.

Martin moved into the office beneath the first-base grandstand and took up the dream that has haunted the Yankees since their last pennant in 1964. He will wear his old uniform with the large No. 1 embroidered on the back and he will chase the Yankees' dream of revival for the rest of this season and all of 1976 while the Yankees continue to pay Virdon for not managing.

"We're not blaming Bill Virdon for a thing," said Gabe Paul, the team's president and the man who pursued Martin to Colorado and back last week. This is just an exciting move that became possible when Martin became available. You don't contemplate things like this, they just happen. No one game or series made us think of changing."

Despite the disclaimer, it seemed clear that the switch had been dictated by George Steinbrenner, the principal partner in the Cleveland syndicate that bought the Yankees from the Columbia Broadcasting System, Inc., two years ago. Steinbrenner was convicted and fined for violating the Federal laws on contributing to political campaigns, and he is now serving a two-year

"suspension" from Yankee affairs under orders of the commissioner of baseball, Bowie Kuhn.

But last Sunday, he watched from the club box alongside the dugout while the Yankees were being held scoreless in both games of their double-header against the Red Sox. He also appeared agitated over his team's inability to score—even with the bases loaded and nobody out—and two days later, Paul set out on his "secret mission" hunting for Martin.

"I was shocked when I was deposed by Texas," Martin conceded, reviewing his melodramatic change of fortune. "They had me doing too many things, like sitting in on board meetings, making trades, running the whole club. Then when my father-in-law telephoned me from Alliance, Neb., and told me the Yankees were trying to reach me, I had a different type of shock.

"I was out there on a mountain in Colorado fishing with my family, and how they ever found me, I'll never know. But I'm very happy, very proud to be coming back to New York. Every manager feels very low when he's fired, and every time they fired me in the past, people said it would be the last time I'd ever manage again."

But for Martin, changing uniforms has been a way of life since the Yankees promoted him from their Kansas City farm club in 1950. He played second base for them for seven seasons and appeared in five World Series, then was traded in 1957, chiefly because he was considered "a bad influence" on Mickey Mantle and other stars.

In the next five years, he played on six teams, then became a phenomenon as a manager. He won the American League's Western title with the Minnesota Twins in 1969 but was dismissed after a series of disputes. He won the Eastern title with the Detroit Tigers in 1972 but again was dismissed after more disputes. And last year he led the Rangers to a strong second-place finish in the West but was dismissed July 21 after yet another wrangle.

"We told Virdon after Friday night's ball-game," Paul said. "He took it like the fine gentleman he is. No, we did not offer him another job. His contract runs through next year and he will be paid in full."

Then Paul recounted the strange odyssey that took him to Colorado trying to track down Martin while the Yankees were trying to escape a disastrous month that involved 18 defeats, 11 victories and numerous injuries.

"We had a tough time getting in touch with Billy," he said. "I left New York on Tuesday night and flew to Chicago. We somehow found a phone number of Billy's father-in-law and we learned that Billy was in Colorado fishing with his family, but Colorado is a big state with a lot of mountains and streams.

"I finally found him near Denver, and we talked a lot Wednesday afternoon and again at breakfast the next morning. He was actually there to give a talk before the American Association all-star game, substituting for Casey Stengel. Nothing much happened, but after I got back to New York on Friday afternoon, he telephoned me around 5 o'clock and said he'd sign."

The bizarre sequence reached unlikely heights when Martin was introduced to Shea Stadium crowd just after Whitey Ford, Mickey Mantle and Joe DiMaggio. He ran onto the field to a standing ovation with some light booing in the background.

"I'm really sorry to see Virdon leave," said Mantle, who is Martin's closest friend. "That happens too much in baseball. But I'm really happy that Billy Martin is the new manager of the Yankees. That's where he's always belonged."

"I feel great for Billy but I feel terrible for Bill Virdon," said Ford, now the pitching coach of the Yankees. "Virdon is a stand-up guy, he treated everybody alike. Mickey's wife told us about it in Dallas yesterday, and we brought Billy's suitcase to New York with us." ◆

Billy Martin in the Yankee dugout.

7 THE BRONX ZOO

In baseball, the spirit of '76—as in 1976—was freedom: freedom for a major league player to sign with another team if his contract had expired, and freedom for George Steinbrenner, his suspension terminated by Commissioner Bowie Kuhn nine months early on March 1, to return to his Yankee Stadium office. Both freedoms would shape not only Yankees history but also the game's history.

After opening the remodeled Yankee Stadium, the retailored Yankees hurried under Billy Martin to their thirtieth American League pennant. Thurman Munson, with a .302 average and 105 RBI, was the American League's most valuable player. Third baseman Graig Nettles's 32 homers led the league. Gabe Paul's trades had obtained outfielders Lou Piniella and Mickey Rivers, first baseman Chris Chambliss, rookie second baseman Willie Randolph, and right-hander Ed Figueroa, a 19-game winner. When the Yankees, in the World Series, were unceremoniously swept by the Cincinnati Reds, the no-longer-suspended Steinbrenner hunted down free agent Reggie Jackson, the marquee slugger.

In 1977 the Yankees turned into the "Bronx Zoo," as reliever Sparky Lyle branded them. Jackson (quoted as saying "I'm the straw that stirs the drink") and Munson got off to a shaky start as teammates. Jackson distrusted Martin, who told reporters he had wanted the Yankees to sign other sluggers. When Martin removed Jackson from a game in Fenway Park for slowly fielding a ball in right field, they appeared about to trade punches in the dugout until Yogi Berra and Elston Howard separated them.

But for all the turbulence, when Jackson, who hit 32 homers and drove in 110 runs, smashed five homers in the World Series, including a memorable trio in the Game Six clincher against the Los Angeles Dodgers at the stadium, the three antagonists suddenly became buddy-buddy-buddy. Jackson, still in his uniform, spent more than half an hour celebrating with Martin in the manager's office. Munson later reminded Jackson not to miss the team's celebratory champagne buffet. But in 1978, after Gabe Paul

★ ★ ★

George Steinbrenner (left) dousing Billy Martin with champagne after the Yankees won the American League pennant in 1977.

returned to the Indians as part owner, and former Indians slugger Al Rosen succeeded him as the Yankees executive vice president, turmoil resurfaced—despite the addition of reliever Rich (Goose) Gossage and shortstop Bucky Dent, and left-hander Ron Guidry's dazzling 25–3 record.

With the team falling further behind the Red Sox in midseason, Jackson was suspended for five days for having bunted unsuccessfully in defiance of Martin's swing-away sign, after having been ordered to bunt earlier in that at-bat. Days later, Martin, still angry at Jackson, uttered to Murray Chass of the New York Times his infamous "one's a born liar, the other's convicted" description of Jackson and Steinbrenner.

Knowing he would be fired, Martin resigned the next day. Rosen quickly hired Bob Lemon, once his Indians teammate as a Hall of Fame right-hander. But later that week, on Old-Timers' Day at the stadium, Steinbrenner announced that Martin had been rehired to be the Yankees manager, but not until the 1980 season. The Yankees soap opera surely couldn't get any crazier—except that it did. The team, once 14 games behind the Red Sox, responded to Lemon's calm leadership with a 48–20 finish that created a one-game play-off for the East Division title, which turned on Dent's three-run homer off ex-Yankees right-hander Mike Torrez into the screen atop Fenway Park's left-field wall. In the World Series, the Yankees beat the Dodgers again as Nettles made several spectacular diving and twisting plays, and Dent, with 10 hits and 7 RBI, was given the MVP Award.

All that success dissolved into sadness on August 2, 1979, when Thurman Munson died in the crash of his $1.4 million Cessna Citation while practicing takeoffs and landings at the Akron-Canton Airport. Without their captain and clubhouse anchor, the Yankees staggered to a fourth-place finish, despite left-hander Tommy John's 21–9 record. In June Lemon was out as manager and—yes—Martin was in again, half a season before his planned 1980 return. But when Martin got into a fight with a marshmallow salesman in a Bloomington, Minnesota, hotel bar in late October, he suddenly was out. Again.

Dick Howser, who had been the third-base coach, was the 1980 manager. And he was a successful manager: his Yankees won 103 games—more than either of the ⟫⟫⟫

≪≪ two recent first-place teams. But when they lost to the Kansas City Royals in the play-offs, Steinbrenner, in perhaps his most shameful decision, used a contrived real-estate opportunity for Howser in order to dismiss him. Martin, now the Oakland manager, was not available to return. The new manager was Gene Michael, a former good field, no-hit Yankees shortstop who had impressed Steinbrenner while serving six lesser front-office assignments. As the seventh manager in the ninth season of the principal owner's regime, Michael would be replaced late in that strike-interrupted 1981 schedule by a familiar face, Bob Lemon. The Yankees wobbled through the American League play-offs but lost the World Series to the Dodgers in six games. Outfielder Dave Winfield, signed to what would be a $23 million deal, had one hit, a single, in 22 at-bats.

Moments after that disappointing defeat, George Steinbrenner issued a statement apologizing "to the people of New York and to the fans of the New York Yankees everywhere" for the Series performance. The players resented the apology: they simply lost; they hadn't done anything to apologize for. Little did the principal owner realize that he should have saved that apology for the next fourteen years, during which the Yankees never got back to the World Series.

March 1, 1976

End of Ban For Yankee Owner

By MURRAY CHASS

COMMISSIONER BOWIE KUHN will lift the two-year suspension of George M. Steinbrenner 3d, principal owner of the Yankees, "in the very near future," a high baseball official said last night.

The official who disclosed the commissioner's intentions did not say when Kuhn would act, but it was believed that it would likely happen within a week. Kuhn was not available for comment.

Steinbrenner was suspended Nov. 27, 1974, because of his Federal conviction for illegal contributions to political campaigns, including those of President Richard M. Nixon in 1972 and several Democratic candidates for Congress.

Thus, when the suspension is lifted, Steinbrenner will have completed slightly more than 15 months of the original 24-month penalty. The reduced term is not unlike time off for good behavior.

There are some observers, though, who would question how closely Steinbrenner followed the restrictions of his suspension. When Kuhn announced the suspension, he declared that the Yankee owner was "ineligible and incompetent" to have "any association whatsoever with any major league club or its personnel."

However, it was widely understood, for example, that when Bill Virdon was dismissed as Yankee manager last August, it was at the direction of Steinbrenner, who reportedly had grown weary of watching Virdon unsuccessfully try to maneuver the team into pennant contention.

Billy Martin had become available, having been dropped by the Texas Rangers only two weeks before Virdon's dismissal, and he was Steinbrenner's kind of man, a manager who was fiery and made things happen.

Steinbrenner, who put together a syndicate that purchased the Yankees from CBS for $10 million in 1973, was indicted in April 1974 on 14 felony counts stemming from his campaign contributions as board chairman of the American Ship Building Company of Cleveland.

He pleaded guilty on Aug. 23, 1974 to two counts for which he could have been sentenced to six years in prison. However, he was fined $15,000, the maximum amount, and American Ship Building was fined $20,000. ◆

April 16, 1976

YANKEES WIN FIRST GAME IN REBUILT STADIUM

By JOSEPH DURSO

FIFTY-THREE YEARS after Babe Ruth opened Yankee Stadium by hitting a home run, the historic old ball park in the Bronx–bought and rebuilt by City Hall– was reopened yesterday before a sellout crowd of 54,010 person and a full house of memories.

The paying portion, which numbered 52,613, paid up to $5.50 for lower box seats to get a glimpse of the stadium after two years of modernizing and they watched the Yankees defeat the Minnesota Twins 11-4.

"There was a great, dark mystery about it when I first came here from Oklahoma," said Mickey Mantle, the former baseball hero, who arrived a quarter-century ago when the stadium was 28 years old. "I still get goose-pimples just walking inside it. Now I think this is about the prettiest ball park I ever saw."

It was pretty all right: gleaming white on the outside, blue and white on the inside, 10 acres of land once part of the estate of William Waldorf Astor, now adorned with a 565-foor electronic scoreboard, hair dryers for the athletes, escalators for the public and executive suites for the brass.

Before their opening game at home, after four on the road this season, the Yankees staged a 45 minute salute to the past–theirs and other tenants of the stadium. They called out onto »»»

Opening Day for the renovated Yankee Stadium on April 15, 1976.

<<< the grass, which seemed a little scruffy despite the two years work, dozens of figures from the days when they were winning 29 American League pennants and 20 world championships.

The dugout bulged with old heroes, and at one time, sitting in a row on the players' benches, were Mantle, Joe DiMaggio, Joe Louis, Yogi Berra, Frank Gifford, Kyle Rote and six members of the 1923 Yankees on hand: Waite Hoyt, Bob Shawkey, Whitey Witt, Oscar Roettger and Hinkey Haines. The winning pitcher in the first game ever played there was Shawkey, and yesterday he was chosen to throw out the ceremonial first ball before Rudy May of the 1976 Yankees threw the first pitch against the Minnesota team.

After all the ceremonies, the national anthem was sung by Robert Merrill of Metropolitan Opera, accompanied by the bands of Lafayette College, Brooklyn College and Greenwich High School.

The stadium's acoustics have been checked out for several weeks by Bob Sheppard, a professor of speech at St. John's University, who has been handling the stadium's public-address system for more than 20 years.

"I've checked the acoustics three times recently," he said in pear-shaped tones. "I made up some Yankee lineups–Gehrig at first base, Tony Lazzeri at second base, Phil Rizzuto at shortstop and Stubby Overmire pitching. The construction crews would be listening and they'd all turn their heads on that one–Stubby Overmire pitching."

Still, to many persons concerned by New York's financial problems, the cost of the stadium's marvels seemed too high for the taxpayers to bear. The current official price tag is $45 million for the stadium, but the projections run up to $100 million for the whole complex.

"After people see it," said George M. Steinbrenner 3d, the chief owner of the Yankees, "They'll be enthused. I can't take credit for it. It was done by the city and the Columbia Broadcasting System when they owned the team. Now we have to make it work." ◆

June 19, 1976

Kuhn Voids Oakland Sales; Finley Threatens to Sue

By JOSEPH DURSO

COMMISSIONER BOWIE KUHN nullified the biggest sale of talent in baseball history yesterday when he ordered the New York Yankees and Boston Red Sox to return the three stars they had bought earlier in the week from the Oakland A's for $3.5 million.

He also may have provoked the biggest series of lawsuits in the sport, which is already embroiled in legal challenges and disputes over the "freedom" of the 600 players in the two major leagues.

His action stunned the baseball world and brought the prompt promise of a lawsuit by Charles O. Finley, owner of the Oakland team, who said the commissioner "sounds like the village idiot."

"We will be taking it to court on Monday," Finley said as soon as the commissioner had canceled the following sales: Vida Blue to the Yankees for $1.5 million and Joe Rudi and Rollie Fingers to the Red Sox for $1 million apiece.

The deals were made last Tuesday just hours before the midnight trading deadline in the big leagues. The next day the commissioner "froze" the sales because "they raise certain questions," and he called the teams' executives to a hearing. It was held Thursday in his office at Rockefeller Plaza, and then the players and their new and old owners waited for what they thought would be a routine decision.

Instead, the onetime Wall Street lawyer dropped a blockbuster. The deals, he ruled, broke no rules of procedure as such, but were "inconsistent with the best interests of baseball, the integrity of the game and the maintenance of public confidence in it."

At the hearing Thursday Finley made a ring-

September 26, 1976

Yanks Bubble in Toasting End to 12-Year Dry Spell

Special to The New York Times

DETROIT, SEPT. 25—The New York Yankees were in the middle of a dinner party given by George Steinbrenner, the team's general partner, when the score of the Boston Red Sox-Baltimore Orioles game was announced tonight.

"It's 1-0 Boston with two out in the bottom of the ninth," came the radio report.

Then came the word: "It's over! The Orioles lose! The Yankees clinch the flag!"

Thurman Munson hugged Willie Randolph. Lou Piniella slapped Oscar Gamble. Steinbrenner clasped hands with Gabe Paul, the general manager, before both doused themselves with champagne. And all of the other Yankees at the Caucus Club left their steaks and began jumping around laughing and shouting, too excited to eat.

New York had captured the Eastern Division title and assured its first postseason appearance since 1964, when, under Manager Yogi Berra, the Yankees won the American League pennant.

"Yeah, it feels just as great," said Yogi, now a Yankee coach, breaking into a wide grin.

And where was Billy Martin? The fiery Yankee manager had one drink and left.

"I'm not celebrating until we get into the World Series," asserted Martin, who had managed teams to the playoffs two previous times and was eliminated each time. ◆

---

ing defense of his transactions, insisting that the players were demanding "astronomical" salaries that would mean "bankruptcy."

"I don't even want them in uniform," he said last night, referring to the three players the commissioner had ordered back to Oakland. "We're not going to use them. We're going to court Monday for an injunction."

But Kuhn stood fast on his general powers to uphold "the best interests of baseball," an authority rarely invoked by any commissioner since Kenesaw Mountain Landis replaced the triumvirate known as the National Commission after the "Black Sox scandal" in the 1919 World Series. ◆

October 15, 1976

YANKEES WIN, 7-6, ON HOMER IN 9TH, CAPTURE FIRST PENNANT IN 12 YEARS

By MURRAY CHASS

WITH A BLOW THAT RIVALED Bobby Thomson's 1951 home run for stunning drama, Chris Chambliss hit a home run on the first pitch of the ninth inning last night and catapulted the New York Yankees to the American League pennant for the first time since 1964.

Chambliss's homer, off Mark Littell, gave the Yankees a 7-6 game victory and 3-2 playoff triumph over the plucky Kansas City Royals in the fifth game of the league's championship series. It sent New York into the World Series, where the Yankees will meet the Reds in Cincinnati ≫≫

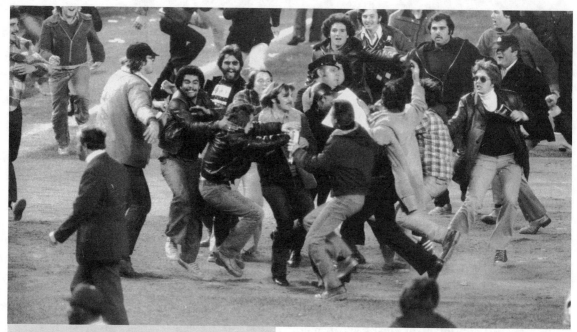

Chris Chambliss holds his batting helmet as a police-man tries to shield him from adoring fans after his 1976 pennant-winning homer at Yankee Stadium.

Reds Triumph, 7-2, for Series Sweep of Yankees

By MURRAY CHASS

HISTORY AND THE CINCINNATI REDS proved to be too strong a combination for the Yankees to overcome last night as the Reds won the World Series by completing a four-game sweep.

The Reds won the fourth game, 7-2, at Yankee Stadium as Johnny Bench hit two home runs and drove in five runs. They became the first National League team in 54 years to win two consecutive Series and the first team to sweep through the three-game pennant playoffs and the Series undefeated.

At the same time, the Reds upheld a Series precedent in which a team that lost the first three games has never come back to win the four-of-seven-game championship.

The Reds, admittedly playing less than their best, had won the first three games of the Series without much difficulty. Their only questionable

---

≪≪ beginning at 1 P.M. tomorrow.

The dramatic drive over the right-center field fence sent a torrent of fans from the sellout crowd of 56,821 onto the field at Yankee Stadium. They massed instantly on the infield and prevented Chambliss from touching home plate. However, the quiet first baseman returned to the field from the clubhouse and, escorted by two policemen, pushed and shoved his way back through the excited throng and touched the plate just to make sure.

Chambliss, whose homer broke championship series records for both hits (11) and runs batted in (8), was the 2-year-old son of a Navy chaplain 25 years ago when Thomson hit the homer that enabled the New York Giants to beat the Brooklyn Dodgers in the final inning of a three-game playoff for the National League pennant.

The home run last night gave the Yankees their 30th pennant and their first in the divisional set-up that was created in 1969, the year the Royals were born as an expansion team. ◆

moment came in the second game when the Yankees briefly managed a 3-3 tie.

"The Reds haven't torn us apart," Thurman Munson, the Yankee catcher and captain, said before last night's game, "but they've beaten us convincingly. I've been embarrassed and I don't like it."

The Yankees didn't like the fact that they were lodged in a position from which no other team ever had extricated itself and won the Series. Fifteen times in the previous 72 World Series one team had won the first three games. That team also won the fourth game 12 times, and in the other three instances, the team lost the fourth game but won the fifth.

Even before Reds left-fielder George Foster caught Roy White's routine fly ball to end the game, the other Reds were running off the field, trying to avoid the crush of humanity they expected to storm out from the stands that had held 56,700 fans.

Some fans did race onto the field and tear up chunks of grass, but nowhere nearly as many as the number that attacked the turf of the $100 million stadium seconds after Chambliss hit his homer last week and gave the Yankees their first pennant since 1964.

Most of the fans filed quietly out of the Stadium after the Yankees had suffered their third four-game sweep in 30 Series appearances.

MARTIN IS EJECTED

Billy Martin, the fiery Yankee manager, wasn't around to see the final out of his first Series as a manager. Bruce Froemming, the first-base umpire, ejected Martin in the top of the ninth inning, just before Bench hit his second homer, a three-run belt off Dick Tidrow that sealed the Reds' triumph.

Bench's first home run, a two-run shot off Ed Figueroa in the fourth inning, vaulted the Reds into a 3-1 lead, and they never trailed again. For his total Series efforts—eight hits in 15 times at bat and six runs batted in—the 28-year-old catcher was named the most valuable player.

Bench wound up with a .533 average for the four games, the fourth best average in the Series' 73-year history. He overshadowed the performance of the Yankee catcher, Thurman Munson, who rapped four straight hits last night, tied a Series mark with six straight hits and finished with a .529 average on nine hits in 17 times at bat.

Martin and George Steinbrenner and Gabe Paul brought—or bought, as some people charge—the Yankees a pennant. But they didn't have enough weapons in their drastically revamped arsenal to overpower the Reds.

The 100th World Series victory will have to wait at least until next year. ◆

November 17, 1976

Yanks' Munson Voted Most Valuable Player

By MURRAY CHASS

THURMAN MUNSON, the captain and most productive hitter on the first Yankee team to win a pennant in 12 years, became yesterday the first Yankee in 13 years to win the American League's most-valuable-player award.

The voting for the award, which once seemed perennial Yankee property, was dominated by the New Yorkers, with competition coming only from the Kansas City Royals, the league's other division champion.

Munson, who batted .302 and drove in 105 runs, led a trio of Yankees who finished among the top five. He received 18 of a possible 24 first-place votes and a total of 304 points. Mickey Rivers was third with one first-place vote and 179½ points, and Chris Chambliss finished fifth with 71½ points, a half-point ahead of Rod Carew of Minnesota.

Munson, who received nothing lower than a third-place vote from the Baseball Writers Association panel (two writers from each league city), is the first Yankee and first catcher in the league to win the award since Elston Howard was named M.V.P. in 1963. »»

<<< Although Munson had fervently hoped he would win this year's award and felt he deserved it, he wasn't certain he would get his wish.

ON FRIENDLIER TERMS

"You know I'm not going to win it on popularity," the catcher said candidly a few hours before the award was announced. "So if I win it, you'll know I deserved it."

Munson, who was the league's rookie of the year in 1970, alluded to a reputation he had built up in his first years in the majors as a player who could be discourteous and sometimes just plain nasty to interviewers. But this past season, he matured in his relationships with people other than his teammates and friends. At the same time, he maintained a batting prowess he had exhibited in 1975.

"I don't feel my season this year was as good as last year's," the 29-year-old Ohioan said, elated nonetheless. "I think it was super in the

Thurman Munson in 1976.

respect that we won the pennant, and defensively my season was better. But offensively, last year I had a hell of a year."

In 1975, Munson batted .318 and drove in 102 runs for a third-place team. He finished seventh in the M.V.P. balloting that was won in a landslide by Fred Lynn of Boston.

Munson, however, received a lucrative four-year contract and also the title of team captain, the Yankees' first since Lou Gehrig.

"This would have been a great year for me even without the award," said the 5-foot-11-inch, 195-pounder his teammates call "Squatty Body." "They named me Yankee captain, I hit the first Yankee home run in the new Stadium, I started in the All-Star Game, we got in the playoffs and I set some records and tied some in the World Series. Now, to get something like this, it sort of capped what I was working for for a long time."

Despite the Yankees four-game demise in the Series, Munson batted .529 (after hitting .435 in the five-game playoff), which was the best average ever compiled by a player on a losing Series team. The M.V.P. voting, however, is closed before the playoffs open.

At the end of the World Series with Cincinnati, Munson became embroiled in a feud with Sparky Anderson, the Reds' manager. Anderson told a news conference following the fourth game that no one should embarrass another catcher by comparing him with Johnny Bench of the Reds.

Munson, who was standing nearby when Anderson said that, took exception to the remarks.

"To me," Munson replied, "to be belittled after the season I had and the game I had tonight [4 for 4] is something I don't enjoy. It's sad enough to lose, but it's tough to have it rubbed in your face."

Anderson sent Munson a letter of apology last week, the same day Munson appeared on a radio talk show in Cincinnati.

"The Cincinnati fans were super," the catcher related. "Quite a few of them said I should be the most valuable player. They also said they didn't think it was right of Sparky to say what he did."

◆

November 28, 1976

Jackson Decides to Play for the Yankees

By MURRAY CHASS

REGGIE JACKSON, the most glamorous member of the first free-agent family in baseball's revolution, has agreed to play for the Yankees.

Yankee officials refused last night to comment on the status of their aggressive quest for Jackson, but a source close to the negotiations said the star had selected New York's American League team from among several high bidders and would come to New York to sign a contract in the next day or two.

Having been the center of hectic negotiations in Chicago last week, Jackson fled to California, where he spent a tranquil couple of days sorting out the offers to him and reaching a decision. Jackson was known to be leaning toward the Yankees when he left Chicago, and, the source said, the 30-year-old slugging outfielder made up his mind yesterday.

One of the offers, from the Montreal Expos, was believed to have approached $3.5 million—a "king's ransom," Charles Bronfman, the Expos' owner, called it.

But Jackson passed up the Expos' dazzling deal and accepted less money to play right field for the Yankees. The Yankee package, presumably for five years, falls short of $3 million.

Jackson was in seclusion in California, although he was said to be preparing to fly to New York today.

George Steinbrenner, the Yankees' principal owner, who handled all the negotiations for his team, could not be reached.

Jackson, who played out his option with the Baltimore Orioles after he had been traded by Finley last April, opted for New York because it is New York. He apparently rejected the Expos' highly tempting offer because he didn't want to play in Montreal and for a last-place team. The Yankees, on the other hand, won the American League pennant last season, and the city they play in has always fascinated him.

"If I played in New York," he has said, "they would name a candy bar after me."

The addition of Jackson to the Yankee lineup improves the team immeasurably. The left-handed outfielder doesn't hit for a high average—he has a .265 career mark—but he has plenty of power, drives in a lot of runs and is as dangerous a hitter as there is in the game.

Steinbrenner met with Jackson in New York last Monday and spent about six hours with him. Part of the time they walked around New York, and Steinbrenner saw what a magnetic personality the former Oakland and Baltimore right fielder has.

Then Steinbrenner flew to Chicago, where he met with Jackson and his adviser, Gary Walker, last Wednesday afternoon. The Yankee owner left Chicago while the high bidders from Montreal, San Diego and Baltimore talked with Jackson. Later that evening the Yankee chief decided to return to Chicago, arrived about 10 P.M. and met with Jackson until 1 o'clock Thursday morning.

Six hours later Steinbrenner, Jackson and Walker were back together, this time for breakfast and another few hours of salesmanship. ◆

October 10, 1977

YANKEES CAPTURE PENNANT, WINNING PLAYOFF FINAL, 5-3

By MURRAY CHASS
Special to The New York Times

KANSAS CITY, Oct. 9—Just as they did a year ago when Chris Chambliss socked a ninth-inning, fifth-game home run, the Yankees rallied in their final turn at bat in the fifth game tonight and won their second consecutive American League pennant.

Trailing by a run, the Yankees struck for three runs in the ninth and edged the Kansas City Royals, 5-3, in the final game of the playoffs. Mickey Rivers singled across the tying run, Willie Randolph sent home the tie-breaker with a sacrifice fly and the third scored on George Brett's wild throw.

The game, which was at its most dramatic at the end, also offered moments of drama earlier. For one thing, Manager Billy Martin benched Reggie Jackson and for another, Brett and the Yankees' Graig Nettles fought at third base in the first inning.

The Yankees will meet the Los Angeles Dodgers in the World Series beginning Tuesday night in New York.

The Yankees seemed bent on ending their own intensely hectic season in failure. They had won the pennant last year and they had spent a million dollars in adding new players, but they kept encountering roadblocks that threatened to destroy their season.

With all of their fights, feuds and personality clashes, they saved their most controversial conflict for the ultimate American League game. Martin, in an unexpected move, benched Jackson because, he explained, Jackson, a left-handed batter, wasn't hitting well (1 for 14 in the playoffs); he has had trouble hitting the left-handed Splittorff (2 for 15 this season) and he has not played well defensively. But it was Jackson whom Martin sent up to pinch hit for Cliff Johnson against the right-handed Doug Bird in the eighth and it was Jackson responding with a single that produced his first run of the playoffs and the run that sliced the Yankee deficit to 3-2.

Through the first seven innings, Jackson said afterward, sitting quietly in the clubhouse, his face teary and sweaty: "I was just hoping for us to win. I wasn't hoping to get in the game. I knew if I got in, we'd be losing."

Jackson had refused to criticize Martin for the move that he learned from Coach Elston Howard two hours and 10 minutes before the game. But, he said, "Sure, I was surprised. You've got to be down, your pride's got to be hurt. I must've talked to 20 to 30 friends and family this afternoon. They said, 'We'll be watching the game and pulling for you.'"

Jackson, however, could only pull for his teammates until the eighth. Then Martin called for him to bat and do something for those friends and relatives and the Yankees.

"I just wanted to get set up right in the box," he said. "Get set up right and let the bat go. I knew I'd hit the ball well if I set up right."

Randolph, who had started the eighth with a single, was at third and Lou Piniella was at first after he had singled. Bird, the Royals' No. 1 relief pitcher, was on the mound, having replaced Splittorff after Randolph's hit, and there was one out.

Jackson took a ball, then fouled off the next two pitches. Then he looped a single to center and Randolph was home with the Yankees' second run. ◆

October 19, 1977

YANKEES TAKE SERIES; JACKSON EQUALS MARK OF 3 HOMERS IN GAME

By JOSEPH DURSO

WITH REGGIE JACKSON HITTING three home runs in three straight times at bat, the New York Yankees swept all those family feuds under the rug last night and overpowered the Los Angeles Dodgers, 8-4, to win their first World Series in 15 years.

They won it in the sixth game of a match that had enlivened both coasts for the last week, and that rocked Yankee Stadium last night as hundreds of fans poured through a reinforced army of 350 security guards and stormed onto the field after the final out.

Thurman Munson (left) and Chris Chambliss (center) welcome Reggie Jackson after his first of three home runs in Game 6 of the 1977 World Series.

«« For a team that already had made financial history by spending millions for players in the open market, the victory in the 74th World Series also brought new baseball history to the Yankees: It was the 21st time that they had won the title, but the first time since they defeated the San Francisco Giants in 1962 toward the end of their long postwar reign. And it marked a dramatic comeback from the four-game sweep they suffered last October at the hands of the Cincinnati Reds.

But for Jackson, the $3 million free agent who led the team in power hitting and power rhetoric, this was a game that perhaps had no equal since the World Series was inaugurated in 1903. He hit his three home runs on the first pitches off three pitchers, and he became the only man in history to hit three in a Series game since Babe Ruth did it for the Yankees twice, in 1926 and again in 1928.

But nobody had ever before hit five in a World Series—let alone five in his last nine official times at bat—a feat that the 31-year-old Pennsylvanian accomplished during the last three games in California and New York.

"Perhaps for one night," Jackson reflected later inside the Yankees' tumultuous locker room, "I reached back and achieved that level of the overrated superstar. I'm also happy for George Steinbrenner, whose neck was stuck out farther than mine."

Steinbrenner's neck was stuck out, and his bankroll extended, because he and his 15 partners had spent a fortune during the last three years to sign Jackson, Catfish Hunter, Don Gullett and other stars of baseball's changing world. And Jackson also stood in the center of the feuding that had embroiled the team and its manager, Billy Martin, who received a bonus and a vote of confidence during the uncertain hours before the Yankees turned their trick.

The Yankees' return to the front rank of the major leagues also was marked by the pitching of Mike Torrez, the 31-year-old right-hander from Kansas, who had unwittingly touched off another family fuss by superseding Ed Figueroa on the mound. Torrez pitched a seven-hitter last Friday night in Los Angeles, where he won Game 3, and a nine-hitter last evening in the Bronx, where he outlasted four Dodger pitchers starting with Burt Hooton.

But this was mainly a night for hitting by both the Yankees and the Dodgers, late of Brooklyn—the teams that once produced the perfect game, the dropped third strike and the Subway Series. And this time they produced another extravaganza before a throng of 56,407 that tossed balloons, paper streamers and firecrackers onto the field and even forced Jackson to leave right field in the ninth inning for a batting helmet to protect his head.

"This is very rewarding," Manager Billy Martin said later, referring to the quarrels his team had surmounted while beating the Kansas City Royals for the American League pennant and then the Dodgers for the World Series. "We had to beat two great teams. I'm proud of our players and what they accomplished this year. What made them overcome all those obstacles? We had five or six guys help patch things up during the season. Reggie? He was sensational."

MARTIN'S DAY TO REMEMBER

For Martin, who lived in the center of the storm surrounding the Yankees this summer, the occasion was rewarding in more ways than one. In a belated bid to bring unity out of chaos, the owners announced during the afternoon that they were rewarding the manager "for a fine job." He received a bonus of perhaps $35,000, a gift of a Lincoln Continental, a subsidy toward his rent and a new assurance that he would stay on the job despite rumors that he would go.

The Yankees also shook down some of the old traditions that had brought them 31 pennants as the monopoly team of baseball for much of the last half-century. The first ball last night was thrown out by Joe DiMaggio, who strode to the pitcher's mound in a blue suit and tossed one to Thurman Munson, one week after he had boycotted the Stadium during a mixup over tickets. And Robert Merrill, a familiar voice in the ball park, sang the national anthem from the grass behind home plate.

But the Dodgers, the champions of the National League twice in the last four seasons, were flanked by celebrities, too. Lillian Carter, the mother of President Carter, attended her third straight game as a self-proclaimed "loyal Dodger fan." And Mayor Tom Bradley of Los Angeles watched from a box alongside the visitors' dugout.

DODGERS BEGIN CRISPLY

When the players got around to the main event, the Dodgers knew full well that only three teams in baseball history had lost three of the first four games in a World Series and then won three straight for the title. Inside one inning, they rattled Torrez for two runs as they fought to force this Series into a winner-take-all finale.

But inside of two innings, the Yankees retaliated on a home run by Chris Chambliss. Then, after Reggie Smith hit one for the Dodgers in the third inning, Reginald Martinez Jackson took charge on three swings of the bat: a home run off Hooton in the fourth inning, another off Elias Sosa in the fifth and another off Charlie Hough in the eighth.

He also knocked in five runs, and later suggested: "Babe Ruth was great. I'm just lucky."

In the fourth inning Munson led off with a single past third base and, on the next pitch, Jackson hammered one into the right-field grandstand.

One inning later, Mickey Rivers singled and Jackson drilled the first pitch beyond the right-field railing past the $15 box seats for his second home run. And now the Yankees were in control, 7-3.

As memorable as that was, Jackson went even farther in the eighth inning when he went to bat for the last time in an unlikely season. For the third straight time, he pounced on the first pitch and bombed it 450 feet into the center-field bleachers for his third consecutive home run, his fourth in his last four swings and his record-breaking fifth in the 74th World Series. ◆

October 19, 1977

SPORTS OF THE TIMES
The Moving Finger Writes, Etc.

By RED SMITH

IT HAD TO HAPPEN this way. It had been predestined sine Nov. 29 1976, when Reginald Martinez Jackson sat down on a gilded chair in New York's Americana Hotel and wrote his name on a Yankee contract. That day he became an instant millionaire, the big honcho on the best team money could buy, the richest, least inhibited, most glamorous exhibit in Billy Martin's pin-striped zoo. That day the plot was written for last night—the bizarre scenario Reggie Jackson played out by hitting three home runs, clubbing the Los Angeles Dodgers into submission and carrying his supporting players with him to the baseball championship of North America. His was the most lurid performance in 74 World Series, for although Babe Ruth hit three home runs in a game in 1926 and again in 1928, not even the demigod smashed three in a row.

Reggie's first broke a tie and put the Yankees in front, 4-3. His second fattened the advantage to 7-3. His third completed arrangements for a final score of 8-4, wrapping up the championship in six games.

Yet that was merely the final act of an implausible one-man show. Jackson had hit a home run last Saturday in Los Angeles and another on his last time at bat in that earthly paradise on Sunday. On his first appearance at the plate last night he walked, getting no official time at bat, so in his last four official turns he hit four homers.

In his last nine times at bat, this Hamlet in double-knits scored seven runs, made six hits and five home runs and batted in six runs for a batting average of .667 compiled by day and by night on two seacoasts 3,000 miles and three time zones apart. Shakespeare wouldn't attempt a curtain scene like that if he was plastered. »»

<<< This was a drama that consumed seven months, for ever since the Yankees went to training camp last March, Jackson had lived in the eye of the hurricane. All summer long as the spike-shod capitalists bickered and quarreled, contending with their manager, defying their owner, Reggie was the most controversial, the most articulate, the most flamboyant.

Part philosopher, part preacher and part outfielder, he carried this rancorous company with his bat in the season's last 50 games, leading them to the East championship in the American League and into the World Series. He knocked in the winning run in the 12-inning first game, drove in a run and scored two in the third, furnished the winning margin in the fourth and delivered the final run in the fifth.

Thus the stage was set when he went to the plate in last night's second inning with the Dodgers leading, 2-0. Sedately, he led off with a walk. Serenely, he circled the bases on a home run by Chris Chambliss. The score was tied.

Los Angeles had moved out front, 3-2, when the man reappeared in the fourth inning with Thurman Munson on base. He hit the first pitch on a line into the seats beyond right field. Circling the bases for the second time, he went into his home-run glide—head high, chest out. The Yankees led, 4-3. In the dugout, the Yankees fell upon him. Billy Martin, the manager who tried to slug him last June, patted his cheek lovingly. The dugout phone rang and Reggie accepted the call graciously.

His first home run knocked the Dodgers' starting pitcher, Burt Hooton, out of the game. His second disposed of Elias Sosa, Hooton's successor. Before Sosa's first pitch in the fifth inning, Reggie had strolled the length of the dugout to pluck a bat from the rack. He was confident he would get his turn. When he did, there was a runner on base again, and again he hit the first pitch. Again it reached the seats in right. a curtain scene like that if he was plastered.

When the last jubilant playmate had been peeled off his neck, Reggie took a seat near the first-base end of the bench. The crowd was still bawling for him and comrades urged him to take a curtain call but he replied with a gesture that said, "Aw, fellows, cut it out!" He did unbend enough to hold up two fingers for photographers in a V-for-victory sign.

Jackson was the leadoff batter in the eighth. For the third time, Reggie hit the first pitch but this one didn't take the shortest distance between two points. Straight out from the plate the ball streaked, not toward the neighborly stands in right but on a soaring arc toward the unoccupied seats in dead center, where the seats are blacked out to give batters a background. Up the white speck climbed, dwindling, diminishing, until it settled at last halfway up those empty stands, probably 450 feet away.

This time he could not disappoint his public. He stepped out of the dugout and faced the multitude, two fists and one cap uplifted. Not only the customers applauded.

"I must admit," said Steve Garvey, the Dodgers' first baseman, "when Reggie Jackson hit his third home run and I was sure nobody was listening, I applauded in my glove." ◆

Reggie Jackson hits his first of three home runs in Game 6 of the 1977 World Series.

October 20, 1977

SPORTS OF THE TIMES
The Two Seasons of Reggie Jackson

By DAVE ANDERSON

NEARLY THREE HOURS AFTER his three home runs had won the World Series for the Yankees and redemption for himself, Reggie Jackson, like almost everyone else, appeared in awe of what he had accomplished. "There's a part of me I don't know," he was saying softly at his locker. "There's the ballplayer in me who responds to all the pressure. I'm not sure I hit three home runs but the ballplayer in me did.

And above all his complex parts, Reggie Jackson is a ballplayer. When he took nearly $3 million from the Yankees, most people scoffed that he wasn't worth it. But he's worth it now. No matter what he does from now on is a bonus. What he did Tuesday night put Reggie Jackson up there with Muhammad Ali winning back the heavyweight title in Zaire, up with Joe Namath and the Jets winning Super Bowl III, up there with Tom Seaver and the Mets winning the 1969 World Series, but to appreciate how the "part of me I don't know" put Reggie Jackson there, it is necessary to remember how another part, his sensitive ego, put Reggie Jackson down so that he might ascend.

"I got to get dressed," he was saying now. "I told some people I'd meet them at 76th and Third."

In the same East Side area, at a sidewalk table at King Arthur's Court in July, he was sipping white wine and saying, "I'm still the straw that stirs the drink. Not Munson, not nobody else on this club."

All the other Yankees had dressed and departed Tuesday night except for Thurman Munson, who was on his way now.

"Hey, coon" called the catcher, grinning. "Nice goin' coon."

Reggie Jackson laughed and hurried over and hugged the captain.

"I'm goin' down to that party here in the ball park," Thurman Munson said, grinning again. "Just white people but they'll let you in. Come on down."

"I'll be there," Reggie Jackson said. "Wait for me."

"I got to make myself go to the ball park," he said in July. "I don't want to go."

"You'll change your mind," somebody told him.

"I don't want to change. I've closed my mind. Remember the thing in Boston," he said, referring to his dugout confrontation with Billy Martin in Fenway Park, "the next day we had a meeting in Gabe Paul's suite and Billy challenged me. He stood over me and said, 'I'll make you fight me, boy.' But there was no way I was going to fight him. I'm 215 pounds, he's almost 50 years old. I win the fight, but I lose.

In the manager's office half an hour earlier, Reggie Jackson and Billy Martin had finished a TV interview together when the slugger overheard the manager talking about punching somebody.

"Anybody fights you, skip," Reggie Jackson said, "he's got to fight the both of us."

"And anybody who fights you," Billy Martin said, "got to fight the both of us."

We can't win this way," he said in July. "The Red Sox hammer. We got nobody who can hammer except me. I should be batting third or cleanup, not sixth. I always hit third or cleanup.

"How far did that last homer go?" the cleanup hitter asked.

"I figured it to be 450 feet," a sportswriter said.

"Make it 475, it sounds better," the cleanup hitter said, laughing. "I hit that one off a knuckler, the first two off fastballs. The general consensus on how to pitch to me is hard and in. On the first one, I knew [Burt] Hooton would pitch me there, but I had an inkling I'd hit one. As soon as they brought in [Elia] Sosa, I got on the phone to Stick [Gene Michael, the Yankee scout] upstairs and asked him about Sosa $\ggg$

because Sosa popped me up with a fastball in spring training. I hit the second one even better than I hit the third, the one off [Charley] Hough's knuckler. Brooks Robinson taught me how to hit a knuckler. Just time the ball."

"Hough said the knuckler didn't move much," somebody said.

"It didn't," Reggie Jackson said, "until I got hold of it."

"I should've signed with the Padres," Jackson said in July. "I'd be happy there. Or with the Dodgers."

"Did you hear," Reggie Jackson was told, "what Steve Garvey said, that after your third homer, he applauded in his glove."

"What a great player Steve Garvey is, what a great man," Reggie Jackson. "He's the best all-around human being in baseball. My one regret about not playing with the Dodgers is not being around Steve Garvey, but I got a security blanket here, Fran Healy [the Yankees' bull-pen catcher]. Before the game he told me I was swinging the bat good."

"I don't need baseball," he said in July, "I'm a businessman. That means as much to me as baseball. I don't need cheers."

"When you hit the third one," a visitor was saying now, "George Steinbrenner had tears in his eyes."

"Get my bat, Nick, please," Reggie Jackson told a clubhouse man. "I started using this bat Saturday after I broke one in Friday's game. Look at the wide grain. The older the tree, the wider the grain, the harder the wood. I think I'll give this bat to George. He'll appreciate. "

"George," somebody said, "ought to put a marker out there halfway up the bleachers where that third homer landed."

"That'd be something. Babe Ruth, Lou Gehrig, Joe DiMaggio, Mickey Mantle and Reggie

---

October 26, 1977

Lyle Wins Cy Young Award in Close Vote

By MURRAY CHASS

SPARKY LYLE, the New York Yankee relief pitcher who handles his job with the coolness and hardness of a hired killer, won the Cy Young Award yesterday as the best pitcher in the American League and instantly became "a screaming maniac."

"I was so nervous when I found out, I couldn't talk," Lyle said minutes after learning of the award. "I can't remember when I was like that."

In becoming the first relief pitcher to gain the honor in the American League, Lyle beat out Jim Palmer, Baltimore's three-time winner; Nolan Ryan of California and Dennis Leonard of Kansas City in the most diversified voting in the 22-year history of the award.

Pitcher Sparky Lyle pitching in 1977.

Jackson. Somehow I don't fit."

"You know what Bobby Vinton sings, 'Color Me Gone,' that's me," he said in July. "Color me gone. I want to hit .300, 30 homers, 50 doubles, drive in 90 runs, be the most valuable player in the World Series, get to win the World Series, and then go. Color me gone."

Thurman Munson appeared. "Hey, nigger you're too slow, that party's over but I'll see you next year," the captain said, sticking out his hand. "I'll see you next year wherever I might be."

"You'll be back," Reggie Jackson said.

"Not me," said Thurman Munson, who has talked of demanding to be traded to the Cleveland Indians. "But you know who stuck up for you nigger, you know who stuck up for you, when you needed it."

"I know," Reggie Jackson said. "But you'll be here next year. We'll all be here." ◆

The 33-year-old left-hander joined Bob Turley (1958) and Whitey Ford (1961) as Yankee winners.

"I finally was in the right place at the right time," Lyle said. "I thank all the starters."

The Yankees, of course, had Lyle to thank, among others, for their success this year. He won 13 games, lost 5 and saved 26 others during the regular season, then was the winning pitcher in the last two games of the playoffs and the first game of the World Series.

"I've been waiting a long time for this," said the irrepressible pitcher, whose 201 career saves are the most in baseball history. "I never thought I'd win it. This is too much to take—the world championship and the Cy Young Award in one year."

Lyle was speaking on the telephone at his Demarest, N.J., home and his wife, Mary, was listening. She reminded him of something else that had happened this year.

"Mary says to say I got married, too," Sparky added. "I don't know where that fits on the list." ◆

April 14, 1978

Jackson Homer Sparks Candy-Bar Shower

By MURRAY CHASS

REGGIE JACKSON'S three-run home run in the first inning and an answering shower of Reggie candy bars from the Yankee Stadium stands made everything that followed anticlimactic yesterday as the Yankees trimmed the unappreciative Chicago White Sox, 4-2, in their home opener.

Ron Guidry pitched an unglamorous 10-hitter, in a performance that did not prompt anyone in the crowd of 44,667 to throw a candy bar or even a stick of bubble gum.

As for the display for Jackson, it evoked contrasting opinions.

"I just appreciated it," Jackson said. "It was a nice gesture."

"It was a very thrilling moment for Reggie," said Lou Piniella, who was the next batter.

"I felt like opening up a candy store," Billy Martin remarked.

"I thought it was silly," said Chris Chambliss, who was to be the hitter after Piniella.

"I think it was horse manure," Bob Lemon, the Chicago manager, said.

The White Sox, from the manager on down, clearly did not appreciate the fans' part in the game.

Wilbur Wood started the Yankees' first inning by walking Willie Randolph. Mickey Rivers singled and that set the stage for Jackson, who with his previous three swings at Yankee Stadium hit three home runs. He took those swings five months and 26 days ago, Oct. 18, 1977, in the sixth and last game of the World Series.

When he rocketed a 2-0 knuckleball from Wood over the right-center-field fence, Jackson had four straight home runs on four straight swings at the Stadium.

When Al Clark, the second-base umpire, ⟫⟫⟫

≪≪≪ signaled home run by waving his right arm over his head, the first candy bars began cascading from the stands. The two-ounce bars had been distributed to all fans before the game.

For five minutes, the fans threw and the grounds crew, plus some fans, picked up the candy from the field.

BETTER THAN WEDNESDAY

"I figured they'd be coming out on the field," said Jackson, who had struck out four times the day before in Milwaukee. "I'm just glad I didn't make an error and have them throw them at me. But I just didn't want anyone to get hurt. Thank God no one did get hurt." ◆

June 18, 1978

GUIDRY FANS 18 ANGELS FOR YANK MARK

By MURRAY CHASS

RON GUIDRY, adding even more drama to what is perhaps the most exciting development of this baseball season—his performance—shattered a 59-year-old club record last night by striking out 18 batters as the Yankees trimmed the California Angels, 4-0.

Almost overshadowed in Guidry's glittering effort at Yankee Stadium was the fact that he gained his 11th victory without a defeat and lowered his major league-leading earned-run average to 1.45 with a four-hitter and his second straight shutout.

The 27-year-old left-hander had a chance to join Nolan Ryan, Tom Seaver and Steve Carlton in a share of the major league strikeout record of 19. However, after he struck out the first two batters in the ninth inning, Don Baylor singled and Ron Jackson grounded into a force play.

'KID WAS OVERPOWERING'

Ryan, the yardstick against whom all strikeout pitchers are measured today, was nearly as close to Guidry as the California batters but, unlike them, he was able to appreciate the performance.

"That kid was overpowering," said Ryan, who watched from the Angel dugout and was not necessarily rooting against Guidry's charge at the record. "Anytime somebody can break that record, I'm all for it. It's just a matter of time. It's going to happen."

If it is broken, Guidry could be the pitcher who does it. Although he averaged only 4½ strikeouts a game in his first eight starts this season, he has struck out 10 or more batters in five of his last six starts and stands only nine strikeouts from Ryan's league-leading total of 113.

"In those early games, I didn't feel strong because I had a bad case of flu in the spring," Guidry explained, his left arm immersed in a tub of ice. "I didn't have that extra foot on my fastball."

In mowing down the Angels, Guidry must have had several extra feet on his pitches. He threw 138 pitches, a remarkably low total for the number of strikeouts he had, and he estimated that 65 percent were fastballs and 35 percent were sliders.

He struck out every Angel at least once, he struck out the side three times, he recorded all nine outs and 12 of 13 on strikeouts in the middle innings, and he broke the Yankee record of 15 that Bob Shawkey set in 1919.

"If you saw that pitching too often," said Joe Rudi, the Angels' cleanup batter who was a four-time victim, "there would be a lot of guys doing different jobs."

"When they start hollering and screaming," Guidry said, "you just get pumped up that much higher. You try harder. I felt I disappointed them

Ron Guidry pitching during his 18-strikeout game against the Oakland Athletics in 1978.

when a guy hit the ball with two strikes. I thought I made a mistake."

On his way from the trainer's room to his locker, Guidry stopped and shook hands with Thurman Munson.

"Thank you for staying in the game," Guidry told the catcher.

Munson, Manager Billy Martin explained, was aching and could have used a night off, but he asked to catch because Guidry was pitching.

"Thurman makes a whole lot of difference," Guidry said. "Most of the pitchers depend on him so much because of his knowledge of the hitters." ◆

July 25, 1978

Martin Resigns; Bob Lemon to Manage Yankees

By MURRAY CHASS
Special to The New York Times

KANSAS CITY, JULY 24—Billy Martin, a tempestuous street fighter who had been dismissed from three previous major league managerial jobs, tearfully resigned today from the one managerial job that he always yearned for— »»

<<< the one with the Yankees.

Bob Lemon, who served as Yankee pitching coach in 1976, was named to replace Martin. Lemon, a Hall of Fame pitcher, was dismissed only 24 days ago by the Chicago White Sox. The 57-year-old Lemon, an easy-going man whose personality is the opposite of Martin's, played with Al Rosen, the Yankee president, in Cleveland.

ROSEN SAYS, 'IT WAS INEVITABLE'

Rosen said that no terms had been determined but that Lemon would manage for "the balance of the season and, I hope, plus." Lemon is to join the team tomorrow.

The end of Martin's stormy relationship with George Steinbrenner, the Yankee owner, came just nine days short of the third anniversary of the manager's return to the team he served as a scrappy second baseman in the 1950's.

Although Martin resigned, there was no question that if he hadn't, he would have been dismissed.

"In view of the events of the past 24 hours," Rosen said two and a half hours after arriving in Kansas City from New York, "it was inevitable that as president of the New York Yankees I could not allow a man to make the statements that were made."

Last night in Chicago, Martin made the statement that ignited the final explosion between the manager and the owner.

After the game with the White Sox, Martin asked to talk to this reporter when the team was at O'Hare International Airport. Later, with another reporter present, Martin referred to Reggie Jackson, just returned from a five-day suspension, and to Steinbrenner, who had been convicted of making illegal campaign contributions in an outgrowth of the Watergate case.

"ONE'S A BORN LIAR"

"The two of them deserve each other," Martin said. "One's a born liar, the other's convicted."

In announcing his resignation on the balcony of the Crown Center Hotel, Martin denied making that remark.

"I don't want to hurt this team's chances for the pennant with this undue publicity," Martin said, reading from a hand-written statement through dark glasses that covered his haggard face. "The team has a shot at the pennant and I hope they win it: I owe it to my health and my mental well-being to resign. At this time I'm also sorry about these things that were written about George Steinbrenner. He does not deserve them nor did I say them. I've had my differences with George, but we've been able to resolve them.

THE TEARFUL FAREWELL

"I would like to thank"—here he started breaking down and crying—"the Yankee management…the press, the news media, my coaches, my players…and most of all"—he began crying more heavily and could not speak for nearly 10 seconds, then gasped out softly—"the fans."

Then, led by Bob Brown, a Kansas City friend who had his arm around the Yankee manager's shoulders, Martin walked quickly down the corridor, his head bowed, his right hand clutching the statement.

Martin's tearful end came in the kind of circus atmosphere that has surrounded the Yankees the last two and a half years.

HOTEL GUESTS TURN OUT

Instead of announcing his resignation in a room, where such things generally occur, he stood on the balcony outside an antique shop—the sign "Antiques" poised above his head—and read the statement while hotel guests—men, women, children—joined the throng of newsmen and television cameramen.

An indoor waterfall, weeping fig trees, holly leaf fern, Chinese evergreen, and philodendron decorated the other side of the balcony.

Before reading his statement, the 50-year-old Martin said he would answer no questions afterward.

"That means now and forever," he said, "because I am a Yankee and Yankees do not talk or throw rocks."

2D YEAR OF 3-YEAR CONTRACT

Martin, however, flung many rocks during his successful managerial tenure—two American League pennants, one World Series championship—with the Yankees. He was in the second year of a three-year contract, one he signed reluctantly because of the clauses that Steinbrenner included.

One of those clauses said Martin couldn't make public comments critical of Steinbrenner or the front office. Last year he was fined $2,500 for a public outburst against the front office over personnel matters.

His latest comment, though, went beyond anything he had said previously because he raised the one aspect of Steinbrenner's life that the owner will not discuss—his conviction.

CONTRACT WILL BE HONORED

Steinbrenner, speaking from his shipbuilding company office in Tampa, said the Yankees would honor the remaining time on Martin's contract. Martin was being paid about $80,000 this season and $90,000 next.

"We have never worked better together than we have the last two or three weeks," Steinbrenner said of Martin. "On learning of the Chicago thing I was shocked. You could have knocked me over.

"The events that have transpired in the last hours have little significance when compared to a man's concern for his own well being. These things along with his family are far more important than the game of baseball.

"I am grateful to Billy for his contributions as manager of the Yankees. He brought us a championship. His apologies over the recent incident are accepted with no further comment necessary. I think Billy knows of our concern for the well-being of his family and himself. We wish him good luck."

Anybody who knows Martin, though, thinks he will work once again with another team, perhaps even as a manager if his health permits. He has been suffering from a liver ailment.

Before today, Martin suffered through a series of near firings in the last year and a half. One of those came exactly one year ago today when Dick Howser, the Yankee's third base coach, was said to be set to replace Martin.

A month before that, Martin nearly came to blows with Jackson in the team's dugout during a nationally televised game in Boston and two days later Martin again was on the brink of dismissal. That day, Jackson went to Steinbrenner and helped convince the owner to retain Martin.

This time Jackson again found himself in the middle because of his five-day suspension for bunting a week ago tonight when Martin ordered him to hit away.

Martin, who seemed to be losing his players' respect this season, was in serious trouble last month when the defending champion Yankees fell eight games behind the Boston Red Sox. Steinbrenner was present at the last game in Boston and was believed to have pressured Rosen to make a change.

However, the following Monday, June 26, Martin met with Rosen and Steinbrenner in Yankee Stadium for two and a half hours and the owner announced afterward that Martin's job was secure for the remainder of the season, although he looked haggard and tired as the season wore on.

Then, during the All-Star break earlier this month, Steinbrenner told Doug Newton, Martin's agent, that if Martin felt he had to resign because of his health he would honor the remainder of the contract and even extend it for perhaps five years with Billy serving as a consultant in the front office.

Meeting with Steinbrenner July 13, Martin said he wanted to stay "and win another pennant and World Series for you, I'll bust my gut for you." ◆

Martin Will Rejoin Yanks As Club's Manager in 1980

By MURRAY CHASS

BILLY MARTIN, who was hired on Old-Timers' Day three years ago to manage the Yankees, was rehired on Old-Timers' Day yesterday to manage the Yankees in one of the most bizarre developments in baseball history.

Stunning and elating Martin's legions of fans at the same time, the Yankees announced that Martin would become the manager again in 1980, succeeding Bob Lemon, who succeeded him when he tearfully and reluctantly resigned last Monday. Lemon, who will manage the rest of this year and next, will become general manager in 1980.

Lemon, who has signed a five-year contract with the Yankees, will replace Cedric Tallis and Tallis will return to his previous duties as vice president and director of scouting.

Martin will serve out the remaining year and a half of his original three-year contract as a consultant to the team president, Al Rosen, and Lemon, the Yankees said, then will manage under a two-year extension of that contract.

The announcement had all the theatrical trappings that George Steinbrenner, the team owner, is so fond of using. Not only was the development shocking, but it also was unveiled instantly on the field at Yankee Stadium before the large Old-Timers' Day crowd, which saw the current Yankees defeat the Minnesota Twins, 7-3.

When Bob Sheppard, the stadium public address announcer, reached Lemon's introduction to the crowd, he announced—scoreboard simultaneously announcing—that Lemon would become the general manager in 1980.

"Managing the Yankees in the 1980 season," Sheppard intoned, "and hopefully for many seasons after that will be No. 1…"

FANS CHEER FOR 7 MINUTES

He didn't have to say "Billy Martin." The crowd screamed and roared and cheered and rose at their seats as the jubilant and resurrected Martin ran onto the field from the Yankee dugout.

For seven minutes, his fans cheered, their voices exploding in a new burst of energy each time the former and future manager waved his cap or bowed, as he did once.

Fans hoisted signs high, saying such things as "Reinstate Billy Martin," "Bring Billy Back" and "Billy, You'll Always Be No. 1."

Martin, beaming, stood next to Yogi Berra in the line of former Yankee players. He embraced Phil Rizzuto, his close friend and former roommate. He trotted over to the other side of the infield and shook hands with Lemon, then returned to his spot next to Berra.

When the cheers finally subsided, the remaining old-timers were introduced—Whitey Ford, Roger Maris, Mickey Mantle, Joe DiMaggio. Mantle and DiMaggio always receive the loudest ovations at these affairs, but their receptions this day were dwarfed by Martin's. It was clearly Billy's day.

It was perhaps the high point of Martin's turbulent life, occurring only five days after he experienced his low point.

The nadir came only 21 hours after he uttered the words that will live in baseball infamy.

"The two of them deserve each other," Martin said of Reggie Jackson and Steinbrenner, speaking to two newsmen in Chicago. "One's a born liar, the other's convicted."

Yesterday, standing before many more newsmen in the press room at Yankee Stadium in his Yankee uniform, Martin, who had denied making that statement, said, "I did say it, I don't know why I said it, I was angered at the time, I had no reason to say it and I feel very bad about it. I'm not afraid to admit it."

The incredible turn of events resulted from many conversations, some in person, most on the telephone, among Steinbrenner, Martin and Martin's agent, Doug Newton.

Billy Martin speaking at a news conference at Yankee Stadium in 1978. At left is Al Rosen, the Yankees' president, and right is George Steinbrenner, the principal owner.

Steinbrenner said he first thought of the idea of rehiring Martin last Monday, the same day Billy resigned.

"Billy Martin came to me after he had resigned," said Steinbrenner, who has produced Broadway shows with James Nederlander and never ignores the importance of showmanship. "What he said to me showed me he was a man who realized he had made a small mistake and it was small in the total picture."

The owner said there are times a person has to be understanding and compassionate and "I didn't feel that what happened was right."

TALKS OF MARTIN'S COMMENTS

He went on to discuss Martin's allusion to his conviction stemming from illegal political campaign contributions, saying his conviction "was part of life, that's what you live with….It's going to come up again and again and again and I should live with it."

Steinbrenner, who flew to New York from Tampa, Fla., Friday night to unleash his surprise package, denied that fan reaction had anything to do with his decision. However, observers saw the timing of the announcement, at least, as a means of placating many disgruntled fans.

The owner talked about Martin's health—he had a liver ailment—and in effect suggested that his 1½-year sabbatical from the daily grind of managing, would give the 50-year-old Martin time to regain his health and his "emotional well-being."

Martin, in beginning his statement, went di-rectly to the problems he and Steinbrenner have had in their stormy three-year relationship.

WAY TO SOLVE PROBLEMS

"George and I in the past," he said, "have had our differences, but we always found a way sometimes to solve them."

Martin, who had met with Steinbrenner twice during the week, called himself a "free spirit" who would "try to do other things George wants me to do."

At the same time, he added, "Steinbrenner said he's going to try to be a little more free spirit, too." Neither Martin nor Steinbrenner would answer any questions after making their statements, but the owner quickly showed he didn't want Martin to be too free.

Riding up to his office on the elevator, Steinbrenner whispered to an aide, "Go stay with Billy and make sure he doesn't say anything." ◆

'78 COMEBACK THAT NEVER APPEARED IN THE TIMES*

By DAVE ANDERSON

IN THE ALMOST DAY-TO-DAY commotion involving Billy Martin, Reggie Jackson, and George Steinbrenner, the 1978 Yankees skidded into fourth place in mid-July, 14 games behind the Boston Red Sox. But when the start of an 88-day pressmen's strike prevented the Times, the Daily News, and the Post from being published on August 10, 1978, the Yankees had climbed into second place, 7 ½ games out, with an overall 63-49 record, including 11-7 since Bob Lemon took over as manager.

"It's more relaxed around here," Bucky Dent said. "We're thinking more about playing the game of baseball. Before, you didn't know what was going to happen."

One of Lemon's first decisions was to tell Jackson, "You're going to hit fourth every day." Stability was typical of Lemon's managerial manner. "I never took the game home with me," he often said. "I always left it in a bar along the way." And with no New York newspapers to fan the few flames that occurred, the Yankees kept winning. On September 7, only 4 games behind, they roared into Fenway Park for a four-game series.

The Yankees won the Thursday opener, 15-3, with 21 hits. The next night they won, 13-2, with 17 hits. On Saturday left-hander Ron Guidry fired a 7-0 two-hitter for a 22-2 record. On Sunday an 18-hit barrage produced a 7-4 victory. Over the four games, the Yankees outscored the Red Sox, 42-9, and out-hit them, 67-30. Willie Randolph was on base 16 times. Dent had 7 r.b.i., Randolph and Jackson each had 6 r.b.i.

More importantly, the Yankees suddenly shared first place and when right-hander Jim Beattie stopped the Tigers, 7-3, in Detroit three days later, they were atop the American League East. Over the weekend, they extended their lead to 3 ½ games when Jackson's homer sparked a 3-2 win over the Red Sox at the Stadium.

But the Red Sox didn't disappear. They won

their last 8 games and when the Yankees lost their season finale, 9-2, to Indians right-hander Rick Waits at the Stadium, the stage was set: Guidry against Mike Torrez, who had joined the Red Sox as a free agent for a two-year $2.7 million contract after winning twice for the Yankees in the 1977 World Series, in a one-game divisional playoff at Fenway Park.

"Wouldn't two out of three games be a fairer test?" Guidry was asked.

"One game's enough," the left-hander said. "I can only pitch one game."

But with Torrez firing a two-hitter through six innings, the Red Sox had 2-0 lead. With one out in the seventh, Chris Chambliss singled and Roy White walked. Pinch-hitter Jim Spencer flied out. Dent, batting ninth, a sure-handed shortstop who had hit only 4 homers and driven in only 37 runs during the season, took a low fastball for ball 1, then fouled the next pitch off his left ankle and fell to the dirt. Trainer Gene Monahan rushed to him and sprayed ethyl chloride on the ankle. After a delay of several minutes, Dent settled into the batter's box again. Torrez threw a fastball inside. Dent swung. The ball soared toward The Wall, the Green Monster, in leftfield.

As he neared first base, Dent was hoping the ball would hit The Wall for a double. As he turned toward second, he saw second-base umpire Al Clark waving his right arm in a circle. The ball had dropped into the net just above The Wall near the foul pole. Home run. The Yankees led, 3-2. Moments later, Mickey Rivers walked and stole second. Thurman Munson doubled. Yankees led, 4-2.

With one out in the Red Sox seventh, George Scott singled. Lemon signaled to the bullpen for Rich (Goose) Gossage, who fired a called third strike past pinch-hitter Bob Bailey. When Rick

Bucky Dent watching his 1978 division-winning home run at Fenway Park.

* The New York Times was on strike from August 10, 1978 to November 5, 1978

Burleson bounced to Dent, the Yankees still had a 4-2 lead.

In the top of the eighth, Jackson smashed a home run into the centerfield bleachers for a 5-2 lead, but the Red Sox narrowed the score to 5-4 in the bottom of the inning on Jerry Remy's double, Carl Yastrzemski's single, Carlton Fisk's single, and Fred Lynn's single. Lemon strolled to the mound.

"You're trying to make me an old man," the manager said, "but I'm already an old man." Gossage smiled, his shoulders relaxed. Butch Hobson flied out. George Scott fanned. But with one out in the ninth, Burleson walked. Remy drilled a liner to right that Piniella, who had snatched Lynn's liner through the low sun's glare in the sixth, appeared about to catch, but he was bluffing. The low sun blinded him. He drifted to where he thought the ball would land. Third-base coach Eddie Yost was waving for Burleson to run, but the Red Sox shortstop hesitated. When he finally realized that Piniella was confused, he ran too late to get to third as Piniella snatched the ball off the grass and threw hard. Burleson, the potential tying run, turned back to second. Remy, the potential winning run, was at first with Jim Rice and Yaz coming up.

Rice lofted a deep, high fly ball above the sun, Piniella caught it. Burleson tagged up and hurried to third. If not for Piniella's bluff on Remy's single, Burleson would've been on third and if Rice had produced a similar flyout, Burleson would have tagged and scored the tying run. Instead, the potential tying run remained on third with Yaz up.

Gossage fired his best fastball. Ball one. The next pitch was just what Yaz was hoping for, a fastball down, but as he swung, the ball exploded toward his hands. He lifted a high pop fly behind third base just in foul territory. "When Yaz was up," Nettles would say later, "I was saying, `Pop it up, pop it up...not to me." Staggering slightly, Nettles settled under it and Yaz watched the ball drop into his glove.

"Gossage didn't beat us," Yaz said. "Piniella beat us with those two plays. If he doesn't ⟫⟫⟫

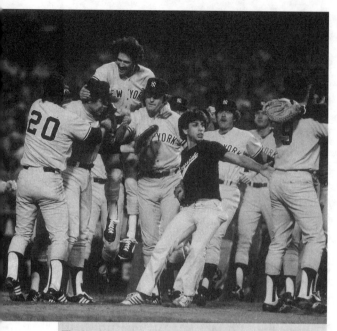

The Yankees celebrate their 1978 World Series victory over the Los Angeles Dodgers.

≪≪≪ catch Lynn's ball and if Remy's ball gets past him, we win by five or six runs."

In one of the most theatrical triumphs in their history, the Yankees won, 5-4, for a 48-20 record after Bob Lemon's takeover and the A.L. East title. They then eliminated the Kansas City Royals, three games to one, in the A.L. Championship Series, and took the World Series from the Los Angeles Dodgers for the second consecutive year, the first team to win in six games after having lost the first two. And guess who turned out to be the Series' most valuable player?

None other than Bucky Dent, who batted .417 with 10 hits, 7 runs batted in and 3 runs scored. When the newspapers reappeared on Nov. 6, what happened during the strike had been engraved into Yankee history. And Red Sox history. ◆

August 3, 1979

YANKEES' THURMAN MUNSON KILLED PILOTING HIS OWN SMALL JET IN OHIO

By JIM NAUGHTON

THURMAN MUNSON, the 32-year-old catcher and team captain of the New York Yankees, was killed yesterday when the plane he was piloting crashed short of the runway while trying to land at the Akron-Canton Airport in Ohio.

Two passengers who were flying with him were taken to local hospitals where they were reported in fair condition.

Mr. Munson's Cessna Citation twin-engine jet crashed outside the perimeter of the airport and came to rest 200 feet north of runway 19 at 3:02 P.M., Eastern daylight time, according to the Akron police.

Federal Aviation Administration officials said that the plane had lost its wings and burst into flames after the crash, resulting in injuries to two occupants and the death of the third.

Anthony Cardarelli, sheriff of Summit County, confirmed that Mr. Munson was the one who was killed.

One of the two passengers, David Hall, 32, of Canton, who first taught Mr. Munson to fly, was reported in fair condition with burns on his arms and hands at the Akron Regional Burn Center at Children's Hospital. The other passenger, Jerry D. Anderson, also of Canton, was reported in fair condition with burns of the face, arms, and neck at Timken Mercy Hospital in Canton.

The F.A.A. authorities said the cause of the crash was unknown. Detective William Evans, who arrived at the scene five minutes after the crash, said witnesses told him the jet began clipping trees as it approached the runway. It touched down just north of Greensburg Road, he said. Motorists had to "brake for the plane," he added. "It's a ≫≫≫

Munson's Career Record

THURMAN LEE MUNSON

Born June 7, 1947, at Akron, O.
Height, 5.11. Weight, 190.
Throws and bats righthanded.
Attended Kent State University, Kent, O.

Led American League catchers in double plays with 14 in 1975 and tied for lead with 11 in 1973.
Named Most Valuable Player in American league, 1976.
Selected by the Baseball Writers' Association as American League Rookie of the Year, 1970.
Named catcher on THE SPORTING NEWS American League All-Star Team, 1973, 1974, 1975 and 1976.
Named catcher on THE SPORTING NEWS American League All-Star fielding team, 1973, 1974 and 1975.
Named American League Player of the Year by THE SPORTING NEWS, 1976.
Received $75,000 bonus to sign with New York Yankees, 1968.

Year	Club	League	Pos.	G.	AB.	R.	H.	2B.	3B.	HR.	RBI.	B.A.	PO.	A.	E.	F.A.
1968	Binghamton	East.	C	71	226	29	68	12	3	6	37	.301	327	53	9	.977
1969	Syracuse	Int.	C-2-3	28	102	13	37	9	1	2	17	.363	81	13	6	.940
1969	New York	Amer.	C	26	86	6	22	1	2	1	9	.256	119	18	2	.986
1970	New York	Amer.	C	132	453	59	137	25	4	6	53	.302	631	80	8	.989
1971	New York	Amer.	C-OF	125	451	71	113	15	4	10	42	.251	547	67	1	.998
1972	New York	Amer.	C	140	511	54	143	16	3	7	46	.280	575	71	15	.977
1973	New York	Amer.	C	147	519	80	156	29	4	20	74	.301	673	80	12	.984
1974	New York	Amer.	C	144	517	64	135	19	2	13	60	.261	743	75	22	.974
1975	New York	Amer.	C-1-O-3	157	597	83	190	24	3	12	102	.318	725	95	23	.973
1976	New York	Amer.	C-OF	152	616	79	186	27	1	17	105	.302	546	78	14	.978
1977	New York	Amer.	C	149	595	85	183	28	5	18	100	.308	657	73	12	.984
1978	New York	Amer.	C-OF	154	617	73	183	27	1	6	71	.297	698	61	11	.986
Major League Totals				1326	4962	654	1448	211	29	110	662	.292	5914	698	120	.982

ALL-STAR GAME RECORD

Year	League	Pos.	AB.	R.	H.	2B.	3B.	HR.	RBI.	B.A.	PO.	A.	E.	F.A.
1971	American	C	0	0	0	0	0	0	0	.000	1	0	0	1.000
1973	American	C	2	0	0	0	0	0	0	.000	5	1	0	1.000
1974	American	C	3	1	1	1	0	0	0	.333	7	0	1	.875
1975	American	C	2	0	1	0	0	0	0	.500	1	1	0	1.000
1976	American	C	2	0	0	0	0	0	0	.000	4	0	0	1.000
1977	American	PH	1	0	0	0	0	0	0	.000	0	0	0	.000
All-Star Game Totals			10	1	2	1	0	0	0	.200	18	2	1	.952

Named to American League All-Star Team for 1978 game; replaced due to injury by Darrell Porter.

CHAMPIONSHIP SERIES RECORD

Estabished Championship Series record for most one-base hits, five-game Series (8), 1976.
Tied Championship Series record for most at bats, five-game Series (23), 1976.
Tied American League Championship Series record for most at bats, four-game Series, (18), 1978.

Year	Club	League	Pos.	G.	AB.	R.	H.	2B.	3B.	HR.	RBI.	B.A.	PO.	A.	E.	F.A.
1976	New York	Amer.	C	5	23	3	10	2	0	0	3	.435	18	6	2	.923
1977	New York	Amer.	C	5	21	3	6	1	0	1	5	.286	24	4	0	1.000
1978	New York	Amer.	C	4	18	2	5	1	0	1	2	.278	22	4	0	1.000
Championship Series Totals				14	62	8	21	4	0	2	10	.339	64	14	2	.975

WORLD SERIES RECORD

Established World Series records for most singles. Series (9), 1976; most assists by catcher, four-game Series (7), 1976; most players caught stealing, four-game Series (5), 1976; most consecutive hits, two consecutive Series (7), 1976-77.
Tied World Series records for most hits, two consecutive games, one Series (7), October 19 and 21, 1976; most consecutive hits, one Series (6), 1976; most hits, game (4), October 21, 1976; most singles, game (4), October 21, 1976; one or more hits, each game, four-game Series, 1976; one or more hits, each game, six-game Series, 1977.

Year	Club	League	Pos.	G.	AB.	R.	H.	2B.	3B.	HR.	RBI.	B.A.	PO.	A.	E.	F.A.
1976	New York	Amer.	C	4	17	2	9	0	0	0	2	.529	21	7	0	1.000
1977	New York	Amer.	C	6	25	4	8	2	0	1	3	.320	40	5	0	1.000
1978	New York	Amer.	C	6	25	5	8	3	0	0	7	.320	33	5	0	1.000
World Series Totals				16	67	11	25	5	0	1	12	.373	94	17	0	1.000

Thurman Munson in the Yankee dugout on July 14, 1979 not long before his death.

<<< miracle people weren't injured during that time of the rush hour."

Mr. Evans said Mr. Hall was in the co-pilot seat, but "Munson had the plane to himself."

"Both victims tried valiantly to get Munson out," Mr. Evans added. He said the two men had about 30 seconds to try to free the Yankee star before the plane "went up in flames." One victim kicked out the emergency door while the other tried to pull Mr. Munson free. They succeeded in removing him from the pilot's seat, investigators said. However, Mr. Evans said that when the door opened "fuel, which was stored in the wing, ignited and engulfed the plane."

The two men tried to free Mr. Munson again, Mr. Evans said, "but the fire got so bad they had to get out. I think some of their clothes were on fire."

Carl Santelli, a friend of Munson's in Canton, said the Yankee star had come in from Chicago at 3 A.M. yesterday. "He said his plane wasn't acting right," said Mr. Santelli, "and he was going out to find out what was wrong with it."

A Cessna spokesman said the plane, which was lettered NY15, corresponding to its owner's Yankee jersey number, was the first Citation in the country to be involved in an accident.

Neal Callahan of the F.A.A.'s Chicago office said the plane "had been engaged in some touch-and-go practice takeoffs and landings" when the crash occurred.

Munson, a native of Akron, often flew home during home stands and road trips to be with his family. A Yankee coach, Elston Howard, said Munson told him he was interested in running a commercial commuter airline and was studying for a special license.

The coach said Mr. Munson wanted to stay as close to his family as possible. "That's why he told me he was flying home on his own plane on off days. He just said, 'Ellie, I want to see my family.' That's what he told me."

Munson, who batted over .300 five times and played on three Yankee pennant winners and two world championship teams, was the first Yankee captain since Lou Gehrig.

In his autobiography, written in 1978, he had described his love of flying. "I have a new love to make things somewhat more pleasant for me this year—airplanes. I studied for my pilot's license and received it during the winter. Now…it's possible to fly from New York to Canton in about an hour and I frequently go home even during home stands."

The police were at his home in Canton, where Mr. Munson's wife, Diane, and the couple's three children, Tracy Lynn, 9; Kelly, 7, and Michael, 4, received news of the crash.

News of the death shocked the baseball world.

The Yankees' principal owner, George Steinbrenner, said in a statement: "There's very little I could say to adequately express my feelings at this moment. I've lost a dear friend, a pal and one of the greatest competitors I've ever known. We spent many hours together talking baseball, and business. He loved his family. He was our leader. The great sport that made him so famous seems so very small and unimportant now."

Billy Martin, the Yankee manager, said: "For those who never knew him and didn't like him, I feel sorry for them. He was a great man, for his family, friends and all the people who knew and loved him, my deepest sympathy. We not only lost a great competitor, but a leader and a husband and devoted family man. He was a close friend, I loved him." ◆

August 6, 1979

The Yankees' Nightmare Season

By DAVE ANDERSON

IN SPORTS, a year is not 12 months, 52 weeks or 365 days. In sports, a year is something a team or an athlete has. In baseball last year the Yankees had a good year, a remarkable year. This year the Baltimore Orioles are having a good year, so far. Back in 1972 the Miami Dolphins were unbeaten going into the Super Bowl game. They won it, so they had a historic year. Had they lost it, they would have had a disappointing year. A team never knows if it has had a good year until the end.

But a bad year is different; a bad year establishes itself early. The Yankees are having a bad year, a nightmare year. Just when they think it can't be any worse, it is.

This is the year the Yankees will never forget. This is the year in which they never made a move toward first place, and now it's too late. But what has already chiseled it into their minds is that this is the year that Thurman Munson died. They will remember his funeral, today in Canton, Ohio, for the rest of their lives.

Whenever they hear somebody mention 1979, all these Yankees will shudder inside and remember the year when Thurman Munson was killed in the crash of his twin-engine jet near the Akron-Canton Regional Airport.

But it was a bad year for the Yankees even before the tragedy. They dropped out of the race in the American League East, never to return, when Rich Gossage missed 12 weeks because of thumb surgery after a clubhouse fight. During that time Bob Lemon was dismissed as manager and Billy Martin was rehired. Mickey Rivers was traded to the Texas Rangers, joining Sparky Lyle in exile there. And there were other injuries—Reggie Jackson's ailing leg kept him out a month, Ed Figueroa is scheduled for arm surgery this week, Rivers had a shoulder separation and Munson was troubled by ailing knees, to name only four. ⟫⟫⟫

««   For the Yankees, their year is over even if their season is not.

Nobody on the Yankees will say the year is over. And nobody should. Anything can happen. But in a sense, anything has already happened. The look on all the Yankees' faces is enough for anybody to know that the year is over. The year ended when they heard that Thurman Munson was dead.

Perhaps more than on anybody else, the look is on Billy Martin's face. It's almost as if a makeup man smudged rouge around the manager's eyes.

"I started crying as soon as I heard, and I cried for hours," he was saying now in his office off the Yankee clubhouse. "I called his wife, and we both started crying. And she told me, 'We lost our friend, Billy, we lost our friend.' Thurman always used to come in to tell me whatever problems he had. His legs were really bothering him this year."

Shaking his head, Billy Martin reached into the wide drawer of his desk and pulled out a snapshot.

"My new granddaughter," he said. "Evie Marie, isn't she beautiful. Somebody dies. Somebody's born."

The manager slid the snapshot into one side of the double frame atop the table behind his desk. In the other side was a large photo of his son, Billy Joe, now 17 years old.

"Thurman used to tell me, 'Isn't it great, Billy, your son looks like you, he walks like you. My son's the same way. He's even got pudgy arms like me. Isn't that a great thrill?'"

The manager puffed on his Sherlock Holmes pipe and shook his head again.

"That damn plane," he said. "At the All-Star break Thurman dropped me off in Kansas City when he flew home from California, and he had problems with the plane on that flight. Up in the air I saw a big flame shoot out of one engine, and I didn't say anything right away because I didn't want to scare his wife. But when we landed, he had to leave the inner part of the engine there to be fixed. And before, when he flew down from Seattle to Anaheim with Nettles and Jackson, he lost the pressure in the cabin. The oxygen masks dropped down. And the altimeter was off. That plane never was right."

Yankees observe a moment of silence commemorating the memory Thurman Munson on August 3, 1979.

Outside, near the door to the trainer's room, the late Thurman Munson's locker resembled a shrine. His pinstripe uniform shirt was on a hanger with the "NY" facing out. His pinstripe pants hung from a hook, like a flag at half-staff. His Yankee cap was perched on the top shelf. And across from his shirt, his catcher's mask was on another hook.

One of the Yankee Stadium security men handed Reggie Jackson a small package that a fan had asked to be delivered to the slugger. Inside was a small ebony cross on a silver chain.

"That's pretty," he said, slipping it over his head. "Somebody knows I'm a Christian."

Then he looked up and resumed talking about the year the Yankees never were in the race.

"The only nightmare is Thurman, the rest is nothing, man," he said. "And someday I'll do something for Thurman, something special for his son. I just hope I get the meaning that God's trying to tell me through this. He'll tell me, too. It takes a big person and a big tragedy for us to feel what God's trying to tell us. But if you walk with God, you'll get through anything. Look at all the messes I've been in, but I always got through 'em."

One of his messes involved his relationship with Munson, who understandably resented the contention by Jackson, shortly after his arrival in 1977, that "I'm the straw that stirs the drink… Munson can only stir it bad." But according to the Yankees' cleanup hitter, time healed that wound.

"We talked about it over a beer a few times," he said. "We got it settled. And hitting in front and behind each other, hitting when it counted, we grew to respect each other."

Bobby Murcer, who returned to the Yankees in late June from the Chicago Cubs, was the Yankees' center fielder when Thurman Munson arrived as a rookie in 1969.

"We were close ever since," Murcer was saying now. "I put him on his jet Wednesday night after the game in Chicago, when he flew back to Canton to spend Thursday with his family. He loved that plane. He was just delighted to be able to fly.

That's all he wanted to do. Every chance he had, he wanted to fly. He wanted my family and me to fly home with him that night and spend Thursday with him, but I had some things I had to do in Chicago where I still have my apartment."

"If you had gone to Canton with him," Murcer was asked, "would you have been up with him in his plane Thursday?"

"No doubt about it," Murcer said, not looking up as he put on his pinstripe uniform. "No doubt about it."

Rich (Goose) Gossage has the look of a guilty man. He knows that if he had been able to pitch, the Yankees probably would be in the race now. But for 12 weeks he was unable to pitch because of that foolish fight with Cliff Johnson, and now the Yankees are out of the race.

"You always want to think positive," he said. "But it seems like not only me, but everybody has had that kind of year when nothing goes right. All year it hasn't mattered how hard you try, nothing seems to work. And now Thurman's death—God, why?"

The husky relief pitcher remembered how his father, once a coal miner in Colorado, had died of emphysema.

"I was a junior in high school, 16 or 17, and I remember thinking I can't see him anymore. And as much as I felt my father's death, at least he had lived his life, a tough life, but he had lived it. Thurman hadn't. It didn't really hit me until I walked into the clubhouse here before Friday night's game and I realized I'd never see him again. It's not quite like losing anybody in your family, but it's the next closest thing. You live with these guys, you travel with these guys. It's almost like a family, and Thurman was like a brother to all of us."

He glanced back at a snapshot of his 14-month-old son, Jeff, that was on his locker wall.

"I owe him more than I realized," he said. "You bring kids into the world, you owe them everything. And you owe your wife everything. And concentrating on baseball, or whatever your job is, you lose a little perspective about ⟫⟫⟫

≪≪ what other things around you are like. And after what's happened to Thurman, we've got a long road ahead of us."

From his royal box high behind home plate, George Steinbrenner, the Yankees' principal owner, thought about the year.

"Three things," he finally said. "One, I was not happy in spring training. I didn't think Bob Lemon had the players running hard enough. And when I asked him about it, he asked me, 'How do you make these guys work?' I told him, 'You're the boss, that's how.' It's not anything against Lem, but I think that lack of conditioning contributed to some of our injuries. Not the Gossage injury, of course, and that's the one that ruined us.

"Two, I don't like to use injuries as an excuse. But if any team ever had a right to claim injuries as a reason for their problems, it's this team.

"Three, the loss of Thurman, because now we don't have our leader. Mel Allen came over to see me the other day and told me that when we made Thurman captain he and a lot of other people couldn't understand why, but now he understands why. And now that he's dead, people are recognizing what a great leader Thurman was."

Last year Ron Guidry had a 25-3 won-lost record with a 1.74 earned-run average. This year he has a 9-7 record with a 2.55 earned-run average, and he will start against the Baltimore Orioles tonight after the Yankees return from Thurman Munson's funeral.

August 7, 1979

Hundreds at Funeral Of Yankees' Munson

Special to The New York Times

CANTON, OHIO, AUG. 6—More than 500 people, including all Yankee team members and many of their wives, attended Thurman Munson's funeral today in the Canton Civic Center. About 1,000 other people waited outside to pay their last respects, and hundreds more lined the five-mile route to the Sunset Hills Cemetery, where Munson was buried.

The funeral procession to the cemetery was escorted by a dozen motorcycle policemen from the Canton City Police Department and the Stark County Sheriff's office.

The 32-year-old Yankee catcher died last Thursday when his private twin-engine jet crashed short of a runway at the Akron-Canton Airport. Munson was a resident of Canton.

At the funeral service, the start of which was delayed by 30 minutes to await the arrival of the charter plane carrying the Yankees from New York, Munson was eulogized as a caring family man, a

great competitor and a man who loved the Yankees.

Immediately after the funeral, the Yankees returned to New York for their scheduled game against the Baltimore Orioles. About a dozen of the players' wives remained to visit with Munson's wife, Diana, and their three children: Tracy, 9, Kelly, 7, and Mike, 4.

The Rev. J. Robert Coleman, pastor of St. Paul's Roman Catholic Church in Canton, who married the Munsons almost 11 years ago, delivered a 20-minute eulogy. Father Coleman also announced that a day-care center had been named for Munson.

'SOMEBODY SPECIAL'

"Everyone has a Munson story to tell because he was somebody special," Father Coleman said in his eulogy. "He was not your ordinary next-door neighbor, 9-to-5 executive; not your ordinary pilot; not your ordinary playing buddy; not your ordinary ballplayer. He was a man who used his

"Strange, that's what this season has been, strange," he was saying. "And all you can say is that what happened to Thurman is the worst thing that's happened so far."

The implication was that the 28-year-old left-hander was wondering what's next for the Yankees this season, wondering what else will befall them in the eight weeks that remain.

"As for myself," he said, "when the season started I was the first one to say that I would not have the record I had last year. I knew that. I knew it wouldn't happen like that again, everything going for me. My stats aren't that far off from last season, but it's not the same. I've been making some great pitches, and guys are hitting them. And when I make a bad pitch, I get punished for it. Last year the outfield would play a hitter one way and somebody would make a good catch. This year they move two steps on a guy and he hits it just over somebody's head."

Back in his office, Billy Martin was still puffing on his Sherlock Holmes pipe.

"That eight-minute ovation for Thurman on Friday night," somebody said. "How rough was it to be down there during that?"

"Rough," the manager replied quietly.

"Were you surprised the fans did that?"

"No, and none of the ballplayers backed off either. I'm going to have 'em stand on the top step of the dugout like that for the national anthem the rest of the season."

The manager puffed on his pipe again. "The funeral is going to be rough, too," he said. ◆

---

time well and, as his wife, Diana, has told me, he spent quality time with her and the children.

"He was very interested in youth, and he liked my inner-city program," Father Coleman went on. "Thurman Munson was a very real person who knew what he really wanted and worked hard to achieve success. He was hard to get to know but yet made real friends. He did what others only dream of doing, because he was not one to sit back and hot-dog at the first stage of activity. You knew where you stood with Thurman Munson, and some people can't take reality. Thurman could. He knew what he wanted, and he worked hard to achieve it. He was hard to get to know, but once you did, he was a great friend."

Lou Piniella, the Yankee outfielder and perhaps Munson's closest friend in baseball, read with a choked voice from Ecclesiastes.

MURCER QUOTES PATRI

Bobby Murcer, another teammate, who was with the Yankees in 1969 when Munson broke in, chose the words of Angelo Patri, a poet and philosopher, to introduce his personal thoughts.

"'The life of a soul on earth lasts longer than his departure,'" said Murcer. "'He lives on in your life and the life of all others who knew him. He lived, he led and he loved.'

"Whatever he was to each one of us, he should be remembered a man who followed the basic principles of life; he lived with his wife, Diana, and his three children; he led his team to two world championships and he loved the game, his friends and, most of all, his family."

Murcer added: "He was No. 15 on the field and he will be No. 15 at the doors of Cooperstown. Loving, living and legend. History will court my friend as No. 1."

More than 200 floral arrangements adorned the McKinley Room, where the service was held, including one in the shape of a Yankee insignia. The flower-bedecked coffin stood under a gold-framed portrait of Munson in his Yankee uniform.

Besides Bowie Kuhn, the commissioner of baseball, the funeral services were attended by many of Munson's friends in baseball, including Joe Torre, manager of the Mets, and many baseball executives, including Lee MacPhail, president of the American League, and Gabe Paul, president of the Cleveland Indians. ◆

August 7, 1979

Murcer Drives In 5 As Yanks Win, 5-4

By MURRAY CHASS

COMPLETING A GRUELING, emotion-racked four days, the Yankees returned somberly from Thurman Munson's funeral in Ohio and rallied last night at Yankee Stadium for a 5-4 victory over the Baltimore Orioles. Bobby Murcer, one of two Yankee players who eulogized Munson, drove in all five runs.

Murcer lashed a three-run home run off Dennis Martinez in the seventh inning and rapped a two-run single off Tippy Martinez in the ninth, enabling the Yankees to overcome a 4-0 lead the Orioles had built against Ron Guidry.

"The first time I got to the mound and I looked around," said Guidry, who gained his 10th victory, "there was something missing."

The Yankees left Newark Airport yesterday morning at about 8 o'clock and returned from Canton at about 2 o'clock. The players felt the same way they did Friday night, their first game after Munson was killed in a plane crash Thursday, no one really wanted to play this game.

Murcer might not have felt like it, but he had a good reason for playing.

"I just know that that's what Thurman would've wanted," said the left fielder who had known Munson since they were youngsters in the Yankee organization in the late '60s. "If he was sitting here and I said I couldn't play, he'd say, 'You're crazy.' I just know that's what he

October 29, 1979

Yanks Oust Martin, Hire Howser

By MURRAY CHASS

BILLY MARTIN, a tempestuous figure in his 11 years as a major league baseball player and 10 as a manager, was replaced by Dick Howser last night as the Yankee manager. It was the second time in 15 months that Martin had lost the job.

The 42-year-old Howser, who reportedly had an opportunity to become manager during one of Martin's several shaky periods in his first Yankee tenure, received a multiyear contract. Howser, a former player for three teams, including the Yankees, was the Yankee third-base coach for 10 years, then left after the 1978 season to become coach at Florida State University.

As a Yankee coach, he managed in one game in the 1978 season, when Martin resigned after an outburst in which he called George Steinbrenner, the Yankee principal owner, a liar.

Steinbrenner declined to discuss the situation last night.

"I have nothing more to say," he commented by telephone from his home in Tampa, Fla., after the club had announced only that Martin, 51, "will not be returning as manager of the Yankees."

His dismissal came five days after he had been involved in an incident with a 52-year-old salesman in a hotel in Bloomington, Minn. Martin was alleged to have hit the man, Joseph W. Cooper of Lincolnshire, Ill., causing a badly cut lip that required 20 stitches. But Martin denied the charge, saying, "He fell and cut his lip."

Steinbrenner, however, was skeptical of Martin's explanation, and a source close to the owner had said that Martin could be dismissed if it turned out he had lied about the incident.

No one was saying that Steinbrenner concluded Martin had lied, but the source said last night, "Obviously, Billy must have hit the guy."

Another source, who was familiar with the incident, gave the following details:

Mr. Cooper followed Martin out of the bar of the Chez Colette restaurant at L'Hotel de France in Bloomington last Tuesday around midnight. As they reached the lobby, Mr. Cooper pushed

would've wanted me to do."

When Murcer stepped to the plate in the seventh inning with runners at second and third and two out, the Orioles already had scored four runs on Lee May's homer and double and Ken Singleton's two-run homer.

"How do you describe how you feel," Murcer said of the homer. "It's the first two-out base hit I've had with men in scoring position in I don't know how long. I don't think I've had one since I've been here."

When Murcer came to bat in the ninth, the same runners were in the same positions, second and third, but there were no outs. Bucky Dent had led off with a walk and raced to third when Tippy Martinez fielded Willie Randolph's bunt and fired it past first base into right field.

Martinez, who had been virtually unhittable in recent relief appearances, got two strikes on Murcer but then threw a fastball closer to the plate than he wanted and Murcer punched it to left field for a single that brought home both runners. An ecstatic Murcer was not too tired to leap into the air after he reached first base.

"Everybody was so tired," he said minutes later, "I think we were playing on the spirit of Thurman. I think that's what carried us through the game. I know it did me."

For most of the Yankees, the day began at about 5 A.M., when they awoke to get the flight to Canton. Bobby and Kay Murcer, and Lou and Anita Piniella flew there Sunday night to be with Diana Munson.

"We were going to leave so she could get some sleep," Murcer said, "but she wouldn't let us leave. She wanted us to stay. So we sat up all night and talked about old times." ◆

Billy Martin kicks dirt on rookie umpire Dallas Parks on August 16, 1979.

Martin from behind. When the manager turned around, Mr. Cooper swung at him and missed. Martin then hit him, knocking him down.

Neither Martin nor any of his advisers could be reached last night to comment on his dismissal or the fight.

It is the fifth time Martin has lost a managerial job. He was ousted after one season in Minnesota, after nearly three seasons in Detroit and after one and a half in Texas. He was just nine days short of completing three years as manager of the Yankees—the job he had said he wanted more than anything else—when he tearfully resigned in Kansas City on July 24, 1978.

In previous months, Steinbrenner had stressed the need for Martin to change if he were to return as manager. He especially said Martin would have to be exonerated in an altercation he had with Ray Hagar, a Nevada sportswriter, last November during an interview at a bar in Reno.

Martin was charged with one count of battery, and Mr. Hagar also filed a civil suit. However, both actions were dropped when Martin apologized publicly to Mr. Hagar last May, and paid him $8,000 in settlement. ◆

January 30, 1982

Yanks Name Nettles Captain

By JOSEPH DURSO

GRAIG NETTLES was named captain of the Yankees yesterday, the sixth in the team's history and the first since his friend Thurman Munson was killed in an airplane crash in August 1979.

"I have no idea what a captain does," Nettles said.

"But it's a great honor, and I hope I can uphold the tradition. Maybe I can help as a liaison between players with problems and the manager or front office."

Nettles, the senior Yankee in terms of service, is 37 years old and entering his 10th season as the team's third baseman. He is the third captain in the last 47 years. Lou Gehrig held the title from 1935 until his death in 1941, and Munson held it from 1976.

The Yankees had long believed that those two were the only captains in the team's history. But they said that recent research discovered that the title was held by Roger Peckinpaugh from 1914 to 1921; Babe Ruth for six days in 1922 until he was suspended for fighting with a fan, and Everett Scott from then until 1925. ◆

November 22, 1980

SPORTS OF THE TIMES
The Food on a Table At the Execution

By DAVE ANDERSON

NEAR THE DOOR of George Steinbrenner's office in Yankee Stadium yesterday, there were two trays of bite-sized roast beef, turkey and ham sandwiches, each with a toothpick in it. As soon as 14 invited newsmen entered his office for the execution of Dick Howser as manager and the transfer of Gene Michael from general manager to dugout manager, Steinbrenner, the Yankees' principal owner, looked around.

"Anybody want any sandwiches?" he asked. "We've got a lot of sandwiches here."

Gene Michael had piled four little roast beef sandwiches on a small plastic plate and he had a cup of coffee. But as he sat against the far wall, under a huge Yankee top-hat insignia and several enlarged photos of memorable Yankee Stadium moments, he was the only one eating when Dick Howser suddenly appeared and walked quickly to a chair in front of the table with the sandwiches.

"Nobody wants a sandwich?" George Steinbrenner asked. "Nobody wants a drink?"

One of the newsmen ordered a glass of white wine from the bartender, but that was all. Then there was a momentary silence as George Steinbrenner, husky in a soft-blue shirt with a navy blue and green striped tie, sat at a big tan vinyl chair behind his shiny round desk. On the desk was a gold numeral one, maybe several inches high, and a small sign announcing, "Lead, Follow or Get the Hell Out of the Way," and a miniature brass ship's telegraph.

"During the season it's always pointed to full speed ahead," he would explain later. "But in the off-season it's on standby."

To the owner's right, about 10 feet away, Dick Howser sat stiffly. His legs crossed, he was wearing a beige shirt, a brown tie, brown pants and brown cowboy boots. He was staring out away from George Steinbrenner, staring blankly at the white draperies that had been drawn across the huge window that overlooks the grassy geometry of the ball field where Dick Howser no longer would work. Most of the time he had his left index finger up against his left cheek, as if to keep from having to look at the Yankee owner who now was discussing the managerial situation that had been simmering for several weeks.

"Dick has decided," George Steinbrenner began, "that he will not be returning to the Yankees next year. I should say, not returning to the Yankees as manager."

Dick has decided. That would be the premise of George Steinbrenner's explanation. Dick has decided. Ostensibly he suddenly decided to go into real estate development in Tallahassee, Fla., and be the supervisor of Yankee scouts in the Southeast after having been the manager for the Yankee team that won 103 games last season, after having been in baseball virtually all his life as a major league infielder, major league coach, college coach and major league manager of baseball's most famous franchise.

But baseball's most famous franchise also has baseball's most demanding owner. When the Yankees were swept in three games by the Kansas City Royals in the American League championship series, George Steinbrenner steamed. And now Dick Howser is in real estate and is a Yankee scouting supervisor.

"At no time," George Steinbrenner said yesterday, "did I lay down rules or commandments that Dick would have to live by if he returned as manager. The door was open for him to return, but he chose to accept this business opportunity. It took so long because he wanted to make sure he was doing the right thing." »»

George Steinbrenner with Gene Michael (left) and manager Dick Howser.

««   All the while Dick Howser stared at the drawn draperies.

"But could Dick," somebody asked George Steinbrenner, "still be the manager if he wanted to be?"

"Yes."

"Dick, why don't you want to be?"

"I have to be cautious here," Dick Howser said staring straight ahead. "But the other thing popped up."

"Were you satisfied that you could have returned without conditions?"

"I'd rather not comment on that," Dick Howser said.

"If you had won the World Series instead of being eliminated in the playoffs," he was asked, "would you have taken this real estate opportunity?"

"That's hard to say."

"Were you fired, Dick?"

"I'm not going to comment on that," the former manager said.

"I didn't fire the man," the owner said.

Maybe not, but it is reasonable to believe that George Steinbrenner suggested that Dick Howser look for employment elsewhere. That way George Steinbrenner could put Gene Michael, whom he considers a more combative manager, in the dugout. Perhaps to soothe his conscience, he disclosed yesterday that Dick Howser would be paid his reported $100,000 salary for each of the remaining two years on this three-year contract.

"I feel morally and contractually obligated to Dick and his wife, Nancy," the owner said. "I took

---

January 27, 1981

WINFIELD AND YANKS REACH AGREEMENT

By MURRAY CHASS

Six weeks after they signed their first contract, George Steinbrenner and Dave Winfield agreed yesterday on an amended one. In one meeting and one telephone conversation, the Yankees' principal owner and his richest-ever free agent worked out a new cost-of-living provision to replace the one from the Dec. 15 contract that could have been worth $23.3 million over 10 years.

"We've reached a final agreement," Steinbrenner said, "but it won't be submitted until the final papers are typed up." Neither Steinbrenner nor Al Frohman, Winfield's agent, would say what method of cost-of-living payment replaced the original one, which would have paid the star outfielder an annual maximum 10 percent cost-of-living raise added cumulatively to his salary.

However, Frohman said the difference in the value of the contract to Winfield would not "run

into the multimillions. It won't run into $8 million or $4 million."

Frohman and Winfield met with Steinbrenner at Yankee Stadium yesterday to discuss the substitute clause. The financial impact of the original clause had eluded Steinbrenner, it was reported, until he read an account of it in The New York Times.

"I'm not embarrassed in the least," the owner said. "It was a matter of a misunderstanding. It's not a foulup on my part, but I take the heat on anything. But we just negotiated it like good partners for the future do."

After their meeting yesterday, Frohman said Steinbrenner had left it up to Winfield and the agent to select the way in which the cost-of-living formula would be altered. Under the cumulative 10 percent formula, Winfield's salary could have soared from $1.4 million in the first year to $3.3 million in the 10th.

Agreeing to a new provision that would bring him less money was not something Winfield had to do. When Steinbrenner discovered what could have been a $7 million oversight, Winfield decided he would accept something less to keep peace for the next 10 years. ◆

him out of Florida State, where he was the base-ball coach and where he could have stayed for life. If it hasn't worked out, maybe it's my fault."

If it hasn't worked out. Until then it had been, "Dick has decided." But perhaps on a slip of the tongue it was, "if it hasn't worked out". Anybody who knew George Steinbrenner knew that all along. And anybody who knew Dick Howser knew that, if given a choice, he would not decide to go into real estate development rather than be the Yankees' manager.

But still George Steinbrenner persisted.

"I think it's safe to say," he said at one point yesterday, "that Dick Howser wants to be a Flor-ida resident year-round, right, Dick?"

Dick Howser didn't even answer that one.

Say this for Dick Howser—instead of going along with George Steinbrenner's party line yesterday, he declined to comment. By not an-swering questions, he answered them. Anybody could see that. And anybody could see through George Steinbrenner's scheme.

"What advice," Dick Howser was being asked now, "would you give Gene Michael?"

"To have a strong stomach," Dick Howser re-plied, smiling thinly, "and a nice contract."

Minutes later, the execution was over. Dick Howser got up quickly and walked out of the room without a smile. Behind his round desk, George Steinbrenner looked around.

"Nobody ate any sandwiches," the Yankee owner said. ◆

October 29, 1981

STEINBRENNER ISSUES AN APOLOGY TO FANS

By JANE GROSS

WHILE THREE SECURITY MEN guarded the glass doors to the Yankees' executives offices, George Steinbrenner remained inside last night drafting a formal apology to the New York fans.

"I want to sincerely apologize to the people of New York and to the fans of the New York Yankees everywhere for the performance of the Yankee team in the World Series," the owner wrote. "I also want to assure you that we will be at work immediately to prepare for 1982. I want also to extend my congratulations to Peter O'Malley and the Dodger organization—a fine team that didn't give up—and to my friend, Tom Lasorda, who managed a superb season, playoffs and a brilliant World Series."

While the statement was being typed and cop-ies made, and while the Dodgers embraced on the field below, Steinbrenner and his security men pushed their way into a crowded elevator heading for the clubhouses. "First I'll talk to our own guys and then congratulate the Dodgers," Steinbrenner said, revealing none of the anger that seemed to lurk in the words of his prepared statement.

"Oh, sure it was disappointing, sure it was," the owner said as the elevator moved toward the base-ment. "It's always tough to lose, but 24 teams are home watching TV. I said it in '76 and I'll say it again—we're the second best team in baseball."

"I expected more from some people but what can you do?" Steinbrenner continued. "I don't have to knock them when they're down. What good does it do to be critical at this point? They answered their own questions. We'll make the necessary changes to see it doesn't happen again."

The guards led Steinbrenner into a side entrance to the home team's clubhouse where he worked his way around the room, stopping at each locker for a few calm, often kind, words. "I just want to get to everybody," Steinbrenner said, as the guards struggled to keep up with their hustling boss.

At Willie Randolph's locker, Steinbrenner em-braced the second baseman wordlessly. >>>

When he reached Andre Robertson, a rookie promoted in the final weeks of the season, he said, "Andre, remember what this feels like." In the shower area, Steinbrenner stopped beside Jerry Mumphrey and spoke quietly to the center-fielder, who was benched for three games of the World Series.

Steinbrenner looked for Reggie Jackson, who is in the last year of his contract and who has talked of playing elsewhere next year, but the rightfielder—0-for-4 last night—was surrounded by reporters. After a stop in Manager Bob Lemon's office, Steinbrenner and his guards moved on to the Dodger clubhouse where the World Series trophy had just been presented.

Steinbrenner's post-game visits to the Yankee and Dodger clubhouses were his first public appearances of the evening. During earlier playoff and World Series games, Steinbrenner had watched from a control booth on the loge level of the stadium, where his every gesture and grimace were visible to reporters and television viewers. Last night, with his left hand still in a cast, Steinbrenner watched the game on television from one of the private offices.

Behind drawn curtains, Steinbrenner was watching the final moments of the loss and near the elevators the guards were preparing for what they feared would be his stormy exit. "He's in there writing a speech," one of them said to the waiting reporters. "He told us to keep this area clear. We have orders before the game, during the game, after the game. Do you think I like this post?"

The glass door opened. Steinbrenner was smiling politely. "It wouldn't do much good to say anything now," he said. "Not now." ◆

Yogi Berra, Who Built His Stardom 90 Percent on Skill and Half on Wit, Dies at 90

By BRUCE WEBER

YOGI BERRA, one of baseball's greatest catchers and characters, who as a player was a mainstay of 10 Yankees championship teams and as a manager led both the Yankees and the Mets to the World Series—but who may be more widely known as an ungainly but lovable cultural figure, issuing a seemingly limitless supply of unwittingly witty epigrams known as Yogi-isms—died on Tuesday. He was 90.

Berra lived for many years in Montclair, N.J., before moving in 2012 to an assisted-living facility in nearby West Caldwell, where he died.

Beloved Yankees catcher Yogi Berra at Yankee Stadium in 1956.

In 1949, early in Berra's Yankee career, his manager, Casey Stengel, said, "Mr. Berra is a very strange fellow of very remarkable abilities."

And so he was. Universally known simply as Yogi, Berra was not exactly an unlikely hero, but he was often portrayed as one: an All-Star for 15 consecutive seasons whose skills were routinely underestimated; a well-built, appealingly open-faced man whose physical appearance was often belittled; and a prolific winner and a successful leader, whose intellect was a target of humor if not outright derision.

That he triumphed on the diamond was certainly a source of his popularity. So was the delight with which his famous, if not always documentable, pronouncements—somehow both nonsensical and sagacious—were received.

"You can observe a lot just by watching," he is reputed to have said about his strategy as a manager.

"If you can't imitate him," he advised a young player who was mimicking the batting stance of a great slugger, "don't copy him."

"When you come to a fork in the road, take it," he said, giving directions to his house. Either path, it turned out, got you there.

"Nobody goes there anymore," he said of a popular restaurant. "It's too crowded."

Whether Berra actually uttered those things, or phrased them precisely the way they were reported, is a matter of speculation. Berra himself published a book in 1998 called "The Yogi Book: I Really Didn't Say Everything I Said!"

The character Yogi Berra may even have overshadowed the Hall of Fame ballplayer Yogi Berra, obscuring what a remarkable athlete he was. He was fearsome in the clutch and the most durable and productive Yankee during the team's most successful era.

Stengel compared Berra favorably to star catchers of previous eras like Mickey Cochrane, Gabby Hartnett and Bill Dickey. "You could look it up," was Stengel's catch phrase, and indeed the record book declares that Berra was among the game's greatest catchers, if not the greatest.

Berra's career batting average, .285, was not as high as that of his Yankees predecessor Dickey (.313), but Berra hit more home runs (358 in all) and drove in more runs (1,430). Berra led the American League in assists five times and from 1957 through 1959 went 148 consecutive games behind the plate without making an error, a major league record at the time.

On defense, he surpassed Mike Piazza, the best-hitting catcher of recent vintage. On offense, Berra and the great Johnny Bench of the Cincinnati Reds were comparable, except that Bench struck out three times as often. Berra whiffed a mere 414 times in more than 8,300 plate appearances over 19 seasons—an astonishingly small ratio for a power hitter.

Only Roy Campanella, who played for the Brooklyn Dodgers and faced Berra in the World Series six times before his career was ended by a car accident, equaled Berra's total of three Most Valuable Player Awards.

Berra's career was punctuated by storied episodes. In Game 3 of the 1947 World Series against the Dodgers, he hit the first pinch-hit home run in Series history, and in Game 4 he was behind the plate for what was almost the first no-hitter and was instead a stunning loss. With two outs in the ninth inning and two men on base after walks, the Yankees' starter, Bill Bevens, gave up a double to Cookie Lavagetto that cleared the bases and won the game.

In September 1951, with the Yankees once again on the brink of a no-hitter, this one by Allie Reynolds against the Boston Red Sox, Berra made one of baseball's famous errors. With two outs in the ninth inning, Ted Williams hit a towering foul ball between home plate and the Yankees' dugout. It looked like the end of the game, which would seal Reynolds's second no-hitter of the season. But the ball was caught in a gust of wind; Berra lunged backward, and the ball deflected off his glove. On the next pitch, Williams hit an almost identical pop-up. This time, Berra caught it, preserving Reynolds' no-hitter. »»»

《《《   In the first game of the 1955 World Series against the Dodgers, the Yankees were ahead, 6-4, in the top of the eighth when the Dodgers' Jackie Robinson stole home. The plate umpire called him safe, and Berra went berserk. The Yankees won the game although not the Series—it was the only time Brooklyn got the better of Berra's Yankees—but Berra never forgot. More than 50 years later, he signed a photograph of the play for President Obama, writing, "Dear Mr. President, He was out!"

During the 1956 Series, again against the Dodgers, Berra was at the center of another indelible image, when he leapt into the arms of Don Larsen, who had just struck out Dale Mitchell to end Game 5 and complete the only perfect game (and only no-hitter) in World Series history.

From 1946 to 1985, as a player, coach and manager, Berra appeared in 21 World Series. He starred on World Series winners in 1947, '49, '50, '51, '52, '53, '56 and '58. He was a backup catcher and part-time outfielder on the championship teams of 1961 and '62. He also played on World Series losers in 1955, '57, '60 and '63. He still holds Series records for games played, plate appearances, hits and doubles.

Lawrence Peter Berra was born on May 12, 1925, in the Italian enclave of St. Louis known as the Hill, which also fostered the baseball career of his boyhood friend Joe Garagiola. Berra was the fourth of five children. His father, Pietro, a construction worker and bricklayer, and his mother, Paulina, were Italian immigrants.

As a boy, Berra was known as Larry, or Lawdie, as his mother pronounced it. As recounted in "Yogi Berra: Eternal Yankee," a 2009 biography by Allen Barra, one day young Larry went with some friends to the movies and were watching a travelogue about India when a Hindu yogi appeared on the screen. His posture struck one of the friends as how Berra sat as he waited his turn at bat. From that day on, he was Yogi Berra.

Berra dropped out of school after the eighth grade. He played American Legion ball and worked odd jobs. As teenagers, he and Garagiola tried out for the St. Louis Cardinals and were offered contracts. But Garagiola's came with a $500 signing bonus and Berra's just $250, so Berra declined to sign.

The St. Louis Browns also wanted to sign Berra but were not willing to pay any bonus. Then, the day after the 1942 World Series, in which the Cardinals beat the Yankees, a Yankee coach offered Berra a minor league contract—along with the elusive $500.

Berra's professional baseball life began in Virginia in 1943 with the Norfolk Tars of the Class B Piedmont League, but World War II put his career on hold. Berra joined the Navy. He took part in the invasion of Normandy and, two months later, in an Allied assault on Marseilles in which he was bloodied by a bullet and earned a Purple Heart.

In 1946, after his discharge, he was assigned to the Newark Bears, then the Yankees' top farm team. He played outfield and catcher and hit .314 with 15 home runs and 59 R.B.I. in 77 games. That September, in his first big league game, he had two hits, including a home run.

Berra became a fan favorite, because of his superior play and because of his humility and guilelessness. In 1947, honored at Sportsman's Park in St. Louis, a nervous Berra said, "I want to thank everyone for making this night necessary."

Berra was a hit with sportswriters, too, although they often portrayed him as a baseball idiot savant. When writers kidded him about his girlfriend, Carmen Short, saying he was too unattractive to marry her, he reportedly responded, "I'm human, ain't I?"

Berra married Carmen in 1949, and the marriage endured until her death in 2014. He is survived by their three sons—Tim, who played professional football for the Baltimore Colts; Dale, a former infielder for the Yankees, the Pittsburgh Pirates and the Houston Astros; and Lawrence Jr.—as well as 11 grandchildren and a great-grandson.

As the earlier jousting over signing bonuses had demonstrated, Berra was a canny negotiator.

His salary as a player reached $65,000 in 1961, substantial for that era.

"He has continued to allow people to regard him as an amiable clown because it brings him quick acceptance, despite ample proof, on field and off, that he is intelligent, shrewd and opportunistic," Robert Lipsyte wrote in The New York Times in October 1963.

At the time, Berra had just concluded his career as a Yankees player, and the team had named him manager. The aging Yankees played listlessly through much of the summer of 1964. A squabble on the bus after a tough loss made it seem to some as if Berra had lost control. Although the Yankees won the pennant, Ralph Houk, the general manager, fired Berra after the team lost a seven-game World Series to St. Louis.

In a bizarre move, Houk replaced him with the Cardinals' manager, Johnny Keane. Keane's Yankees finished sixth in 1965. Berra, meanwhile, took a job as a coach for the Mets under Stengel. The team floundered until 1969, when the so-called Miracle Mets, with Gil Hodges as manager—and Berra coaching first base—won the World Series.

After Hodges died, before the start of the 1972 season, Berra replaced him. That summer, Berra was inducted into the Hall of Fame. But the Mets finished third in 1972. The following season, they were well under .500 and in sixth place when Berra supposedly uttered perhaps the most famous Yogi-ism of all.

"It ain't over till it's over," he said (or words to that effect).

Lo and behold, the Mets got hot and won the National League's Eastern Division title. They beat the Reds in the League Championship Series before losing to the Oakland Athletics in the World Series.

Berra was rewarded with a three-year contract, but the Mets finished fifth in 1974. The following August, with the team in third place, Berra was fired.

He returned to the Yankees as a coach, and in 1984 the owner, George Steinbrenner, named him to replace Billy Martin as manager. The team finished third that year, but during spring training Steinbrenner promised him that he would finish the 1985 season as manager. But after a 6-10 start, Steinbrenner fired Berra, bringing back Martin. Not only did Steinbrenner break his word, but he sent an underling to deliver the news.

For 14 years, Berra refused to set foot in Yankee Stadium. In January 1999, Steinbrenner tried to make amends, admitting that he should at least have had the decency to fire Berra face to face.

To welcome him back into the fold, the Yankees held a Yogi Berra Day on July 18, 1999. Don Larsen threw out the ceremonial first pitch, which Berra caught.

Incredibly, David Cone of the Yankees pitched a perfect game that day. It was, as Berra may or may not have said in another context, "déjà vu all over again." ◆

8 THE MATTINGLY YEARS

Slumps in baseball usually involve hitters or pitchers, not teams. Certainly not the Yankees—the proud Yankees, the majestic Yankees with their trays of World Series rings, their museum of Hall of Fame players and personalities. But for fourteen seasons following the loss of the 1981 World Series, the Yankees stayed in a serious slump.

They never won an East Division title. They were second four times, third twice, fourth twice, fifth four times, and a lowly seventh once. Maybe they would have finished first in 1994, but we'll never know. With a 70–43 record in Buck Showalter's third season as manager, they had a six-and-a-half-game lead when a labor dispute terminated the schedule on August 11. Commissioner Bud Selig later canceled the postseason play-offs and the World Series. The next year the Yankees made the play-offs before losing a taut five-game division series to the Seattle Mariners.

With the arrival of Joe Torre and Derek Jeter in 1996, the Yankees would be proud and majestic again, but over the fourteen seasons of the slump Don Mattingly and Dave Winfield were about all that Yankees fans had to cheer about.

Mattingly won the American League batting title in 1984 with a .343 average. He was voted Most Valuable Player in 1985, when he had 35 home runs, 145 RBI, and 211 hits. While earning 10 Gold Gloves at first base, the man known as "Donnie Baseball" had a .307 career average, but an ailing back gradually restricted his power and wrecked his Hall of Fame potential. Winfield, who had been drafted out of the University of Minnesota as a tight end by the Minnesota Vikings and as a power forward by both the Atlanta Hawks and the Utah Stars, had six seasons of at least 100 RBI and anywhere from 24 to 37 home runs before leaving to solidify his Cooperstown credentials with the Toronto Blue Jays in the 1992 World Series.

Two other future Hall of Famers, base-stealer Ricky Henderson and knuckleball right-hander Phil Niekro, appeared briefly in pinstripes during the slump. Another eventual Cooperstown resident, five-time American

★ ★ ★

Don Mattingly acknowledges the cheers of the crowd after receiving one of his many standing ovations at Yankee Stadium.

League batting champion Wade Boggs, arrived in 1993. But the slump is mostly remembered for the arrivals and departures of managers and general managers in George Steinbrenner's ever-revolving door.

During the slump, Steinbrenner had thirteen managers du jour, notably three hirings of Billy Martin, always available but always vulnerable. In order, the dugout managers were Bob Lemon (for the second time), Gene Michael, Clyde King, Martin (for the third time, after having served twice during the Bronx Zoo years), Yogi Berra, Martin (for the fourth time), Lou Piniella, Martin (for the fifth and last time), Piniella again, Dallas Green, Bucky Dent, Stump Merrill, and Buck Showalter. The nine general managers, in order, were Cedric Tallis, Murray Cook, Clyde King, Woody Woodward, Lou Piniella, Bob Quinn, Syd Thrift, Quinn again, Pete Peterson, and Gene Michael. Notice that Michael, Piniella, and King did both jobs at different times.

As absurd as many of those changes were, Steinbrenner branded himself as insensitive with the way he dismissed Yogi Berra as manager. Berra had guided the Yankees to a 51–29 finish and a respectable third place in 1984, leading Steinbrenner to declare in 1985 that "Yogi will be the manager all year"; but after a 6–10 start, he angrily phoned Clyde King, the general manager who was with the team in Chicago, and ordered King to tell Yogi he was fired.

Steinbrenner had not been man enough to tell Yogi himself. Understandably seething, Yogi announced he would no longer visit Yankee Stadium as long as Steinbrenner owned the franchise. Yogi had always been among the most popular Yankees, but now he was beloved. (He would boycott the stadium until 1998, when Steinbrenner eventually apologized, personally and with television cameras rolling). Yankees fans suffered another loss when Billy Martin, the popular but troubled five-time manager, was killed in a crash in 1989 while driving his pickup truck on an icy road in upstate New York on Christmas Day. Steinbrenner, meanwhile, made more news than his team. Although he was pardoned by President Ronald Reagan for his 1974 conviction, his attempt to discredit Winfield's foundation by dealing with gambler Howard Spira led to his 1990 ban from baseball by Commissioner Fay Vincent. But that three-year ban turned out to be a turnaround for the franchise. »»»

<<< In Gene Michael's return as general manager, who now could make a decision without having to worry that the principal owner might disagree, he traded for outfielder Paul O'Neill and left-hander Jimmy Key and supervised the free-agent signing of third baseman Wade Boggs. Unlike many of his predecessors, who had to comply with Steinbrenner's wishes, Michaels did not trade the best prospects in the farm system for quick-fix players on other teams. Bernie Williams would emerge in 1993 as a center fielder to remember. In 1994 O'Neill was leading the American League with a .359 average and Key was a 17-game winner when the labor dispute ended the season in August, and with it the Yankees' opportunity for a division title and beyond.

More important, during Michael's administration, the Yankees signed the young players who would develop into the "Core Four" of future World Series triumphs. Mariano Rivera, a skinny 20-year-old right-hander from Panama, joined the Gulf Coast League Yankees in Tampa, Florida, in 1990. That same year the Yankees drafted Jorge Posada, a chunky 19-year-old catcher from Puerto Rico, and Andy Pettitte, an 18-year-old left-hander out of San Jacinto Junior College in Texas. With the sixth choice in the first round in 1992, they selected Derek Jeter, a skilled 18-year-old shortstop out of Kalamazoo Central High School in Michigan. Michaels never traded any of the four, and for a while Steinbrenner wasn't eligible to intrude.

Nobody realized it at the time, but thanks to the nurturing of those four players, the last few years of the slump weren't so bad after all.

January 27, 1982

SPORTS OF THE TIMES
The Odd Couple Breaks Up

By GEORGE VECSEY

IT BEGAN AS A LOVE AFFAIR, and it ended the way love affairs often do, with the biggest truths known but unspoken. Openly and adoringly, Reggie Jackson once carved his initials in the apple tree. Reggie loves the Yankees. Five years later, George Steinbrenner no longer wanted Reggie Jackson around—probably not even as a designated hitter. If he had, Steinbrenner would have been able to keep him.

With as much dignity as possible under the circumstances, Reggie Jackson found a new home, new promises, and a four-year contract with the California Angels. Paul Simon says there are 50 ways to leave your lover, but Reggie found the 51st: free agency.

No matter what Jackson said yesterday at Anaheim Stadium, he would never have been in Orange County yesterday if George Steinbrenner had wanted him. But Steinbrenner's eyes had long ago grown cold and distant, hoping Jackson would pack his bags without making a scene and not even stay in the same neighborhood, the Yankees' own division.

At the end, there was a seven-paragraph publicity release, with Steinbrenner praising the way Jackson and his agent had conducted negotiations, and citing Jackson's good qualities for the Hall of Fame. It was like Rhett Butler telling Scarlett he would write her a letter of recommendation if she ever wanted an office job in Atlanta.

It had started so passionately. Jackson was young when the Oakland A's won five straight division championships, but he knew there must be something more to life than the braying of Charles O. Finley's pet mule. Reggie made his break, Baltimore, but his heart was set on New York.

Riding through New York City in the Orioles'

bus one day in 1976, Jackson entertained his temporary teammates by speculating which penthouse would one day be his: Should he live on Riverside Drive or Central Park West or Fifth Avenue?

Reggie let himself be romanced by other clubs in the fall of 1976, a whirlwind courtship while his agent, Gary Walker, who does not believe in airplanes, followed Reggie around in a motor home, to make sure the club owners' intentions were honest.

It was all over the day George Steinbrenner strolled Reggie around the East Side. Memory is a little blurred by now, but the impression is that there were violinists on street corners, waiters pouring champagne as George and Reggie waited for the lights to change. There may even have been a Yankee general manager ringing the bells in the tower of St. Patrick's, which is what general managers do when they work for George.

Steinbrenner held nothing back as he wooed Reggie in public. That's the way love affairs go at the beginning. For five years the couple had a love affair, right out in the open. There is no need to catalogue all the spats and the reconciliations. Sometimes Jackson came to regret ever coming to New York, came to feel the city and the team were against him. Sometimes he owned New York. For five years Reggie Jackson was as charismatic and heroic as any Yankee has ever been, but that was hardly enough for a man with a high Intelligence Quotient and an even higher Ego Quotient. He had to be in the middle of everything.

Picture Reggie in a World Series game, hitting a sacrifice fly to deep center field. He passes first base and watches the outfielder catch the ball. He stands motionless, inspects the futile throw to the infield, follows his teammate's progress to home plate and the dugout. Then Reggie turns and waits until the "1" flickers on the Yankee line in the scoreboard. Satisfied that everybody else in the ballpark has done the job, Reggie is now content. He claps his hands once, and consents to jog back to the dugout, allowing the game to continue. He is having a love affair with

baseball and the Yankees and, like many lovers, with himself.

The affair could have survived all the little indiscretions like the annual lateness to spring training. George and Reggie savored those scenes, like couples who enjoy throwing dishes around the love nest, because it is so much fun to make up.

The affair could not survive Reggie turning 35. It wasn't his temperament and it wasn't his salary, it was the wrinkles and the gray hairs in his batting average. Last spring Jackson struggled to raise his batting average to .200. He lost his supreme confidence; his muscles were still in the right places, but for the first time in his career he felt mortal. It showed in his eyes.

When the baseball players went on strike in June, Reggie was the Yankee representative who informed the other players: "Go home, the season's over." Of all the Yankees, Jackson 〉〉〉

Reggie Jackson and owner George Steinbrenner watch batting practice before Game 3 of the ALCS against the Oakland Athletics in 1981.

≪≪ seemed the most relieved at a break in the schedule. He made jokes about needing a mid-summer vacation, but he wasn't smiling.

When the strike ended, Steinbrenner sent Reggie to the doctor to see if Jackson needed glasses or Geritol or plastic surgery or a shrink. Kind words might have sufficed, but the owner had already turned cold. More than ever, Jackson began referring to the owner in obscene and furious tones. Hell hath no fury like a superstar scorned.

The rage produced better baseball from Reggie Jackson, including one marvelous clutch home run in the final game of the Eastern Division playoffs—a "one more time" for Reggie to stand in the batter's box and lovingly inspect the beauty of a long one, deep to right.

When the season ended, Jackson cleaned out his locker, but that was just a call for attention. All he wanted was a word that he was still Reggie Jackson, that he was still Mr. October, that the violinists and the champagne and the bells of St. Patrick's would always be there for him. But Steinbrenner has been working late at the office this winter, bringing in new people named Griffey and Collins.

Reggie and George never threw dishes at each other this January. One day it was all over. Yesterday Reggie Jackson moved across the country, to California, to start over again, the way people do when love dies. He was hardly out of the house when George started redecorating. ◆

April 12, 1982

YANKEES LOSE BY 7–6 AND 2–0 TO WHITE SOX

By MURRAY CHASS

FIVE DAYS AFTER they were supposed to begin their season, the Yankees finally opened yesterday, and what was the big hurry? The Yankees, thwarted by snow in three previous attempts to open, unveiled their radically altered team at Yankee Stadium, and the debut was a flop. The Chicago White Sox, the only other major league team that had not played any games because of bad weather, swept a doubleheader, winning the first game, 7–6, in 12 innings, and the second, 2–0, in nine.

Rich Gossage, the fourth Yankee pitcher in the game that Ron Guidry had started, gave up the decisive run in the opener as Bill Almon lashed a towering triple and scored on Ron LeFlore's single. In the second game, in which Tommy John pitched well but lost, Britt Burns and Salome Barojas stopped the Yankees on five hits. Tony

Bernazard doubled home one run and scored the other as Steve Kemp singled.

The Yankees didn't do much hitting in the first game, either, after Dave Winfield's two-run homer off Jerry Koosman in the sixth inning tied the score at 6-6. Dennis Lamp, pitching four and two-thirds innings, and Kevin Hickey, working one and two-thirds, permitted the Yankees only one hit.

At the end of a day of futility, George Steinbrenner declined comment on the initial performance of the team he has reconstructed, subtracting power and adding speed. Yankee fans, though, commented. Periodically during the second game, some of them chanted, "Reggie, Reggie, Reggie," recalling the not-so-long-ago days when Reggie Jackson's presence meant power hitting.

"I didn't hear them," Dave Winfield said, smiling, when asked about the fans. "Maybe they heard them upstairs." The executives upstairs, along with the players and fans, were disappointed in the results. The players were also confused about the constant personnel maneuvers, which have left many of them uncertain about their roles. ◆

April 20, 1982

YANKS DISMISS LEMON AND NAME MICHAEL MANAGER

By MURRAY CHASS

DESPITE HIS AVOWAL that Bob Lemon would manage the Yankees for the entire 1982 season, no matter what the team's record, George Steinbrenner dismissed Lemon yesterday for the second time in three years. Gene Michael, whom Steinbrenner dismissed as manager last September, will replace Lemon only 14 games into the season.

The change, announced at Yankee Stadium at 8 o'clock last night, is the eighth in the 10 seasons that Steinbrenner has been the principal owner of the Yankees. Six of the changes have occurred in the last four years, and three of the managers involved—Michael, Lemon and Billy Martin—have held the job twice.

The Yankee players were gone, following their 3–1 victory over Detroit, by the time the move was disclosed. However, the players generally and Rich Gossage specifically have blamed Steinbrenner for the team's problems.

"If they're talking about changing managers," the usually lowkey Gossage said before leaving, "I don't know that that's what we need."

Lemon, who succeeded Martin as Yankee manager in July 1978, and was in turn succeeded by Martin in June 1979, replaced Michael last Sept. 6. That change came after Michael had publicly complained that Steinbrenner should dismiss him or quit threatening to do so. It was widely believed that Lemon would not return this season, but on successive days in December, the Yankees announced that Lemon would be retained for 1982 and Michael would return as manager in 1983.

"There will be no change this year," Steinbrenner said at the time, for any reason other than possibly Lemon's health. "I wouldn't care how the team is doing. I'm not going to make a change in 1982 unless it's dictated by something other than how the team is doing."

Gene Michael, who replaced Bob Lemon as manager of the NY Yankees, holding a news conference in 1982.

The Yankees have not been doing well this season. They gained their sixth victory yesterday by stopping Detroit's eight-game winning streak, but that was not enough to deter Steinbrenner from making the move that came as no surprise.

"No one is more appreciative of Lem's great loyalty to the organization than I am," Steinbrenner said in a statement. "He has always been loyal to the Yankees and to me in whatever role he has been asked to assume. It is just that I feel it is in the best interests of the club that this change be made now. I have discussed it with Lem —he understands my feelings even though I had >>>

≪≪ promised him the entire season."

The players, however, feel that it has been the constant change of personnel that has prevented them from playing effectively. The Yankees have made five trades that have affected the roster in the last month. Gossage discussed the consequences of these kinds of changes.

"I'm depressed," he said after combining with Rudy May and Shane Rawley for a three-hit shutout of the Tigers. "It's very depressing around here. It's no fun. It's getting worse all the time. I've never seen anything like this. It started in the World Series last year and it's gone straight through to spring training and up to now. "It's tough enough in New York with the fans. If you're not performing, the fans will get on your butt. You don't need Steinbrenner on your butt, too. The pressures of the game are tough enough." But every guy comes in here looking at the lineup to see if they're in it. Guys come in here every day and don't know who's playing. Guys go up to hit looking over their shoulder. What kind of baloney is that? I come in here and see the way guys look and see the way guys feel. I tell you, it's going to be a long year."

The players generally have been confused since the season began, not only not knowing who would be in the lineup from day to day but also not knowing who would be on the team from day to day. None of the players seems to attribute those uncertainties to the manager. The prevailing belief is that Steinbrenner is directing the operation, not only in the front office but also on the field. ◆

May 8, 1982

Yankees Reach Cable Accord

THE YANKEES YESTERDAY concluded their prolonged negotiations for cable-television rights by reaching agreement with SportsChannel, according to a source with knowledge of the negotiations.

No details of the deal were available, but last week a source familiar with the negotiations said SportsChannel had offered the Yankees a 15-year deal for more than $100 million.

It is expected that SportsChannel will carry about 40 games this season and in each of the next two seasons, and that WPIX will televise 100 games each year. However, beginning in 1985, after the WPIX contract expires, the ratio is to be reversed. ◆

January 12, 1983

MARTIN TO MANAGE A THIRD TIME

By MURRAY CHASS

PROCLAIMING THE START of a "new era for the third time," George Steinbrenner introduced Billy Martin yesterday as the new manager of the Yankees. Both men said things would be different this time because they had learned from their past experiences.

"We've had the experience twice," Steinbrenner, the Yankees' principal owner, told a news conference at Yankee Stadium. "That's a plus, not a negative. We've done this before and I'd rather take my chances with someone I've been down the road with before rather than someone new."

Martin, 54, is anything but new to the Yankees. Steinbrenner hired him for the first time in 1975 to replace Bill Virdon, then hired him in 1979 to replace Bob Lemon.

In between, in July 1978, Martin resigned under fire. Five days later, the Yankees announced he would return in 1980, but Steinbrenner brought him in to succeed Lemon in June 1979, and he was dismissed before the 1980 season even began.

This time Martin replaces Clyde King, the third of the Yankees' three managers last season. No details of Martin's agreement with Steinbrenner were announced, but the length of the contract was believed to be five years.

"It's a long-term contract and it's a lot of money, a lot of dollars," a beaming Martin said. "When George called and wanted me to come back, it was exciting," Martin added. "It's great, and it's going to be good." The relationship between the two self-described headstrong and intense men was so good yesterday that they even played out a skit for their audience that was reminiscent of the television commerical they once made together.

"I'll be handling all the trades," Martin said at one point, standing at the cluster of microphones behind a table and in front of a banner with the Yankee logo.

"What do you mean?" answered Steinbrenner, sitting a few feet away.

"There will be no phone calls in the dugout," Martin continued, ignoring his boss.

"What do you mean?" Steinbrenner repeated, this time more forcefully. "That's not right. I'm handling the trades."

Martin: "That's not the way we said, George."

Steinbrenner, bolting out of his chair: "I have the right to call you in the dugout anytime I want."

Martin: "George, that's not the way it's going to be, George."

Steinbrenner: "Damn right it is and if you don't like it, you're fired."

"You haven't hired me yet," Martin said, rel-

ishing the punch line.

The orchestration was not unusual for Steinbrenner, who has directed, in one way or another, all 10 of the managerial changes in the 10 years he has been owner.

To be technical, Steinbrenner did not dismiss Martin July 24, 1978. Martin tearfully resigned after commenting to two newsmen the night before that Reggie Jackson and Steinbrenner "deserve each other."

"One's a born liar," Martin said, "the other's convicted." He was alluding to Steinbrenner's plea of guilty to a charge of making an illegal contribution to President Nixon's campaign in 1972.

Steinbrenner did get rid of Martin in October 1979, after Martin was involved in a fight with a salesman in a Bloomington, Minn., hotel, then initially denied it.

In trying to explain why they were reuniting after two separations, both men made comments yesterday that had a familiar ring, recalling things they had said after the first separation.

Steinbrenner: "Billy and I are going to deal more directly than in the past. I think both of us have learned. I think this will be for a long time."

Martin: "George and I will be working very close. I'll be talking with him quite a bit. This is going to be great because I'll be working directly with him."

Steinbrenner: "There were no holds barred in our conversations and that's never been done before. The lines of communication are open like they've never been open before. It's a one-on-one situation, which it's never been before."

Martin: "The talks that we've had tell me everything will be good. I don't think anyone will put a wedge between us. In the past, we weren't talking to each other. We were going around—something he read I said, something I read he said." ◆

March 1, 1983

YANKS' MATTINGLY ROOKIE ON THE MOVE

By MURRAY CHASS

FORT LAUDERDALE, FLA., FEB. 28—The Yankees, in the free agent era, have not produced the caliber of rookies who dotted the major leagues last season, players such as Steve Sax, Johnny Ray, Cal Ripken Jr., Kent Hrbek and Dave Hostetler. This season Don Mattingly hopes to change that pattern.

Mattingly, 21 years old, is the youngest player competing for the first-base job. But he has the minor league record and the confidence to indicate that he may be ready for the majors.

The other entrants are Ken Griffey, the favorite, who began working at first today; John Mayberry, the closest the Yankees have to an incumbent at the position: and Steve Balboni, whose potential was tarnished in a .187 Yankee September.

"Griffey was one of my idols when I was a kid watching Cincinnati on television," Mattingly said before today's workout. "It's a tough thing watching a guy in the World Series, and four or five years later you're trying to get his job. But I have to tell myself I want that job. I have to support my family, too.

"That's one thing you have to forget—you're a young kid and they're way up there. You have to bring them down to your level. They're people, just like anybody else. I have to feel proud of my performance. If I'm a little shaky and think the other guy's great, it's not going to help me any."

Mattingly, a left-handed hitter who is 5 feet 11 inches tall and weighs 185 pounds, was the club's 19th-round choice in the June 1979 amateur free agent draft. The club's No. 1 choice was Todd Demeter, also a first baseman. Demeter, however, has languished in the Class A level of the minors for four seasons while Mattingly has moved past him, batting .349, .358, .314 and .315 in four seasons, the last at Columbus of the

Don Mattingly played for the Yankees from 1982 to 1995.

Class AAA International League last year.

"I thought I was going to be drafted higher than 19th," said Mattingly, an Indiana native. "But I felt the No. 1 guy has to hit the same pitchers, and that makes us equal. Demeter and I are different players. He has a big swing, he hits the ball a mile that way. I have a shorter swing, I make contact, I don't strike out that much. I don't like walking back to the dugout."

He struck out only 24 times in 476 times at bat last year, an average of one every 20 times. In competing for the job, Mattingly returns to the position he played in high school. Because he joined the Yankee organization the same time as Demeter, he was moved to the outfield. Last year he made the International League all-star team as an outfielder.

"Before spring training," he said, "they told me I was going to have a chance to play first. I'm working hard and I just want to show them what I can do." ◆

May 1, 1983

MARTIN SUSPENDED FOR 3 GAMES

By MURRAY CHASS

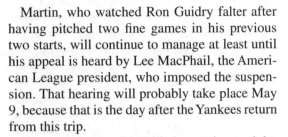

ARLINGTON, TEX., APRIL 30— Billy Martin, who only last week was fined $5,000 for his behavior toward umpires, was suspended today for three games for kicking dirt on an umpire in the Yankees' game with Texas Friday night. Martin, however, immediately appealed the suspension and was on hand to direct the Yankees to a 6–3 loss to the Rangers tonight.

George Steinbrenner was also at the game and afterward called the Yankees "futile at this point," adding "there's a pretty good chance changes will be made."

Martin, who watched Ron Guidry falter after having pitched two fine games in his previous two starts, will continue to manage at least until his appeal is heard by Lee MacPhail, the American League president, who imposed the suspension. That hearing will probably take place May 9, because that is the day after the Yankees return from this trip.

Martin had no trouble with the umpires tonight. He twice emerged from the dugout to discuss matters with them but did so quietly and politely.

"You wouldn't know which team has the big payroll if you watched that tonight," Steinbrenner said in a low key way after watching the Yankees lose for the 11th time in 20 games. "I've been pretty quiet, but I'm getting to the end of my patience. I promised I wouldn't single out any players, and I won't, but they know who they are. I can lose this with the kids from Columbus. Some guys are really a disappointment so far, but I'm not going to mention names."

Steinbrenner said he came to Texas to meet with Martin "because I'm concerned for him." He was referring to the suspension and, saying that other managers kick dirt on umpires, com- >>>

Yankee manager Billy Martin and umpires didn't always agree.

‹‹‹ plained that "It can't be a selective prosecution."

Martin's suspension resulted from the culmination of three disputes he had with umpires in the Yankees' 8–3 loss to the Rangers Friday night. One involved Drew Coble's out call on Roy Smalley on an attempted steal of home, the second on Mark Johnson's interference call against Graig Nettles at second base and the third Johnson's ruling that Parrish's hit to left-center field was not a ground-rule double.

One pitch after the double, in the Rangers' half of the third inning, Martin raced onto the field, his hat turned backward, and first yelled at Coble. After he was ejected, he kicked dirt at the umpire's legs.

"It shouldn't have happened to begin with," Martin said. "I shouldn't have been thrown out of the game at all. He told me to turn my hat around on the bench. He has no right to do that. I can wear my hat on the bench any way I want. He said, 'Fix your hat.' Then when I went out, he said, 'You're out of the game for wearing your hat that way.' That's when I kicked the dirt. Dirt kicking is no more embarrassing than getting kicked out of a game as far as I'm concerned. He's harassing me."

Coble said he told Martin that he couldn't come out of the dugout wearing his hat backward, not that he couldn't wear it on the bench backward. ◆

July 5, 1983

RIGHETTI PITCHES FIRST YANKEE NO-HITTER SINCE 1956

By MURRAY CHASS

DAVE RIGHETTI, who last year at this time was banished to the minors because of his disappointing efforts, pitched the Yankees' first no-hitter in 27 years in a 4–0 victory over the Boston Red Sox at the Stadium yesterday.

Righetti, 24 years old, walked four batters and struck out nine, including seven of the first nine who came up. He gained his second shutout in six days after having had none in his first 60 starts in the majors.

He stymied the hot-hitting Red Sox so effectively that they hit only two balls that remotely had a chance to become hits, one in the fourth inning and the other in the sixth. Bert Campaneris, the third baseman, and Roy Smalley, the shortstop, turned those plays into routine outs, so that when Righetti struck out Wade Boggs, the major league leader in hits, for the final out, he had his prized no-hitter.

"For one split second, I was blank," Righetti said after having registered his 10th victory against 3 defeats. "I didn't know whether I should jump around or not. I just kind of looked at Butch and I saw him coming, and I said, 'Oh, geez!' I just leaned on him and held onto him. I didn't want to fall on the ground."

The exuberant scene as the catcher Butch Wynegar and the rest of his teammates mobbed Righetti was the first of its kind for the Yankees since Don Larsen pitched a perfect game against the Brooklyn Dodgers in the fifth game of the 1956 World Series. Allie Reynolds pitched the last Yankee no-hitter in a regular-season game, against Boston Sept. 28, 1951.

Righetti, who was born two years after Larsen's perfect game, established a milestone of his own. This was the sixth no-hitter at the Stadium in the 59 years the Yankees have played there, but the first by a left-hander.

Righetti's first milestone as a Yankee came in 1981, when he was named the American League's rookie of the year. However, in the middle of last season on June 27, the principal owner George Steinbrenner was disappointed with his pitching and sent him to the Columbus farm team, where he remained for three weeks.

There has been nothing disappointing about Righetti this season. He said he felt he deserved to be added to the American League All-Star team after Ron Guidry had to withdraw because of a bad back. He was not added because he was pitching yesterday, and league officials felt he would not be ready to work again by tomorrow night. Ironically, he pitched only because Guidry's injury had forced a change in the rotation.

He faced a Boston team that in the first three games of the series had amassed 25 runs and 38 hits, including 9 homers. "They've been hitting the ball too good," Righetti said after the game. "I said I was going to go out and shut them down. That's what I did the first three innings."

During the Yankee eighth, Righetti, who goes to the clubhouse between innings, made an extra visit to fortify himself with a fresh piece of gum. When he emerged from the dugout for the critical ninth, the crowd of 41,077 saluted him with a standing ovation.

"I was nervous, definitely, without a doubt," Righetti said. "'Everybody was nervous. They were making me nervous. I didn't look in the dugout because I didn't want to get more nervous. But I calmed down. I was enjoying the fans. I was enjoying being a Yankee."

No one had pitched a no-hitter since Nolan Ryan of Houston did it against the Los Angeles Dodgers Sept. 26, 1981. But Righetti was three outs away. The Red Sox had not gone hitless since 1968.

Righetti did not start the ninth on a positive note; he walked Newman, a .190 hitter. Hoffman was next, and Righetti recalled that two years ago Hoffman ended his no-hit bid with a single to right in the seventh inning.

After throwing a two-strike pitch away from the right-handed Hoffman for a ball, Righetti threw a fastball inside, and Hoffman grounded it to short. It looked as if it could result in a double play, but Robertson's throw to first pulled Don Mattingly off the base.

Remy now stepped to the plate and swung at the first pitch, grounding it between first and second, where Robertson fielded it and threw to first for the second out.

The fans, who had roared with every strike and out, now stood and cheered as Boggs came to bat. Boggs, with 101 hits so far this season, said he wanted to hit the ball "where they ain't."

As Wynegar, the catcher, prepared to give Righetti the sign for the 2-2 pitch to Boggs, he thought he would call for Righetti's best pitch, a fastball. But at the last second, "for some reason," he said, he changed to a slider.

"I don't think he expected that," Righetti said of Boggs. Boggs missed the slider, and Righetti's 132d pitch of the game was his last, the one that clinched his no-hitter. ◆

Dave Righetti celebrates his no-hitter with Butch Wynegar.

July 25, 1983

BRETT HOMER NULLIFIED, SO YANKEES WIN

By MURRAY CHASS

BASEBALL GAMES often end with home runs, but until yesterday the team that hit the home run always won. At Yankee Stadium yesterday, the team that hit the home run lost.

If that unusual development produced a sticky situation, blame it on pine tar. With two out in the ninth inning, George Brett of the Kansas City Royals hit a two-run home run against Rich Gossage that for several minutes gave the Royals a 5–4 lead over the Yankees. But Brett was called out by the umpires for using an illegal bat, one with an exces-sive amount of pine tar. The ruling, after a protest by Billy Martin, the Yankees' manager, enabled the Yankees to wind up with a 4–3 victory.

"I can sympathize with George," Gossage re-marked after the game, "but not that much."

The outcome, which the Royals immediately protested, is certain to be talked about for years to come, because it was one of the more bizarre finishes any game has ever had.

"I couldn't believe it," Brett said, infinitely more calm than when he charged at the umpires after their controversial call. "It knocks you to your knees," added Dick Howser, the Kansas City man-ager. "I'm sick about it. I don't like it. I don't like it at all. I don't expect my players to accept it."

What the Royals refused to believe or accept was that the umpires ruled the home run did not count because Brett's bat had too much pine tar on it.

Pine tar is a sticky brown substance batters apply to their bats to give them a better grip. Baseball rule 1.10 (b) says a bat may not be covered by such a substance more than 18 inches from the tip of the handle. Joe Brinkman, the chief of the crew that umpired the game, said Brett's bat had "heavy pine tar" 19 to 20 inches from the tip of the handle and lighter pine tar for another three or four inches.

The umpire did not use a ruler to measure the pine tar on Brett's 34 1/2-inch bat; they didn't have one. So they placed it across home plate, which measures 17 inches across.

When they did, they saw that the pine tar exceeded the legal limit. The four umpires conferred again, and then Tim McClelland, the home plate umpire, thrust his right arm in the air, signaling that Brett was out. His call prompted two reactions:

Brett, enraged, raced out of the dugout and looked as if he would run over McClelland. Brinkman, however, intercepted him, grabbing him around the neck. "In that situation," Brinkman said later, "you know something's going to happen. It was quite traumatic. He was upset."

Gaylord Perry of the Royals, who has been long accused of doing things illegal with a baseball, tried to swipe the evidence, according to Brinkman.

"Gaylord got the bat and passed it back and tried to get it to the clubhouse," Brinkman said. "The security people went after it, but I got in there and got it. Steve Renko, another Kansas City pitcher, had it. He was the last in line. He didn't have anyone to hand it to."

Why the stadium security men went after the bat was not clear.

"I didn't know what was going on," Howser said. "I saw guys in sport coats and ties trying to intercept the bat. It was like a Brink's robbery. Who's got the gold? Our players had it, the umpires had it. I don't know who has it—the C.I.A., a think tank at the Pentagon."

Umpire Joe Brinkman (right) collars George Brett after Brett was ruled out after using a "pine tar" bat on July 24, 1983.

Brinkman, when asked about the stadium security's bat force, said, "Maybe if it had been reversed, the bat might be gone." The umpires declined to show the bat, which they said was on its way to the American League office. Presumably, Lee MacPhail, the league president, will study the bat and measure the pine tar, then rule on the Royals' protest.

Martin, who has had a few violent encounters with umpires himself, was as peaceful and as smug as he could be about the whole incident.

"We noticed the pine tar on his bat in Kansas City," he said, alluding to the team's visit there two weeks ago. "You don't call him on it if he makes an out. After he hit the home run, I went out and said he's using an illegal bat."

"It's a terrible rule, but if it had happened to me I would have accepted it," Martin said. "It turned out to be a lovely Sunday afternoon."

But the umpires obviously thought Martin did have a case, although Brinkman acknowledged that pine tar, unlike cork or nails, has no effect on the distance a ball will travel.

"I was aware of the rule," Brett said, "but I thought it couldn't go past the label. Some umpires, when they see the pine tar too high, will say, 'Hey, George, clean up your bat.'"

Why was the pine tar that high on Brett's bat?

"I don't wear batting gloves," Brett explained, showing his calloused hands. "I like the feel of raw skin on raw wood. But you also don't want to hold the bat where pine tar is, so you put it up higher on the bat, get some on your hands when you need it, and then go back to the bottom of the bat. Where I hit that ball, it was on the meat part of the bat, about five inches from the end. There's no pine tar 29 inches from the handle. That ball wasn't even close enough to the pine tar to smell it."

Brett said he especially liked the bat, not for the pine tar but for the kind of wood with which it was made. He called it a seven-grainer ("the fewer grains a bat has, the better it is") and said it is the best bat he has ever had.

"I want my bat back," he said. ◆

July 29, 1983

KANSAS CITY WINS PINE-TAR PROTEST

By MURRAY CHASS

THE GEORGE BRETT home run that was, then wasn't, is. The case of Brett's pine-tarred bat slipped in another direction yesterday when Lee MacPhail, the American League president, upheld a protest by Brett's team, the Kansas City Royals. He overruled the umpires at the game, who had canceled the two-run home run Brett hit in the ninth inning at Yankee Stadium last Sunday on the ground that he had too much pine tar on his bat.

MacPhail's ruling marked the first time he had upheld a protest in his 10 years in office, a period in which perhaps 50 cases of protest had been sent to him. It also wiped out the Yankees' 4–3 victory and created a game that is suspended with the Kansas City Royals leading, 5–4, with two out in their half of the ninth. MacPhail acknowledged that Brett had pine tar too high on his bat, which made the bat illegal. But he based his decision reinstating the home run on other factors, including what he and rules-makers saw as the intent of the pine-tar rule and his belief that "games should be won and lost on the playing field, not through technicalities of the rules."

◆

August 19, 1983

RESUMED GAME ENDS IN 5–4 YANKEE LOSS

By MURRAY CHASS

TWENTY-FIVE DAYS, one upheld protest and two court decisions later, the Yankees and the Kansas City Royals completed a baseball game last night. The finish was anticlimactic.

Four batters—one for the Royals, three for the Yankees—batted, and four made outs. In 9 minutes 41 seconds, the pine-tar game that grabbed the attention of baseball fans throughout the country was over. The Royals won it, 5–4, on the two-out, two-run home run that George Brett hit

October 1, 1984

MATTINGLY WINS A.L. BATTING TITLE

By MURRAY CHASS

THE THING DON MATTINGLY wanted to do most yesterday, other than get a bunch of hits, was relax. "When I woke up this morning," he related, "my wife gave me a big smile and said 'I love you.' I couldn't ask for more than that."

But given the relaxation he wanted, Mattingly took more. He lashed four hits in the Yankees' 9–2 victory over Detroit and snatched the American League batting championship from Dave Winfield, who had only one hit.

Mattingly, who entered the final game of the season trailing Winfield by 2 points (or more precisely 1.57 points), finished with a .343 average to .340 for Winfield.

The 23-year-old first baseman, playing his first full major league season, blooped a single to left field in the first inning, lined a double against the right-field wall in the third, lined a double along the right-field line in the fourth, flied to center in

in the ninth inning July 24.

The home run was challenged by Manager Billy Martin of the Yankees, then disallowed by the umpires because, they agreed, Brett had too much pine tar on his bat. That meant Brett was out, the game was over, and the Yankees had won, 4–3.

But the homer was reinstated four days later by Lee MacPhail, the American League president, after the Royals protested, meaning that now the Royals led, 5–4, and the game had to be completed.

Brett was not present for the finish nor was his controversial bat. He flew to New York from Kansas City with the team yesterday afternoon but did not accompany the Royals to Yankee Stadium. He and three other members of the team, including Manager Dick Howser, had been ejected by MacPhail for their heated reaction to the umpires'

ruling that bizarre Sunday afternoon. Brett broke that bat in Milwaukee two weeks ago, and it probably will wind up in the Hall of Fame.

Whereas Brett was the hero, or antihero, of the first part of the game, Dan Quisenberry was the man of the moment for the Royals this time. The league's best relief pitcher this year, Quisenberry threw 10 pitches and retired Don Mattingly on a fly to center field, Roy Smalley on a fly to left field and Oscar Gamble on a grounder to second base.

When the game resumed, Martin had, by necessity, altered the July 24 lineup. Ron Guidry, a pitcher who is an excellent athlete, was in center field, replacing Jerry Mumphrey, who was traded to Houston last week. Mattingly, who throws left-handed, was at second base in place of Bert Campaneris, on the disabled list. ◆

Don Mattingly, the 1984 American League batting champion.

the fifth and bounced a bad-hop single to right in the eighth, clinching the title with that last hit. Winfield grounded into a force play, walked, bounced an infield single, lined to center with one of the hardest hit balls he's had in the past two weeks and forced Mattingly in the eighth.

"Someone said if I didn't get a hit the last time up and Winfield did, he would've won by two-thousandths of a point," Mattingly said. "Right then I knew there was no way I could be a loser. Neither of us could be a loser. But I guess it's the American way—someone has to win and someone has to lose."

If Mattingly had made an out in the eighth and Winfield had stroked a hit, Winfield would have finished at .34215 and Mattingly .34163, a winning margin of .52 of a percentage point for Winfield. However, after taking a strike and a ball from Willie Hernandez, Mattingly rapped a bouncer between first and second.

"I thought he was going to get it," Mattingly said, "but then it took a bad hop and got past him."

Winfield, batting next, hit a bouncer to third, and Howard Johnson forced Mattingly at second. As Mattingly walked to the dugout, the fans roared in salute. Then Mattingly re-emerged from the ⟩⟩⟩

⟨⟨⟨ dugout and walked to first base, where he and Winfield clasped hands, then walked off the field together as the crowd roared.

"It was good that we could come off together," Mattingly said. "Dave has been a great person through this whole thing. He handled himself like a gentleman. I have great respect for him. It's good that we're going to be teammates the next few years at least."

Winfield had left the clubhouse by the time it was opened after the game. Mattingly, though, related how they had talked a couple of weeks ago about the attention and the pressure their contest had created. "We agreed there was no need for friction," Mattingly said.

For a long time, there was no contest. On July 12, following the first game after the All-Star break, Winfield had a 39-point lead, .371 to .332. And once they began running one-two on a daily basis, Winfield led for 94 of 100 days until Sept. 21 in Detroit. Mattingly grabbed the lead that night and held it until last Friday night at Yankee Stadium. Mattingly hadn't exactly been crushing the ball, but Winfield was slumping and most of the hits he was getting were infield bouncers.

"Basically, I wanted to get a hit every time up," Mattingly said. "After the first hit, I wanted to get a hit the second time. After the second hit, I wanted to get three hits. As long as I got a hit every time up. . ."

He didn't finish the sentence, but he did finish his quest with a flourish. ◆

April 23, 1985

HENDERSON ARRIVES

By MALCOLM MORAN

RICKEY HENDERSON's bumpy road to Yankee Stadium grew even bumpier yesterday. His weekend had begun with anxiousness over the rehabilitation of his sprained left ankle, the worst injury he has experienced. He wondered about how limitations from the lingering effects of the injury might complicate his effort to meet the expectations that were waiting in New York. He felt that his 493 stolen bases have overshadowed his other abilities and distorted his anticipated role.

In the Yankee clubhouse, cameras were there to capture his first buttoning. People expected him to say how good it was to be a Yankee, home at last. At that moment, his salary of $1.3 million for this season, part of a five-year package of $8.6 million, just wasn't enough to make him want to answer questions.

An optional practice was scheduled to begin at 2 P.M. Because of the rough flight it was 2:25 when Henderson walked in the door.

When a small crowd of questioners quietly began to form a semicircle, Henderson spoke his first words as a Yankee in the Bronx.

"I dont need no press now, man," he said.

That is not how one goes about having a candy bar named after oneself, but then, Henderson does not have that in mind. Everyone knew that the game Henderson plays is different from Reggie Jackson's.

"See, my career, to me, does not depend on running," he said in Florida. "My career depends on me playing, if I can play the game. Because I can hit. People say 'base-stealer,' and they really don't understand a base-stealer. A base-stealer has got to know how to hit. If he don't know how to hit, he's not a base-stealer. There are a lot of guys who can run real fast, outrun me. Being a base-stealer is a different thing.

"You've got to know how to get on base, or you can't steal a base. That's what I do. That's what I work hard on, getting on base and hitting. I don't even work on stealing. If I can't run as well as I've been running in my career, or if something happens that I'm a little sore, I feel I can hit, and get on base, and make things happen." ◆

April 29, 1985

BERRA DISMISSED; MARTIN REHIRED

By MICHAEL MARTINEZ

CHICAGO, APRIL 28— George Steinbrenner, who said two months ago that Yogi Berra would be the Yankees' manager for the entire 1985 season no matter what, dismissed Berra today, just 16 games into the season, and brought back Billy Martin for his fourth term.

Martin, who was removed as Yankee manager at the end of the 1983 season and named a special scout, will join the team in Arlington, Tex., Monday, where the Yankees open a three-game series against the Texas Rangers.

The appointment of Martin marks the 12th managerial change since Steinbrenner led a group

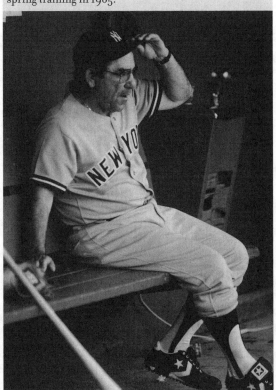

Manager Yogi Berra watches batting practice during spring training in 1985.

that purchased the Yankees from CBS in 1973.

The task of informing Berra of his dismissal was given to Clyde King, the Yankee general manager, who spoke with Steinbrenner by telephone during the Yankees' game with the Chicago White Sox. According to King, Steinbrenner had decided to dismiss Berra even before the contest ended in a 4–3 Yankee defeat, the team's third straight loss.

King notified Berra of his dismissal shortly after the game. Steinbrenner also telephoned Berra an hour later in the visiting clubhouse at Comiskey Park.

"Today's game had no bearing on what happened," King said afterward. "Mr. Steinbrenner said he hoped to see Yogi go out a winner. Mr. Steinbrenner said he didn't sleep last night. He said he agonized all night over this."

Steinbrenner issued a statement through the Yankee publicity department, announcing the dismissal. Steinbrenner was quoted as saying, "This action has been taken by the Yankees, and we feel that it is in the best interests of the club." It also said that Steinbrenner told King "he would rather fire 25 players than to fire Yogi, but we all know that would be impossible."

Berra, who remained behind closed doors for nearly a half hour after receiving the news, smiled when reporters finally entered the small office. His son, Dale, had already spent several minutes with his father and emerged with tears in his eyes.

"I'm in a very good mood," Yogi Berra said. "This is still a very good ball club, and they're getting a good manager in Billy Martin. I don't think my players laid down on me."

Martin, reached in Texas tonight, said he was confident he would be able to survive as manager this time. "We're good friends now," he said of his relationship with Steinbrenner. "We're closer now than we've ever been before. It helps when you don't have to go through three or four people."

Berra refused to criticize Steinbrenner. "He's the boss," Berra said. "He can do what he wants. I'm used to this. This is the third time I've been fired. That's what this game is—managers are hired to be fired. I know it's an old saying, »»»

◀◀◀ but that's what it is."

Berra had been dismissed twice before, once by the Mets, whom he managed from 1972 to 1975, taking them to the World Series in 1973, and by the Yankees, whom he managed to a pennant in 1964 but lost in the World Series.

Asked if he would accept another position with the club, Berra said: "I don't know. He hasn't asked me yet. My contract says I don't have to do anything.

"Right now, I'm just gonna go home and play golf."

Berra said he felt no relief that the turmoil of the last three weeks, which included continual criticisms from Steinbrenner over the team's play and what he termed "lack of discipline," was over.

Berra shook his head. "I'd still like to stay here," he said. "But like I said, he's the boss."

At the same time, Berra intimated that the team had yet to play at its full capacity. "We had injuries at the beginning of the season," he said. "We've got two or three guys who are still in spring training."

Did he feel he was treated fairly by Steinbrenner?

"I don't know if I did or not," he answered. "But I still think this club is gonna turn itself around."

Few players were willing to discuss Berra's sudden dismissal. Several, including Dave Winfield, Willie Randolph and Don Baylor, three of the most outspoken members of the team, refused to comment. But Baylor, after reading the prepared statement that had been handed out to reporters, kicked over a trash can in the clubhouse.

The team left after the game for Texas, but Berra was not on board the charter flight. He walked through the clubhouse, saying goodbye to players and wishing them well. They stopped at his son's locker. "Are you going home?" Dale asked. "Yeah," said Yogi. "Home." ◆

November 4, 1985

PINIELLA ANSWERS THE BOSS'S CALL

By IRA BERKOW

ALLENDALE, N.J.— Yes, Lou Piniella had said, "the owner and I have an interesting relationship."

Piniella is the new manager of the New York Yankees, and the owner he referred to was none other than George Michael Steinbrenner 3d, keeper of the trapdoor down which Yankee managers regularly disappear.

Steinbrenner understandably strikes fear into the hearts of some Yankee managers, some Yankee players, and assorted other Yankee employees. But Lou Piniella, when playing for the Yankees from 1974 to 1984, wasn't necessarily among those quaking numbers.

"I know," Steinbrenner said a few years ago, "that a guy like Lou Piniella writes on the blackboard in the locker room when I'm in New York, 'Col. Klink's in town,' or 'Attila the Hun has arrived.' But I don't mind. I chuckle about it."

Though Piniella will touch upon such literary efforts when asked about them now, he perceives that it is best not to go into detail; after all, he is starting a new and highly visible and historically perishable job for the good Colonel, or Mr. Hun, as the case may be.

Piniella got back at the owner in little ways. The owner has also had a concern with his own waistline, and if he wasn't quite Col. Blimp, he wasn't quite Col. Beanpole, either. When he came through the clubhouse door, Piniella would yell out, "Hide the Hershey bars!"

Despite all this, the owner and the player became quite friendly, and developed not only a mutual respect and liking, but a partnership, too. Piniella, now 42 years old, was born and raised and lived in the offseason in Tampa, Fla., the headquarters for Steinbrenner's American Ship Building Company. Each is interested in horse racing—Steinbrenner owns a race track in Tampa and race horses, and Piniella has been known on occasion to peruse a form chart. They bought two horses together, and one, Flip 'N' Hold, has had modest success around New York tracks.

Several years ago, Steinbrenner and his family moved to Tampa from Cleveland. And two years ago, Piniella and his family—his wife, Anita, and their three children, Louie Jr., 16, Kristi 13, and Derrick 6—moved north to Allendale.

"Tampa," said Piniella, with a smile, "wasn't big enough for both George and me."

But Yankee Stadium has been. When Piniella, serving both as player and hitting instructor, was unable to shake a shoulder injury that hampered his batting swing, he retired as a player on June 17, 1984. He became the hitting coach exclusively. By last winter, Steinbrenner was saying that Piniella was a Yankee manager of the future.

Last Sunday, he became the Yankee manager of the present. ◆

Manager Lou Piniella (left) listens to George Steinbrenner at Yankee Stadium in 1986.

November 21, 1985

MATTINGLY WINS M.V.P. AWARD IN LANDSLIDE

By MURRAY CHASS

DON MATTINGLY, who did just about everything this year except put the Yankees into the play-offs, achieved a runaway victory yesterday in the voting for the American League's most valuable player award. In so doing, Mattingly became the first person to stop the Kansas City Royals in a postseason contest.

Mattingly easily defeated George Brett, who led the Royals into the playoffs and then the World Series championship. Mattingly became the first player on a non-championship team to win the award since Jim Rice of the Boston Red Sox won in 1978.

In the voting, conducted before the postseason by a panel of 28 members of the Baseball ⟫⟫

≪≪ Writers Association of America, two from each league city, Mattingly received 23 first-place votes and 5 second-place votes for a total of 367 points. Brett, whose September slump might have cost him votes, was named first on five ballots, second on 20 and third on three for a total of 274 points. They were the only players named on all 28 ballots.

In only his second full season in the majors, Mattingly, 24, led the majors with 145 runs batted in, batted .324 (third in the American League) and hit 35 home runs (fourth in the league). He also led the majors in doubles (48) and led the league in total bases (370) and extra-base hits (86). Defensively, he led American League first basemen with a .995 fielding average.

"I never dreamed of putting those kinds of numbers up," Mattingly said at a Yankee Stadium news conference last night. "There's no way you can say I'm going to get 140 or 150 R.B.I. and over 30 homers."

Yet, last spring, on the night that the Yankees renewed Mattingly's contract for the 1985 season, he angrily said his time would come. "I'll have the hammer next time," he said.

He said yesterday that he had made his spring remarks out of frustration over his failure to achieve what he thought he was worth as 1984 batting champion, but when reminded of the "hammer" comment, he said, "I guess I do have it now." ◆

September 30, 1987

Mattingly Breaks Grand-Slam Record

By MURRAY CHASS

IN EACH OF HIS first three full seasons in the major leagues, Don Mattingly did something to distinguish himself. In 1984, he won the American League batting championship. In 1985, he led the league in runs batted in and was named the most valuable player. Last season, he led the league in five offensive categories and broke the Yankees' record for hits with 238.

Mattingly distinguished himself this season in July, hitting home runs in eight consecutive games and tying the major league record. Then last night, he gained more distinction and more glamour, hitting his sixth grand slam of the season and setting a major-league record.

The third-inning shot, off Bruce Hurst, carried 11 rows into the third tier of the right-field stands and powered the Yankees to a 6–0 victory over the Boston Red Sox.

There is nothing enigmatic about Mattingly. In his brief major-league career, he has strung together a series of remarkable feats, utilizing all the important aspects of a hitter's game. He hits for average and he hits for power. His two feats of power-hitting this season are among the most remarkable achievements of any home-run hitter.

"It feels good to do this, to do something nobody in the game has done," Mattingly said after a 12-year-old fan, Mike Smith of the Bronx, handed the first baseman the ball he had retrieved while attending his 67th game of the season. "All the players who have played, it's surprising that nobody did it. You don't go after records. I just try to hit the ball hard."

Mattingly, who approached his time at bat in the third inning with a .217 career average against the left-handed Hurst with no home runs, stepped to the plate after the Yankees loaded the bases on singles by Roberto Kelly and Rickey

Henderson and a walk to Willie Randolph. He had batted the previous night with the bases loaded in the ninth inning, but hit a sacrifice fly.

This time he had a count of one ball and two strikes when Hurst threw him a change-up.

"I just wanted to try to stay on the ball," Mattingly explained. "I didn't want to pull off. He got me with two changeups the first time."

Hurst's change-up did not get Mattingly this time. He lofted the ball high in the air and it descended in the upper deck in right field.

Perhaps just as remarkable as the record is the fact that before this season, Mattingly had never hit a grand slam in the majors.

"I can't explain it," he said. "I basically haven't done anything different other than try to hit the ball hard. Before, I would hit a sacrifice fly with the bases loaded. Now, I think of hitting the ball hard. Consequently, if I get the ball in the air, it carries."

When Mattingly went to bat against Mike Mason of Texas on May 14, he had a career record of 13 hits in 52 at-bats with only one extra-base hit with the bases loaded. He hit a grand slam against Mason that day and subsequently hit grand slams against John Cerutti of Toronto on June 29, Joel McKeon of Chicago on July 10, Charlie Hough of Texas on July 16 and Jose Mesa of Baltimore last Friday night. The grand slam against Mesa tied the record shared by Ernie Banks of the Chicago Cubs (1955) and Jim Gentile of Baltimore (1961).

Interestingly, four of Mattingly's grand slams —the first three and the sixth—came against left-handed pitchers, whom Mattingly has found easier and easier to hit.

The home run was Mattingly's 29th of the season and raised his runs-batted-in total to 114, his second highest total in the majors, surpassing last season's total by one. His batting average is .330.

If he had one regret about his record-breaking grand slam, it was that Dave Winfield was the next hitter.

"I just wish Winnie had hit this one,' Mattingly said of his teammate, who needs four R.B.I. to reach the 100 plateau for the sixth successive season. "I told him I'd move the runners along. I moved them too far." ◆

Don Mattingly's "Grand Slam" swing.

October 20, 1987

Martin Manager for 5th Time

By MICHAEL MARTINEZ

BILLY MARTIN, who came and went four times as Yankee manager in a 10-year span that began in 1975, was brought back for a fifth term today in another shakeup by the team's owner, George Steinbrenner. Lou Piniella, who has been the manager for the past two seasons, was named general manager by Steinbrenner.

Martin, who is 59 years old, spent the last two years as one of the team's television broadcasters and as a consultant to Steinbrenner. His hiring marks the 14th managerial change in the 15 years Steinbrenner has owned the team. Martin managed the Yankees for most of the 1985 season, then was dismissed in favor of Piniella, the man he will replace.

Piniella, who had one year left on his two-year contract to manage the team, had confided to friends that he neither expected—nor wanted—to return to fulfill the deal.

The club said that Piniella had agreed to a multiyear contract as general manager, replacing Woody Woodward.

Woodward said tonight that he asked Steinbrenner to replace him four weeks ago. "I felt like the demand of the schedule I was asked to keep was not one I wanted to continue," he said. "I wanted to see what was out there." Woodward would not disclose how the remaining two years on his contract were settled.

The announcement on Martin did not come as a surprise. The former manager's return was expected since late in the season, after the Yankees dropped from the American League East race, and after Piniella incurred Steinbrenner's wrath by not making himself available for a telephone call from the owner during an August trip.

Because Piniella has had no front-office experience, Steinbrenner is expected to hire someone to assist him in contract negotiations and with major league and labor-agreement rules. Steinbrenner has said that person could be Bill Bergesch, who was dismissed by the Cincinnati Reds.

Martin's off-and-on tenure with the Yankees, which began in August 1975 when he replaced Bill Virdon, has been marked by a number of stormy incidents.

He resigned under fire in July 1978. Stein-

November 1, 1987

YANKEES TO STAY IN NEW YORK CITY

By SAM HOWE VERHOVEK

NEW YORK YANKEE BASEBALL in the Bronx, a 64-year tradition that spans 22 world championships, will continue for at least 45 more years under terms of an agreement announced last night.

The accord to keep the Yankees in New York City, disclosed by officials for the team, the city and the state at a news conference at Yankee Stadium, ended 15 months of negotiations and headed off a possible move of the club to New Jersey.

"The Bronx Bombers will remain the Bronx Bombers well into the 21st century," said a beaming Mayor Koch, who announced the agreement before leaving today on a trip to Nicaragua.

Under terms of the pact to extend the Yankees current lease until 2032, the city and state are to jointly finance about $90 million in improvements in and around Yankee Stadium. The improvements are to include construction of a Metro-North railroad station and a 3,200-space parking garage as well as refurbishing parts of the Stadium, upgrading streets and highway access around it and construction of two or three city parks within about 15 blocks of the ballpark.

The new $8 million train station, near the Harlem River, would provide access to the Stadium on all three Metro-North train lines. It would be

brenner brought Martin back in June 1979, then dismissed him after the season when the manager had a fight with a marshmallow salesman outside a hotel bar in Bloomington, Minn.

Martin was back again in 1983 and remained the entire season, suffering his next dismissal after growing unrest among the players prompted Steinbrenner to make a change.

His fourth term began 16 games into the 1985 season when he replaced Yogi Berra, who had replaced him. The season culminated in a series of bizarre events, climaxed by a vicious barroom fight at a Baltimore hotel with Ed Whitson, a Yankee pitcher.

Piniella replaced Martin and became the first manager since Martin in 1976-77 to manage the team two consecutive full seasons. His teams won 179 games and finished second in 1986 and fourth last season in the American League East. Only three other managers - Dave Johnson of the Mets, Sparky Anderson of the Reds and Jimy Williams of the Blue Jays - won more games in that time.

Martin has managed the Yankees for more games, 874, than any manager under Steinbrenner. Piniella is second with 324 games. In a statement issued through the team's publicity de-partment, Martin said he was "anxious" to return.

"I want to bring back the winning tradition that our fans expect from the Yankees," he said, "and I look forward to working with Lou to accomplish that." ◆

Billy Martin in his fifth term as Yankee manager.

the first time that railroad commuters have direct access to the Stadium, as well as to the general area around the Bronx County Courthouse, at 161st Street and the Grand Concourse, which officials have long targeted for a renaissance.

The new parkland is intended to make up for a large section of Macombs Dam Park, near the Stadium, that would be torn up to make room for the parking garage.

The garage, which will cost about $50 million, will be financed by revenues from the parking fees, according to Vincent Tese, the chairman of the state Urban Development Corporation, who was widely credited with keeping the talks on track.

The principal owner of the Yankees, George M. Steinbrenner 3d, said in signing the agreement that he had never wanted the team to leave the Bronx. However, he added that at one point he believed the team might be forced to relocate.

He declined to say to where he thought the team might have moved.

The announcement came only three days before a vote in New Jersey on a $185 million bond issue to build a baseball stadium near the Meadowlands Sports Complex.

Officials of the New Jersey Sports and Exposition Authority, which operates the complex, said last week that, based on a telephone poll conducted at its request, the measure was in trouble. The poll showed 46 percent of the respondents opposed and 39 percent in favor. ◆

October 8, 1988

Green Replaces Piniella As Manager

By MURRAY CHASS

GEORGE STEINBRENNER, as expected, changed managers yesterday for the 16th time in his 16 years as the Yankees' principal owner. Steinbrenner dismissed Lou Piniella for the second time in 355 days and replaced him with Dallas Green, a former major league pitcher, manager, general manager and club president. Green received a two-year contract.

Steinbrenner's move came after he met with Piniella in Tampa, Fla.

Piniella, who was replaced by Billy Martin last Oct. 19 after two years as manager, has a three-year, $1.2 million contract that he signed after agreeing to replace Martin on June 23. It was not known immediately if Piniella would remain with the Yankees in another capacity.

He instantly became a candidate for other managerial vacancies, especially the ones in Houston and Seattle, where Woody Woodward is the Mariners' general manager. Piniella worked closely with Woodward when he was the Yankees' general manager.

Steinbrenner's selection of Green came as no surprise. If Piniella had rejected the chance to return in June, Green would have become the manager then.

When Piniella replaced Martin, the Yankees had a 40–28 record and were in second place, two and one-half games from first. Under Piniella, the Yankees had a 45–48 record and slipped to fifth place on the last two days of the season, finishing three and one-half games out. For the seventh consecutive season the Yankees failed to win the American League East championship.

"I thought Lou did a great job holding them together," Green said in a telephone conference call from his farm in West Grove, Pa. "The pitching broke down a little bit, and we had some physical problems that hurt us at times."

Why, then, did Steinbrenner feel a change was necessary?

"The bottom line with Mr. Steinbrenner is winning," Green said, "and apparently he wasn't satisfied with the way Lou went about it or the results."

Green, who compiled a 20–22 record as a major league pitcher in the 1960's, mostly with Philadelphia, managed the Phillies to the World Series championship in 1980, becoming only the fourth rookie manager to win the Series. He moved to the Chicago Cubs one year later as general manager and took on the duties of president three years after that. The Cubs dismissed him a year ago, citing philosophical differences.

Speaking of Steinbrenner, he said: "George and I go back a lot further than people realize. When I was a minor league player in Buffalo, who do I run into in a couple of my favorite haunts but George Steinbrenner? Later, I attended a lot of meetings in behalf of the Cubs that Mr. Steinbrenner was at. I've listened to him talk. I've been in conversation with him. I think I know him and I think he, in turn, knows me."

Green, 54 years old, cited his varied baseball background as a reason why he could possibly succeed where others have failed.

"All of those things," he said, "have given me an insight that perhaps I'll be able to accomplish some of the things that maybe some of the other guys haven't been able to do. What I intend to do is instill in this team the discipline that I think is necessary in today's baseball to get things done. If that doesn't work, I'll probably go the way of all Yankee managers."

Green, the type of disciplinarian Steinbrenner likes, said the owner would allow him to bring in his own coaches. The 1988 coaching staff, he said, would not return.

Because Green has front-office experience, it was thought that he might gain authority over personnel decisions and trades. He said he would discuss such matters with Steinbrenner and General Manager Bob Quinn but that he would not have final say. ◆

August 19, 1989

Steinbrenner Does It Again: Green Out, Dent In

By MURRAY CHASS

DETROIT, AUG. 18—George Steinbrenner, saying his mushrooming differences with Dallas Green had become personal, today made the 17th managerial change in his 17 seasons as owner of the Yankees. Steinbrenner dismissed Green and replaced him with Bucky Dent, the man who will forever live in Yankee history for the playoff home run he hit in 1978.

The owner, who has employed 11 different men for a total of 18 managerial tenures, met with Green late this morning at the team hotel in suburban Dearborn, Mich., and told him of his decision. Just before the meeting, he called Dent in Columbus, Ohio, to tell him, "We're going to offer you the job."

After the meeting, he called Dent again and, according to the new manager, said, "My plane will be there at 12:30; be on it."

Steinbrenner, at a brief news conference at the hotel, gave no reason for the change, saying only: "I have nothing critical to say about Dallas Green. Perhaps some things I did disappointed him and things he did disappointed me. But we're close friends."

But in a subsequent telephone interview, Steinbrenner elaborated on his reasons for the move, although his version differed from what Green told reporters.

Green said that at their meeting, the owner told him he was going to dismiss four of the manager's six coaches. Green related that he told Steinbrenner: "That's not the professional way to do it; that's not the baseball way to do it, and you're not going to do it here. It's only going to lead to more agitation. >>>

Bucky Dent managed the Yankees from 1989 from 1990.

⟨⟨⟨ Why don't you just fire the manager and then make all the coaching changes you want."

Steinbrenner said the coaching changes were a secondary matter.

"It had nothing to do with coaching changes," said the owner, who arrived here late Thursday night intending to make the change. "I came here on the basis of what was happening with the relationship. I just felt I wanted to make a change. I felt we had been friends for a lot of years—some 30 years—and it started getting personal. I was beginning to read in the papers he was saying a lot of personal things. I told him it was very disappointing to me. He was upset with me and I was upset with him. Life's too short for that."

The two admittedly strong-willed men began aiming public remarks at each other early this month. As has often happened in Steinbrenner's relations with his managers, the public dispute escalated.

The owner especially took exception to a remark attributed to Green the other day that said the Yankees didn't know anything about Jeff Peterek, a rookie Milwaukee pitcher who helped beat them, because they didn't have any scouts on the road, a thinly veiled criticism of Steinbrenner.

"We had reams of information on the kid," Steinbrenner said.

Dent, at 37 years old the youngest manager in the American League, has managed in the Yankees' minor league system for five years, the last three at Columbus, Ohio. How long did he expect to manage, the new manager was asked before tonight's game against the Detroit Tigers. Steinbrenner did not announce a specific term for Dent.

"Who knows?" responded Dent, who as a player watched Steinbrenner make five in-season managerial changes, including two in 1982. "I'm going to do the best job I can. I know the ground rules here. I played here."

Green never played for the Yankees. In fact, when he was hired last Oct. 7, he became the owner's first manager with no previous Yankee connection.

"The reason I took the New York thing was the city and the Yankees were such a great thing in baseball—or had been," said Green, who previously served as manager of the Philadelphia Phillies and general manager and president of the Chicago Cubs. "It was an ego thing. I thought I could bring something to the Yankees I thought they needed to bring them back to a championship situation."

As the season progressed and the Yankees struggled, falling to sixth place three weeks ago, the owner and the manager seemed to have overrated their players. Green would, at times, criticize some of the players for not playing the way he thought they were capable of, and Steinbrenner would criticize some of the coaches for not working hard enough. The owner began extending his criticism to Green earlier this month, although he reiterated that Green's job was safe for the rest of the season. Steinbrenner's criticism of the coaches was seen as his way of getting to Green.

"I think he knows it," Green said, discussing what his reaction would be to dismissal of any of his coaches. "We've said it enough."

In the wholesale dismissals today, Steinbrenner dismissed Charlie Fox, the dugout coach; Pat Corrales, the first-base coach; Lee Elia, the third-base coach, and Frank Howard, the hitting coach. He retained Billy Connors, the pitching coach, and John Stearns, the bullpen coach.

Connors and Stearns, who joined the Yankees as part of Green's carefully selected team, said they had considered leaving with Green, but he urged them to stay.

Howard was offered the managing job at Columbus, but rejected it. "There are things far more important than managing Columbus," said Howard, expressing loyalty to Green. He was as obviously angry about the developments as the other dismissed coaches.

Added to Dent's staff were Mike Ferraro for first base, Gene Michael for third base and Champ Summers as the hitting instructor. Summers had been coaching with Dent at Columbus.

Michael and Ferraro, both of whom will repeat coaching roles they have had in the past, had been scouting for the Yankees.

"It was something that probably would have had to happen anyway," Green, who was in the first year of a two-year, $700,000 contract, said of his departure. "The constant agitation we had in the press was a deciding factor. He didn't want it. He knew I wasn't going to buckle under."

As he has done with previous dismissed managers, Steinbrenner asked Green to remain with him in another, undisclosed, capacity, presumably as an evaluator of talent. Asked why he wanted Green to remain with him, Steinbrenner said: "He'll tell me not what he thinks I want to hear but what he thinks. I don't always get that."

When Green was asked if he would manage the Yankees again, as Billy Martin did four times after his first departure and Michael, Bob Lemon and Lou Piniella each did a second time, he said emphatically: "No, no, no, no, no. No Dallas II here."

Can a good baseball man manage the Yankees?

"Only if he succumbs to the will of George Steinbrenner," Green said. Can anyone manage the Yankees? "Anybody can manage," he said, "but for how long? Bucky will be fired. You could book it." ◆

December 26, 1989

BILLY MARTIN KILLED IN CRASH ON ICY ROAD

By MURRAY CHASS

BILLY MARTIN, the combative baseball manager who was celebrated for his ability to motivate players but was notorious for fighting with them and others, was killed yesterday in a traffic accident near Binghamton, N.Y. He was 61 years old.

According to the sheriff's office in Broome County, Mr. Martin was a passenger in a pickup truck driven by William Reedy, 53, a longtime friend of Mr. Martin from Detroit. The accident occurred at 5:45 P.M. near Mr. Martin's home.

Mr. Reedy was charged with driving while intoxicated, said Sheriff Anthony Ruffo. The sheriff said the truck was owned by Mr. Martin.

The Associated Press quoted witnesses as having said the pickup truck skidded off the icy Potter Hill Road in Fenton, continued 300 feet down an embankment and stopped at the foot of Mr. Martin's driveway. The authorities said neither Mr. Martin nor Mr. Reedy was wearing a seat belt.

Mr. Martin was taken to Wilson Memorial Hospital in Johnson City, N.Y., where efforts to revive him failed, said Michael Doll, a hospital spokesman. Mr. Doll said Mr. Martin was pronounced dead at 6:56 P.M. of severe internal injuries and possible head injuries. Mr. Doll said an autopsy would be done today at the hospital.

Mr. Reedy was listed in serious condition with a broken hip and possible broken ribs at Wilson Memorial.

Sheriff Ruffo said Mr. Reedy had been charged with driving while intoxicated and would be arraigned Jan. 4 in Fenton town court. The sheriff said Mr. Reedy took a blood alcohol test after the accident, but the sheriff did not disclose the results of the test.

Word of Mr. Martin's death spread quickly to current and former Yankee associates.

"It's shocking; it makes me sick to my stomach," said Lou Piniella, who is the Cincinnati Reds' manager but who spent as much time in a Yankees' uniform with Mr. Martin as anyone. "He was a friend," Mr. Piniella said. "I played for him. I coached for him. I had a special relationship with him. I talked to Billy in Nashville just a couple of weeks ago. He said he was going to be more involved with the team. He was ⟫⟫⟫

«« going to go to more Yankee games, help evaluate the team in spring training. He was enthused about doing these things."

An unconfirmed rumor in the last two months had Mr. Martin poised to become the Yankees' manager a sixth time, replacing Bucky Dent if the team did not start the 1990 season successfully.

Mr. Martin had been serving as a special adviser to George Steinbrenner, the owner of the Yankees, with whom he had a love-hate relationship. The two always seemed to get along better when Mr. Martin was not managing the Yankees than when he was. Mr. Steinbrenner denied yesterday that he had had managerial plans for Mr. Martin again.

"No way," the owner said by telephone from Tampa, Fla. "He was too happy doing what he was doing. He was coming upstairs. He was going to be there more than ever before. He was enthused about the coming season. In the past, it was a hit-and-miss thing, but he was going to be working a lot. I must have talked to him 20 times in the last month and a half."

Mr. Dent, in Florida, said that Mr. Martin had "his ups and downs, but he was a Yankee, heart and soul."

"He was a winner and nobody can fault him for that," Mr. Dent said.

Mr. Martin had lived near Binghamton since his last managerial tour with the Yankees ended on June 23, 1988. He managed the Yankees five times, a major league record for a single team, and also served as manager of the Minnesota Twins (1969), the Detroit Tigers (1971–73), the Texas Rangers (1973–75) and the Oakland Athletics (1980–82).

Considered one of the most brilliant game managers of his time until his last two or three stints with the Yankees, Mr. Martin won the World Series with the Yankees in 1977, the American League pennant with the Yankees in 1976 and division titles with Minnesota in 1969, Detroit in 1972 and Oakland in 1981.

The fiery Mr. Martin was especially adept at

motivating players, though some said he did this through intimidation. Some of his former players said it was always easier to win, than to lose and face Mr. Martin's wrath. Players in a losing Martin clubhouse often resembled mourners at a funeral.

Virtually all of his managerial jobs ended in controversy, but none as storied as his departures from the Yankees. Mr. Martin resigned the first time, in 1978, a day after saying of Reggie Jackson, his right fielder, and Mr. Steinbrenner: "The two of them deserve each other. One's a born liar; the other's convicted."

Billy Martin's death shocked Yankee fans and players.

Mr. Steinbrenner dismissed him the four other times, usually after Mr. Martin had been engaged in a fight. In 1979, it was with a marshmallow salesman; in 1985, one of his own players, Ed Whitson, who broke Mr. Martin's arm in a furious fight at a Baltimore hotel; in 1988, in the men's restroom at a topless bar in Texas.

Between the bar fight and his dismissal last year, Mr. Martin threw dirt on an umpire in one of his many on-field disputes. His action drew a three-day suspension and a threat from the lawyer for the umpires' union that the umpires would eject Mr. Martin from every game in which he dared step out of the dugout. Mr. Martin was gone as the Yankees' manager a few weeks later.

Alfred Manuel Martin was born in Berkeley, Calif., on May 16, 1928. His Italian grandmother called him Belli, Italian for pretty, and it evolved into Billy. He grew up fighting.

"I didn't like to fight," he once explained, "but I didn't have a choice. If you walked through the park, a couple kids would come after you. When you were small, someone was always chasing you. I had to fight three kids once because I joined the Y.M.C.A. They thought I was getting too ritzy for them."

Mr. Martin overcame his fighting long enough to become a baseball player with the Yankees. Then he resumed his fighting in that arena. He had fights with Clint Courtney, a catcher for the St. Louis Browns, in 1952 and 1953. He and several teammates, including Mickey Mantle and Yogi Berra, were involved in a fight at the Copacabana nightclub in New York in 1957. In 1960, he broke the jaw of a Chicago pitcher, Jim Brewer, and Mr. Brewer later won $10,000 in a lawsuit. As a manager, in 1969, Mr. Martin knocked out one of his players, Dave Boswell, who was fighting another player.

Mr. Steinbrenner always explained his desire to have Mr. Martin as his manager by saying that Mr. Martin was a dynamic personality, which was needed in New York, and he put "fannies in the seats." The two, however, fought fiercely as owner and manager.

When he made a change, Mr. Steinbrenner often said he was doing it for Mr. Martin's health. Conversely, it was always a sign that the owner was getting ready to hire Mr. Martin again when he began remarking on how healthy Mr. Martin looked.

Last night, Mr. Steinbrenner related a story Mr. Martin had told him about the way Mr. Martin's mother viewed the owner. Mr. Martin's mother died recently.

"When I first hired him," Mr. Steinbrenner related, "his mother called me and asked for an autographed picture, and I sent it. He told me that 'every time you'd fire me, my mother put the picture in the john. When you hired me, she put it above her dresser.'"

Mr. Martin is survived by his fourth wife, the former Jilluan Guiver, whom he married on Jan. 25, 1988, and by a son, Billy Joe Martin, and a daughter, Kelly Ann Martin, both from previous marriages, and one grandchild. ◆

August 5, 1990

Steinbrenner Banned

By CLAIRE SMITH

WHEN GEORGE STEINBRENNER was ordered by Commissioner Fay Vincent to give up operational control of the New York Yankees last week, Americans who treasure baseball as the national pastime and those with a stake in the game as a business both had reason to feel relieved. One of the most demoralizing eras in a fabled franchise's history had ended.

Steinbrenner was barred from a role in the Yankees' management not because he was tyrannical or because his organization was inept. He was banished because he had consorted with a gambler, Howard Spira, to run a clandestine investigation of the outfielder Dave Winfield, Steinbrenner's nemesis. The Yankees owner admitted as much when he accepted Vincent's ban on Monday.

But while Vincent's action was aimed solely at protecting the sport from the taint of Steinbrenner's dealings, baseball will surely welcome an important side effect: an overhaul of the Yankees' image as a laughingstock and a renegade in the baseball world.

"They are one of the premier, recognizable sports franchises in the world," said John Schuerholz, general manager of the Kansas City Royals. "They still have that reputation, despite what has happened in the last several years or so. But definitely it's for all of our best interests to have the Yankees be a viable and competitive team. If they are, it can only be great for our game."

Baseball measures its well-being by the success of franchises in the major cities. And no team's aura has enhanced the game more than that of the Yankees.

Steinbrenner came close to irreparably damaging the reputation of baseball's most lucrative franchise. His dictatorial dismissals, demotions and banishments left executives of other teams wondering whom on the Yankees they could deal with. A bemused official once asked, "Who do you call if you want to make a trade with the Yankees?"

Frank Robinson, manager of the Baltimore Orioles and president of the Baseball Network, a group of former players who have pressed baseball on affirmative action, was once asked if it bothered him that not one black or Hispanic candidate had been interviewed for the job of Yankees manager through 18 managerial changes in 18 years.

"Nah," he said. "We don't even consider them a part of baseball. That's a renegade team. George just keeps hiring and firing the same people over and over again."

Such disdain showed again in 1988, after Steinbrenner had just secured a $500 million, 12-year television deal from the MSG cable network. Not every executive quaked at the notion of a free-agent market suddenly flooded with Yankee dollars.

"I don't know what drives the man to say and do the things he does, except he's the owner and has that perceived right," Dallas Green said before he was dismissed as manager last August. "Whether he, down deep, thinks he knows more baseball than anybody on earth, I don't know. My only comeback is if we're dealing with somebody who really looks at what happened in the past, he should learn from the past. The interference isn't right."

Steinbrenner did not listen to Green, or to anyone. The Yankees ceased being considered seriously as a pennant contender.

Eventually even the free-agent market could not help the Yankees. Early on, Steinbrenner won praise for restoring the pride of the Yankees, with lavish spending to lure Reggie Jackson, Catfish Hunter, Goose Gossage and their winning ways to New York.

But the acclaim stopped when the winning did, and as top free agents, with an occasional exception, spurned the Yankees. The pitcher Floyd Bannister once told the Yankees not to bother making an offer. Last year the Yankees offered Mark Langston, another free-agent pitcher, $18 million. He signed with the California Angels for $2 million less.

The Yankees are now at a critical stage. They must choose a new general partner. They are said to be leaning toward Steinbrenner's choice, his son Hank. No matter who it is, Steinbrenner's successor will represent an opportunity to plot the course back into baseball's fold.

"It's going to take time," said Green. "It's going to take some hard work and some good baseball people to get that thing right. There's despair throughout the organization." ◆

March 1, 1991

Mattingly Named Captain

By MICHAEL MARTINEZ

FORT LAUDERDALE, FEB. 28—One day earlier, Don Mattingly walked into the Yankees' training camp to begin a new season with the same old bad back. Today, with rain interrupting the second day of workouts, he took on another major task.

Looking for leadership on a club filled with young players, Manager Stump Merrill officially named Mattingly the 10th Yankee captain in team history. He becomes the first captain since Ron Guidry in 1989.

Merrill made the announcement to the team this morning, but he discussed the idea with Mattingly in conversations during the off season.

"It had a chance to sink in," said Mattingly, who had told none of his teammates of Merrill's decision. "It's one of the biggest thrills and biggest honors for me in baseball. I take it seriously."

So did the players, who offered their congratulations to Mattingly before beginning a shortened workday. They weren't asked to vote, but it is clear they would have chosen the first baseman, whose seven full seasons make him the senior member of the team.

"Who else could you name captain?" asked Randy Velarde, the infielder. "When you think of the Yankees, who do you think of? Don Mattingly. It's ideal that Stump did it."

The announcement was one that Mattingly openly welcomed, but it is also something else to shoulder besides his back troubles. Without him, the Yankees are surely doomed to repeat their 95-loss season of 1990; with him, they can hope for a first-step recovery.

"This year is more challenging because a lot of things are up in the air, a lot of people are saying what I can and can't do," said Mattingly, who turns 30 in April. "I've got a lot to prove—mainly that I can stay healthy—and the only way I can do it is out on the field."

Mattingly, who finished the season with a career-low .256 average, said he did not believe his captaincy would create an additional burden. More than anything, he said, he intends to act as a liaison between players and management.

"I don't think I'll do anything different," he said. "If players have problems, I can act as a window between them and Stump. I've watched guys like Willie Randolph and Ron Guidry and Graig Nettles, and they never did things differently. They just tried to keep it loose and fun. I'll lead by example. I'm not a talker. What's a leader anyway? I think it's anybody who goes about his job consistently." ◆

August 18, 1991

SPORTS OF THE TIMES
The New Yankee Clippers Aren't Very Sharp

By IRA BERKOW

ALL OVER TOWN, wherever you went—to the coffee shop, to the bank, to Seymour, the guy brandishing the clippers at the third chair, and even, if you happened to pop in, to the Mayor's staff meeting at City Hall—the question being asked was, "Will he or won't he?" And also, "Why should he?"

This was on Friday after the bombshell the day before when Yankee management forced its star player, Don Mattingly, to remain on the bench during a game instead of manning his post at first base because it had asked him to trim his locks—no, demanded it—and he had refused.

"This wasn't any kind of stand for freedom, or anything," Mattingly said Friday, "it's just that they put me into a corner, and I guess the competitive nature in me came out."

Mayor David N. Dinkins, like many others, didn't get management's position. "I understand rules are rules," he said, "but it is not inappropriate to inquire as to the rationale for a rule, and that one beats me. I want to know, can he take two and hit to right?"

The Yankees have a rule about their personnel being well-groomed. There are no specifics in all this, and obviously one man's well-groomedness is another man's mess. Before it was trimmed yesterday, Mattingly's hair was short on top but a little long in back—scraggly, admittedly, when wet with sweat, but hardly what you'd call bushy.

It reminded some of the Case of Oscar Gamble, which happened in spring training about 15 years ago. Gamble was a new Yankee outfielder whose hair style was such that he wore his baseball hat about two feet over his head. The Yankees refused to give him a uniform until he had his Afro felled.

The Mattingly controversy, like the Gamble case, had little to do with grooming, and much more to do with power. The team is going lousy and there has to be a reason. It certainly can't be the players that Stick Michael, the general manager, has helped assemble. And it certainly can't be the stratagems that Stump Merrill, the manager, has employed. So it has to be something else. And Stick or Stump hit on it: Eureka, it's that long hair.

Not just Mattingly, but a few other Yankees, too. If they look like one, maybe they'll play like one. (The crazy thing is, the Yankees should want everyone to play like, if not look like, Mattingly.)

Hair is an old sheargoat. Control someone's hair and you control his mind, goes a theory. You manipulate him by sapping his psychological strength, his sense of identity. That seems the symbolism in the tale of the clipped Samson.

In the same way, the first thing a private receives in the Army is a full hedge pruning. He goes into the barber shop a person and comes out a billiard ball.

Meanwhile, the retaining of one's locks has often been taken as rebellion. Never more so than in the 1960's, when a musical dealing with tresses was a Broadway hit. Authority figures in the person of football coaches and baseball managers and assorted school officials felt they were in a death struggle with self-expression.

Beatniks and hippies, it seemed to some, threatened our homes, our families, the well-being of an ordered and respectable society.

Arguments abounded. Long hair, it was recalled, had an honorable history. Besides Samson, there were Jesus, Shakespeare, Henry VIII, Louis XIV, George Washington, Buffalo Bill, Sitting Bull, Tarzan, Toscanini and Einstein ("Uh, Professor, the members of the academy believe you might be getting a little shaggy around the ears and. . . ."). Entertainers included Valentino, the Beatles and Lassie. In sports, the irrepressible and sometimes thickly thatched Joe Namath led the way.

Don Mattingly before he cut his hair.

As if this weren't enough, examples of bad bald guys, or short-haired ones, anyway, were trotted out: Mussolini, Mao Zedong, Al Capone, Fu Manchu, Dr. No, Professor Moriarty, Flat Top (whose hair was cut like an aircraft carrier) and Odd Job.

Somehow, the republic managed to survive. Then all this came back on Thursday.

Mattingly's action seemed to mirror a belief put forth years ago by Supreme Court Justice William O. Douglas about the right at specified times to defy a bad law. "It has its roots," Douglas said, "in our traditions of individualism and in our mistrust of the uncontrolled powers of the state."

When Mattingly, still unshorn, walked into the Yankee dressing room Friday, there were shouts of appreciation from teammates for his independence.

Management had backed down. Mattingly played, and got two hits. The Yankees won. Stick and Stump, meanwhile, watched the game with fresh haircuts. And thus the problem was solved. Turned out it was their hair that was too long. ◆

October 30, 1991

Showalter at Helm

By JACK CURRY

TWENTY-TWO DAYS after he was dumped onto baseball's rapidly growing unemployment line, Buck Showalter was hired back yesterday and given a superior position as the new manager of the Yankees.

After the Yankees turned left and right and scratched their heads while searching for someone to replace Stump Merrill, they settled on the man who coached at third base for the last two years and has been affiliated with the organization since he was 21 years old. Excluding the last three weeks, of course.

In signing a one-year contract, the 35-year-old Showalter became the youngest manager in the majors and the youngest for the Yankees since 1914. The move left Gene Michael groping for words, for the Yankee general manager had said the next manager would have major league experience. When he was asked if Showalter had been his first choice, Michael chirped, "He is now."

It was quickly apparent why the Yankees' limited partners made a smart move on Oct. 18, when they strongly suggested to Michael that he consider Showalter ahead of retread candidates like Doug Rader and Hal Lanier. At yesterday's news conference at Yankee Stadium, the new manager looked polished while discussing what the club must do to avoid losing 90 games for the third straight season.

"I have thoughts about what went wrong here," said Showalter. "But you keep getting back to the Al Davis theory. Just win. Winning takes care of a lot."

Showalter appeared to say all the right things and made an uncomfortable situation comfortable for all parties. He even said Michael had done him a favor by letting him go as coach because he could then entertain the calls that came from other teams.

Seattle interviewed Showalter for the Mariners' manager's post, which was filled by hiring Bill Plummer yesterday, and three other teams spoke to Showalter about coaching positions. But »»»

《《《 11 days after Michael told Showalter to look elsewhere, the Yankee executives told Michael what to do and started a process that turned Showalter into the 20th Yankee manager since 1973, including the multiple terms of Billy Martin, Lou Piniella, Bob Lemon and Michael himself.

Though the Yankees seemed to make the correct choice, problems may still exist. The club did not express much faith in Showalter by giving him a one-year contract worth about $225,000, but the new manager tried turning the touchy topic into a positive.

"I'm on a one-year contract," Showalter said. "That means we're on a one-year plan."

Michael claimed the one-year contract was an organizational policy and did not believe it was an issue, saying that was what the club "gave the last two guys." Both Merrill and Bucky Dent, the last two guys, are no longer around.

The Yankees remain a team immersed in conflict and confusion. Since Showalter was not Michael's choice, the relationship may be troubling. The limited partners stripped away Michael's first chance to hire a manager and put him under the microscope. How will Michael deal with another manager who was not his selection? He did not defend Merrill, who was also not his hire, when players criticized him last year.

Both the general managing partner, Robert Nederlander, and the chief executive officer, Leonard Kleiman, insisted yesterday Michael was standing on solid footing. Nederlander called Michael, "the best baseball man in the country" and Kleinman said the general manager "had done a wonderful job." ◆

Manager Buck Showalter and George Steinbrenner during batting practice.

July 25, 1992

Vincent Grants March 1 Return To Steinbrenner

By MURRAY CHASS

ALMOST TWO YEARS after George Steinbrenner received a lifetime ban from baseball, Commissioner Fay Vincent said yesterday that the Yankees' owner could return unconditionally to active duty with the club next March 1.

Mr. Vincent's announcement would appear to end the seemingly ceaseless Steinbrenner saga, but the owner could still stumble. There have been bizarre twists before. In late July 1990, the commissioner at first imposed a two-year suspension that would have ended next Wednesday, but Mr. Steinbrenner negotiated a lifetime ban, a choice he tied to other interests, including his role as an officer for the United States Olympic Committee.

Mr. Steinbrenner was disciplined after an investigation by the commissioner showed that the Yankees' owner had paid $40,000 to Howard Spira, a self-proclaimed gambler, after Mr. Spira gave the owner information aimed at discrediting Dave Winfield, then one of Mr. Steinbrenner's star players.

The agreement under which Mr. Steinbrenner stepped aside as the Yankees' managing partner will remain in effect until March 1.

"So if one were to violate that agreement, obviously all bets are off," Steve Greenberg, baseball's deputy commissioner, explained yesterday. "But I don't anticipate that happening."

On the other side of that issue, Mr. Vincent indicated he might make exceptions to the stipulations of the agreement, depending on Mr. Steinbrenner's behavior.

"We need evidence of good will and peace and quiet, and we'll judge the future as it unfolds," the commissioner said by telephone from his summer home in Cape Cod. "I have no intention of changing the agreement, but that doesn't mean developments couldn't warrant it."

When Mr. Vincent originally imposed the discipline, on July 30, 1990, he stipulated that it was to be a two-year suspension. But in a meeting that day, Mr. Steinbrenner asked for an alternative penalty that resulted in an agreement under which Mr. Steinbrenner permanently relinquished his role as managing partner.

In an affidavit he filed later in a lawsuit, Mr. Steinbrenner explained his decision in semantical terms by saying he "felt that I could not have it declared publicly that I had been 'suspended.'" He feared, he continued, that a suspension would "cause great harm to my reputation and put in jeopardy" his position as a vice president of the U.S.O.C., whose Committee officials subsequently said the type of penalty would not have mattered to them.

Serving in his Olympic capacity yesterday, Mr. Steinbrenner was in Barcelona, Spain, yesterday and said early in the day that "my only concern now is with the Olympic team."

But the Yankees have never been a distant concern for Mr. Steinbrenner, and his effort to return to the team has been constant. In a meeting with the commissioner last May 19, Mr. Steinbrenner asked to be permitted to return this month. Mr. Greenberg said yesterday that Mr. Steinbrenner might have been allowed back next month "but for the litigation—the year and a half of litigation had an effect."

Mr. Steinbrenner and others associated with him filed three lawsuits stemming from the commissioner's 1990 investigation and action. Once Mr. Steinbrenner asked to be permitted to return, Mr. Vincent told him the lawsuits would have to "disappear" before he would consider his request.

This is the second time in Mr. Steinbrenner's 20-year tenure as the Yankees' principal owner that he has been allowed to return early from a commissioner's disciplinary action. Bowie Kuhn suspended him for two years on Nov. 27, 1974, for his role in making illegal contributions to the re-election campaign of President Nixon. He was reinstated after 15 months. ◆

November 4, 1992

Kelly Traded to Reds for O'Neill

By JACK CURRY

THE YANKEES SCRAPPED their glorious plans involving Roberto Kelly yesterday and traded their once-untouchable outfielder to the Cincinnati Reds for power-hitting right fielder Paul O'Neill.

Joe DeBerry, a minor league first baseman, also came to New York in the deal, which essentially centered on the 29-year-old O'Neill, a .259 career hitter with 96 home runs and a contract through 1994, being swapped for the 28-year-old Kelly, a .280 career hitter with 56 home runs and an opportunity to become a free agent after next season.

In recent years, the Yankees had labeled Kelly as someone they would not trade because of his potential to be their next superstar. They spoke

Paul O'Neill, a 'quality left-handed bat.'

glowingly of Kelly as an integral part of their outfield of the future and raved about his combination of power and speed. Apparently, the Yankees grew impatient.

"We were looking for left-handed bats because I didn't think we had enough," said General Manager Gene Michael. "I always said we were too right-handed. I feel this is a quality hitter and Yankee Stadium should be conducive to his hitting."

In O'Neill, the Yankees are getting a player who struggled this past season after compiling his best career numbers in 1991. O'Neill batted .246 with 14 homers and 66 R.B.I. in 1992, after hitting .256 with 28 homers and 91 R.B.I. the year before.

The Yankees will lose one of their main sources of speed without Kelly, who had a decent season in 1992, when he hit .272 with 10 homers and 66 R.B.I. But he failed to have the breakout season the Yankees expected and the team was not pleased with his attitude after he was shifted from center field to left field when Bernie Williams was promoted full-time to center. In 638 career games with the Yankees, Kelly batted .280 with 56 homers, 258 R.B.I. and 151 stolen bases.

Lou Piniella, the former Yankee and Reds manager, who knows both players well, advised Michael about the trade, and it is doubtful Michael would have made it if Piniella did not give a superb report on O'Neill.

O'Neill, a regular for six years in Cincinnati after growing up in Columbus, Ohio, said he was at first "shocked" by the trade. He said he had not given much thought about being traded from the team of Marge Schott, one of the eccentric owners in baseball, to the team of George Steinbrenner, one of the outspoken owners in baseball.

"Everybody hears the horror stories," he said about playing in New York. "I hope there are some good ones too." ◆

December 11, 1992

Yankees Finally Get It Right and Land a Lefty

By JACK CURRY

THE YANKEES FINALLY DID IT. After a dreadful experience at the winter meetings, where they unsuccessfully chased expensive free agents, they finally signed a pitcher on their wish list last night as Jimmy Key agreed to a four-year contract worth $17 million.

Key, who is represented by his wife, Cindy, responded to the lucrative proposal from a cruise ship where he is on a weeklong vacation. The Yankees' managing partner, Joseph Molloy, personally wooed Key as the team's chief negotiator.

Desperate to add another reliable pitcher to their erratic rotation, the Yankees had staggered home from baseball's winter meetings in Louisville, Ky., after a dreadful and unsuccessful week of chasing expensive free-agent pitchers like Greg Maddux, David Cone, Doug Drabek, Jose Guzman, Greg Swindell and Chris Bosio. So it was essential for them to seduce Key and pair him with Jim Abbott to give them two left-handers and a sounder rotation.

The soft-spoken Key, who turns 32 in April, is one of only two major leaguers to win at least 12 games in each of the last eight seasons. He comes to the Bronx after nine seasons in Toronto and brings a career record of 116–81, including an 8–1 mark at Yankee Stadium.

"I'm excited about getting a player of his background and with his track record coming to New York,"said Manager Buck Showalter, in a telephone interview from Pace, Fla. "As important as that is, I'm excited that he wanted to come to play in New York."

What a concept. Key, who lives in Tarpon Springs, Fla., and does not seem like a big-city type, told former Blue Jays teammate David Cone that playing in New York would not bother him, unlike Maddux and Barry Bonds, who snubbed Yankee offers. The signing certainly came as no surprise after George Steinbrenner expressed his desire earlier yesterday to see Key pitching at Yankee Stadium.

"I think Key is a guy I would have wanted as much as anybody," said Steinbrenner, in a telephone interview from Tampa, Fla. "I like Jimmy Key. He would have been one of my first choices. If we can get him, I think that our rotation will be all right."

After enduring frustrating negotiations with Maddux and Bonds, the Yankees were able to celebrate as their rotation began to take shape with Abbott likely to be the ace followed by Melido Perez, Key and then Sam Militello for the fourth or fifth slot. That situation depends on whether the Yankees sign free agent Ron Darling, the former Met who is quite interested in returning to New York. And there could be more. The Yankees are intrigued by free-agent catcher Terry Steinbach, and they will meet with third baseman Wade Boggs's agent today in Tampa.

Even though the Yankees signed Key, the sour taste of the meetings in Louisville will remain for some time.

The Yankees envisioned Bonds, the two-time National League most valuable player, anchoring their lineup and Maddux, last season's National League Cy Young Award winner, anchoring their rotation, and they were willing to invest $71 million to corral them. But the Yankees were miffed when Bonds suddenly grew fond of San Francisco and signed a six-year, $43.75 million contract to play there, and they were devastated when Maddux accepted $6 million less than they offered to play in Atlanta.

"We'll find a way to win without them," Steinbrenner said. ◆

September 5, 1993

SPORTS OF THE TIMES
The Leather That Saved a No-Hitter

By GEORGE VECSEY

IT TOOK AWHILE to get into this no-hitter by Jim Abbott on a clammy September afternoon because Abbott was putting down these Cleveland Indians so ordinarily, with the odd walk thrown in.

It took a desperate defensive act by Wade Boggs to wake up Yankee Stadium.

Abbott lulls people with his burly athlete's body and his competitive, even slightly pugnacious, pose on the mound. He never carries himself like a curiosity, with the rudimentary right hand of his. He juggles a fielder's glove and with his left hand he fires sinking fastballs.

This has been a trying season for this big Olympic hero of 1988. He started yesterday with a 9-11 record and a 4.31 earned run average. But yesterday he was throwing the way Jim Abbott can. And the outs were so unspectacular that the game just sort of rolled along.

It got good only in the seventh inning. Albert Belle spanked a grounder toward "the hole"—the badlands where the shortstop and the third baseman sometimes converge and sometimes do not.

The shortstop, Randy Velarde, had a chance to get his glove on the ball but much less of a chance to throw out Belle.

The third baseman was Wade Boggs, from the Red Sox. The old professional lunged to his left, dived to stop the medium-velocity grounder, went to his knees and came up throwing, hard and straight, to first, where Don Mattingly made the easy stretch. It wasn't even close.

"Every no-hitter takes a bit of luck," Abbott said. "The draw you get on certain days." Yesterday, the luck was created by Wade Boggs, transforming a clammy September afternoon with one lunge, one stab of his glove. ◆

September 15, 1994

All the Magic Is Gone From the Numbers

By JACK CURRY

THE SEASON that could have been special for the Yankees, the season that might have ended their 12-year post-season drought and the season that they often conceded might never be duplicated officially ended yesterday without a resolution on the field. When Bud Selig, the acting commissioner, canceled the remainder of the baseball season, the Yankees were left to wonder what might have been.

They possessed the finest record in the American League at 70–43, they had the top hitter in the league in Paul O'Neill, they had perhaps the elite pitcher in the league in Jimmy Key and they had a wonderful chance to rumble to the World Series for the first time since 1981.

But their terrific achievements will now be stashed away, stuffed into record books that focus on a season turned meaningless because of a protracted labor dispute.

"It's a very terrible day," said the majority owner George Steinbrenner. "It's a very depressing day because we were doing so well and it looked like we were going to win our division. To have that not happen is real hard."

Although the cancellation had become more of an inevitability in recent days, the somber mood that had enveloped the Yankees offices in the Bronx grew even drearier, even gloomier yesterday. Even while the players and the owners seemed to be at separate ends of the Grand Canyon during negotiations, there was always a chance for a settlement and a chance for the Yankees to resume playing with a six and a half game lead over the second-place Baltimore Orioles.

That possibility vanished yesterday.

"I can't believe what's happened," said O'Neill. "All along, I've been waiting for a call to tell me to come back and play. Now, who knows when that will be?

"Nobody is going to run onto the field to end it this year. It's weird. There's no doubt in my mind we had a chance to win this thing."

General Manager Gene Michael was depressed, too. "You wake up with this sick feeling," he said. "It's like losing five or six games in one day. It's a tough thing to go through."

The voices of the Yankee officials told the stories of frustration. Steinbrenner's was gruff, reflecting his aggravation that potential losses could escalate into the high millions. Michael's voice was despondent as he explained how he detested coming to work during the strike and wondered if he will be able to assemble such a quality team again.

Manager Buck Showalter sounded lethargic as he spoke about Don Mattingly still not being able to participate in the playoffs, and as he tried to ignore the World Series dreams that had been erased. He declined to designate the Yankees the American League East champions.

"I made no secret about saying all year that I thought we surrounded ourselves with pretty special people," Showalter said. "We'll never know now what they could have done."

Or how it would have felt in the Bronx in October 1994.

"It's the greatest feeling in the world to have your team in the World Series," Steinbrenner said. "It's the greatest thrill you'll ever know in your life. You see the look on people's faces and you realize just how incredible it is. We lost that."

On those October evenings when the World Series would have been played, it will be difficult for the Yankees to avoid being angry. They won 70 of 113 games, they focused on advancing to the playoffs and they had a balanced and cohesive team. Now they are a scattered bunch, and Mattingly, their symbol of October futility, the veteran star who has hinted at retirement if the work stoppage dragged too far into next season, has still not secured a post-season at-bat.

The Yankees will almost certainly have a new look when they play their next game because only six players are under contract for 1995.

"We'll never know how good we could have been," said catcher Jim Leyritz. "We have four or five free agents who might not be back. As dominating as our team was, it's unfortunate we'll never find out whether we could have dominated the National League, too."

While Steinbrenner and others wait for meaningful negotiations, hopes for a meaningful season officially died yesterday.

"It bothers me that we won't be remembered 10 years from now for having won anything," General Manager Gene Michael said. "We were good enough to win this thing. We had the kind of makeup to win it all. It's a downer." ◆

April 27, 1995

All Is Forgiven at Delayed Opener

By BRUCE WEBER

BASEBALL RETURNED to New York City yesterday afternoon, bringing with it the balm to soothe tens of thousands of heartsick fans. The crowd for opening day at Yankee Stadium—50,245, about 6,500 fewer than last year—arrived early and stayed late, witnesses to the first professional baseball game in the city since a players' strike shut down the game last August.

In between they saw the Yanks hold off the Texas Rangers, a satisfying start to a season in which the New York team is expected to excel. But more than that, the returning fans seemed to relish the sheer pleasure of being in the ball park on a sunny day, as if it were a kind of medicine for an undiagnosed malady.

"I didn't want to come back, but I did," said Will Damiano, who stood outside the Bronx ball park with his 7-year-old son, William, on his shoulders. "I didn't want to ruin my son's baseball fever." Mr. Damiano identified himself as a die-hard Mets fan, and he had no reason he could name for going out to Yankee Stadium yesterday. "Still," he said, "I'd be disappointed if not too many people came. I like the crowd."

He spoke quietly, but apparently with some authority, on behalf of the fans that milled on River Avenue for more than two hours before the game, filling the bars and memorabilia shops that had been empty for months.

The Yankee Doodlers, a strolling brass band, perhaps best caught the mood (or maybe they were merely paid to help create it) when they played a rousing rendition of "Happy Days Are Here Again" outside the stadium before the game. Two little girls walked past them singing a tune of

their own: "Take Me Out to the Ball Game."

Even Mayor Rudolph W. Giuliani, who threw out one of the first pitches (Gov. George E. Pataki threw out another), felt no need to make a politic early exit; he stayed to the end of the Yankees' 8–6 victory.

"It was sort of like a lovers' feud," the Mayor said about the relationship between the game and its fans, which had clearly been sundered by the eight-month-long strike. "It's all over now."

There were, of course, detractors. Sign-wielders proclaimed sentiments like "We're Here But We're Not Happy" and "R.I.P. Baseball 1869–1994." Behind third base, several rows of fans were decked out in neon yellow hats with "Replacement Fan" inscribed across the crown.

There is something about baseball that encourages reflection. Even those who were having the

Joe DiMaggio throws the ceremonial first pitch at the 1995 home opener.

bitterest experiences at the ball park yesterday succumbed. These were the dozen or so major league umpires picketing in front of the park. The umpires, in the midst of a contract dispute, have been locked out by the American and National Leagues, replaced for the time being by non-major league umps.

"Umps get especially psyched up for opening day; it stinks being out here," said Mark Hirschbeck, an umpire for eight years.

For yesterday's opening day in the Bronx, Yankee fans were already in midseason form, exhibiting their reputations for both baseball expertise and roughhouse. Several fights broke out in the farther reaches of the stadium, particularly in the right-field bleachers, where a small klatch of spectators tossed beer cups and, in one case, a baseball at the neighboring box seats.

Still, few fans overall were unruly, and most just seemed baseball-shrewd. Perhaps the biggest cheer of the day was not for either of the two Yankee home runs, but for a rarer, much-tinier moment, a brilliantly placed bunt single by Pat Kelly.

As for the frequently voiced notion that the strike has turned off a whole new generation of baseball fans, the opposite view was delivered by Thomas Allessandro, 10, of Old Bridge, N.J., who sat in the upper deck with his father, Richard.

Thomas spent most of the afternoon firing high-pitched enthusiasm at the Yankees, quoting their better statistics at high volume, and pleading for the players to repeat their past performances.

They left in the sixth inning to get home in time for Thomas to play in his own Little League game.

"I've been working on my fastball lately," Thomas said. "I jam right-handed hitters with that. But my best pitch is a slider."

As his father led him down the aisle, Thomas motioned at the diamond below. "I can't wait till I'm out on that field myself," he said. ◆

October 9, 1995

THE YANKEES' RUN AGROUND IN SEATTLE

By JACK CURRY

SEATTLE, OCT. 8—There were so many hurdles and obstacles for the Yankees in the last six weeks. Again and again, the Yankees leaped over them. Until tonight. Until Edgar Martinez's two-run double off Jack McDowell in the 11th inning lifted the Mariners to a dramatic 6–5 victory in the decisive game of their American League Division Series. Their exciting season is over.

The Yankees snatched a 5–4 lead in the top of the 11th on Randy Velarde's run-scoring single against Randy Johnson, but Seattle rallied quickly in the bottom of the inning against McDowell. Joey Cora reached first on a nifty bunt single along the first-base line, Ken Griffey Jr. singled him to third and McDowell, whose specialty was supposed to be retiring Martinez, could not. The Yankee killer doubled down the left-field line, scoring Cora from third and enabling Griffey to speed home from first. The relay was late. The stunned Yankees walked off the field for the last time this season.

The 57,411 fans at the Kingdome were ecstatic because the Mariners qualified for the American League Championship Series, which begins here on Tuesday against the Indians, by winning the last three games of the series against the Yankees. The Mariners rushed onto the field and fireworks erupted above them after they became only the fourth team to rally from a two-game deficit in a three-of-five-game playoff series. The home team won every game in this classic series.

"For the fans and for baseball, it was one hell of a series," said David Cone, who blamed himself for not protecting a 4–2 lead in the eighth. "Both teams laid their guts out on the line. There were guys who were willing to blow their arms out. Randy and Jack would have pitched all night."

McDowell, who pitched in relief on one day of rest, had tears in his eyes as he stood before »»»

《《 his locker in the somber clubhouse. So did Wade Boggs. So did a handful of other players who saw their season end with such a jolt after they had botched three separate leads in the critical game. Instead of advancing to the A.L.C.S., the Yankees boarded a plane to uncertainty.

"It's the greatest feeling in the world when you get in," Boggs said in reference to the playoffs, "and it's the worst feeling in the world when you leave."

"We have absolutely nothing to be embarrassed about," Velarde said.

After his first post-season appearance ended on a sour note, Don Mattingly was sullen as he discussed the wonderful plays, wonderful games and wonderful memories. "Everything about it was great," said Mattingly, who finished with 10 hits and a .417 batting average in the series. "Except that we lost."

Cone will probably wonder for months about his 3-2 forkball to Doug Strange in the eighth inning. After Ken Griffey Jr.'s record-tying fifth post-season homer trimmed New York's lead to 4-3, Cone walked Tino Martinez with two out. It was his first walk of the game. He then allowed Jay Buhner's single and walked pinch-hitter Alex Diaz to load the bases. Showalter did not summon a reliever because his bullpen had been abysmal, with a 6.14 earned run average in four games. This was Cone's game.

Strange pinch-hit for Dan Wilson and Cone threw a strike before throwing three straight balls. Cone rebounded to throw a second strike, but he elected to throw a 3-2 forkball that bounced. It forced in the fourth run. Cone slumped over with his hands on his knees before being replaced by Mariano Rivera.

His bat and helmet discarded, Don Mattingly returns to the dugout after striking out in the 10th inning of Game 5 of the 1995 ALDS, his final at bat as a Yankee.

"I'd be lying if I told you that I wouldn't second-guess myself," said Cone, who threw 147 pitches and said he would have thrown 180. "If you second-guess yourself, you won't last long in this game. It takes some guts to go with that pitch in the first place. I just keep thinking if I get that out, we go to the ninth with a one-run lead."

Pursuing their first trip to the A.L.C.S. since 1981 and trying to overcome their mishandling of a 2-0 series lead, the Yankees were distraught after they surrendered leads for the second straight game and lost for the ninth time in 10 games at the Kingdome.

Despite losing two leads, the Yankees needed three outs in the 11th to keep their season alive. McDowell, who wound up pitching one and two-thirds innings as Manager Buck Showalter eschewed his closer John Wetteland, could not secure even one out in the decisive inning. Edgar Martinez, who finished with 12 hits in 19 at-bats (.636) and 10 runs batted in in the series, ripped what McDowell called "a horrible split-finger" to send the Yankees home and keep the Mariners playing for at least four more games.

"There's not really any solace to be taken from this," McDowell said. "There's only one team left standing and that's all that matters. When you put the uniform on in spring training, that's what you play for. The rest is a waste."

The Yankees did not secure the wild-card berth until the final day of the regular season and the Mariners did not win the American League West until a day later, so it was fitting that the two teams battled in a fifth game that extended into extra innings. Maybe it was also fitting that McDowell and Johnson, two aces, finished the game in relief.

"That's what it should come down to," said Showalter. "Two warriors going at it."

Johnson came into the game in the ninth inning and retired the first six batters he faced before Mike Stanley walked to open the 11th. Kelly was inserted as a pinch-runner and Tony Fernandez adeptly bunted him to second base. Then Velarde, who had 18 hits in 39 career at-bats against the dominating Johnson, rapped the single that helped the Yankees go ahead, 5-4. It was their last lead of the season and maybe the last time they will ever be together.

"That's what hurts," Boggs said. "You're hugging guys and when they walk out the door, you don't know if you'll ever see them again."

George Steinbrenner paraded around the clubhouse after the game and shook hands with players. Surprisingly calm, Steinbrenner said he was "proud" of the Yankees and that "frustration will set in later." He declined to discuss the futures of Manager Buck Showalter or General Manager Gene Michael, whose contracts are up at the end of the month. "Let's not start any of that," said Steinbrenner. "Let's stay where we are here and now." ◆

9 THE TORRE JETER RIVERA ERA

When the Yankees announced that Joe Torre would be their new manager in 1996, a Daily News headline called him "Clueless Joe." Understandably. Over fourteen seasons in three earlier dugout opportunities with the New York Mets, the Atlanta Braves, and the St. Louis Cardinals, he guided only the 1982 Braves to the postseason, where they were quickly swept. His win–loss record, at 894–1,003, was more than 100 games under the .500 mark. Yes, he had been quite a player. As a catcher–third baseman with the Braves, Cardinals, and Mets, he was a nine-time All-Star with a 1971 season to remember—a .363 batting title with 230 hits, 137 RBI, and the National League's MVP Award. But his only American League experience involved six years as a television analyst for the California Angels before he managed the Cardinals. How and why had the Yankees hired him?

The answer: Arthur Richman. A Yankees senior media adviser who had been the Mets' traveling secretary when Torre was the manager, Richman recommended Torre to Gene Michael, the jack-of-all-front-office-trades, who touted him to George Steinbrenner. Michael thought that Torre, as a "New York guy" who had grown up in Brooklyn and managed the Mets, could handle the New York stress— and the Steinbrenner stress—that surrounded the job.

None of Steinbrenner's other managers handled it better. Torre proved he knew not only how to manage the Yankees but also how to manage Steinbrenner. In his first five seasons, the Yankees won four World Series, including three in a row. The Yankees would lose two World Series, but, before Torre's 2007 departure in a contract dispute, each of his twelve teams always made the postseason (10 first-place American League East titles, two wild cards). His regular-season record with the Yankees was 1,173–767, which lifted his career mark to 2,067–1,770. His postseason record was 75–44, including 21–11 in the World Series, 27–14 in American League Championship Series, and 27–19 in American League Division Series.

Torre's 4–2 record in World Series ranked third among Yankees managers: Joe McCarthy was 7–1, and Casey

★ ★ ★

Joe Torre and Derek Jeter.

Stengel was 7–3. Oddly, their common denominator was that each joined the Yankees with a National League background. McCarthy had been a career minor league infielder before managing the Chicago Cubs for five seasons, notably to the 1929 pennant. Stengel had been an outfielder with the Brooklyn Dodgers, Pittsburgh Pirates, Philadelphia Phillies, New York Giants, and Boston Braves before managing the Dodgers and the Braves.

Torre's arrival in 1996 coincided with the debut of shortstop Derek Jeter and bullpen right-hander Mariano Rivera, each certain of a bronze plaque at the Hall of Fame. Left-hander Andy Pettitte and catcher Jorge Posada joined Jeter and Rivera to form the "Core Four" of Torre's teams as prominent names came and went through free agency, trades, or minor league development: first basemen Tino Martinez, Cecil Fielder, and Jason Giambi; second basemen Chuck Knoblauch, Alfonso Soriano, and Robinson Cano; third basemen Scott Brosius, Aaron Boone, and Alex Rodriguez; outfielders Hideki Matsui, Johnny Damon, Gary Sheffield, and Bobby Abreu; designated hitters Darryl Strawberry, Ruben Sierra, Chili Davis, and David Justice; pitchers David Cone, Dwight Gooden, Jeff Nelson, Mike Stanton, Ramiro Mendoza, David Wells, Roger Clemens, Orlando Hernandez, Mike Mussina, Randy Johnson, and Chien-Ming Wang.

Torre's success coincided with Brian Cashman's rise to power in the front office. Originally hired as an intern out of Catholic University, where he was a second baseman on the baseball team, Cashman was assistant farm director, then assistant general manager to Gene Michael and Bob Watson, before his 1998 promotion to general manager at age 31—the second youngest GM in baseball history. After decades of Steinbrenner's hectic changes, Torre and Cashman provided a continuity of command that the principal owner admired. During the 2000 American League Division Series, Steinbrenner was sitting in the mostly empty Yankees dugout at the stadium after batting practice when he said, "Joe and Cash are a great combination." The Yankees went on to win a third consecutive World Series, the fourth of Torre's tenure. They lost in 2001 to the Arizona Diamondbacks and in 2003 to the Florida Marlins, but even after their 2004 collapse from a 3–0 lead in the ⟫⟫⟫

<<< American League Championship Series with the Red Sox, that "great combination" endured. In earlier years, Steinbrenner probably would have turned the dugout and the front office upside down. Instead, Torre got a three-year extension for $19.2 million, making him the highest-paid manager in history, and upstairs Cashman remained in charge. When the Angels, for the second time in four years, eliminated the Yankees from the postseason in 2005, Steinbrenner growled, but the "great combination" continued. Cashman not only got a $5.4 million three-year contract, making him the highest-paid general manager in baseball, but he also was granted full authority over the Yankees' entire baseball operations, notably the minor leagues and the draft.

In both 2006 and 2007 the Yankees did not get to the World Series, much less win it. With Steinbrenner's health and influence waning, the owner's sons, Hal and Hank, dominated the franchise's thinking. When Torre's contract came up for renewal after the 2007 season, he felt "insulted" by a cut in salary with incentives. He resigned. Cashman hired Joe Girardi, a studious catcher in Torre's first four seasons, to usher the team into the new Yankee Stadium across East 161st Street in the Bronx.

The "great combination" was no more. Brian Cashman was more firmly established than ever, but Joe Torre took his Hall of Fame résumé to the Los Angeles Dodgers, whose Brooklyn ancestors were the Yankees' nearly annual World Series rival when he, curiously, was a Giants fan growing up in Brooklyn.

October 1, 1994

Another Award for Jeter

DEREK JETER, the Yankees' top prospect, has received yet another honor. The 20-year-old shortstop, who was voted Baseball America's minor league player of the year, has been named USA Today Baseball Weekly's minor leaguer of the year. Jeter hit .344 with 68 runs batted in and 50 stolen bases for three Yankee farm clubs this season.

Runners-up for the award included outfielder Ruben Rivera, another Yankee minor leaguer and shortstop Alex Rodriguez who was promoted to the Seattle Mariners during his first season in professional baseball. ◆

November 3, 1995

Yet Another Era Begins as the Yankees Hire Torre

By JACK CURRY

JOE TORRE WANTED to be wanted as a manager. Even if it was by George Steinbrenner, who has routinely been a manager's worst friend for 23 seasons. But Steinbrenner wanted Torre to replace Buck Showalter so desperately that the Yankees did not even interview another candidate.

Yesterday, Torre got what he wanted and so did Steinbrenner as the Yankees introduced their new manager at the Stadium Club, where 12 months earlier Showalter was toasted as American League manager of the year.

Why was the respectable but hardly overwhelming Torre a unanimous choice for the job? Why would he want to manage for Steinbrenner? And why was General Manager Bob Watson saying Wednesday night that he was still considering candidates, when Torre had already accepted the position for two years with a contract worth $1.05 million?

These were among the questions swirling around Yankee Stadium yesterday as the Yankees christened a new era by presenting an old face to New York fans.

"If you were thinking of retiring, you could never think of retiring if you were offered the New York Yankee job," said Torre, who grew up in Brooklyn, played and managed the Mets in Queens and now will report to work in the Bronx. "This is a once-in-a-lifetime situation. For Billy Martin it wasn't, but it is for me. When you walk into Yankee Stadium, you get goosebumps."

But what about when you walk into Steinbrenner's office?

"When you get married, do you think you're always going to be smiling and have a great relationship?" reasoned Torre, who has been married three times. "I have a wonderful relationship with my wife and we don't agree on things. To have an opportunity to win, it is worth all the negative sides you want to talk about."

Honest, intelligent and personable, the 55-year-old Torre was inundated with questions about Steinbrenner, who did not attend the news conference and did not return telephone messages. He knows Steinbrenner can make his life nightmarish, but like the other 13 people who served as manager under the Boss (some more than once), he thinks he can handle the heat.

"Hopefully, you go out and win, and when you win everybody's happy," Torre said. "I like to see smiles on people's faces. I worked for Ted Turner and Anheuser Busch. Those people are used to winning. They get very impatient when they don't, and I can understand that. I do, too."

In following Casey Stengel, Yogi Berra ⟫⟫⟫

Bob Watson (right) introduces Joe Torre as the Yankees manager at a news conference in 1995.

<<< and Dallas Green as managers of both the Yankees and the Mets, Torre replaces Showalter, who is gone after four years in which he rebuilt the team and earned a spot in the playoffs this season.

Although Watson awkwardly tried to depict Showalter as a candidate for the Yankee job—along with Sparky Anderson, Gene Lamont, Chris Chambliss and Butch Hobson—it is obvious that Torre was Steinbrenner's only choice as he changed managers for the 20th time since taking over the team in 1973.

Watson never spoke to Showalter as the Yankees waited for his contract to expire before signing Torre. Why was Torre such a commodity?

"I did not bring in any other candidates after speaking to Joe," Watson said. "I really feel this is the right man to lead the Yankees."

Torre said he was driving to a golf course in Cincinnati on Wednesday when his pregnant wife beeped him to inform him that Watson had called, and the swift process of hiring a manager began. Torre traveled from Cincinnati to Tampa, Fla., met with Watson, Steinbrenner and Gene Michael, the former general manager, for an hour, and accepted the job. He did not even feel as if he had been interviewed, only courted.

But why would Torre take the pressure-filled job when he claimed that he did not need to work? Torre, who was dismissed from a $550,000-a-year job as manager of the St. Louis Cardinals last June 16, interviewed for Michael's vacant general manager slot last month but felt the $350,000 salary was too low. For slightly more, the man who replaced Whitey Herzog in St. Louis gets to field phone calls and lineup suggestions from Steinbrenner.

A nine-time All-Star who batted .297 with 252 homers in his 18-year career, Torre has an 894–1,003 career record in 14 seasons managing the Atlanta Braves, the Mets and the Cardinals.

"When Bob called me, the realization of what the Yankees organization means hit me," Torre said. "I was in the office where the World Series trophy sits. That's what it's all about for me. It's one missing piece to my puzzle in my career." ◆

May 15, 1996

SPORTS OF THE TIMES
Gooden's No-Hitter

By DAVE ANDERSON

PAUL SORRENTO SWUNG, the pop-up soared into the sky above Yankee Stadium and on the mound Dwight Gooden soared into the sky with it.

At age 31, after having been suspended throughout the 1995 season for having repeatedly violated his substance-abuse treatment program, after having struggled through spring training, after having been on the brink of being released by the team two weeks ago until David Cone missed a start because of a shoulder aneurysm that required surgery, Gooden pitched a no-hitter last night in the Yankees' 2-0 victory over the Seattle Mariners.

"One day at a time," he has often said recently of his struggle with alcohol and drugs for the last decade. "One day at a time."

And before 31,025 rooters on a cool Bronx evening, it was one pitch at a time, one batter at

Dwight Gooden being carried off the field at Yankee Stadium after pitching his first no-hitter.

a time, one out at a time, one inning at a time. When he watched Sorrento's pop-up settle into shortstop Derek Jeter's glove, he jumped into the air and pumped his right fist.

"I'm dedicating this to my father," he said later.

"He's having open-heart surgery tomorrow."

His father, Dan Gooden, will undergo surgery in Tampa, Fla., where Gooden was raised and still lives.

"The operation is at 9 o'clock," the reclaimed right-hander was saying now at his locker. "I'm on a 7 o'clock flight in the morning."

"I want to be there when he comes to in the recovery room."

But last night, as he pitched a no-hitter, Dwight Gooden had turned Yankee Stadium into his own recovery room. ◆

June 17, 1996

Mel Allen Is Dead at 83; Golden Voice of Yankees

By RICHARD SANDOMIR

MEL ALLEN, the exuberant Alabaman who turned "How about that!" and "Ballantine Blast" into common parlance during a glorious reign as the voice of the Yankees, died yesterday at his Greenwich, Conn., home some time after watching the Yankees' game with the Cleveland Indians, his sister, Esther Kaufman, said. He was 83 years old.

Allen, who had open heart surgery seven years ago, had been ill over the past year. "But he was rallying and planning to go back to work," said Mrs. Kaufman, who had lived with her brother since 1977. The cause of death had not been determined.

Educated as a lawyer, Mr. Allen called Yankees games on radio and then on television from 1939 to 1964—from the last days of Lou Gehrig to the last gasp of the Yankee empire. He bled pinstripe blue and welcomed listeners with his trademark greeting, "Hello, everybody, this is Mel Allen!"

His garrulous, infectious style bonded him to fans but made Yankee haters loathe the team more. He did not think of himself as a Yankee booster, but he became as intimately identified with the team's fortunes as almost any player.

Recently, he said: "Some guy once said to me, 'When I tune you in, I know you'll say something positive about the Yankees.' But there's a difference between partisanship and prejudice. I gave other players their due."

Mr. Allen's voice, distinctly Southern but a perfect fit for the Bronx, became synonymous with baseball's rhythms, its lazy summer afternoons, chilly Octobers and shadows creeping over Yankee Stadium's greensward.

His manner contrasted with the cool objectivity of Walter (Red) Barber, the legendary voice of the Brooklyn Dodgers who joined Mr. Allen with the Yankees from 1954 to 1964. In 1978, the two men —fire and ice—were the first inductees into the National Baseball Hall of Fame's broadcasting wing.

In all, he called 20 World Series and 24 All-Star Games, and was present for nearly every major Yankees event: Joe DiMaggio's 56-game hitting streak in 1941 (the home portion), Mickey Mantle's tape-measure swats and Roger Maris's 61 home runs. He dubbed Joe DiMaggio "Joltin' Joe," and Tommy Henrich "Old Reliable." Through his "Ballantine Blasts" and "White Owl" wallops, Mr. Allen may have sold more beer and cigars than any sportscaster of his time.

He introduced Lou Gehrig at his July 4, 1939, farewell and Babe Ruth at his sad 1948 adieu. Mr. Allen recalled seeing Mr. Gehrig, the stricken Yankee captain, ravaged by amyotrophic lateral sclerosis, shuffle into the dugout one day in 1940.

"Lou patted me on the thigh and said, 'Kid, I never listened to the broadcasts when I was playing, but now they're what keep me going,'" said Mr. Allen, who was then 27. "I went down the steps and bawled like a baby."

It was in 1949, when DiMaggio hit four home runs in four games after a long absence because of a heel injury, that Mr. Allen shouted, "How about that!" each time DiMaggio homered. The phrase immediately caught on with fans. ◆

July 5, 1996

Yankees Stir Strawberry Into the Mix Again

By MURRAY CHASS

RISING OUT OF THE OBSCURITY of an independent minor league in the Upper Midwest, Darryl Strawberry will return to the Yankees, most likely next week after the All-Star Game break, for his second last chance in less than a year.

Ten days after their general manager declared repeatedly and emphatically that Strawberry didn't fit, the Yankees reached agreement with the wayward slugger late Wednesday evening and announced his latest comeback yesterday. Although the general manager, Bob Watson, tried hard to explain his change of mind, it seemed clear that it was George Steinbrenner, the principal owner, who performed the rescue operation.

"George is genuinely interested in being part of a story that will have a happy ending," a member of the Yankees' family said of the owner's effort to rescue Strawberry from the Northern League, where he batted .435 and hit 18 home runs in 29 games for the St. Paul Saints.

In Strawberry's new contract, which will cost the Yankees less than $400,000 for 1996, Steinbrenner holds an option for next season. He signed Strawberry last season, too, but opted not to exercise an option for a $1.8 million salary for this season. Buck Showalter, the 1995 manager, displayed little interest in having Strawberry in the lineup in the last two months of the season, but the current manager, Joe Torre, said he expected to use the left-handed hitter with 297 career home runs as the designated hitter against right-handed pitchers.

In the past 18 months, Strawberry has served a 60-day suspension from baseball for testing positive for cocaine, served a six-month home confinement sentence for Federal income tax evasion and failed to make a $300,000 payment to his former wife, Lisa, for child and spousal support by an agreed-upon deadline.

Strawberry, in fact, faced a trial in Los Angeles municipal court today on a charge of "willful failure to provide," a misdemeanor that carries a maximum one-year prison sentence.

But in a telephone news conference yesterday, Strawberry said from Columbus, Ohio: "That situation has been worked out. I don't think I have that hanging over my head anymore."

His representative, Eric Grossman, a New York lawyer, confirmed that the matter had been "taken care of" and said the hearing had been canceled. He also acknowledged that the Yankees were taking care of the back payments via a signing bonus they were giving Strawberry.

Under an agreement reached in Los Angeles, Strawberry will pay his former wife $260,000, which he will get from the Yankees. His salary will be at the rate of $300,000, meaning that if he joins the Yankees in Baltimore next Thursday, he will earn 44 percent of that total, or $132,787.

Resolving the payments problem was a high priority for Steinbrenner in signing Strawberry, a person familiar with the negotiations said, explaining that the owner did not want the support payments to act as a potential distraction for the player the Yankees hope will provide the power they have lacked. Strawberry, 34, has virtually no assets of his own, the person said. ◆

October 10, 1996

Winning With a Boy's Help, Yankees Make No Apologies

By JACK CURRY

ONE OVERZEALOUS 12-YEAR-OLD helped the Yankees rejoice on a day when all of their runs except Bernie Williams's game-winning homer were somewhat tainted. Still, after beating the Baltimore Orioles, 5–4, in 11 innings yesterday, the Yankees refused to apologize.

They won their first American League Championship Series game in 15 years, and did it with an assist from 12-year old Jeff Maier, a New Jersey boy with a keen eye and a quick glove. The young fan lived out every kid's dream, bringing his mitt to Yankee Stadium and getting a chance to use it. In the bottom of the eighth inning, Maier reached over the wall in right field to scoop a ball hit by New York's Derek Jeter away from Baltimore's right fielder and into the stands.

The Orioles screamed for interference, but it was ruled a home run. Although the umpire later second-guessed his call, the home run stood, the Yankees had tied the score at 4–4 and were on their way to a dramatic Game 1 victory.

Jeter wants to meet the boy to thank him and "Good Morning America" telephoned his house in Old Tappan, N.J., minutes after the game to try to schedule him on the show. The Orioles, who were rightfully perturbed, saw the incident as another indignity at the hands of a team that has now beaten them 11 out of 14 times this year.

Who could blame the Orioles? Leading off the bottom of the 11th, Williams rocked Randy Myers's 1-1 slider deep into the left-field seats. It was his fourth home run this October, and it vaulted the Yankees to their fourth straight come-from-behind triumph in the post-season. The Yankees were delirious, and Jeff Maier was delighted.

"It's unbelievable," Maier said. "It's pretty cool."

Darryl Strawberry soaked in the evening's strange events, the start of what is expected to be a riveting series, and mused, "They'll be talking about this one for a long time."

"Do I feel bad?" asked Jeter. "We won the game. Why should I feel bad? Ask them that."

Asked if New York's third one-run victory in the post-season was tainted, Andy Pettitte, the Yankee starter who gave up four runs in seven decent innings, snapped: "Ain't nothing tainted about this as far as I'm concerned. We're up, 1–0. Nothing else matters." »»»

Twelve-year-old Jeffrey Maier scoops a home-run ball in the right field stands.

<<<   Pettitte is right. Nothing else does matter.

The Yanks never expected to receive a run batted in from a fan. It came when they needed it most, trailing by a run. Jeter hit a towering fly ball to right off Armando Benitez that Tony Tarasco positioned himself to snare by backing up against the fence. Tarasco was waiting for the ball to descend into his glove when Maier dipped his glove down about two feet and scooped the ball over the fence as it glanced off his arm. Umpire Rich Garcia signaled for a homer and Tarasco and the Orioles fumed.

Television replays clearly showed that without interference, the ball would have hit near the top of the fence or Tarasco would have caught it to put the Orioles four outs away from a 4–3 victory. But Maier was stationed in the walkway in front of the first row and, as kids sometimes do, he got in the way. The Yankees are fortunate he did.

"It was like a magic trick," explained Tarasco. "I was getting ready to catch it and suddenly a glove appeared and the ball disappeared. When the kid reached over the wall, the kids' glove was very close to mine. We almost touched gloves. Obviously, I was camped underneath it and ready to catch it."

Garcia, who did not think Maier interfered with Tarasco, said he thought the ball was leaving the Stadium and that the right fielder did not have a chance to snare it. After watching the replay, he was asked if he still thought Jeter deserved a homer.

"Well, after looking at it, no," he said. "At the time I saw it, I never saw anybody touch the ball and I thought the ball was out of the ball park." ◆

October 14, 1996

YANKEES IN SERIES AFTER 15 YEARS IN WILDERNESS

By JACK CURRY

BALTIMORE, OCT. 13—With awesome power and precise pitching, the Yankees continued their stunning superiority over Baltimore today to create this picturesque scene at Camden Yards: a 6–4 victory that secured the elusive American League Championship and the Yankees' first World Series appearance since 1981. There will be more meaningful baseball played in the Bronx in October. The season is alive.

The scenes keep getting prettier and prettier for the Yankees, a team that made first place its permanent home during the regular season and made stylish comebacks its modus operandi in the post-season. The Yankees unveiled the basic rout today as they ripped three homers off Scott Erickson during a six-run third inning fueled by second baseman Roberto Alomar's inexplicable error and cruised through Game 5 while waiting to uncork countless bottles of champagne.

Darryl Strawberry and Cecil Fielder, two power hitters who did not even join the reassembled Yankees until July, and Jim Leyritz, who was playing only because he is Andy Pettitte's personal catcher, each slugged homers and disappointed most of the sellout crowd of 48,712. The Orioles are officially finished after losing three straight games at home, going a shocking 0–9 against New York at Camden Yards this season and losing the league championship series by four games to one.

"No question about it, this is the most exciting thing that has ever happened to me in this sport," said Manager Joe Torre, who will be involved in a World Series for the first time in his 32-year baseball career. "It's not even close."

No matter the outcome of the National League Championship Series, Torre will face a team he formerly managed and played for: the Atlanta Braves or the St. Louis Cardinals, who beat the Braves in St. Louis tonight, 4 to 3, and lead the N.L. series by three games to one. The World Series begins Saturday at Yankee Stadium.

With dance music pumping in the clubhouse, the Yankees exchanged their gray uniforms for white T-shirts and white caps that declared them American League champions. The players instantly soaked the new additions to their wardrobe by reaching into a tub filled with bottles of Champagne and spraying anyone who moved in the cramped, humid setting. Torre cried after the last out, but any tears were replaced by smiles in a clubhouse filled with families, friends and euphoria.

"This is a special group," said Strawberry, who swatted three home runs in the last two games. "This is probably the most special group of players I've ever been around."

A grinning Fielder added: "This team worked hard and never quit. We always believed," while an equally excited Leyritz said, "It's a very emotional feeling."

After the Yankees snatched a 6–0 cushion in the third, Pettitte made certain the Orioles would remain stymied as he pitched eight typically reliable innings in limiting them to two runs and three hits. It was appropriate that New York's best pitcher thrived on the most critical day of the season. Most critical, that is, until the World Series.

The Yankees have five days without a game so they can regroup and ponder the pursuit of the 23rd championship in their 94-year history. After playing and managing in 4,272 games, Torre is four victories away from a World Series ring.

"I never felt comfortable, as a player or manager, watching the World Series," said Torre. "I always shut off the celebrations. To me, it was like watching someone else eating a hot fudge sundae."

Not anymore. Pass the spoon to Torre, whose team was adamant about wanting the next game played at the Stadium to be a World Series contest. The Yankees did not want to loosen their stranglehold on the sputtering Orioles. They succeeded.

The Yankees' 10 homers set a league championship series record for five games as they hit one more than the Orioles, who set a major league record with 257 homers in the regular season. Their three straight road victories marked only the second time it has happened in a league championship series. Their dominance over the Orioles, who finished second to them in the American League East, must have set a record for aspirin sales in Baltimore.

"They didn't let us make things happen, and that's an attribute of a great team," said Baltimore's Davey Johnson, whose team was 4–14 against the Yanks. He weaved through a maze of players and reporters to congratulate Torre, saying, "I want you to come out on top."

"Wow, this is really it," said Wetteland. "I don't get too wrapped up in emotions on the field. This is a case where a 12-year-old boy who has dreamed about playing in the World Series came out today." ◆

October 24, 1996

Yankees Are Puttin' On The Leyritz

By DAVE ANDERSON

ATLANTA, OCT. 23—Whether the Yankees or Braves win this World Series, last night's fourth game is the one that will be remembered and dissected in the years to come. And in all the bars now and to come.

More than anybody else, Jim Leyritz will be remembered for this 8–6 Yankee victory. His three-run homer in the eighth lifted the Yankees into a 6–6 tie after the Braves had jumped into a 6–0 lead, but Joe Torre didn't even shake Leyritz's hand.

"I didn't have time," the Yankee manager said. "I had to get Mariano Rivera up in the bullpen."

That's what this game was like. Nobody had time to look back because they were too busy looking ahead.

"I hit a slider out," Leyritz would say of Mark Wohlers's pitch. "He hung a slider, and I hit it out."

Leyritz lauded Torre for "giving me the respect I didn't get the last couple of years," a slap at Buck Showalter, the previous Yankee manager. "That respect gave me the confidence to do what I've been able to do.

What he's done is hit big homers, notably the homer that ignited the Yankees' pennant-clinching victory in Baltimore.

"The thing about Jimmy," Torre said, "is that he's able to hit the ball out of the ball park. When he was running around the bases, I thought of the homer he hit in the 15th inning in the division series last year."

With its revolving door of pitchers and pinch-hitters and pinch-runners and managerial double-switches, the Yankees' victory in 10 innings is why baseball in October is the best game of all.

It's also why baseball is better without the designated hitter than with the d.h.

Without the designated hitter, Wade Boggs was Torre's last pinch-hitter when he stepped into the batter's box against Steve Avery in a rare game-on-the-line confrontation: a left-handed batter against a left-handed pitcher.

With two out, Avery, no longer in the Braves' rotation because of a damaged stomach muscle, had walked Tim Raines, then allowed a single to Derek Jeter.

Bobby Cox, the Braves' manager, hurried to the mound as right-hander Brad Clontz, more shaky than reliable in recent outings, threw in the bullpen.

"No, no, no," the tomahawk choppers chanted. "No, no, no."

The choppers didn't want Clontz and neither

Jim Leyritz's sixth inning home run ties Game 4 of the 1996 World Series. The Yankees went on to win the game, 8-6.

did Cox, who ordered Avery to walk Bernie Williams intentionally to load the bases, a risky strategy that moved Raines, the go-ahead run, to third base where he could score on a wild pitch or, heaven forbid, a walk.

And, after Avery had a count of one ball and two strikes, Boggs walked, forcing in the lead run. Moments later, first baseman Ryan Klesko's error allowed Jeter to score. And the tomahawk choppers were chopping up Cox, as they will forever more.

Why had he walked Williams intentionally?

"He's their best hitter," Cox said.

Why had he brought in Mark Wohlers to pitch the eighth after Mike Bielecki had stopped the Yanks in the sixth and seventh?

"It was the smart thing to do," he said.

But, in retrospect, not the right thing to do. But that's baseball. And that's why baseball is better without the d.h., when managers must make moves in a few seconds, moves that would make a chess master ponder for several minutes.

"A lot of things went wrong for us tonight," Cox would say later. "We'll bounce back."

And, in retrospect, just about everything went right for the Yankees as Joe Torre used seven pitchers, five pinch-hitters and a pinch-runner as well as his reserve catcher, Leyritz, who entered the game in the bottom of the sixth after Torre had sent up Paul O'Neill as a pinch-hitter for Joe Girardi.

Leyritz is known mostly as Andy Pettitte's catcher. And when the World Series resumes tonight in what will be the last game in the soon-to-be-leveled Atlanta-Fulton County Stadium, he will be in the lineup as Pettitte's catcher in the left-hander's rematch of the World Series opener with right-hander John Smoltz.

But whatever happens tonight and Saturday night in Yankee Stadium, and maybe Sunday night there too, it won't upstage the theater of what was the longest World Series game ever -- 4 hours 17 minutes.

The longest and one of the best. ◆

October 27, 1996

A RETURN TO GLORY

By JACK CURRY

FROM EVERY POIGNANT MOMENT to every marvelous play to every memorable rally, the Yankees' season unfolded like some unbelievable baseball fairy tale. Again and again, the Yankees outdid themselves in inspiration and in achievement, and last night at Yankee Stadium the Yankees provided a joyous conclusion to their special story.

The thrilling journey ended in happiness when the Yankees stopped the Atlanta Braves, 3–2, in Game 6 at Yankee Stadium to win the World Series and make one of New York's most unforgettable teams even more noteworthy. The Yankees overcame a 2–0 deficit in the series with four straight stylish victories against the defending champions. So, the best team in baseball resides in the Bronx for the first time since the Yankees won the World Series in 1978, and will be toasted with a parade on Tuesday morning.

It was appropriate that the Yankees clinched the 23d title in franchise history with the same winning formula that helped them reach the World Series. Jimmy Key gave them an effective start into the sixth. Four relievers followed him, with John Wetteland making it a typically tense finish by allowing a run in the ninth before stranding Braves on first and second when he induced Mark Lemke to pop out to third baseman Charlie Hayes.

Bernie Williams and Derek Jeter, their twin Mr. Octobers, and Joe Girardi, who made a late cameo appearance, each drove in a run off Greg Maddux in a three-run third that supplied enough offense. Maddux and the Braves looked mortal, and the Yankees looked special.

"You could not have written a better script," Girardi said. "This was the way we won all year. This game was the season in a nutshell. I truly feel blessed."

So did Joe Torre and the Yankees. Torre finally experienced his first title after 32 years of futility as a player and manager and he burst out ⟫⟫⟫

≪≪   onto the field and joined the pile of players behind home plate. The 56,375 fans roared as the sound system exploded with Frank Sinatra's "New York, New York" and Torre led a spine-tingling victory lap around the Stadium that will be remembered for years.

"I wanted to go into the stands and thank all 60,000 fans," Tino Martinez said. "If I could have, I would have."

"The ground was shaking," Paul O'Neill raved. "I mean, it was shaking. I've never seen that happen before."

Wade Boggs was the most daring Yankee because he hopped on the back of one of the mounted horses and allowed the police officer and the horse to ride him around the Stadium. Boggs disembarked after his second time on a horse in his life, raced to the plate, waved his cap to the fans and was the last Yankee to leave the field.

"That was the final piece to the puzzle," Boggs said. "I don't know why I did any of that stuff, but it felt terrific. This was a great send-off."

With 23 championships, the Yankees are tied with hockey's Montreal Canadiens (23 Stanley Cups) for the most titles for any professional team. The Yankees quickly and easily avenged being embarrassed by the Braves by a combined score of 16–1 in the first two games in the Bronx and did not let Maddux dominate them as thoroughly as he had in a 4–0 victory in Game 2.

"This team never quit," Torre said. "This team was always ready."

"You have fun this winter," said Atlanta Man-

The Yankees celebrate their first World Series championship since 1978.

ager Bobby Cox, as he hugged Torre in his crowded office. "You deserve it. Good going. I love you."

Everyone loved Torre and the Yankees last night when more than 200 reporters, family and friends squeezed into their Champagne-drenched clubhouse. There were hugs and high-fives in every nook and cranny. The Yankees wore new hats and shirts declaring them the World Series champions.

"This is great for New York," said George Steinbrenner. "There's just something special when the Yankees win the World Championship. It's special for New York when the Yankees are the best team in baseball."

The Yankees are the best because they suffocated the Braves with stellar pitching and were not intimidated by Maddux. Key held the Braves to one run and five hits in five and one-third innings and David Weathers, Graeme Lloyd, Mariano Rivera and Wetteland continued the bullpen brigade that carried the Yankees throughout the post-season by surrendering two hits and one run and sending the 56,375 fans and all of New York into a frenzy.

With a 3–1 lead in the ninth, Wetteland, who had four saves, and was named the most valuable player, allowed three singles to slice the score to 3–2 with runners on first and third and two outs. But, after Hayes almost made a splendid catch as he tumbled into the third base dugout for a foul popup, Wetteland got Lemke to hit one that stayed in fair territory and the Yankees had their victory.

"I got the ball and I'm not telling anyone where it is," Hayes said. "I'm going to hold onto that ball forever. I have already asked our video guy to make me a 90-minute tape of me catching that ball. Just me and the catch. Nothing else."

"This is a New York team," said David Cone. "This is a comeback team. This is a team that New York can really relate to. This is a great team."

This is a fairy-tale team. This is a championship team. ◆

October 27, 1996

SPORTS OF THE TIMES
The Yankees Got Better And Better

By GEORGE VECSEY

THE OLD CHAMPIONS are the champions once again. For the 23d time since they got the hang of it, the Yankees have won the World Series, this time with a 3–2 victory over the Atlanta Braves last night that could have stopped a few hearts that were not certifiably just out of the shop.

Everything went well in the Bronx on this balmy late October night of nights. Aside from derisive and vulgar variations on the dopey Atlanta tomahawk chop, the vast majority of fans behaved themselves, perhaps wanting to keep themselves sober and out of a detention pen to see the first world championship for the Yankees since 1978.

This was a different Yankee team from those swashbuckling warriors who fought among themselves and watched managers come and go. On this team, young stars like Bernie Williams and Derek Jeter blossomed, and management kept bringing in mature old hands.

Charlie Hayes, an itinerant who came over on Aug. 30 so the Pirates could trim their payroll, dived headfirst into the opposing dugout to try to catch a pop-up last night, and then did catch the final foul pop moments later.

"I wanted that ball, I wanted every ball," Hayes said in the Champagne-spattered clubhouse. "I've failed so much in this business. As a batter, you know you'll fail 70 percent of the time. But this time I was in the right place at the right time."

Many of these players wound up in the right place at the right time. This was not by accident. The World Series has returned to New York also because Bob Watson and Joe Torre, the general manager and the manager, were willing to consider the Yankees as a work in progress. »»

≪≪ Torre, the native son from Brooklyn, had captivated the New York area—even Met fans and diehard New York Giants and Brooklyn Dodgers fans who still think 1954 and 1955 are coming back. The human drama of one Torre brother, Rocco, dying in midseason and another Torre brother, Frank, receiving a heart transplant on the Series' off day, made Joe Torre even more sympathetic.

Last night's game was a textbook example of the depth and versatility of this team. Torre decided that Paul O'Neill needed to play the outfield, twanging hamstrings and all, and O'Neill started the stunning three-run rally off Greg Maddux, who had mystified the Yankees in the second game. When Jimmy Key ran out of gas, Torre went to the deepest bullpen in baseball, starting with David Weathers and Graeme Lloyd, both of whom had been acquired during the season, and had been dreadful.

The joke, of course, is that Watson's job is in jeopardy with George Steinbrenner because of the flap over Lloyd, the lanky left-handed relief pitcher who showed signs of a damaged elbow when he came over from Milwaukee

So last night Lloyd got a tough hitter, Ryan Klesko, to polish off the sixth inning. Then came the heavy arsenal of Mariano Rivera and John Wetteland, the man with the sweat-ringed cap

---

November 5, 1996

Jeter Captures Rookie of the Year

By JACK CURRY

DEREK JETER was supposed to be the question mark on the Yankees this season, even according to Manager Joe Torre. Could the rookie handle playing shortstop? Could he succeed in New York? What would happen to the Yankees if the youngster floundered?

Imagine how ludicrous those concerns seem now.

Jeter's stylish play forced those questions to vanish faster than World Series tickets. The only question Jeter had to answer yesterday was where he planned to display his newest trophy, the American League rookie of the year award he won in a landslide.

The 22-year-old Jeter garnered all 28 first-place votes in becoming the fifth American Leaguer since the award's inception 50 years ago to be a unanimous choice for the honor.

No one was surprised. Not even the normally humble Jeter.

After Jeter homered off Cleveland's Dennis Martinez and made a nifty over-the-shoulder catch in the Yankees' season opener, he immediately became a strong candidate for the award.

When the glorious season progressed and Jeter became a special and instrumental part of the Yankees' magical ride, it became more obvious that he would be named the premier rookie.

"I'm still dreaming," Jeter said yesterday. "The way New York has embraced us after the championship, I can't put it into words. This is still a dream. I hope we can do it a few more years."

Jeter was the first Yankee to win the award since Dave Righetti in 1981, the second-youngest Yankee to be voted the award after Tony Kubek (21 years old in 1957) and the eighth Yankee over all.

"Unanimous?" joked Jeter. "I must have had some of my family voting in it."

It was another wondrous day for Jeter, who hugged his father, Charles, during a news conference at Yankee Stadium and thanked "Mr. Steinbrenner" and "Mr. Torre" for having patience with him. Jeter even suggested that the Yankees could have demoted him to the minor leagues after he had an uneventful spring, but that was never a consideration. The Yankees wanted him to learn

who often makes things interesting.

Cecil Fielder, Hayes and Luis Sojo were in the lineup at the end. In the three-game sweep in Atlanta, Torre had used Fielder and Hayes ahead of the incumbents Tino Martinez and Wade Boggs, risking anger from the two deposed players and second-guessing from millions of baseball savants.

Before the fifth game in Atlanta, you could pick up the unflappable poise of Fielder and Hayes. Hours before game time, while most Yankees rested in their clubhouse, Fielder and Hayes sat in the dugout, savoring the feel of being in the lineup. They chatted with reporters. This was fun. Why not take a look around? With

people like this, World Series are won.

Watson brought in Fielder on July 31 in a trade for Ruben Sierra and a minor leaguer and cash. Fielder recognized this might be the right place and the right time for him. "The city is nuts," he said the other day. "You go outside, everybody's giving you high-fives. It's like, 'You gotta beat those guys,' and I'm saying, 'Hey, wait a minute, you don't understand, those guys are professionals, too.'"

The Yankees were professionals who improved markedly late in the season. Bob Watson and Joe Torre were as responsible as any player. ◆

Derek Jeter receiving his Rookie of the Year award in 1996.

on the job and he did. Quickly and emphatically.

"We had a lot of guys who were valuable," said Torre. "I don't think we had one guy, player-wise, who was more valuable than him."

Torre said last February that he hoped Jeter would bat .250 and play dependable defense. The rookie exceeded those goals by hitting .314—the highest among the 10 shortstops voted rookies of the year—with 10 homers, 78 runs batted in, 104 runs scored and 22 errors in 157 games.

He evolved into perhaps the Yankees' premier player following the All-Star Game break, batting .350 with 6 homers and 40 R.B.I. to finish the regular season with a flourish, clinch the rookie

award and secure a $10,000 contractual bonus.

"His hitting blew me out of the tub," said Torre, a former National League batting champion. "I never expected anything like that. I said something about him hitting .250. Someone told me he'd hit more than .250. I said fine."

Though the rookie voting is completed when the regular season ends, Jeter was even more impressive in the pressure-packed October as veterans like Wade Boggs, Paul O'Neill and Tino Martinez struggled for the Yankees. Jeter had a .361 average in the post-season—including one unforgettable homer against Baltimore that was helped by an overzealous 12-year-old—with 3 R.B.I. and 12 runs scored. Jeter combined with Bernie Williams as twin Mr. Octobers and helped usher the Yankees to their first World Series title since 1978, never looking like a player who would be a college senior right now.

"It's tremendous," said Charles Jeter. "Derek is doing what he wants to do. I'm most proud of the way he carries himself beyond the baseball end. As a parent, I'm proud of the way he handled himself."

When Jeter was asked what would inspire him in 1997 after a grandiose debut, he responded: "To come back. It was incredible. The parade. How the city took to us. I want to be back year after year. There's nothing else I'd rather do than win some more." ◆

October 8, 1997

This Time Around, the Breaks Betrayed the Yankees

By JACK CURRY

THE CUSTODIAN CARRIED one gallon of white paint, a paint brush and a ladder around Yankee Stadium yesterday. Using methodical strokes across a white cinder block wall, he painted over the blue "1996," then painted over the blue words "World" and "Champions" until all that remained was the Yankees' interlocking NY. It is still a proud symbol, but it is no longer the symbol of the best team in baseball. Not after Monday night.

"It's a shame," the workman muttered. "I hate having to do this. That darn game killed me."

He was not alone. It was that sort of depressing day at the Stadium. Glum players trudged into the clubhouse, emptied their lockers, packed cardboard boxes and vanished, some not knowing whether they would return next season and some knowing they definitely would not. It was a day when the players tried not to reflect on the numbing 4–3 defeat to the Cleveland Indians in Game 5 of the division series, which was akin to asking a 7-year-old not to think about trick-or-treating on Halloween.

"I thought we were going to win the whole thing," David Wells said. "My stomach was hurting because I thought we were going all the way. I really thought this was going to be a storybook finish."

There were no storybook finishes in 1997. Maybe the Yankees used up their magic during an inspirational dash to the World Series championship in 1996.

There was a laundry list of agonizing developments that worked against the Yankees in their series with Cleveland: Mariano Rivera permitting the stunning homer to Sandy Alomar in Game 4 when the Yankees were four outs away from the American League Championship Series; Omar Vizquel's decisive hit glancing off Ramiro Mendoza's glove; Jaret Wright's deflecting Joe Girardi's hit-and-run liner and turning it into a dazzling double play in the second inning of Game 5; Jim Thome's sweet diving stop and terrific throw from his knees on Paul O'Neill's grounder in the seventh inning of the final game, and O'Neill's missing a game-tying homer in the ninth by 5 feet.

"The breaks we got to help us win a world championship last year are the same breaks they got to help send us home this year," O'Neill said.

The Yankees must get ready for next season because they will have a revised look. Cecil Fielder, Wade Boggs, Charlie Hayes, Tim Raines and Pat Kelly will almost certainly not wear pinstripes again, while the outlooks for Dwight Gooden, who has a $3 million option, and Darryl Strawberry are murky. But the Yankees should field a very talented team that contends again and might even improve if George Steinbrenner

Defeat sinks in for Derek Jeter, seated, and Tino Martinez after the Indians eliminated the Yankees in the 1997 playoffs.

spruces up the roster by adding Robin Ventura at third or Chuck Knoblauch at second.

"We'll win it next year," Steinbrenner said in the sullen clubhouse Monday. "Mark that down."

The bleary-eyed Torre actually perked up when he was told of Steinbrenner's vow. Ten minutes after the 1997 season ended for the Yankees, Steinbrenner was talking about winning in 1998. Then the custodian could switch back to blue paint next October.

"Second place is not an option, and that's fine," Torre said. "I expect to win, too. It makes it tougher when you expect to win when you don't know who your players are. When the Boss says that, it means he's going to get you the players." ◆

February 4, 1998

Cashman: Ahead of the Game at 30

By MURRAY CHASS

IN THE SPRING OF 1989, the Yankees were talking to the Atlanta Braves about a trade for Jeff Blauser just before Blauser began a nine-year run as the Braves' shortstop. Suddenly, Bobby Cox, the Braves' general manager, encountered a problem.

Calling a reporter who covered the Yankees, Cox, in a fit of frustration, said, "I've been talking to Bob Quinn every morning, but I called Quinn this morning and he said he isn't in charge anymore, so who do I call now?"

General managers of other teams have had the same problem for years. When they want to discuss a trade with the Yankees, they don't know whom to call. Is it the general manager or is it George Steinbrenner or is it the current top Steinbrenner adviser in the Yankees' office in Tampa, Fla.?

Asked that question yesterday, Brian Cashman gave a firm reply. "Please call me," he said upon his appointment as Steinbrenner's latest general manager. "I am the guy. If someone wants to reach out and they're wondering who to reach out for, that man is me."

In naming the 30-year-old Cashman to succeed Bob Watson, who resigned yesterday, Steinbrenner has found himself a new "bright young executive." That was the owner's term for some of his baseball people in the mid-1980's, none of whom stayed around long, leaving either of their own volition or of Steinbrenner's.

Cashman is the second-youngest general manager in baseball history, but he accepted the job yesterday with far more pragmatism and candor than many of his predecessors.

When Watson, for example, was asked about an hour before he was named general manager 27 months ago about reports that he would be named, he denied even knowing that the Yankees had interest in him for the position.

When Cashman was asked yesterday about his strength as a talent evaluator, he quickly said: "It's not a strength. I'm an administrator. I'm a good listener. I would not pass myself off as an evaluator of talent."

Like just about every one of his predecessors, Cashman also said he knew what he was getting into. Unlike most of the others, though, he had reason to say it.

"I have not been given any false expectations," he said. "I know some people have come in here and said it's going to be different. I've been here. I know what to expect. There will be good times; there will be tough times. I understand George. I understand what he wants. I know there will be phone calls when I don't want them."

As a Yankee employee for nine years and a front-office intern three years before that, Cashman has experienced Steinbrenner up close and personal. Steinbrenner, in reality, is his own general manager, unlike any owner. Others become involved in negotiations for high-priced contracts, but who else calls general managers about a trade for a second baseman or a pitcher?

What other organization, too, is run from a distance of a thousand miles? The Yankees' ⟫⟫

≪≪ minor league operation is based in Tampa, and the fiefdom that Steinbrenner has allowed to exist there has often created havoc for the general manager in New York.

Cashman spoke candidly of his views of that set-up, too. Asked about problems with the geographical division of club executives, he said: "I know there have been times in the past; there's no question there's been one. I'd be misleading anybody if I said otherwise." But the new general manager, who once worked in the Tampa office, also said: "I think Tampa's a good thing. Obviously, I would prefer to have people in the office every day up here. But we do talk on the phone. I have to reach out. I have to rely on those people a great deal and I've done that up to this point and I'll continue to do that. Right now there isn't a Tampa–New York problem. Not with me and I don't think there's one with Tampa with me either." ◆

March 7, 1998

Defector From Cuba Will Join The Yanks

By BUSTER OLNEY

FORT LAUDERDALE, FLA. MARCH 6—Orlando Hernandez, a Cuban defector and the older brother of the World Series star Livan Hernandez, agreed last night to a four-year, $6.6 million contract with the Yankees.

Once the Yankees arrange for a visa for Hernandez, who is living in Costa Rica, the team is expected to develop him deliberately in its farm system, in an attempt to avoid the mistakes made in the rapid promotion of Hideki Irabu.

Hernandez's agent, Joe Cubas, said that he intends to fly to Costa Rica on Sunday to have the player sign the deal, and the paperwork will be given to the American League office on Tuesday. It will take at least a week for Hernandez, who is known as El Duque, to appear at the Yankees' camp.

As negotiations with Hernandez's representatives have progressed, Yankees officials have said they view him as a No. 4 or No. 5 starter or middle reliever, with the experience and ability to advance to the major leagues sometime late in the 1998 season. Hernandez's actual age is in some dispute; some baseball officials have obtained old baseball cards that show him to be 32, while Cubas told Yankees officials that the player is 28. Last week, Brian Cashman, the Yankees' general manager, jokingly said that if he signed Hernandez, he would maintain that the player was 28 years old.

Based on a strong recommendation from Lin Garrett, the club's director of scouting, the Yankees are gambling that placing Hernandez in reserve now will pay off in the future, when Torre is searching for help.

Hernandez was once a top pitcher on Cuba's national team. Under suspicion that he would defect, however, he was suspended from baseball. He has said he was constantly threatened and harassed by Cuban officials. On Dec. 26,

1997, Hernandez, his wife and three friends slipped off a remote beach in a 20-foot sailboat and reached a small deserted island. After three days on Anguilla Cay, the group was spotted by a Coast Guard helicopter.

Hernandez was offered asylum in the United States, but chose to take up residence in Costa Rica instead, improving his bargaining power. Had he come to the United States, he would have been subject to the amateur draft, rather than enjoying free agency. ◆

Orlando Hernández, nicknamed "El Duque."

April 11, 1998

Babe, Mickey and Joe D Never Saw One Like This

By BUSTER OLNEY

JOE DIMAGGIO threw out the first ball at the Yankees' home opener yesterday, and the 10 pitchers who followed him on the mound labored to match his effort. DiMaggio worked fast and threw a strike. Most of the other pitchers did neither.

Home openers are supposed to be memorable, and the Yankees' 17–13 victory over Oakland certainly was, as a house painted with polka dots might be. Big leads were lost, rallies were perpetual, pitchers entered and departed with dizzying regularity on a sunny and chilly afternoon. The sheer absurdity of the 4-hour-6-minute game—witnessed by a crowd of 56,717, the largest regular-season turnout since the renovated stadium opened in 1976—actually became its most interesting quality.

"It's always fun to win a game," said Paul O'Neill, who watched the parade of hits, runs and relievers from right field. "But this is one of the ugliest games I've ever been a part of."

Said Jose Cardenal, the Yankees' first-base coach, "This has got to be the most brutal game I've ever seen in my life."

Many records were set and challenged, among them most runs scored in one game in the 75-year history of Yankee Stadium and most runs scored by the Yankees in a home opener since 1955. The Yankees drew 12 walks and accumulated 16 hits. Tino Martinez hit his first home run of the season and drove in five runs, and George Steinbrenner, the Yankees' principal owner, bragged afterward about his team's incredible offense and its ability to recover from a deficit of five runs.

There was little praise for the pitching or the pace of the game. Two hours and one minute after David Cone opened the game with a high fastball to Rickey Henderson, the Yankees and Athletics had completed exactly four innings. »»

«« Cone and his counterpart, Oakland's Jimmy Haynes, each got through the first inning without a run. But the Athletics scored five runs on four hits in the second, a solid advantage until Haynes suddenly couldn't throw a strike. He walked two of the first three hitters he faced in the Yankee second and started shaking his head.

Two years ago, when Haynes pitched for Baltimore, the Orioles sent him home with two weeks to play in the season because they were worried about his response to stress. Haynes flunked his Yankee Stadium stress test yesterday, giving up two runs in the second inning and walking the first two hitters of the third, before Martinez tied the score with his home run. After Darryl Straw-

berry walked and stole second, Art Howe, the Oakland manager, called for a reliever—the first of the game's eight pitching changes. The game slowed to a crawl.

"It was a fiasco out there," said Jason Giambi, Oakland's first baseman. "You almost pitied anyone who went to the mound. Guys were throwing out hits like it was a joke, like there were no fielders out there."

Some of the 56,717 rubberneckers watching from the stands began deserting the stadium in the fifth inning, having watched nearly three hours of baseball. Others stayed and kept themselves warm by standing in long lines at the concession stands and the restrooms. Some yelled

to Steinbrenner that more restrooms are needed. "Stop drinking the beer," Steinbrenner replied in jest. All things considered, Martinez said, "the fans hung in with us pretty good."

Jim Dougherty (0–1), Oakland's third pitcher, promptly lost his team's 13–12 lead in the bottom of the fifth, giving up a two-run double to Martinez and a run-scoring single to Strawberry. With four runs across, the Yankees led, 16–13.

Mike Buddie walked Oakland's Rafael Bournigal, the No. 9 hitter, to open the sixth. More groans from the stands, and Graeme Lloyd started warming up in the Yankees' bullpen. At some point, Torre turned and asked outfielder Tim Raines, "When is the last time you pitched?"

"In Little League," Raines responded, laughing.

With two out in the inning, Torre again left the dugout to call for a replacement for Buddie, the 11th of 16 times a coach or a manager trekked to the mound yesterday. Derek Jeter, the shortstop, gathered near second base with his fellow infielders Chuck Knoblauch and Scott Brosius. Maintaining concentration, Brosius said later, became something of a problem. Jeter said, "It seemed like we were playing a doubleheader."

Finally, Lloyd applied sanity to the game, closing out the sixth, shutting out Oakland in the seventh and retiring the first hitter in the eighth, before being relieved. Fans who remained roared their appreciation. Pushing across a run in the seventh, the Yankees completed the scoring.

Inside the Yankee clubhouse, Buddie, one of only three rookies on this team, was getting ice on his arm when he realized late in the game that he would be credited with a victory, his first in the majors. He had pitched one and a third innings, allowing two hits, a walk and a run.

"Not the textbook win," Buddie said. "Not what I imagined my first win would be."

But then, who would have imagined this home opener? ◆

Tino Martinez is greeted by Paul O'Neill (left) and Bernie Williams (center) after hitting a home run.

RAREST GEM FOR YANKEES' WELLS: A PERFECT GAME

By BUSTER OLNEY

NERVOUSNESS GNAWED at David Wells in the seventh inning yesterday, when he began realizing that he might pitch a perfect game. He wanted the roaring Yankee Stadium crowd of 49,820 to remain silent, and he desperately needed his superstitious Yankee teammates to speak and ease the mounting tension.

But nobody would oblige him, save for David Cone, who removed his good-luck sunglasses and approached Wells. "I think it's time," Cone said, his delivery perfectly dry, "to break out the knuckleball."

Wells burst out laughing at the notion of going to such an unpredictable pitch, and though he found himself shaking in the ninth inning, his fingers numb to the feel of his final pitch to Minnesota's Pat Meares, he completed the 15th perfect game in major league history, beating the Twins, 4–0. Twenty-seven batters, 27 outs; no hits, no walks, no errors. The only other perfect game at Yankee Stadium, and the only other one by a Yankee, came on Oct. 8, 1956, when Don Larsen beat the Brooklyn Dodgers in Game 5 of the World Series.

When Meares's soft fly ball dropped into the glove of right fielder Paul O'Neill, the burly and balding Wells bent down and thrust his left fist into the air, and then again. "This is great, Jorge, this is great," he yelled to catcher Jorge Posada, over and over.

After Wells hugged other Yankees and rode off the field on the shoulders of his tallest teammates, Darryl Strawberry and Bernie Williams, and after he emerged from the dugout to acknowledge one last and long salute from the crowd, a phone call awaited him. Don Larsen was on the line, and he confirmed to Wells that yes, the only two pitchers to throw perfect games in Yankee ≫≫

Stadium attended the same high school, Point Loma High of San Diego. Larsen, Class of '47; Wells, Class of '82.

"Right now, I'm the happiest man on earth," Wells said later, seeming genuinely humbled.

Larsen said: "He won't forget it. He'll think about it every day of his life, just like I do."

Larsen's perfect game was considered improbable, given the circumstances and his career as a journeyman pitcher. Wells's is incredible, for many of his managers and pitching coaches have regarded him as entirely imperfect.

Wells, who turns 35 on Wednesday, grew up in San Diego raised by his mother, Eugenia Ann Wells, known as Attitude Annie. For years she dated a chapter president of the Hell's Angels,

called Crazy Charlie, and Wells can remember bikers coming to his Little League games, rewarding his strikeouts and victories with a few dollars. He told friends his father was dead, but he did not know for sure.

When Wells was 22, he dreamed that his father lived in West Virginia. When he asked his mother about this, she produced a telephone number. Soon after, Wells met his father for the first time.

Managers and coaches thought Wells's baseball ability was extraordinary and admired his ability to pitch well in important games. But many have been confounded by Wells's lack of attention to details, his expanding girth, and the maverick personality that led him, for instance, to an appearance on Howard Stern's radio show last Friday.

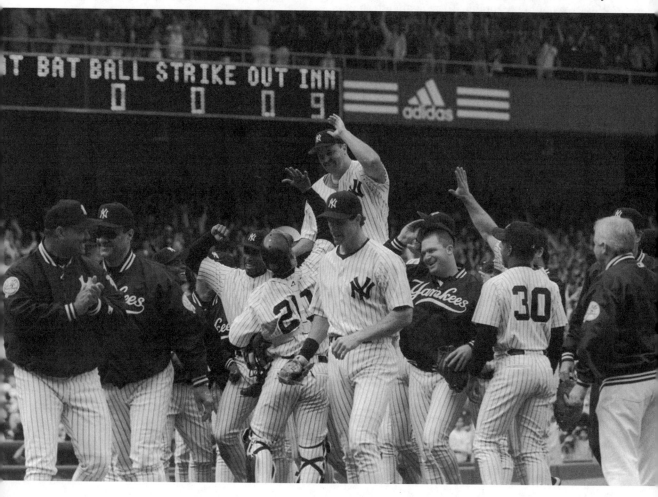

When Stottlemyre watched Wells warm up before yesterday's game, he was stunned by the alacrity of the left-hander's fastball, the sharp break of his curve, his overall command. Trying to play down his astonishment, Stottlemyre told Wells to keep his concentration. When Stottlemyre returned to the dugout, Torre asked, "How did it go?"

Stottlemyre replied, "Wow."

The possibility of a no-hitter was on their minds already, then, when Wells retired the first nine hitters easily. The closest the Twins came to a hit in the first three innings was when Javier Valentin, their catcher, hit a long fly ball down the left-field line that drifted foul by 20 feet or so.

Wells struck out all three hitters in the third inning; he would finish with 11 strikeouts. He generally pitches high in the strike zone, and the zone of the plate umpire, Tim McClelland, worked in his favor, with McClelland calling strikes on fastballs that appeared high and slightly outside.

Torre, who was in the stands the day Larsen pitched his perfect game, began to wonder about Wells's chances in the fourth inning. The crowd, unusually large because of a Beanie Baby giveaway, began to stir in the fifth inning, when Wells reached a two-strike count on Ron Coomer and then finished him off with a curveball.

Wells struck out the first two hitters in the sixth, and the inning ended with an easy fly to center field, and now the secret was out. Everybody knew: Wells was working on a no-hitter. He walked into a wall of cheers as he left the mound.

But his teammates seemingly ran from him, lest they violate baseball's long-held tradition that no one should mention a no-hitter in progress. Wells wanted to speak to his catcher, but Posada escaped to the other end of the dugout. Wells sat down next to Strawberry, and Strawberry got up and walked away. "They were killing me, man," Wells said.

Wells returned to the mound for the seventh, and Matt Lawton flied to center. Eight more outs to go. Brent Gates reached out and smashed a grounder toward right field, but first baseman Tino Martinez, positioned perfectly, fielded the ball and outran Gates to the base. Wells then fell behind in the count, three balls and one strike, to Paul Molitor, one of only 21 players to accumulate 3,000 hits in his major league career. If the perfect game was ever in jeopardy, if Wells was in danger of issuing a walk, Torre thought, this was the moment.

But Wells threw two straight fastballs and Molitor took one for a strike and swung and missed at the other. Six outs left.

Cone, a fellow pitcher and a friend, understood that Wells needed conversation, and while the Yankees batted in the seventh, he made his suggestion about the knuckleball. "I can't tell you how much that helped me," Wells said.

Wells dropped his glove down in the clubhouse after the eighth. "It's getting a little hairy out there," he said to Cone, who complained, in response, that Wells still had not thrown a knuckleball. Again the crowd roared for Wells as he strolled to the mound for the ninth inning, the top button of his jersey undone as always. Jon Shave hit a high fly to right. Valentin flailed at a curveball for strike three. Posada could not breathe. Wells was shaking, struggling to feel the ball. Meares fouled a fastball straight back, the infielders lurching expectantly. Then Meares reached out and poked a high fly to right, where O'Neill waited.

The great thing about David Wells, Sparky Anderson once said about the player he managed with the Detroit Tigers, is that he will always be a kid at heart. When O'Neill squeezed the ball, Wells began jumping around, perfectly happy. ◆

David Wells is carried off the field by his teammates after his perfect game.

July 6, 1998

Blending Talent and Karma, The Yankees Court History

By BUSTER OLNEY

THE LAST TIME a major league baseball team won 61 of its first 81 games, Theodore Roosevelt was President of the United States, Franklin and Eleanor Roosevelt were newlyweds and a precocious child named George Herman Ruth, later known as the Babe, had just left his father's saloon in Baltimore for a school for wayward boys. The last time until yesterday, that is, when the Yankees defeated the Baltimore Orioles to make their record 61–20, equaling the midseason marks of the 1907 Chicago Cubs and the 1902 Pittsburgh Pirates.

The Yankees of 1927 are generally considered to be the greatest team in baseball history, its lineup graced by the famed Murderers Row; that group won 57 of its first 81 games. Whether the Yankees of 1998 will be compared favorably to the 1927 Yankees, the 1961 Yankees, the 1976 Cincinnati Reds or any of baseball's other great teams will depend on whether they win the World Series, and whether they continue to win at such an astounding rate during the regular season.

The 1998 Yankees set a 114-48 regular-season franchise record.

They are on a pace to win 122 games, which would shatter the 20th-century record of 116 victories set by the Chicago Cubs in 1906.

"We should be proud," said David Cone, who is one of three Yankee pitchers with 10 or more victories. "It's a great start. It's a great accomplishment to be named with the best teams of all time."

Joe Torre, the Yankees' manager, has a lineup stocked with stars, like right fielder Paul O'Neill, but also with capable veteran role players, like Darryl Strawberry, and a pitching staff that includes the likes of Cone and David Wells, who pitched a perfect game on May 17.

Beyond the obvious talent, however, the Yankees seem to possess a karma; good things happen for them. Orlando Hernandez, the defector from Cuba who has been a wild success, was promoted to the big leagues last month only because a Jack Russell terrier belonging to Cone's mother bit the pitcher on the hand, forcing him to miss a start. Yesterday, the Yankees scored the only run of their game against Baltimore when Chad Curtis was hit by a pitch with the bases loaded.

"They have their own little 'Truman Show,'" said Scott Erickson, the losing pitcher yesterday, referring to the movie about a man who doesn't know his life is scripted to perfection. "Everything goes right for the Yankees."

Branch Rickey, the legendary baseball executive, once said that luck is the residue of design, and this Yankee team resulted from the evolution of the methods of George Steinbrenner, the team's principal owner.

For years, Steinbrenner invested heavily in free agents and traded away his organization's top prospects. Through this approach, the Yankees were left with an aged team and a barren farm system. But Steinbrenner placed more emphasis on developing prospects, and his executives, in turn, concentrated on scouting the personalities of prospective Yankees, as well as their talents.

The farm system regenerated and now the Yanks are built around home-grown players, like shortstop Derek Jeter, center fielder Bernie Williams and reliever Mariano Rivera. They already had O'Neill and Tino Martinez, hitters who seethe with intensity.

Before this season, they added Scott Brosius, a likable and respected third baseman, who Torre says maintains his focus from pitch to pitch as well as anybody he has ever seen, and Chuck Knoblauch, a leadoff hitter who engages opposing pitchers in a tireless tug-of-war almost every time he bats.

"I've never seen a team that is as focused as this one," said Steinbrenner, whose teams won championships in 1977, 1978 and 1996.

"Sesame Street" producers might consider using the Yankees as an example of selflessness. Joe Girardi, the regular catcher when the Yankees won the World Series two years ago, tutors Jorge Posada on a daily basis, even as Posada has assumed more of Girardi's playing time. Tim Raines and Strawberry, superstars when they were younger, are sometimes removed for pinch-hitters and must share playing time. "You're talking about real professionalism," Cone said earlier this year. "Those guys want to play as much as anybody, but what is most important to them is winning. That's what everybody is all about here, is winning."

Brosius said, "The core of the team is the team." ◆

July 25, 1998

SPORTS OF THE TIMES
It's Time For Yogi to Get Over It

By HARVEY ARATON

THE TOWN OF MONTCLAIR, N.J., will have its second Hall of Fame baseball player tomorrow when Larry Doby is inducted in Cooperstown, N.Y. Not coincidentally, his neighbor in the leafy suburb happens to be on the Veterans Committee that voted him in more than a half-century after he integrated the American League.

Doby, in fact, ran into Yogi Berra recently and asked him if he was nervous back in 1972 when Berra made his own induction speech. Not really, Berra said. It is doubtful Doby will be either, given the odds and insensitivity he has stared down for much of his 73 years.

As the folksy master of the faux pas, Berra has himself become a national symbol of sporting valor for his refusal to set foot in Yankee Stadium for as long as George Steinbrenner remains the Yankees' owner. Recently, Sports Illustrated even asked Berra to pose for a cover story on the most principled people in sports. Berra, to his credit, said no.

He has never made his personal stand a public crusade, the way others have for him, usually around Old-Timers' Day, which is at Yankee Stadium today. When Steinbrenner fired Berra as manager after a handful of games in 1985, Berra said that's it, he was going home to Montclair and wouldn't be back. That is his choice, which he is certainly entitled to, but the reality is that he is not hurting Steinbrenner, only depriving nostalgic fans the privilege of seeing No. 8 once more inside the grand ball park. He is unwittingly sending the wrong subliminal message that Steinbrenner, above all, is the Yankees.

Berra should get over the firing, and next year walk back into a stadium that is owned in part by tax-paying Yankee fans, not the man who holds its sweetheart lease. Go home again. Stand alongside Joe DiMaggio and Whitey Ford and Willie Randolph and, yes, Jim Bouton, all of whom were the Yankees, the way Paul O'Neill, Derek Jeter and David Cone are now.

Yankee Stadium was Berra's house long before Steinbrenner knew his way out of Ohio. Berra should at least once in his remaining years experience the cheers, the looking up at the owner's box to let Steinbrenner know that banishing the manager from the dugout does not chase true greatness from the field.

They are not close friends, but Doby, for one, could tell Berra about the emotional rewards of holding his ground, of standing tall. When he was a young boy in Camden, S.C., rich white Northerners would stable their horses there during the winter. Once or twice a year, they would ride in or out of town, tossing pennies into the street for poor black children to chase. Doby has said that while he often watched this procession, he never once moved a muscle to pick up a coin.

He learned early not to jump at the bait, and when he joined the Cleveland Indians in July, 1947, he ignored the foul taunts, just as Jackie Robinson did in Brooklyn, beginning three months earlier. Doby played 13 years in the major leagues, won two home-run titles, was a seven-time All-Star, yet for 50 years, couldn't shake Robinson's shadow. The racist, ignorant and indifferent never defeated him, though. Never made him acquiesce, or run.

After retirement, Doby managed briefly, worked for major league baseball, for the Baseball Assistance Team and with inner city kids. He campaigned for others, never himself. Whatever came his way, he was happy for that. If the Hall of Fame ever called, he would be honored to go.

There is power in his presence, Doby apparently understands. He goes to Cooperstown today knowing that he never sold himself out for pennies and always waited patiently to make a real score. You can't change history, can't undo the bad that's already been done, but there is no significant achievement in just going away. Nothing gained, Yogi, by giving up the time and place that is rightfully yours. ◆

September 26, 1998

Victory Establishes A.L. Mark

By BUSTER OLNEY

JOE TORRE made his way through the clubhouse shaking hands last night, the first manager in the 98 years of the American League to congratulate his players on 112 victories.

The Yankees' won–lost record is 112–48 after they beat the Tampa Bay Devil Rays, 6–1, before 32,447 at Yankee Stadium. That's one more victory than the total won by the 1954 Cleveland Indians, who won 111 games in a 154-game season. The Yankees have two games to play. They will fall short of the major league record of 116 victories, set by the 1906 Chicago Cubs, but that hardly diminished the feelings of Torre or some of his players.

"It's astounding, and it's really a credit to my ball club," Torre said. "They've come to play every day."

Torre grew up in Brooklyn, as a fan of the New York Giants, and what he remembers most about the 1954 Cleveland Indians is that the Giants swept Cleveland in four games in the World Series. He acknowledged the A.L. record—and then immediately changed the subject to the playoffs, which begin on Tuesday. ◆

September 28, 1998

Batting Title for Williams

By BUSTER OLNEY

BERNIE WILLIAMS came into the season fearful that his impending free agency might be a distraction. It appears to have been more of a motivation. Williams went 2 for 2 yesterday, improved his batting average to .339 and won the American League batting title.

Williams began the day leading Boston's Mo Vaughn by only .33602 to .33553. Before the Yankees' game started, Vaughn grounded out in Boston's home game against Baltimore, lowering his average to .3349.

Vaughn homered in his second at-bat, singled in his third at-bat and made an out his fourth time up, leaving his average at .3366; it was determined that Vaughn would have to play into extra innings to catch Williams, who had two singles and a sacrifice fly. "I really made a great effort to try to not let it bother me," Williams said.

All of this information was relayed to Joe Torre, the Yankees' manager, who then decided to remove Williams in the bottom of the sixth inning. Once the Yankees made their move, Vaughn was taken out of the Red Sox lineup, a concession.

"It felt great, absolutely," Williams said. "It's such a great feeling when you add your name to the list of players who've accomplished this feat." ◆

Bernie Williams won the 1998 American League batting title with a .339 average.

October 22, 1998

YANKS SWEEP SERIES, ASSURE LEGACY

By BUSTER OLNEY

SAN DIEGO, OCT. 21—The Yankees have been a team greater than the sum of its parts all year, and when they secured their own corridor in history tonight, it was appropriate that a pitcher who had struggled in recent weeks pushed them over the finish line.

Andy Pettitte, dropped to the back of the Yankees' rotation for the World Series, applied the final piece to their mosaic tonight, pitching seven and a third shutout innings and outdueling Kevin Brown in a 3–0 victory over the San Diego Padres in Game 4. In achieving their first Series sweep since 1950 and seventh in their history, the Yankees wrapped up their 24th championship and the second in the last three years.

The Yankees set an American League record with 114 victories in the regular season, then eliminated Texas, three games to none, Cleveland, 4–2, and San Diego, 4–0. The Yankees finished the year with 125 victories and 50 losses in the regular season and post-season combined, shattering the previous record of 118, Their winning percentage of .714 is the third best in history for World Series

winners, behind the 1927 Yankees (.722) and the 1909 Pittsburgh Pirates (.717).

Scott Brosius, named the most valuable player in the Series, sensed as the ninth inning began that he would make the final play, and so it was: The Padres pinch-hitter Mark Sweeney grounded to third base, and after Brosius threw to first for the final out, he raised his hands into the air. Mariano Rivera, the Yankees' closer, dropped to his knees near the mound, and the other Yankees embraced and piled around him.

The catchers, Joe Girardi and Jorge Posada, jumped and high-fived each other, and they all hugged. Chuck Knoblauch, the smallest Yankee, was lifted off his feet over and over. The Padres' relievers walked off the field as the Yankees celebrated, and Rivera turned and embraced Trevor Hoffman, San Diego's closer, just before the Yankees retreated to their clubhouse to spray each other with Champagne—the good stuff, as promised by the Yankees' principal owner, George Steinbrenner.

"This is as good as any team I've ever had," Steinbrenner said, his hair slick from Champagne. "This is as good as any team that's ever played the game."

Said right fielder Paul O'Neill, a member of the 1990 Cincinnati Reds, the last team to have swept the World Series: "This is a special team. The things we accomplished won't be done for a long time."

Players gathered in the clubhouse to hoist Champagne bottles and chant the name of Darryl Strawberry, who is recovering at his New Jersey home following the removal of a cancerous tumor. Then they called out Brosius' name, but Brosius was not there to hear it—he was in the family

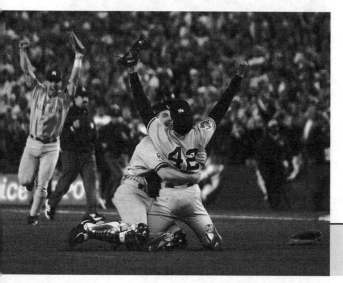

After Tino Martinez (left) secured the final out, in Game 4 of the 1998 World Series, catcher Joe Girardi and Mariano Rivera embraced.

room, to spend time with his family, including his father, who is being treated for cancer.

With the clubhouse packed, many of the players went back onto the field to yell and scream and hug again. Tino Martinez, cigar in hand, walked to the mound with his wife at his side and saluted the brigade of Yankees fans who gathered above the visitors' dugout. O'Neill hugged Derek Jeter. Hideki Irabu wandered aimlessly, cigar in hand. Pettitte grabbed teammates and thanked them. "I tend to think about the bad things," Pettitte said. "So this is definitely very gratifying for me."

Jeter's shirt and face were wet from Champagne, a bottle in one hand and a cigar in the other. "I'm a little young to know about the teams back in the early 1900's," said the 24-year-old Jeter, "but we were 125 and 50, and there's not too many teams that can say that."

Just one. ◆

January 6, 1999

Yogi and the Boss Complete Makeup Game

By HARVEY ARATON

LITTLE FALLS, N.J., JAN 5.—Let the record show that a celebrated grudge held for nearly 14 years was dropped here a few minutes after 5 this evening when a contrite George Steinbrenner arrived at Yogi Berra's doorstep and thanked the self-exiled Yankee great for the opportunity to make this day necessary.

The Yankees' principal owner traveled from his home in Tampa, Fla., to the museum named for Berra on the campus of Montclair State University to apologize, finally, for how he fired Berra as the team's manager 16 games into the 1985 season. The news of Berra's dismissal was delivered by Clyde King, another member of Steinbrenner's organization, and Berra vowed after that never to again set foot in Yankee Stadium as long as Steinbrenner owned the team. This evening, Steinbrenner walked up to the front entrance of the museum, where Berra awaited him with his hand outstretched.

"Hello, Yogi," Steinbrenner said, cautiously.

"You're 10 minutes late," Berra quipped.

The man known as the Boss and the Hall of Fame catcher then ducked into a small office, accompanied by Berra's wife, Carmen. According to Mrs. Berra, Steinbrenner took Berra's hand, looked him in the eye and said: "I know I made a mistake by not letting you go personally. It's the worst mistake I ever made in baseball."

Berra replied, "I made a lot of mistakes in baseball, too." Then he gave Steinbrenner a tour of his museum, which formally opened last month, and coyly said he would strongly consider returning to the Stadium sometime next season, possibly on opening day or Old-Timers' Day, which is later in the summer. "I told him what he needed to do," Berra said. "He apologized. We'll see."

The overwhelming feeling was that Berra would now go back. "Fourteen years, it was time," said Suzyn Waldman, the WFAN radio host who is close to Steinbrenner and who helped arrange the meeting and a subsequent interview for a live show at the museum last night.

Carmen Berra said she believed Steinbrenner's visit had nothing to do with business and everything to do with a clear conscience. "With the year 2000 coming, everyone is thinking about the future, about peace, about making things right," she said.

Along those lines, Steinbrenner admitted that the death of Mickey Mantle in 1996 and the near loss of Joe DiMaggio last month made him feel a sense of urgency in making amends. "There ⟩⟩⟩

<<< was a missing piece," he said, alluding to the recent record-setting, 125-victory Yankees season, and it was Berra. "He's got to forgive me and come back," he told Carmen Berra in a private moment, perhaps with the thought that Berra return to help raise the team's championship banner on opening day next spring, and make 1998 complete.

Berra, surprisingly, seemed to enjoy the public nature of the event, often tweaking Steinbrenner. He praised the Yankees' current managerial staff and told Steinbrenner not to interfere or he wouldn't show up for another 14 years. But mostly, he enjoyed being host to Steinbrenner, ushering him around the museum. "He's very proud of this," Carmen Berra said.

Though this was the house that Berra built and he, at 74, is six years older than Steinbrenner, he seemed like the wandering son returning to a paternal embrace, when the two men hugged at the door, and said goodbye. Steinbrenner, clutching a copy of Berra's latest book of original "Yogisms" and a Berra Museum shirt, said, "I'll talk to you soon."

The door closed. Berra, who coined the expression "It's not over till it's over," turned back. "Fourteen years," he said, smiling. "It's over." ◆

February 19, 1999

Yankees Add a Legend

By BUSTER OLNEY

TAMPA, FLA., FEB. 18—In their most significant deal since the purchase of Babe Ruth 79 years ago, the Yankees traded today for Roger Clemens, regarded as perhaps the greatest pitcher of his era. The Yankees won the World Series and a record 125 games in 1998, and now with Clemens they may be even better in 1999.

In return for Clemens, the Yankees traded the popular starting pitcher David Wells, who threw a perfect game at Yankee Stadium last May 17, to the Toronto Blue Jays, along with two other players, Graeme Lloyd, a relief pitcher, and Homer Bush, an infielder.

It was a shocking deal that came together in less than 10 hours and brought the Yankees the only five-time winner of the Cy Young Award, given annually to a league's best pitcher.

"You can equate this with getting a Michael Jordan," said George Steinbrenner, the Yankees' principal owner, drawing a comparison with the basketball icon. "We're getting a man who makes it a notable day in Yankee history."

Clemens, known as the Rocket, is already something of a legend: a contentious, hard-throwing right-hander who routinely tries to intimidate hitters by aiming his fastball at them. Clemens is 36, with a history of some arm and back problems, but he has shown no recent signs of wear: he was named the American League Cy Young Award winner in each of the last two seasons and had a 20–6 record last year, leading the league in victories, strikeouts and earned run average.

With him, the Yankees will be overwhelming favorites to win the World Series again. "The Yankees," a Toronto executive said, "are in a league of their own." ◆

March 11, 1999

Torre Has Prostate Cancer

By BUSTER OLNEY

TAMPA BAY, FLA., MARCH 10—Joe Girardi sat silently at the front of a Yankees team bus this morning, an island among teammates who cheerfully anticipated the return of Darryl Strawberry to baseball this afternoon in an exhibition game against the Red Sox. This was supposed to be a good day.

But Girardi wondered how he would tell teammates the words Joe Torre had just asked him to relay—that Torre, who managed the Yankees to World Series championships twice in his first three seasons with the team, has prostate cancer.

Torre told others in the organization that his doctors believed they had detected the cancer in its early stages, and he underwent further diagnostic tests today that will help determine the course of

After his prostate cancer treatment in 1999, Joe Torre jokes with his bench coach, Don Zimmer.

treatment. The Yankees announced that Torre will leave the team for an unspecified period.

"I feel fine," the 58-year-old Torre said in a statement released by the Yankees today, "and am looking forward to taking care of this problem and getting back to work."

George Steinbrenner, the Yankees' principal owner, told reporters this afternoon that today's test results were encouraging. "We might see Joe in the next two to three weeks," he said. "Joe Torre will come out of this like a champion."

The Yankees have not named a temporary replacement for Torre, and officials within the organization are hopeful he can continue as manager this season. His coaching staff will collaborate on the day-to-day workings of spring training, but if Torre is forced to miss days or weeks of the regular season, Don Zimmer, the Yankees' bench coach, now in his 51st >>>

《《 year in the game, is expected to take over.

So as Strawberry went 1 for 4 in his first game since the discovery last October that he has colon cancer, the mortality of mankind once again was apparent in the Yankees' family.

Torre's brother, Frank, required a heart transplant during the 1996 World Series. A week ago, the Hall of Fame pitcher Jim (Catfish) Hunter, stricken with the terminal illness named after the former Yankees star Lou Gehrig, arrived here to be with old friends. Early Tuesday, the legendary Joe DiMaggio died at age 84 after battling lung cancer and pneumonia. And Joe Torre learned late Tuesday night that a biopsy confirmed he has cancer.

After learning of the cancer Tuesday night, Torre told Steinbrenner, and this morning he called Bob Watson, the team's former general manager. Watson had surgery for prostate cancer in 1994, before joining the Yankees and sharing in the 1996 title. Now, Torre told Watson, we have something else in common.

Players had noticed a change in Torre's demeanor in recent days: usually upbeat, Torre had become quiet and reserved, and they all learned why this morning. Torre informed his coaches of the diagnosis at the Yankees' complex before two squads of players departed for exhibitions here against the Red Sox and in Bradenton against the Pirates. Others remained behind to work out. He called Girardi, Paul O'Neill and David Cone into his office separately and asked them to tell the players of his condition.

Girardi said he told Torre, "Joe, our prayers are going to be with you and we're going to do everything we can to be right alongside you, and you tell me what you need and we're here for you."

O'Neill expressed hope that the cancer had been caught at an early stage. "He said he had no indication of it whatsoever," O'Neill said.

Girardi told one squad once it arrived here, O'Neill told the other squad when it reached Bradenton, and Cone told those who stayed behind to work out. Girardi said his teammates were quiet, sad, almost too accustomed to these sort of meetings now.

"After what happened to Straw," said Tino Martinez, "you're ready for anything."

Chris Chambliss, who managed the Yankees' squad here today, spoke to reporters after Girardi did and mentioned that although any form of cancer is bad for the body, prostate cancer is one of the more treatable forms. The players seemed to hang on these words. Three times, Derek Jeter said, "From what I understand, he's going to be all right."

The Yankee players are so intense and dedicated that for a few days or weeks they could probably manage themselves. But it was clear today how much they would miss Torre if he could not manage for a substantial period of time.

"He's been a tremendous leader for us," Girardi said. "He's just really in tune with what this club needs and when it needs it and why it needs it."

Martinez said: "He's just as big as any player on this team. We need him back."

Torre became manager of the Yankees before the 1996 season, and as Steinbrenner is fond of pointing out to reporters he was not, at first, a popular choice in the news media or among fans. But the Yankees responded to Torre's leadership—in tense situations, he seems to become more calm, and his team played this way—and they won the American League East and then came back from two games down to beat Atlanta in the World Series.

As it touched others. "He's a guy who played the game," Jeter said. "He knows what it's like to succeed, what it's like to fail. He's a players' manager, and everybody loves him."

Girardi echoed the sentiment. "Everybody loves Joe," he said, "because Joe treats us the way we want to be treated." ◆

July 19, 1999

ON DAY MADE FOR LEGENDS, CONE PITCHES PERFECT GAME

By MURRAY CHASS

IN AN IMPROBABLE SETTING, David Cone performed an improbable feat yesterday. He pitched the Yankees' second perfect game in little more than a year, and he did it playing in front of Don Larsen, who pitched a perfect World Series game for the Yankees in 1956.

Larsen was at Yankee Stadium to help celebrate Yogi Berra Day, and after Larsen threw the ceremonial first pitch to Berra, Cone took command of the mound and retired all 27 Montreal batters he faced as the Yankees clubbed the Expos, 6–0. It was only the 16th perfect game in major league history.

Following David Wells's perfect game against Minnesota by one year, two months and one day, Cone made the Yankees the first team to pitch perfect games in successive seasons and the first to have three perfect games to their credit.

"I probably have a better chance of winning the lottery than this happening today," an exuberant Cone said. "What an honor. All the Yankee legends here. Don Larsen in the park. Yogi Berra Day. It makes you stop and think about the Yankee magic and the mystique of this ball park."

When the foul pop-up lofted by Orlando Cabrera, the ninth batter in the Expos' lineup, on Cone's 88th pitch of the day descended softly into third baseman Scott Brosius' glove for the 27th out, Cone dropped to his knees and grabbed his head, "in disbelief," he said. Joe Girardi, the catcher, was the first to reach him.

"I just put a bearhug on him and took him down," Cone said. "I didn't want to let go. Somebody dragged me off him. I wasn't going to let go. That's how good I felt about Joe Girardi and what he means to me not only professionally but personally."

After hugs and high-fives all around, Girardi,

Chuck Knoblauch and Chili Davis hoisted Cone into the air and carried him toward the dugout. Once finished acknowledging the roar of the crowd of 41,930, thrusting first his right hand holding his cap into the air and then his left with his glove still on it, the 36-year-old right-hander reached Manager Joe Torre's office and was handed the telephone.

"Boomer's on the phone," Cone said, meaning Wells, with whom he became close before Wells was traded to Toronto during the off season. "He welcomed me to the club and said he was going to fly in and party with me tonight, so I'm expecting him any minute."

Working in 98-degree heat, Cone threw only 20 called balls and increased the velocity of his fastball as the game progressed. He had the Expos lunging at sliders the entire game. Unable to hit his sliders or his fastballs with authority, they struck out 10 times and hit 13 balls into the air, nine to the outfield, four that remained in the infield. The Expos made only four outs on ground balls.

But the fourth grounder was the ball that »»

David Cone reacts to the "disbelief" of his perfect game.

‹‹‹ nearly shattered Cone's brilliant, dominating performance. With one out in the eighth inning, Jose Virdo rapped a grounder up the middle that had every chance to scoot into the outfield for a single.

"I went 2-0 on him," said Cone, who had not thrown two balls with his first two pitches to any other batter. "I said, 'I got to go for it here. I'm just going to challenge him.' I got the better part of the middle of the plate and he hit it hard up the middle and I thought, there it goes."

But second baseman Knoblauch ranged far to his right, speared the ball with a backhanded grab and traveled another four steps on momentum before he stopped, turned, planted his feet deliberately and, unlike many times this season, fired a perfect throw to first for the 23d out.

Brad Fullmer, the next batter, took a strike, fouled off the next pitch with a checked swing, then took strike three for the third out of the eighth inning. The fans roared as Cone walked slowly to the dugout.

Cone said that around the middle of the game he fought the urge to think about what he was accomplishing. But then came the sixth inning.

"I went out in the sixth," he related, "and said the heck with it; I'm going to throw fastballs and try to get through the inning quickly and it happened. Then I'm thinking O.K., here we go, the last three innings. That's when you really pick it up a notch and try to go for it."

In his 13-year career, Cone has won the Cy Young award once and has been a 20-game winner twice, but he has also experienced the down side. His worst time occurred early in the 1996 season, when he was found to have an aneurysm in the upper part of his right arm. Surgery eliminated the problem, but he had no guarantee that he would continue his career or continue to be successful in it.

That September he returned and pitched seven innings against Oakland without allowing a hit. But he was not allowed to try to complete the no-hitter.

"I've wondered if I'd ever get a chance again," Cone said yesterday. "Going into the latter innings today, that was running through my mind, about how many times I've been close and how this might be the last chance I get. My heart was pumping. I could feel it through my uniform."

Throwing quick-biting sliders like he said he used to throw, Cone achieved his quest. He did not surprise Felipe Alou, the manager of a young and inexperienced Expos team. Asked when he thought Cone might do something special, Alou said, "When I wrote the lineup and saw that we didn't have anybody who faced him." ◆

October 28, 1999

YANKEES SWEEP BRAVES FOR 25TH TITLE

By BUSTER OLNEY

ROGER CLEMENS was traded to the Yankees on the first day of spring training, and on the last day of the World Series he became a Yankee. He and his teammates heard all year how the team wasn't as good as the record-setting Yankees of 1998, but when it came to achieving any team's ultimate goal—winning the World Series—the Yankees, and Clemens, were every bit as good.

Clemens shut out the Atlanta Braves into the eighth inning last night and the Yankees went on to win, 4–1, at Yankee Stadium, clinching a four-game sweep, the Yankees' 25th championship of the century and their third title in four years. The Yankees' victory was their 12th consecutive in the World Series, tying a record. Mariano Rivera was named the most valuable player after three scoreless appearances in relief.

Rivera threw the last pitch of the Series in the bottom of the ninth inning, and when Keith Lockhart popped a fly ball to left field, the Yankees lurched out of their dugout, waiting for the ball to come down. Catcher Jorge Posada began running toward the mound, where Rivera stood and stared, emotionless, watching left fielder Chad Curtis settle under the ball and make the catch.

And then they went crazy. Rivera raised his arms, turned and embraced Posada, and third baseman Scott Brosius joined them. They all gathered in a circle behind the mound, while security officials and mounted police officers began rushing onto the field. Clemens, jacketed, ran onto the field, arms raised. Paul O'Neill, who only hours earlier had learned in an early-morning phone call that his father, Charles O'Neill, had died, was the last of the position players to join the happy scrum, pausing at second base to step on the bag superstitiously.

They began trading hugs, Manager Joe Torre joining, and it was in those moments, some of them said later, that the gravity of all they endured this year began to hit them. Brosius's father had died, and so had the father of the infielder Luis Sojo, and Torre was found to have prostate cancer. They had worn the No. 5 in a black sphere on one shoulder, after Joe DiMaggio died in March, and late in the season, a black armband was added following the death of the Hall of Fame pitcher Catfish Hunter. "We're all family here," Brosius said.

As O'Neill traded embraces, he burst into tears, and with his head down, he rushed off the field, seeking seclusion. His teammates gathered in the Yankees' clubhouse to spray champagne—Derek Jeter doused the principal owner, George Steinbrenner—and share their joy.

With his Yankee-blue undershirt soaking wet, Clemens pushed through the crowd of reporters and teammates with a bottle of champagne in each hand, a son under each arm, grinning broadly. No one can ever say again that he has never won a championship.

Mike Stanton, a longtime friend of Clemens, found the pitcher amid the happy humanity. "Hey, you finally got a ring," Stanton said. "About time."

And Clemens grinned, having pushed the Yankees over the finish line that had seemed so distant all summer. ◆

Yankees Win (Queens), Yankees Win (the Bronx); Clemens Beans Piazza

By BUSTER OLNEY

THE DAY BEGAN with Mets and Yankees fans cheering together for Dwight Gooden at Shea Stadium but culminated with the Mets' best player lying dazed on the ground of Yankee Stadium, his teammates shouting furiously at one Yankee in particular.

This one-day, crosstown ride through history was supposed to be about MetroCards and the E-ZPass, but after Roger Clemens beaned Mike Piazza in the second inning last night, it become something ugly. For the first time, there is real anger in the inter league rivalry between the Yankees and the Mets.

Chuck Knoblauch whacked a three-run homer that was nearly caught as the Yankees beat the Mets, 4–2, in the second game to sweep the day-night doubleheader.

But the Mets are simmering. Piazza was found to have a concussion after having X-rays, and some of the Mets—notably Manager Bobby Valentine—are convinced Clemens hit Piazza intentionally.

"We've handed his lunch to him every time we've played him, so the first hitter he throws at his head, the third hitter he throws at his head, and the fourth hitter he hits him in the head," Valentine said. "My player who had pretty good success against that pitcher got hit in the head."

Clemens said: "I didn't hit Mike on purpose. I was going to pitch him inside. That was my game plan going in."

Valentine: "I've seen him try to hit guys in the head before."

The hostility began with what might have been a misunderstanding in the very first inning. Clemens whipped a fastball past the ⟫⟫⟫

◀◀◀ Mets' Lenny Harris to open the game and received the ball back from catcher Chris Turner. Clemens turned his back toward the plate, and suddenly the umpires were asking for the ball, and it was thrown out of play.

Many pitchers do not like it when hitters ask for a ball change in the middle of an at-bat, and Clemens may have thought that the Mets' lead-off hitter had done just that. In fact, the Hall of Fame had requested the baseball used with the game's first pitch, and the umpires had forgotten to retrieve it immediately. Regardless, Clemens fired his next pitch, a fastball, in the vicinity of Harris's head, the hitter ducking backward. To the Mets, it appeared to be an overt attempt to intimidate them.

Piazza led off the second against Clemens. Both are destined for the Hall of Fame, but Piazza dominated Clemens in previous encounters: 7 hits in 12 at-bats, including three home runs. "Everybody knows Mike's had success against me, obviously," Clemens said. "I wanted to pitch him inside."

Clemens threw a fastball inside that Piazza watched—strike one—and threw another fastball, 92 miles an hour. Piazza realized the ball was coming at him and began ducking, but it hit him solidly on the helmet, just above the bill. He

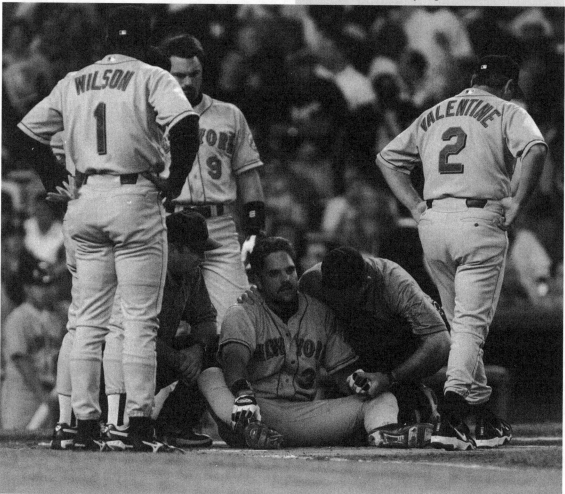

Mike Piazza of the Mets being treated by trainers after being hit in the helmut by Roger Clemens.

fell onto his back, eyes closed and then open, his expression blank.

There was a rush from the Mets dugout, and as Piazza was being tended to, Valentine walked back and forth, glancing in the direction of Clemens. John Stearns, the Mets' bench coach, was more obvious, yelling and holding up two fingers: twice they thought Clemens aimed fastballs at their hitters. Clemens squatted in front of the mound, looking down. "I was shaken after I hit him," he said. "That was not the way I wanted to get him out."

Yankees Manager Joe Torre defended Clemens, saying he has encouraged him to pitch inside. "To hit somebody in the head—we don't do that," Torre said. "Why? Mike hadn't had a hit in the series, and we're not going to stir that up."

Piazza eventually rose, woozy, and walked off unsteadily, replaced by a pinch-runner. When play resumed, Valentine and the Mets' Derek Bell and perhaps others screamed profanities at Clemens. The Mets players stood at the railing at the front of the dugout, poised, just in case. Retaliation seemed inevitable.

Tino Martinez led off the bottom of the second against Glendon Rusch, and with his second pitch to Martinez, Rusch hit him on the backside with a fastball. Message sent. Martinez glanced at Rusch, flipped his bat away and jogged to first, while 55,821 roared.

Doug Eddings, the plate umpire, warned both teams against further brushbacks. Valentine argued more, again making the point that Clemens had thrown two brushback pitches, while Rusch had hit one batter. Later, Clemens threw inside to Bell. "Sounds like three for one to me," Valentine said.

Clemens pitched into the eighth, throwing well, and Mariano Rivera recorded his second save of the day. There were no more incidents, which does not guarantee bad blood won't rise again today. "I hope not," Torre said. ◆

July 11, 2000

Posada's Father Basks as Teachings Pay Off

By JACK CURRY

ATLANTA, JULY 10—The father told his 8-year-old son to put down the aluminum bat and use a wooden one. The son resisted. The father repeated why the son would benefit from using a wooden bat. The son frowned, he cried, he refused to give up the aluminum bat. But the boy finally acquiesced because he would not have been allowed to play otherwise.

The father also told his son, who was a natural right-handed batter, that he needed to bat left-handed for five years without interruption. Again, the son was upset. Calmly yet sternly, the father explained why it was important to be a switch-hitter. Tears gathering in his eyes, the boy moved to the other batter's box and stayed there until he was 13.

These scenes happened in Rio Piedras, P.R., and Jorge Posada Sr. proudly told these stories Sunday about his son—the catcher for the Yankees, who will participate in the All-Star Game on Tuesday night. The father arrived here today from Puerto Rico and admitted that when the American League opposes the National League at Turner Field, he will still see images of the skinny boy who did not initially understand his strict baseball lessons.

"I always used to tell him to remember what we were doing and to remember that it was for the future," Posada Sr. said. "Now I ask him, 'Do you remember?'"

The Yankee catcher remembers. Merely mentioning his father's name caused the 28-year-old to grin and then caused his eyes to moisten. He remembers not being able to use an aluminum bat, but he is appreciative now since he never had to adjust to wood. He remembers feeling feeble as a left-handed hitter, but he now realizes how marketable a solid switch-hitting ⟫⟫⟫

<<< catcher is in the major leagues.

"I wouldn't be here if it wasn't for him," Posada said. "I was a project of his."

While Posada sat behind a table in a hotel ballroom with the other A.L. All-Stars today, he reminisced about watching All-Star Games when he was 13.

As giddy as Posada was, he obviously belongs on this team after batting .309 with 14 homers and 41 runs batted in and flourishing in his first year as the full-time starter.

"When you come from where he did last year, where everyone was asking the question 'What's wrong with Jorge?' it's special," said Joe Torre, the A.L. manager, who selected Posada as a reserve behind Ivan Rodriguez, who was chosen in the fans' balloting. "To see him on the All-Star team is great."

Posada told Derek Jeter before the season that one of his personal goals was to make the All-Star team. He told his father that, too, and it made Jorge Sr. happy. When Posada was asked how he is similar to his father, he responded: "Workaholics. I watched him work three jobs when I was a kid, so I had to be the same way."

The father rarely travels to New York to watch the son because he hates the traffic and because he wants his son to rest, not play tour guide for him. The father usually watches the Yankees on television, but he needed to see the All-Star Game in person and needed to see the continued improvement of his son, his project.

"I wanted him to think about what we were doing and remember it," Posada said. He paused and then said, "He remembered everything." ◆

Jorge Posada.

October 12, 2000

El Duque Doing What He Does Best

By DAVE CALDWELL

ORLANDO HERNANDEZ was asked last night through a translator how he planned to celebrate his birthday, and a smile tickled the corner of his mouth like a leftover dab of frosting. He said there would be a party late last night on the Yankees' long flight to Seattle, and it sounded as if that would be plenty for him.

El Duque, who turned either 31 (according to the Yankees) or 35 (according to other documentation) yesterday, had already given his teammates and a city aching for a Subway Series a better gift than any he could have received. With another superb postseason pitching performance, Hernandez had given the Yankees their hope back.

"When he takes the mound," right fielder Paul O'Neill said, shaking his head almost in disbelief, "you feel like you're going to win."

The Yankees have not done anything but win when Hernandez pitches in the postseason. He allowed the Seattle Mariners only one run and six hits in eight innings yesterday, and the Yankees ended their offensive stupor with seven runs in the bottom of the eighth for a stunning 7–1 victory. The American League Championship Series is now tied at one victory apiece.

"He does this time and time again," Yankees Manager Joe Torre said, "and I know you're not surprised at it, but you still marvel at it."

Hernandez is 7–0 in the postseason in his three-year major league career. He is the first Yankee to do that, and the first major leaguer to do that since Orel Hershiser, who needed 11 years to win his first seven postseason games. Hernandez has allowed only eight earned runs in 59 1/3 postseason innings.

"I believe I'm going to do my job and hold the other team, and our hitters are going to go out there and score some runs," Hernandez said. ◆

October 21, 2000

SUBWAY SERIES
Roll 'Em: Yanks and Mets Ready for a Wild Ride

By BUSTER OLNEY

THE SUBWAY SERIES begins tonight and the participants will be greatly relieved, because when the Yankees' Andy Pettitte throws the first pitch to the Mets' Timo Perez in Game 1, they will all be temporarily bunkered from the bombardment of ticket requests.

Desperation to see the first World Series between city rivals in 44 years is setting in, and no connection is too remote. The Mets' general manager, Steve Phillips, received a call yesterday from the batboy of the Class A Columbia Mets—the 1983 Columbia, S.C., Mets, a team for which Phillips played. "So he hasn't seen you in 17 years, and you want tickets?" the secretary for the general manager asked the former batboy.

It has been 16,083 days since the end of the last Subway Series, when the Yankees shut out the Dodgers in the final game of the 1956 World Series, and a city is on edge. It has been five days since the Mets, who have lived in the shadows of their Bronx big brothers for most of the last decade, clinched the National League pennant. It's been four days since the Yankees, the nearest thing to a dynasty that baseball has seen in a quarter-century, wrapped up the American League.

The players are eager. "There is a lot of build-up," Yankees pitcher David Cone said, "almost like a Super Bowl atmosphere."

The Mets must break through against a tough, veteran Yankees team that fought back from a late-season slump to survive two playoff trials, and seems to be gaining momentum. The Yankees have won 12 consecutive World Series games; if the Yankees win Game 1, their streak will set a record.

"They know how to win," Leiter said, "and they've certainly shown it by winning championships." »»

Yankees and Mets fans at a Subway Series rally at Bryant Park in 2000.

The Series is filled with top players capable of performing at the highest level. Rivera, the Yankees' closer, has allowed one run in 10 World Series appearances. Piazza is one of the greatest offensive players of his generation, and the Yankees will try to pitch around him. Hernandez, who could start two or more games in this series, has pitched in 10 postseason games and the Yankees have won all of them.

But both teams were sired by the same city, and the clans that follow them are distinct and divided. Yankees fans screamed at Leiter in downtown Manhattan the other night—"Just don't go to Madison Square Garden right now," Leiter advised some Mets followers—and Cone has walked around the city and been impressed by all the baseball caps, both with the interlocking N's and Y's but absolutely dissimilar to the fans who wear them.

As the Yankees finished batting practice yesterday afternoon, some of the Mets began to filter from their dugout and onto the field for their workout. Some coaches from the two teams chatted, and there were a few waves across the field by the players, but mostly, there was little contact. The Mets took infield practice and batting practice. Second baseman Edgardo Alfonzo stood behind the cage, stoic, a blank expression.

Why so quiet? "What do you think I'm feeling inside?" Alfonzo asked, his face splitting into a grin. "I'm about to play in my first World Series. I'm just trying to keep my emotions inside."

Alfonzo, and a city, will let loose tonight. ◆

October 23, 2000

SUBWAY SERIES
Clemens Throws a Bat, Dominates the Mets

By BUSTER OLNEY

ROGER CLEMENS threw fastballs that reached 99 miles an hour, but drew even more attention for firing a broken bat in the direction of the Mets' Mike Piazza last night, pitching eight shutout innings and heightening the emotions of the Subway Series that is being controlled by the Yankees.

Facing Piazza for the first time since hitting the Mets catcher in the head with a fastball in July, Clemens sparked an astonishing bench-clearing incident in the first inning by hurling the broken bat. But Clemens retreated to a private room in the clubhouse, refocused and continued his recent postseason domination, allowing only two hits and striking out nine in a 6–5 victory over the Mets in Game 2 of the World Series at Yankee Stadium.

Clemens shut out Seattle on one hit in Game 4 of the American League Championship Series nine days ago, and in his last two games, opposing hitters are 3 for 55 (.055) against Clemens, with 24 strikeouts.

But Clemens and his manager, Joe Torre, became animated when questioned after the game about Clemens's intent when he threw the bat at Piazza. "There was no intent there," Clemens said repeatedly. Torre said: "It was just emotional. Should he have done it? No."

Clemens's beaning of Piazza three and a half months ago has hovered over this Series, and the Mets' hostility toward Clemens has never really dissipated. Everything Clemens did last night would be seen by the Mets through the prism of that incident.

Clemens wore linebacker's eyes to the mound. He wears a mouthpiece when he pitches, and his lower jaw was locked, his chin pushed forward, except when he cursed, either at himself or the batter, or at no one in particular.

Timo Perez faked a bunt on Clemens's first pitch and Clemens breathed two words, one syllable apiece, verbal aggression. He shook his head between pitches, talked aloud, his inner frenzy and his fastball both gaining speed. He struck out Perez »»

Roger Clemens fires Mike Piazza's broken bat toward him during Game 2 of the 2000 World Series.

◀◀◀ with fastballs, all of them 97 m.p.h., and twice he threw 98-m.p.h. fastballs to Edgardo Alfonzo, before finishing off the second baseman with a 94-m.p.h. splitter—a stunning speed for that diving pitch.

When Piazza was announced as the next hitter the crowd of 56,059 roared, the culmination of 106 days of anticipation for the first confrontation between the two men since Clemens beaned Piazza on July 8. The pitcher pumped two fastballs for strikes. Then, after throwing a ball out of the strike zone, Clemens fired inside, shattering Piazza's bat into at least three pieces.

The ball went foul and the barrel of the bat bounced toward Clemens, who fielded it as he would a grounder, then turned and fired the fragment sidearm toward Piazza, the bat head skimming and skittering along the ground just in front of Piazza.

Piazza was stunned, and he turned and stared at Clemens, moving toward the pitcher, turning the bat handle in his hand, stepping across the base line. The Mets coaching staff and players immediately rushed from their dugout. Clemens held his hand up, as if to ask the umpire for a new ball, but then came face to face with Piazza, appearing to tell Piazza that he thought the barrel was the ball.

Piazza said in July that he had lost respect for Clemens, and having just seen a bat go flying across his path, Piazza was stunned. He shouted at Clemens, asking him what his problem was. Then the Mets' bench coach, John Stearns—who had tried to confront Clemens the day after the beaning—bulled his way toward the pitcher, screaming. The two hordes of Yankees and Mets were bunched together, some pushing, the group turning slowly, like a satellite image of a hurricane.

Torre grabbed Stearns, who used to play for him, and tried to calm him down, and gradu-

ally, as Clemens and Piazza were separated, the situation came under control without punches. After Piazza grounded out to second, the crowd was still murmuring while Clemens stopped and talked to the plate umpire, Charlie Reliford, explaining his actions.

What he told Reliford is close to what he said after the game—that he had thrown the bat without knowing where Piazza was, and when he looked up, he was surprised to see Piazza standing where he had thrown the bat. "I had no idea that Mike was running," Clemens said. "No idea."

Piazza was unsure, even after the game, about what happened, calling it bizarre. For an inning afterward, Mets Manager Bobby Valentine asked his players what had happened, because he hadn't seen Clemens throw the bat. There was no consensus, Valentine said, among his players, and Valentine said that if he had seen the incident, he might have handled it differently, asking the umpires for clarification on whether Clemens should have been ejected.

Clemens went into the clubhouse after that first inning, and sat alone for more than five minutes. "I knew I had to get control of my emotions quickly," he said later.

The Yankees led, 6-0, in the ninth, and Clemens was removed, having thrown 112 pitches. But the Mets started creeping back, Piazza ripping a two-run homer off Jeff Nelson, and three batters after left fielder Clay Bellinger caught Zeile's fly ball at the fence in left, Jay Payton crushed a three-run homer off Mariano Rivera.

The Yankees' closer finished the game, however, leaving the Mets to figure out how to beat the Yankees, and leaving everyone to wonder what the heck Clemens was thinking about when he caught Piazza's broken bat. ◆

Mariano Rivera celebrates the Yankees' third straight World Series championship with his teammates.

October 27, 2000

SUBWAY SERIES; In 5 Games, a Third Straight World Series Trophy

By BUSTER OLNEY

THE YANKEES MAINTAINED their pre-eminence in New York last night, finishing off the Mets in the Subway Series by rallying in the ninth inning of Game 5, and established their place among the greatest baseball dynasties by winning their third consecutive title.

Luis Sojo slapped a rolling single off the Mets' starting pitcher, Al Leiter, with two outs in the top of the ninth to score Jorge Posada with the tie-breaking run, and when the throw home bounced off Posada and rolled into the Mets' dugout, Scott Brosius also scored. The Yankees won, 4–2, at Shea Stadium, finishing off a breathless World Series in which three games were decided by one run, two others by two runs.

When Mike Piazza flied out to deep center field to end the game—coming within 15 feet or so of hitting a game-tying home run—center fielder Bernie Williams dropped to a knee in prayer, then jumped and hugged left fielder Clay Bellinger, as teammates rushed from the Yankees' dugout to swarm the infield, to join the closer Mariano Rivera, and Derek Jeter, the World Series most valuable player, and the rest.

Some players lifted Manager Joe Torre onto their shoulders and carried him off the field; the principal owner, George Steinbrenner, watching the final out in the clubhouse, burst into tears. "The Mets gave us everything we could want," he said, "and it was great for New York."

The Yankees recovered from seven »»

◀◀◀ consecutive losses at the end of the regular season and scares in the first two rounds of the playoffs to become the first team since the 1972–74 Oakland Athletics to win three consecutive championships, the first team since the advent of free agency, a change that has made it far more difficult for teams to maintain continuity.

After winning the World Series 25 times in the 1900's, the Yankees have won again.

The Mets advanced further into the postseason than they had in more than a decade, and there will be some solace in that. But for their fans, this is the worst imaginable fate: not only did the Mets lose the World Series, but they were also beaten by their cross-city rivals; this was the big brother whipping the little brother in a snowball fight and then rubbing his face in the slush, an indelible memory that can be mitigated only by revenge that may not come for years, or may never come.

"There are a lot of heavy hearts in that clubhouse," Mets Manager Bobby Valentine said, "and I have a heavy heart with them."

Steinbrenner has been emotional after each of the championships, but never more than he was last night, his mouth turned down as the championship trophy was handed to him, his words halted, tears running out of his eyes. It was a hard year for the Yankees, Torre said time and again as they straggled through the regular season, through the playoffs. They played poorly early, there were trade talks about Sammy Sosa and Juan Gonzalez, until David Justice and Denny Neagle and others all came over and contributed and stabilized the team, before that late-season slump made them all doubt, just a little, about whether this was possible.

"I'd be lying if I said this one wasn't more gratifying," Jeter said. "I mean, we struggled this year. We had tough times."

Posada said, "They don't get old, I'm telling you that."

A half hour after the game, many of the Yankees began to stream out of the clubhouse and onto the field, their shirts soaked with Champagne, and they held the championship trophy aloft, Roger Clemens and O'Neill and others. Fans who remained at Shea Stadium chanted O'Neill's named and thanked him, thanked all of them. Four titles in five years, a city's dynasty. ◆

November 30, 2000

Mussina Reaches Agreement

By JACK CURRY

THE FIERCE COURTING of Mike Mussina was virtually complete last night as the Yankees reached an agreement in principle with the free-agent pitcher on a six-year contract for about $87 million. By yesterday afternoon the Yankees were prepared to hold a news conference, and Arn Tellem, Mussina's agent, was flying from California to New York to attend it.

The imminent addition of Mussina makes the Yankees prohibitive favorites to win their fourth straight World Series title as he will join Roger Clemens, Andy Pettitte and Orlando Hernandez in a remarkable rotation. The Yankees also feel that Mussina's signing could have a domino effect and enable them to sign David Cone to a modest deal and complete their five-man rotation.

By adding Mussina, the rich Yankees will get richer. After having won the World Series with a payroll of $112 million, the Yankees moved swiftly to land Mussina, one of the two marquee free-agent pitchers with Mike Hampton. Manager Joe Torre met face to face with Mussina, Derek Jeter, Paul O'Neill and Pettitte telephoned him and the Yankees gave a pitcher who will be 32 next week a hefty six-year deal. Mussina, who was 11–15 with a 3.79 earned run average last season, was 147–81 in his 10 seasons with the Orioles. ◆

September 19, 2001

Triumph And Cheers Greet Yanks After 9/11

By BUSTER OLNEY

CHICAGO, SEPT. 18—Flag-waving fans wiped away tears and loudly sang "God Bless America," and when first baseman Paul Konerko failed to scoop a throw out of the dirt and allowed the Yankees to score a first-inning run, the fans came together in heart and soul again. They groaned, in perfect harmony.

They booed an umpire's mistake and the ejection of a Chicago coach and player, and they gave a Bronx cheer when the same umpire got a call right. Teammates shared smiles and laughs and high-fives. Yankees pitcher Orlando Hernández jumped over the first base line to and from the dugout for good luck, as always, and he blurted angry words when he couldn't throw strikes.

The respite lasted nine innings, and the Yankees, playing their first game since the Sept. 11 horror, romped over Chicago, 11–3; Alfonso Soriano, Jorge Posada and Shane Spencer hit homers. But White Sox fans didn't seem to take it personally. "We love you, New York!" a man bellowed through silence as the colors were marched onto the field before the game, and other fans among the crowd of 22,785 roared approvingly.

The Yankees stood on the foul lines before the game and wore the hats of the New York Fire and Police Departments, as the Mets had in Pittsburgh on Monday night. There was a moment of silence, the national anthem was sung and fans chanted "U.S.A.!" Several Yankees wept; Manager Joe Torre thought of children and returned to his office to compose himself before the game started.

"People responded so great," Bernie Williams said. "I never heard White Sox fans rooting for us."

The Yankees had won 9 of their last 10 games before everything stopped last week, and once they resumed tonight, it was as if nothing had changed. Chuck Knoblauch singled on the seventh pitch of the game, Derek Jeter singled, Tino Martinez pulled a single to right field, and Jeter crossed the plate with the game's first run, slapping Posada's outstretched hand. The atmosphere in the dugout was the same, Torre reported: the chatter, the feeling of confidence.

Hernández jogged out to pitch the first inning and, after he reached the rubber, he marked the spot where his front foot should land, as he always does. The Yankees threw the ball around the infield, and Scott Brosius smiled as he flipped the ball to Hernández, nodding: Let's go. And Hernández dominated the White Sox, spinning sliders and curves, flopping change-ups, allowing two hits and no runs in seven innings.

The Yankees piled on runs in the last innings, Posada crushing a grand slam in the seventh, Jeter finishing the game with three hits. The Yankees reduced their magic number for clinching the American League East to seven, and with the playoffs set to begin in three weeks, the perception of the Yankees as a talented and successful team will not change for some.

But judging by the reception the Yankees received here tonight, others will see the interlocking N and Y on the caps of the Yankees, the words "New York" extended across their road jerseys, and it's inevitable that the Yankees will be viewed as representatives of a devastated and resilient city.

Some players began to sense this as they walked among firefighters and emergency workers last Saturday. Men and women laboring amid the World Trade Center rubble kept telling the players to make the city proud, to keep playing well.

"The people who have been down there going through the 12-hour days and looking for something to lift them up," Mike Mussina said, "and maybe feel good for even a brief period of time; we're going to be one of those outlets they can look to for a little motivation and to take their minds off of what everybody's been going through."

Brosius, who just three days ago sounded unsure of what to expect when the team played at Yankee Stadium, is now greatly looking forward to that day. "I think it's going to be like ⟫⟫⟫

<<< a big, giant family reunion," he said. "It's not in any way forgetting what is going on, or minimizing the tragedy. It's just a matter of coming together. Fans have taken to our team, and certainly guys on the team have taken to the city."

Brosius continued: "This could be a year where they could possibly attach more pride than they normally do, which is saying a lot because there's a lot of pride in all the New York teams that go into the playoffs. If we get that opportunity, certainly the farther that we went into the playoffs, New York might grab onto it."

Everybody is ready to move on, Torre said, "and baseball is what we do." It's a form of relief, he said. If only for nine innings, nine loud and emotional innings. ◆

October 14, 2001

JETER'S PLAY

By MURRAY CHASS

OAKLAND, CALIF.— One hit, one defensive play. The combination enabled the Yankees to continue playing and avoid their briefest postseason appearance since 1980.

That year the Yankees lost the American League Championship Series to the Kansas City Royals in three games. This year they lost the first two games of the division series to the Athletics and were on the brink of being swept. But Jorge Posada hit a home run in the fifth inning, and Derek Jeter made a defensive play two innings later that saved the lead and the 1–0 victory for the Yankees.

In the seventh inning Terrence Long ripped a two-out double into the right-field corner that looked as if it might produce the tying run. Jeremy Giambi, younger brother of Jason, the Athletics' star, was at first base when Long threatened to spoil Mike Mussina's budding shutout. Giambi had singled to right with two out for only the third hit against Mussina.

As Giambi neared third, Ron Washington, the third-base coach, waved him home. It was the Athletics' best scoring opportunity.

Shane Spencer, the right fielder, raced into the corner and retrieved the ball. He turned and threw to the infield. But he overthrew Alfonso Soriano, the second baseman, who serves as the first relay man on that play. Worse, he also overthrew Tino Martinez, the first baseman, who serves as relay man No. 2. He is the backup, just in case the throw eludes Soriano.

Teams do not practice plays where they have a third relay man. As Giambi said later, "Usually there's a double cut and if someone overthrows it, it's the catcher picking up the ball."

In this instance, though, the ball didn't bounce or roll to Posada. Jeter, the Yankees' ubiquitous shortstop, raced across the infield, grabbed the loose ball near the first baseline and, with his momentum taking him away from the plate, turned and flipped the ball to Posada.

Giambi came racing down the third-base line. Hernandez, doing what the on-deck hitter is supposed to do when there is a play at the plate, signaled for Giambi to slide.

"I told him to slide," Hernandez said. "I don't know if he saw me or not. I waved and yelled. I was trying to yell, but it was too loud, so I just put my hand out and told him to go down."

Giambi did not slide. He tried to leap over Posada's tag, and Kerwin Danley, the plate umpire, called him out.

"I didn't know he missed the cutoff man," Giambi said. "I was picking up Washington. I was coming in and was getting ready to make

Jorge Posada, taking the backhanded flip from Derek Jeter, before turning to tag Jeremy Giambi at the plate.

some contact with Posada. He hadn't got the ball yet so I figured I had a better chance to try to run through the bag and beat him to the bag."

Hernandez and Giambi knew that Jeter made a great play. "I think if he let it go, the ball would hit me," Hernandez said. "He made a great play to pick it up and throw how he was. That was really hard to do."

Giambi said the play showed the "kind of instincts Derek Jeter has on the field, the kind of player he is."

A minute later Giambi talked about how the Yankees had won four of the last five World Series and that "they know how to play in the playoffs. It seems when their backs are against the wall they step up to the occasion." Asked if Jeter's play was an example of how the Yankees rise to the occasion, Giambi said: "It's no question. They know how to get it done." ◆

October 17, 2001

How Much Is Left In the Tank?

By WILLIAM C. RHODEN

HALF AN HOUR AFTER the Yankees defeated Oakland to win their division series, General Manager Brian Cashman stood in the clubhouse, stunned, weary and elated.

"I refuse to be surprised by this club," he said. The team he helped put together had set yet another benchmark, becoming the only team to prevail after losing the first two games of a division series at home. This was the end of one crazy crisscross day and the beginning of another. The team arrived in New York from Oakland early Monday morning. Now, in the time between Monday night and yesterday morning, the team was simultaneously granting interviews and packing and preparing for a flight back west, this time to Seattle.

Cashman lives in two worlds, the world on the field of emotion, muscle and pride, and the world upstairs of trades and cuts, of cold decisions designed to keep the machine rolling—who stays, who goes, who takes their place. This is probably the winter Cashman, his own future with the Yankees still not nailed down, makes tough decisions or risks suffering the fate of franchises who stayed put too long.

"You can't help it," he said. "It gets into your head. That's why my office is three levels above this clubhouse, where that stuff doesn't filter in."

Five days ago, the consensus was that the Yankees were aging and had come to the end of their run. Roger Clemens, 39, was forced to leave Game 1 against Oakland with an injury; David Justice, 35, and Paul O'Neill, 38, were not hitting.

Today, as if by magic, Yankees fans sense that their team is all the way back and rolling toward another World Series.

This time, the Yankees' second wind is dependent on the presence of Derek Jeter. Jeter has refused to let the Yankees be eliminated this postseason. We overuse that phrase, but not this time. In a span of 72 hours, Jeter used athleticism and rare instincts to compensate for tired Yankee legs and sore arms.

On Saturday in Game 3, when a crucial throw to the plate was off-line and overthrown, Jeter raced like a sprinter to run the ball down, snared the ball like a football receiver, shuttled it to the catcher like a quarterback. The runner was out, like magic.

In Game 5, Jeter chased down a foul pop, called Scott Brosius off the play, leaped, extended himself, made the catch and tumbled into the stands headfirst. "Postseason is basically pitching and defense," Jeter said. "You've got to limit the other team to only three outs an inning."

The catch in foul territory may have been the final psychological blow to the A's and served notice to surging Seattle that it will have to expend this type of effort—at the very least—to be successful against New York.

"We're not going home unless somebody beats us," Jeter said. ◆

October 23, 2001

SPORTS OF THE TIMES
Winners, By Knockout

By GEORGE VECSEY

THE OLDER YANKEES NOTICE, and so does the mayor. Through all the rollicking postseason times of the past seven years, it has never been quite this loud, never quite this happy.

Strangers were high-fiving strangers as they walked down the ramps of the old ballpark last night. They were chortling and skipping and singing along to Sinatra's upbeat version of "New York, New York" as if they had inhaled pure oxygen.

The giddiness level seems higher than it has ever been after the Yankees dispatched the Mariners, 12–3, at Yankee Stadium to win yet another American League pennant.

"I've never heard the crowd this enthusiastic," said Mayor Rudolph W. Giuliani, who has been a real hero in the important business of keeping the city going.

"There's no question this city needs a lift," the mayor said in the clubhouse with just the slightest reek of Champagne. "The World Series is going to be played here."

The Series is coming here because the old guys and the young guys who had seemed suspect a month ago were now doing exactly what Yankee teams have done in other Octobers, but this time it seems like pure joy.

The fans have shown a need for release ever since the terrorist attacks of Sept. 11. Nobody has called for the Yankees to win for the city because that would be a burden the players do not need, but there is definitely a link between the performers and their audience.

"The Yankees and the NY we wear on our cap when we play the games, we feel we are representing more than the Yankees now, with what New York and the rest of the country have gone through since the 11th of September," Joe Torre said before last night's game.

Then he added, "I don't think it would be fair for me to say that that's been our motivation because we've done this before this tragedy, and we've always been a highly motivated team."

"But for sure they are in our thoughts regularly," Torre said of the uniformed workers at the center of the horror.

Even for the fans who may be a degree or two removed from ground zero, these games have presented a potential for momentarily forgetting.

"New York needs this," George Steinbrenner, the owner, said Sunday night. "This is good for the city, but we haven't won this yet."

He would not be complacent last night, even with the fans making the Stadium rock with their feet and their voices. By winning at home, the Yankees gave their best starters a few days to rest up before matching the buzz saw of Curt Schilling and Randy Johnson.

The World Series against Arizona will come soon enough. In the past, Yankee fans greeted each October victory with a swagger. All those gloomy legends amassed in the monuments behind center field and all those booming pregame history film clips seem to induce a bristling sense of entitlement.

"It's not the uniform," Lou Piniella of the Mariners asserted before last night's game. "You can put purple and green on this bunch over there, and they are going to play well."

The poor Mariners won 116 games during the regular season, then had the misfortune of running into three-quarters of a century of tradition, plus one extremely talented team in the present tense.

And afterward, Piniella volunteered that in the middle of the whipping he was taking, he had looked around at the happy fans and felt good for the city where he used to play.

The Yankees imposed their real or imaginary mystique in only three of their six postseason games in the Stadium, but Alfonso Soriano's game- >>>

<<< ending homer on Sunday and last night's early cluster of runs touched off a lighthearted celebration.

Maybe it's the balmy weather. The Stadium turns more ominous when true fall sets in. The feet and hands are colder. The first couple of beers turn people sour and aggressive. The extra layers of clothing cause people to bump into each other in the narrow alleyways built back in 1923, when people were smaller and, dare one say it, more self-controlled.

Now that the Yanks have settled it in front of the home folks, the ever-present Challenger, the nonreleasable American bald eagle, can point toward next Tuesday's third game and the Sunshine Boys tandem of Yogi Berra and Phil Rizzuto can store up their energy for their nightly stint of throwing out the first pitch.

They've got the big-game routine down pat in the Bronx. Once you get through the barricades, there is the feeling of a city that hopes this happy little party has no curfew. ◆

November 5, 2001

In Final Twist, Yankees Fall in Ninth

By BUSTER OLNEY

PHOENIX, Nov. 4— The Yankees' dynasty was about to be passed down intact, and all that was needed was three outs from Mariano Rivera, who had not failed in the postseason in 1,479 days.

They had a 2–1 lead tonight in the bottom of the ninth inning of Game 7 of the World Series. Alfonso Soriano, the youngest Yankee, had hammered an eighth-inning homer off Arizona's Curt Schilling, and Paul O'Neill and other Yankees had gathered at the dugout railing, preparing to rush the field, to charge Rivera and hug him and congratulate each other on a fourth consecutive world championship, their fifth in six years.

The prospect of failure was nothing any of them considered; this was Mariano Rivera.

An excited mob formed on the infield minutes later, between first and second base, but the player in the midst of the maelstrom was Arizona's Luis Gonzalez.

Rivera walked off, head down, after allowing a game-tying double to Tony Womack and a game-winning single to Gonzalez with the bases loaded and one out. Arizona won Game 7 with a stunning 3–2 victory, ending a World Series filled with stunners.

The Yankees had won Games 4 and 5 after hitting game-tying home runs with two outs in the ninth, and they lost the decisive game after coming within two outs of becoming the first team in almost 50 years to win four consecutive championships.

Derek Jeter sat in the dugout for a minute or so after Gonzalez's hit, staring onto the field, and Manager Joe Torre remained at the railing, watching the Diamondbacks celebrate, before he turned slowly and retreated to the Yankees' clubhouse.

Rivera answered questions quietly, politely, without regret; he had broken bats on all three hits he allowed in the bottom of the ninth. "I did everything I could," he said.

A half-hour before the Yankees' pregame meeting today, Torre deferred to others in the clubhouse, who, by and large, view this World Series as an end of an era. O'Neill and Luis Sojo are retiring, Tino Martinez and others may not return. The Yankees may continue to win in the years to come, but next year, only four prominent players from the 1996 championship will be with the team.

Roger Clemens started Game 7, allowing one run in six and a third innings and striking out 10. He almost singlehandedly kept the Yankees in the game while the lackluster offense slowly came to life against Schilling.

In the top of the eighth, Schilling tried fooling Soriano with an off-speed pitch, and Soriano swung and lifted the ball toward left field. The Yankees' players bounced happily around the dugout, feeling as if they had the run they needed. They had Rivera, this they knew.

Rivera struck out three of the four batters he faced in the eighth inning, his fastball overwhelming the Arizona hitters. He had not blown a postseason save since Game 4 of the 1997 division series, when Cleveland's Sandy Alomar Jr. hit a game-tying home run. Rivera had 23 saves in 23 chances since that game. Preparations for the celebration were being made in the Yankees' clubhouse.

In the bottom of the ninth, Mark Grace singled. David Dellucci was inserted as a pinch-runner as the Diamondbacks prepared for a sacrifice. Damian Miller bunted in front of the plate and Rivera—one of the best fielding pitchers in the game—charged the ball, with catcher Jorge Posada screaming for him to throw to second base. Rivera threw wide, past Jeter, the ball bounding into center field. The whole inning would have been different, Rivera suggested, if only he had been able to make that throw.

Arizona had runners at first and second and nobody out, the fans screaming. Jay Bell tried another sacrifice and bunted in front of the plate, and Rivera threw to third, successfully getting a forceout.

Midre Cummings entered the game as a pinch-runner at second base for Miller. Rivera tried jamming Womack with a cut fastball, the pitch he has dominated hitters with over the last four years. Womack swung and his bat broke, and he lofted a double down the right-field line, scoring Cummings and tying the score, as Bank One Ballpark erupted. Bell stopped at third. Torre and players in the Yankee dugout stood at the railing impassively.

Craig Counsell then came to bat, and Rivera nicked him with a fastball, loading the bases. The Yankees' infielders and outfielders moved in, trying to cut off the run.

Gonzalez was next, and Rivera fired a cutter inside. When Gonzalez fisted a looper toward short, Jeter raised his glove instinctively.

But the ball was far too high for him to reach, too far in for any outfielder to catch. Bell scored, his arms extended, and the Diamondbacks rushed toward Gonzalez.

Torre watched the bedlam; so did O'Neill, his career at an end. Martinez glanced over his shoulder at Gonzalez, his childhood friend. Rivera walked off the field, head down.

Torre hugged O'Neill, and he spoke to his players briefly, told them how proud they should be. Most of the Yankees seemed at peace. It was a great World Series, Scott Brosius said, great games against a great team, "and you just can't assume you're going to win every game, every time. It just doesn't happen that way."

For most of six years, it did, for the Yankees. ◆

October 6, 2002

SPORTS OF THE TIMES
Angels Leave Yankees Soundly Beaten

By GEORGE VECSEY

ANAHEIM, CALIF., OCT. 5—In harrowing times this season this promising season now emphatically over—people would remind Derek Jeter of the wondrous things the Yankees had accomplished.

"Some of us have," Jeter would reply softly.

He was not being snide or self-aggrandizing, merely pointing out that this year's Yankees team was different from last year's Yankees team —considerably so.

Maybe Jeter saw it coming down the pike, the 9–5 thumping by the onrushing Anaheim Angels, who outplayed the Yankees for the third straight game and clinched the American League Division Deries this afternoon at Edison Field.

"No team has played better against us," Jeter said graciously, referring to the seven fat years in which he had played shortstop and Joe Torre had managed and the Yankees had won four World Series.

The walloping means there will be no fifth straight pennant that would have tied the major league record. But on a much more visceral level, it also means that Anaheim played solid baseball and showed no trace of fear, not even of the gray road uniforms with "New York" across the chest.

"We won the first game and they came back in every game," Jeter said, sitting at his locker while Anaheim celebrated winning its first postseason series in the 42 years of the franchise. He seemed weary and resigned, like a man who had seen it coming.

"A loss is a loss," he said. "The season's a failure." ◆

June 4, 2003

Steinbrenner Appoints Jeter Captain of the Yankees

By TYLER KEPNER

CINCINNATI, JUNE 2—Derek Jeter has been an established Yankees star for years, and the highest-paid player on George Steinbrenner's team since February 2001. But Steinbrenner, the principal owner, waited until today to make official what the players in the clubhouse already knew: that Jeter is the captain of the Yankees.

Steinbrenner did not show up for the announcement at Great American Ball Park before the Yankees lost to the Cincinnati Reds, 4–3, choosing instead to stay in Tampa, Fla., to

Derek Jeter, the Yankees' 11th captain.

oversee today's amateur draft. But it was Steinbrenner's decision alone, and he appointed Jeter at this moment— on the road, with the team still shaking off a slump—for a reason.

"I think he can hopefully pull them together," Steinbrenner said in a telephone interview today. "I think he can give them a little spark. I just feel it's the right time to do it. People may say, 'What a time to pick.' Well, why not? He represents all that is good about a leader. I'm a great believer in history, and I look at all the other leaders down through Yankee history, and Jeter is right there with them."

Jeter became the 11th captain—Babe Ruth, Lou Gehrig and Thurman Munson are among the others—and the first since Don Mattingly retired after the 1995 season. Steinbrenner discussed the appointment with Jeter last weekend in Detroit and again this morning. "He just says he wants me to be a leader, like I have been," Jeter said. "The impression I got is just continue to do the things I've been doing."

Steinbrenner was not ready to make the appointment over the winter, when a question about it prompted his famous rant about Jeter's supposed lack of focus. Jeter's measured response to the criticism made an impression on Steinbrenner, who thinks Jeter can help Manager Joe Torre as a leader.

"He's a young man that's handled it very well," Steinbrenner said. "He said what he thought. He's always available, ready to face the questions, win or lose. I think he can be a big help to Joe Torre. I think he and Joe will work great together."

Steinbrenner has been eager to fix something with the Yankees since their 3–12 skid last month. He has expressed doubt about the effectiveness of Torre's coaching staff and has had almost no contact with Torre this season. He did not consult him on the Jeter decision.

Torre said he did not want to play down Jeter's honor but did not think Jeter could help him do his job better, as Steinbrenner had suggested.

"I don't see my job being any different, as far as helping," Torre said, "because I don't know

what he could tell someone if they have a question to ask me. It can't be a negative, but I don't think players are going to listen to him more now that he's captain. He's always had that respect."

The day after the Yankees were swept by Texas two weeks ago, Jeter spoke at a team meeting in Boston. Jeter was injured during the Yankees' hot start, and according to catcher Jorge Posada, he challenged his teammates. "What I saw on TV is this, and when I got here, I don't see the same thing," Jeter said.

Jeter is able to get his message across in private conversations and group settings, said Posada, who has long considered him the captain. "When he needs to talk, people are going to listen," Posada said.

It is a great responsibility, one that could put Jeter, even without a C on his jersey, in Steinbrenner's sights when things go wrong.

Jeter dismissed that idea.

"I don't see how it would," Jeter told reporters. "I talk to you guys every day."

But dealing with the news media is just one aspect of Jeter's new role. Steinbrenner is putting his faith in Jeter, and that always carries significant demands. In the statement the team released, Steinbrenner used his favorite quotation from Gen. Douglas MacArthur: "There is no substitute for victory."

Cajoling his teammates to victory will clearly be a mandate for Jeter.

"You do what your gut tells you," Steinbrenner said. "My gut tells me this would be a good time for Derek Jeter to assume leadership. He is a great leader by the way he performs and plays. I told him I want him to be the type of cavalry officer who can sit in the saddle. You can't be a leader unless you sit in the saddle. I think he can." ◆

October 17, 2003

Old Hero, and Newest, Carry New York to the Series

By TYLER KEPNER

As THE BIGGEST HIT of Aaron Boone's life sailed into the seats down the left-field line, Mariano Rivera raced for the mound and knelt there, kissing the dirt and thanking God. Boone danced around the bases, raising his arms, beaming, grinning wildly. And there was Rivera, overcome with joy, the kind of mystical October euphoria that has sometimes seemed out of reach for these Yankees, celebrating in his own way.

"Today," Rivera said, "we played like a champion."

Rivera had worked three heroic innings, proving again that for all of the Yankees' problems, he is the biggest reason they are headed back to the World Series. Boone's home run this morning sent them there, coming on the first pitch from the Boston Red Sox' Tim Wakefield in the bottom of the 11th inning.

The Yankees rode Rivera's effort and Boone's blast to a 6–5 victory in Game 7 of the American League Championship Series, completing a stirring comeback against their tortured century-old rival. Boone, who had struggled for months and was not in the starting lineup last night, accomplished the unthinkable: a sudden strike to win the pennant, an instant spot in the pantheon of Yankee legends.

"It took a while," Boone said he told third-base coach Willie Randolph after the homer. "But I showed up."

Boone was not even in the game in the eighth inning, when a nightmare was five outs from becoming a reality for the Yankees. The Red Sox, spellbound for years by the most powerful mythic force in sports, were that close to stealing a pennant from Babe Ruth's house.

For the Red Sox, there is a new villain to curse for the ages. The signs Yankee fans sometimes wave can be updated: Babe, Bucky, Buckner, Boone. The homer by Boone will rank in Boston heartbreak with the sale of Ruth, the 1978 homer by Bucky Dent to lift the Yankees to the A.L. East title and the error by Bill Buckner in the 1986 World Series against the Mets.

Boone's older brother, Bret, was in the broadcast booth covering the game for Fox. Bret Boone, the second baseman for the Mariners, was direct in a conversation with Aaron after Game 6. Aaron was 2 for 16 in the series, and Bret told him he stunk.

"But you never know," Bret Boone said. "You get a big hit, everyone forgets about the bad at-bats. And that was as big as any hit you could get right now."

The chance for something even greater will come on Saturday, when the Yankees return to the stage they have dominated for eight decades. Boone is new to the team, coming over in a trade with Cincinnati in July. But as he spoke with reporters in the clubhouse, Champagne soaking his body, shaving cream smeared on his face, Boone had become a Yankee.

Rudolph W. Giuliani, the former mayor, approached Boone and hugged him. "Welcome to New York," Giuliani said. ◆

October 17, 2003

YANKS SEND RED SOX REELING

By JACK CURRY

EVERY OTHER YANKEE scampered to the plate to swarm Aaron Boone and celebrate his game-winning homer in an epic 6–5 victory in 11 innings over the Boston Red Sox this morning, but Mariano Rivera sprinted to the mound and collapsed as if it were an altar. He wanted to be by himself, on his knees, with his thoughts, thanking God.

While Boone danced around the bases and the Yankees and their fans were in an utter state of delirium, their impenetrable closer was 60 feet 6 inches away. He was in his own world, which was appropriate because that is where Rivera is as a postseason closer. In his own world, far away from any other humans—far, far away.

"I was thanking the lord," said Rivera. "You don't know. I had a lot of conversations with the man. I was thanking him for getting us through this game. This was his game."

This was Rivera's game and the Yankees' game, too. It is no surprise that Rivera, the most significant difference between the two evenly matched teams, was the most significant difference in the most important moments of the series and was named the series' most valuable player. He pitched three dominant innings, his longest outing since April 2000, and uncorked 48 pitches, his second-most in the postseason, and seemed as if he could have thrown 48 more. On and on, Rivera goes, like the best windup toy in the store.

"I didn't feel anything," Rivera said. "I felt great out there."

The Yankees had Rivera, and the Red Sox did not have anything like him, which is the main reason the Yankees won the decisive game of the American League Championship Series and why they will play the Florida Marlins in Game 1 of the World Series. There are other reasons why Red Sox fans will curse the Yankees, like Boone becoming an alliterative nightmare for them in joining Bucky, Buckner and Babe, but, really, they should send the most venom toward Rivera because he is the pitcher who separates the Yankees from other teams.

"He's old Mr. Reliable," said the pitching coach, Mel Stottlemyre. "He's there when we need him in situations like this. Most of the time, he's good enough."

Good enough? How about great enough? Roger Clemens, who was spared from seeing his career end with an erratic start, joked that Manager Joe Torre might want to start Rivera after what he did in Game 7. Willie Randolph, who was the first person to reach Rivera on the mound and had to lift his 180-pound body off the dirt before he could hug him, called him a "tremendous" pitcher who gives everyone around him endless confidence.

How emotional was Rivera? How consumed by the moment? After weeping on the mound, he cried some more between spraying and sipping Champagne. Shockingly, Rivera, who has four World Series rings, said this postseason victory ranks first among all of them? First? "We were down by four runs," Rivera said. "Buddy, you can't forget that." ◆

Aaron Boone connects for the pennant-winning home run in 2003 ALCS against the Red Sox.

October 27, 2003

SPORTS OF THE TIMES
Yankees' Fall Gives Rise to Hope Elsewhere

By GEORGE VECSEY

FOR SOME REASON, the eyes picked up Dontrelle Willis running in from the outfield bullpen. Well, he did not exactly run. He skipped, he leaped, he gamboled, he frolicked, a couple of steps forward, a leap in the air, and back to earth again, rushing toward a place he had never imagined a few short months ago.

And finally he heaved himself into the pile of Florida Marlins celebrating on the hallowed mound in hallowed Yankee Stadium.

Despite all the clichéd film clips on the Yankees' scoreboard, somebody had indeed come into their house and filched the World Series.

This is the third straight season when, improbably, an outsider has won the World Series. (In baseball, 29 teams are outsiders.) All the celebrations have been giddy. Beating the Yankees will do that. The Yankees are still the target, more than any other team in North American sports. Beat them and you have done a very big thing. But you can beat them as they are constituted.

The Diamondbacks stunned the Yankees in the seventh game of the 2001 World Series. The Angels dispatched the Yankees in the first round last year and went on to outlast the Giants. And the

---

February 15, 2004

Yankees Closing Deal For Rodriguez

By TYLER KEPNER;
Murray Chass contributed reporting

IN A TRADE that would join the most celebrated franchise in baseball with perhaps the best player in the game, the Yankees and the Texas Rangers have agreed in principle to a deal that would bring Alex Rodriguez to New York for Alfonso Soriano and a player to be determined, according to several people familiar with the discussions. The deal is all but complete, they said.

The commissioner's office and the players union must approve the trade, and the teams were working on administrative details last night, baseball officials said. "It has reached the commissioner's office," said Sandy Alderson, Major League Baseball's executive vice president for baseball operations, who declined further comment.

Rodriguez has seven years and $179 million remaining on the 10-year, $252 million contract he signed in December 2000. The Rangers would include money in the mid-$60 million range that would reduce the Yankees' average annual payments to Rodriguez from $25.5 million to about $16 million.

Rodriguez has performed as the Rangers hoped, leading the American League in home runs in each of the past three seasons and winning the Most Valuable Player award last year. But the Rangers have finished in last place each season and are desperate to shed his contract.

On Oct. 26, about 12 hours after the Yankees lost the World Series to the Florida Marlins, Rangers officials called Yankees General Manager Brian Cashman to gauge his interest in trading for Rodriguez. Irritated by the timing and confident in his own star shortstop, Derek Jeter, Cashman passed.

The Boston Red Sox, bitter rivals of the Yankees, reached their own deal for Rodriguez in December, only to have the trade quashed when the players union rejected the restructuring of

Marlins beat the Yankees in this year's Series, fair and square, four games to two, concluding with that masterly complete game by Josh Beckett in a 2–0 victory Saturday night.

Parity has come to Major League Baseball. And amen to that. The Marlins' triumph probably has less to do with the dribs and drabs of revenue sharing that Selig has imposed than with the mystery of human endeavor. Professional football seeks parity through sharing network revenue and certain tilts of the schedule. Pro basketball tends to dynasties, based on superstars. Hockey favors brilliant goalies and resilient systems. Now baseball has more than a glimmer of hope.

Put 30 teams into the mix and sometimes the other guy will get it right, not necessarily the team with the $180 million payroll.

Maybe the television ratings this year reflected the hope that people sensed in this, the third straight season in which the Yankees did not win the World Series. Try telling George Steinbrenner that this is ''good for baseball,'' but it is.

Joe Torre and Derek Jeter were magnanimous in their praise of the Marlins. They had seen good baseball prevail. The Marlins were a better defensive team by far. Watching the Yankees' middle infielders and three of their four regular outfielders brought home the reality of how ordinary their defense was.

Three straight World Series have made the point. The Yankees are not invincible. Other baseball cities can dare to hope for exuberance and youth and talent, like Dontrelle Willis, bounding joyously into the pack in late October. ◆

Rodriguez's contract. But with more financial might than the Red Sox and the lesson of Boston's failed trade to guide them, the Yankees were privately confident their deal would not fail.

"It is not going that route again," said one person involved in the talks. "That's been clear from the start."

The impetus for the Yankees' deal came on Jan. 16, when third baseman Aaron Boone seriously injured a knee while playing pickup basketball and Cashman could not find a replacement. Rodriguez, sensing an escape from what had become a gilded prison in Texas, decided he would shift from shortstop to third base if the Rangers dealt him to the Yankees.

It was no small concession from Rodriguez, who has won Gold Gloves for fielding excellence at shortstop the past two seasons. But Rodriguez has never played in the World Series, and according to one person familiar with the trade talks, he told the Rangers' owner, Tom Hicks, through an intermediary early last week that he wanted to be traded to the Yankees. ◆

Joe Torre (left) with Alex Rodriguez and Derek Jeter at the news conference announcing Rodriguez's arrival.

July 2, 2004

Dust Settles in 13th, and Yankees Sweep

By TYLER KEPNER

ONLY THE CALENDAR kept last night's game at Yankee Stadium from standing among the most electrifying in baseball history. There were battered heroes and brushback pitches, missed opportunities and clutch hits. There was Alex Rodriguez playing shortstop and Gary Sheffield playing third base.

And in the end, with Derek Jeter at a hospital after crash-landing in the seats for a game-saving catch an inning earlier, there was John Flaherty, the last man on the bench, rifling the game-winning hit down the left-field line in the bottom of the 13th inning for a 5–4 victory.

In the top of the 12th, Jeter was the Yankees' only hope. Trot Nixon's soft fly ball was falling fast, and no other fielder was close to it. From his position at shortstop, Jeter raced to his right and added to his legend.

With two outs and a runner at third, a hit would have given the Red Sox the lead. But there was Jeter, sprinting and swiping the ball from the air in fair territory. Unable to stop his momentum, he tumbled into the seats, spikes high, several rows back.

"Greatest catch I've ever seen," Rodriguez said. "It was unbelievable. He's just so unselfish. He put his body in a compromising spot. It was hard to watch."

Rodriguez followed Jeter in and waved for help. As a trainer went onto the field, Jeter emerged from among the fans—his fans—and stood above them for a moment as he climbed a wall to get back on the field. There was blood on his jersey, blood on his right cheek, blood on his chin. It was Jeter to the rescue.

Jeter left Yankee Stadium for X-rays on his right cheek. The Yankees said he sustained a laceration of his chin, a bruised right cheek and a bruised right shoulder. Jorge Posada said Jeter had stitches on his chin. "He said he's playing tomorrow," Posada said. ◆

October 21, 2004

Back From Dead, Red Sox Bury Yanks

By TYLER KEPNER

THEY HAD BEEN RELIABLE caretakers of a cosmic curse, feasting for decades on the gift that kept on giving: Babe Ruth, purchased from the Boston Red Sox in 1920, and all the championship karma he brought with him.

The rules were very simple. The Yankees won and their rivals lost, often painfully, eternal justice for the worst deal in baseball history. The Red Sox still have not won a World Series in 86 years. But they got there last night, playing the Babe's game in the house that he built.

With a barrage of four home runs—all pulled into the right-field seats, where Ruth once took aim—the Red Sox eliminated the Yankees with a 10–3 victory in Game 7 of the American League Championship Series at Yankee Stadium.

The Red Sox became the first team in baseball history to win a best-of-seven series after losing the first three games, and they will play host to the Houston Astros or the St. Louis Cardinals in Game 1 of the World Series at Fenway Park on Saturday.

"There's no curse," said Red Sox catcher Jason Varitek, who leapt on reliever Alan Embree after Ruben Sierra grounded to second base for the final out. "The curse, in my opinion, was just being outplayed. That team outplayed us over the years."

This series was different. For the Yankees, whose $180 million payroll is the highest ever for a baseball team, it was a devastating failure. They had beaten the Red Sox in Game 7 of last October's A.L.C.S., rallying from a three-run deficit to capture an 11-inning thriller. But losing the rematch hurt worse than any victory.

"Without question," Derek Jeter, the Yankees' captain, said. "We haven't won in a while. We've been losing here the last few years. Every year is a different group. This group just didn't get it done."

In Game 4 on Sunday, the Yankees were three

Willie Randolph, Joe Torre and Mel Stottlemyre suffer in silence.

outs from a sweep, seemingly on their way to the World Series, and possibly their first title since 2000. But Boston came back to win consecutive extra-inning showdowns, then stifled the Yankees behind Curt Schilling on Tuesday night.

Last night, Derek Lowe was the pitching star, allowing one hit over six innings despite pitching on two days' rest. And Johnny Damon, the shaggy-haired leadoff man batting .103 through the first six games, slammed two homers and drove in six runs.

The Yankees had done their best to channel their ghosts. Bucky Dent, who homered to slay the Red Sox in 1978, threw the ceremonial first pitch to Yogi Berra. The game was played on Mickey Mantle's birthday. George Steinbrenner, the impatient principal owner, showed up in the clubhouse some six hours before the first pitch, apparently spreading good cheer.

"He was very supportive," Manager Joe Torre said.

The good feelings undoubtedly have passed. Steinbrenner will probably order a reconstruction of the team, which won 101 games during the regular season but folded when it mattered most.

"I want to congratulate the Boston team," Steinbrenner said at about 1:15 this morning when he was leaving the stadium. "They did very well. They have a great team."

Yankees third baseman Alex Rodriguez, who was 2 for 17 in the four losses, said: "This is obviously crushing for us."

Rodriguez was not the only Yankee to fall flat in the final four games. Gary Sheffield was 1 for 17, and Tony Clark was 3 for 19 as a replacement for John Olerud, who severely bruised a bone when he stepped on a bat in Game 3.

Before the game, Torre had said he was searching for the team that won 101 games in the regular season.

"We just need to see the team that we've come to know and love tonight, not to go out there worried about making mistakes," he said.

In the end, they made the biggest mistake of all, performing one of the most stupefying collapses in sports history and losing their grip on their own history.

The nerd kissed the homecoming queen. Paper beat scissors; scissors beat rock. Charlie Brown kicked the football. The Red Sox beat the Yankees for the American League pennant. ◆

October 9, 2005

SPORTS OF THE TIMES
Johnson's Prison of Pinstriped Expectations

By DAVE ANDERSON

WHEN THE YANKEES clinched the American League East in Boston a week ago for the left-hander Randy Johnson's 17th victory, Joe Torre told him, "This is why we got you here."

Winning the division was certainly one reason the Yankees traded for Johnson, now 42, and signed him to a two-year contract extension worth $16 million a year through 2007. But there was another reason, the real reason, the Yankees spent all last off-season figuring out how they could get him in a trade with the Arizona Diamondbacks, as he soon learned.

"When I first got here," he recalled at his off-day news conference Thursday at Yankee Stadium, "they said there's two seasons here, and I go, 'Really?' They said, the regular season and the postseason."

Randy Johnson understood his responsibility. And with the Yankees returning to Yankee Stadium on Friday night for Game 3 against the Los Angeles Angels in their American League division series, Johnson appeared ready to justify that $16 million. He had 263 career victories. He was third on the career strikeout list, behind Nolan Ryan and Roger Clemens. With a 17–8 record and a 3.79 earned run average, he was unbeaten in his last eight starts. He was 11–2 at the Stadium this season. And in his previous 13 starts, left-handed hitters were only 4 for 54 against him (.074), with one extra-base hit and no runs batted in.

But in a misty drizzle Friday night, it was as if another Randy Johnson were wearing that pinstriped uniform with No. 41 on the back.

Unable to get an out in the fourth inning, he was battered for nine hits and five earned runs. Garret Anderson, the Angels' best left-handed hitter, swatted a three-run homer and a triple off him. When Torre, the Yankee manager, removed Johnson, boos followed him down the dugout steps. And when the 11–7 loss was over, and the Yankees trailed the best-of-five series by 2–1, Johnson talked about how he had had "bad location" and how his slider "found too much of the middle" of the plate.

But why, for a pitcher with a 3–0 record in the World Series (in 2001 against the Yankees) and a 2–1 record in league championship series, does Johnson have a woeful 2–7 record in division series?

Although not charged with Friday night's loss, he had been the losing pitcher in seven consecutive division series starts since winning twice, once in relief, for the Seattle Mariners against the Yankees in 1995.

Johnson described it as "just one of those games," but a $16 million pitcher isn't supposed to have one "of those games" in the

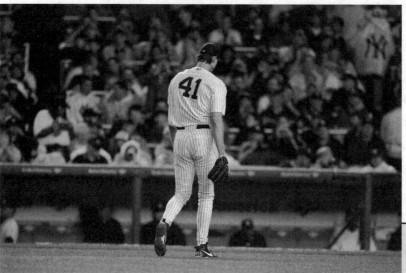

Randy Johnson walks off after being battered by the Angels in the 2005 ALCS.

playoffs. And yet in his years with the Mariners, the Houston Astros and the Diamondbacks, he had several "of those games" in the division series.

In two starts for the Mariners in 1997, he allowed 8 earned runs in 13 innings. In two strong starts for the Astros in 1998, he allowed only 3 earned runs in 14 innings, but in three starts for the Diamondbacks in 1999, 2001 and 2002, he allowed 15 earned runs in 22⅓ innings.

"There's no rhyme or reason," Johnson said Thursday, "other than this year is a different year, and I feel like there's a lot of reserve energy in my tank."

But on Friday night he wasn't even the same pitcher who had struggled for much of the season, who was an erratic 11–8 after an Aug. 21 loss in Chicago.

"I watched some video," he said, "and realized on a split-screen with some Arizona footage and tape here that mechanically some things were not the same as they had been. The reason I wasn't consistent was because my arm angle was dropping down. The reason my arm angle was dropping down was because I was rushing towards home plate. The reason I was rushing towards home plate was because I wasn't staying back over the rubber. It was just a chain reaction."

With his mechanics in sync and with the glow of having pitched the A.L. East clincher for a 5–0 record against the rival Red Sox, he assumed he would pitch well against the Angels, but maybe he assumed too much.

And even though Randy Johnson insisted there was no rhyme or reason for his problems in so many division series, his record is a strange 2–7 that doesn't even reflect Friday night's failure. And for an eventual Hall of Fame pitcher, that's an unremovable stain on his career. ◆

October 11, 2005

A Feeble Finish From the Yank's Premier Player

By JACK CURRY

ANAHEIM, Calif., Oct. 10—There was nothing Alex Rodriguez could say to change what had happened against the Los Angeles Angels and nothing he could do anymore about the five games that had just slipped in and out of his baseball career like a recurring nightmare.

Was that the $252 million man at third base for the Yankees? Was that the player who is supposed to be one of the best in baseball? Could that have been the powerful Rodriguez slipping and sliding through another October?

Even Rodriguez admitted, in a quiet corner of a cramped clubhouse, that he had flopped, that he was one of the reasons the Angels halted the Yankees, 5–3, in Game 5 of their American League division series Monday night and marched into the A.L. Championship Series against the Chicago White Sox.

"I played great baseball for a year," Rodriguez said. "I played like a dog for five games."

As Rodriguez was peppered with questions, he had a glazed look, almost as if he wondered if this was really happening to him and the Yankees again. Rodriguez was still wearing his soiled uniform, perhaps hoping that there would be a Game 6 on Tuesday. Rodriguez would have loved a do-over.

But, of course, Rodriguez knew there would be no more baseball for him in 2005 and one less chance for him to try to snatch his first World Series ring with the Yankees. So far with the Yankees, when the calendar shifts to October, Rodriguez does not look like an intimidating force anymore. He looks rattled.

"It's one of those things you can't figure out," he said. "I felt good and I saw the ball. I just had a bad series."

It was a very bad series. Rodriguez finished with 2 hits in 15 at-bats, he did not hit any homers after clubbing 48 during the regular season and he did not drive in any runs after driving in 130 during the season. The Yankees waited and waited for Rodriguez to do something. They are still waiting. ◆

October 8, 2006

Mighty Yanks Fizzle

By TYLER KEPNER

DETROIT—They have won almost 600 games over six regular seasons, spending nearly $1 billion on salaries. They have imported some of the biggest stars in baseball, created their own cable network, set attendance records at their ballpark and broken ground on a new one.

But the one thing that used to define the Yankees, the boast spelled out across the marquee at Yankee Stadium, has escaped them. The Yankees no longer win championships.

Another year is over, and another chance is gone. The Yankees shuffled meekly from the postseason stage on Saturday, falling to the Detroit Tigers, 8–3, in Game 4 of their American League division series at Comerica Park.

"Everyone in that locker room is disappointed," Manager Joe Torre said. "They outplayed us. They outpitched us. There's not much else you can say."

The Yankees, who have ruled October for much of baseball history, are a first-round casualty for the second season in a row, their season expiring when Robinson Canó grounded to second base against Jamie Walker.

The Yankees have not won the World Series since 2000. Two stars from that team, Derek Jeter and Jorge Posada, batted .500 in this series. The rest of the Yankees hit .173.

Their plight was personified by Alex Rodriguez, who batted eighth on Saturday for the first time in more than 10 years. He went 0 for 3 with an error and was 1 for 14 in the series.

Rodriguez realized the fans' worst fears about him, folding in the very part of the season that mattered most. Since the Yankees took a three-games-to-none lead over Boston in the 2004 A.L.C.S., he has 5 hits in 46 postseason at-bats. Rodriguez has no runs batted in in his past 12 playoff games.

After the game, Rodriguez was the last Yankee to leave the clubhouse. Inevitably, the winter will be filled with talk that he should be the first Yankee to leave the team.

"I've never run from problems," said Rodriguez, who can veto any deal. "I'm part of the solution. I don't want to go anywhere, and when we do win, it will be much more gratifying."

Brian Cashman, the general manager, watched from the stands and said he was stunned. This team, he believed, had that special something, that championship moxie he had seen before.

"At least I thought it did," Cashman said. "They fought all year. You've got to continue to earn that every day, and we did not here in October. Turned out to be a hell of a regular-season team, no more."

The Yankees are gone, ousted again from a tournament that once seemed to be their birthright. Now is the time for their new fall ritual, the one without ticker tape or heroes. The season of blame is upon them. ◆

October 18, 2006

Yankees at Tearful Ceremony for Lidle

By DAMON HACK

COVINA, CALIF., OCT. 17—A few minutes past 9 a.m. on a hilltop to the east of Los Angeles, three small aircraft appeared in the sky above the Forest Lawn Memorial Park and Mortuary.

The flyover signaled the start of the memorial service for Cory Lidle, the Yankees pitcher who died last Wednesday when his plane, a Cirrus SR20, crashed into a high-rise building on the Upper East Side. Lidle and his flight instructor, Tyler Stanger, were killed. The cause of the crash has not been determined.

For several seconds, the hum of engines lingered above the service. The morning was crisp and the clouds were lifting. It was a day Lidle might have chosen for flying.

"He would," Mike Lieberthal, a catcher for the Philadelphia Phillies and a former teammate of Lidle, said Tuesday. "And I was one guy who would have gone up with him."

The 34-year-old Lidle, who played for seven major league teams, was honored by several hundred family members, friends and baseball associates in a tearful ceremony that recalled his athletic feats as a high school pitcher who later made his major league debut with the Mets in 1997.

But he was mostly remembered as a husband to his wife, Melanie; as a father to his 6-year-old son, Christopher; and as a laid-back son of Southern California who liked poker and cheeseburgers.

Several members of the Yankees' organization attended the service, including General Manager Brian Cashman, Manager Joe Torre, shortstop Derek Jeter, pitcher Jaret Wright, the special adviser Reggie Jackson and first baseman Jason Giambi, who attended South Hills High School in West Covina, Calif., with Lidle and later became his teammate with the Oakland Athletics and the Yankees.

"That was our dream," Giambi said of the goal of becoming a professional that he shared with Lidle. "For a team and an area to produce big-league ballplayers, it was exciting. We always reminisced about the old times." ◆

Cory Lidle, shown pitching in September of 2006, was killed when the small aircraft he owned crashed into a residential building in New York City.

May 7, 2007

Clemens Returns

By TYLER KEPNER

IT WAS A NEWS BULLETIN delivered before 52,553 fans on a glorious spring day at Yankee Stadium, where the season is suddenly alive with hope again. The man with more victories than any living pitcher was holding a Yankees microphone, addressing the crowd with a splash of the high drama that has punctuated his career.

"Thank y'all," said Roger Clemens, who was wearing a business suit, a crew cut and a Yankees World Series ring as he stood in a box above home plate. "Well, they came and got me out of Texas, and I can tell you it's a privilege to be back. I'll be talking to y'all soon!"

Then Clemens pumped his fist as Yankees General Manager Brian Cashman crouched behind him, beaming. For a $28 million salary—prorated based on the date he is added to the major league roster—Clemens has returned to the Yankees, who trail the Boston Red Sox by five and a half games in the American League East but got a pitcher both teams wanted.

"Make no mistake about it," Clemens, who hopes to be ready by late May, said later at a news conference. "I've come back to do what they only know how to do here with the Yankees, and that's win a championship. Anything else is a failure."

The Yankees acquired Clemens in a trade from Toronto in 1999, then watched helplessly as he retired after the 2003 World Series, his fourth in five years with the team.

Clemens, who turns 45 in August, changed his mind and kept playing, joining his hometown Houston Astros for three more seasons. Cashman tried to sign Clemens in March and consummated this deal Friday night, when he talked with the Yankees' team president, Randy Levine, and chief operating officer, Lonn Trost, about how Clemens might make a grand entrance.

"We thought, 'Wouldn't it be great if he showed up and announced it himself on the scoreboard?'" Cashman said, reflecting on the day in a telephone interview last night. "It just seemed like it would be a real nice touch, and only someone of his type of stature could really pull it off. It was one of those neat moments in Yankee history. I got goose bumps. He's just such a presence." ◆

Roger Clemens announces his return to the Yankees from the owner's box at the Stadium.

October 20, 2007

Torre Says Yankees' Offer Showed Lack of Trust

By TYLER KEPNER

RYE BROOK, N.Y., OCT. 19—His duties now include cleaning the garage, shopping for groceries and cooking dinner. With no job lined up for next summer, Joe Torre said he may see the major horse races or show up at Wimbledon. His charitable work will continue.

But Torre's itinerary, in his new life as the former manager of the Yankees, does not include a trip to Yankee Stadium. His personal assistant will pack up his photos and books and cigars.

"I walked out of there, and I'm not going back," Torre said Friday. "I just leave the memories."

Torre rejected the Yankees' contract offer on Thursday, but in a news conference Friday at the Hilton Rye Town, he said he felt rejected by them. The wound is fresh, and Torre could not even say if he would throw out a ceremonial first pitch sometime after the Yankees open their new ballpark in 2009.

"If somebody wants you to do a job, and it takes them two weeks to figure out, yeah, 'I guess we should do this,' you're a little suspicious," Torre said, adding later, "If somebody wanted me to manage here, I'd be managing here."

Torre acknowledged that the $5 million the Yankees offered him was generous. But he said he felt insulted by the framework of the deal, which was heavily tied to incentives and not open to negotiation.

In a meeting Thursday in Tampa, Fla., the Yankees offered one year and Torre intimated that he wanted two. A team that spends lavishly for players was unwilling to give a second year to Torre, who reached the postseason in each of his 12 seasons but had not won a World Series in either of his last two contracts.

The structure of the Yankees' proposal rewarded Torre with a $1 million bonus for each postseason round the team would achieve in 2008. But if he did not reach the World Series, he would not have exceeded this season's $7.5 million salary.

"The fact that somebody is reducing your salary is telling me they're not satisfied with what you're doing," Torre said. "I think it was just the way it was offered, more so than the numbers involved. Two years would have opened the door to have more discussions, and it never happened."

Torre said he would leave it to reporters to interpret whether the Yankees made him an offer they knew he would turn down. In a meeting that included the team's principal owner, George Steinbrenner; his sons, Hank and Hal; his son-in-law, Felix Lopez; Randy Levine, the team president; General Manager Brian Cashman; and Lonn Trost, the chief operating officer, Torre said he sensed that only one or two people wanted him back.

One supporter, Torre said, was Cashman, who talked Steinbrenner out of firing him after the Yankees' 2006 playoff loss. Cashman was less vocal in his support this time, but he said he was not the only person who hoped Torre would accept.

"Everybody in that room wanted him back; I have to disagree with him there," Cashman said Friday night. "Joe knows I'm an ally because there's a bond there. But I've got to speak for everybody else in the room, and they did want him back, too."

As Steinbrenner cedes control to his sons, he is more intent on seeking consensus for major moves. Levine said all of the executives wanted Torre back.

"Every single one of us made that offer with the hope that he would return," Levine said. "We were all disappointed that he did not accept it. Reasonable people can differ."

Asked why the Yankees would not negotiate, Cashman said there were pressure points for both sides that made the deal unworkable. "It's just complicated, given the dollars," Cashman said.

This was not the first time the Yankees had talked about a new contract for Torre. Early in spring training, Torre indicated he would ⟫⟫⟫

<<< be willing to accept a one-year contract extension.

Steve Swindal, who was then Steinbrenner's son-in-law, said a pay cut would be mandatory, but in any case, the Yankees wanted to wait until the season was over. After a third consecutive first-round knockout, they would not give Torre the kind of deal he got last time, after winning six pennants in eight seasons.

The new offer would have kept Torre as the majors' highest-paid manager, and while Torre bristled at the idea of incentives, ownership saw them as a way for him to exceed his 2007 salary. Cashman said the incentive package would probably not be part of a new manager's contract.

Torre said Cashman told him about the offer on Wednesday night and warned that the Yankees were unlikely to adjust it. But Torre said he wanted to fly to Tampa anyway.

Cashman flew home on Wednesday and flew back with Torre on Thursday. On the flight, Torre said, Cashman asked him, "Are you going down to make a deal or to say goodbye?" Torre said he did not know.

The meeting was brief—20 minutes, Torre said—and although Steinbrenner was there, it was his younger son, Hal, who presented the offer and the rationale. Torre had incentives built into the contract he signed after the 2001 World Series, but he disputed the idea that he needed financial motivation to win in the postseason.

"I've been there for 12 years and I didn't think motivation was needed," Torre said. "I just didn't think it was the right thing for me, and I didn't think it was the right thing for my players. Any pressure that was caused by thinking the manager's going to lose his job, I didn't think we needed."

Torre said that, besides Cashman, he had little backing among the Yankees' hierarchy.

Joe Torre during a his farewell news conference at the Hilton Rye Town on October 19, 2007.

"If something goes wrong, I understand a lot of questions are going to be asked," Torre said. "But I'd like to believe the support should come from the organization that, 'He knows what he's doing.' It's not the money that is going to be the determining factor. It's just going to be the commitment and trust—because you can't have one without the other—to manage the ball club."

Then Torre thanked Steinbrenner for trusting him to manage his team for 12 years. It is Steinbrenner's team, after all, and in winning more games for it than any manager besides Joe McCarthy, Torre is now an important part of its past.

Torre had played for each of the three teams he managed before Steinbrenner hired him, but he never played for the Yankees. "I still feel very much like a visitor to this whole organization," he said.

Now Torre is a visitor again, officially, a proud and wounded one with no plans to stop by anytime soon. ◆

10 THE GIRARDI YEARS

The new Yankee Stadium before its 2009 opening day.

The new Yankee Stadium opened in 2009 as a pin-striped palace of the present, a memorable museum of the past, and a timeless tribute to George M. Steinbrenner III's often tempestuous reign.

For more than a decade, the principal owner finally got it right. With his health fading, he was content to let a different 'Joe' and the same 'Cash' do most of the heavy lifting. Awaiting his 11th season as general manager, Brian Cashman was the primary voice in hiring Joe Girardi as the new manager in 2008 following Joe Torre's departure. Yes, a Yankee general manager was starting his second decade in the job. In earlier eras during Steinbrenner's reign, the general manager was not always around to start his second season. But even before Spring training began in 2008, the dark cloud of performance-enhancing drugs cast a shadow on the Yankees and ex-Yankee righthander Roger Clemens, the seven-time Cy Young Award winner.

When the Mitchell Report, Major League Baseball's investigation into P.E.D.'s, identified Clemens as a user of steroids and human growth hormone and his former personal trainer, Brian McNamee, as his supplier, both were summoned to appear before a Congressional hearing. Also identified was Yankee lefthander Andy Pettitte, who admitted to Mitchell Report investigators that he used human growth hormone in 2002. He later told the Congressional committee that he also used H.G.H. in 2004, a year before MLB banned it. During a news conference at Spring training in 2008, Pettitte apologized "to everybody" for his use.

At the Congressional hearing in February, 2008, McNamee said under oath that Clemens repeatedly used P.E.D.'s when both were with the Yankees and the Toronto Blue Jays. Confronted with McNamee's words, Clemens, under oath, denied that he never used steroids or human growth hormone. When informed of Pettitte's testimony on a videotape that Clemens had told him of his use of steroids and H.G.H., Clemens insisted that Pettitte, his longtime Yankee and Houston Astros teammate, had "misremembered." Six months later, Clemens was indicted by a Federal grand jury in Washington on charges that he lied to Congress. When the perjury case went to trial in July of 2011, the Federal judge declared a mistrial, ruling that the government prosecutors had presented inadmissible testimony (the Pettitte videotape) that would prejudice the jury against Clemens. >>>

★ ★ ★

<<< In the confusion of the Clemens situation, the Yankees new 'Joe and Cash' combination did not succeed right away. When the 2008 season ended with the last game at the old Stadium across 161st Street, the Yankees had an 89-73 record. Not bad for other teams, not good for the Yankees. Third place meant no playoffs, no shot at the World Series, no post-season revenue. Two or three decades earlier, both Cashman and Girardi would have been dishonorably discharged quickly, but Steinbrenner and his sons, Hal and Hank, had learned that patience and poise were more important than panic. When the glitzy new Stadium opened in 2009, the Yankees had reloaded. Cashman spent a total of $423.5 million on reinforcements: $161 million over seven years for lefthander C.C. Sabathia, $82.5 million over five years for righthander A.J. Burnett, $180 million over eight years for first baseman Mark Teixeira.

Early in 2009, that dark cloud reappeared. Alex Rodriguez, the third baseman who had signed a 10-year $275 million in December 2007, confessed in a television interview to having used illegal drugs from 2001 to 2003 when he was with the Texas Rangers but didn't know what he took. About a week later, in a news conference at the Yankee training base in Tampa, Fla., he identified the drug as "boli," believed to be the street name in the Dominican Republic for Primobolan. Surgery on his right hip kept him on the disabled list until early May, but he responded with 30 homers and 100 runs batted in, then streaked through the post-season with a .365 average, 6 homers and 18 RBI as the Yankees won their 27th World Series title in a six-game triumph over the Phillies that gilded the new Yankee Stadium and allowed George Steinbrenner to bask as the boss of the reigning champions until his death on July 13, 2010.

Over his tenure of more than 37 years, longer than that of any other Yankee owner by 13 years, Steinbrenner's teams, as described on his plaque in the Stadium's Monument Park, "posted a major-league best .566 winning percentage, while winning 11 American League pennants and seven World Series titles, becoming the most recognizable sports brand in the world." Some international soccer clubs would argue with such self-acclaim and, as the future beckoned, the Yankees, ownership, front office, manager, and players knew they hadn't burnished that brand lately.

In that 2010 season the Yankees reached the American League Championship Series but lost to the Rangers in six games. In 2011, after Derek Jeter drilled his 3,000th hit and Mariano Rivera cherished his record 602nd save for a team with the A.L.'s best record, the Yankees lost the Divisional Series to the Detroit Tigers in a decisive fifth game at the Stadium. But as the 2012 season approached, Girardi and Cashman, who signed a new three-year contract, were both on the job. Awaiting the 2017 season, Cashman has been there longer than any other Yankee general manager—longer than the hallowed Hall of Fame executives Ed Barrow of the Babe Ruth-Lou Gehrig era, and George Weiss of the Joe DiMaggio-Mickey Mantle eras. In the years to come, Brian Cashman, no matter where he is, no matter who the Yankee dugout manager is, will be remembered as the general manager of the Derek Jeter-Mariano Rivera era.

October 30, 2007

Girardi Is Choice as Manager

By TYLER KEPNER

WHEN THE YANKEES needed a big hit to propel them to victory in the clinching game of Joe Torre's first World Series, it was Joe Girardi who got it. A triple to center field off Greg Maddux sparked the Yankees to the 1996 title that started their dynasty.

Eleven years later, Torre is gone, Alex Rodriguez has opted out of his contract and the rival Boston Red Sox are atop the baseball world. The Yankees need Girardi again, this time as the manager to steer them back to the World Series.

The Yankees expect to formally name Girardi as Torre's successor today, according to Hank Steinbrenner, the son of the principal owner, George Steinbrenner. General Manager Brian Cashman spent much of yesterday completing the contract with Girardi, who won three World Series as a Yankees player in the 1990s and was the 2006 National League manager of the year for the Florida Marlins. Girardi was a broadcaster for the YES Network this season.

"The baseball people felt Girardi was very sharp," said Hank Steinbrenner, who relied on Cashman to make the recommendation. "He answered all their questions just about perfectly. All three candidates did very well, but Girardi —it was obvious he was on top of a lot of stuff."

Don Mattingly and Tony Peña, coaches on Torre's staff, also interviewed for the job, which opened Oct. 18 when Torre rejected the Yankees' one-year offer for a guaranteed $5 million. Torre led the Yankees to 12 consecutive playoff appearances, but they have not won the World Series since 2000.

Two officials familiar with the Los Angeles Dodgers' plans said the Dodgers were likely to fire Manager Grady Little and hire Torre as their manager.

The Yankees have not won an American League pennant since 2003, when their loss in the World Series to the Marlins prompted George Steinbrenner to ask Mattingly to join the coaching staff. Mattingly did so with the hope of succeeding Torre, and he said through his agent that he would leave the organization, the only one for which he has worked.

"Don was extremely disappointed to learn today that he wasn't the organization's choice to fill the managerial vacancy," said a statement from the agent Ray Schulte.

The statement thanked Steinbrenner for his "initial faith" and concluded by saying Mattingly had informed the Yankees that he would not accept a coaching position within the organization for next season.

Hank Steinbrenner did not say if Mattingly was offered another position in the organization, ›››

◀◀◀ but he implied that the option was open.

"It was a very difficult decision for everyone concerned, ownership and the baseball people," Hank Steinbrenner said. "We love Donnie. We always want him to be an integral part of our organization."

Mattingly, who forged a strong bond with Torre, may have a far more enticing opportunity. If the Dodgers hire Torre, he would make Mattingly part of his coaching staff. A job with the Dodgers would be a natural fit for Mattingly, whose son Preston was a first-round pick by the team in 2006.

Mattingly congratulated Girardi in his statement, and in a telephone interview, Peña did the same. But unlike Mattingly, Peña reiterated that he would be open to staying on the coaching staff, a topic he touched on in a conversation with Cashman. ◆

December 14, 2007

Former Trainer Puts Yankees Stars Under Microscope

By JACK CURRY

ROGER CLEMENS has long been known for his intense workouts, sessions that helped him pitch effectively into his mid 40s and receive acclaim as one of the most dominant pitchers ever. Andy Pettitte, Clemens's close friend and Yankees teammate, adopted those workouts. But both pitchers may have been harboring secrets about an unsavory aspect of their regimen.

Brian McNamee, a former strength and conditioning coach for the Yankees who later was also a personal trainer for both pitchers, told investigators for George J. Mitchell that he had injected Clemens with steroids and had injected Pettitte with human growth hormone. Mitchell released his report on the use of performance-enhancing drugs in baseball on Thursday.

Mitchell's report, about 400 pages, devotes roughly 2,500 words to Clemens, who has 354 career victories and seven Cy Young Awards. Pettitte, who has 201 victories and four World Series rings, is mentioned in a much briefer passage.

It was a depressing day for the Yankees, whose sustained run of success was smudged by the revelations. The team said it was reviewing the report and had no comment. In addition, Chuck Knoblauch, Mike Stanton and David Justice, who were part of a combined seven championship teams with the Yankees, and other Yankees were also cited for using performance enhancers. Justice denied the allegations.

Still, the most glaring names were Clemens and Pettitte, the big brother and little brother pitching tandem from Texas. Clemens, who fancies himself

Roger Clemens works out with trainer Brian McNamee during the 2001 season.

as the John Wayne of pitchers, and Pettitte, whose personality is more like that of Andy Griffith, have denied that they used enhancers.

Rusty Hardin, Clemens's lawyer, said Clemens denied the allegations and was outraged that his name was included in the report. Harden called McNamee's statements "uncorroborated" comments from a "troubled and unreliable" witness, who was threatened with prison.

While Hardin said Clemens was repeatedly tested for those substances and never tested positive, McNamee alleges that Clemens used steroids before baseball tested for them.

Randy Hendricks, Pettitte's agent, said Pettitte would comment after consulting with his advisers and the players' union. Clemens did not respond to a message left at his home. A text message and a voice message left with Tom Pettitte, Andy's father, were not returned. Laura Pettitte, Andy's wife, called the situation "hurtful."

Because Clemens had such a commanding presence and he was Pettitte's mentor, there was often a feeling around the Yankees that Pettitte would follow Clemens's lead in most situations. Clemens started working with McNamee while he was with the Toronto Blue Jays in 1998, more than a year before Pettitte began training with McNamee.

McNamee, a former New York police officer, started his career with the Yankees as a bullpen catcher in 1993. He was reticent then, and even as McNamee gained more attention for working with Clemens and Pettitte, he remained quiet, even guarded.

But in interviews with Mitchell's investigators, McNamee offered vivid details about injecting Clemens and Pettitte.

He described how Clemens asked him about steroids around June 8–10, 1998. Just before Clemens inquired, McNamee, who was working for the Blue Jays, said that he and Clemens had attended a luncheon with Jose Canseco. Canseco told Mitchell's investigators that he had several discussions with Clemens about the benefits of the drugs Deca-Durabolin and Winstrol.

McNamee told Mitchell that Clemens said he could not inject himself and needed help. Later that summer, McNamee said, Clemens asked him to inject him with Winstrol, which Clemens provided.

McNamee told Mitchell that Clemens said the steroids "had a pretty good effect on him" and that Clemens's pitching dramatically improved. On June 10, 1998, Clemens was 6–6 with a 3.27 earned run average. He finished the season going 14–0 with a 2.29 E.R.A.

Before the 1999 season, Clemens was traded to the Yankees. McNamee was reunited with Clemens a year later, when, at Clemens's urging, the Yankees hired him as their assistant strength and conditioning coach. McNamee said he injected Clemens four to six times during the 2000 season with testosterone and four to six times with H.G.H. Late in the 2001 season, McNamee said, he injected Clemens at least four times with Sustanon or Deca-Durabolin.

McNamee, who was not rehired by the Yankees after the 2001 season, said Clemens never asked him about performance enhancers again. He continued as a personal trainer for Clemens through the 2007 season.

"He has not been charged with anything, he will not be charged with anything and yet he is being tried in the court of public opinion with no recourse," Hardin said of Clemens.

Pettitte trained with McNamee after the 1999 season through last season. McNamee said Pettitte asked him about H.G.H. after the 2001 season, but that McNamee advised against it.

During 2002, Pettitte was on the disabled list for almost two months with elbow tendinitis. McNamee said Pettitte asked him again about H.G.H. while he was rehabilitating.

So, McNamee said, he injected Pettitte two to four times with H.G.H. that was obtained from Kirk Radomski, the former Mets clubhouse attendant who was found guilty of steroid distribution last April. When Pettitte was asked last May if he had heard of Radomski, he said he had not. ◆

February 14, 2008

Clemens Vs. McNamee

By DUFF WILSON

WASHINGTON — Roger Clemens and Brian McNamee kept a tight grip on their contradictory accounts of illegal drug use in a dramatic show-down Wednesday before a Congressional panel whose 40 Democrats and Republicans seemed to line up and take sides on a partisan basis.

In a four-hour hearing in which Mr. Clemens and Mr. McNamee shared the same table but never seemed to directly look at each other, Mr. Clemens continued to insist, under sometimes strenuous questioning, that Mr. McNamee never injected him with steroids and human growth hormone, as Mr. McNamee maintains.

Missing from the witness table but present nonetheless was Mr. Clemens's friend and for-mer teammate, Andy Pettitte, who in an affidavit, along with a separate one submitted by his wife,

provided some of the most difficult moments of the day for Mr. Clemens. Both affidavits stated that Mr. Clemens, in the past, had talked to Mr. Pettitte about Mr. Clemens's use of H.G.H.

Mr. Clemens, in repeated questioning about Mr. Pettitte's sworn statements, said several times that Mr. Pettitte "misremembers" the con-versations that they had.

Other moments tested Mr. Clemens, too, particularly when he was asked about whether he attempted to coach a witness—his former nanny—before she spoke earlier this week to lawyers for the panel, the House Committee on Oversight and Government Reform. The hear-

Roger Clemens, flanked by his lawyers, at the House committee hearing in Washington.

ing ended with the committee chairman, Henry A. Waxman, Democrat of California, pounding the gavel sharply to keep Mr. Clemens from interrupting him, but with the committee drawing no immediate conclusions as to who was being truthful. That question may well be left to the Department of Justice, which could pursue charges against Mr. Clemens or, less likely, Mr. McNamee for lying under oath.

The hearing revealed a political fracture more common to instances in which presidents are being investigated, not pitchers with Hall of Fame credentials. Many Democrats took aim at Mr. Clemens, and many Republicans targeted Mr. McNamee for untruths or partial truths he has acknowledged in past statements.

Sitting between them, mostly silent, was a lawyer who had worked with former Senator George J. Mitchell on his 20-month investigation on the use of performance-enhancing drugs in baseball. The lawyer, Charles P. Scheeler, said he and fellow investigators still stood by the Mitchell report, including the section in which Mr. McNamee stated that Mr. Clemens took steroids and human growth hormone on 16 occasions in 1998, 2000 and 2001.

Until now, the committee's investigation of drug use in baseball had seemed to be bipartisan. In 2005, the panel held a widely publicized hearing in which the slugger Mark McGwire declined to answer most questions about steroid use. That hearing was led by Tom Davis, Republican of Virginia, who now heads the committee minority and who at one point Wednesday used the word "lynching" to describe the questioning of Mr. Clemens.

But Mr. Waxman, an aggressive investigator of the Bush administration, pressed hard on Mr. Clemens, stating flatly that he did not believe some of Mr. Clemens's account. And that led to the flareup at the end of the hearing, with Mr. Clemens interrupting Mr. Waxman's final summary of the damaging statements by Mr. Pettitte.

"Doesn't mean he wasn't mistaken, sir," Mr. Clemens said of Mr. Pettitte. Mr. Waxman hit the gavel sharply once to silence him. "Doesn't mean he wasn't mistaken, sir," Mr. Clemens repeated.

Mr. Waxman also apologized to Mr. McNamee at the end of the hearing for questions, from Republican committee members, that accused Mr. McNamee of being a drug dealer.

Jeff Novitzky, the I.R.S. special agent who has investigated steroid cases against prominent athletes, including Barry Bonds and Marion Jones, sat with two other federal agents in the second row, behind chairs reserved for Mr. McNamee's friends. He will presumably be involved in any Justice Department investigation of the matter.

Pettitte and Chuck Knoblauch, another former teammate of Mr. Clemens and a client of Mr. McNamee, have acknowledged what Mr. McNamee said about them was true, Mr. Waxman noted during the hearing, leaving only Mr. Clemens challenging the Mitchell report.

As for Mr. Pettitte's affidavit, it stated: "In 1999 or 2000, I had a conversation with Roger Clemens in which Roger told me he had taken human growth hormone." Mr. Pettitte also said he reminded Mr. Clemens of that statement during a conversation in 2005 and that Mr. Clemens said he had misunderstood the earlier reference, that he was talking about his wife, Debbie, using H.G.H.

Mr. Waxman said Debbie Clemens has acknowledged trying H.G.H. in 2003 but not as early as Roger Clemens's first conversation with Mr. Pettitte in 1999 or 2000. Asked to explain that discrepancy Wednesday, Mr. Clemens said his conversation in 1999 or 2000 with Mr. Pettitte had been about a television program in which three older men talked about using H.G.H., not about his own use. And he said he did not remember any 2005 conversation with Mr. Pettitte in which he mentioned his wife's use of H.G.H.

Elijah E. Cummings, Democrat of Maryland, spoke directly to Mr. Clemens near the end of the hearing. "It's hard to believe you, sir," he said. "I hate to say that. You're one of my heroes, but it's hard to believe you." ◆

February 19, 2008

Pettitte Apologizes to His Fans

By JOE LAPOINTE

TAMPA, FLA.—In a one-hour news conference Monday that neither he nor the Yankees could have ever wished on themselves, a composed Andy Pettitte apologized for using human growth hormone in 2002 and 2004, said there was no other drug use he was concealing and revealed an awkward breakdown in his communications with Roger Clemens, his friend and former teammate.

Pettitte said he had used H.G.H. not to gain a competitive advantage but to recover from injuries while with the Yankees in 2002 and with the Houston Astros in 2004. He said H.G.H. was not forbidden by baseball when he used it, although he acknowledged it was wrong to use it without a medical prescription.

"I am sorry," Pettitte said at the news conference, which came as he reported four days late to spring training, with the Yankees' permission. "I know in my heart why I did things. I know that God knows that. I know that I'm going to

Andy Pettitte's longtime teammate Derek Jeter (left) supported the Yankee lefthander's apology for using human growth hormone in 2002 and 2004.

have to stand before him one day. The truth hurts sometimes and you don't want to share it. The truth will set you free. I'm going to be able to sleep a lot better."

The presence of Derek Jeter, Jorge Posada and Mariano Rivera was a reminder of just how much Pettitte has meant to the Yankees. But the presence of two lawyers representing Pettitte was a reminder of just how entangled he has become in Clemens's adamant challenge to the Mitchell report.

Shortly after the Mitchell report's findings on performance-enhancing drugs in baseball were released on Dec. 13, Pettitte admitted to using H.G.H. several times in 2002, as the personal trainer Brian McNamee had asserted in the report. Clemens, however, has disputed McNamee's assertions that he had injected Clemens with steroids and H.G.H. on at least 16 occasions between 1998 and 2001.

Clemens's denials ultimately led each pitcher, and McNamee, to give a sworn deposition to a Congressional panel earlier this month. In a nationally televised hearing last week, a Pettitte affidavit, read aloud, put him at odds with Clemens. In the affidavit, Pettitte also acknowledged using H.G.H., supplied by his father, in 2004.

But it was the recollection of conversations with Clemens that created drama. In particular, Pettitte said in the affidavit that Clemens told him in 1999 or 2000 that Clemens had used H.G.H. Clemens disputed Pettitte's account as well as Pettitte's recollection of a conversation about H.G.H. the two men had in 2005, saying Pettitte had "misremembered" in both instances.

Pettitte's lawyers have advised him not to discuss specifics of his conversations with Clemens. When he was asked Monday about their different versions of conversations, Pettitte said, "I'm just not going to go there." Pettitte said he did not watch the hearing and had not talked with the 45-year-old Clemens recently.

"I hope the friendship with Roger will still be there," said Pettitte. "I love the guy like a brother." ◆

March 2, 2008

The Best Deal the Yankees Never Made

By TYLER KEPNER

TAMPA, FLA.—The Yankees' hitters are so accomplished that there is little room for wonder. Some are chasing hallowed career numbers, others are fading with age. Few conjure awe about feats unseen, potential still untapped. It is the nature of a veteran lineup.

Robinson Canó is different. At 25, with only two full seasons in the majors, his star is ascending, his talent tantalizing.

"If he starts like he finished last year, he could win the batting title," said the Yankees' hitting coach, Kevin Long. "I mean, he could run away with it—with 30 homers. That's what we're looking at. I think he could be real special."

Long has believed this, he said, since he first saw Canó at Class AAA in 2004. That was the year the Yankees tried to trade Canó three times, only to keep him and quickly reap the benefits.

Since his promotion to the Yankees in 2005, when he bumped Tony Womack a month into Womack's two-year contract, Canó has led all major league second basemen in hits. He has made one All-Star team and batted .314 with 48 homers in 414 games. In 489 minor league games before that, he hit .277 with 41 homers.

"I can't tell you that anyone thought he was going to be the premier player at his position he is now, or has a chance to be," General Manager Brian Cashman said. "Right now, you could argue that he's the second-best second baseman in the majors, behind Chase Utley."

Trades not made, and offers not accepted, are part of baseball lore. In 1997, the Yankees wanted Pedro Martínez, who had priced himself out of Montreal. They offered a young catcher, Jorge Posada, and a third baseman, Mike Lowell. The Expos opted for Boston's offer of pitchers Carl Pavano and Tony Armas Jr. »»»

Robinson Canó.

≪≪≪   Posada and Lowell have had long and productive careers. Pavano and Armas have not. The Yankees would have liked a young Martínez, but they are glad they still have Posada.

So it is with Canó. He was never offered cheaply, but only luck spared him from leaving.

"Sometimes, I heard about getting traded and I thought, 'Oh, God, I don't want to get traded; I want to be here,' " Canó said. "I love being a Yankee. This is where I started my career, and I want to end it right here, too."

With a new contract that could tie him to the Yankees through 2013, Canó may be on his way. Yet before the 2004 season, he was offered in the trade that sent Alfonso Soriano to Texas for Alex Rodriguez. The Rangers passed on Canó for a different infielder, Joaquín Árias, who has played only briefly in the majors.

In June 2004, when Kansas City shopped Carlos Beltrán, the Yankees shifted Canó to third base to showcase him. They offered Canó and

---

March 30, 2008

SPORTS OF THE TIMES
Looking Out My Window Into the Past and the Future

By WILLIAM C. RHODEN

As we anticipate the final months, weeks and days of Yankee Stadium, the memories — mountains of memories—can be overwhelming.

Every morning, I look out my bedroom window at two Yankee Stadiums: the old one to my right, the new one to my left. What an awesome sight: looking across the river at the Yankees' past, present and future. The new stadium is like that freshly purchased baseball glove that requires years of line drives and ground balls to be sufficiently broken in. The old stadium bursts at the seams with collective experiences.

Sweet memories.

My favorite baseball season was 1996, the year the Yankees won the World Series, ending a protracted run of darkness. Their success invigorated the neighborhood. Everything was Yankees, Yankees, Yankees before the season began, when the Boss, on top of his game, made the bold move to jettison popular names: Showalter, Stanley and Velarde.

There was Dwight Gooden's no-hitter, the acquisition of Darryl Strawberry, the death of Manager Joe Torre's younger brother and the news that his older brother was undergoing a long-awaited heart transplant. Twelve-year-old Jeffrey Maier made the catch heard around the world, and the seven days of the World Series were a roller coaster of crushed feelings and humiliation, washed away by the ecstasy of four straight wins.

One of my neighbors, Jesse Williams, remem-

catcher Dioner Navarro, but the Royals sent Beltrán to Houston in a three-team deal that got them third baseman Mark Teahen, catcher John Buck and pitcher Mike Wood.

Cashman said Canó's contract, which guarantees him $30 million over four years, would be a good value if Canó simply stayed at his current level of performance. But the Yankees believe he can become better, and he is eager to show them.

"I don't think, Oh, well, I got a contract," Canó said. "I want to go get another one. I'm going to prove to the Yankees that I deserve the money, prove that I can get better and that money isn't going to change anything." ◆

---

bered how the excitement of that 1996 season brought him back to baseball. He died a few years ago, but his insights encapsulate my feelings about the time and about Yankee Stadium.

"I've found myself going back to the old times," Mr. Williams said. "I'm hanging on every pitch, standing up, then sitting down. The baseball strike pushed me away from baseball; the Yankees have pulled me back."

My home is in Harlem — on Sugar Hill — where life is sweet. I've mastered the art of following Yankees games by listening to Yankee Stadium sounds: Bob Sheppard. Crowd cheers. Organ. Canned noise. Metallica. Frank Sinatra.

As the new Yankee Stadium goes up, there's excitement mixed with dread over that inevitable D-Day, when the old stadium comes tumbling down. On the other hand, if Yankee Stadium has taught us anything, it's that life, like baseball, is all about cycles. ◆

September 21, 2008

Echoes in the Bronx; Yankees Add Member to Family

By BILLY CRYSTAL

MAY 30, 1956, was the first time I walked into Yankee Stadium. My dad, and my two older brothers and I holding hands so we wouldn't get separated, my 8-year-old heart pounding as I saw the field for the first time.

Mantle hit it off the facade that day, my first game.

Fifty-two years later, it, and all the other great moments I've witnessed there, are as fresh in my mind as if they just happened. But that's Yankee Stadium, and why I will miss it so.

Saying goodbye to it is saying goodbye to a huge part of my life. The bond of my late father and his boys, the way he taught us about the game, its intricacies, its glory, its failures, the plays that are made, the ones that aren't. How to read a box score and recreate a game.

If stadiums are the cathedrals of baseball, or in my case synagogues, then I have been worshiping at the same place for over half a century. The Stadium has been the safe room of my house of memories. Who would have thought that I would become a good friend of Mantle and his family? Who would have thought that Joe Torre would become one of my closest friends and would have me, still an O.K. player, work out with the team before World Series games because he felt it relaxed his players? Who would have thought I would get to recreate the old stadium to perfect detail when I directed "61*"? As I got older I appreciated it more.

As life got more difficult, I needed it more. I was on my way to Game 4 of the 2001 Series, Yankees vs. Diamondbacks, when my mother had a stroke.

The doctors at the hospital told us to go home, not to exhaust her as she strained to make sense of what had happened. I wasn't sure what to do with myself. How can you be, when your mother ⟫⟫⟫

isn't sure who you are? I am not a religious man, though I love my religion. Praying doesn't come easily to me.

I went to the Stadium that afternoon because it made sense. I went to the area where we sat that day in 1956.

Alone among the 55,000 seats, I prayed. I sat there saying to myself, "Dad, if you're here, help me get through this." Mr. Steinbrenner saw me. He was the first one I told about her illness. A few moments later, he handed me an auto-graphed team ball. "Give this to her from me." Joe Torre personalized one to her as well. She passed away a week later.

George had Bob Sheppard recite her name on Old Timers' Day as a member of the Yankee family who had left us. It sounded as if God him-self announced her name in heaven. Our entire family were George's guests that day. We will never forget him for that.

The sun shines a little differently on this part of the Bronx. It has a theatricality to it that is simple and spectacular. I was a boy here, a teen-ager here, a father, and now a grandfather here. To me, it was never the awesome place of the Babe, Joe D. and Mickey after it was renovated. The pillars were gone, the facade was gone, yet the ground was still the same, the aura of past moments hovering always. It was still ours.

I will miss this park because no matter how great the new one is, I won't be able to look over and see my dad and me and my brothers sitting there, in the sun, eating a hot dog and learning how to keep score.

Billy Crystal, a native New Yorker, is an Emmy and Tony Award-winning actor, writer and director. ◆

September 22, 2008

A Full House and a Crowded Stage Mark Yankee Stadium's Closing Night

By TYLER KEPNER

IT WILL ONLY GROW with time, like Lou Gehrig's farewell, Don Larsen's masterpiece and Reggie Jackson's third home run in a World Series game. Untold thousands will say they were there the night the curtain fell on baseball's grandest stage.

It happened Sunday night in the Bronx, when Yankee Stadium hosted a baseball game for the last time. It went out the way it opened, with a victory, this one by 7-3 over the Baltimore Ori-oles. Babe Ruth hit the first home run, in 1923, and José Molina hit the last, a two-run shot to left that broke a tie in the fourth inning.

The Yankees held off elimination with the vic-tory, the eighth in their final nine games at Yan-kee Stadium. Andy Pettitte, the winning pitcher, worked into the sixth inning, waving his cap to the fans, who never stopped cheering until he took a curtain call.

"The way I feel emotionally right now, and just physically so drained, it feels like a huge postseason win for us," Pettitte said, standing on the infield grass after the game. "I kind of feel embarrassed saying that, because unless a mira-cle happens, we're not going to the postseason. But it was special."

Manager Joe Girardi compared it to the sev-enth game of the World Series, because the Yankees could not afford to lose, and it felt that way for many reasons. From the bunting along the upper deck, to the United States Army Field Band, to the mix of excitement and anxiety bub-bling up in the guts of the uniformed Yankees, there was no doubt this night would be special.

"I feel as nervous as I was before a playoff game," said Bernie Williams, back in pinstripes at last, one of more than 20 former Yankees who returned for the pregame ceremonies.

Yankee legends and fans join in the ceremonies at Yankee Stadium's last game.

The Yankees opened the gates seven hours early, allowing fans to stroll the warning track for one last walk in the park. Closer to game time, the team unveiled the American League championship flag that was raised on the first opening day, in 1923.

Bob Sheppard recorded an introduction, promising to be there to christen the new Yankee Stadium next April 16. A team of stand-ins, dressed in old-time uniforms, processed into center field, representing some of the late Yankees legends. They might as well have come in from the cornfields; the "Field of Dreams" overtone was palpable.

One by one, the living greats took their positions, all to heartfelt cheers. The children of other standouts — Randy Maris, Michael Munson, David Mantle and others — took their fathers' places.

Willie Randolph slid into his position, second base, and rubbed dirt on his jersey, reveling in his return to the Yankees. Whitey Ford pretended to lift out the pitcher's rubber. The fans reprised chants that rang through the walls years ago — "Bob-by Mur-cer!" "Ti-no! Ti-no!" and so on.

Many of the stars not there were shown on the video board in right-center field — Rickey Henderson and Chuck Knoblauch, Sparky Lyle and Orlando Hernández. No mention of Roger Clemens.

The bench was so stuffed that some of the Yankees sat on the dugout roof to watch. Jorge Posada stood on the field, taking photos with a digital camera, just another fan with rich memories of a stadium that always seemed to give his team an edge.

"Especially in 2001," Posada said. "We were helped by Yankee Stadium, the fans coming here, playing for something more meaningful."

The former players mingled in the clubhouse before the game, in full uniform, right down to Yogi Berra's stirrups. Current Yankees scurried around collecting snapshots and autographs.

"It's remarkable," said Phil Coke, a rookie pitcher with three weeks in the majors. "Totally and completely blows my mind. I turn around and look over and see Goose Gossage walking around our clubhouse. Wow."

Derek Jeter said he would miss the walk from the clubhouse to the dugout — down a tunnel, with the Joe DiMaggio sign hanging above. "I want to thank the good Lord for making me a Yankee," it says, and Jeter tapped it before every game. Jeter would not say, but there seems to be a strong chance the sign will be his.

On Saturday night, Jeter said, he spoke with Jackson about their shared emotions. Both built their legends at Yankee Stadium, but they agreed they would be filled not with sadness, but with pride for having been a part of history.

"Make sure you enjoy this," Jeter said his parents told him recently. "You don't want to look back and wish you'd done something different."

Jeter's parents and sister joined him on the field before the first pitch, as two of George Steinbrenner's children presented him with a crystal bat for breaking Gehrig's record for hits at the Stadium. »»»

«« Jeter would get no more hits on Sunday, going 0 for 5, but he went down as the last Yankee ever to bat at Yankee Stadium, with a groundout to third in the eighth inning. Girardi pulled him for defense with two outs in the top of the ninth, so the fans could give one last curtain call.

It was Jeter who had the memorable line in 2006, when the Yankees broke ground on the new $1.3 billion Yankee Stadium, saying that the ghosts from the old place would simply move across the street. Others are not so sure.

Alex Alicea, a 37-year-old fan from Union City, N.J., brought his 16-month-old son, Justin, on Sunday. As he walked the warning track before the game with his wife and son, he lamented the passing of the game's shrine.

"I would have been happy being 80 or 90 years old and still coming to this stadium," Alicea said. "The new stadium is beautiful, but I don't know if the ghosts are going to be there. You can feel that, standing here — Babe Ruth, DiMaggio. It's not going to be the same."

There was a sense of sadness and loss amid the celebration. Berra, who had dismissed the renovated Stadium as nothing like the original, nearly broke down at a pregame news conference as he invoked the names of former teammates who have died.

He made jokes, too, saying he wanted to take home plate, and complaining that the yellowed, wool uniform he was given did not quite feel authentic. But Berra, born two years after the Stadium opened, seemed to feel he was losing a part of himself.

"It will always be in my heart, it will," he said, adding later, "I'm sorry to see it over, I tell you that."

The ceremonial first pitch was thrown by Julia Ruth Stevens, the daughter of the Babe, who beamed as she bounced her toss to Posada. "To Be Continued ..." it said on the scoreboard, beneath a photo of a winking Bambino.

In Ruthian style, the Yankees went ahead twice on home runs. Johnny Damon hit the first, a three-run shot in the third inning that erased a 2-0 Baltimore lead.

When the Orioles tied it in the fourth, Molina came up in the bottom of the inning with a man on second and one out. He had just two homers in 259 at-bats, but he lifted his third onto the netting above the retired numbers, pumping his fists as he put the Yankees ahead, 5-3, with the last homer the Stadium will ever see.

"Nobody thought it was going to be me," Molina said. "We have A-Rod, we have Abreu, we have Giambi, we have so many guys that can hit home runs, and look who it was — the guy that probably nobody expected."

After a leadoff single in the sixth, Pettitte gave way to four relievers, with Mariano Rivera at the end. He worked a 1-2-3 inning, with Cody Ransom making the final putout at first base on a grounder by Brian Roberts at 11:41 p.m. Ransom put the ball in Rivera's glove, and Rivera earmarked it for Steinbrenner.

"Mr. George, he gave me the opportunity and he gave me the chance," Rivera said. "The least I can do is give the ball to him."

As horses carried police onto the field, several Yankees and Orioles gathered at the mound to scoop dirt as souvenirs. Soon, all of the Yankees converged there. Jeter took the microphone, praising the fans as the greatest in the world.

"And we are relying on you to take the memories from this stadium, add them to the new memories to come at the new Yankee Stadium, and continue to pass them on from generation to generation," Jeter told the crowd.

Then all of the Yankees lifted their caps to the crowd and took a final lap around the field, waving all the way, to the sounds of Sinatra. Not much has gone according to plan for the Yankees this season, but that worked just right.

"It was more the people than the stadium," Williams said. "You talk about the magic and the aura, but what really made the Stadium was the fans. Concrete doesn't talk back to you. Chairs don't talk back to you. It's the people that are there, that root for you day in and day out. That's what makes this place magical." ◆

September 24, 2008

Yankees Can't Delay the Inevitable

By TYLER KEPNER

TORONTO, SEPT 27—Joe Girardi went to Yankee Stadium on Monday, the day after the final regular-season home game, to board the team bus to the airport. Girardi, the Yankees' manager, noticed that sprinklers were watering the grass.

Maybe the Yankees want to keep the color in their lawn so they can slice it up and sell it. But Girardi saw a noble purpose. "To prepare," he said in the dugout before Tuesday's game, hopeful as ever for a miracle.

Four hours later, from the same vantage point, Girardi saw the end come when the out-of-town scoreboard on the right-field wall flashed the final score of the Cleveland–Boston game. The Red Sox had beaten the Indians to clinch a playoff spot and eliminate the Yankees.

Mariano Rivera was on the mound at the time, closing out Mike Mussina's 19th victory, a 3–1 decision over the Toronto Blue Jays.

"It's really devastating," Alex Rodriguez said, adding later: "There's absolutely no excuse for a team with this talent to be going home. It's hard to believe right now that we're out. As inconsistent as we were, to have an opportunity this late in the season just makes it that much more frustrating."

The Yankees have won 9 of their last 10, pushing their record to 86–71. But the Red Sox are 92–65, a record the Yankees cannot match. They will miss the postseason for the first time since 1993, two years before Rivera and Derek Jeter started their major league careers.

"The best teams make it and the hottest team wins, and we weren't one of the best teams," Jeter said. "Over 162 games, I think there's no flukes. The teams that make it to the postseason deserve to be there, and we weren't one of those teams." ◆

November 21, 2008

Hal Steinbrenner Is Named the Yankees' Boss

By JACK CURRY

HAL STEINBRENNER, the younger and more reserved of the Steinbrenner sons, was given control of the Yankees on Thursday in a unanimous vote by Major League Baseball owners. George Steinbrenner, the Yankees' principal owner, asked Commissioner Bud Selig to pursue the change last month.

While Hank Steinbrenner, George's older son, has been much more talkative about the Yankees in his frequent interviews, Hal has been more involved in the daily operations of the team. It is Hal, not Hank, who deals with team executives and spends considerable time in the Yankees' offices in New York.

"I realize it's a great responsibility," Hal Steinbrenner said. "My dad is, needless to say, a tough act to follow. But I'm going to do it to the best of my ability and give it my all every day."

George Steinbrenner's health has declined, so he is no longer the demanding owner who was deeply involved in every decision. When Hal Steinbrenner was asked about the timing of his designation, he referred to how his father's approach as an owner had changed.

"He's been slowing down for the last couple of years," Hal said. "Really, for the last couple of years, I have been intimately involved with all aspects and all departments of the company. It's what I've been doing day to day. My duties aren't really going to change and my work isn't really going to change much. It's as much a procedural thing within the family at this point." ◆

December 19, 2008

The Yankees Welcome $243.5 Million of Pitching

By TYLER KEPNER

THERE WAS A CHRISTMAS TREE on the mound at the old Yankee Stadium on Thursday, a fitting metaphor for what took place at the condemned baseball shrine. With the new stadium under construction—and the old one still months from demolition—the Yankees wrapped their new purchases in pinstripes and hoped for a happy new year.

After missing the playoffs for the first time since 1993, the Yankees are giving themselves no excuses for their debut season at the new Yankee Stadium. They introduced C. C. Sabathia and A. J. Burnett to the news media and made clear the expectations that come with a combined $243.5 million in salary.

"You're looking at a very strong rotation," Manager Joe Girardi said, "and that's what you have to have to compete in late October."

The news conference was perhaps the last event to be held at the original Stadium, where the removal of seats will begin in March and demolition could start next summer. By then, the Yankees hope to be back atop the American League, with their revamped rotation leading the charge.

Sabathia threw the most pitches in the majors last season, and Burnett threw the most in the American League. They combined for 35 victories, and neither is yet 32 years old. The Yankees rewarded Sabathia with a seven-year, $161 million deal—a record for a pitcher. Burnett received $82.5 million for five years. ◆

The Yankees acquired C.C. Sabathia and A.J. Burnett in 2008.

February 8, 2009

Rodriguez Said to Test Positive in 2003

By MICHAEL S. SCHMIDT

ALEX RODRIGUEZ, who is the highest-paid player in baseball and is widely viewed as the most talented, tested positive for performance-enhancing drugs in 2003, according to two people familiar with the results.

Rodriguez tested positive while he was playing shortstop for the Texas Rangers and on his way to winning the first of his three Most Valuable Player awards. A year later, he joined the Yankees and moved to third base. He is now in the second year of 10-year contract that will pay him at least $275 million.

The disclosure is the latest blow for Major League Baseball, which is confronting the fact that two of its best players over the past 25 years —Barry Bonds and Roger Clemens—are in legal jeopardy because of statements they made under oath that they never used performance-enhancing drugs. Rodriguez's positive test result was first reported by SI.com, the Sports Illustrated Web site.

Until now, Rodriguez had never been publicly linked to a positive drug test. His 2003 test occurred as Major League Baseball began testing for steroids for the first time under guidelines in which the results were to remain anonymous with no penalties imposed.

But in 2004, the 104 positive tests from a year earlier were seized by federal authorities in conjunction with their investigation into the Bay Area Laboratory Co-operative, the California company known as Balco that has long been accused of supplying performance enhancers to Bonds, the career home run leader.

Now Rodriguez has been added to the mix, although because the test took place before baseball imposed any penalties, he is not in danger of a suspension. Nor is he ensnared in any legal proceedings. Nevertheless, the positive test could affect his status in the game and could create a major distraction for him and his teammates with spring training set to begin this week.

At 33, Rodriguez has hit 553 career home runs and is on a course to eventually break Bonds's career mark of 762. Rodriguez was viewed as the sport's antidote to Bonds, who is widely suspected of taking performance-enhancing drugs.

But now many fans may be tempted to argue that there is little difference between Bonds and Rodriguez and Mark McGwire, who was baseball's single-season home run king a decade ago but whose image suffered greatly when, at a 2005 Congressional hearing, he refused to answer questions about steroid use.

Rodriguez has long denied any use of performance-enhancing substances. Still, the disclosure that he tested positive in 2003 did not come as a shock to people in baseball. Fairly or unfairly, his name has been linked more than once to possible drug use, if for no other reason than his tremendous home run numbers. ◆

February 18, 2009

As Team Looks On, Rodriguez Details His Use of Steroids

By TYLER KEPNER

TAMPA, FLA.—Eight days after admitting his steroid use in a television interview, Alex Rodriguez offered more details in a news conference after his arrival at Yankees spring training camp on Tuesday. With dozens of teammates standing nearby and roughly 200 reporters watching, Rodriguez said he and a cousin had obtained the drugs in the Dominican Republic and injected them for an energy boost.

"My mistake was because I was immature and I was stupid," Rodriguez said. "I blame myself. For a week here, I kept looking for people to blame, and I keep looking at myself."

Nick Swisher (left), C. C. Sabathia, Joba Chamberlain and Brett Tomko (right) at the Alex Rodriquez news conference.

In his interview last week, which followed the revelation by Sports Illustrated that he tested positive for a banned substance in 2003, Rodriguez said he used illegal drugs from 2001 to 2003 but did not know what he took. On Tuesday, he identified the drug as "boli" but did not name the cousin.

"I knew we weren't taking Tic Tacs," Rodriguez said.

Rodriguez said he injected himself with the drug twice a month for six months a year, yet said he did not know if he was using it properly or whether it was safe. Rodriguez, who was 25 years old in 2001 and had already signed a 10-year contract for $252 million, repeatedly said he was young at the time of his drug use.

"It goes back to being young and being curious," Rodriguez said. "I realized after my neck injury in '03 that I was being silly and irresponsible and I decided to stop. And I was a young guy."

Rodriguez began the news conference by reading a prepared statement and took questions for about 30 minutes. He paused for 38 seconds near the start when he tried to address his teammates, from stars like Derek Jeter to rookies like Phil Coke. "Thank you," Rodriguez finally said.

"I saw tears in his eyes," said Manager Joe Girardi, who sat at a table with General Manager Brian Cashman and Rodriguez. "I thought he was disappointed that it's come to this. For him to look over and see his teammates, he was moved. I think he really felt like they were part of his family."

The Yankees are tied to Rodriguez through 2017, after signing him to a 10-year, $275 million contract in December 2007, when Hank Steinbrenner was more visible atop the organization. (Steinbrenner attended the news conference but his brother, Hal, did not.) Rodriguez has stressed that he has been clean since joining the Yankees in 2004, and said he had never taken human growth hormone.

It is not clear what substance Rodriguez was referring to when he said that he had used the drug "known on the streets as boli or bollee." Rodriguez said his cousin bought the drug legally in the Dominican Republic.

"I've never heard of this name for a drug," Gary Wadler, an internist and member of the World Anti-Doping Agency, said in a telephone interview. "It seems to me that it sounds like it could be Primobolan."

SI.com, which first reported 10 days ago that Rodriguez tested positive in 2003, said that testosterone and the anabolic steroid Primobolan were found in his urine sample.

Rodriguez said he was reckless with how he took the drug, saying he consulted no one besides his cousin and did not even know if he derived an edge.

"I'm not sure what the benefit was," he said. "I will say this: when you take any substance, especially in baseball, it's half mental and half physical. If you take this glass of water and say you're going to be a better baseball player, if you believe it, you probably will be. I certainly felt more energy, but it's hard to say."

Rodriguez said he was eager to start playing again, and he pledged to his teammates that they would have "the best season of our lives." But the issue of his steroid use, and the verbal abuse he could take from fans, will be a sobering backdrop. "This thing is not dying," Cashman said. "The shelf life of this is a lot longer. The story itself will follow him for quite some time."

Girardi, a natural optimist, said he believed Rodriguez because he knew him so well. But even Girardi conceded that Rodriguez must earn back the trust of others.

"I think a lot of people are going to say, 'Prove it to me,' " Girardi said. "That's what happens when trust is broken." ◆

March 2, 2009

Yankees' Mattingly Was the Man to Teixeira as a Boy

By JACK CURRY

THE AGING POSTER is encased inside a flimsy plastic frame and hangs on the wall of what used to be a boy's bedroom. The boy became a man and moved out, but the poster has survived. He has made sure of that.

Twice, the man's parents took down the poster and tried to spruce up the room, making it more suitable for guests. Both times, the man returned home for the holidays and hung it in the same spot.

It is still hanging, even with the frame having lost one of its sides.

The poster features Don Mattingly as a Yankee, and it has a prominent spot in Mark Teixeira's old bedroom in Severna Park, Md. Whenever Teixeira visits his parents, he climbs the stairs to his room. The first thing he sees upon walking through the door is the poster.

"He was my guy," Teixeira said.

Somehow, a baseball-obsessed boy who grew up in Maryland and loved the Orioles peered into the other dugout to find his prototypical player. While Teixeira, the Yankees' new first baseman, adored Baltimore's Cal Ripken, too, he ⟫

«« gravitated toward the man whose job he now has. He gravitated toward a Yankee.

Could a first or second grader be astute enough to become a Mattingly devotee? John Teixeira, Mark's father, said his son was. John said Mark sat in his seat and watched entire games as a 3-year-old, studying at-bats and letting other kids worry about ice cream in plastic helmets.

"I think his interest in Mattingly had to do with the way Mattingly played the game," John Teixeira said. "He probably played the game the way no one else played it. He worked very hard and he carried himself professionally."

Since John was a Navy pilot, he preached discipline to Mark, especially in baseball. John and Margy, Mark's mother, repeatedly told their son that baseball was flooded with failure and that there was a proper way to respond to it. The Teixeiras expected Mark to be calm and respectful, the same attributes he detected in Mattingly. If Mattingly did not throw his bat or preen or argue with umpires, there was no need for him to do those things, either.

During Mark's childhood, he attended at least one Yankees–Orioles game a year at Memorial Stadium and then Camden Yards. On those days, Teixeira wore a Yankees shirt and cap and was treated like the enemy in his own backyard. Camden Yards was not littered with Yankees fans the way it often is now, so Teixeira's allegiance to Mattingly was unusual.

Whenever Teixeira could secure No. 23 on teams, he did it because it was Mattingly's number. It was Teixeira's number at Georgia Tech and with the Texas Rangers, his first team. Mattingly's 23 is retired, so Teixeira is wearing 25.

In 2002, Teixeira was still a minor leaguer when he played an exhibition game against the Yankees in Tampa, Fla. John Teixeira remembered how his son played only one inning, but acted as if he had socked three homers because he spoke with Mattingly for the first time.

"We were waiting for Mark, and the first thing he said was: 'Did you see me? I got to meet Don Mattingly,' " John Teixeira said. "He was like a little kid all over again."

Three years later, Teixeira had blossomed into an All-Star first baseman who hit 43 homers, drove in 144 runs and won a Gold Glove. That was also the year Buck Showalter, the Rangers' manager and former Yankees manager, helped arrange a lunch for Teixeira with Mattingly.

Teixeira said he and Mattingly met at a restaurant near the Ballpark in Arlington, Tex., and spoke about baseball, nothing but baseball, for 90 minutes. He recalled how Mattingly advised him to "not sweat an 0-for-12" slump and stay composed during those bleak stretches. Ever since, Mattingly said Teixeira was one of the first players he checked in the box scores.

"I've always kept an eye on him," Mattingly said. "I'm excited that he's with the Yankees. He's one of those everyday guys a team can count on. I think he'll do great there."

Now that Teixeira is the $180 million Yankee, he said it was a "cool twist" that the Maryland kid who loved Mattingly was playing for Mattingly's old team. Teixeira has autographed Mattingly jerseys in glass frames hanging in his homes in Arizona and Texas. But it is the poster, the flimsy poster, that best reflects a boy's attachment to his guy. ◆

In their new $1.5 billion stadium, the Yankees recreated the look of the original frieze that is meant to evoke the 1923 design.

April 15, 2009

A Distinctive Facade Is Recreated at New Yankee Stadium

By RICHARD SANDOMIR

NO FEATURE OF THE ORIGINAL Yankee Stadium defined its architectural look more than the gently curving frieze that crowned the upper deck. The elegant topping of the three-tiered House That Ruth Built oxidized early in its life, but the green patina only made it more memorable.

The frieze cast an unusual shadow on the field in late afternoons and became a part of history when Mickey Mantle hit a home run to right field in 1963 that nearly hit the top of it.

Someone—the architects at Osborn Engineering in Cleveland or the Yankees' visionary owners, Jacob Ruppert and Tillinghast L. Huston—intuitively understood magnificence.

"The shape of it came from out of nowhere,"

said John Pastier, an architectural critic and expert on stadiums. "It was quite original. It's not like they copied a classical design."

Philip Lowry, the author of "Green Cathedrals," a well-regarded survey of baseball stadiums, said via e-mail, "Just as shiny bumpers are the jewelry of a car, the third-deck frieze was the ornamental jewelry of Yankee Stadium." He called it unique among stadiums and ballparks that generally "followed a functional rather than an ornamental design."

The frieze lasted 50 years, until it was stripped away during the New York City's 1974–75 renovation and replaced by an ersatz version beyond the outfield fence and above the bleachers. »»

≪ "That was a horrible architectural mistake," Lowry wrote.

Yankees executives tell the story that Cary Grant suggested adding the outfield frieze to George Steinbrenner, either before the renovation or in 1976 (although photographs showed the imitation facade in place by opening day that year).

But Marty Appel, the Yankees' assistant public relations director in the early '70s, said that Michael Burke, who ran the Yankees for CBS and served briefly under Steinbrenner, "got huffy" when he saw there was no frieze in the renovation plans but knew the new upper deck could not accommodate it. So it went into the outfield.

"The design was in place by the time George bought the team," Appel said.

As if to atone for past sins, the Yankees have recreated the look of the original frieze in their $1.5 billion stadium that is meant to evoke the '23 design. The first was made of copper—although the Osborn blueprint calls it Toncan metal, which suggests a copper-iron alloy—but the new one is steel coated with zinc to protect it from rusting and two layers of white paint.

(A vigorous online discussion of the frieze's composition—with photographs and frieze diagrams and talk of old copper trade magazines—has ensued on baseball-fever.com.)

"Our challenge was to make the frieze aesthetically comparable with the original," said Carla Da Costa, a senior director of Tishman Speyer, the stadium's developer.

The new version looks very much like the old one, although its details are less intricately drawn than Osborn's original. It is made of 38 connected panels, all 11 feet deep, 12 feet high and most of them 40 feet long. With the columns between each panel, the frieze weighs 315 tons.

Unlike the original, the new frieze is more than a distinctive decorative touch; it is part of the support system for the cantilevers beneath the upper deck and for the lighting above it.

April 15, 2009

First Pitch at Yankee Stadium? Yogi, of Course

By TYLER KEPNER

IF THE YANKEES HAD PICKED anybody else to throw out the ceremonial first pitch at their new stadium Thursday, it just wouldn't have seemed right. Yogi Berra, 83 years young, will do the honors before the Yankees host Cleveland at 1:05 p.m.

The team also announced that Kelly Clarkson would sing the national anthem, a selection that should be popular with Derek Jeter, a confessed "American Idol" addict. The pregame ceremony will begin at 12:10 p.m. with the West Point Marching Band performing John Philip Sousa's "Washington Post March" and "Stars and Stripes Forever." Those choices are meaningful: before the original Yankee Stadium's opener on April 18, 1923, Sousa performed on field with the Seventh Regiment Band.

The home plate and pitching rubber to be used Thursday are the same set that closed out the old Yankee Stadium in September. When the game is over, the plate and the rubber will be moved to the Yankees Museum, located in the ballpark.

In case they missed anybody, the Yankees will have 40 of their alumni on hand for the opener. Here's the list:

The frieze was so critical to Billy Crystal's film "61*"—which followed Mantle's and Roger Maris's chase to beat Babe Ruth's single-season home run record—that it was digitally recreated.

"It's the top of the cathedral, it's your first visual memory of the stadium," said Ross Greenburg, a co-executive producer of the film and the president of HBO Sports. "We had those dramatic wide shots with Mickey at the plate and the facade in the background."

The frieze is also a prominent graphic element on YES Network programming and has become as notable a symbol of the team as the interlocking NY logo and the top hat and bat logo.

"It symbolizes the heart and legacy of the Yankees," said Randy Levine, the team's president. "It distinguishes Yankee Stadium. It's inspiring."

But it is never likely to turn green. ◆

Luis Arroyo, Jesse Barfield, Yogi Berra, Ron Blomberg, Bobby Brown, Horace Clarke, Jerry Coleman, David Cone, Chili Davis, Bucky Dent, Al Downing, Dave Eiland, Ed Figueroa, John Flaherty, Whitey Ford, Joe Girardi, Rich "Goose" Gossage, Ken Griffey Sr., Ron Guidry, Charlie Hayes, Rickey Henderson, Reggie Jackson, Tommy John, Jim Kaat, Don Larsen, Hector Lopez, Tino Martinez, Lee Mazzilli, Gene Michael, Jeff Nelson, Graig Nettles, Paul O'Neill, Joe Pepitone, Willie Randolph, Bobby Richardson, Mickey Rivers, Buck Showalter, Bill "Moose" Skowron, Luis Sojo, Mel Stottlemyre, Ralph Terry, Bob Turley, David Wells, Roy White, Bernie Williams, Dave Winfield. ◆

April 17, 2009

A Good Day Spoiled in the Bronx

By TYLER KEPNER

THE YANKEES CONTROLLED everything they could about the first game at their sparkling Bronx palace Thursday. Dozens of storied players hugged the infield dirt before the game. Yogi Berra tossed the first pitch. Crisp new flags for every team ringed the frieze, like colorful candles on a white birthday cake.

It was a celebration of Yankee glory, and even the weather cooperated. As the pregame performer John Fogerty would say, the sun came out and there was new grass on the field. The only problem was the game.

The Cleveland Indians, who won the final playoff series at the old Yankee Stadium, blistered the home team, 10–2, before 48,271 fans. The bullpen allowed nine runs in the seventh inning after C. C. Sabathia, the new $161 million starter, could not complete six.

The original Yankee Stadium opened with a Babe Ruth homer and a victory over the Boston Red Sox, foretelling decades of dominance. The Yankees can only hope Thursday's rout was not an omen.

"It's not how you want to start out a new stadium," Manager Joe Girardi said. "But one game is not going to make the history of this Yankee Stadium and this year."

Sabathia uncoiled for the first pitch to Grady Sizemore—a 94-mile-an-hour fastball for Ball 1—at 1:09 p.m. Sizemore then grounded out to first, just as Baltimore's Brian Roberts did last Sept. 21 on the final play at the original stadium.

Ruth's famous homer landed beyond right field, and the bat he used to hit it greeted the first Yankees hitter Thursday. When Derek Jeter came up against Cliff Lee in the bottom of the ⟫⟫

≪≪ first, he found Ruth's brown bat stretched across the plate. Jeter picked it up and playfully tried to keep it, offering his model to the bat boy.

The Ruth bat, on loan from a collector, seemed to bestow a blessing on the batter's box from the Yankees' highest god. But Jeter flied out.

The Yankees did have the first home run, at least, by Jorge Posada, to straightaway center with two outs in the fifth. It cleared the blue fence, bouncing in front of the retired numbers in Monument Park. The fans—including David Wells, the former Yankees pitcher who sat in the bleachers with his old admirers—prompted Posada to take a curtain call.

The mound had seemed like hallowed ground before the game, when the Yankees greats Whitey Ford and Don Larsen scooped dirt from it after the ceremony. But the Yankees' poor showing there sent many fans to the exits, including some from the seats that cost $2,625 a game.

There were no prices so extravagant at the old Stadium, which still stands across the street, alone with its memories. Its successor has the looks, but a lot to learn about drama. ◆

September 25, 2009

The Taskmanager Loosens Up

By TYLER KEPNER

JOE GIRARDI'S HAIR is the color of steel, buzzed close to his scalp, suited for the military. The reason is that anything else would look frizzy. But the haircut, it seems, has always informed the narrative. Girardi must be rigid and humorless, cold and disciplined, a taskmaster in pinstripes.

There is some truth to the caricature. Girardi's Little League coach in Peoria, Ill., Dave Rogers, once told him to wear a tube sock around his elbow at night to prevent a sore arm. He followed orders for years.

"He did that until he met Kim," said Rogers, 64, referring to Girardi's wife. "Kim even asked me, 'Can you tell him to take that ridiculous sock off?' But he never had a sore arm."

The regimented lifestyle has worked for Girardi, who has guided the Yankees to a playoff berth in his second season as their manager. But

he has not been so strict as to ignore professional failings. He looked within himself last winter after a disappointing debut.

"You have this plan that it's going to go this way and this way, and it always veers off," Girardi said last week, before a game in Seattle. "You've got to be willing to adjust."

It would be wrong to say Girardi has changed his personality. Far from his stereotype as a drill sergeant, he is actually relentlessly upbeat, bounding from task to task, radiating energy. He was the same way last year.

This season, though, the optimism seems more grounded in reality. A better team has accounted for much of the difference.

"I think he's backed off, maybe let his coaches do a little more, but I'm searching," starter Andy Pettitte said. "He definitely seems a little bit more relaxed, but a lot of that has to do with us winning 97 games. We've played so well in the second half, it's just been a great atmosphere."

The better mood has been by design, and it would not have happened if Girardi had not been as perceptive as he was about last season. He admitted this spring that he had waited too long to jolt a sluggish Robinson Cano, waiting until September to pull Cano from the lineup for loafing after a grounder.

Cano responded with a torrid finish, made a mechanical adjustment with the hitting coach Kevin Long, and carried his momentum into this season. Through Wednesday he was tied for second in the league in total bases, behind his teammate Mark Teixeira.

"I think players become stronger and better if they have to fight their way out of it, as opposed to you rescuing them," Girardi said, explaining that he did not want to embarrass Cano. "Maybe if I would have done it sooner, maybe he would've had a better year. I can't tell you, but since we've done it, he's played extremely well. You have to evaluate what you do, and the other thing is you have to know the players. And it takes time."

Manager Joe Girardi made changes in his managerial approach during the 2009 season.

Cano said Girardi was right to bench him last season. The manager, Cano said, had seen what he could not see about himself. There have been no obvious concentration lapses this season—and, to Cano, no change in Girardi.

"He's been the same as last year," Cano said. "Always talks to everybody."

Girardi has emphasized communication, between himself and his players and especially among the players themselves. Last off-season, he and the bench coach Rob Thomson decided spring training was too long, and they thought of ways to break the monotony while fostering a sense of team.

One day, Girardi canceled practice and took the team on a field trip to a pool hall for a two-on-two tournament. Girardi carefully selected the pairs, and the winners were Mariano Rivera, the veteran closer, and Phil Coke, a rookie setup man.

Five months later, when Coke was mad at himself for allowing six runs to the White Sox, Rivera took him to dinner in Chicago. Newcomers have also picked up on Girardi's cues.

"A lot of players were brought in who followed up on what Joe was trying to do," Johnny Damon said. "Whether it was C. C. Sabathia taking guys to basketball games or A. J. Burnett having people over for a Fourth of July party, everybody feels like a big family."

To that end, Girardi has designated one day roughly every month for players to bring their daughters to the clubhouse. He reminds the players to dress in back rooms so girls can roam freely around the locker room, just as their brothers do.

Communication is essential, Girardi said, and that is the basis for the harmonious clubhouse he runs. That and the winning, of course, which Burnett punctuates by slamming a pie in the face of a player who ends a game with a hit.

In this area, too, Girardi makes his feelings clear. The ritual amuses him, and though he has never smashed a pie on a player, he knows he may be a target.

"A. J. told me they're going to get me," Girardi said. "And I said I want banana cream." ◆

October 5, 2009

Yankees 10, Rays 2
Rodriguez Does the Math, and It Adds Up to 2 Records

By TYLER KEPNER

ST. PETERSBURG, FLA.—Before batting practice at Tropicana Field on Sunday, Alex Rodriguez explained a reason for his success this season. When he missed the first five weeks after hip surgery, Rodriguez said, he realized he could not compile his usual dazzling statistics. It sharpened his focus on the everyday.

A few hours later, though, an improbable circumstance intruded. It was the sixth inning of the Yankees' eventual 10–2 victory against the Tampa Bay Rays, and Rodriguez was down to what he figured was his last at-bat. He needed two homers and seven runs batted in to reach 30 and 100 for the 13th time.

"I just didn't think it was realistic at all, so therefore it wasn't even a goal," Rodriguez said. "I kind of had conceded that."

Rodriguez had agreed to more days off recently, allowing his hip to rest before the playoffs. But when he drove a ball to the left-field seats with two on in the sixth, he suddenly had 29 homers and 96 R.B.I.

"I may have one shot," Rodriguez said he told his teammate Eric Hinske. "We load the bases, I might pop one, you never know."

Rodriguez was only joking, but the chance came around. Later that inning, with two outs and two on, Andy Sonnanstine intentionally walked Mark Teixeira, who was tied with the Rays' Carlos Pena for the American League home run lead, at 39. Rodriguez promptly smoked a grand slam to right-center, and raised his fist as he rounded first base.

The home run established two records for Rodriguez. He is the first player to have 13 seasons of 30 homers and 100 R.B.I. And he is the first A.L. player to drive in seven runs in an inning. Fernando Tatis holds the major league mark with two grand slams in an inning for St. Louis in 1999.

It also provided symmetry to Rodriguez's regular season. He homered with his first swing in Baltimore on May 8, and did it again with his last swing.

"It's magical," the hitting coach Kevin Long said. "He comes in his first game in Baltimore and hits a home run, and then this last game he hits a grand slam. You just shake your head at the things he's able to do."

The Yankees expect extraordinary feats from Rodriguez, who is finishing the second season of a 10-year deal that could exceed $300 million. It is a heavy investment by the team's principal owner, George Steinbrenner, who greeted the team in the clubhouse before the game.

The Yankees have been a close team this season, and after a rocky spring in which he admitted to using steroids, Rodriguez has fit neatly into the dynamic. Considering his past, it might have been his most unlikely achievement of all.

"I think it's fair to say I hit rock bottom this spring, between the embarrassment of the press conference and my career being threatened with my hip injury," Rodriguez said. "My life and my career was at a crossroads, and I was either going to stay at the bottom or I was going to bounce back." ◆

October 12, 2009

YANKEES 4, TWINS 1; EXORCISING DEMONS

By TYLER KEPNER

IT TOOK FIVE YEARS of wandering, five years of wild spending and first-round heartbreak and changes both awkward and grand. But the Yankees are back in the American League Championship Series, back where it all went off course in 2004, back with the World Series in reach.

They got there by sweeping the Minnesota Twins in the division series with a 4–1 victory in Game 3 on Sunday, closing the Metrodome for baseball. Alex Rodriguez, as dangerous now as he was lost in past Octobers, slammed a tying home run for the second game in a row, driving in six runs while batting .455 in the sweep.

"It's just a better team," General Manager Brian Cashman said. "We've got a deeper pitching staff, we're better defensively, better offensively, better bench, better camaraderie, all of it."

A better Rodriguez counts for a lot, too. His homer came with one out in the seventh inning off the former Yankee Carl Pavano, just after the Twins had taken a lead for the third game in a row. Two batters later, Jorge Posada drove another homer off Pavano to put the Yankees ahead.

The Yankees will host the Los Angeles Angels in Game 1 of the A.L.C.S. on Friday at Yankee Stadium. The last time the Yankees were in the A.L.C.S., they blew a three-games-to-none lead against Boston, the low point of the Joe Torre era.

Now the Yankees have a new manager, Joe Girardi, a new ballpark and new stars like C. C. Sabathia. He can start Game 1 against the Angels on normal rest because the Yankees won this series so quickly.

"We'll celebrate tonight," said Sabathia, drenched in Champagne in the clubhouse. "We know we've got a long way to go. The Angels are a tough team, and we'll see what happens."

The Twins outhit the Yankees, .257 to .225. But the Yankees crunched six homers, the Twins none, and their pitchers had a 1.55 earned run average.

The Yankees also had more strikeouts than innings pitched, the first time they have done that in the postseason since the 2001 World Series.

"It's just pitching," Posada said. "Doing things right when it counts. It's simple, it really is. The winning equation doesn't really change. You've just got to keep on pitching."

Pettitte was just as stingy. He was perfect through four innings, ending that stretch with five strikeouts in his last eight batters. Mauer struck out on three pitches to end the fourth, missing Pettitte's signature cutter.

"That's a pesky team," Mark Teixeira said of the Twins. "That's a team that can score in a lot of different ways, and he kept them down all night."

For the third game in a row, the Yankees' starter worked at least six innings, allowing one earned run. The lack of such lockdown pitching doomed the Yankees to first-round losses in 2005, 2006 and 2007 and contributed to their 2004 collapse.

"People can say whatever they want about home runs and big hits," Rodriguez said. "I mean, if you don't pitch and you don't defend, you are not going to win."

The rotation is stronger now, and a relaxed Rodriguez is a devastating offensive force. The combination has brought the Yankees back, and earned them a chance at the World Series. ◆

November 5, 2009

BACK ON TOP, YANKEES ADD 27TH TITLE

By TYLER KEPNER

A SLIVER OF TIME for other teams is an epoch for the Yankees, who define themselves by championships. For eight seasons, they led the majors in victories, payroll and drama. They built a ballpark, created a network and expanded their brand around the globe. But they did not win the World Series.

Now they have done it. There is a 27th jewel in the Yankees' crown and a peaceful, easy feeling across their empire. The Yankees captured their first title since 2000, humbling the defending champion Philadelphia Phillies on Wednesday, 7–3, in Game 6 of the World Series at Yankee Stadium.

Hideki Matsui homered, with his six runs batted in tying a World Series record, and Andy Pettitte ground through five and two-thirds innings for his second victory in five days. Mariano Rivera collected the final five outs, getting Shane Victorino to ground out to end it.

"They persevered and they were determined, a lot like the '98 team," General Manager Brian Cashman said, referring to the best Yankees team of modern times. "They had the attitude that nothing was going to stop them. But they had to prove it, and they proved it."

They did it on the eighth anniversary of Rivera's lowest moment, when he blew Game 7 of the 2001 World Series in Arizona. The Yankees lost the World Series again two years later, to Florida, and they did not return until this season, fortifying their roster with free agents around the core

The Yankees celebrate their 2009 World Series championship.

of Rivera, Pettitte, Derek Jeter and Jorge Posada.

"We play the game the right way," Jeter said on the podium behind second base, cradling the Commissioner's Trophy. "And we deserve to be standing here."

Pettitte became the second pitcher to win all three clinching games of a postseason. The other was Boston's Derek Lowe in 2004, when the Yankees lost a three-games-to-none lead to the Red Sox, fumbling away a pennant and plunging into a postseason funk. Pettitte was gone that autumn, part of a three-year sojourn to his Houston hometown. Otherwise, Pettitte, Rivera, Jeter and Posada have been Yankees since 1995, through dynasty and drought and back to the top. The have each earned five championship rings, one more than Babe Ruth won for the Yankees.

It is the seventh championship for the principal owner George Steinbrenner, 79, who was not at Yankee Stadium on Wednesday.

"It's been a while—it's been nine years," said his son, Hal Steinbrenner, the managing general partner. "I just talked to him today. He was a little bit excited and nervous, as we all were. But this team, they fought and they fought and they fought. They never gave up."

Matsui has done more than raise the Yankees' profile in Japan. He has been steady and efficient for seven seasons. His ravaged knees have made him a full-time designated hitter and called into doubt his future as he comes to the end of his contract. But if this was his last game as a Yankee, he made it his best.

Decorated champions embraced new ones, christening the ballpark the way they all expected. The championship was back to the Bronx, where the Yankees believe it belongs.

"This is what the Steinbrenner family has strived for year after year and tried to deliver to the city of New York," Manager Joe Girardi said. "To be able to deliver this to the Boss, to the stadium he created and the atmosphere he created around here, it's very gratifying to all of us." ◆

July 14, 2010

GEORGE STEINBRENNER, 1930–2010; A Legacy of Championships From the Man Who Hated to Lose

By RICHARD GOLDSTEIN

GEORGE STEINBRENNER, who bought a declining Yankees team in 1973, promised to stay out of its daily affairs and then, in an often tumultuous reign, placed his formidable stamp on 7 World Series championship teams, 11 pennant winners and a sporting world powerhouse valued at perhaps $1.6 billion, died Tuesday morning at a hospital in Tampa, Fla., where he lived. He was 80.

The cause was a heart attack, the Yankees said. Mr. Steinbrenner had been in failing health for several years.

His death came eight months after the Yankees won their first World Series title since 2000, clinching their six-game victory over the Philadelphia Phillies at his new Yankee Stadium, and two days after the team's longtime public-address announcer, Bob Sheppard, died at 99.

A pioneer of modern sports ownership, Mr. Steinbrenner started the wave of high spending for players when free agency arrived, and he continued to spend freely through the Yankees' revival in the late '70s and early '80s, the long stretch without a pennant and then renewed triumphs under Joe Torre as manager and General Manager Brian Cashman.

The Yankees' approximately $210 million payroll in 2009 dwarfed all others in baseball, and the team paid out millions in luxury tax and revenue-sharing with small-market teams.

In the frenetic '70s and '80s, when general managers, field managers and pitching coaches were sent spinning through Mr. Steinbrenner's revolving personnel door (Billy Martin had five stints as the manager), the franchise became known >>>

George Steinbrenner's Yankees earned seven World Series titles and 11 pennants.

<<< as the Bronx Zoo. In December 2002, Mr. Steinbrenner's enterprise had grown so rich that the president of the Boston Red Sox, Larry Lucchino, frustrated over losing the pitcher Jose Contreras to the Yankees, called them the "evil empire."

But Mr. Steinbrenner—who came to be known as the Boss—and the Yankees thrived through all the arguments, all the turmoil, all the bombast. Having been without a pennant since 1964 when Mr. Steinbrenner bought them, enduring sagging attendance while the upstart Mets thrived, the Yankees once again became America's marquee sporting franchise.

Despite his poor health, Mr. Steinbrenner attended the opening game at the new Yankee Stadium in April 2009, sitting in his suite with his wife, Joan (pronounced Jo-ann). When he was introduced and received an ovation, his shoulders shook and he cried.

He next appeared at the Yankees' new home for the first two games of the World Series, then made his final appearance at the 2010 home opener, when Joe Girardi, the manager, and Derek Jeter, the team captain, came to his suite to

present him with his 2009 World Series championship ring.

After the World Series victory, Girardi said, "To be able to deliver this to the Boss, to the stadium he created and the atmosphere he created around here, it's very gratifying to all of us." Mr. Steinbrenner, the Yankees' principal owner and chairman, had ceded increasing authority to his sons, Hal and Hank, who became co-chairmen in May 2008. Hal Steinbrenner was given control of the team in November 2008 in a unanimous vote by the major league club owners.

Mr. Steinbrenner lived year-round in Tampa, but he became a New York celebrity and a figure in popular culture. He was lampooned, with his permission, by a caricature in the sitcom "Seinfeld," portrayed by the actor Lee Bear, who was always photographed from behind at the Boss's

George Steinbrenner signing autographs at Yankee Stadium in 1994.

desk while Larry David, the show's co-creator, provided the voice. George Costanza (Jason Alexander) became the assistant to the team's traveling secretary, whose duties included fetching calzones for Mr. Steinbrenner.

Mr. Steinbrenner also appeared in a Visa commercial with Jeter, calling him into his office to admonish him. "You're our starting shortstop," Mr. Steinbrenner said. "How can you possibly afford to spend two nights dancing, two nights eating out and three nights just carousing with your friends?" Jeter responded by holding up a Visa card. Mr. Steinbrenner exclaimed "Oh!" and the scene shifted to Mr. Steinbrenner in a dance line with Jeter at a night spot.

Mr. Steinbrenner was the central figure in a syndicate that bought the Yankees from CBS for $10 million. When he arrived in New York on Jan. 3, 1973, he said he would not "be active in the day-to-day operations of the club at all." Having made his money as head of the American Shipbuilding Company, based in Cleveland, he declared, "I'll stick to building ships."

But four months later, Michael Burke, who had been running the Yankees for CBS and had stayed on to help manage the franchise, departed after clashing with Mr. Steinbrenner. John McMullen, a minority owner in the syndicate, soon remarked that "nothing is as limited as being a limited partner of George's."

Mr. Steinbrenner emerged as one of the most powerful, influential and, in the eyes of many, notorious executives in sports. He was the senior club owner in baseball at his death.

Yankee Stadium underwent a major renovation in the mid-1970s, but that did not satisfy Mr. Steinbrenner. He cast an eye toward New Jersey, pressed for a new stadium in Manhattan and ultimately got a $1.5 billion stadium built in the Bronx, alongside the original House That Ruth Built.

He found new revenue streams from cable television, first in a longtime deal with the Madison Square Garden network and then with the creation of the Yankees' YES network. The franchise also engineered lucrative marketing deals,

notably a 10-year, $95 million apparel agreement with Adidas.

Mr. Steinbrenner usually adored his players but at times insulted them. He called outfielder Paul O'Neill "the ultimate warrior." (Steinbrenner idolized Generals MacArthur and Patton.) But he derided the star outfielder Dave Winfield, calling him Mr. May, pointedly contrasting him with Reggie Jackson, who had been known as Mr. October for his clutch hitting in the postseason.

Mr. Steinbrenner was twice barred from baseball, once after pleading guilty to making illegal political campaign contributions. By October 1995, when he was fined for complaining about the umpires in a playoff series with the Seattle Mariners, Mr. Steinbrenner had accumulated disciplinary costs of $645,000.

When he was not phoning his general managers and managers with complaints or advice, he meddled in the smallest matters of ballpark maintenance. He was often portrayed by the news media as a blowhard and a baseball know-nothing.

"George is a great guy, unless you have to work for him," Lou Piniella, who managed the Yankees twice in the 1980s, told Sports Illustrated in 2004. Mr. Steinbrenner saw himself as sticking up for the everyday New Yorker, though the price of Yankees tickets kept rising.

"I care about New York dearly," he told Sports Illustrated in 2004. "I like every cab driver, every guy that stops the car and honks, every truck driver. I feed on that."

He helped many charities and individuals in need and as a board member was a major fundraiser for the historically black Grambling State University in Louisiana.

George Michael Steinbrenner III was born on July 4, 1930, the oldest of three children, and reared in the Cleveland suburb of Bay Village. His father, Henry Steinbrenner, graduated from the Massachusetts Institute of Technology with a degree in naval architecture and engineering and starred as a collegiate hurdler before taking over the family's maritime shipping business.

Young George tried to please his father »»

⟨⟨⟨ by taking up hurdling and running a home-based business that raised chickens and sold their eggs.

"He was a tough taskmaster," Mr. Steinbrenner once said of his father. "You know, if I ran four races in track, won three and lost one, he'd say, 'Now go sit down and study that one race and see why you lost it.'"

His mother, Rita, offered a contrasting presence. "It was my mom who gave me compassion for the underdog and for people in need," Mr. Steinbrenner was quoted by Bill Madden in "Steinbrenner: The Last Lion of Baseball" in an apparent reference to his many charitable endeavors.

Mr. Steinbrenner attended Culver Military Academy in Indiana in the mid-1940s. His father, who idolized the Yankees' Joe DiMaggio and Bill Dickey, took him to Cleveland to watch Indians games, especially when the Yankees came to town. "We were in awe of the Yankees," Mr. Steinbrenner said.

Mr. Steinbrenner graduated from Williams College in Massachusetts with a degree in English. He served as an Air Force officer, coached high school football and basketball in Ohio, and was briefly an assistant football coach at Northwestern and Purdue.

He returned to Cleveland in 1957 to join the family's shipping firm, Kinsman Marine Transit, which carried Great Lakes cargo. He also operated the Cleveland Pipers basketball team.

In 1967, Mr. Steinbrenner began obtaining stock in the American Shipbuilding Company, based in Lorain, Ohio. He eventually took it over, merging it with Kinsman. By the time he gained control of the Yankees six years later, the company had greatly strengthened its operations.

Gabe Paul, a veteran baseball executive who helped arrange Mr. Steinbrenner's purchase of the Yankees, and Lee MacPhail, the holdover general manager from the CBS years, were expected to make the personnel decisions when Mr. Steinbrenner arrived.

But he quickly became immersed in baseball decisions, spending large sums to end the long pennant drought, starting with the acquisition of the star pitcher Catfish Hunter. Meanwhile, he ran into trouble in a matter far beyond the ball fields.

In November 1974, Commissioner Bowie Kuhn suspended him for two years—a term later reduced to 15 months—after he pleaded guilty to two charges, one a felony and the other a misdemeanor: conspiring to make illegal corporate contributions to President Richard M. Nixon's 1972 re-election campaign, and trying to "influence and intimidate employees" of his shipbuilding company to lie to a grand jury about the matter. He was fined $15,000 in the criminal case but given no jail time.

"Everybody has dents in his armor," Mr. Steinbrenner told The New York Times in 1987. "That's something I have to live with." President Ronald Reagan pardoned him in January 1989, during his final days in office.

When free agency arrived as a result of an arbitrator's decision in 1975 that nullified the reserve clause, which had bound players to their teams, Mr. Steinbrenner stepped up his spending.

The Yankees signed the slugger Reggie Jackson and the ace relief pitcher Goose Gossage, and they won the World Series in 1977 and 1978.

Mr. Steinbrenner changed managers and general managers with abandon, punctuated by the bizarre comings and goings of Martin. The oddest sequence began on July 24, 1978, when Martin resigned as manager, presumably a step ahead of being fired, after saying of Jackson and Mr. Steinbrenner: "The two of them deserve each other. One's a born liar; the other's convicted," a reference to Mr. Steinbrenner's guilty plea in the illegal-contributions case.

Only five days later, on Old-Timers' Day at Yankee Stadium, Martin was introduced as the Yankees' manager for 1980. Instead, he returned in June 1979, replacing the fired Bob Lemon, only to be fired himself a month after that season ended.

Another furor arose in 1985, this one surrounding Yogi Berra, the Yankees' Hall of Fame catcher, who had become the manager. After declaring that "Yogi will be the manager the entire season, win or lose," Mr. Steinbrenner fired him with the team off to a 6–10 start. Berra, furious, refused to set foot inside Yankee Stadium until Mr. Steinbrenner apologized 14 years later. By 1990, he had switched managers 18 times and hired 13 general managers.

Then came more trouble. In July 1990, Commissioner Fay Vincent ordered Mr. Steinbrenner to step aside as the Yankees' managing partner for making a $40,000 payment to a confessed gambler named Howard Spira in return for Mr. Spira's seeking damaging information about Winfield. Mr. Steinbrenner had been displeased with Winfield's performance on the field, and the two had feuded over contributions Mr. Steinbrenner was to make to Winfield's philanthropic foundation.

Mr. Steinbrenner resumed control of the Yankees in 1993, and three years later, they were World Series champions, beginning a long run of dominance.

By the 1990s, with free agents becoming ever more expensive, Mr. Steinbrenner acknowledged the need to develop the Yankees' minor league system. The Yankees swept to championships with homegrown talent like Jeter, center fielder Bernie Williams, catcher Jorge Posada and pitchers Andy Pettitte and Mariano Rivera. But they also assumed more than $100 million in payments owed to Alex Rodriguez, who arrived in a trade with the Texas Rangers, and obtained the high-priced Jason Giambi, Roger Clemens and Randy Johnson.

In 2002, an investment group that included the Yankees formed the YES network to carry many games and broadcast Yankees-related programming. YES had $257 million in revenue in 2005, for the first time surpassing MSG as the country's top regional sports network, according to Kagan Research.

The Yankees' management achieved stability in the last decade as the team captured World Series championships in 1996 and every year from 1998 to 2000. But the Yankees faltered after that in their bid for another World Series title, and when they were knocked out of the playoffs by the upstart Detroit Tigers in 2006, speculation arose that Mr. Steinbrenner would fire Torre.

Torre, the manager since 1996, and Mr. Cashman, the general manager since 1998 and a frequent object of Mr. Steinbrenner's criticism, stayed on.

But in October 2007 in a newspaper interview, Mr. Steinbrenner threatened to fire Torre if the team did not advance beyond the first round of the playoffs. The Yankees were eliminated by the Cleveland Indians in that round, and soon afterward, Torre departed after rejecting a one-year contract extension with a cut in his guaranteed salary.

Even in his earliest days running the Yankees, Mr. Steinbrenner acknowledged that he seemed to rule through fear. "Some guys can lead through real, genuine respect," he told Cleveland magazine in 1974, "but I'm not that kind of a leader."

Always fastidious about his own grooming, he insisted that his players shun unruly hair and beards, displaying something of the disciplinarian he had been at home, with his children. He admitted he had been overbearing and even verbally abusive toward them. His daughter Jennifer said in 2004 that her brothers had absorbed the brunt. "Let's put it this way: he had very high expectations of us," she said.

In addition to his wife, Joan, his sons Hal and Hank, and his daughter Jennifer Steinbrenner Swindal, Mr. Steinbrenner is survived by his daughter Jessica Steinbrenner; two sisters, Susan Norpell and Judy Kamm, and several grandchildren.

In his later years, Mr. Steinbrenner spent most of his time in Tampa. He had divested himself of most of his business interests. American Shipbuilding filed for bankruptcy in 1993, but he owned a stud farm in Ocala, Fla., and had entered six horses in the Kentucky Derby over the years. In April 2010, Forbes magazine estimated the Yankees' value at $1.6 billion. The Red Sox had the second-highest value among major league teams, according to Forbes, far behind the Yankees at $870 million, with the Mets third at $858 million.

In his last years, Mr. Steinbrenner seemed to mellow some. He cried in public on several occasions, including the time he walked past a group of West Point cadets who cheered >>>

⋘ for him at the Yankees' 2004 home opener. He cried again in a television interview that day.

"This is a very important thing that we hold the string to," he said of the Yankees, his voice cracking. "This is the people's team."

In building it into a fabulously successful and exceedingly lucrative enterprise, he never lost sight of his credo. As he told The New York Times in 1998: "I hate to lose. Hate, hate, hate to lose." ◆

July 12, 2010

Bob Sheppard, Voice of the Yankees, Dies at 99

By RICHARD GOLDSTEIN

BOB SHEPPARD, whose elegant intonation as the public-address announcer at Yankee Stadium for more than half a century personified the image of Yankees grandeur, died Sunday at his home in Baldwin, on Long Island. He was 99.

From the last days of DiMaggio through the primes of Mantle, Berra, Jackson and Jeter, Sheppard's precise, resonant, even Olympian elocution—he was sometimes called the Voice of God—greeted Yankees fans with the words, "Good afternoon, ladies and gentlemen, and welcome to Yankee Stadium."

"The Yankees and Bob Sheppard were a mar-riage made in heaven," said Paul Sheppard, a 71-year-old financial adviser. "I know St. Peter will now recruit him. If you're lucky enough to go to heaven, you'll be greeted by a voice, saying: 'Good afternoon, ladies and gentlemen. Welcome to heaven!' "

In an era of blaring stadium music, of public-address announcers styling themselves as entertainers and cheerleaders, Sheppard, a man with a passion for poetry and Shakespeare, shunned hyperbole.

"A public-address announcer should be clear, concise, correct," he said. "He should not be colorful, cute or comic."

Sheppard did not feel strong enough to attend the ceremony marking the final game at the old Yankee Stadium on Sept. 21, 2008, but he announced the Yankees' starting lineup that night in a tape recording. His recorded voice still introduces Derek Jeter at the plate, a touch the Yankees' captain requested to honor Sheppard.

"He's as much a part of this organization as any player," Jeter said Sunday. "Even though the players change year in and year out, he was the one constant at Yankee Stadium. He was part of the experience." Sheppard was the chairman of the speech department at John Adams High School in Queens and an adjunct professor of speech at St. John's University while becoming a New York institution as a public-address announcer.

"I don't change my pattern," he once said. "I speak at Yankee Stadium the same way I do in a classroom, a saloon or reading the Gospel at Mass at St. Christopher's."

On May 7, 2000, Bob Sheppard Day at Yankee Stadium, the Yankees outfielder Paul O'Neill reflected on Sheppard's aura.

"It's the organ at church," O'Neill told The Record of Hackensack, N.J. "Certain sounds and certain voices just belong in places. Obviously, his voice and Yankee Stadium have become one."

Robert Leo Sheppard, who was born on Oct. 20, 1910, gained a passion for his calling while growing up in Queens.

"My father, Charles, and my mother, Eileen, each enjoyed poetry and music and public speaking," Sheppard told Maury Allen in "Baseball: The Lives Behind the Seams." "They were very precise in how they spoke," he said. "They measured words, pronounced everything carefully and instilled a love of language in me by how they respected proper pronunciation."

Sheppard played first base at St. John's Prep and at St. John's University, where he was also a quarterback.

While he was in high school, two Vincentian priests put him on the path toward a career in speech education.

"The combination there of one, the fiery orator, and the other, the semantic craftsman, probably presented a blending I wanted to imitate," he once recalled.

Sheppard earned a bachelor's degree in English and speech at St. John's and a master's degree in speech from Columbia before serving as a Navy officer during World War II. He became a speech teacher at John Adams upon his return and served as the public-address announcer for the Brooklyn Dodgers and the New York Yankees of the All-America Football Conference.

He was hired by the baseball Yankees in 1951, and soon fans were hearing Sheppard's pronunciation of "Joe Di-Mah-ggio."

"I take great pride in how the names are pronounced," Sheppard said. He seldom entered the clubhouses, but made certain to check directly with a visiting player if he had any doubt on the correct way to pronounce his name.

"Mick-ey Man-tle" was a favorite of his, but as Sheppard once told The Associated Press: "Anglo-Saxon names are not very euphonious. What can I do with Steve Sax? What can I do with Mickey Klutts?"

He enjoyed announcing the name of the Japanese pitcher Shigetoshi Hasegawa and the names of Latin players, particularly pitcher Salome Barojas and infielder Jose Valdivielso.

Sheppard feared he would trip over his pronunciation of Wayne Terwilliger, an infielder who played at Yankee Stadium with the Washington Senators and Kansas City Athletics in the 1950s. "I worried that I would say 'Ter-wigg-ler' but I never did," he recalled.

But there was at least one flub.

When the football Giants played their first game at the Meadowlands, against the Dallas Cowboys in October 1976, Sheppard told the crowd: "Welcome to Yankee Stadium."

On Bob Sheppard Day — during his 50th year with the Yankees — he was honored at a home-plate ceremony in which Walter Cronkite read the inscription on the plaque being unveiled for Monument Park behind the left-field fence. It stated in part that Sheppard "has announced the names of hundreds of players — both unfamiliar and legendary — with equal divine reverence."

George Steinbrenner, the principal owner of the Yankees, said in a statement: "For over a half-century, fans were thrilled to hear his unforgettable voice and players were thrilled to hear ⟩⟩⟩

«« his majestic enunciation of their names. Bob Sheppard was a great member of the Yankees family and his death leaves a lasting silence."

He leaves behind his second wife, Mary; two sons, Paul and Chris; and two daughters, Barbara and Mary. His first wife, Margaret, the mother of all four children, died in 1959. He also leaves four grandchildren.

Sheppard had his imitators, most notably the ESPN broadcaster Jon Miller.

"One day when my wife Mary and I were down in St. Thomas, we went into a restaurant," Sheppard told The Village Voice in 2002. "I told the waitress, 'I'll have the No. 1. Scrambled eggs, buttered toast and black coffee. No. 1.' My wife looked at me and said. 'You sound like Jon Miller's imitation.' I wasn't conscious of the fact that I was ordering the same way I'd introduce Billy Martin." ◆

Bob Sheppard in the public-address announcer's box.

July 9, 2011

JETER REACHES 3,000, AND IT'S A BLAST

By TYLER KEPNER

THE PURSUIT OF A SPORTS MILESTONE can seem like a march to the inevitable. Fans have known for years that barring a catastrophic injury, Derek Jeter would reach 3,000 career hits. The only question was how.

Jeter, the Yankees' captain, answered it Saturday with a performance that ranks among the greatest of his decorated career. He slammed a home run in the third inning for his 3,000th hit, and capped a five-hit day with the go-ahead single in the eighth inning of a 5–4 victory over the Tampa Bay Rays at Yankee Stadium.

Even for Jeter, who dreamed he would be the Yankees shortstop and grew up to lead the team to five championships, the script seemed almost implausible.

"If I would have tried to have written it and given it to someone, I wouldn't have even bought it," Jeter said. "It's just one of those special days."

The 3,000th hit, off a full-count curveball from the left-hander David Price, was Jeter's first over the wall at Yankee Stadium since last June. His five hits matched a career high he had reached only twice before in the regular season, in 2001 and 2005.

Christian Lopez, 23, a fan from Highland Mills, N.Y., caught the ball in the left-field seats

Derek Jeter saluting the crowd after his 3,000th hit.

Berra and DiMaggio, Mickey Mantle, all those guys, and none of them have 3,000," Rivera said. "And then here comes Derek Jeter, for so many years."

Jeter became the 28th player to reach 3,000 hits, but only the second to do so with a home run, after Tampa Bay's Wade Boggs in 1999. Only Ty Cobb, Hank Aaron and Robin Yount joined the club at a younger age than Jeter who turned 37 on June 26.

However the rest of his career plays out, Jeter—whose 5-for-5 day raised his career average by a point, to .313—will be known most for relentless consistency, for churning out hits at a rate few have matched. Jeter has 10 seasons with at least 190 hits. Only Rose and Cobb, who rank first and second on the career list, have more such seasons.

"I take a lot of pride in going out there every single day and trying to be as consistent as possible," Jeter said. "I think that's probably the most difficult thing to do in our sport. Playing well gets you here. Consistency keeps you here. That's the thing that I've always tried to focus on."

Jeter was only 20 when he rapped his first hit, a single off the Mariners' Tim Belcher at the Seattle Kingdome on May 30, 1995. It was only appropriate that the 3,000th hit come in the Bronx, where Jeter broke Lou Gehrig's franchise record with 2,722 hits in 2009.

Passing Gehrig was a stirring moment, even if it had little resonance outside Yankee Stadium. With 3,000 hits, Jeter has passed a revered number in the game's history, leaving an indelible mark in style. ◆

and returned it to Jeter, who became the first player with 3,000 hits for the Yankees.

Jorge Posada, Jeter's close friend and a teammate for 17 years, wrapped Jeter in a hug at home plate, with reliever Mariano Rivera joining the embrace.

"You're talking about from Babe Ruth to Yogi

September 19, 2011

RIVERA GETS HIS RECORD 602ND SAVE

By BENJAMIN HOFFMAN

JUST BEFORE 10:30 A.M. Monday, Mariano Rivera walked into the Yankees' clubhouse in street clothes. Less than 15 minutes later, he was dressed and ready to go. By 4:30 p.m., he had passed Trevor Hoffman as the major league career leader in saves with 602.

In many ways, it was just another day in the life of a famously modest player who, over the course of a decade and a half, has put his signature on the ninth inning in a way no other pitcher has.

When it was over, after Rivera had gotten a called third strike against Minnesota's Jason Parmelee to finish a 1-2-3 ninth and preserve a 6–4 victory, and after he had been mobbed by his teammates, his longtime catcher, Jorge Posada, joined with Alex Rodriguez to push Rivera back out to the mound so the crowd could salute him one more time.

Asked to describe that moment, Rivera, seated with his three sons, said: "Oh my God. For ≫≫

Mariano Rivera surrounded by teammates after his record 602nd save.

<<< the first time in my career, I'm on the mound alone. There's no one behind me, no one in front of me. I can't describe that feeling because it was priceless."

Rivera entered the eight-game homestand needing just one save to break the record. With the Yankees holding a 6–4 lead late in the game, the only question was whether their relentless lineup would add a couple of runs to the lead and take away the save opportunity.

But the Yankees did not, and when Rivera took the mound in the ninth, the crowd—somewhat sparse by Yankees standards because the contest was a makeup game against a last-place team—

urged him on. Efficient as always, Rivera complied, getting Trevor Plouffe to ground out to second base and Michael Cuddyer to fly out to right. Then came the called strike three, the 177th time Rivera has completed a save with a strikeout.

For a good part of the game, the Yankees and starting pitcher A. J. Burnett kept the fans guessing about whether Rivera would have a shot at history. At first, it seemed the Yankees' lead would be too large for a save situation (the maximum is three runs to start an inning). Then it seemed the Twins might actually tie the score or go ahead.

The announced attendance was 40,045, although the crowd was nowhere near that large.

And the fans who did show up were so determined to witness history that they cheered in the bottom of the eighth when Nick Swisher grounded into a double play to keep the Yankees' lead at 6–4.

"I didn't think I'd ever hear the day that people would cheer for us to make outs," Girardi said, laughing.

For his part, Rivera said he was amazed to hear that reaction.

"It's unbelievable," he said. "I wanted to pitch, but I didn't want my teammates to do bad. When I saw that I thought: 'These fans are crazy. We need to score some runs.' But at the same time, I appreciated it because they wanted me to pitch." ◆

January 24, 2012

Tearful Posada Says He'll 'Forever Be a Yankee'

By DAVID WALDSTEIN

IN THE LATTER INNINGS of his career, Jorge Posada faced the painful but inevitable slide of an aging star. Younger and more productive players pushed him lower and lower down the batting order, ultimately resulting in the only real public feud he had with his team.

But on Tuesday at Yankee Stadium, Posada was in the middle of another impressive lineup, with Derek Jeter, Mariano Rivera, C. C. Sabathia, Hal Steinbrenner, Joe Girardi, Brian Cashman, Diana Munson and Willie Randolph seated in front of him; his wife and children at his side; and the five World Series trophies that he contributed to as the Yankees' catcher behind him.

An emotional Posada announced his retirement after an illustrious 17-year career, wiping away the tears as he recounted his career and thanked everyone who helped and supported him, including his closest friend on the team, the star shortstop he came up with in the minor leagues.

"I want to thank my teammates throughout the years," Posada said, choking with the emotion, "especially Derek Jeter, who helped me stay focused and positive. Thank you, buddy."

Certain to garner Hall of Fame consideration in five years, Posada finishes his career with 275 homers, 1,065 runs batted in, a .273 batting average, 5 All-Star selections and 5 championship rings.

In a novel and poignant touch by the Yankees, Munson, the widow of Thurman Munson, came to the podium and recounted how a meeting with Posada in the dugout in 1997 brought her back to baseball nearly two decades after her husband died.

"I am so honored," she said, "to have loved two Yankee catchers in my life." ◆

October 18, 2012

$200 Million Yankees Give Their Poorest Effort

By DAVID WALDSTEIN

DETROIT—When it mattered most, $200 million could barely buy a hit.

The Yankees, the richest and most accomplished team in baseball, were swept from the postseason on Thursday, embarrassed and undone by a staggering and costly display of ineptitude at the plate.

Alex Rodriguez, with 647 career home runs and a $29 million salary for the 2012 season, managed a single hit against Detroit, and then was unceremoniously benched as the Tigers ran off four straight victories. Robinson Cano, widely regarded as one of the most talented players in baseball, endured an 0-for-29 streak that now stands as a major league record for postseason failure, and batted just .075 in the playoffs.

The Yankees, who led the major leagues in home runs during the regular season with 245, failed to score a single run in 20 straight innings against Detroit, scored in just 3 of 39 innings overall and never had a lead in any of the ⟫⟫⟫

«« four games. The same offense that produced the second-most runs (804) in baseball
during the regular season could barely manage
a bloop single as the Yankees suffered their first
postseason sweep since 1980 and only the fifth in
their mostly glorious 27-championship history.

But there was no glory this year. Their futility
continued to the very end as they managed just
two hits on Thursday while the Tigers pounded
them, 8-1, to capture the American League
Championship Series. ◆

September 22, 2013

The Sun Sets on Forever

By TYLER KEPNER

SUMMER IS OVER. It ended on Saturday, the day
before the Yankees honored Mariano Rivera,
who brought a sense of calm to their tense empire as no other pitcher has. When Rivera took
the mound Sunday, just a sliver of sunlight remained on the back slope of the hill.

"You can't script it better," his former catcher
Jorge Posada had said in the early innings, while

Andy Pettitte toiled on that mound one last time.
"I'm super happy for both of them. They're
at Yankee Stadium and the best crowd in the
world."

The scripts were so reliable once, when they
were young. The Yankees welcomed four rookies in 1995, and together they won four titles in
five seasons and another in 2009. Despite months
of evidence that things are different now, Sunday
promised something special, as past champions
gathered to salute the great Rivera.

"Baseball, while you're doing it, you think
it's going to last forever," said Joe Torre, the
Yankees' manager for 12 seasons. "Some guys

just drop out and move on, and when you get everybody together, it just conjures up all those memories."

A ceremony that felt like Old-Timers' Day and a Hall of Fame induction promised one last gilded outcome. But as hard as these bruised Yankees have fought this season, they just did not have it in them.

They lost, 2-1, vanquished by unfamiliar rookies named Adrianza and Noonan and Perez. The Yankees now trail in the playoff race by four games with six to play.

"No regrets; it has been wonderful," Rivera said, reflecting after the game with his wife, Clara, by his side. "The only thing is I wish we can be in a different position than where we are now."

The last time they missed the playoffs, the Yankees, at least, could expect things to turn. Nothing stopped them from spending wildly for free agents, and Derek Jeter, Rivera, Pettitte and Posada were still around to support Robinson Cano and Alex Rodriguez.

Jeter, naturally, had an honored role at Rivera's tribute, escorting his wife and children onto the field.

"To America, that has given me the pleasure since I left my country 23 years ago," Rivera said, in his closing remarks to the fans. "That's why America's a great country. Your Yankees are a great organization, and you guys, fans, are the best. So let's play ball. We gotta go. I love you guys. Thank you very much."

Rivera meant that the Yankees had a game to play. But with 652 saves, he does have to go, and Pettitte, too, and Jeter soon enough. Nothing lasts forever, and nobody knows what comes next. ◆

Mariano Rivera during a ceremony before his last game at Yankee Stadium.

February 11, 2014

Tanaka Welcomes Biggest Stage

By TYLER KEPNER

NOBODY SELLS HOPE like the Yankees. Nobody has such easy access to it. With their money and their marquee, they are a magnetic draw to an overseas sensation like Masahiro Tanaka, who buttoned up a No. 19 pinstriped jersey on Tuesday, tugged on that famous navy blue cap and proclaimed, in English, "I'm very happy to be a Yankee."

To Tanaka's right, on a dais before more than 200 reporters in a dining hall at Yankee Stadium, the team's top executives clapped in delight. After missing the playoffs with an ancient, brittle roster, they had faced the prospect of a long, cold, lonely winter if they wanted to adhere to the goal of reducing their luxury-tax rate. Instead, they invested $470 million, and the penalties, in new talent.

"We know what our fans expect," Hal Steinbrenner said. "They expect us to field a championship-caliber team, every year, as best we can. I think we've got a very good team. We have to stay healthy; that's a given. But with a normal year of injuries, we're going to be a force."

Steinbrenner may be right. At worst, the point is debatable, but that really does not matter. What matters is that the Yankees are interesting again—and for pure baseball reasons, not the dark specter of an Alex Rodriguez controversy.

How many homers will Brian McCann send over the inviting right-field wall? How will Jacoby Ellsbury energize the top of the lineup—and how will he play against his old team, the champion Boston Red Sox? How will Carlos Beltran perform on this side of town?

Admit it. If you're a baseball fan, you're interested in those story lines. You will tune in again and maybe even buy tickets. And of all the stories, none is as compelling as Tanaka's.

At 25, he is by far the youngest impact player on the Yankees. He showed a star's flair ⟫⟫⟫

Masahiro Tanaka, standing next to Manager Joe Girardi, being introduced in a private dining room on ground level of Yankee Stadium.

≪ with his arrival Sunday at John F. Kennedy International Airport on a rented 787 that transported only six passengers, including his pop-star wife and his poodle. It cost him an estimated $200,000.

Tanaka said Tuesday that he chose such an extravagance because he wanted to arrive in top physical condition and had few other options. He mostly slept on the flight, anyway.

A more telling revelation was his reason for joining the Yankees. Tanaka sidestepped a question about the offers from other teams; the Yankees have already said that they outbid the field with their seven-year, $155 million deal. Money mattered, of course, but so did the stage.

"I've heard this place could be very harsh to you at times," Tanaka said through an interpreter. "I just wanted to put myself, though, in this environment and try and see where I can get to with my ability."

No pitcher in major league history has posted a record as dazzling as Tanaka's for the Rakuten Eagles last season: 24 wins, no losses.

The Yankees have cautioned against overhype. Pitchers from Japan must get used to the hitters, a slightly larger ball and a less rigorous throwing program.

Tanaka is the only notable addition to a pitching staff that lost Andy Pettitte and Mariano Rivera and has questions everywhere.

He would not label himself an ace, but he seems to share his new fans' expectations.

"When I take the mound," Tanaka said, "I feel like I like to win every single game." ◆

August 23, 2014

Joe Torre Is Honored

By ANDREW KEH

IT WAS JUST BEFORE THE start of the 1996 baseball season, and Joe Torre, who had just been hired to manage the Yankees, needed a new uniform number.

He wanted a single digit, and with his new team, there were only two choices: No. 2 or No. 6.

Neither number particularly spoke to Torre, so he called his wife, Ali, who noted that he had worn No. 9 over the last nine years of his playing career. Why not flip it around?

"We turned 9 around and made it 6," Torre said early Saturday afternoon, smiling at the memory. "That's how scientifically we did that."

The Yankees unveiled a plaque honoring former manager Joe Torre that currently hangs in Monument Park.

Torre on Saturday became the 18th person to have his number retired by the Yankees. While the stands at Yankee Stadium were still filling before the team's 5-3 win over the Chicago White Sox, Torre stood in Monument Park, beyond the centerfield fence, and unveiled a plaque with his likeness and the No. 6 that would be added to the celebrated collection there.

"When you know the neighborhood you're in out there, it's pretty cool," Torre said of Monument Park. "It's unbelievable. I mean, this is the Yankees. You start talking about number retirements. This is the New York Yankees." ◆

September 26, 2014

Derek Jeter's Memorable Final View at Shortstop

By TYLER KEPNER

BOSTON—He got cowboy boots in Texas, a surfboard in California and adulation everywhere. But the one gift Derek Jeter wanted most from his final season was the same thing he has wanted since he was a boy growing up next to a baseball field in Kalamazoo, Mich.

Jeter wanted the best view in New York City. He wanted something that cannot be bought and something he can never have again. In the end, it meant everything to him.

"I want to take something special from Yankee Stadium," Jeter said late Thursday night. "The view from shortstop here, tonight, is what I want to take from it."

So that was where Jeter went, after the spine-tingling ending to his New York baseball career, when his signature hit—opposite-field single, first pitch—beat the Baltimore Orioles 6-5 in the bottom of the ninth inning. He raised his arms in triumph, smiled widely, embraced teammates past and present. And then he went for a walk.

The point of baseball is to go home. Jeter, who understands the game as well as anyone ever has, did just that. He went to his home, shortstop, the position he played his entire career, never straying for even an inning to another spot. He will hit this weekend in Boston, he said, out of respect for the fans there, and the rivalry but he will not play shortstop again. This was it.

For the last time as an active player, Jeter stopped at the edge of the outfield grass and squatted there for a moment, his head bowed, his back to the pitcher's mound, his hat near his face. He said a prayer.

"I basically just said thank you, because this is all I've ever wanted to do, and not too many people get an opportunity to do it," Jeter said later. "It was above and beyond anything that I've ever dreamt of. I don't even know what to say. ≫≫

‹‹‹ I've lived a dream since I was 4 or 5 years old, and part of that dream is over now."

Jeter chose his words carefully; he always does. Only part of his dream is over. He has belonged to the Yankees for more than half his life, but he is only 40. He has started his own publishing imprint. He wants to own a baseball team, someday, and to start a family.

He said it had felt strange to be present, in a way, at his own funeral this season, to show appreciation for the tributes while forcing himself not to focus on what he is losing. The emotions have been there all along.

"I have 'em," Jeter said. "I try to hide 'em. I try to trick myself and convince myself that I'm not feeling those particular emotions, whether it's nerves, whether I'm injured, pain. I just try to trick myself that I don't have it."

When his teammates presented him with a painting in a private ceremony before Thursday's game, Jeter had to look away. He did not want the ball hit to him at shortstop, he said, a new and unsettling feeling. He forgot his elbow guard, misplaced a batting glove, called out plays to the second baseman with nobody on base. He ducked back to the clubhouse bathroom during the game, he said, and cried where nobody could see him.

Jeter said these things in two 20-minute news conferences, after Thursday's game and before Friday's, that were easily the most introspective and revealing he has ever been in public. He was confessional and self-deprecating, reflective and raw. Basically, he was spent—emotionally, for sure, and probably physically, too.

Someone asked Jeter on Thursday how he defined Frank Sinatra's "My Way," the song he chose as his personal anthem in his farewell Gatorade commercial and over the stadium loudspeakers after his winning hit. Usually quick with his answers—he gets many of the same questions, and thus has many automated responses—Jeter paused to think this over.

"I know there's a lot of people that have much more talent than I do throughout the course of my career, not just now," he said, finally. "And I can honestly say I don't think anyone played harder. I don't. Maybe just as hard, but I don't think anyone had more of an effort. Every single day I went out there and tried to have respect for the game and play it as hard as I possibly could. And I did it here in New York, which I think is much more difficult to do. And I'm happy for that."

His next Twitter or Instagram post will be his first. His professionalism has compelled him to be the face of the team, and the sport. Extreme self-confidence has helped, too, even at the end, as a .255 hitter with 3,465 hits.

"I still feel as though I could play," Jeter said. "I just don't want to. I want to call it a career."

Derek Jeter celebrates after his ninth-inning hit during his last game at Yankee Stadium.

He was gracious, to the end, a grown-up in a child's game. In his postgame interview on the field, he congratulated the Orioles and wished them well in the playoffs.

Even Jeter, who does not like watching baseball on television, said he wanted to see this game again. He said he might host a screening for friends and family. He willed his way through it in a daze.

"I'd like to see how it went, because I think I missed a lot of it," he said Friday.

The replay will not let him down. For two decades, Jeter was a better show than anything on Broadway, a character of grace and skill whose story seemed too good to be true. Except it was. His final act was the only game he ever played in New York with the Yankees eliminated from playoff contention. Yet he made it unforgettable.

"Take a good look," said Buck Showalter, the Orioles' manager, who brought Jeter to the majors with the Yankees in 1995, "because there's not going to be many like this to come our way again." ◆

February 17, 2015

Exchanging Sword for Pen, Rodriguez Apologizes

By DAVID WALDSTEIN

TAMPA, FLA.—PREPARING to make a highly scrutinized return to baseball after a long suspension for drug use, Alex Rodriguez issued a brief, handwritten statement Tuesday to say he was sorry for his behavior.

It was Rodriguez's first public comment on the matter since he issued a defiant statement in January 2014, the day his suspension went into effect. Back then, he said the charges against him were false. Thirteen months later, writing in cursive in an apparent attempt to add a personal touch, Rodriguez demonstrated some contrition.

While not directly admitting to the use of performance-enhancing drugs, the matter at the heart of his suspension, he tacitly acknowledged that the record 162-game penalty against him had been warranted and said that the misdeeds had been his own.

"To the fans," his statement began. "I take full responsibility for the mistakes that led to my suspension for the 2014 season. I regret that my actions made the situation worse than it needed to be. To Major League Baseball, the Yankees, the Steinbrenner family, the players association and you, the fans, I can only say I'm sorry.

"I accept the fact that many of you will not believe my apology or anything that I say at this point," the statement added. "I understand why, and that's on me."

The statement on Tuesday echoed similar apologies Rodriguez had already made to Major League Baseball, the Yankees and the players association earlier this month, not only for using drugs provided by Bosch but also for the combative and litigious approach he took while initially trying to avoid a suspension. ◆

October 7, 2015

Upstart Astros Outshine Yankees

By TYLER KEPNER

THE YANKEES FACED elimination at home against an upstart team and a dominant pitcher on three days' rest. It felt like 2003, except this time at the start of the postseason, not the very end. Dallas Keuchel played the role of Josh Beckett in Tuesday's wild-card game in the Bronx, and now the Yankees' season is over.

The Houston Astros bounced around on the Yankee Stadium grass, surviving baseball's knockout round with a 3-0 victory and earning a division series date with the Kansas City Royals. »»»

《《《 Twelve Octobers ago, it was Beckett and the Marlins clinching the World Series at the old stadium, squeezing the life from the Yankees and muting their fans. The Yankees responded with a late-winter trade for Alex Rodriguez, who has helped them reach the playoffs nine times.

Rodriguez led the Yankees to a title in 2009, and in all his other postseasons with the team, he has hit .202. He was 0 for 4 on Tuesday, and Keuchel retired him with runners in scoring position to end the first and sixth innings. Rodriguez, 40, had a strong comeback season, but the Yankees' utter dependence on him—especially against left-handers after Mark Teixiera's broken leg—was their failing, not his.

Even if the Yankees wanted to, they could never retrench. They are blessed and burdened by a philosophy that demands they always go for it. ◆

August 13, 2016

Under Dark Skies, Alex Rodriguez Ends Complicated Career

By TYLER KEPNER

THE PINSTRIPED ODYSSEY of Alex Rodriguez was an action-packed thriller, a cautionary tale, a pathetic farce and a story of redemption, all in one. The postscript—starting as a coach and adviser, leading to places unknown—must still be written. But a dozen uproarious volumes closed for good on Friday.

Rodriguez made his final playing appearance for the Yankees, who beat the Tampa Bay Rays, 6-3, and will officially release Rodriguez on Saturday morning. Batting third as the designated hitter, Rodriguez went 1 for 4 with a run-scoring double, a strikeout and two groundouts to shortstop. He played third base for the first out of the ninth inning—a strikeout—and then left to applause and hugs from his teammates.

After the last out, as the other Yankees waited for him on the first-base line, Rodriguez strode back to third base—the spot where he stood when the Yankees won their last World Series. He scooped a handful of dirt, put it in his back pocket and waved to the stands.

"That's where we won the world championship in 2009," he told the crowd from the field in a postgame interview. Then his daughters rushed to the field and embraced him, and the remaining fans from the crowd of 46,459 stood and cheered.

"I've given these fans a lot of headaches over the years," Rodriguez said, referring to his two admissions of steroid use, one resulting in a yearlong suspension in 2014. "I've disappointed a lot of people. But like I've always said, you don't have to be defined by your mistakes. How you come back matters, too—and that's what New York is all about."

Manager Joe Girardi broke into tears at his postgame news conference, saying that he and Rodriguez had been through a lot and that he wished he could have given him more playing time lately.

"I have really strong feelings for him," Girardi said, "and this has been extremely hard."

Rodriguez enthralled and enraged in equal parts, and his farewell ceremony was almost eerily appropriate. Fierce winds whipped the flags atop the stadium. Darkening clouds drew closer and closer. A tarp covered the infield. There were no folding chairs, no podium—but there were dignitaries.

Reggie Jackson escorted Rodriguez's mother onto the field. Starlin Castro and Didi Gregorius, young infielders Rodriguez has mentored, brought out his sister and brother. Then Mariano Rivera appeared, to raucous applause, taking Rodriguez's daughters out to greet him.

"Alex," said Paul Olden, the public-address announcer, "you spent 12 of your 22 seasons with the Yankees. . . ."

At that precise moment, a thunderclap boomed over the Bronx. The sound repeated a few minutes later, again as Olden cited Rodriguez's 12 years in New York.

After a video message from Lou Piniella, Rodriguez's first manager with the Seattle

Mariners, the Yankees hurried through a gift presentation. Jennifer Steinbrenner Swindal gave him a base autographed by teammates; Hal Steinbrenner held up a framed 2016 jersey.

By then the clouds had burst, sheets of rain pelting the field, and everyone scurried back to the safety of the dugout and clubhouse tunnel. No time for a tearful farewell speech, though none was planned.

His final hit came in the first inning—with the crowd chanting "Let's go, A-Rod!"—against Chris Archer, a hard-throwing right-hander with a wicked slider. He connected on a 2-2, 96 m.p.h. fastball, lashing a blistering low liner to the gap in right-center field.

The hit was Rodriguez's 3,115th (20th on the career list) and his 1,275th for extra bases. Only five players have more extra-base hits, and none need a first name to be instantly recognized: Aaron, Bonds, Musial, Ruth and Mays.

It would be Rodriguez's final hit as a Yankee—No. 1,580 for the team, outside the franchise's top 10—but not his last at-bat. He led off the fourth inning and bounced out to shortstop, then ended the fifth by striking out on a slider.

In the bottom of the seventh, Rodriguez would take his final at-bat as an active Yankee with two outs and the bases empty against reliever Ryan Garton. The fans rose to their feet, many viewing the moment through the camera on their cellphones. But there was little suspense.

Rodriguez swung at the first pitch, a fastball at 90 m.p.h., and chopped a grounder to shortstop Matt Duffy, who threw him out at first. His season average—for the Yankees, at least—is frozen at .200, his career mark at .295.

Perhaps more swings remain, for the Marlins or another team. But Rodriguez knows he has a job to do with the Yankees. He is leaving the field but might not really go anywhere.

"With all my screw-ups and how badly I acted," he said, "the fact that I'm walking out the door and Hal wants me as part of the family, that's hitting 800 home runs for me." ◆

Alex Rodriguez was honored in a ceremony with his family before playing his last game for the Yankees.

September 18, 2016

The Silver Lining in Pinstripes: Gary Sanchez

By BILLY WITZ

BOSTON—IN RECENT weeks at Yankee Stadium, sprouting up through the thicket of pinstriped No. 2 jerseys and other remnants of the Derek Jeter era, there have been signs that Yankees fans are wrapping themselves in something other than nostalgia.

Now speckling the crowds are Gary Sanchez T-shirts and No. 24 jerseys, evidence, it would seem, that fans are investing emotionally and financially—those licensed jerseys retail for $129.99—in the team's slugging rookie catcher.

There is one T-shirt, though, that neatly captures what Sanchez has brought to the Yankees, who for more than a decade have been chasing yesterday, throwing money at players for what they have done, not what they might do.

It is a knockoff of the street artist Shepard Fairey's iconic portrait of Barack Obama before the 2008 presidential election. Instead of Mr. Obama, it is Sanchez who gazes up confidently, above the block letters "HOPE."

With the Yankees sliding out of playoff contention for another season, this one at least will be ending with brighter prospects ahead.

When the team jettisoned Alex Rodriguez, Mark Teixeira announced his retirement, and several top veterans, including Carlos Beltran, were dealt to bolster the farm system by early August, it cleared the way for a number of prospects to audition.

There have been ups and downs, as might be expected of players finding their way, but Sanchez has been a revelation. With a third-inning home run Sunday night, he has hit 16 homers and driven in 30 runs in 41 games. The American League player of the month in August, he has also been dynamic defensively, rifling throws to all bases at just about any time.

Sanchez, 23, did not necessarily sneak up on anyone. The Yankees signed him as a 16-year-old from the Dominican Republic for $3 million, the most they have bestowed on an amateur international free agent.

A year ago at the trade deadline, General Manager Brian Cashman told teams that pitcher Luis Severino, first baseman Greg Bird and outfielder Aaron Judge were off limits. But he listened to offers for Sanchez.

"I'm glad for my sake that I didn't do it," Cashman said.

The infusion of youth gave the Yankees a jolt that unexpectedly carried a disappointing, listless team back into playoff contention by early September. The clubhouse music became more lively when it was turned over to Judge, and the veterans say they have been reinvigorated by the rookies' enthusiasm and naïveté.

Yet Sanchez, who has had the greatest impact, carries himself like an old hand. Naturally reserved and quietly confident, he gives interviews (conducted mostly through an interpreter) that reveal as little as his businesslike home run trots: head down and carried out with an absence of ebullience.

Sanchez has lived with his wife, Sahaira, and their 2-year-old daughter, Sarah, at his in-laws' home in Yonkers since he was recalled. Sanchez's grandmother, aunt and brother also live in New York, he said.

Just how the Yankees will proceed in their rebuilding remains uncertain. Will Judge, the behemoth right fielder who has shown prodigious power and an alarming proclivity to strike out, develop into another potential cornerstone? Will Bird, who showed promise late last season, be the same player when he returns next spring from shoulder surgery?

Asked how he would assess Sanchez's place next season, Manager Joe Girardi expressed little interest in peeking into the future, but he said the value the Yankees place on Sanchez was already evident.

"We're showing you how much faith we have in him by hitting him third in the lineup and giving him a lot of responsibility," Girardi said. "He's catching a lot. He's D.H.-ing. And that will continue because he's playing at an extremely high level. We think he's a really good player, and he's shown that so far."

It is a sentiment fans are beginning to share while watching the Yankees finish out this season, carried along by Sanchez and, whether they own a particular T-shirt or not, the audacity of hope. ◆

December 7, 2016

A Perfect 10. Just Add 2.

By BILLY WITZ

THE YANKEES WILL retire Derek Jeter's No. 2 jersey and honor him with a plaque in Monument Park on May 14, Mother's Day, making official what had been expected long before he retired after the 2014 season.

The retirement of Jeter's jersey brings the Yankees' total of retired uniform numbers to 21, the most in baseball, and means that every Yankees number from 1 to 10 will have been retired.

In numerical order, Billy Martin wore No. 1; Babe Ruth No. 3; Lou Gehrig No. 4; Joe DiMaggio No. 5; Joe Torre No. 6; Mickey Mantle No. 7; Yogi Berra and Bill Dickey, both catchers, No. 8; Roger Maris No. 9; and Phil Rizzuto No. 10. ◆

E P I L O G U E
by Dave Anderson

The Yankees march into a future that demands they be as successful as they were in their past.

The wealthiest franchise has the money to entice some of baseball's best free agents and develop its share of its best prospects. But in winning 27 World Series and 40 American League pennants, they have relied not merely on some of the best or a share of the best, but the best of the best—Babe Ruth, Lou Gehrig, Joe DiMaggio, Yogi Berra, Phil Rizzuto, Mickey Mantle, Whitey Ford, Catfish Hunter, Reggie Jackson, Goose Gossage—all Hall of Famers, as well as future Hall of Famers Derek Jeter and Mariano Rivera. In the dugout, four managers—Miller Huggins, Joe McCarthy, Casey Stengel and Joe Torre earned a bronze plaque in Cooperstown. Two of their general managers, Ed Barrow and George Weiss, reside there and George Steinbrenner, the principal owner who thought he was the general manager, might join them sooner or later.

But the Yankees can't rest on their laurels or bask in their bronze. With all their rings and pennants and wealth, the Yankees have created a responsibility to themselves and to their fans to buy, find and hire the best of the best players, managers and executives in order to continue to be baseball's best of the best.

INDEX

Illustrations are indicated in **bold**.

S

Y

Z

PHOTO CREDITS